DATE DUE			
SEP 0 9 2014			

EARLY AMERICAN HISTORY

An eighteen volume series reproducing over three hundred of the most important articles on all aspects of the colonial experience

EDITED WITH INTRODUCTIONS BY
PETER CHARLES HOFFER
UNIVERSITY OF GEORGIA

A Garland Series

AMERICAN PATTERNS OF LIFE

Selected Articles on the Provincial Period of American History

EDITED WITH AN INTRODUCTION BY

PETER CHARLES HOFFER

Garland Publishing, Inc.
New York & London
1988

Library of Congress Cataloging-in-Publication Data

American patterns of life.

(Early American history)
Includes bibliographical references.
1. United States—History—Colonial period, ca. 1600–1775.
I. Hoffer, Peter C. II. Series.
E188.5.A44 1988 973.2 88-4185
ISBN 0-8240-6240-X (alk. paper)

The volumes in this series are printed on
acid-free, 250-year-life paper.

Printed in the United States of America

CONTENTS

Preface

Shortly before he died, Richard Hofstadter, one of the foremost students of American national history, began a study of American ways in 1750. He had found profound similarities and notable differences among the settlements, but the book his wife Beatrice completed and published was only a preliminary report of his findings.[1] This volume of essays continues that project. Certainly the thirteen mainland colonies were poised at a critical moment in their courses, at peace with the world, productive and populous, yet still willingly dependent upon mother country and empire. What was American about them? What bound them together? In what ways were they similar?

The foregoing volumes of this series have stressed the regional differences in Great Britain's North American Empire. By the provincial period, between 1689 and 1763, the West Indies, the Lower South and the Upper South, the Middle Colonies and New England all had distinct domestic economies, roles in the imperial economic system, patterns of labor use, ethnicity, residence, and religious affiliation. All of the colonies within these regions were separate legal jurisdictions, originating in crown land grants or charters. Cooperation among the colonies was tenuous and temporary at best. Within each colony were localities—western and eastern settlements, mountain frontiers and coastal plantations, dispersed farms and urban conglomerations—each with its own political agenda, economic needs, and cultural priorities. Within these localities, kin stretched upward into clan and downward into families. In many ways the heart of settlement was its smallest unit: the nuclear family. Families gave structure to towns and parishes; families took in servants and apprentices; shops and farms were run by families.

All of these units, in Robert Wiebe's words, operated in a segmented society, under a logic of their own devising.[2] Yet there were powerful commonalities pulling these different and dispersed colonists together. All were tied to a world market, not merely because the empire was a vast mercantile project, but because almost all American farmers produced staples of some kind for export. Even the subsistence farmers of New England contributed the labor of their children to the building and outfitting of ships for the Atlantic and African trades. The frontier families' furs and skins went abroad, as did the coastal farmers' rice and indigo. All of these farmers had common interests: defense against the enemies of the British Empire, insufficiency of credit and currency, replacement of land, and extension of political autonomy. Common opportunities and common problems turned the closed segments of settlement into networks of trade, travel, and political activity.

Peter Charles Hoffer
University of Georgia

Notes

1. Richard Hofstadter, *America at 1750: A Social Portrait* (New York, 1973).

2. Robert H. Wiebe, *The Segmented Society: An Historical Preface to the Meaning of America* (New York, 1975), 15.

Eighteenth Century Medicine in America

BY RICHARD H. SHRYOCK

ONE sometimes wishes that the history of our early medicine had been recorded by the patients, rather 1
than by physicians or other learned gentlemen. Those who were ill in Colonial days underwent stern experiences. They were first exposed to the pharmacopeia—no mean hazard in itself. Dr. Holmes later described this situation by observing that:

> The mines have been emptied of their cankering minerals, the vegetable kingdom robbed of all its noxious growths, the entrails of animals taxed for their impurities . . . and all the inconceivable abominations thus obtained thrust down the throats of human beings.

In combination with such dosings, the Colonial patient was subjected to the age-old depletion procedures—bleeding, sweating, and the like. If all this was of small avail, there was no telling what bizarre expedients might be employed. Cotton Mather, in writing to Dr. John Woodward of the Royal Society in 1724, reported the following case history:

> The wife of Joseph Meader . . . had long been afflicted with that miserable *Distemper* known as the *twisting of the guts*. Her physician advised her to swallow a couple of *Leaden Bullets;* upon which after some time, her Pain was abated and the use of her Limbs returned to her.

But, added Mather, "attempts to *swallow Bullets* have not always terminated so well." He recalled a case in which the bullet entered the lung, and added sagely enough: "From which and from other unhappy Experiments, I think, I should endure abundant, before I tried such a remedy."

Upon first encountering such practice, one wonders how our ancestors of only two centuries ago could have submitted to it. Of course, they wanted to believe that it was "good for what ailed them;" and this faith was often sustained by recovery—by the *post hoc, ergo propter hoc* fallacy. But to the modern reader, there seems at first glance no rhyme or reason in that complex thing which was eighteenth century medicine.

2 First glances are superficial, however, and it is well to look into the matter with more care. Upon further examination, this medicine will be found worthy of some respect; not only as a part of the culture of the times, but because it was in a real sense the precursor of present science. It was in the eighteenth century that the foundations of modern medicine were established; and if American medicine illustrates only the difficulties experienced in laying these foundations, it is still a part of the larger story.

In discussing early American medicine, one must keep in mind (1) the nature of European medicine during the seventeenth and eighteenth centuries, and the means by which this was transmitted to the Colonies, and (2) the social and intellectual circumstances in America which impinged upon medicine once it was established here. For the sake of clarity, the analysis may be broken down into the conventional categories of the history of the public health, of professional institutions, of science, and—last but not least—of medical practice.

The public health in seventeenth- and eighteenth-century England was nothing to boast of from the modern viewpoint. We all know that the country was ravaged by serious epidemics, notably of smallpox and of the plague. It is a truism that death rates were relatively high and life expectancy at birth correspondingly low. One aspect of the transit of Europeans to America which is not usually exphasized, is

the fact that they brought with them all their more or less domesticated diseases. Once on this side, moreover, they engaged in a free exchange of their infections with those of the Indians and Negroes; with the result that America served as a melting pot for afflictions heretofore peculiar to three separate continents. This fact helps to explain the toll taken by epidemic diseases among the Colonial populations of all three races. The Indians suffered most; so much so, indeed, that their resulting mortality probably made easier the 3
European occupation of our North American seaboard.

Since few specific diseases were recognized prior to 1800, it is difficult to identify those which harassed the Colonies before that time. The evidence indicates, however, that malaria and the usual respiratory and intestinal infections were responsible for most of the tragic reports in Colonial sources. The most feared epidemics were those of smallpox and diphtheria (European in origin) and of yellow fever (probably of African origin). Why plague failed to make the Atlantic passage is not clear. There were also serious endemic conditions of a non-infectious character, such as scurvy—a reminder of the dietary deficiences of our ancestors.

Threatened by ever-present illness, Europeans turned for protection to their folk medicine, to physicians, and to the major institutions of Church and State. Certain of these protective patterns do not concern us here, but it should not be forgotten what a role they played in the actual practice of the masses. In the ordinary vicissitudes of illness, the Colonial as well as the English family looked to its folk lore; which involved a blend of home remedies, astrology and other occult practices, and (in America) of notions taken over from Indian "medicine men." They also turned to prayer; a practice which, in one's more cynical moments, might be termed theological prophylaxis and therapy. Yet, apart from the human sympathy which may be accorded this behavior, who can be sure that their faith—whatever its rewards—did not at least have some of the merits now ascribed to psychosomatic medicine?

Governments, in their effort to protect the public health, were handicapped by the state of contemporary medical science. Since epidemics occasioned the chief fear, it was against them that officials took action. Medicine had inherited two theories as to the transmission of epidemics:
4 (1) that these were carried by airs, waters, and food and therefore called for sanitary controls; and (2) that they were transmitted by contagion and therefore indicated isolation, notification, and the destruction of animals. Orthodox medicine tended to uphold the classical emphasis upon sanitation, which was revived during the Renaissance and led in Elizabethan England to the adoption of a respectable sanitary code. This was reflected in Colonial towns by sporadic efforts at street cleaning, inspection of foods, and the like.

Popular feeling, however, leaned towards the medieval contagion theory and was reinforced between 1650 and 1750 by experience with plague and with smallpox. As a result, governments introduced port quarantines, isolated homes, ordered the destruction of animals during epidemics, established pesthouses, and so on. All of these practices were resorted to in Colonial towns, which sometimes even enforced quarantines against neighboring communities.

Town and county authorities in the Colonies also had to assume, against the background of the Elizabethan poor laws, responsibility for sick paupers. Various devices, such as outdoor financial relief or boarding out with the lowest bidders, were employed. The insane were the most troublesome problem here. Boston provided indoor relief in the form of an almshouse as early as 1665; and in 1732 the Philadelphia Almshouse set up an infirmary which in theory provided "state medicine" to the poor. In practice, however, the care given in this and other early institutions was merely custodial in nature. The same was true of the sick who were isolated in town pesthouses.

Since the main defense against disease was resort to private medical practitioners, governments had long been looked to in Europe for some control over this professional personnel. The authorities, in turn, sought the advice of professional organizations in matters of education and 5
licensure. In the England of 1700, the London College of Physicians was authorized to control licensing. This elite body limited its certification to the graduates of Oxford and Cambridge, and so never approved enough men to meet the needs of a tenth of the population. The consequent vacuum was partly filled by licentiates of the apothecaries guild, and by the 1700's apothecaries made up the ranks of ordinary practitioners. Surgeons, overseen by the Surgeon's Guild, were viewed as an inferior group in comparison with the licensed physicians. Since there was no real interference with all sorts of irregulars and quacks, these various forms of licensing meant little in practice.

Hence it is not strange that, in the distant Colonies, governmental control over medical practice almost disappeared. There were occasional acts which reflected the tradition of licensing; for example, the Massachusetts law of 1649 which limited practice to those approved by "such as are skillful in the same art," or by "at least some of the wisest and gravest then present." In the nature of the case, such regulation was vague and ineffective. Most Colonial legislation or court action concerning physicians related to the size of fees rather than to the quality of service.

Some English physicians, including a few university men, came to the Colonies in the 1600's, and introduced the rudiments of respectable practice. Thereafter, the more ambi-

tious students "read medicine" (which was all that was done in the English universities) and apprenticed themselves to older practitioners. Others, who had a flair for the art or were inspired by selfish motives, simply launched themselves into practice. Not until after 1700, did any number of provincials go abroad for formal training. All degrees of reliability were thereafter represented in the Colonial setting; from that of men holding the M.D. from
6 Leyden or Edinburgh, down to the pretense of the most outrageous quacks.

The concept of licensing was never entirely forgotten, and there is evidence that it eventually attracted some support. During the 1760's, New York became the first province to set up a council to license physicians—a body which, incidentally, contained no member of the profession. There is no evidence, however that, this effort—or that of a number of other states during the ensuing half century—was really effective. The general state of things was outlined in the remarks of a New York critic who declared, just before the Revolution, that:

> Few physicians among us are eminent for their skill. Quacks abound like locusts in Egypt. . . . This is the less to be wondered at, as the profession is under no kind of regulation. . . . Any man at his pleasure sets up for physician, apothecary, and chirurgeon. No candidates are either examined or licensed, or even sworn to fair practice.

Against this background, occasional practice by clergymen was not surprising and probably had its merits. Ministers were frequently the only ones who could "read medicine," since before 1700 the greater part of the literature was in Latin. Clerical practice survived incidentally in rural areas well into the eighteenth century—as it did also in England—and traces can be found as late as 1850. Rural conditions in the Colonies also had the effect of imposing all functions upon the general practitioner, so that English distinctions between physicians, surgeons, and apothecaries disappeared.

The lack of a well-trained and licensed profession in the Colonies is usually ascribed to isolation and primitive surroundings. But it must be recalled that English conditions were little if any better. One may therefore attribute the situation in some degree to a lack of respect for medical learning. It was only in large towns that a European degree became an asset after 1700, and it was in these centers that 7
ambitious doctors founded medical institutions both to aid practice and to improve their own status. Philadelphia affords an excellent illustration of these developments between 1750 and 1800; where in imitation of London precedents, leading physicians established the Pennsylvania Hospital, the first native medical school, and the College of Physicians. Patronized by prosperous families, these men acquired wealth and so commanded respect for their social position as well as for their professional standing.

This was not the equivalent, however, of awe for medical learning. The impulse behind the founding of the first hospitals was not primarily a desire to bring medical science to the masses—this, such as it was, could be secured at home. Men sought rather to provide decent care of the poor in terms of charity and of humanitarianism. The truth is that the medical science of the time was unable to guide practice into any more effective channels than those followed by any clever empiric. Exceptions need to be made only in the cases of surgery and of obstetrics. The learned physician was actually more dangerous to his patients in some ways than was the self-trained man. In view of these circumstances, it is not surprising that the masses saw little difference between doctors of one sort or another.

What, then, was the nature of this eighteenth-century medicine which reached Americans through Latin and English texts, through the *Transactions* of the Royal Society and the early British medical journals, and through direct training in European schools? There is no more complex period in the history of medicine: it may be interpreted, with equal regard to the sources, as an era of lingering medievalism or as an epoch of progress. Perhaps we may characterize the century, as historians are apt to do with any confusing interval, as an era of transition.

8 In many respects eighteenth-century medicine was far removed from the medieval. Metaphysical perspectives had been discarded, and occult elements had largely disappeared from practice. Although Hippocrates and Galen were cited by physicians, this was because the classic literature still had something to offer; and there was no longer much veneration for authority as such. The respect for original observations which had been inculcated by Bacon was further encouraged by British philosophic empiricism associated with Locke and later with Hume. Precept was closely associated with achievement; the record of eighteenth-century medical investigations was no trivial one. Without reviewing all the various lines of development, let me call attention to one major trend in research which was to lay the foundation for medical science as we now know it.

It is often said that the revival of the Greek anatomic tradition during the Renaissance was the starting point of modern medicine. Actually, it was the combination of this revival with the introduction of new methods of observation (not, themselves, primarily of classical origin) which made all later progress possible. I refer to experimentation, to the use of instruments for aiding the senses, and to quantitative procedures. It is unnecessary to labor the value of experimentation and of measurements in the physiologic research of the seventeenth and eighteenth centuries. One need only recall Harvey and Haller in this connection.

There was little concern about physiologic experimentation in America until Rush encouraged it for a brief time among his students during the early national period. Sporadic interest in experimenting in other fields had appeared earlier than this, however, as in the chemistry of Winthrop the Younger or the immunology of Boylston and Cotton Mather. The latter, moreover—whom I would seriously suggest was the first significant figure in American
medicine—employed quantitative procedures in demonstrat- 9
ing the value of inoculation. His figures became a part of the data on which was based the later development of the calculus of probabilities.

Immunology, however, was largely empirical at this stage and was tangential to the major trend in research. This was the continued study of anatomy, a knowledge of which was essential to physiology. But quite apart from this, anatomic investigations revolutionzed the concepts of pathology and with these the whole approach to problems of disease. Here one should recall that, along with a sound tradition in anatomy, the moderns had inherited from Greece a speculative pathology in which illness was ascribed either to impurities in the body fluids (the humoral theory) or to conditions of tension in the vascular and nervous systems.

This type of pathology involved little recognition of distinctions between different forms of illness. Although a number of distinct diseases had long been known because of their obviously peculiar symptoms (skin infections, "consumption," gout, and so on), most forms of illness were not recognized as specific and were treated as involving only a state of the body "system." The chief concern was to find cures for these generalized conditions. The humoral theory indicated the common depletion procedures (bleeding, sweating); while the tension thesis called for the use of stimulants and narcotics. The therapy of both schools was reinforced by the employment of the traditional pharmacology—an accumulation in which a little sense was imbedded in a great mass of nonsense. Although there was much talk of the effect of each drug or concoction upon the humors or upon tension, most of these materials were actually of empirical origin and their employment was simply added to depletion procedures for good measure.

This sort of therapy was followed in the Colonies as in Europe, and it was not only ineffective but involved real danger. The more enthusiastic a practitioner was about his pathologic theory, the more was he apt to carry it to logical extremes in heroic practice. Lacking a concept of specific diseases, practitioners could not even recognize the few specifics which had been stumbled upon. Because cinchona bark clearly aided in some fevers, it was tried in all. Whereupon some physicians decided that, since it was supposed to be good for everything, it was really good for nothing.

The speculative pathology not only confused ordinary therapy, but also blocked any development of major surgery. If illness was located in impure body fluids, there was little that surgery could do in the nature of the case. After all, one cannot operate on the blood. Hence surgery remained until after 1800 a matter of superficial emergency measures, such as amputations and the treatment of fractures. Yet the knowledge of anatomy and the instruments necessary to major surgery were available long before this time.

There was no way out of this maze until pathology could be made a natural science. Instead of inquiring what would cure diseases, men must first learn what the diseases were. For only when distinct forms of illness were identified, could one look for their specific causal factors—which would in turn provide clues for their specific cures. Yet the hope of finding immediate remedies was a natural one: it was shared alike by suffering patients and by busy doctors. At this point one encounters an important social influence. The only men who investigated disease were practitioners: there were no scientists who, as in astronomy, could give themselves primarily to research. And just because they were practitioners, physicians who attempted investigations were pressed for time and asked the wrong questions of Nature.

Fortunately, however, a few medical men of the seventeenth century realized—for reasons not entirely clear—
that diseases must be discovered before rational cures could 11
be found. Sydenham, for example, gave an impetus to the study of diseases as such. Unfortunately, these at first could be identified only by symptoms (as we still do with the common cold), and symptoms were endlessly confusing. Here, at last, the anatomic tradition began to bring order out of chaos. For the study of normal anatomy led, by internal logic, to the investigation of pathologic anatomy. And by 1760, Morgagni of Padua made it clear that this structural, localized pathology—correlated with symptoms—would yield an identification of specific conditions. Observations made at autopsies, correlated with the antemortem, bedside data, began to break down such vague, symptomatic notions as "inflammations of the chest" into the specific concepts of bronchitis, pneumonia, pleurisy, and so on. Eventually, these distinctions made possible a search for distinct causal factors: a line of development which was successfully exploited by medical bacteriology during the ensuing century.

The significance of research in pathologic anatomy seems never to have been realized in eighteenth-century America. The ideas behind it were doubtless noted in the Colonies by a few individuals who read European works; indeed, the matter was in part explained by Dr. Thomas Bond in a famous lecture at the Pennsylvania Hospital in 1766. But the occasional autopsies performed in American towns reflected only a fear of foul play or a medieval-like curiosity about things in general. Language barriers may have had something to do with the prevailing indifference to Morgagni's work. Perhaps, also, the pragmatic outlook of Americans played a role: pathologic anatomy offered no immediate aid to practice. The busy American doctor wanted therapeutic short-cuts, and had no time for a meditation on the circumstances of death.

12 Meantime, even before pathology began to identify diseases, there was some speculation as to the causal factors (etiology) of such conditions as were recognized. Here the Greek tradition ascribed much illness to poisons or miasms circulating in the air—the theory upon which their sanitation was predicated. But a new instrument of observation—the microscope—had introduced observers after 1660 to the world of the animalculae. A few men suspected that these little "insects," gaining access to the body, might be the causes of disease. The theory could not be proved in the 1700's, not only because microscopes were imperfect but also because the diseases which would have been checked in this connection were not yet clearly recognized. But speculation and attempted demonstration had meaning: they kept the idea alive until it could be made workable, and occasionally suggested a rational approach to practice.

Did this promising "germ theory" reach the American Colonies? Until recently, we would have doubted it. As far as I know, no prominent physicians so much as mentioned it in the eighteenth century. It is therefore surprising to find that the whole animalcular theory was calmly accepted by none other than Cotton Mather as early as 1723. I am indebted to my student, Mr. O. T. Beall, for this knowledge of Mather's views;[1] as contained in the latter's unpublished manuscript, *The Angel of Bethesda*, which was

[1] Mr. Beall plans to proceed with a thorough study of Mather's medicine.

kindly made available by the American Antiquarian Society. Mather, to be sure, combined this new concept with much of the old speculative pathology. But he viewed the animalcular hypothesis as a most promising one; and, in addition, had some notion of its implications for medical practice. Incidentally, the *Angel*—rarely noticed heretofore by medical historians—seems to have been the first systematic treatise on medicine ever prepared in this country.

Several questions immediately occur. Why was this 13
pioneer American work never published? Failing publication, did it exert any influence? And why was it a theologian and historian, rather than a physician, who prepared this study and who accepted a new theory of etiology a full century before any medical men seem to have done so?

The failure of Americans to participate in the investigation of either pathologic anatomy or the "germ theory" simply reflected their indifference to medical research in general. There were a few notable exceptions, such as the experiments in immunology at Boston with which Mather was associated. But it is remarkable how seldom original studies were undertaken, even by the faculties of the first medical schools. Benjamin Rush lost his interest in experimental physiology and chemistry, after having picked it up at Edinburgh. Dr. John Morgan, of the College of Philadelphia, visited Morgagni at Padua but was not inspired to attempt pathologic studies. Indeed the only American who made serious contributions in pathology, William Charles Wells of Charleston, did his work after fleeing to London as a loyalist. He shares with Franklin and Benjamin Thompson the top honors in Anglo-American science, and was in my opinion as versatile as either of the other two in scientific matters. Not only did Wells do basic work in physics and in medicine, but in an odd moment he tossed off the first known presentation of the Darwinian theory of biologic evolution.

The very fact that these leaders all worked for years in London, suggests that the European center provided stimuli which were rarely present in the American setting. There is no need to explain this contrast here, so far as science in general is concerned, other than to say that it was not simply the result of pioneer conditions on this side. The explanation is more complex than that. But it is, in any case, a mistake to confuse professional progress in eighteenth-
14 century American medicine—which certainly took place—with scientific advances. Boston, New York, and Philadelphia could boast by 1790 of medical institutions comparable to those of London, but no such research was under way in them as was being cultivated in the metropolis.

Although Americans rarely participated in research, they had no difficulty in becoming involved in the confusions and uncertainties of the medical science of that era. This is the other side of the eighteenth-century story. The traditional controversy in speculative pathology related to the humoral versus the tension theory. The influence of Boerhaave at Leyden at first encouraged the humoral tradition among Americans; but Rush later revived the tension theory with vigor. In therapy, men had long been divided between those who advocated leaving cures to Nature and those who demanded interference with Nature. The Dutch influence early in the century promoted some reliance on Nature and correspondingly mild treatments; while Rush and his followers later came to distrust Nature and to demand heroic treatments. From the present viewpoint, American therapy thus went from bad to worse between 1750 and 1800.

A disconcerting phenomenon of this age was the manner in which objective advances in physical science seemed only to revive and complicate speculation in medicine. Thus Newtonian physics, which had systematized dynamics and astronomy, encouraged physicians to go and do likewise

in physics. But the only "systems" they could find were the revived pathologic speculations, which represented so many short-cuts across fields of yet unrecognized complexity. The prestige of Newton's physics also encouraged some to urge that all medical problems could be solved by mathematical or physical approaches. This iatro-mathematics had American advocates in Mather (interesting, in a theologian) and in Cadwallader Colden of New York. Mather, who denounced uncertainties and disagreements in medicine as 15
roundly as would Jefferson nearly a century later, urged that the causes and cures of diseases be sought "mathematically" by a study of the "*Laws of Matter and Motion.*" While there was a sound instinct in this advocacy of quantitative procedure, it was of little help at the time; and meanwhile it involved a debate with those who held that biologic phenonema were too complex for quantification.

Related to this issue was the controversy between the vitalists and the mechanists; for the vitalists were inclined to minimize quantitative methods, and the mechanists to favor them. The most active center of the debate was at the University of Halle (1694), where Stahl was the champion of the vitalistic "sensitive soul," and Hoffmann the advocate of a mechanistic conception of the body. Actual research on nervous mechanisms (promising in themselves) only encouraged Hoffman to ascribe illness to tensions—in other words, to revive this ancient type of pathologic theory. Hoffmann influenced Cullen at Edinburgh, whence Rush brought the thesis to Philadelphia after 1765. The latter subsequently elaborated it into the most popular and also most dangerous "system" in America. In order to overcome tension, he urged that a patient sometimes should be relieved of three-fourths of all the blood in his body!

Here, again, we have what was in a sense retrogression. It will be noted that German influence on American medi-

cine was largely indirect; although a few German doctors came to the Colonies, and various Americans read German works either in Latin or in the vernacular. Only Pennsylvania was directly influenced by German theory or practice. This is well illustrated in the person of Henry Melchior Muhlenberg. Trained at Halle in the days of Stahl and Hoffmann, Muhlenberg avoided extreme support of either of their theories; though his emphasis upon psycho-somatic
16 relationships suggests the impact of Stahl's vitalism on his thought. Coming to America in order to organize the Lutheran churches, the German leader found time to practice medicine on a considerable scale—employing the remedies of Halle in combination with religious exhortation. His approach was different from that of earlier clerical physicians, however, since his university training had introduced him to the spirit of the *Aufklärung*. He rejected crude empiricism and the occult, and practiced only in the absence of those whom he considered as qualified physicians.[1]

A final illustration of the way in which sound investigations often confused medical thought before 1800, is afforded by Rush's advocacy of a tension pathology. It was actually the early effort to identify specific diseases—so desirable in itself—which led him to revert to this ancient speculation *via* Hoffmann and Cullen. For early identification, as noted, was based upon symptoms alone; and these—with their innumerable combinations—had led by the 1780's to lists of over 1500 so-called diseases. Rush decided that order could be restored here only by reverting to the other extreme, in holding that there really was only one disease; that is, an all-pervading hypertension in the vascular system. He failed, as did his compatriots, to see that there was a middle way out of the maze—the correlation of symptoms with pathologic findings which has been mentioned.

[1] I am indebted to my student, the Rev. Mr. W. E. Fisher, for this data on Muhlenberg.

Various other examples of the medical confusion caused by even valid research could be cited; for example, the controversy over the relative values of acids and of alkalies as drugs, which was occasioned by studies in chemistry. The truth is that medicine, as already suggested, was unable to use effectively the scientific developments in physics, biology, and chemistry—or the improved methods which made these possible—until it had first discovered with what it was dealing. Its primary subject was human illness, and this was a 17
far more complex phenomenon than were those handled by the physical disciplines. All biologic sciences must first go through a taxonomic stage, since their data must be put in order before they can be employed in research on an analytic level. In botany, this was a matter of identifying and classifying species; in medicine, it involved discovering the diseases. Prior to this, physicians could only accept unverified theories; yet on these theories they based a practice which affected the very lives of the entire population.

Notice that it was again a social factor—the fact that patients could not wait for a sound science—which made it impossible to pursue the internal logic of medicine in an orderly manner. Botanists could postpone theories about the origin of species until a large number of these had been found; but physicians must have their pathologic theories at once if they were to attain any rational approach to practice. Under these circumstances, objective studies in physical science or even in special branches of medicine only enlivened speculation. This was the general picture of American medicine in the eighteenth century. Fortunately, amidst all this confusion, a few Europeans continued the pathologic studies which eventually provided medicine with a sound taxonomy. Such research was on the right track by the end of the eighteenth century; but few physicians—and practically no Americans—were even aware of this.

We should not be too severe, in retrospect, in judging the Americans on this score. All of them were immersed in practice and were handicapped, in addition, by the demand for immediate, practical results which has been noted. Perhaps we should recall the better practitioners as men who were at least devoted to their patients and to their art, and who—in the larger towns—labored successfully to improve the status of their guild. These achievements would prove of value even to future science; since when European re-
18 search was later imported to these shores, it was essential to have here a profession capable of making the most of it.

Currency Finance: An Interpretation of Colonial Monetary Practices

E. James Ferguson*

THE accepted view of the financial and monetary history of the American colonies needs revision. It owes too much to the influence of nineteenth-century scholars who were themselves partisans in currency disputes. In their own day, William G. Sumner, Albert S. Bolles, Charles J. Bullock, and Andrew M. Davis stood for "sound money" against inflationist movements. One of their chief aims was to show the disastrous effects of wandering off the straight line of a sound-money policy.[1] Hence, they studied those colonies whose money depreciated and relied on the opinions of such eighteenth-century controversialists as Dr. William Douglass, Thomas Hutchinson, and others in whose views they concurred.[2] With the notable exception of Andrew M. Davis, who did a

* Mr. Ferguson teaches at the University of Maryland. The present study is a phase of work in progress on a financial history of the United States from 1775 to 1793.

[1] See a review by Curtis Nettels of Richard A. Lester, *Monetary Experiments, Early American and Recent Scandinavian* (Princeton, 1939), in *English Historical Review*, LVI (1941), 333.

[2] The treatment of the colonies in William Graham Sumner, *A History of American Currency* (New York, 1874) is hardly a serious effort, and the same can be said of the earlier work of William M. Gouge, *A Short History of Paper Money and Banking in the United States, Including an Account of Provincial and Continental Paper Money*, 2nd ed. (New York, 1835). Of considerably greater merit are two studies of particular colonies: Joseph B. Felt, *An Historical Account of Massachusetts Currency* (Boston, 1839) and Henry Bronson, "An Historical Account of Connecticut Currency, Continental Money, and the Finances of the Revolution," New Haven Historical Society, *Papers*, I (1865), 1-192 (separate pagination following page 170). Early works displaying another bias are Henry Phillips, *Historical Sketches of the Paper Currency of the American Colonies, Prior to the adoption of the Federal Constitution* (Roxbury, Mass., 1865-1866) and John H. Hickcox, *A History of the Bills of Credit or Paper Money Issued by New York from 1709 to 1789* (Albany, 1866). The book by Phillips includes surveys of several colonies, written by different authors.

The case against paper money as drawn by nineteenth-century historians rested heavily on the data and opinions supplied by William Douglass, *A Discourse Concerning the Currencies of the British Plantations in America* (Boston, 1740). This treatise came out of a bitter controversy and was highly partisan. A careful reading shows how deeply the local situation in New England colored Douglass's attitudes

scholarly work on Massachusetts,[3] they were interested in the colonies chiefly as background to the financial history of the Revolution. Their works in the latter field incorporated study in primary sources and were generally accepted as authoritative.[4]

The pattern they stamped on historical interpretation still survives in its major outlines. Recent books sometimes modify their harsher judgments and bring in new material, but the interpretation rests largely on the story they told of paper money in Massachusetts, Rhode Island, and the Carolinas. These were the provinces where depreciation created a
20 major problem. Neglect of other colonies whose experiments were more

---

and his judgment of the situation in other colonies. Even in the case of New England, he correctly attributed depreciation to the uncontrolled emissions of one province, Rhode Island. His observations on other colonies are not reliable.

[3] Andrew M. Davis, *Currency and Banking in the Province of the Massachusetts-Bay,* American Economic Association, *Publications,* 3rd ser., I (1900), no. 4. Davis was a careful and honest scholar, but his main concern was to expose the evils of fiat money. He relied, for example, on the testimony of Thomas Hutchinson and Douglass, although his chapter on sources listed without comment works by Franklin and Thomas Pownall, as well as secondary accounts, which gave quite another view of colonial currency. It must be said, however, that these sources related to provinces outside New England and therefore lay beyond the immediate scope of his study. See *ibid.,* I, 413-435.

The same year that Davis's essay came out, Charles J. Bullock published *Essays in the Monetary History of the United States* (New York, 1900), which included a general survey of colonial currency and more detailed treatment of North Carolina and New Hampshire. The latter studies were based on research in primary sources and are of value.

[4] Charles J. Bullock, *The Finances of the United States from 1775 to 1789, with Especial Reference to the Budget* (Madison, 1895), University of Wisconsin, *Bulletin, Economics, Political Science and History Series,* I (1895), no 2; William Graham Sumner, *The Financier and the Finances of the American Revolution,* (New York, 1891); Albert S. Bolles, *Financial History of the United States from 1774 to 1789* (New York, 1879). None of these works gives much space to the colonies. Bolles dismisses their financial history as a "dark and disgraceful picture" and, in another place, writes: "nowhere had the experiment [paper money] worked satisfactorily except in Pennsylvania." *Ibid.,* 29, 56-57. It is interesting that Bolles made an exception of Pennsylvania. His later book, *Pennsylvania, Province and State* (Philadelphia, 1899), praises the paper money system of that province. See *ibid.,* I, 243-251, 262-265, 396-398. Had he studied other colonies at first hand, he might have altered his general conclusions.

Another influential work published at the turn of the nineteenth century was Davis R. Dewey, *Financial History of the United States* (New York, 1903). Dewey was circumspect, avoiding gross errors of fact or judgment in his treatment of colonial and Revolutionary finance. His reliance on existing secondary works molded his interpretation into the customary formula.

fortunate conveys the impression that paper money typically depreciated and was harmful to the community.

A correlated idea is that paper money was significant mainly as a ground of conflict between colonial debtors and creditors. No doubt this view is more readily accepted because it fits in with the Turner hypothesis. Here again, Massachusetts furnishes the prime example. The land bank controversy of 1740 is portrayed as a struggle of creditors against debtors, coastal merchants against back-country farmers. Other instances can be found in the early history of South Carolina.

While the debtor-creditor thesis has logical probability and a founda- 21
tion in fact, it is nonetheless inadequate when viewed in a perspective embracing the whole development of the American colonies. Historians generally concede, for example, that in most provinces, a propertied aristocracy dominated the government. The debtor-creditor thesis, broadly considered, affords no sufficient explanation for the fact that in the half century before the Revolution, these aristocratic bodies regularly and persistently issued paper money.[5] The thesis is also at odds with the fact that in the middle provinces, at least, mercantile groups strongly opposed the act of Parliament which prevented the colonies from making paper money a legal tender in private transactions. On the assumption that serious internal conflict existed between debtor and creditor, the stand taken by merchants would be inexplicable.

Several accounts of individual provinces appearing in the last few decades appraise the fiat money methods of the colonies in their setting. As the authors have stayed close to primary sources and have extended their range beyond New England, they depict a more successful use of paper money.[6] The collective influence of these works has not been as

[5] Conflict between colonial debtors and British creditors may explain the interest of wealthy planters and merchants in currency expansion, but even this proposition needs careful investigation. The extent to which British merchants as a whole favored restriction of colonial currency varied with conditions in the colonies to which they traded.

[6] Cf. Kathryn L. Behrens, *Paper Money in Maryland* (Baltimore, 1923), in Johns Hopkins University, *Studies in Historical and Political Science*, 41, no. 1; Clarence P. Gould, *Money and Transportation in Maryland, 1720-1765* (Baltimore, 1915), in Johns Hopkins University, *Studies in Historical and Political Science*, 33, no. 1; Carl Lotus Becker, *History of Political Parties in the Province of New York, 1760-1776* (Madison, 1909), in University of Wisconsin, *Bulletin, History Series*, II, no. 1. Historians of Pennsylvania all praise the colony's paper money. Winfred T. Root, *The Relations of Pennsylvania with the British Government, 1696-1765* (New York, 1912), is not

great as one might suppose. Curtis P. Nettels has added a general study of monetary affairs; unfortunately, it covers only the period before 1720, when the colonies were just beginning to employ paper currency.[7]

There are signs, however, that the dogmas which have prejudiced research are giving way. Fiat money is now the rule, and most economists have ceased to believe that currency must be convertible into gold or silver. Governments freely manipulate currency, as a means of economic control. In this frame of reference, the ways of the American colonies acquire new significance. An economist, Richard A. Lester, explores their use of paper money in the attempt to curb economic depression.[8] He finds
22 that their tactics were analogous to those of the New Deal and bore some ancestral relationship to present-day Keynesian doctrine. The most promising effort, however, is an unpublished doctoral dissertation by Leslie Van Horn Brock,[9] which displays a grasp of colonial usages and attitudes

---

enthusiastic, but see Bolles, *Pennsylvania, Province and State,* and Isaac Sharpless, *Two Centuries of Pennsylvania History* (Philadelphia, 1900). Isaac S. Harrell, *Loyalism in Virginia* (Durham, 1926), is the best discussion of that province yet in print, though it is very brief. William Roy Smith, *South Carolina as a Royal Province, 1719-1776* (New York, 1903), is most extensive. Historians of North Carolina have left the subject very vague. Except for the early study included in Bullock's *Essays in the Monetary History of the United States,* which is somewhat lacking in coherence, there is no satisfactory treatment published. For an abbreviated pamphlet see Mattie Erma Parker, *Money Problems of Early Tar Heels,* issued by the North Carolina Historical Commission (Raleigh, 1942). Herbert L. Osgood, *The American Colonies in the Eighteenth Century* (New York, 1924), gives money and finance far less attention than they merit, although his brief treatment is well-considered. The other multi-volumed histories leave the subject virtually untouched. Other works will be cited in discussing particular colonies.

[7] Curtis P. Nettels, *The Money Supply of the American Colonies Before 1720* (Madison, 1934), in University of Wisconsin, *Studies in the Social Sciences and History,* no. 20.

[8] Lester makes the colonies appear more self-conscious in attempting to regulate prices by currency manipulation than they probably were, but his provocative essays, though based on limited research, have nevertheless opened a new approach to colonial economic history. Richard A. Lester, "Currency Issues to Overcome Depressions in Pennsylvania, 1723 and 1729," *Journal of Political Economy,* XLVI (1938), 324-375; and "Currency Issues to Overcome Depressions in Delaware, New Jersey, New York and Maryland, 1715-1737," *ibid.,* XLVII (1939), 182-217. Lester recapitulates this material in *Monetary Experiments, Early American and Recent Scandinavian.*

[9] The Currency of the American Colonies, 1700 to 1764 (Doctoral Dissertation, University of Michigan, 1941). Brock's conclusions fully support those advanced in this paper. See *ibid.,* 528-563.

seldom found in older studies. When such works as these attract more notice, other scholars may be persuaded to explore a field which is rich in implications for social and economic history.

Until more evidence is brought together, any general conclusions must be tentative. The formulations attempted in this paper are, therefore, exploratory and subject to correction. It seems possible, however, to qualify older interpretations and point out the tendency of future research. An effort will be made to show that in the middle colonies, from New York to Maryland, paper money was successful. Secondly, it will be argued that except in New England and the Carolinas, paper money did not 23
engender any great conflict between broad classes of the population. Finally, the system of paper money will be described in general terms and an attempt made to define the essential features of "currency finance."

In judging the success of paper money, the first question is whether it depreciated. The answer cannot always be explicit. Different authors do not mean exactly the same thing by the word *depreciation*. Older historians were inclined to go by the rate of exchange. If currency passed below its legal rate[10] in trade for hard money or in the purchase of bills of exchange, they considered that it had depreciated and inferred that too much had been issued or that people lacked confidence in fiat money. This was certainly true in colonies like Rhode Island, Massachusetts, and the Carolinas, where currency sank to low levels. In colonies where fluctuations in the value of money were only moderate, however, a discount on currency in exchange for specie or sterling bills did not necessarily imply that the currency was unsound. Historians of such provinces refer to

[10] Colonial accounts were kept in terms of pounds and shillings. In the seventeenth century, provincial governments began enacting laws which placed a higher value on Spanish and other coins than these coins were worth in British sterling. In an effort to attract hard money, the colonies vied with one another in raising the legal value of foreign coin. To preserve some kind of uniformity, the Board of Trade prepared a royal proclamation, issued in 1704, which allowed the colonies to fix a value of up to £133 on coins worth £100 in sterling. The crown thus sanctioned a double standard, by which the pound in America might be valued less, in terms of silver, than the British pound. At the so-called proclamation rate, £100 sterling was worth £133 in colonial proclamation money. Evading royal and Parliamentary restrictions, however, the colonies raised the legal value of coin even higher.

When they came to issue paper currency, the colonies placed different values on their bills (in terms of coin or silver). In some colonies the proclamation rate was maintained and colonial "current money" passed legally at £133 to £100 sterling. In other colonies the legal ratio was as high as £178 to £100 sterling. For a discussion of this matter, see Nettels, *Money Supply*, 162-181, 229-249.

paper money as stable, even though its value sometimes sank in relationship to specie.

It was normal to discount currency somewhat in exchange for hard money. First of all, the colonies sought to attract foreign coin by giving it a high legal value. They fixed such rates that hard money equivalent to £100 British sterling was legally worth from £133 to around £175 in the currency of different provinces.[11] This was the legal rate. But hard money ordinarily commanded a premium beyond this, for it had more uses than paper. It was more negotiable in payments to foreigners and in inter-colonial transactions.

24 Besides a general preference for hard money, other factors sometimes worked to bring about a further discount on paper money. Detailed information on the processes of colonial trade is lacking, but it appears that most payments to Britain were made in bills of exchange, that is, drafts payable in Britain which the colonists procured largely by shipments of cargoes. The availability of sterling bills in America depended on the condition of trade. When British purchases fell off and the colonies shipped less than would pay for their imports, sterling bills became scarce and expensive, and people sought hard money to make payments abroad. Specie and bills of exchange rose in value relative to paper money. On the other hand, there were times during the French and Indian War when the colonies enormously increased the volume of their domestic currency, yet the exchange with specie remained constant or even improved because large British expenditures, decreased importations, and a greater supply of specie at hand reduced the need for hard money.[12] Circumstances beyond the control of colonial governments affected the rate of exchange, regardless of how scrupulously the colonies managed their paper money or how good its credit was at home.

[11] It should be understood that the term *specie* was used in a double sense in the eighteenth century. It denoted a standard of value, legally established by the colonies. Thus, at the proclamation rate, £133 specie would equal £100 sterling, or an equivalent amount of silver. But the term also meant actual silver or gold, i.e., hard money. When the latter meaning is intended, the phrase "in specie" will be used, or the sense otherwise clarified by the context.

[12] Exchange rates are discussed in Anne Bezanson, Robert D. Gray, Miriam Hussey, *Prices in Colonial Pennsylvania* (Philadelphia, 1935), 314-336. A contemporary analysis may be found in the valuable public letters of Robert Carter Nicholas, provincial treasurer of Virginia, "Paper Money in Colonial Virginia," *William and Mary Quarterly,* 1st ser., XX (1911-1912), 254-256. See also Jerman Baker to Duncan Rose, February 15, 1764, *ibid.,* 1st ser., XII (1903-1904), 241.

The most accurate test of the stability of paper money would be its value in exchange for commodities sold in colonial markets. An adequate price study exists for Pennsylvania, and there is some information for a few other colonies.[13] Unfortunately, this kind of data is fragmentary, and historians usually have to depend on scattered figures and the casual remarks found in contemporary letters.

The weight of evidence suggests, however, that in the middle colonies fluctuations were not great enough to impair the credit or utility of paper money. Historians agree that Pennsylvania "maintained the system without fear of repudiation and to the manifest benefit of the province."[14] 25
It appears that for the half century before the Revolution, the domestic price level was more uniform than in any succeeding period of equal length.[15] The emissions of New Jersey and Delaware are said to have been stable and to have passed usually at par with that of Pennsylvania.[16] New York's currency was highly regarded, and the colony's ability to keep its bills at par was a "subject for special commendation."[17]

[13] Arthur H. Cole, *Wholesale Commodity Prices in the United States, 1700-1861* (Cambridge, 1938), has price studies for Boston, New York, Philadelphia and Charleston.

[14] Sharpless, *Two Centuries of Pennsylvania History,* 115-116, 119, 134-136; Bolles, *Pennsylvania, Province and State,* I, 243-251, 262-265, 396-398. Favorable testimony can be found in nearly all commentators, modern or contemporary. See Adam Smith's famous observations on the subject in *Wealth of Nations,* Modern Library ed. (New York, 1937), 311.

[15] According to Lester, "Currency Issues in Pennsylvania," 373. See the concluding chapter in Bezanson, *Prices in Colonial Pennsylvania.*

[16] Richard P. McCormick, *Experiment in Independence, New Jersey in the Critical Period, 1781-1789* (New Brunswick, 1950), 190-191, 233-234; Brock, Currency of the American Colonies, 93-99, 391-409; Lester, "Currency Issues in Delaware, New York and Maryland," 185-186, 192, 199, 216; Phillips, *Historical Sketches of Paper Currency,* I, 67-76; Richard S. Rodney, *Colonial Finances in Delaware* (Wilmington, 1928), 23.

[17] Becker, *Political Parties in New York,* 66-67; Lester, "Currency Issues in Delaware, New Jersey, New York and Maryland," 207, 216; Brock, Currency of the American Colonies, 66-74, 336-353. Nettels, *Money Supply,* 273-274, refers to New York's early bills as depreciated. His statement appears to rest on a decline in the rate of exchange occurring about 1717. The general opinion in colonial times, however, was that New York had a very sound currency. Even A. M. Davis admitted that New York as well as Pennsylvania were "partially immune from the severe penalties paid by the New England colonies for their infatuation." Davis, *Currency and Banking in Massachusetts-Bay,* 427. See Edmund B. O'Callaghan, ed., *Documents Relative to the Colonial History of the State of New York* (Albany, 1853-1887), VII, 884-885. Clarence W. Loke, The Currency Question in the Province of New York, 1764-1771 (Master's thesis, University of Wisconsin, 1941), Appendix D, sur-

Maryland's first emission of 1753 depreciated, even though well-secured, apparently because tobacco remained the primary medium of exchange. Later her bills rose in value and by 1764 were reported "locked up in the Chests of the Wealthy" for the sake of the interest falling due on them.[18] Thereafter, in spite of heavy additions, the bills held their value. "As a colony," writes a modern scholar, "Maryland had solved the problem of a paper currency."[19]

The provinces further south had trouble with their currency. Until 1755, Virginia supplemented the hard money in circulation with tobacco notes, which passed in local exchange and payment of taxes. But the
26 coming of the French and Indian War forced the colony to emit paper money. The bills held their value until 1760, when a sharp break in tobacco prices marked the onset of a long and severe depression. For the next several years, planters could hardly sell their crops, and prices stayed very low. A shortage of the planter balances ordinarily arising from tobacco sales in Britain caused bills of exchange and specie to grow scarce, and their value rose in terms of the currency offered by planters obliged to make payments to British creditors. Virginia currency was discounted as much as 50 per cent to 60 per cent in purchase of bills of exchange. Although specie was extremely scarce, the colony did not put aside its plans to retire war-time paper emissions, and it probably contributed to the easement of conditions that the treasurer of the province, John Robinson, restored some £100,000 to circulation through secret loans to hard-pressed planters. Robinson's defalcations probably occurred in 1765 and 1766. It appears, however, that the decline in Virginia's currency in these and pre-

---

veys newspaper price quotations for tea, pork, wheat, sugar, and molasses, finding them stable from 1760 to 1775.

Writing generally of the middle colonies, Lester says: "In all, except Maryland for the first few years, the exchange value of the currency seems not to have fallen more than about 30 per cent in terms of gold and silver for any year during the period of fifty or sixty years that these colonies were on a paper standard prior to the Revolutionary War." "Currency Issues in Pennsylvania," 325.

[18] Jerome Baker to Duncan Rose, February 15, 1764, *William and Mary Quarterly*, 1st ser., XII (1903-1904), 240.

[19] Behrens, *Paper Money in Maryland*, 9-58; Gould, *Money and Transportation in Maryland*, 87-105. The Maryland legislature reported in 1787 that more than £238,000 in colonial currency and above £200,000 issued by the Revolutionary convention passed at par with specie until August, 1776. Address of the Maryland House of Delegates to their Constituents [1787], Broadsides, Portfolio 28, no. 24, Rare Books Division, Library of Congress.

ceding years owed little to Robinson's private emissions, but was rather the result of trade depression. In the last years of the decade, the value rose, and by 1771 it was reported that the British merchants who had formerly complained of paper money were among its warmest advocates.[20]

In the Carolinas, depreciation was severe, though it occurred for the most part early in the eighteenth century, when these colonies were thinly populated and undeveloped. Clearly, however, the legislature of North Carolina did little to sustain its first emissions, and the bills steadily depreciated. In 1748, they were called in to be exchanged for new bills at the
rate of 7½ to 1. The new bills fluctuated thereafter around a point con- 27
siderably below their nominal value, but were rising towards the end of the colonial period, when the British government kept the legislature under close rein.[21]

A different situation prevailed in South Carolina, where all the depreciation occurred before 1731. The infant colony was then under heavy financial strain resulting from war. Debtor elements found the depreciation to their liking, however, and tried to maintain the downward trend. They were overcome after a bitter struggle. The currency was stabilized in 1731 at the rate of 7 to 1 of sterling, which remained unchanged until the Revolution. During its maturity, the province had a stable currency and a record of successful management.[22]

[20] There is no good modern account of Virginia's financial history. Two published contemporary sources are "Paper Money in Colonial Virginia" and letters to the assembly's English agent, "Proceedings of the Virginia Committee of Correspondence, 1759-67," *The Virginia Magazine of History and Biography*, X(1902-1903), 337-356; XI (1903-1904), 1-25, 131-143, 345-357; XII (1904-1905), 1-14, 225-240, 353-364. The recent biography by David John Mays, *Edmund Pendleton, 1721-1803* (Cambridge, 1952) has a vivid story of these years of depression, told as an incident of the long-term decline of the tobacco planters. Mays has a full account of the Robinson affair. *Edmund Pendleton*, I, 142-149, 174-188. See also Brock, Currency of the American Colonies, 467-497; George Louis Beer, *British Colonial Policy, 1754-1765* (New York, 1907), 179-188.

[21] The most coherent account of North Carolina's finances is in Brock, Currency of the American Colonies, 106-113, 428-446, Table 22. Brock draws from Bullock, *Essays on Monetary History*, 125-183.

North Carolina's paper money suffered, among other things, from the fact that commodities were employed as a tender in all transactions and "in the public mind were the 'money' of the province." Parker, *Money Problems of Early Tar Heels*, 7-8. Also, like Virginia and Maryland, North Carolina established public warehouses, whose receipts for deposits of tobacco constituted another medium of exchange.

[22] About £106,500 in legal tender bills circulated without any provision for redemption. The government met annual expenses by issuing "public orders" and

Constancy of value was not, in many minds, the sole test of a currency.. Another criterion is suggested by the remark of Thomas Pownall, that in spite of the depreciation in New England, "it was never yet objected that it injured them in trade."[23] Thomas Hancock, one of the greatest merchants in America, seems at one time not to have been altogether convinced that paper money was an unmitigated evil, though he had dealt in a depreciated medium all his life. Of the legislation which placed Massachusetts on a sound money basis, he said: "This d——d Act has turn'd all Trade out of doors and it's Impossible to get debts in, either in Dollars or Province Bills."[24] No study has been made of the economic
28 effects of depreciation in the provinces where it occurred. It is possible that a steady and continuing inflation was not wholly injurious to an expanding country whose people seldom had fixed incomes or large stores of liquid capital.

Even if stability is taken as the sole rule in judging the success of colonial currency, the record is not entirely black. The depreciation in New England was mainly the fault of Rhode Island, whose emissions flooded the unitary economy of that area and undermined the currency of her neighbors. Elsewhere, North Carolina was the leading offender. The colonies, it must be said, did not have complete freedom to act. Each of them felt, in varying degree, the weight of British authority, which was always cast on the side of moderation in the use of currency. Nevertheless, the predominating fact was not the failure of paper money but its success and good credit—in the colonies from New York to Maryland, and in Virginia, as well as in South Carolina during its later development.

"tax certificates" which, although not legal tender in private transactions, functioned as a supplemental currency. This additional paper passed at par with the legal tender bills. Smith, *South Carolina as a Royal Province*, 228-279; Robert L. Meriwether, *The Expansion of South Carolina, 1729-1765* (Kingsport, Tenn., 1940), 8-9; Brock, Currency of the American Colonies, 115-127, 446-462; Alexander Hewatt, *An Historical Account of the Rise and Progress of the Colonies of South Carolina and Georgia* (London, 1779), II, 58; Cole, *Wholesale Commodity Prices*, 52-53; Osgood, *American Colonies in the Eighteenth Century*, 371-383.

Georgia was undeveloped as a colony, and her monetary affairs will not be discussed.

[23] Pownall also observed that the trade of North and South Carolina went on as usual, in spite of depreciation. Thomas Pownall, *The Administration of the Colonies*, 4th ed. (London, 1768), 220, 221.

[24] Quoted by William T. Baxter, *The House of Hancock* (Cambridge, 1945), 112. This book is a valuable addition to economic history.

Serious conflicts between debtors and creditors did not arise when paper money stayed near par value. Ideally, perhaps, men of property would have preferred a circulation of coin or a currency backed by precious metals. Practically, however, most of them shared the popular belief that there was no alternative to the existing system. "Contrary to the traditions that historians have perpetuated," writes a modern student of economic thought, "a critical analysis of the contemporary literature indicates that the proponents as well as the critics were not poor debtors or agrarians, but for the most part officials, ministers, merchants, and men of substance and learning in general."[25]

29

Pennsylvania's currency was esteemed by all classes and regarded as having contributed to the growth and prosperity of the colony. In his widely read work on colonial affairs, Thomas Pownall wrote that there "never was a wiser or a better measure, never one better calculated to serve the uses of an encreasing country . . . never a measure more steadily pursued, nor more faithfully executed for forty years together."[26] Merchants and traders of Philadelphia formally opposed the restraining act of 1764 which prevented the colonies from making paper money legal tender.[27] As colonial agent in England, Benjamin Franklin fought the enactment of the law and afterward wrote pamphlets urging its repeal.[28] Franklin joined other colonial representatives and English merchants to argue the case for repeal before British ministers and members of Parliament. By 1767, the American agents planned to secure the introduction

[25] Joseph Dorfman, *The Economic Mind in American Civilization* (New York, 1948-1949), I, 142. Dorfman's comment must be given additional weight in view of the fact that most of the spokesmen he considers were from New England.

[26] Pownall, *Administration of the Colonies,* 185. Pownall referred to Pennsylvania's land bank.

[27] See a merchant petition in Samuel Hazard, *The Register of Pennsylvania* (Philadelphia, 1828-1835), II, 222-223. John Dickinson wrote against the restraining act, giving high praise to Pennsylvania's paper money system. [John Dickinson], "The Late Regulations Respecting the British Colonies on the Continent of America, Considered . . . ," *The Political Writings of John Dickinson* (Wilmington, 1801), I, 54-58.

[28] Franklin's views are well known. He had long been an advocate of paper money, though he did not favor making it legal tender in private transactions. See Albert H. Smyth, ed., *The Writings of Benjamin Franklin* (New York, 1905-1907), II, 133-155; Carl Van Doren, ed., *Letters and Papers of Benjamin Franklin and Richard Jackson, 1753-1785* (Philadelphia, 1947), 125-135. Franklin's opinions, as well as his effort to get the restraining act repealed, are treated in Lewis James Carey, *Franklin's Economic Views* (New York, 1928), 1-24.

of a repealing act into Parliament. They gave up the idea only when it became known that Parliament would very likely insist that the price of such a concession must be the surrender by the colonies of permanent revenues to the crown.[29]

Franklin told the House of Commons that restrictions on paper money were among the leading reasons why the American provinces had become alienated from the mother country.[30] In 1774, the First Continental Congress cited the restraining act among the violations of colonial rights.[31]

New York merchants also protested the restraining act. The assembly appointed a committee of New York county members, whose duties
30 included corresponding with other provinces and the colonial agent with respect to the act.[32] Governor Moore espoused the cause and repeatedly asked the Board of Trade to sanction an emission on the terms desired by the province.[33] The assembly refused aid to British troops unless the crown approved a currency bill, and, according to Carl Becker, opposition to the Townshend Acts had one of its sources in this grievance. Popular unrest was stilled not only by the repeal of the duties, but also by a special act of Parliament which allowed the colony to issue paper money.[34]

Public opinion in Maryland, according to historians of the province, was nearly unanimous in favor of paper money. Among the beneficiaries of the currency system were many of the most prominent men of the

[29] Carey, *Franklin's Economic Views*, 19-24; Van Doren, *Letters of Franklin and Jackson*, 196-197; Verner Crane, "Benjamin Franklin and the Stamp Act," Colonial Society of Massachusetts, *Transactions, 1933-1937* (1937), 57-58; Franklin to Joseph Galloway, June 13, 1767, Smythe, *Works of Franklin*, V, 25-28; Osgood Hanbury and Capel Hanbury (London commissioners for the Maryland Bank of England stock) to Charles Hammond, George Steuart, and John Price, May 6 and May 21, 1767, Black Books, V, 19, 20, Maryland Hall of Records, Annapolis.

[30] John Bigelow, ed., *The Complete Works of Benjamin Franklin* (New York, 1887-1888), III, 418.

[31] Worthington C. Ford and others, eds., *Journals of the Continental Congress, 1774-1789* (Washington, 1904-1937), I, 71.

[32] Becker, *Political Parties in New York*, 26-27; Hickcox, *Bills of Credit Issued by New York*, 43-46. Two memorials of the legislature are printed in *Journals of the Votes and Proceedings of the General Assembly of the Colony of New York, 1743-1765* (New York, 1766), II, 779, 799. Mercantile objection to the restraining act is noted by Arthur M. Schlesinger, *Colonial Merchants and the American Revolution, 1763-1776* (New York, 1918), 55-56.

[33] O'Callaghan, *New York Colonial Documents*, VII, 820-821, 878, 884-885, VIII, 1, 72, 169-170. Lieutenant-Governor Colden also pressed the legislature's demands. *Ibid.*, VIII, 189, 206.

[34] *Ibid.*, VIII, 189; Becker, *Political Parties in New York*, 26, 69-80, 88.

colony, who received loans from the government. The list included a "surprising number" of merchants. After Parliamentary restrictions were laid down in 1764, all classes concurred in the need for further emissions, and Maryland's agents in London tried to get the act repealed.[35]

In spite of the notorious depreciation which afflicted North Carolina's emissions, paper money does not seem to have been a major factor in the sectional antagonisms of that colony. Both houses of a legislature presumably dominated by the "court house ring" petitioned the crown in 1768 to approve paper money legislation. At a time when the Regulator Movement in the backcountry had begun to split the colony into warring 31
factions, Governor Tryon added his pleas to those of the legislature. His letters to the Board of Trade repeated familiar arguments, which, coming from less responsible sources, have often been dismissed as the pretence of debtors trying to evade their obligations. He said a larger circulating medium was necessary and that much distress arose from the lack of it.[36]

In South Carolina, the early struggle between debtors and creditors was never quite forgotten, but in time the memory grew so dim that the contemporary historian, David Ramsay, could write: "From New-York to Georgia there had never been in matters relating to money, an instance of a breach of public faith."[37] On the basis of his personal recollection, no doubt, he wrote that the use of paper money "had been similar from the first settlement of the colonies, and under proper restrictions had been found highly advantageous."[38] Another historian of the province, Alexander Hewatt, an extreme foe of paper money at the time he wrote, acknowledged the benefit of currency emissions to a "growing colony" like South Carolina, provided they were kept within bounds.[39]

[35] Gould, *Money and Transportation in Maryland,* 105, 109; Behrens, *Paper Money in Maryland,* 45, 47-48.

[36] William L. Saunders, ed., *The State [and Colonial] Records of North Carolina (Goldsboro,* 1886-1907), VII, 679, 680, 681, 682, VIII, 11-12.

[37] David Ramsay, *The History of the American Revolution* (Dublin, 1793), 437.

[38] *Ibid.,* 432. A modern historian remarks that the crown had so long protected Charleston merchants against inflation they had become "oblivious of danger." Smith, *South Carolina as a Royal Province,* 279. See *ibid.,* 234-235.

[39] Writing after the inflation of the Revolution, Hewatt said the colonies would have been better off if they had never known paper money. But elsewhere in his history, he acknowledged that South Carolina's first emissions were "absolutely necessary" to pay war expenses and that paper money supplied a circulating medium which the colony's economic growth required. Hewatt, *An Historical Account of South Carolina and Georgia,* I, 155-156, 205-206, II, 54-58.

Virginia's treasurer, Robert Carter Nicholas, expressed the view of a conservative planter. In a public defense of the government's conduct in emitting paper money, he declared that the outbreak of the French and Indian War had made it absolutely necessary. Sufficient funds could be obtained in no other way, and, though hesitant at first, the assembly found no other course open. Nicholas himself knew well the dangers of a paper medium and was conversant with the arguments against it, including the pamphlet of William Douglass, its ardent foe in New England. But Nicholas believed that the evils discovered in some places did not arise from paper money as such. "They have been chiefly, if not totally owing,"
32 he wrote, "either to these Bills of Credit not being established upon proper Funds, or to a Superabundance of them or to some Mismanagement." Granting a risk was involved, Nicholas believed that many countries had derived great benefit from paper money. He thought it had been helpful to Virginia.[40]

Nicholas's opinion was much like that of a conservative New York merchant, John Watts, who was highly critical of the restraining act of 1764. Like many others, Watts thought the act would virtually put an end to paper money. "The use of paper money is abolished as an evil," he complained, "when, properly treated, it is the only medium we have left of commerce and the only expedient in an exigency. Every man of estate here abominates the abuse of paper money, because the consequences fall upon himself, but there is just the same difference in the use and abuse of it as there is in food itself . . ."[41]

The writings of the post-Revolutionary era contain many allusions to the success of paper money in colonial times and the esteem in which it was then held. In 1786, a correspondent to a New York newspaper recalled how easily the provinces had maintained their paper money systems:[42]

Before the commencement of the late war, when public faith was still in possession of vestal chastity, divers of the states, then provinces, had large sums in circulation at full value, depending on funds calculated to redeem only five to ten per centum per annum of the amount issued; consequently it must

[40] "Paper Money in Colonial Virginia," 232-233, 244-247, 251, 254.

[41] Quoted in Leonard Woods Labaree, *Conservatism in Early American History* (New York, 1948), 51. See also pp. 48-55. In discussing conservative opinion on paper money, Labaree, like so many historians, draws heavily on New Englanders for expressions of hostility.

[42] "Thoughts on Banks and Paper Money," *Daily Advertiser*, February 2, 1786.

> be from ten to twenty years before the whole would be redeemed; and yet, tho' the money drew no interest . . . it circulated freely and at its full nominal value on a perfect equality with specie . . .

As this article appeared, the New York Chamber of Commerce made the same point in declaring its opposition to a paper money issue contemplated by the legislature. The Chamber of Commerce acknowledged that paper money had worked well in colonial times, but argued that this should not be taken as evidence that it would succeed under changed conditions.[43]

An observation frequently made in these times was put down by David Ramsay in his *History of the American Revolution*. Noting that Conti- 33
nental currency held its value during the first year or two of the war, even though it had no security behind it, Ramsay explained: "This was in some degree owing to a previous confidence, which had been begotten by honesty and fidelity, in discharging the engagements of government."[44] Alluding to the same fact, Financier Robert Morris observed: "There was a time when public confidence was higher in America than in any other country."[45]

The inflation of the Revolution destroyed that confidence, at least among propertied men, for they believed that paper money could never be a reliable instrument in an era when the whims of the people dictated, as they said, the policy of the government. A great proportion of the people, however, never lost the old affection for paper money. "From the earliest settlement of America," declared a petition composed in 1785 for presentation to the Pennsylvania legislature, "most of our improvements have been aided by the medium of paper currency . . . and your petitioners are persuaded that . . . public faith might be restored, and the ancient system revived, to the great ease of the inhabitants and emolument of the community."[46] Such an appeal invoked common knowledge.

It becomes clear that paper money occupied an important place in colonial affairs not because it embodied the aims of a particular class, but because it rendered important services to the community.

The circumstances which led to the adoption of paper money are well

[43] *Ibid.*, March 3, 1786.

[44] Ramsay, *History of the American Revolution*, 437. Ramsay's opinion of the trustworthiness of state governments was entirely different. See *ibid.*, 439-441.

[45] Francis Wharton, ed., *The Revolutionary Diplomatic Correspondence of the United States* (Washington, 1889), IV, 607.

[46] *Pennsylvania Packet*, March 4, 1785.

known. There was not enough hard money to provide a medium of trade for domestic transactions. Gold and silver coins flowed outward in purchase of British commodities and while in the colonies circulated mainly among merchants. Much business was done on the basis of book credits and debits,[47] but specie was nearly always in short supply. Economic depression intensified the problem, for when cargoes did not raise enough to meet debts owed abroad, specie had to be shipped. Domestic trade became almost wholly barter. People who had specie could get an exorbitant premium, and those forced to make payments in hard money faced difficulty. Provincial governments could not collect taxes. The inhabitants
34 felt the need of a medium of exchange which, unlike specie, would not "make unto itself wings and fly away."[48]

The colonies, therefore, adopted paper money. It was issued by two different processes. The first method, in point of time, was the direct emission of fiat money by the government to pay expenses, particularly the costs of war. The other method, which we shall consider immediately, was the emission of money through a loan-office or "land bank."

The land bank was the primary social legislation of colonial America. It was a method of putting currency into circulation and at the same time affording loans to farmers which they could scarcely obtain from other sources. Provincial governments set up loan offices which advanced currency to farmers at low rates of interest, taking mortgages on real property as security. An individual could usually get only a limited sum. He repaid the loan in annual installments over a period of years. Frequently, though not always, the bills were legal tender in private transactions; in any case, they were almost always accepted in payments to the govern-

[47] Baxter, *House of Hancock*, affords a valuable discussion of business practices.

[48] The quotation is from a circular printed (1779) in *Journals of the Continental Congress*, XV, 1057. The circular continues: "It [paper money] remains with us, it will not forsake us, it is always ready at hand for the purpose of commerce or taxes and every industrious man can find it."

The general problem of the currency is treated in many places. For a brief discussion, see Nettels, *Money Supply*, 202-203. Among contemporary sources, the preambles to money acts sometimes furnish an elaborate justification for the emission. Much testimony of the same kind is reproduced in the two articles by Richard A. Lester already cited. Pownall, *Administration of the Colonies*, 177-187 analyzes the problem at length. For comment on Britain's failure to appreciate the legitimate needs of the colonies, see Oliver M. Dickerson, *American Colonial Government* (Cleveland, 1912), 320; Phillips, *Historical Sketches of Paper Money*, I, 75; Charles M. Andrews, *The Colonial Period of American History* (New Haven, 1938), IV, 350-352.

ment for taxes, land, etc. As the annual installments due on the principal came back into the loan office, the bills were cancelled and retired, though they were often reissued, or successive banks established to keep up a continuous flow of loans. The colonies thus developed a medium of exchange out of "*solid* or *real* property . . . melted down and made to circulate in paper money or bills of credit."[49]

The land banks of the middle colonies were, from all accounts, markedly successful. Pennsylvania managed one almost continuously after 1723 without mishap. For more than twenty-five years before the French and Indian War, the interest received by the government from 35
money out on loan supported the costs of provincial administration, without the necessity of direct taxes. Relative freedom from taxation probably contributed to Pennsylvania's remarkable growth.[50]

Other middle colonies also obtained good results. New Jersey enacted three separate loans up to 1735, and the interest enabled the government to exist without direct taxation for sixteen years before 1751. Delaware issued land bank notes from 1723 to 1746, with apparent benefit to the province.[51] New York extended its land bank of 1737 until the last install-

[49] The quotation is from Address of the Maryland House of Delegates to their Constituents [1787], Broadsides, Portfolio 28, no. 24, Rare Books Division, Library of Congress.

[50] Robert Morris wrote, in 1782, of the "notorious" fact that farmers made 12 per cent on borrowed capital, which he said equalled profits in trade or the professions. It is not clear whether he spoke generally or merely alluded to the exceptional conditions which prevailed during the Revolution. *Journals of the Continental Congress,* XXII, 430.

On Pennsylvania's land bank, see above, notes 14 and 15; also, Lester, "Currency Issues in Pennsylvania," 357, 369; Brock, Currency of the American Colonies, 74-84; Pownall, *Administration of the Colonies,* 185-186; Van Doren, *Letters of Franklin and Jackson,* 81.

A search of the Pennsylvania statutes confirms the fact that the province long existed without direct taxes and even without substantial duties on imports. A property tax was passed in 1717 and no other enacted until after the outbreak of the French and Indian War (1755). See James T. Mitchell and Henry Flanders, comps., *The Statutes at Large of Pennsylvania, 1782-1801* (Harrisburg, 1896-1911), III, 128-138, 408-417, V, 201-212, 352-361.

[51] McCormick, *Experiment in Independence,* 190-191; Brock, Currency of the Colonies, 93-99, 391-409; Phillips, *Historical Sketches of Paper Currency,* 67-76; Lester, "Currency Issues to Overcome Depressions in Delaware, New Jersey, New York and Maryland," 183-199.

Donald L. Kemmerer, *Path to Freedom, the Struggle for Self Government in Colonial New Jersey, 1703-1776* (Princeton, 1940), is not sympathetic with the popular passion for paper money, though he leaves no doubt that New Jersey's experiments were successful.

ment of the principal fell due in 1768, at which time all classes demanded its renewal. The bank was reinstituted in 1771 by virtue of the special act of Parliament, of which mention has already been made. Governor Tryon's report in 1774 showed that the interest from loans comprised about half the revenue of the province, an amount which nearly matched expenses in time of peace.[52]

The notes which Maryland issued on loan in 1733 fell considerably below par, but later rose to nominal value. A modern historian writes:[53]

> Considering the peculiar benefits to grain and tobacco culture, the conveniences
> 36 offered to trade, the exceptionally high exchange that the bills maintained throughout most of their life, and the faithful redemption of every shilling at face value, it is hardly too much to say that this was the most successful paper money issued by any of the colonies.

A new bank was instituted in 1769, and the notes stayed at par until the Revolution.[54]

Virginia never adopted a land bank. In North and South Carolina, land banks figured in the early depreciation of paper money, and it became the settled policy of the British government to disallow acts for their establishment. Similarly, as is well known, the land banks of the New England colonies, particularly those of Rhode Island, contributed to the decline of currency in that area and brought on the first statutory regulation of paper money by Parliament.

This system of agricultural credit so widely practiced in the colonies would seem to be a subject of considerable importance for social and economic history, yet it has not received the attention it deserves. The economist, Richard A. Lester, offers a general view of the use of land bank emissions to curb depressions, and it may be added that such a background of experience explains why even after the financial chaos of the Revolution, the common people still looked to paper money for relief from hard times. But the subject has further ramifications. Agriculture's need for credit facilities has been a constant factor in American history

52 *The Colonial Laws of New York from the Year 1664 to the Revolution* (Albany, 1894), II, 1015-1040, IV, 708-710; O'Callaghan, *New York Colonial Documents,* VIII, 452-454.

53 Gould, *Money and Transportation in Maryland,* 111.

54 *Laws of Maryland made since M,DCC,LXIII . . .* (Annapolis, 1787), November sess., 1769, Chapter XIV; Behrens, *Paper Money in Maryland,* 46-58.

and a source of political unrest. Banks have served commerce and industry; until lately, agriculture remained at a disadvantage. It should be an interesting fact that colonial governments loaned money to farmers at low rates of interest. But no analysis has been made of the effects of land bank loans in the domestic economy, nor has anyone yet approached the general subject with sufficient breadth of view to place it in its relationship to the main currents of American development.[55]

The revenue problems of colonial governments were lessened by land bank emissions; taxes were more easily collected when citizens had access
to money. During the frequent wars of the eighteenth century, however, 37
the provinces developed another use of paper money. They emitted it to pay governmental expenses. The procedure became a rationalized system of public finance.

Provincial revenues were normally small and inflexible. Officials drew fees rather than salaries, and the few public services were performed mainly by local government. Such provinces as Pennsylvania and New York spent no more than £5,000 a year apart from war expenses.[56] Taxation was adjusted to limited needs. Imposts and excise taxes usually afforded a maintaining fund, while direct levies on polls and property raised what else was needed. None of these revenues could be freely expanded. Heavy duties on imports tended to drive off trade or cause smuggling. Direct taxes were often hard to collect and slow coming in.[57]

Colonial governments found it difficult or impossible to borrow money

[55] Earl Sylvester Sparks attempts it in the first chapter of his *History and Theory of Agricultural Credit in the United States* (New York, 1932), 1-19, but falls short of a contribution because the accounts upon which he relies are so few and one-sided.

[56] A State of the annual Expense of the several Establishments of the British Colonies in North America . . . C. O., 323/19, f. 13, Public Record Office (London), photostats, Library of Congress. Massachusetts had the highest costs, about £18,000 in 1760. South Carolina's peace-time expenditures the same year were £8,000. The other colonies spent less than £5,000. Bolles, *Pennsylvania, Province and State,* I, 376, reports a statement of William Penn in 1775 that Pennsylvania's ordinary expenditures were £3,000. £5,000 was the cost of government in New York, exclusive of expenses originating in war, as late as 1774. O'Callaghan, *New York Colonial Documents,* VIII, 453-454.

[57] Two informative tax studies on provinces with contrasting economies are: Charles H. J. Douglas, *Financial History of Massachusetts from the Organization of the Massachusetts Bay Colony to the American Revolution* (New York, 1892), in Columbia University, *Studies in History, Economics and Public Law,* I, no. 4, and Percy Scott Flippin, *The Financial Administration of the Colony of Virginia* (Baltimore, 1915), Johns Hopkins University, *Studies in Historical and Political Science,* 33, no. 2.

from their own citizens. Private capital was tied up in lands or commodities.[58] No banks or business corporations existed with liquid capital which could be enlisted in the public service.[59] When a war or other emergency required large outlays, colonial governments knew no alternative but to issue paper money.[60] Massachusetts hit upon this device in 1690, and eventually all the colonies took it up. "Currency finance" became the regular mode of financing government during war and often, as well, in time of peace.

Practice varied in details, but over the period in which the colonies experimented, they regularized their procedure in something like a system
38 conducted on the basis of known principles. The one exception was Massachusetts, which went on a sound money basis in the 1750's.[61] Elsewhere, methods fall into a pattern that can be described in general terms.

The essential feature of the system was that it avoided dealing in hard money. During a war, for instance, colonial legislatures printed, from

[58] Robert Morris wrote in 1781: "To expect loans within the United States presupposes an Ability to lend, which does not exist in any considerable number of the inhabitants. The personal property, not immediately engaged either in commerce or the improvement of lands, was never very considerable." Wharton, *Revolutionary Diplomatic Correspondence*, IV, 532-533.

[59] The absence of commercial or banking corporations is emphasized by Joseph Stancliffe Davis, *Essays in the Earlier History of American Corporations* (Cambridge, 1917). See the chart of early corporations and their types, *ibid.*, II, 22-23.

[60] Brock, for example, writes of the methods by which the colonies financed their participation in the French and Indian War: ". . . the colonies' only means of timely and adequate exertion was the issuance of bills of credit. No colony succeeded in supplying the funds by any other method. This was obvious to men in all classes at the time, but has been lost sight of since, because later writers, filled with the enthusiasm of those embarked on a sacred crusade for 'sound' money, have found it more convenient to write the history of colonial currency everywhere from the well-publicized happenings at certain periods in New England, and more particularly in Rhode Island, than to examine the facts elsewhere." Currency of the American Colonies, 466-467.

[61] Massachusetts anticipated future revenue mainly by issuing treasury notes, which bore interest in specie. It is difficult to tell from accounts now available just how far in practice her methods resembled or differed from those of other colonies. Massachusetts, however, was probably better able than any other province to deal in specie. In an earlier period, at least, Boston was the "coin center" of North America. Curtis P. Nettels, "The Economic Relations of Boston, Philadelphia and New York, 1680-1715," *Journal of Economic and Business History,* III (1930-1931), 201-202. See also Nettels, *Money Supply,* Chapter IV. Massachusetts's finances after 1749 are treated in Davis, *Currency and Banking in Massachusetts-Bay,* 233-252. A contemporary analysis is to be found in a letter of Governor Bernard to the Board of Trade, Aug. 1, 1764, C.O. 323/19, f. 33-35, Public Record Office.

time to time, the money needed to pay their expenses. Usually, the act which authorized the emission also appropriated sufficient taxes to withdraw the money from circulation. If expenses were large, the taxes for several years ahead might be pledged to the redemption of money issued during a single year.[62]

The credit of the bills depended on several interrelated factors. Regardless of any promise on the face of the notes, the basic security was the fund assigned to withdraw the money. The holder had to be certain that all taxes and payments to the government taken together would be enough to create a general use for the bills and ensure a demand for them. He 39
must rest easy in the knowledge that withdrawals would be continuous and that future governments would have the ability and the will to collect taxes. As this money was created and upheld by political acts, confidence in government was essential to its value.[63]

Meanwhile, the value of the money was sustained by its current usages, as in paying fees, buying land from the province, or use in ordinary trade. So long as there was no great reason to question it, the people accepted currency in day-to-day transactions because it was the recognized medium of exchange. Colonial legislators, however, knew something about the quantity theory of money and understood that the amount must not exceed too far the requirements of trade at existing price levels, else depreciation would occur regardless of guarantees.

The system appears to have worked against the accumulation of public debt. The debt at any particular time consisted of bills of credit in circula-

62 The currency legislation in the Pennsylvania statutes gives a good picture of the uses and adaptations of currency finance, as well as the operation of a land bank. See Mitchell and Flanders, *Statutes at Large of Pennsylvania,* III, 324-338, 389-407; IV, 38-51, 98-116, 150-152, 322-326, 344-359; V, 7-15, 45-49, 201-212, 243-261, 294-302, 303-308, 337-352, 379-396, 427-443, 456-462; VI, 7-22, 226-229, 311-319, 344-367.

63 An enlightening discussion of the theory of currency finance may be found in "Thoughts on Banks and Paper Money," New York *Daily Advertiser,* February 2, 1786. Dorfman, *Economic Mind in America,* I, 141-178, samples formal theorizing on the subject of money.

Certain exceptions to the system here outlined, besides that of Massachusetts, may be noted. Part of Maryland's direct emissions, as well as her first land bank notes, were backed by Bank of England stock, purchased with the income from a permanent export duty on tobacco. See Behrens, *Paper Money in Maryland,* 20-21, 46-58. Although the facts are not clear, Connecticut appears to have paid interest in specie on some of her notes. Henry Bronson, "An Historical Account of Connecticut Currency," 66-84. North and South Carolina paid annual administrative expenses by issuing various kinds of warrants instead of paper money.

tion; to retire it, the government levied taxes payable in the certificates of indebtedness themselves. If the debt was large, paper money was apt to be correspondingly plentiful and widely distributed. The people were taxed in a medium readily accessible to them.[64] As withdrawals reduced the supply of currency and it became concentrated into fewer hands, the debt was by that token rendered less onerous, until at some point the taxes imposed to cancel it could be discontinued and the remaining currency left in circulation.[65] Under the benign operation of currency finance, the facility with which the public debt could be retired was in rough proportion to its size.

40 Other means than currency were used to anticipate future income. Colonial governments, and to a much greater extent the state governments of the Revolution, issued various kinds of warrants and certificates which, though often given an extensive circulation, did not serve as a medium of exchange to the same degree as paper money. With certain exceptions, however, these notes were issued and redeemed on the same terms as currency. In spite of variations, therefore, it is possible to trace a basic pattern in the financial methods employed by the colonies. They met expenses by issuing a paper medium, whether currency or certificates, directly to individuals in payment for goods and services. They redeemed this paper not by giving specie to those who held it, but by accepting it for taxes or other payments to the government. This was the system of currency finance.

It was not a system which would stand the strain of a prolonged and expensive war. Nonetheless, it sufficed for the wars in which the colonies engaged. During the French and Indian War, for example, New York emitted £535,000. Pennsylvania, whose currency normally stood at

[64] A circular issued by Congress in 1779 well expressed the distinction which contemporaries made between the ease of paying public debts by withdrawals of a paper medium and the hardship imposed on the taxpayer by having to redeem them in specie. The circular contrasts the happy circumstances of the United States with the difficult situation which Britain must face when the war is over and debts must be paid. America's debt, it is said, may be cancelled by withdrawals of paper money that is within the country and available to the people; whereas Britain "will find her national debt in a very different situation . . . she must provide for the discharge of her immense debt by taxes to be paid in specie, in gold or silver perhaps now buried in the mines of Mexico or Peru, or still concealed in the brooks and rivulets of Africa or Indostan." *Journals of the Continental Congress,* XV, 1057.

[65] A growing economy would absorb ever larger quantities of unredeemed paper.

£80,000, issued £540,000. Virginia authorized £440,000.[66] Other colonies made extraordinary contributions. The Board of Trade estimated that the North American provinces spent £2,500,000 sterling beyond their ordinary costs of government. About £800,000 of this represented expenditures of Massachusetts, the sound money colony. The remainder of £1,700,000 sterling consisted almost entirely of currency or certificates issued in the expectation that they would be retired only by acceptance for taxes and other payments to the government.[67] In spite of the volume of this paper, little or no depreciation appears to have resulted in most provinces.[68] The colonies benefited from expenditures of the home government, and from 41
large British subsidies which put specie in their hands.[69]

Debt retirement was rapid after the war. Virginia's currency was down to £206,000 by 1767, according to the treasurer's report, and though two small post-war emissions restored some money to circulation, only £54,391 was afloat in 1773.[70] Pennsylvania, no longer tax free, made regular withdrawals until the Revolution. In New York, an acute shortage of currency existed by 1768.[71] Elsewhere, the provinces quickly freed themselves of their debts. A speaker in the House of Commons observed in 1766 that they had already retired £1,755,000, and that most of the remaining debt of £760,000 could be written off within two years.[72]

How much this happy situation was due to British subsidies is hard to

[66] Brock, Currency of the American Colonies, Tables XV, XVIII, XXVIII; An Account of the Tender and Amount of the Bills of credit . . . in . . . Pennsylvania since . . . 1749, C.O. 323/19, f. 85, Public Record Office; "Proceedings of the Virginia Committee of Correspondence," *Virginia Magazine of History and Biography,* XI (1903-1904), 355-357.

[67] A State of the Debts incurred by the British Colonies in North America for the extraordinary Expences of the last War . . . C.O. 323/19, f. 19, Public Record Office. Massachusetts issued non-interest-bearing notes to soldiers, which seem to have had a considerable circulation. *Ibid.,* f. 33-35. See also cancellations listed in regular reports in *The Acts and Resolves of the Province of Massachusetts Bay* (Boston, 1869-1922), XV-XVIII.

[68] The total amount did not circulate at any one time, as withdrawals were continuous even during the war. Serious depreciation occurred in New Hampshire and North Carolina. See C.O. 323/19, f. 29, Public Record Office; Brock, Currency of the American Colonies, 437, 476-477.

[69] See Beer, *British Colonial Policy,* 52-57.

[70] "Paper Money in Colonial Virginia," 228, 234.

[71] *Journal of the Votes and Proceedings of the General Assembly of New York . . .,* 799; O'Callaghan, *New York Colonial Documents,* VII, 820-821, 843-845.

[72] T. C. Hansard, publisher, *Parliamentary History of England* (London, 1806-1820), XVI, 204; C.O. 323/19, f. 19, Public Record Office.

know. During the war, Parliament granted over £1,150,000 sterling for distribution among the American colonies, a sum which was nearly half of the £2,500,000 estimated as their war expenses. Even so, when one compares their real expenditures during the war with the sums involved in their ordinary fiscal operations, it appears that they made what was for them a most unusual effort, and the ease with which they retired their debts must in some measure be attributed to the peculiar facility offered by the methods of currency finance.[73]

British policy on matters pertaining to colonial currency is a subject which has scarcely been touched. No doubt it was a factor of greater
42 importance in imperial relations than is commonly understood. From the one considerable treatment available,[74] it appears that most of the time the British government acknowledged the necessity of colonial emissions. Before 1740, the Board of Trade was "reluctantly sympathetic and essentially reasonable" in sanctioning both land bank loans and direct emissions. The Board, however, always opposed making currency a legal tender in private transactions, even though it approved laws for this purpose. Generally speaking, the Board tried to regulate colonial issues by ensuring that the amounts were reasonable, that funds for redemption were adequate, and that emissions were withdrawn within a limited period of time. Control was exerted largely through instructions to governors, who were ordered to refuse assent to laws which did not have a clause suspending their execution until approved by the crown.[75]

Supervision was not effective and lapsed almost completely during frequent periods of war. As currency emissions were the only way the provinces could furnish aid, governors were permitted to approve acts without a suspending clause, provided the Board's other stipulations were satisfied. The colonies took advantage of their bargaining position, however, to procure the governors' assent to laws which did not comply with

[73] Lawrence H. Gipson, "Connecticut Taxation and Parliamentary Aid Preceding the Revolutionary War," *American Historical Review*, XXXVI (1931), 731. Though Gipson overstates the case, he argues forcefully that British subsidies enabled Connecticut to remain solvent during the war and pay her debts afterwards with ease. Unfortunately, there is no complete account of the British subsidies to individual colonies, nor the way in which these subsidies were used.

[74] Brock, Currency of the American Colonies, 168-243, 476-508, 520-527, 558-563.

[75] Examples of the Board's instructions may be found in Leonard W. Labaree, *Royal Instructions to British Governors, 1670-1776* (New York, 1935), I, 218-238; O'Callaghan, *New York Colonial Documents*, VI, 949; VII, 463-464.

the Board's requirements. Neither governors nor the crown could afford to scrutinize too closely the modes by which assistance was rendered.

War still hindered the enforcement of policy, but British control tightened after 1740. Rhoce Island's emissions were a flagrant abuse. The Board also appears to have been more susceptible to complaints of British merchants, some of who claimed injury from legal tender laws. The same mercantile and creditor interests carried their appeals to Parliament, with the result that after 1750 the standing instructions of the Board of Trade were given statutory effect.[76]

The act of 1751 applied only to New England. It did not abolish the 43
paper money system even in that area, as is sometimes supposed, but merely established rules for carrying it on. Bills already in circulation were to be retired in strict accord with the terms of the issuing acts. When these were withdrawn, no paper money was to be legal tender. The provinces were allowed to emit bills from year to year to pay governmental expenses, provided they committed taxes sufficient to redeem them within two years. This clause was flexible enough to accommodate a moderate expansion of currency. In event of war or other emergency, all curbs were relaxed as to the amount which could be issued, provided enough taxes were appropriated to redeem the bills within five years. The act of 1751 left the colonies outside New England undisturbed. Within New England, its major effect was to prohibit legal tender laws and to rule out land banks.[77]

The restraining act of 1764 came at the end of the French and Indian War, when the colonies had large sums outstanding. As first drafted, it would have placed all the provinces under the curbs imposed on New England. In its final form, it merely prohibited legal tender laws and required that existing legal tender currencies be sunk at their expiration dates.[78] Many colonies protested, in the belief that the legal tender feature was an essential prop to their money. Experience was to show, however, that the restriction did not materially impair the workings of the currency system.

There is more than a hint that by this time Britain's policy as to paper

[76] Besides the work by Brock already cited, see Dickerson, *American Colonial Government*, 314-319.

[77] 24 Geo II, C-53, Danby Pickering, comp., *The Statutes at Large from Magna Charta to the End of the Eleventh Parliament of Great Britain, Anno 1761* (London, 1762-1807), XX, 306-309.

[78] 4 Geo III, C-34, *ibid.*, XXVI, 103-105; Van Doren, *Letters of Franklin and Jackson*, 116, 139, 169.

money was subordinated to the larger purpose of securing a permanent civil list, and that attempts were being made to trade approval of colonial emissions for the grant of a fixed revenue to the crown.[79] Even so, the colonies made headway against British restraints, though they could not again pass legal tender laws. New York was permitted to renew its land bank in 1771. After a long struggle, New Jersey exacted consent for the establishment of a land bank in 1774. Pennsylvania continued to emit currency and in 1773 renewed its land bank. Maryland issued £173,733 to pay war debts and over half a million dollars to finance improvements and to establish a land bank.[80] Virginia's council annulled two land bank acts
44 passed by the lower house, but the province emitted £40,000 for other purposes. North Carolina, closely confined by the British government, issued treasury notes and debenture bills, while South Carolina emitted "public orders" and "tax certificates," which were in effect a non-legal tender currency.[81]

Parliament in 1773 legalized colonial monetary practices as carried on under the restrictive acts of 1751 and 1764. A question had arisen as to how far the prohibition of legal tender applied. To clarify the matter, Parliament passed an explanatory act which declared that the prohibition ruled out only those laws which made currency legal tender in private transactions. The colonies were allowed to make it legal tender in payments to the government. In stating the latitude permitted by existing law, Parliament defined the essential workings of the currency finance system. The act is worth quoting because it verifies the general survey given above:[82]

[79] Brock makes the most of this point, although he covers in detail only the period to 1764. Currency of the American Colonies, 409-411. See also Phillips, *Historical Sketches of Paper Currency*, I, 69-71; Dickerson, *American Colonial Government*, 316.

[80] 10 Geo III, C-35, Pickering, *Statutes at Large of Great Britain*, XXVIII, 306. *Colonial Laws of New York*, V, 149-170; *Acts of the General Assembly of the Province of New Jersey . . .* (Burlington, 1776), 419-441 (act of March 11, 1774); Mitchell and Flanders, *Statutes at Large of Pennsylvania*, VII, 100-107, 204-211; VIII, 15-22, 204-220, 264-283, 284-300, 417-423, 447-455; *Laws of Maryland made since M,DCC,LXIII*, November sess., 1766, Chapter XXVI; November sess., 1769, Chapter XIV; November sess., 1773, Chapter XXVI.

[81] "Paper Money in Colonial Virginia," 236-237, 262; Phillips, *Historical Sketches of Paper Currency*, I, 206-208; Parker, *Money Problems of Early Tar Heels*, 13; Smith, *South Carolina as a Royal Province*, 275-279; Brock, Currency of the American Colonies, Tables XXIV, XXVI, XXVII.

[82] 13 Geo III, C-57, Pickering, *Statutes at Large of Great Britain*, XXX, 113-114. See also Brock, Currency of the American Colonies, 525-527.

> Whereas the want of gold and silver currency in several of his Majesty's colonies and plantations in America may make it necessary, as well for the publick advantage as in justice to those persons who may have demands upon the publick treasuries in the said colonies for services performed, that such publick creditors should be secured in the payment of their just debts and demands, by certificates, notes, bills, or debentures, to be created and issued by the authority of the general assemblies . . . on the securities of any taxes or duties given and granted to his Majesty—for and towards defraying expences incurred for publick services; and that such certificates, notes, bills or debentures, should be made chargeable on the publick treasurers of the said colonies
> and received and taken by them as a legal tender in discharge of any such 45
> duties or taxes, or of any debts whatsoever, due to the publick treasuries . . . be it enacted . . . That . . . any certificates, notes, bills or debentures which shall . . . be voluntarily accepted by the creditors of the publick . . . may be made . . . to be a legal tender for the publick treasurers . . . for the discharge of any duties, taxes, or other debts whatsoever . . .

Had the Revolution not occurred, Britain might have reached a solution of colonial monetary problems. As early as 1754, Richard Jackson and Franklin exchanged plans to form one or more land banks based on capital loaned from the Bank of England or subscribed by private investors. It was expected that land bank notes would provide a circulating medium for the continent. Later, when the Stamp Act was under discussion, Franklin and Thomas Pownall broached a similar scheme, as an alternative way of gaining a revenue from the colonies. They envisaged a continental land bank with a branch office in each province, centrally managed in Britain. The bank was to issue legal tender notes on loan at 5 per cent interest, the principal to be repaid over a period of ten years. The notes would circulate as currency throughout the American colonies. Franklin and Pownall pressed this scheme for three or four years.[83]

By 1767, it appears that the Secretary of Trade concurred in the idea that the restraining act of 1764 should be modified to permit the colonies to establish loan offices which would emit legal tender notes valid for all transactions except payment of sterling debts. A bill for this purpose was

[83] Van Doren, *Letters of Franklin and Jackson*, 41-54; Carey, *Franklin's Economic Views*, 19-20; Verner Crane, "Benjamin Franklin and the Stamp Act," Colonial Society of Massachusetts, *Transactions*, XXXII, 58-59; Pownall, *Administration of the Colonies*, 186-187, 230-253. See [John Dickinson], *Political Writings of John Dickinson*, I, 58.

being prepared and the ground laid for its introduction into the House of Commons, when the colonial agents learned that the Commons would probably seize the opportunity to declare the income arising from the loan offices subject to the appropriation of the crown. As the colonial agents could not risk this outcome, they gave up the project. Saying he had hoped to make better use of his plan for a continental land bank, Pownall published the details of it in the 1768 edition of his *Administration of the Colonies*.[84]

Any solution of the money problem under British auspices was forestalled by the Revolution. When it was too late, the British government
46 instructed its peace commissioners of 1778 in a number of schemes which might have borne fruit if attempted earlier.[85]

A view of the evidence suggests that generations of historical scholarship have fostered a mistaken impression of the monetary practices of the colonies. The efforts of the American provinces to create a medium of exchange, erect a system of agricultural credit, and equip their governments with the means of incurring and discharging responsibilities, hardly constitute a "dark and disgraceful" picture; nor, on the whole, is the record one of failure. Most of the colonies handled their currency with discretion and were successful in realizing the purposes associated with its use. Except for New England, where depreciation had given it a bad name, paper money was the "ancient system," which had long served well the needs of trade and the ordinary processes of government. Although mindful of its dangers, men of property accepted it as useful and necessary. In time of war, all the colonies but one were fully prepared to adopt the methods of currency finance as the only way of meeting an emergency. Emissions might then be over-large, as the Revolution was to prove, but the common need precluded any nice regard for the effect on contracts.

[84] See preceding citation, also Franklin to Joseph Galloway, June 13, 1767, Smythe, *Works of Franklin*, V, 25-28; Osgood Hanbury and Capel Hanbury to Charles Hammond, George Steuart, and John Brice, May 6 and May 21, 1767, Black Books, V, 19, 20, Maryland Hall of Records.

[85] Samuel E. Morison, ed., *Sources and Documents Illustrating the American Revolution, 1764-1788*, 2nd ed. (Oxford, 1929), 195-197, contains the instructions.

Statistical Method and the Brown Thesis on Colonial Democracy

John Cary[*]

With a Rebuttal by Robert E. Brown[†]

Professor Robert E. Brown's study of the American Revolution in 47
Massachusetts has been one of the most influential works in Revolutionary historiography during the last decade.[1] Following its publication in 1955, reviewers expressed cavils or even serious reservations, but several prophetically praised it as a book that would make historians take a fresh look at some old ideas. In fact, Brown's study continues to provoke discussion at historical meetings, but it has never been critically analyzed.[2]

Middle-Class Democracy and the Revolution in Massachusetts falls into two parts. In the first six chapters, Professor Brown attempts to refute the argument that the Revolutionary movement was a fight against control of provincial politics by a local aristocracy, as well as against England.[3] He

* Mr. Cary is a member of the Department of History, Lehigh University, Bethlehem, Pennsylvania.

† Mr. Brown is a member of the Department of History, Michigan State University, East Lansing, Michigan.

[1] Robert E. Brown, *Middle-Class Democracy and the Revolution in Massachusetts, 1691-1780* (Ithaca, 1955). Page citations to this work are included in the text, rather than in separate footnotes.

[2] The best reviews of Brown's book were by: Clifford K. Shipton in *Political Science Quarterly*, LXXI (1956), 306-308, who pointed out that an internal revolution began in Massachusetts in 1766; Richard B. Morris in *American Historical Review*, LXII (1956-57), 636-637, who criticized Brown's use of wills; and Robert J. Taylor in *Mississippi Valley Historical Review*, XLIII (1956-57), 111-113, and Raymond P. Stearns in *William and Mary Quarterly*, 3d Ser., XIV (1957), 100-103, both of whom questioned Brown's use of the word democracy. Roy Lokken dealt more fully with Brown's anachronistic use of the word democracy. Referring to the presentism in his thought, Lokken notes that Brown bases his definition of democracy "on observation of the twentieth-century scene" and on the striking phrase "of the people, by the people, for the people." Roy N. Lokken, "The Concept of Democracy in Colonial Political Thought," *Wm. and Mary Qtly.*, 3d Ser., XVI (1959), 570.

[3] Brown's chief target is James Truslow Adams's *Revolutionary New England, 1691-1776* (Boston, 1927), but he lists (p. 2*n*) a number of textbooks with which he disagrees.

argues that colonial society, politics, and economic life were democratic. In the second part of his book, Brown denies that the Revolution had anything at all to do with who should rule at home, and presents his own view of the causes of the war, arguing that it was brought on by a determined effort by Great Britain to destroy the democratic institutions of the colonies. Thus, the validity of his conclusions in this second part of the book depends upon the success with which he establishes his thesis that Massachusetts was democratic.

One of the most striking aspects of Professor Brown's book is the presentation of important conclusions in mathematical percentages, which
48 are, in some cases, based upon statistical samples. He concludes, for example, that 90 per cent of the people in colonial Massachusetts were farmers, that 98 per cent of them were Congregationalists, and that 95 per cent of the adult males were qualified voters. (pp. 20, 37, 402, 403) Brown also uses a number of quotations from contemporary sources to prove that Massachusetts was democratic, but a large part of any evaluation of his thesis must be an examination of his statistical techniques.

Looking first at economic conditions, Brown argues that there was widespread "economic democracy"—which he equates with property holding—in Massachusetts. He concludes that "90 per cent of the people were farmers, most of whom owned their own farms." (p. 20) As evidence, Brown describes the property holdings of eighteen men (pp. 14-15, 41-43), and shows that Northampton had many middle-class farmers. He argues that virtually any Massachusetts town would demonstrate these generalizations. This may be true, but we are given no reason for believing so, and are asked to accept on faith the contention that Northampton is representative of all towns in Massachusetts. Some modest conclusions might be drawn from such evidence, but is it safe to argue, on the basis of so limited a sample, that 90 per cent of the people were farmers, most of whom owned their own farms?

Brown extends his thesis that Massachusetts was democratic before the Revolution to religious and educational institutions, but his argument is unconvincing. His chapter on religion and education is most disappointing, because he studies these subjects in much the way he does the suffrage—confining his attention to a discussion of statutes, number of church members, and legal provisions for education. A historian of structures rather than of ideas, he ignores entirely theology, sermon literature, and the content of the educational curriculum, the study of which is of vital importance in answering the question of whether religion and education were aristocratically dominated or oriented. Charles S. Grant, in his study of Kent, Connecticut, found that both education and religion tended to be aristocratic.[4]

Brown claims that there were many democratic practices in the Congregational Church, and that "some 98 per cent of the people were Congregationalists." (p. 403) Such a percentage would be astounding, even if he meant to say that 98 per cent of all church members, rather than of the people of the colony, were Congregationalists. In any case, this conclusion may be dismissed, for no evidence is given to support it. As to democratic religious practices, he writes, "There were some elements of democracy, however, in this religious law of 1692. For one thing, individual churches were to exercise and enjoy all their privileges and freedoms respecting 49
divine worship, church order, and discipline." (p. 103) This certainly is evidence of local autonomy in Congregationalism, an obvious tautology, but it is not evidence of democratic elements in Congregationalism, unless we are to assume that local control is synonymous with democracy.

While Professor Brown feels that it is important to establish the fact that religion, education, and economic life in Massachusetts were democratic, his principal effort is devoted to proving that this was also true of the colony's political institutions. This is a key part of his thesis, since in the second part of his book, he interprets virtually all British policy as designed to curtail or destroy colonial political democracy. If he does not successfully establish the democratic nature of political institutions, his views as to the causes of the war are unsupported.

In his chapters on the eighteenth-century suffrage, Brown reads the word democracy by the light of a definition that differs from that used by many other colonial historians. If one believes, as Brown seems to, that eighteenth-century men used this word to mean that nearly all adult males could vote, one may easily conclude that Massachusetts was a democracy in this sense of the word. If, however, a student believes, as a great many do, that by democracy or the democratic part of government the colonists often meant no more than the elected lower house, he will find less evidence of democracy in Brown's quotations. Lokken has demonstrated the anachronism in reading "adult male suffrage" where the documents read "democracy."[5]

[4] Charles S. Grant, *Democracy in the Connecticut Frontier Town of Kent* (New York, 1961), 155, 162, 167.

[5] Lokken also criticizes Brown's use of sources, declaring that "Brown's uncritical use of Hutchinson's and Adams's prejudiced evaluation of the Massachusetts politics of their time, unfortunately, hardly merits recognition as a study of the political ideas current among the colonists of eighteenth-century America." Lokken, "Concept of Democracy," 569*n*. An excellent article that appeared after mine was

In a section designed to prove that colonials believed that most people could vote, Brown quotes Francis Bernard as saying that the colony was democratic in most respects and Thomas Hutchinson as saying that the Massachusetts towns were absolute democracies. An examination of the sources indicates that Bernard meant no more than that the General Court was elected, rather than appointed, and that Hutchinson meant that there was no aristocratic body to check the town meeting and that the only monarchic or executive element was the moderator.[6] Neither man is concerned here with the question of how many people were eligible to vote, either in town meeting or in province elections. To imply, as they did, that
50 any branch or element of the government overbalanced the other elements, was to impugn these governments in the minds of many eighteenth-century men, who believed so wholeheartedly in an Aristotelian balance of all three.

Brown musters other evidence for his argument that the "needy part of the province" or those "of low condition among the plebeians" could influence the General Court on such issues as a fixed salary or the Land Bank scheme. Such phrases, however, tell us nothing about property ownership or the extent of colonial suffrage. Much of Brown's testimony here comes from conservatives—from Dr. William Douglass, Benjamin Lynde, Jr., Francis Bernard, William Shirley, a British officer who feared anything that smacked of leveling, and from Thomas Hutchinson again and again. (pp. 53-55) In many cases, these writers used such terms as "the democracy" and the "lowest order" simply to impugn the character of their opposition, and one may not accept these terms as descriptive of the political order in the colony.

Aside from such quotations from contemporaries, many of which are of questionable value, Brown rests his conclusions concerning colonial suffrage upon a study of Massachusetts wills, tax lists, and disputed election returns. He argues, first, that the wills show that most adult males had property worth at least £40 sterling or £53.4.0 lawful money. More than 90 per cent or, as he says in another place, 95 per cent of them owned this much property and would have been qualified voters, assuming that they met other requirements such as residency. This conclusion seems intended to be a statistical one and should, of course, be based upon a reliable sta-

completed is J. R. Pole, "Historians and the Problem of Early American Democracy," *American Historical Review*, LXVII (1961-62), 626-646.

[6] Brown, *Middle-Class Democracy*, 57, 58; Francis Bernard, *Select Letters on the Trade and Government of America* . . . (London, 1774), 43; Massachusetts Archives, XXV, 226, Massachusetts Statehouse, Boston, Mass.

tistical sample, in lieu of using team research to execute the arduous task of checking all extant wills.[7] In his chapter on the province franchise, Brown uses only about fifty wills in deciding how many people could vote. This seems like an unfortunately small sampling of the thousands of Massachusetts wills that survive. More important, however, than the numbers, is the degree to which these fifty wills are representative of the records available.

One disturbing aspect of Brown's choice of wills is that he draws all of them from three seaboard counties. One might almost say two counties, for he cites only five Middlesex County wills as evidence that many adult men had enough property to qualify to vote. One can sympathize with 51
Professor Brown's difficulties. The probate records of Essex and Suffolk counties are well-preserved, well-organized, well-indexed, and convenient to use. Those of Middlesex are extensive, but are not so conveniently organized and may quickly lead one to despair. This, however, is an obstacle to be surmounted, rather than avoided by going to the convenient, but not necessarily representative, records of Essex and Suffolk.

More serious than the inadequacy of the sampling of Middlesex wills is the complete absence of evidence from the southeastern counties and from western Massachusetts. Suffolk and Essex counties may be typical of all of Massachusetts—maritime and agricultural, urban and rural, eastern and western—but Brown offers no convincing reason for believing this to be true. In the prerevolutionary period, Massachusetts had fourteen counties, five of which were in Maine or on islands off the coast. Clearly it is untenable to conclude that 95 per cent of the colony's adult males could vote on the basis of a study of the wills of two of the colony's nine principal counties. What we have in this chapter of *Middle-Class Democracy and the Revolution in Massachusetts* is a study of the franchise in two seaboard counties, rather than of the entire colony of Massachusetts Bay.[8]

It is also important to ask whether Brown's records are representative even of the two counties he has studied. Again, the answer is that they may be, but we have no way of knowing for certain that they are. Brown discusses the property holdings of a number of men without telling us how he selected these particular wills. Did he use a random number system?

[7] Brown, *Middle-Class Democracy,* 37, 402. Brown uses the term sample in referring to his evidence. If he did not mean his wills to represent adequate statistical samples, the evidence is nonetheless inadequate as support for the precise percentages he gives.

[8] See n. 14 below on Brown's failure to use the evidence offered in the one study that has been made of the suffrage in western Massachusetts. No writer seems to have studied the suffrage in the southeastern counties.

Did he study all wills for particular years or in particular volumes? No answer is given to these questions. Brown groups his records in three categories—wills of town workers and artisans; wills of men who owned small or average-sized farms; and wills of captains, gentlemen, and esquires. This, of course, raises the further question as to whether the wills he selected are representative of these classes.

Aside from supporting the general conclusion that most men could vote, this grouping is designed to show several things. First, that most men who owned land, even small farms, possessed enough property to qualify as voters and that many farmers were wealthy. Second, that many artisans and town workers were not only voters but had more property than some
52 aristocrats. Third, that some people whom we normally think of as being of the upper class were debtors or had so little property that they were not qualified voters. Brown's table of small and average farms includes the wills of sixteen men, all of whom were Essex County men except two. Even of Essex County, this is a less than satisfactory sample. Brown argues that, even if a farmer owned no real estate, he would have been able to vote on the basis of his personal estate. As proof that virtually all farmers had enough personal property to vote, he cites only two examples, both of whom are Middlesex County men. (p. 27)

For his table of town workers and artisans, Brown draws his evidence entirely from the Essex and Suffolk records. Since the colony's major towns were in these counties, it is more justifiable to rely upon these counties for conclusions as to the wealth of the colony's workers than to use these counties as representative of the colony's farm population. However, in this table, he uses only fifteen wills of town workers and artisans for his conclusions that most of these workers could vote and that those who had little property "were few compared with those who were property owners." (pp. 28, 18) These fifteen wills may be a fair sample of the hundreds of workers in these two counties during the fifteen years preceding the war, but we have no reason for believing this to be the case. Brown does not indicate why he chose the wills of these particular workmen, four of whom owned more than £240 of property at death and only one of whom had less than the £40 necessary to vote. I have studied a larger sample of the wills of a particular town, Marblehead, for the two years from October 1769 through September 1771, and found that thirty-one men had estates of less than £53.4.0 lawful money and only twenty had estates larger than this.[9] If we were to accept these fifty-one wills as representative of that town, we would have to conclude that a majority of the adult men

[9] Essex Probate Records, CCCXLVI-CCCXLVII, Essex County Courthouse, Salem, Mass.

were disfranchised and discard Brown's statement that those who had little property "were few compared with those who were property owners." Future studies of the suffrage in other colonies that use wills as evidence, might be more valuable if, instead of listing the names and estates of a few farmers or workers, they were to summarize the total number of men in representative counties in particular years who left enough property to qualify as voters.

Brown's study of thirteen gentlemen, esquires, captains, and doctors leads him to conclude that there were some aristocrats who had "much less property than the small farmers." Almost any farmer and many artisans, he says, had more property than the gentlemen he studied. (pp. 53
31-32) This, of course, is different from saying that farmers and artisans had more property than *most* gentlemen, as Brown has studied only thirteen of the latter. Here he points out that some of these gentlemen were insolvent debtors, not something, incidentally, that is necessarily connected with voting rights, but he does not call attention to such insolvency when it appears in the wills of farmers like Joseph Harrington. (pp. 32, 26) He says that not one of four captains whose wills he studied had real estate and not one was worth more than £130. This is a contrast to the six mariners whom Brown includes in his list of town workers. Five of these mariners had enough property to vote, and three of them owned real estate. (pp. 28-29) Brown seems to use the term mariner to mean sailor, ignoring the fact that this is a general word, used in the eighteenth century for both sailors and captains. Thus, Brown chooses to classify John Hewett, worth £248.18.10, as a sailor rather than as a captain and include him with the town workers rather than the aristocrats, despite the fact that he owned a sloop. The town workers thus gain one sleek, fat artisan, while the four hungry captains are left to represent their class with their petty fortunes. Edward Stone, who had real estate of £100 is designated in his own will as both captain and mariner, but Brown classifies him as a mariner, not mentioning that he was a captain who might have been grouped with the gentlemen instead of the town workers.[10] In this way the artisans gain another qualified voter and the four captains remain a forlorn little group. The wills of the other four mariners he studied do not indicate whether they were captains, but if we were to claim them, by defining mariner as captain, we should have ten captains, nine of whom could vote, and Professor Brown would be left without a sailor on deck—or rather on the voting lists.

Finally, it is interesting to note how easy it is to choose different wills

[10] Brown, *Middle-Class Democracy*, 28; Suffolk Probate Records, LXXII, 17, Suffolk County Courthouse, Boston, Mass.

from those elected by Professor Brown and reach opposite conclusions. One need not even range over several volumes of wills in two counties. In a cursory turning of pages in a single volume of the Suffolk Probate Records, I found the following seven wills: Benjamin Blackman, yeoman, £20.5.2; John Kenney, yeoman, £28.16.6; Ebenezer Eaton, feltmaker, £3.18.6; Joshua Thornton, housewright, £27.16.2; Mr. Samuel Allen, merchant, £1683.9.8; William Robinson, gentleman, £1472.15.4; and Ebenezer Storer, Esq., £1900.10.1, plus a Negro man, furniture, and a warehouse.[11] Here we have four small farmers and artisans, none of whom owns even enough property at death to qualify as a voter, and three gentlemen, the poorest of whom is worth nearly £1500. Conclusion: only
54 43 per cent of the population could vote, and voting was confined entirely to the upper class, with 100 per cent of Massachusetts farmers and artisans being disfranchised by property requirements. Such figures are not only unrepresentative of Massachusetts, but are probably atypical of the volume from which they are drawn. Indeed, my own examination of the Suffolk and Essex probate records suggests that Professor Brown's wills are more representative than these seven. The question, however, is how we can tell whether my evidence or Brown's or anyone else's is typical, when we are given no notion as to how it was selected. Returning to our four captains, we find a further illustration of how truth varies with the evidence used. Brown mentions that none of these four owned real estate and the wealthiest of them was worth only £129.2.1. (p. 32) His conclusion is that most farmers and many artisans were wealthier than some captains. In a single volume of Essex wills, I found three captains, all of whom had real estate and who left total estates ranging from £300 to £700.[12] My conclusion: few farmers and almost no artisans had as much property as the captains I studied. In actuality, of course, neither of these inadequate samples proves anything at all about social classes or suffrage in colonial Massachusetts.

Looking now at the wills of several towns in the two counties Professor Brown studied, we find—on the basis of a limited sampling—different percentages than he did of the adult males eligible to vote. I examined the wills of adults males in Marblehead, Salem, and Ipswich for a two year period from October 1769 through September 1771, and those wills of adult males in Suffolk County that are recorded in the first 330 pages of volume 72 of the records, a volume used by Brown. I found that only two of twenty-six adult males of Salem and only one of twenty-six from Ipswich had so little property that they could not vote. These records appear

[11] Suffolk Probate Records, LIX, 85, 126-127, 127-128, 130-133, 163, 186-187, 241.
[12] Essex Probate Records, CCCXLVI, 203, 217, 246.

to substantiate Brown's conclusions, though only for those two towns in that period. In the Suffolk records, however, we find that only 30 of 41 adult males who left wills in the period examined had sufficient property to vote. This is 73 per cent, rather than 95 per cent. The Marblehead wills reveal that only 20 of 51 men had enough property to vote; in other words, only 39 per cent of them were eligible, far from Brown's figure.[13] Totaling all of these wills, we find that 99 of 144 men studied would have been able to meet the property qualifications at their deaths. This means that 68 per cent, rather than 90 to 95 per cent, of them would have been able to vote.

In judging the reliability of such figures, several things should be kept 55
in mind. Though a larger sample than Brown's, this is not necessarily a representative one. This information, like Brown's, tells us nothing about property holdings in other parts of the colony. It might be that long-established families in Ipswich had built their fortunes over several generations, while the settlers in the western counties had little personal property and real estate of less than £40 value.[14] Many farmers in the West may have lacked the silver porringers, pewter plates, and modest libraries that added to the personal estates recorded in the wills of wealthy farmers in the eastern counties. Also, wills indicate only how much property a man owned at death. It might be that some of these men, who accumulated enough property to qualify as voters by the time they died, were disfranchised for the first ten or twenty years of adult life.

Perhaps the most important flaw in this evidence, and in Professor Brown's, is the failure to determine how many adult men left wills. In some periods, the poorer class of people do not make wills. Having more property, a higher rate of literacy, and greater acquaintance with the law, the rich are more likely to provide for the final distribution of their property than are the poor. If this was true in the colonial period, it would make Professor Brown's evidence less trustworthy, for the records of a large class of people who did not have £40 sterling might not appear in the probate records he relies upon. The law required that intestate estates

[13] Suffolk Probate Records, LXXII, 1-330; Essex Probate Records, CCCXLVI and CCCXLVII, 1-200. The records indicate when the deceased was a minor or insane, and I have omitted the wills of such persons, as well as those of women.

[14] Robert J. Taylor believes that most disfranchisement would occur in the eastern seaports, and that land prices in the West were so cheap that few farmers in that area would not have qualified as voters. He reaches this conclusion by comparing the estimated adult population in certain towns with the tax lists. For the most part, Brown cites Taylor only to disagree with him, and makes no use of the evidence in Taylor's appendix in discussing the extent of suffrage in Massachusetts. Robert J. Taylor, *Western Massachusetts in the Revolution* (Providence, R. I., 1954), 36-37.

be probated and some of them were, but we do not know how many of them were. If inventories of the property of all adult men are found in colonial probate records, as Brown assumes, and we discover that 90 of 100 men left estates of at least £40, we may conclude that 90 per cent of the men in that county could vote. Suppose, however, there were 80 adult men whose estates were never inventoried, all of whom had less than £40 of property. In that case, 90 of 180, or only 50 per cent, would have been qualified voters. Professor Brown does not consider the question of how many adult males left wills, a point crucial to his evidence. Until this question is answered by comparing death records with wills, the probate records are somewhat suspect sources as to the extent of colonial suffrage.

56 Town tax lists and disputed election returns are other sources Brown uses to support his estimate of the percentage of adult males who were eligible voters. His evidence on two disputed elections seems convincing, but his information on a third, Weston, reveals the difficulties involved in using tax records. Chilton Williamson points out the great risk of error in interpreting tax lists and says that they are often "the basis for more than one set of inferences."[15] Brown notes that there were 216 polls listed on the Weston tax records of 1772 and that 133 votes were cast in the election of 1773. He estimates that 25 per cent of the 216 men listed for polls would be between 16 and 21 years of age and thus ineligible for voting, leaving 162 adult men in the town. He then says that, if the 133 voters of 1772 included every eligible voter in Weston, over 80 per cent of the adult men must have been qualified voters. But he finds even better support for his thesis in the valuation list of 1774, which, he says, lists 154 eligible voters, thus boosting to about 95 the percentage of adult males who had enough property to qualify as voters. (p. 46)

I differ sharply with Professor Brown in interpreting these lists. For one thing, there seems to be no need to *estimate* that there were 162 adult males in town by deducting 25 per cent from the 216 polls on the 1772 list. The Weston lists do not include the names of minors; their polls are listed behind the names of their fathers or guardians. Thus, the male names on the 1772 list are all adults, and there are 175 of them, rather than 162, which lowers Brown's percentages somewhat. Secondly, Brown calls the 1774 record a list of eligible voters, and assumes that every one of the 154 names on it was that of a voter. In my opinion, the 1774 list includes all of the adult males in town and was, as its editor points out, drawn specifically to be used at the polls to check upon property qualifications.[16]

[15] Chilton Williamson, *American Suffrage; from Property to Democracy, 1760-1860* (Princeton, 1960), 23.

[16] Weston. *The Tax Lists, 1757-1827* (Boston, 1897), pp. iii, 72-76, 83-84.

The list of 1774 is a list of eligible voters only in the sense that all adult males living in Weston are on it, with minors and nonresidents being omitted; it does not mean that every man listed had sufficient property to qualify as a voter. These records of Weston do not list taxes paid, but the value of a man's real and personal property, with some of the lists including faculty (income from one's profession) and money at interest. In fact, they seem to provide a rare opportunity to discover the exact property holdings of every adult male in a Massachusetts town. From them we can tell just how many men in Weston had estates of at least £40, with no need to deduce the size of their estates from the taxes paid.

One thing that is not clear is whether the Weston lists are in sterling or 57
in lawful money. Looking first at the 1774 list (which actually includes 159, rather than 154 names), if we assume that the list is in lawful money, we find that only 53 adult men had estates of at least £53.4.0, and were qualified voters, as compared to 106 who had smaller estates. If the list is in sterling, 75 men had estates of £40 and 84 men would have have been unable to meet the property qualifications. In other other words, only 33 per cent, or at best 47 per cent, of the adult men of Weston met the property qualifications. Much the same is found to be the case in 1757, 1768, 1772, and other years. The lists of 1772 record 175 adult men in the town. If these lists are in lawful money, only 57 men had sufficient property to vote, while 118 could not meet the property qualifications. If the 1772 lists are in sterling, 78 men had at least £40 of property and 97 did not. The fact that many more people, 133 altogether, voted in the election of 1773 than were qualified suggests that the town officials, who knew all of these men intimately, paid little or no heed to property qualifications. Elsewhere in his book, Brown notes that Hutchinson said that anyone with the appearance of a man was allowed to vote in Boston, with little or no inquiry into property owned. This probably was even more true in a small town like Weston, where everyone knew everyone else. But to say that most adult men in Weston *did* vote, including many who were technically unqualified, is quite different from Brown's conclusion that nearly all of them *were qualified* to vote.

If I am correct in my interpretation of the Weston lists, these findings graphically point up the need to study more than the statistics. The intimate social relations of a group as small as the population of a New England town may well have made our study of property qualifications largely beside the point. Most of these men were members of the same militia company, sat in the same meetinghouse, traded at the same store, and swapped cattle and even breeches with each other. It is worth considering whether the closeness of the lives of 175 men in Weston led them to ignore province laws and allow anyone to vote who was a good neighbor. Charles S. Grant indicates that this was precisely what happened in Kent, Connecticut. Men were admitted as freemen who had no property, and most or all town inhabitants, including propertyless hired hands, rather than only qualified voters, were admitted to the town meeting. "Humble and unqualified men," Grant found, who would not have qualified as voters under Connecticut law, were elected to town offices.[17]

In chapters 7-15 of his book, Brown presents his own view of the causes of the War of Independence. This part of his thesis has received less attention than his study of the suffrage, though it is quite as important. His
58 general argument is that the war was caused by a British attempt to undermine American democracy. He believes most British legislation passed between 1763 and 1775 was designed to accomplish this, and interprets nearly every colonial squabble after 1691 as involving democracy. He says "democracy was in part the reason" for Governor Shirley's difficulties in getting restrictions on paper money, and argues that a conflict over the quartering of troops grew out of "the inevitable clashes between a democratic society" and the aristocratic philosophy of Englishmen. (pp. 134, 167) Disputes over the outfitting of a province ship, the right of the governor to issue charters to colleges, the chartering of a Congregational society to rival the Society for the Preservation of the Gospel in Foreign Parts, and the Sugar Act—all of these and more, Brown interprets as involving the preservation or destruction of colonial democracy. (pp. 186-187, 188-189, 203) In none of these cases does Professor Brown show how democracy was involved, or why one should see in a dispute over who had the power to tax or quarter troops anything more than a colonial-imperial dispute. Are we to believe that the protests of colonial peoples today against French or Belgian troops in their countries are caused by deep traditions of democracy in Tunisia or the Congo?

In our own time, many people feel that any imperial control is undemocratic, but men of the eighteenth century did not necessarily think as we do, and colonists protested against such control because it violated their concept of the British colonial constitution, rather than because it subverted democracy. When the colonists phrase, as they invariably do, their

[17] Grant, *Democracy,* 109-110, 130, 131. McCormick found the suffrage restrictions to have been liberally construed in colonial New Jersey and discovered only one case in which the authorities inquired into, "or attempted to enforce, any suffrage qualifications." Richard P. McCormick, *The History of Voting in New Jersey: A Study of the Development of Election Machinery, 1664-1911* (New Brunswick, N. J., 1953), 22-23, 62.

protests in terms of violations of Magna Charta, the Massachusetts Charter, and the rights of Englishmen, one must offer some strong evidence for his assumption that they really meant to say that Britain was destroying American democracy. To read current political beliefs into an earlier period is often to obstruct rather than to aid our understanding of it. For example, Brown says that the instructions of 1764 to Boston's representatives attacked the Sugar Act "both as a restraint on trade and as a tax that threatened democratic government." (pp. 207-208) Actually, the instructions do not mention "democratic government" and the emphasis in them is upon the "Charter Right to Govern and Tax ourselves" and upon "our British Privileges which . . . we hold in common with our Fellow Subjects 59
who are Natives of Britain."[18]

It appears, in fact, that it is only by interpreting authors as talking about democracy when they are not doing so that Professor Brown is able to maintain his thesis. He argues that, following the Tea Party, members of Parliament condemned Massachusetts, and particularly Boston, "for the democracy there." Here is the evidence he adduces for this conclusion: "Lord North blamed Boston . . . where, he said, the colonies and Britain were now considered as two independent states. One member thought that . . . British laws would never be obeyed until Britain had 'destroyed that nest of locusts.'" (pp. 320-321) Is Lord North condemning democracy or a spirit of independence—two rather different things? Is the other member quoted concerned about "the democracy there" or disobedience to British laws—again two different things which Brown confuses repeatedly?

One other similar example is important because it makes clear the monism in Professor Brown's approach to historical study. He argues that Hutchinson "expressed the idea that the conflict was not an internal lower-class movement for more democracy. The authority of Parliament to make any laws for the colonies was now denied as freely as Parliament's right to tax had previously been, he declared." (p. 246) Is it logical to conclude, from Hutchinson's statement that the colonists denied parliamentary authority, that Hutchinson was also saying there was no internal conflict? It is, perhaps, if we believe in a monistic interpretation: it had to be a war for independence *or* an internal revolution. But it is quite possible for Hutchinson to have said that the colonists were challenging Parliament's power without wishing to imply anything at all about internal conflict.

Professor Brown's interpretation is interesting, but it is an interpreta-

[18] Boston. *A Report of the Record Commissioners of the City of Boston Containing the Boston Town Records, 1758 to 1769* (Boston, 1886), 121-122.

tion without adequate evidence to support it. His argument that the War of Independence was caused by a British attempt to subvert the democratic institutions of the colonies is based upon the study of a single colony, and depends upon reading a struggle for democracy into issues and documents which most historians interpret in colonial-imperial terms. In the case of Massachusetts, his thesis fails because he does not offer sufficient proof that the colony's institutions were democratic. His analysis of religious and educational institutions does not prove that they were democratic, because he ignores some of the most important materials for determining whether they were. Because of his sampling techniques, his conclusions as to the
60 extent of land ownership and the number of men who were qualified voters are unreliable.

If he has not resolved the question of how many people owned enough property to vote, Brown has certainly made us aware of the total lack of evidence on this subject in the work of earlier historians. One can, however, question the wisdom of pursuing this line of enquiry at much greater length. Perhaps colonial historians have come to think of the issue of suffrage as centering upon property holdings more than it did. Though the property requirement was discussed by John Adams and some others (mostly after 1776, it seems), it is not clear that the eighteenth century viewed the property qualification as one overwhelming issue. It was a relict in Massachusetts of a provision that had developed in England, and may have been observed more in the breach than in the practice. The colonists seem to have been confronted by the more general question of who should vote—Negroes, whites, householders with families, bachelors, Trinitarians, and the like.[19] Earlier historians were responsible for this distortion of the subject of colonial suffrage and for the polarization of colonial social classes into propertied and nonpropertied. It would, however, seem prudent for the new generation of historians simply to reject the earlier formulation of the question, which is too limited to give us a full understanding of the practical politics or political institutions of the period. Further monographs showing that 40 or 75 or 90 per cent of the people could vote will not tell us whether colonial society and politics were democratic or whether there was an internal revolution in eighteenth-century America. The important questions, which it is hoped future studies will tell us more about, are who actually voted and why people voted as they did, rather than simply how many people were qualified to exercise the suffrage.

[19] Williamson, *American Suffrage*, 15-16, 115.

A New Look at Colonial Militia

John W. Shy*

THE subject of the militia has produced some passionate writing by American publicists, soldiers, and historians. Defenders of the militia—those who believe that a universal military obligation is the proper way to defend a society—are fond of stressing that only when free men must themselves fight to protect their liberty are they likely to remain free. The colonial militia, in particular, represents the happy uniqueness of America, where Englishmen in the seventeenth century revived this military relic of the middle ages just as in Europe it was sinking beneath the superiority of the politically dangerous mercenary army on the battlefield. Critics of the militia—many of them professional soldiers—point a different moral, one that rests on the apparent inefficiency of militia in combat, and on the way that the myth of defense by militia led again and again to tragic unpreparedness for war.

There is one point, however, where critics and defenders appear to agree: it is on the assumption that the militia, especially the colonial militia, is a fairly static institution; once its simple theory of organization has been described, there seems little need to watch it as closely for signs of deviation and change as one would watch, say, political institutions. Historians have tended to go along with this assumption, as they have generally accepted the major tenets of both defenders and critics; in short, the militia is usually regarded as both politically healthy and militarily inefficient, but in any case relatively uncomplicated.[1]

* Mr. Shy is a member of the Department of History, Princeton University. A version of this article was presented at the annual meeting of the Southern Historical Association, Miami Beach, Florida, Nov. 8, 1962.

[1] Even the best military historians have done this, at least by implication. See Walter Millis, *Arms and Men* (New York, 1956), chap. 1, especially the first sentence; or Louis Morton, "The Origins of American Military Policy," *Military Affairs*, XXII (1958), 75-82. Daniel Boorstin, author of the most provocative essay yet written on the subject, says: "Allowing for some variations, there was an impressive uniformity in the way colonists organized (or failed to organize) their defense." *The Americans: The Colonial Experience* (New York, 1958), 356, in the part entitled "A Nation of Minute Men."

My aim is simply to raise a question about this conventional view; and to suggest that the early American militia was a more complicated—and more interesting—institution, that it varied from province to province, that it changed through time as the military demands placed upon it changed, and that these variations and changes are of some historical importance.[2] My motive is not to bolster either the Pentagon or the House Armed Services Committee in their latest disagreement over the concept of the citizen army, or even to provide a new key to the reinterpretation of the American Revolution, but only to offer ways of thinking about our early military history, and of more satisfactorily relating that history to the
62 general history of colonial America.

It is not difficult to understand why the militia has been treated in terms of an unvarying sameness; one has only to read the laws to know the answer. In 1632 the Virginia Assembly told every man fit to carry a gun to bring it to church, that he might exercise with it after the service.[3] One hundred forty-four years later, the legislature of Revolutionary Massachusetts ordered men between the ages of sixteen and fifty to be enrolled in the militia, to provide their own weapons and equipment, and to be mustered and trained periodically by their duly commissioned officers; that is, the same thing Virginia had said if in less sophisticated language.[4] In other ways, the laws are much alike. Certain minor groups of men are exempted from duty. In time of emergency, individuals may be impressed or levied or drafted—the word varies—from their militia companies for active service. In most cases, the law provides that anyone so drafted can be excused by paying a fine, sometimes also by finding an able-bodied substitute. The one case of a clear legal difference—that company officers are elected by their men in New England while they are appointed by governors elsewhere—turns out on inspection to have made little difference in practice. As in the case of colonial politics, men of the "better sort" usually

[2] It is emphasized that what follows are hypotheses suggested by research done in another connection, and are intended to stimulate further inquiry. Professor Clyde R. Ferguson of Kansas State University discussed these hypotheses, when they were presented as a paper, knowledgeably and perceptively. While not accepting some of his views, I have profited by his criticism, as I have by that of Professor Wesley Frank Craven.

[3] William Waller Hening, ed., *The Statutes at Large: Being a Collection of All the Laws of Virginia* . . . (Richmond, 1810-23), I, 174.

[4] *Acts and Resolves, Public and Private, of the Province of Massachusetts Bay* (Boston, 1869-1922), V, 445-454.

appear in office whatever the process of selection; military organization and social structure seem as yet undifferentiated.

In the beginning, of course, this is true quite literally; social and military organization were the same thing. When John Smith wrote of "soldiers," he meant only those inhabitants who at that moment had guns in their hands and who had been ordered to help Smith look out for danger. But military change in Virginia began very early. To make everyone a soldier when men were still concerned about starving was to ensure that no one would be much of a soldier, as Virginia learned several times. First, a few forts and garrisons were established, either by appropriated funds or, more often, by land grants. Then Negroes, and later most inden- 63
tured servants, were excused from militia duty.[5] Indian policy had a direct bearing on military organization. For a time, Virginia attempted to treat all Indians as hostile, *ipso facto*.[6] But the military requirements of such a policy were too great, demanding large forces to make almost continuous raids into Indian country.[7] The policy was changed, and the system of defense changed with it; henceforth, Virginia relied on a buffer of friendly Indians, on several forts along the frontier, and—after Bacon's Rebellion—on a few dozen paid, mounted soldiers who "ranged" between the forts—the first rangers of American history.[8]

The year of Bacon's Rebellion, when both Chesapeake and New England colonies waged war against the Indian, affords a convenient opportunity for comparison. Though there are many similarities in the way Virginia and Massachusetts responded to this danger, differences are equally evident and may be more important. Virginia had fewer enemies to contend with, and yet suffered political breakdown in the process of fighting the war, while Massachusetts did not. Governor William Berkeley's strategy of defense, which called for five hundred soldiers in the pay of the colony, required a level of taxation that most Virginia planters believed they could not bear. When Nathaniel Bacon and his followers later reshaped strategy, they called for a thousand soldiers, but planned to use

[5] Philip A. Bruce, *Institutional History of Virginia in the Seventeenth Century* (New York, 1910), II, 5-6. Bruce says slaves were excused, but Hening, ed., *Statutes at Large*, I, 226, says "negroes."

[6] Wesley Frank Craven, "Indian Policy in Early Virginia," *William and Mary Quarterly*, 3d Ser., I (1944), 73-76.

[7] See the manifestly impracticable laws in Hening, ed., *Statutes at Large*, I, 140-141, 292-293.

[8] Bruce, *Institutional History*, II, 101-120.

them in raiding and plundering the Indian settlements; thus, Virginians would get not only the satisfaction of hitting back at their tormentors, but also the chance to make a burdensome war profitable.[9] The change from Berkeley to Bacon is more than a little reminiscent of European mercenary armies of the sixteenth and early seventeenth centuries, when a government often lost control of a war while trying to wage it more effectively. Massachusetts and Plymouth lost many more lives than did Virginia in 1675-76, but their governments never lost control of the war. Crucial to New England success was its ability to draft large numbers of men when and where they were needed. Of course there were grumbling and evasion
64 as war-weariness set in, but the point is that Boston could do it and apparently Jamestown could not.[10]

The reasons for this difference are not altogether clear. There is always danger of neglecting the effect of the particular economic and political situation in each colony while making a military comparison. There is also the possibility that if danger to Virginia had been greater, it might have unified and invigorated that colony. But it would seem that the principal factor is the different pattern of settlement. New England towns were more scattered than Chesapeake farms, but each town had a capacity for armed resistance that was lacking in an individual plantation. A town could bear the burden of a military draft and still hope to maintain itself against attack, while the loss of a man or two from a single, remote household often meant choosing between abandonment or destruction. Despite shortages and complaints, a New England town could usually house and feed a company of soldiers besides its own, thus acting as an advanced military base. Even the meetinghouse, large and centrally located, often doubled as the "garrison house," strong point and refuge in case of attack. New England promised its soldiers plunder in the form of scalp bounties, profits from the sale of Indian slaves, and postwar land grants, but such promises were contributory, and not essential as they were in Virginia, to the procurement of troops. The contrast between New England and the

[9] Hening, ed., *Statutes at Large*, II, 326-336, 341-350. See the discussion in Wilcomb E. Washburn, *The Governor and the Rebel: A History of Bacon's Rebellion in Virginia* (Chapel Hill, 1957), 35-63.

[10] Douglas Leach, *Flintlock and Tomahawk: New England in King Philip's War* (New York, 1958), emphasizes that New Englanders disliked the draft, but also makes it clear that many of them were drafted. See especially pp. 45-46, 103-104, 123, and 185-187.

Chesapeake can be exaggerated, because many New England towns were destroyed or abandoned during King Philip's War. But there remains an important difference: the clustering of manpower and the cohesive atmosphere in the town community gave New England greater military strength.

This point about the importance of atmosphere can be sharpened by adding the case of New York to the comparison. The Dutch West India Company made the initial error of promising protection to the settlers of New Netherland, and it never thereafter could correct its mistake, although it tried.[11] Organized solely as a commercial enterprise, the colony acquired 65
a social heterogeneity and an attitude toward war that subverted militia organization. The English conquest in 1664 brought the stereotype militia law, but it also brought a small garrison of regulars that tended to perpetuate the Dutch atmosphere of military dependency. Moreover, an accident of geography gave New York not the two-hundred-mile frontier of Massachusetts or Virginia, but a single center of danger—the Anglo-Dutch city of Albany, a city constantly torn by internal disputes. More straggling in its pattern of settlement than Virginia, and with much less of the sense of community that makes men fight for one another, New York depended for protection on its diplomatic and commercial connection with the Iroquois Confederation rather than on an effective militia; in time of trouble, it had to call for help.[12]

By the end of the seventeenth century, the principal threat to the British colonies was changing. Europeans—French and Spanish—became the main danger. Virginia found itself so little troubled by the new threat, and her Indian enemies so weak, that militia virtually ceased to exist there for about a half century, a time when a handful of semi-professional rangers could watch the frontier. When the Tuscarora momentarily menaced Virginia in 1713, Governor Alexander Spotswood had little success in ordering out the militia. He then tried to recruit two hundred volun-

[11] E. B. O'Callaghan and B. Fernow, eds., *Documents Relative to the Colonial History of the State of New-York* (Albany, 1853-87), I, 153-154, 389, 392, 397, 427-428, 438; II, 112.

[12] Jasper Danckaerts, who saw a New York militia muster in 1680, wrote: "I have never seen anything worse." Bartlett Burleigh James and J. Franklin Jameson, eds., *Journal of Jasper Danckaerts, 1679-1680* (New York, 1913), 239. Shortly thereafter he was favorably impressed by the Boston militia; *ibid.*, 271. For New York's continuing troubles with militia, see O'Callaghan and Fernow, eds., *Doc. Rel. Col. Hist. N.-Y.*, III, 373, 478; IV, 185, 870-879, 968; V, 60, 253.

teers from the counties along the frontier ("for those that are far enough from it are little inclined to adventure themselves"), but soon learned that frontiersmen were understandably reluctant to leave their homes in time of danger. Spotswood, finally convinced that he could not make war, made peace.[13]

During the same period, the frontiers of Massachusetts were under sporadic attack by French-supported Indians. After the loss of Deerfield in 1704, the colony developed a net of what have been called, in another time and place, "strategic villages," from Hadley to Wells in Maine, each protected by its own militia, and augmented by provincial troops who used
66 horses in the summer, snowshoes in the winter, to connect the towns by patrols and to conduct raids into Indian country.[14] Clearly the New England militia was retaining much of its vitality.

But it was not just the prevalence or absence of an external threat that determined military change. As New England bore the brunt of war with France, South Carolina occupied the post of danger against Spain. The Carolina militia came in from the country to repulse a Spanish attack on Charleston in 1706, and it rallied—with some help from North Carolina and Virginia—to save the colony during the Yamassee War in 1715, though not before most of the outlying settlements had been abandoned. But South Carolina came to have a more scattered population than either Virginia or New York. In 1720, the Council and Assembly complained to the British Board of Trade that it was difficult to react to any sudden danger because the colony's 2,000 militiamen were spread over 150 miles.[15] In

[13] Spotswood to the Lords Commissioners of Trade, Sept. 14, 1713, in R. A. Brock, ed., *The Official Letters of Alexander Spotswood . . .* (Richmond, 1882-85), II, 37. In a long report to the Board of Trade in 1716 (*ibid.*, 194-212), Spotswood proposed the abandonment of the militia system in Virginia in favor of a force that would comprise only one-third of the available military manpower, but would be paid by a tax on the other two-thirds who would be excused from service. Spotswood's proposal has a certain similarity to the modern American Reserve and National Guard. He was certain that most Virginians would be happy to pay a small tax to avoid traveling 20 or 30 miles to muster, but foresaw opposition from "Persons of Estates," who "would not come off so easily as they do now." As Spotswood saw it, under the militia system, in practice "no Man of an Estate is under any Obligation to Muster, and even the Servants or Overseers of the Rich are likewise exempted; the whole Burthen lyes upon the poorest sort of people."

[14] Governor Joseph Dudley to the Board of Trade, Apr. 8, 1712, in Cecil Headlam, ed., *Calendar of State Papers, Colonial Series, America and West Indies, July, 1711-June, 1712* (London, 1925), 257-258.

[15] The Council and Assembly of South Carolina to the Council of Trade and

1738, Lieutenant Governor William Bull reported to the Board that, brave as the Carolinians might be, an effective defense was, as he phrased it, "Inconsistent with a Domestick or Country Life."[16]

Bull neglected to mention South Carolina's other major difficulty in defending itself—slavery. Under the earliest militia law, officers were to "muster and train all sorts of men, of what condition or wheresoever born." In the Yamassee War, four hundred Negroes helped six hundred white men defeat the Indians.[17] But as the ratio of slaves to whites grew rapidly, and especially after a serious slave insurrection in 1739, Carolinians no longer dared arm Negroes; in fact, they hardly dared leave their plantations in time of emergency. The British government tried to fill the gap, first by organizing Georgia as an all-white military buffer, then by sending a regiment of regulars with Oglethorpe in 1740. But increasingly the South Carolina militia became an agency to control slaves, and less an effective means of defense.[18]

Elsewhere the new, European threat of the eighteenth century called forth responses that went far beyond the original conception of militia. War against France and Spain required larger forces, serving for a longer time and traveling greater distances. These were volunteer forces, paid and supplied, often armed and clothed, by the government. The power of the governor to raise and command the militia accordingly came to mean less and less, while the military role of the legislature grew larger. The shift in power from royal governor to colonial Assembly had many causes, but the change in the character of warfare was not the least of them.

Less important perhaps, but also less obvious, was the changing character of recruitment in the eighteenth century. So long as military service

---

Plantations, Jan. 29, 1719/20, *ibid., January, 1719 to February 1720* (London, 1933), 319.

[16] Lieutenant Governor William Bull to the Board of Trade, May 25, 1738, Egremont Papers, Public Record Office 30 (Gifts and Deposits), Piece 47, XIV, 55-56, Public Record Office, London.

[17] Contents of the First Charter of South Carolina, 1663, Thomas Cooper and D. J. McCord, eds., *Statutes at Large of South Carolina* (Columbia, 1836-41), I, 29; "Journal of the . . . Yemassee War," *Year Book—1894, City of Charleston, So. Ca.* (Charleston, n.d.), 323 et passim.

[18] In a memorial to the King, Apr. 9, 1734, the Governor, Council, and Assembly argued that the presence of three Negroes for every white man made provincial self-defense impossible. *Cal. State Papers, Col., Amer. and W. Indies, 1734-1735* (London, 1953), 173-175.

was nearly universal, one might imagine that volunteers for active duty necessarily must have been militiamen who received a reminder of their military obligation along with a little tactical drill at the militia muster, three or four times a year. This, it would appear, is not wholly true. There were several classes of men, whose total number was growing after 1700, who fell outside the militia structure. These classes were: friendly and domesticated Indians, free Negroes and mulattoes, white servants and apprentices, and free white men on the move. These were precisely the men who, if given the chance, were most willing to go to war. As the militia companies tended in the eighteenth century to become more social than mili-
68 tary organizations, they became the hallmarks of respectability or at least of full citizenship in the community. Evidence gathered so far is not full nor does it admit of any quantitative conclusions, but it does indicate that a growing number of those who did the actual fighting were not the men who bore a military obligation as part of their freedom.[19]

It is difficult to believe that the colonial volunteers of the eighteenth

[19] For Negroes, see Benjamin Quarles, "The Colonial Militia and Negro Manpower," *Mississippi Valley Historical Review*, XLV (1959), 643-652. For servants, see Richard B. Morris, *Government and Labor in Early America* (New York, 1946), 279-290, which shows that a considerable number of servants fought in the 18th century, despite the protests of their masters; and Abbot E. Smith, *Colonists in Bondage; White Servitude and Convict Labor in America, 1607-1776* (Chapel Hill, 1947), 279, which shows that servants were not usually mustered into the militia during the 18th century. There is scattered evidence for the existence of migratory free white men not enrolled in the militia: Nathaniel B. Shurtleff, ed., *Records of the Governor and Company of the Massachusetts Bay in New England* (Boston, 1853-1954), V, 242; *Colonial Laws of New York from the year 1664 to the Revolution* (Albany, 1894-96), I, 454; Governor Dudley to the Council of Trade and Plantations, Nov. 15, 1710, in Headlam, ed., *Cal. State Papers, Col., Amer. and W. Indies, 1710-June, 1711* (London, 1924), 268, where Governor Dudley reported that all his "loose people" had gone in the expedition to Nova Scotia; Smith, *Colonists in Bondage*, 281-282, which discusses the impressment of vagrants; Colonel George Washington to Governor Dinwiddie, Mar. 9, 1754, in R. A. Brock, ed., *The Official Records of Governor Robert Dinwiddie . . .* (Richmond, 1883-84), I, 92, where George Washington complains that his soldiers in 1754 are "loose, Idle Persons that are quite destitute of House and Home." For Indians, either as allies or as individual recruits, examples abound. Perhaps the over-all tendency was exemplified by the New York Assembly in 1711; when asked to provide 600 men for the expedition against Canada, it voted 350 "Christian" volunteers, 150 Long Island Indians, and 100 Palatine Germans, who were not only outside the militia system but recently had been disarmed for their unruly behavior. In addition, 100 more Palatines were sent by the Assembly as recruits to the four British regular companies stationed in the province.

century had more in common with the pitiable recruits of the contemporary European armies than with the militia levies of an earlier period; nevertheless, changes in the social composition of American forces between about 1650 and 1750 were in that direction. By impressing vagabonds in 1740, the Virginia Assembly filled its quota of men for the expedition against Cartagena. Six years later, when Governor William Gooch sought to recruit volunteers for another expedition, he found few men willing to enlist, the usual sources apparently depleted by the previous draft.[20]

Perhaps the vital change was in the tone of active service: with more social pariahs filling the ranks and military objectives less clearly connected
to parochial interests, respectable men felt not so impelled by a sense of 69
duty or guilt to take up arms. Only when a war approached totality (as in the Puritan crusade to Louisbourg in 1745, when an impressive percentage of Massachusetts manpower served in the land and sea forces) might the older attitude appear. Otherwise fighting had ceased to be a function of the community as such. It seems never to have crossed the introspective mind of young John Adams that he was exactly the right age to serve in the Seven Years' War, and he was shocked when a friend expressed envy in 1759 of the heroic warriors who had begun to win victories in North America.[21]

In fact, volunteer units so constituted could perform well under certain circumstances, but generally suffered from low morale and slack discipline. At least one British general in the Seven Years' War understood that there were two kinds of provincial troops: those levied from among the militia on the basis of a legal military obligation, and those who were recruited for all the wrong reasons—money, escape, and the assurance of easy discipline.[22] It is instructive to note that before Pitt's promise of reimbursement permitted the colonial governments to pre-empt the recruiting market with high pay and enlistment bounties, British regiments, despite their notoriously low pay and harsh discipline, enlisted about 7,500 Americans after

[20] Richard L. Morton, *Colonial Virginia* (Chapel Hill, 1960), II, 526-527, 535.

[21] L. H. Butterfield and others, eds., *The Adams Papers: Diary and Autobiography of John Adams* (Cambridge, Mass., 1961), I, 110 et passim.

[22] In a private letter to the Earl of Loudoun, Feb. 25, 1758, Major General James Abercromby urged that the provincial troops be improved "by drafting them out of the militia, in place of whom they send out at an extravagant premium the rif-raf of the continent." Loudoun Papers, No. 5668, Henry E. Huntington Library, San Marino, Calif.

Braddock's arrival.[23] Again in 1762, when the colonies themselves used supplementary bounties to recruit regulars for General Jeffery Amherst, almost 800 enlisted.[24] There are hints that some of these recruits—for the provincial as well as the regular regiments—were Indians and Negroes, and better evidence that many of the white men were second-class citizens of one sort or another.[25]

The generally low opinion acquired by most British officers of the American fighting man, an opinion that later would have disastrous consequences for them, originated with the kind of provincial units they saw during the Seven Years' War. Even when Massachusetts and Virginia re-
70 sorted to the draft to fill their quotas, they now provided first for the impressment of "strollers," and "idle, vagrant, or dissolute persons."[26] Once the British had seen the American encampment at the head of Lake George in 1756—"nastier than anything I could conceive," reported one officer—most provincial regiments were relegated by the British command to an auxiliary function, becoming toward the end of the war "hewers of wood and drawers of water," as James Otis put it.[27] This was ignoble and backbreaking work, often on short rations, so that low morale and poor discipline declined still further. Add to this the frequency of epidemics among the Americans, whose officers probably had never heard of the elementary rules of field sanitation set down by Dr. John Pringle in 1752 and could not have enforced them even if they had. Contributory to certain

[23] Stanley M. Pargellis, *Lord Loudoun in North America* (New Haven, 1933), 108-109.

[24] J. C. Webster, ed., *The Journal of Jeffery Amherst* (Toronto, 1931), 331. Pargellis, *Loudoun*, 111, gives the lower figure of 670 based on the report enclosed in Amherst to Samuel Martin, Nov. 1, 1762, Amherst Papers, War Office 34, LXXIV, fol. 176, Public Record Office. But a comparison of this report with the list in Amherst's *Journal* shows an increase in the number of recruits supplied by Massachusetts, Rhode Island, Connecticut, and New York, suggesting that the former document is an incomplete report.

[25] In 1761 Governor Thomas Fitch of Connecticut went so far as to propose the enlistment of French prisoners of war, then in his colony, in the provincial forces. Jeffery Amherst to Thomas Fitch, Apr. 15, 1761, Connecticut Historical Society, *Collections*, XVIII (Hartford, 1920), 109-110.

[26] The words are those of Massachusetts (*Acts and Resolves*, IV, 193) and Virginia (Hening, ed., *Statutes at Large*, VII, 70), respectively.

[27] James Otis, *The Rights of the British Colonies Asserted and Proved* . . . (Boston, 1764), 58. Lieutenant Colonel Ralph Burton was the officer disgusted by the American camp; to Lord Loudoun, Aug. 5, 1756, Loudoun Papers, No. 1424, as quoted in Pargellis, *Loudoun*, 95.

kinds of disease was the absence—not the presence—of women among the provincial troops. These poor creatures—ridiculed in the drawings of Hogarth and maligned by the Puritan clergy—at least kept some semblance of cleanliness about the camp, hospitals, and person of the British regular.

Because the Seven Years' War in America was primarily an attack on Canada with New England supplying most of the provincial troops, it was the Yankee in particular who came to be regarded as a poor species of fighting man. This helps explain the notion of the British government that Massachusetts might be coerced without too much trouble in 1774. The government and most British officers failed to understand that those pro- 71
vincials who had mutinied, deserted, and died like flies during the Seven Years' War were not militia units; those who did understand the difference apparently failed to see that the New England militia had not decayed to the extent that it had elsewhere. Even after Bunker Hill, General Thomas Gage seems still to have been somewhat confused: "In all their Wars against the French," he wrote to the Secretary of State, "they never Shewed so much Conduct Attention and Perseverance as they do now."[28]

It would be wrong, I am sure, to push either of the arguments advanced herein beyond certain limits. A good deal of research remains to be done before these comparisons are fully established, or perhaps modified. But the main points seem to me clearly borne out by the evidence turned up so far. The approach to early American warfare that promises new insight into the nonmilitary facets of colonial history—into political behavior, social structure, economic activity, even religious belief—is the approach that emphasizes regional diversity and continual change.

[28] Gage to Dartmouth, June 25, 1775, in Clarence E. Carter, ed., *The Correspondence of General Thomas Gage* (New Haven, 1931-33), I, 407. Though the hypotheses advanced in this article are meant to apply only to the colonial period, the author being willing to admit that the Revolution brought rapid and extensive changes, there remains at least a trace of persistent difference between Virginia and Massachusetts after 1775. In 1777, Jefferson opposed a draft from the Virginia militia: "It ever was the most unpopular and impracticable thing that could be attempted. Our people even under the monarchial government had learnt to consider it as the last of all oppressions." Adams, in reply, agreed that it was "only to be adopted in great Extremities." But he added: "Draughts in the Massachusetts, as they have been there managed, have not been very unpopular, for the Persons draughted are commonly the wealthiest, who become obliged to give large Premiums, to their poorer Neighbours, to take their Places." Jefferson to Adams, May 16, 1777, and Adams to Jefferson, May 26, 1777, in Lester J. Cappon, ed., *The Adams-Jefferson Letters: The Complete Correspondence between Thomas Jefferson and Abigail and John Adams* (Chapel Hill, 1959), I, 4-5.

THE
HUNTINGTON LIBRARY
QUARTERLY

VOLUME XXX, NUMBER 1 NOVEMBER 1966

The Role of Newspapers in Early America "In Defense of Their Own Liberty"

By Lawrence H. Leder

The dominant factor in shaping and expressing public opinion in eighteenth-century America was the newspaper, and it forms the only source for evaluating what the "average colonist" thought about the issues of the day. If we wish to understand popular attitudes, as differentiated from the views of the elite, we must turn to what the people read. The high degree of literacy in the colonies, coupled with the wide circulation of the newspapers, leads to the conclusion that the press must have been a potent force in focusing and defining eighteenth-century attitudes.[1]

Before we can fully accept this thesis, however, we must contend with the disturbing view, recently expressed, that freedom of the press did not exist in colonial America. Although prior licensing of newspapers had been abandoned as English policy in 1695, it is argued, every printer had hanging over his head the threat of either a seditious libel prosecution under common law or a prosecution for breach of legislative privilege. Thus eighteenth-century America did

[1]Richard L. Merritt, "Public Opinion in Colonial America: Content-analyzing the Colonial Press," *The Public Opinion Quarterly*, XXVII (1963), 356-358, 362-365. Although imprecise, Merritt's figures suggest that by 1775 there was one issue of a newspaper for every 65 colonists. For the press's influence, see also Paul M. Spurlin, *Montesquieu in America, 1760-1801* (Baton Rouge, 1940), p. 42.

Research for this paper was facilitated by grants from the LSU Research Council and the American Council of Learned Societies.

not "produce or inherit a broad concept of freedom of speech or press," and the words themselves were neither meaningful nor effective.[2] If this were true, the press's influence in forming public opinion would be severely lessened, and its usefulness as a gauge of public attitudes would be diminished.

The existence of prosecutions of printers can be documented by court records and legislative journals and, viewed only in this way, a bleak and dismal picture of repression is presented. But a more realistic approach is to look at the newspapers themselves and see what they had to say about the issue. If the press were truly subdued by the threat of official action, that would be reflected in their statements on their own freedom, or such statements would not appear at all.

A few printers were prosecuted in colonial America,[3] but it is of greater interest to determine whether their cases were the rule or the exception. It can be contended that such prosecutions merely indicated the failure of the eighteenth century to understand freedom fully, not the full absence of any understanding of the subject. If the press of eighteenth-century America sought consistently to define its own freedom and if those definitions became increasingly precise and widespread, a fair case may be made for this freedom's existence as a working concept.

Perhaps the basic dilemma is to find and apply an adequate definition. The difficulty of the meaning and nature of freedom is still with us, and we should not be shocked that it plagued our ancestors; rather, we should be encouraged that they were concerned with it. Carl Becker illustrated the difficulty rather well: "The nature of freedom and responsibility," he explained, "is such that they cannot be discussed, still less dealt with, to any good purpose separately. Freedom unrestrained by responsibility becomes mere license; responsibility

[2]Leonard W. Levy, *Legacy of Suppression: Freedom of Speech and Press in Early American History* (Cambridge, Mass., 1960), p. 86.

[3]More printers were attacked by legislatures than by courts or governors (ibid., pp. 20-21). But Levy's source also suggests: "And yet it would be most unfair and misleading to give the impression that the many severe and sometimes cruel dealings of the various assemblies with violators of privilege represent simply a clash of personalities with no principle behind it. If this were all, it would not be worth relating. The rights of English freemen were voiced over and over again by the various assemblies, and there is no reason to doubt the sincerity of these utterances" (Mary Patterson Clarke, *Parliamentary Privilege in the American Colonies* [New Haven, 1943], p. 130).

unchecked by freedom becomes mere arbitrary power. The question, then, is . . . how they can be united and reconciled to the best advantage."[4] An eighteenth-century jurist could not have phrased the problem better.

Before proceeding further, some stipulations as to the limits of this paper are in order. Only materials appearing in American newspapers (and occasionally magazines) and written by Americans have been considered. No essays or letters lifted without comment or modification from the English press have been included. They were frequently picked up as cudgels with which to beat the opposition
74 over the head, with no thought being given to the finer points of theory involved; or at least such thought cannot be demonstrated. Only papers published before 1762 have been used, so as to determine the ideas in the mainstream of American thought before it became polluted by the imperial crisis. Until the end of the Great War for Empire, Americans had not challenged the basic framework of their own political thinking—their loyalty to crown, country, and constitution.

Newspapers long existed in the American colonies before they engaged in any speculations on their own freedom. The absence of such discussion in the first three decades has been puzzling, but it is probably explained by the fact that each urban area, until the population expanded adequately, could support but one newspaper, usually an official one that depended on governmental contracts for economic survival.[5] Not until newspapers began to compete with one another did the question of their freedom arise. Then, as the newcomer sought to break into the monopolistic situation, it found its

[4] *Freedom and Responsibility in the American Way of Life* (New York, 1953), pp. 2-3.

[5] Some parallels can be drawn between population expansion and newspaper multiplication, though they are only tentative because of the inexactness of population statistics. Boston's first continuous paper, the *News-Letter*, began in 1704; its second, the *Gazette*, in 1719; its third, the *Courant*, in 1721. Boston's population in 1700 was 6,700; by 1722 it increased to 10,567. Philadelphia's first paper, the *American Weekly Mercury*, started in 1719; the second, the *Gazette*, in 1728. The city's growth was rapid; it had 1,200 houses in 1708 and 2,400 by 1731. New York City's first paper, the *Gazette*, began in 1725; its second, the *Weekly Journal*, in 1733, followed by the *Post Boy* in 1734. Its population jumped from 1,460 adult males in 1723 to 2,628 males over ten in 1731 and 3,253 males over ten in 1737. For the newspaper data, see Clarence Brigham, *History and Bibliography of American Newspapers 1690-1820* (Hamden, 1962), passim. For the population figures, see Evarts B. Greene and Virginia D. Harrington, *American Population before the Federal Census of 1790* (New York, 1932), pp. 22n, 96-98, 117.

audience among the opposition faction, and it challenged both the government and the subservience of its longer-established competitor.

Such a situation existed in Boston, where the first competitive newspaper began operation in 1721. James Franklin's *New-England Courant* took up the cause of freedom, though in a most guarded way. A letter allegedly coming from "P[ortsmout]h New-Hampshire" and signed "Tom. Penshallow" complained: "As for freedom of speech, it is utterly suppressed among us, and I suppose we shall be hanged for our thoughts.... It is whispered, that we are to have a law prohibiting the reading [of] your Courants ... because your paper 75
sometimes sets forth the rights and liberties of mankind."[6]

Having labeled himself as the enunciator of liberty, James Franklin quickly collided with the Massachusetts authorities. In the summer of 1722, he published a "high affront" to the General Court and was jailed for the balance of the legislative session. Young Benjamin Franklin, the anonymous author of the Silence Dogood letters, responded to the high-handed treatment given his brother by including in one of his letters an extract on freedom of thought from the *London Journal*.[7]

Pretentious behavior continued to be the *Courant's* target, and James Franklin attacked religious hypocrisy and cast some aspersions on the recently departed governor in 1723. The House of Representatives immediately ordered that the paper be supervised by the provincial secretary, and Franklin ignored the order.[8] He argued that, if he violated any law, he should be "presented by a grand jury and a fair tryal brought on."[9] The *Courant's* editor was then arrested for contempt, and his younger brother became nominal editor. Young Benjamin stated his position succinctly: "It is a vulgar error which some have entertained, and which it concerns every true Englishman to obviate, that there must be no complaint made of the proceedings of the legislative power."[10] There matters rested for the moment.

[6]Dec. 11-18, 1721 (No. 20).

[7]*The Papers of Benjamin Franklin*, ed. Leonard W. Labaree et al. (New Haven, 1959-), I, 27.

[8]Ibid., p. 47.

[9]The *New-England Courant*, Jan. 28–Feb. 4, 1722/3 (No. 79).

[10]Ibid., Apr. 29–May 6, 1723 (No. 92).

Philadelphia was the next urban center to acquire a competitive newspaper, and the newcomer was Benjamin Franklin, who established the *Pennsylvania Gazette* in 1728. His Boston experience must have left its mark, for he was concerned about the abuse heaped on printers for publishing materials disliked by those in authority. The business of printing, he editorialized, "has chiefly to do with mens opinions." Consequently, everything a printer did would "probably give offence to some, and perhaps to many." But the printer did not necessarily agree with everything he set in type, nor did he try to limit his columns only to those things of which he personally ap-
76 proved. Franklin's argument, simply enough, was that the printer was a craftsman who should not judge the merits of the ideas he printed, but merely their physical appearance. If the printer turned critic, "the world would afterwards have nothing to read but what happened to be the opinions of printers."[11]

But Franklin begged the question. Who would accept the responsibility shirked by the printer? Andrew Bradford's longer-established *American Weekly Mercury* sought to answer that by defining the proper limits of the press. "In all countries where liberty only reigns," wrote an essayist, "every man hath a privilege of declaring his sentiments with the utmost freedom; provided he does it with a proper decency, and a just regard to the laws." The last phrase imposed the traditional limitations of common-law prosecution, but coupled with it was a broader theme: "All governments, under whatever form they are administered, ought to be administered for the good of the society; and when they are otherwise administered, they cease to be government, and become usurpation. . . . even the most despotick have this limitation to their authority." Although, the writer continued, the despotic prince did not have to contend with written constitutional limits, "there is still this tacit condition annexed to his power, that he must act by the unwritten laws of discretion and prudence, and employ it [power] for the sole interest of the people, who give it to him."[12] Suddenly, the definition took on added dimensions, although it was clearly not libertarian, when "just regard to the laws" was joined to the concept of limited government.

[11]June 3-10, 1731 (No. 134). This was modified and reprinted in the *South Carolina Gazette*, Oct. 7-14, 1732 (No. 39).

[12]Mar. 30–Apr. 6, 1732 (No. 640).

New York City's first competitive newspaper was John Peter Zenger's *Weekly Journal*. Although Zenger's famous trial immediately comes to mind, it has been analyzed often and well enough by others and it needs no further comment here.[13] What is of greater interest is the furor aroused in the press by Zenger before and after his trial. He clearly established himself as the opposition printer in the early issues of his paper. His publication of Gordon and Trenchard's "Cato Letters," two of which dealt with freedom of the press, really began New York's inquiry into this area of freedom.[14]

Zenger's own correspondents soon took up the battle cry, and he published one letter that dealt with the problem specifically and in absolute terms. "The liberty of the press," it announced, "is a liberty for every man to communicate his sentiments freely to the public, upon political or religious points; it is either this or nothing." Those who feared to expose their pet doctrines to public analysis, the author continued, knew that their ideas stood upon a "very weak foundation," or they were "friends to Popery and arbitrary power."[15]

Zenger continued to publish the "Cato Letters," and one of them finally evoked a response in William Bradford's longer-established *New-York Gazette*. "But here is the fallacy, here lies the imposition upon the people," wrote the Bradford essayist, "it would here be insinuated, that to punish the licentiousness of the press, would be to take away the liberty of the press. . . . Tis the abuse not the use of the press that is criminal, and ought to be punished."[16] As the voice of government, this essay expressed the traditional attitudes and left undefined the distinction between use and abuse.

Interestingly enough, an answer came from Charleston, South Carolina, where Lewis Timothy's *Gazette* printed a careful analysis of the problem as its lead editorial in his first issue. The idea was simple and powerful: "Neither do I see how any restraint can be put upon the press, in a nation that pretends to liberty, but what is just sufficient to prevent men from writing either blasphemy or treason."

13Livingston Rutherfurd, *John Peter Zenger* (New York, 1904); Vincent Buranelli, *The Trial of Peter Zenger* (New York, 1957); *A Brief Narrative of the Case and Trial of John Peter Zenger*, ed. Stanley N. Katz (Cambridge, Mass., 1964).

14The *New-York Weekly Journal*, Nov. 12 and 19, 1733 (Nos. 2 and 3).

15Ibid., Jan. 14, 1733/4 (No. 11).

16Jan. 28–Feb. 4, 1733/4 (No. 432).

Zenger quickly reprinted this, noting it was worthy of repetition and that it could not be deemed seditious "because it is the government's paper." The same editorial, slightly amplified by a new introduction, appeared that same week in Andrew Bradford's *American Weekly Mercury* in Philadelphia.[17]

The concentric circles widened and the discussion of freedom of the press expanded. A series of articles appeared in the *American Weekly Mercury;* the first advocated an absolute freedom, but did not define terms; the second hit at the real problem.[18] "We must carefully distinguish between liberty and licentiousness," the essayist
78 warned, for "the extreams that separate liberty from license are closer than most men imagine." He began his definitions with negative reasoning: to call into question the king's right to his realm and dominions, or to challenge his private or public life was "treasonable license." Liberty did not include the subversion of fundamental points of religion and morality. Neither did it include a "license of traducing those gentlemen who are appointed our lawful governors; when they behave themselves well, they ought to be treated with all the respect and gratitude, that's due from an obliged people; should they behave themselves ill, their measures are to be remonstrated against in terms of decency and moderation, not of fury or scurrility." Nor should the "'sacred veneration" due "the upright dispensers of the law" be altered or destroyed.

Turning to a more positive approach, the essayist concluded: "by freedom of the press, I mean a liberty, within the bounds of law, for any man to communicate to the public, his sentiments on the important points of religion and government; of proposing any laws, which he apprehends may be for the good of his country, and of applying for the repeal of such, as he judges pernicious. I mean a liberty of detecting the wicked and destructive measures of certain politicians; of dragging villany out of its obscure lurking holes, and exposing it in its full deformity to open day; of attacking wickedness in high places, of disentangling the intricate folds of a wicked and corrupt administration, and pleading freely for a redress of grievances. I mean a lib-

[17]*South-Carolina Gazette*, Feb. 2, 1733/4 (No. 1); it was reprinted in the *New-York Weekly Journal*, Mar. 4, 1733/4 (No. 18), and the *American Weekly Mercury*, Mar. 5-12, 1733/4 (No. 741).

[18]Mar. 21-28 (No. 743), Apr. 18-25, 1734 (No. 747).

erty of examining the great articles of our faith, by the light of scripture and reason."

Although Zenger immediately reprinted this statement in his own *Journal*, it raised more questions than it answered.[19] Such broadside treatment bothered at least one of Zenger's correspondents. "But how any man can with great satisfaction see that liberty [of the press], the essential liberty of the constitution, enjoyed in so unconfined a manner, that some men continue to abuse it . . . with impunity," the writer questioned, "is too deep and intricate for me to understand, unless the person seeing this abuse with so great satisfaction be himself the abuser of it: For I cannot conceive how any man can see a liberty, and an essential liberty of a constitution, abused with impunity, and see that abuse with great satisfaction, too, except himself be the abuser, or some of his friends."[20]

This distinction between what is abuse and use, of course, is the key issue. William Bradford's *New-York Gazette* sought to clarify it. "I must own," wrote a reader, "that no restraint ought to be put upon the press, but what is sufficient to prevent the grossest abuses of it, abuses that dissolute society, and sap the very foundation of government . . . but with regard to abuses of a less flagrant nature, I had rather see such permitted, than the liberty itself abridged."[21]

The response in Zenger's *Journal* sharpened the issue: "I hope by freely he means without the fear or danger of being punished. When they can so write, it will then be felicitas, and rara felicitas temporum." It is true, the author admitted, "that abuses that dissolve society, and sap the foundations of government, are not to be sheltered under the umbrage of the liberty of the press: But if those in power will term a trifling song, or anything of so minute a nature, a dissolving of society, and sapping of the foundations of government; if they will fix determinate meanings to sentences and even blanks, which the authors have not fixt, and to which other meanings can with equal justice be applyed; I would be glad to know wherein this liberty of writing consists?"[22]

[19] The *New-York Weekly Journal*, Apr. 15, 1734 (No. 24).

[20] Ibid., Oct. 21, 1734 (No. 51).

[21] Oct. 21-28, 1734 (No. 470).

[22] The *New-York Weekly Journal*, Nov. 4, 1734 (No. 53).

This interesting and potentially fruitful dialogue was interrupted by Zenger's arrest for seditious libel in November 1734. Although the focus shifted to the courtroom, our attention remains fixed on the continuing debate in the newspaper columns. Lewis Morris, James Alexander, and Andrew Hamilton all involved themselves in the printer's defense, and they aimed their arguments at winning freedom to criticize for themselves. But in so doing, they phrased their arguments in an appealing fashion and, as a result, made them convenient tools for others to use.

The debate began anew when Jonathan Blenman of Barbados
80 penned a series of newspaper essays which were reprinted in pamphlet form and given wide distribution. He desired to destroy the mistaken doctrine that freedom of the press is a "license to write and publish infamous things of their superiors and of all others, at their pleasure, provided they write and publish nothing but what is true." He acknowledged the subject's right to complain to magistrates, parliament, and the king, but he flatly denied the right "of complaining to the neighbors." The press, Blenman declared, is "a two-edged weapon, capable of cutting both ways, and is not therefore to be trusted in the hands of every discontented fool or designing knave. Men of sense and address (who alone deserve public attention) will ever be able to convey proper ideas to the people, in time of danger, without running counter to all order and decency, or crying fire and murder thro' the streets, if they chance to wake from a frightful dream." Moreover, the right of complaining to the public, even by men of sense and address, is limited to a people in a sovereign state subject to no superior; "this is far from being the case of colonies," he concluded.[23]

Blenman found his match in a series of essays by James Alexander in the *Pennsylvania Gazette*. Alexander probably felt impelled to respond to the criticism because he had master-minded Zenger's defense; and he probably chose the Philadelphia newspaper because Hamilton, who had been the defense attorney, was undergoing a strenuous assault by his Pennsylvania enemies because of his role in the trial. Blenman's legalistic arguments proved a potent weapon that

[23]Jonathan Blenman, *Remarks on Zengers Tryal, Taken out of the Barbados Gazette's* (Philadelphia, 1737), pp. 3, 33-34.

had to be blunted. The result was what one authority has cited as the major American contribution to the libertarian theory of the press.[24]

Alexander's arguments began with a statement that republics and limited monarchies derived their strength "from a popular examination into the actions of the magistrates," a privilege which "in all ages has been and always will be abused." Security for the government official, he argued, came not from repression of criticism, but from the knowledge that "impartial posterity will not fail to render him justice." Freedom of speech and press would be abused—"these are the excresciencies of liberty"—and "they ought to be suppressed." But, he queried, "to whom dare we commit the care of doing it?" To give this to a magistrate would place too much power in his hands—"under pretence of pruning off the exuberant branches, he frequently destroys the tree."

Tracing the doctrine of seditious libel from Augustus Caesar to the days of the Stuarts, Alexander dwelt on the famous case of Algernon Sydney and concluded that a grave danger "attends a law for punishing words." There is little security for men when "a judge by remote inferences and distant inuendos may construe the most innocent expressions into capital crimes." Rather suffer an inconveniency, he warned, "when it cannot be removed without introducing a worse."

Alexander concluded on the theme that it was every man's duty to "expose the evil designs or weak management of a magistrate." "To suppress inquiries into the administration is a good policy in an arbitrary government. But a free constitution and freedom of speech have a reciprocal dependance on each other; that they cannot subsist without consisting together."[25]

The debate, once narrowly focused between Governor Cosby and his opponents in New York, had now spread out and become something far more important. New ideas had been broached which could not be suppressed, and they reappeared in the most unusual places

[24]Levy, p. 321.

[25]The *Pennsylvania Gazette*, Nov. 10-17, 1737 (No. 466), Nov. 17-24, 1737 (No. 467), Nov. 24-Dec. 1, 1737 (No. 468), Dec. 1-8, 1737 (No. 469); reprinted in the *New-York Weekly Journal*, Dec. 19, 1737 (No. 215), Dec. 26, 1737 (No. 216), Jan. 2, 1737/8 (No. 217), Jan. 17, 1737/8 (No. 219).

and contexts. Moreover, each time they were applied, they were further refined.

One illustration of this was the proposal by Andrew Bradford and John Webbe to publish a magazine in Philadelphia. In the initial announcement, Webbe assured his prospective subscribers that the magazine would adhere to freedom of the press. Its pages would be open to all contenders, but "would carefully avoid contributing to the licentiousness of the press." By this, he meant "defamatory libelling, as it comprehends the ideas of falsehood and scandal combined together." After citing Hamilton's arguments in Zenger's defense, Webbe proceeded to scriptural evidence. "We are there commanded
82 to pay obedience to governors, yet not to all generally, but only to those who use their authority for the punishment of evil doers and for the praise of them that do well . . . . Where the end of government is perverted, it is criminal in any man to acquiesce under it." He qualified his libertarianism with a plea for practicality: should a people "be reduced to the unhappy necessity of making such public remonstrances . . . [it was hoped] that the management of them might always be reserved for men of skill and address. It is not for every puny arm to attempt to wield the club of Hercules."[26]

Freedom as a whole served as the topic for an extended essay by Jeremiah Gridley in the *American Magazine and Historical Chronicle* published in Boston by Rogers and Fowle. Among his assertions was this: "In a state of nature, I had a right to read Homer, or Virgil, or Horace. . . . And therefore under a government instituted to support my life and property and civil interests, I retain my liberty to read them still. For from what source can such a society derive a right to hinder my studies, recreations, or amusements, which do not affect the ends of society?" While the last clause limited his concept of freedom, Gridley later strengthened it with a nautical allusion. After declaring that men by entering society actually acquired a liberty of speaking their "sentiments openly concerning such matters as affect the good of the whole," he continued: "Where-ever therefore he perceives a rock upon which there is a probability that the vessel may split, or if he sees a shoul or sand that may swallow it up, or if he foresees a storm likely to arise, his interest is too deeply concerned not to

[26]The *American Weekly Mercury*, Oct. 30–Nov. 6, 1740 (No. 1088).

give notice of the danger. And the right he has to life and property gives him a right to speak his sentiments. If the pilot of the ship refuses to hear, or if the captain will take no notice, yet 'tis certain they acquire no right to punish the well-meant information, nor to stop the mouth of him who thinks he decries danger to the whole ship's crew."[27]

The Boston *Independent Advertiser* sharpened the awareness of freedom with a conscious effort to define terms. "Perhaps no words have been more misunderstood or perverted," stated an essayist, "than the words loyalty and sedition. The former I take to signify a firm and inviolable attachment to a legal constitution, the latter, all ten- 83
dencies, machinations, and attempts to overset a legal constitution." It was a great mistake, he continued, "to imagine that the object of loyalty is the authority and interest of one individual man, however dignified by the applause or enriched by the success of popular actions.... The true object of loyalty is a good legal constitution, which as it condemns every instance of oppression and lawless power, derives a certain remedy to the sufferer, by allowing him to remonstrate his grievances, and pointing out methods of relief when the gentler arts of persuasion have lost their efficacy."[28]

This author had certainly glimpsed a significant idea. By clarifying the term to which loyalty and sedition must of necessity refer, he weakened the case for seditious libel. When the subject is loyal to an inanimate object, a document, or a set of generally accepted rules, rather than a personality, we have achieved the modern democratic state. Although no other newspaper reprinted this particular essay, none sought to rebut it. Indeed, the same idea would crop up again in different dress before the end of our period.

Still another variation on this theme was supplied by James Parker in the *New-York Gazette*. "How can any branch of our liberties be said to be safe," he argued, "if we have not the liberty of complaining of any attempt to take it away? Though liberty be a joint stock, in respect to the nation, yet every individual has his property therein; and the security he has for't, is his right of appealing to the public, if its invaded, or taken away." "False and foolish complaints are often

[27] I (1744), 556-557.

[28] Aug. 8, 1748 (No. 32).

brought," Parker admitted, "but then they are brought to no purpose, or, at least, the bringing them answer no ill purpose. On the contrary, the contempt with which they are treated, manifest the candour and impartiality of the public; and this ought not therefore to be set up as an argument for suppressing that tribunal"—meaning the press.[29]

This theme soon spread. The *New-York Mercury* published an item which the *Pennsylvania Gazette* immediately picked up. "The licentiousness of the press is, in the eyes of some people, an extraordinary grievance, and oblique threats are thrown out, that as it de-
84 serves, so it will meet with a restriction. Be that day far from us! . . . But the press may be abused. What is there then that may not? The Bible may be abused, the laws may be abused, the constitution may be abused, yet we have a birthright in them all, and we should be miserable if they were taken from us."[30]

A more sophisticated and thorough analysis appeared shortly thereafter in the "Watch Tower #10." published in the *New-York Mercury* and reprinted in the *Virginia Gazette*. "The most interesting objects of knowledge to men in society are religion, either natural or revealed, and government. To the study of which, the downright priest, and despotic ruler, generally claim an exclusive right. It is, however, the proper business of an intelligent being, to investigate those relations of his existence, which either bestow on him some privileges or subject him to certain duties . . . . If no law can be binding upon the subject, without his consent, he has surely a right to divulge his sentiments, either relating to the conduct of the person intrusted with the execution of the laws; or of those, who, intrusted with certain powers for the public good, convert them to private and sinister uses; such persons being all creatures of that constitution or body of laws, to the making of which his assent was absolutely necessary . . . ."

"It is true," continued the "Watch Tower," that "by a variety of adjudged cases, in our law-books, the publication of any writing which charges a person in office, with the commission of a crime, or exposes him to popular odium and reflection, is not the less libellous

[29]Supplement, Oct. 2, 1754 (No. 505).

[30]The *New-York Mercury*, Dec. 9, 1754 (No. 122); reprinted in the *Pennsylvania Gazette*, Dec. 12, 1754 (No. 1355).

for being true. Which piece of law is founded upon this reason, that tho a libel be true, yet it may tend to stir up sedition, or cause a breach of the peace; and therefore the law relating to libels, may sometimes be wholesome. But as every general rule admits of some exceptions, so in particular cases, a state may be ruined by the persons to whom the management is committed, for want of timely notice to those whose interest, were they apprized of the danger, would urge them to the utmost exertion of their abilities in its support. And if a people can be presumed to have a right in any instance to oppose the undue measures of an arbitrary ruler, when they strike at the very vitals of the constitution, they are certainly justifiable in opposing them not only with the pen, but even with the sword. And then, what becomes of the reason upon which the above law, relating to libels, is founded?" Libel charges in lesser matters could easily be avoided because an official could be calumniated by "a writing that inveighs against a particular order of men, and does not descend to individuals of that order." Such a writing "is no libel."[31]

Once again an essayist had hinted at the way to destroy the weapon of seditious libel. The theme enunciated earlier in the *Boston Independent Advertiser* had been repeated seven years later. If officeholders are the creatures of the constitution, and if men's loyalties were to that instrument rather than to the person exercising the office, seditious libel as a repressive device loses its value. Although the "Watch Tower" essayist did not pursue this as closely as the earlier article had, he went even further, in a sense, by arguing that the people have a right to oppose arbitrary rulers by sword as well as pen.

The sharpening of definitions continued. An article by "W.K." in the *Boston Gazette, and Country Journal* took an even more absolute view and incorporated freedom of speech and thought as well. "Without freedom of thought, there can be no such thing as wisdom; and no such thing as public liberty, without freedom of speech: Which is the right of every man as far as by it he does not hurt and controul the right of another; and this is the only check which it ought to suffer, the only bounds which it ought to know. . . . That men ought to speak well of their governors is true, while their governors deserve to

[31]The *New-York Mercury*, Jan. 27, 1755 (No. 129); reprinted in the *Virginia Gazette*, Mar. 7, 1755 (No. 217).

be well spoken of; but to do public mischief, without hearing of it, is only the prerogative and felicity of tyranny."[32]

The theme of freedom was expanding rapidly. James Parker, it is asserted, wrote a piece for the *Connecticut Gazette* which went even further. "It is no wonder," the essay began, "that a darling so carefully guarded and powerfully supported, should sometimes grow wanton and luxurious, and misuse an indulgence granted it, merely to preserve its just freedom inviolate: It has been tho't safer to suffer it to go beyond the bounds that might strictly be justified by reason; then to lay the least restraint on it, lest thereby, it should lose the salutary in-
86 fluence for which it is so highly esteemed by Britons . . . . And this the rather, because a stretch of liberty in the press, cannot be attended with any very bad consequences, as the restraint of it may; because it carries the means of restraining, or reducing itself to its proper boundaries; for the freedom of animadversion, even upon the press itself, being included in the liberty thereof, its extravagances must soon be suppressed, and it must be reduced to the limits prescribed by reason." The true definition of freedom, the author emphasized, was that "none can complain, that the same liberty was not allowed impartially to every one. Whoever was displeased at any thing that has been published, might have made his objections as public as the cause of them."[33]

This, indeed, was true freedom of the press. The article attributed to Parker was not alone in its view that the government had no power to restrain or punish printing. The *Boston Gazette* elaborated on it in 1756 and in 1758. "'Tis true, where there is liberty, there may be licentiousness. But this is as true of every other liberty as that of the tongue or pen. And if 'tis reasonable our tongues or pens should be subjected to the controul of appointed inspectors, lest they should be misused; 'tis reasonable that our liberty, in all other instances, should be restrained in like manner; that is, we ought to be enslaved to prevent our making an ill-use of our freedom." Two years later, the same paper returned to the argument: "Every Britton . . . has therefore a right to think for himself on all public affairs, and if he pleases to think aloud:—This privilege like all others should be used with discretion, but not to have it at all, or never to improve it, is the same thing . . . .

[32] Apr. 21, 1755 (No. 3).
[33] Feb. 7, 1756 (No. 44).

Let both sides then speak freely, and by the collision, the sparks of truth may leap out."[34]

At the very close of the period, Weyman's *New-York Gazette* prophetically summed up the newspapers' views of their own freedom and utility. "It is to this bringing grievances before the tribunal of the public that we owe every good law that has been passed within our memory; and though it may be true that there are many grievances still unredressed, against which long complaints have been often made; yet this is no just objection. For tho' they are not yet redressed, they may and will be in time.... But there is another very good effect which may be looked upon as certain, though we can afford no proof of it; it is this, that many more grievances we should have had, if this remedy was not always in our power; and many more grievances we certainly shall have, if ever it is taken from us; which under the English constitution we have no reason to fear; because that constitution can fear nothing from it."[35]

"The persistent image of colonial America," wrote the most recent investigator in this field, "as a society in which freedom of expression was cherished is an hallucination of sentiment that ignores history."[36] He is correct, but only in part. It was a society in process of learning the value of such freedom and defining, albeit haltingly at times, its meaning. By the 1760's, however, it had developed a viable definition, one which was circulated widely enough to permit a conclusion that it had attained public acceptance. By defining the object of loyalty more precisely, the press had blunted the weapon of seditious libel; by identifying itself with the forces of self-government, it had reduced the need for legislative repression; by urging that its columns be open to all, it had safely channeled criticism. The way now was open for the newspaper, despite occasional efforts to repress its exuberance, to become a basic political force in the imperial crisis of the 1760's and 1770's. Although the hysteria of the revolution would jeopardize this definition, its speedy and easy recovery is more worthy of note than the aberration.

[34]The *Boston Gazette, and Country Journal*, Apr. 26, 1756 (No. 56); Jan. 2, 1758 (No. 144).

[35]Feb. 22, 1762.

[36]Levy, p. 18.

Congregation, State, and Denomination: The Forming of the American Religious Structure

Timothy L. Smith*

THE history of religion in America has seemed to most of its students a story best told in terms of the differences among denominations. To Philip Schaff's generation of church historians these differences seemed the outcome of varying doctrinal traditions. The Presbyterians were Calvinists, the Methodists Arminian; Baptists insisted upon a believer's church, while Anglicans revered the apostolic succession; hence the variations in their development.[1] Shortly after World War I, another group of students set out to explain denominational patterns by means of sociological and economic analysis, following the example of the German scholar Ernst Troeltsch. They identified as "right wing" communions those in which liturgy and confessionalism were predominant—Roman Catholic, Lutheran, Anglican, and German Reformed. These represented the old social classes whose status, whether gentlemen, yeomen, or peasants, had traditionally been determined by their relationship to land. The Presbyterians, Congregationalists, and Friends, by contrast, ministered to the rising bourgeoisie, and the Methodists and the Baptists to the workers whom the commercial revolution had deprived of both status and property.[2]

More recently still, Winthrop Hudson and Sidney Mead have proposed a context of interpretation which places the emphasis upon the emergence of denominationalism itself. First in Cromwell's England but more dramatically in colonial America, they have told us, Protestant dissenters came to see their communions not as established "churches" on one hand, or "sects," on the other, but as members of a family of related

* Mr. Smith is a member of the Department of History, the University of Minnesota.

[1] See Philip Schaff *et al.*, eds., *The American Church History Series* (New York, 1893-98).

[2] Representative works are H. Richard Niebuhr, *The Social Sources of Denominationalism* (New York, 1929); and Liston Pope, *Millhands and Preachers; A Study of Gastonia* (New Haven, 1942).

religious bodies called "denominations." All were heirs of a common faith and a common duty, and after the War for Independence all became partners in the task of remaking American society in the image of evangelical Protestantism. Denominationalism, thus conceived, is the opposite of sectarianism; for it admits no claim to an exclusive possession of saving truth.[3]

Mead and others have explained the origin of this new system of religious order as in some degree a necessary adjustment of religious traditions to the fact of cultural diversity, as in part a response to the enactment of legal toleration, and, finally, as an effort to find a common front against the threat of barbarism and infidelity on the frontier. My aim in this essay is a modest one, namely, to show how denominations emerged out of the needs of congregations in a society where mobility even more than diversity made voluntary association the rule of religious life. Indeed, I think that all three of the denominational interpretations of American church history described above would gain new usefulness and precision from a fresh consideration of the nature, problems, and role of religious congregations in New World communities.

A combination of factors drew the European peasants away from their ties to heath and cottage, to village custom and parish church. The commercial revolution, beginning in the fourteenth and fifteenth centuries, transformed agriculture, affecting first the lower Rhine Valley and southern England, then, in widening circles century by century, the rest of Europe. An immense growth of population at the same time pressed in upon the available space. Poverty became a spreading plague which respected no national boundaries. The sons of both yeomen and gentry who lost out in the scramble for land at home slowly turned toward vacant territories elsewhere: east beyond the Elbe, west to North Ireland, the West Indies, and the continent of North America, and later, to South America, Africa, and Australia.[4] Those who joined the great migrations were not simply lured by free land. The world of their fathers had begun

[3] Sidney E. Mead, "Denominationalism: The Shape of Protestantism in America," *Church History*, XXIII (1954), 291-292, and *passim;* Winthrop S. Hudson, "Denominationalism as a Basis for Ecumenicity: A Seventeenth-Century Conception," *ibid.*, XXIV (1955), 32-33, and *passim.*

[4] Wallace Notestein, *The English People on the Eve of Colonization, 1603-1630* (New York, 1954), 11-21, 48-50, 58-60, 71-85; Marcus Lee Hansen, *The Atlantic Migration, 1607-1860; A History of the Continuing Settlement of the United States*, ed. Arthur M. Schlesinger (Cambridge, Mass., 1940), 3-24.

to come apart long before, laying upon them the insecurity and the restless ambition that prepared them for the exodus.[5] America was only one of several promised lands which beckoned to such men. Some of them saw the vision of Canaan earliest in spiritual or apocalyptic form, as Karl Mannheim has made plain in *Ideology and Utopia*.[6] It ought not to surprise us, therefore, that when John Bunyan's England and the Rhineland which still remembered Muenster sent pilgrims to the American wilderness, they journeyed with both earth and heaven in view.[7]

The ambitions and decisions of individuals distinguished this migration sharply from the *Volkwanderungen* of the Middle Ages. Single persons and small family units floated free of the web of community which
90 had once enfolded their lives. Young people, more young men than women, and the landless ones at that, chose colonization most readily, whether in desperation to escape the clutch of poverty or in the hope of finding a better chance beyond the seas.[8] What they seem to have wanted most was not the New Jerusalem but the old village and the familiar community their fathers had known, but reconstituted in such a way as to enable each man to own land outright, as his more fortunate cousins in Europe had managed to do. In the seventeenth century, on both sides of the Atlantic, peasants strove to become free farmers, yeomen to become gentlemen. Neither class realized how much and how long such strivings had contributed to the disruption of traditional patterns of life in the Old World, and how much more difficult they would make the task of creating stable communities in the New.[9]

Family life in the early American settlements was especially lonely and insecure. In Virginia, it hardly existed at all at the beginning, since few women went to the colony until after the leaders of the London Company realized that their chance for profit lay in agriculture and trade, not gold. They hastened then to encourage families to emigrate, and sent out for

[5] Hansen, *Atlantic Migration*, 26-29, and *passim;* Wilbur K. Jordan, *Philanthropy in England, 1480-1660; A Study in the Changing Pattern of English Social Aspirations* (London, 1959), 54-74.

[6] Karl Mannheim, *Ideology and Utopia* (New York, 1936), 191-200.

[7] Perry Miller, *Errand Into the Wilderness* (Cambridge, Mass., 1956), 1-15.

[8] Mildred Campbell, "Social Origins of Some Early Americans," James M. Smith, ed., *Seventeenth-Century America; Essays in Colonial History* (Chapel Hill, 1959), 63-69.

[9] Mildred Campbell, *The English Yeoman under Elizabeth and the Early Stuarts* (New Haven, 1942), 68-78, 103-104, 289-296.

the single men already there a shipload of at least technically marriageable maids. The "families" which some of these began at once to rear were not children of their own, but youngsters twelve years of age and older gathered off the streets of London and sent out at the same time to be apprenticed to planters in Virginia. Additional cargoes of both women and apprenticed children came in succeeding seasons, to form perhaps the most artificially contrived families known to history. One is not surprised to find how few of the women survived. Of 140 brought over in the years 1620-1622, 105 were in their graves by 1625.[10] In New England, also, disease and unmanageable anxiety took a pathetic toll. Fifty of the passengers of the *Mayflower* died within seven months of their departure from Old Plymouth, among them all but a handful of the women and 14 of the 26 married men.[11] In Charlestown, a little later, the children whom John Winthrop's diary praised for showing neither "fear or dismayedness" during the long voyage, and who joyfully gathered strawberries and wild roses the June afternoon they came off the ships, found their summer days filled with weary toil and their nights with multiplying fears.[12] With winter came illness and death. "There is not a house," Thomas Dudley wrote, "where there is not one dead."[13]

With the loneliness and the danger came also to these fragmented families what seemed by Old World standards an oppressive burden of hard work. Gone was the material heritage of the European village—the cottages and garden plots, the dam and the mill, the oven and threshing floor, the sheds and fences, roads and bridges which man and beast required. Even if the land had not lured tradesmen from their crafts, reconstructing the specialization of skills and the extensive division of labor that the colonists had known in Europe would have taken a generation. Nor had they found room aboard the ships for many of the tools and utensils they required. Homes had to be built at once, and crude furnishings—if possible, at least, a bed—fashioned out of materials found

[10] Julia C. Spruill, *Women's Life and Work in the Southern Colonies* (Chapel Hill, 1938), 9-10.

[11] William Bradford, *Of Plymouth Plantation, 1620-1647*, ed. Samuel E. Morison (New York, 1952), 77.

[12] John Winthrop, *History of New England from 1630 to 1649 . . . from His Original Manuscripts . . .* , ed. James Savage (Boston, 1853), I, 11-13, 31, 117, 119-120.

[13] *Ibid.*, 43, 47-49, 52-53, 57-58. Alice Morse Earle quotes Dudley's statement in *Child Life in Colonial Days* (New York, 1899), 2.

nearby.[14] Fields must be cleared and planted and laboriously tended, and boats built by unaccustomed hands for fishing and for trade. They must soon begin the arduous toil of making linen cloth, using spinning wheels and looms also constructed on the spot. These would replace the garments which, brought over from Europe or meted out by masters at the end of the servant's term of indenture, were so quickly worn to shreds.[15] The tasks of the family had thus multiplied enormously, but the hands to perform them were fewer. The old people and the maiden aunts who might have borne a share had not ventured across the sea. And the servants whom better-off families brought along struck out on their own as soon as law and circumstances permitted.

92 Little wonder that when respite came briefly from loneliness, danger, and toil, or when illness interrupted the busy round of life, weary minds threw a bridge of memory across the Atlantic and longed for the order and security of the villages they had left behind. In such moments was bred a deep hunger for kinship and community in the new settlements which they now must call home.[16] But how did one create community, when the only kind he had known seemed a natural inheritance, not a human contrivance? The pattern of life in the European village and town had been marvelously intricate. Habits so deeply ingrained as to require little conscious thought regulated word, work, and worship. To each person and family belonged usually a status in the neighborhood, and a set of duties and privileges to fit it. To fashion new and equally secure relationships in the American wilderness seemed a task beyond mere human capacity. Simply to sign a compact aboard the *Mayflower*, or to create by decree a parish in Virginia, or to plat a Swiss township in Carolina, was not enough.

To men reared in an age of faith, this crisis of community inevitably seemed a religious one. They took it for granted that the church congre-

[14] John Brickell, *The Natural History of North-Carolina . . .* (Raleigh, 1911), 37; Alexander S. Salley, Jr., ed., *Narratives of Early Carolina, 1650-1708* (New York, 1911), 175-176.

[15] Anonymous, *American Husbandry*, ed. Harry J. Carman (New York, 1939), 66-67, n. 1; Brickell, *North-Carolina*, 32-33, 51, 265-267; F. J. F. Schantz, *The Domestic Life and Characteristics of the Pennsylvania-German Pioneer . . .* (Lancaster, Pa., 1900), 14-28.

[16] "Letter of John Jones, 1725," Albert C. Myers, ed., *Narratives of Early Pennsylvania, West New Jersey, and Delaware, 1630-1707* (New York, 1912), 454-455; Ann Maury, ed., *Memoirs of a Huguenot Family* (New York, 1872), 378-380.

gation must be the nucleus of all their new associations. Awe and reverence alone seemed to them able to generate the mystic force required to knit erstwhile strangers into units of belonging. They simply could not have dealt with the problem in a purely instrumental way, as modern Americans do, when with all the paraphernalia of P.T.A.'s, community centers, Kiwanis clubs, and backyard barbecues we lace ourselves into suburban togetherness.

Herein lies the meaning of the exaggerated emotions which characterized congregational life in the New World. In Virginia, it was not simply the heritage of reformation piety which, as Perry Miller has suggested, turned men's minds to God. The anxieties awakened by their taking leave of England and their arrival in America, strangers to one another and in a strange land, also played a part. Likewise in New England, the solemn ceremonies of church founding and church joining bespoke a search for long lost community as well as a testimony to newfound grace. Later, Pennsylvania pietism, though originally imported from Europe, was nurtured by the need which both British and German immigrants felt for personal identity, for recognition and response, in a threatening wilderness.[17]

John Winthrop's account of the troubles in the church at Watertown in 1631 and 1632 makes plain how the search for brotherly fellowship initially took precedence even over the concern for Puritan orthodoxy. The trouble began when Elder Richard Brown maintained, after a debate and decision of the congregation to the contrary, that "the churches of Rome were true churches." The people of Watertown invited Winthrop and other of the magistrates to sit with them in council on the matter. After a lengthy discussion, the divided flock "agreed to seek God in a day of humiliation, and so to have a solemn uniting." Meanwhile, they permitted the elder to retain both his opinions and his office. The strife continued, however, and the next year the congregation gave those who refused to take communion with Brown the choice of submission or excommunication. Eventually, to be sure, Brown was discharged from the eldership—not for his opinions, however, but on account of "his passion and distemper in speech, having been oft admonished."[18]

[17] Miller, *Errand*, 99-140; Philip Alexander Bruce, *Institutional History of Virginia in the Seventeenth Century . . .* (New York, 1910), I, 13-27; Ola E. Winslow, *Meetinghouse Hill: 1630-1783* (New York, 1952), 20-30.

[18] Winthrop, *History*, ed. Savage, I, 70, 81, 97, 113-114.

In all the colonies, the early congregations were exceedingly fragile institutions. They were too new in their personnel, and too unstable in their structure to bear unaided the responsibility laid upon them to nurture a sense of spiritual kinship in the neighborhood or to provide for the education of children. None was, as far as I have been able to discover, a bodily transplantation from Europe, with pastor, elders, or deacons, and lesser officers intact and with each communicant bearing in his heart the memory of his place in the village status system at home. Those about whose history this legend clings—as, for example, the founders of Plymouth and Dorchester in early Massachusetts, the Baptist company which settled first in Rehoboth and then in Swansea after the Restoration, or the
94 Welsh Friends who a bit later colonized Merion, Pennsylvania—were at most only fragments of churches recently "gathered" in Europe.[19] More typical, indeed, was a great diversity of background, especially in the larger towns like Boston, New Amsterdam, Philadelphia, and Charleston.

The Boston church, organized in midsummer 1630 among the ill and troubled settlers who were soon to flee the reeking squalor of Charlestown Hill, received new members each time a ship from England anchored in the harbor.[20] John Cotton arrived in 1633, with some of his former parishioners as well as others from East Anglia, desiring to "sit down where they might keep store of cattle." Their pastor was soon persuaded to become teacher in the church at Boston, however, and to allow his own flock to be scattered throughout the town.[21] Cotton began his ministry in the Puritan city with a brave statement on the sovereignty of the congregation. He wound up some years later at the head of the movement which imposed synodical order on the New England churches. In the interim, of course, Mistress Anne Hutchinson had arrived and, gathering about herself a coterie of true believers, had nearly torn the Boston congregation and community to shreds. Her movement, and the response of

[19] Dorchester Antiquarian and Historical Society, *History of the Town of Dorchester, Massachusetts* (Boston, 1859), 17-19; Thomas Prince, *A Chronological History of New England, in the Form of Annals* (Edinburgh, 1887-88), IV, 60; Isaac Backus, *A History of New-England, With Particular Reference to the Denomination of Christians Called Baptists*, 2d ed. (Newton, Mass., 1871), I, 283-286; and James J. Levick, M.D., "John Ap Thomas and His Friends: A Contribution to the Early History of Merion, Near Philadelphia," *Pennsylvania Magazine of History and Biography*, IV (1880), 305-306, 312, 314, 319.

[20] See Winthrop, *History*, ed. Savage, I, 36-37; and Charles F. Adams, *Three Episodes of Massachusetts History . . .*, rev. ed. (Boston, 1894), I, 234-236.

[21] Winthrop, *History*, ed. Savage, I, 133, 128-132, 137.

the clergy and magistrates to it, reflected both the consistencies and the contradictions between Puritan ideals of social order and personal religious experience, to be sure. But it also owed something, I believe, to the simple fact that this and other Massachusetts congregations were composed of persons new to one another, and in a new land. Many were profoundly disturbed by the hazards, known and unknown, which lay before them, and by the memory of the ordeal of migration which they had just passed through. They fell easy prey to the emotionalism and the egotism of the magnetic personalities whose teachings highlighted their sense of social and spiritual estrangement.[22]

The situation in New Amsterdam was even more confused, but completely typical of the tenuous character of congregational life in the Middle Colonies. When Jonas Michaelius administered the first communion on Manhattan Island in 1628, the fifty whom he admitted to the sacrament were a motley group indeed. Part were Dutch and part French-speaking Walloons. Some came on their first confession of faith and some by church certificate. A larger number, however, having either misplaced their certificates of membership or neglected to bring them to America, "not thinking that a church would be formed and established here," were admitted on the testimony of persons who had known them in Europe.[23] Matters improved but slowly in succeeding years, chiefly because the Dutch West India Company persisted for two decades more in policies suitable only for the operation of a trading post. All the residents were under contract to the company, and enjoyed none of the municipal liberties which in Holland were the backbone of Dutch freedom. The discontinuity between congregation and community proved disastrous. Little sense of social unity developed, and almost no commitment to a common dream of the colony's future. The education of children and young people inevitably suffered.[24]

The Friends and other dissenters who first settled West New Jersey were chiefly English in origin and shared a similar religious outlook. But the individual members of each congregation were drawn from widely

[22] Adams, *Three Episodes,* I, 366-367, 273-274, 392-394, 428-429; Perry Miller, *Orthodoxy in Massachusetts, 1630-1650* (Boston, 1959), xiv-xvi, xx, 157-168.

[23] "Letter of Reverend Jonas Michaelius, 1628," J. Franklin Jameson, ed., *Narratives of New Netherland, 1609-1664* (New York, 1909), 124-125, 259-260.

[24] *Ibid.,* 119-120.

separated villages and towns in Britain.[25] Similarly, at Germantown, the Mennonite Francis Daniel Pastorius found the problem of establishing a sense of community among the mechanics and weavers who comprised the original settlement almost unmanageable. They were natives of various localities in the Rhineland and represented every shade of religious opinion. Pastorius described the ship on which he came over as a veritable "Noah's Ark" of different faiths. In his own household of servants were those who clung, he said, "to the Roman, to the Lutheran, to the Calvinistic, to the Anabaptist, and to the Anglican church, and only one Quaker." The legal bond of the community which he tried to fashion was William Penn's rule requiring corporate settlement. Its spiritual heart proved to be
96 nationality—Pastorius's accent on German municipal law and the use of the German language in church, school, and social discourse.[26]

Once established, however, the seventeenth-century congregations found that other factors besides diversity of origin restricted their ability to bring solidarity to the neighborhood or security to family life. One was that the churches, like the villages whose corporate life they helped to sustain, were subject to constant attrition from the removal of their members to new lands nearby. The larger number of these migrants were poor men, chiefly latecomers or servants who had completed their terms of indenture. Such persons needed even more than others the anchor of faith and communal discipline. In each colony they helped create a second tier of towns whose organic life was as unstable as the first. Charles Francis Adams's description of the origin of the Braintree congregation and Ola Winslow's account of the long search for seven worthy "pillars" for the church in Dedham make this fact clear.[27] An equally troublesome hindrance was the divisive nature of the Christian faith itself, especially those radical versions of it which took root in the New World. Congregations preoccupied with fencing the Lord's table were not creating a community so much as playing odd man out. When the odd men proved to be citizens

[25] "The Present State of the Colony of West New Jersey, 1681," Myers, ed., *Narratives of Early Pennsylvania*, 194, and *passim*.

[26] "Circumstantial Geographical Description of Pennsylvania, by Francis Daniel Pastorius, 1700," *ibid.*, 381, 387-388, 396, 407, 414, 438-439, and J. Franklin Jameson's introduction to the document, 355-359.

[27] Adams, *Three Episodes*, II, 585-586; Winslow, *Meetinghouse Hill*, 37-49; see also John Demos, "Notes on Life in Plymouth Colony," *William and Mary Quarterly*, 3d Ser., XXII (1965), 264-268; and for the example of Duxbury, Nathaniel B. Shurtleff, ed., *Records of the Colony of New Plymouth in New England . . .* (Boston, 1855), I, 41, 44, 84-85.

whose political and financial privileges were restricted, or who differed from the majority in language or national origin, control of the congregation by a clan of first settlers could undermine the unity of a neighborhood.[28]

The religious congregation, therefore, like the family, suffered profound shock from the fragmentation and uprooting which migration to the New World involved. Yet its responsibility for the welfare of its members had greatly increased. Here, again, the tasks were many but the hands to perform them were few.

The seventeenth-century settlers turned instinctively to the political authorities for aid, regardless of the theory of church-state relationships they had held in Europe. The earliest American tradition became, therefore, not religious liberty, but state control. The difficulties which beset the first attempts of congregations to establish community life on a religious basis largely explain this development. The actions of provincial governments and county courts in ecclesiastical, moral, and educational matters aimed not at displacing the family and the congregation by a "secular" authority but at supporting their efforts to stabilize behavior in a mobile and remarkably pluralistic setting. Nor was the establishment of democracy or aristocracy the primary issue, for the experience of the first settlers was limited to a hierarchical status system, and they expected nothing different here. To them, as Bernard Bailyn has pointed out, the larger problem was the threat of social disorder, of barbarization, which hung over their common enterprise.[29] They believed the creation of a Christian community was the only reliable protection from this threat.

At its initial meeting in 1619, for example, the Virginia House of Burgesses gave attention first to legislation requiring church attendance, forbidding idleness, gaming, drunkenness, and "excesse" of apparel, and laying heavy penalties upon adulterers, gossipers, and sowers of dissension. Succeeding sessions extended such godly watch-care to other matters as well. Here, as later in New England, the full power of the law supported a weakened church in the task of cementing neighborhoods together.[30] Soon, however, tobacco planting encouraged a scattering of

[28] Edmund S. Morgan, *Visible Saints: The History of a Puritan Idea* (New York, 1963), 64-66; B. Katherine Brown, "Freemanship in Puritan Massachusetts," *American Historical Review*, LIX (1964-65), 882-883, and *passim*.

[29] Bernard Bailyn, *Education and the Forming of American Society: Needs and Opportunities for Study* (Chapel Hill, 1960), 22-29.

[30] "Proceedings of the Virginia Assembly, 1619," Lyon G. Tyler, ed., *Narratives*

families which made the development of cohesive congregations virtually impossible.[31] Thereafter, Virginia's illness, as contemporaries saw clearly, was the "scattered planting" which tobacco culture and bound labor made profitable. *Virginia's Cure,* as the title of a tract of 1662 put it, was the recovery of community by a forced-birth process. The author proposed that the generosity of Londoners be tapped for funds to build a town in every county of the colony, where planters might be directed to gather with their families and servants on weekends for worship and the instruction of the young.[32] The idea seems absurd, until we reflect that this is exactly what intensive agriculture, communal settlement, and the Puritan instinct for organization made possible in New England during
98 these years.

In the Middle Colonies, the diversity of religious traditions was from the outset a barrier to effective state action. In 1649, Johannes Megapolensis, having ended his tour of duty as pastor at Killiaen Van Rensselaer's settlement on the Hudson River, agreed to take charge of the struggling Dutch church in New Amsterdam. Megapolensis spent the remainder of his life there trying with Peter Stuyvesant's help to create a religious basis for communal solidarity. He urged the Classis of Amsterdam to request that the trading company close New Netherland to Jews and Quakers, and prohibit Lutheran ministers from exercising their office there. He also proposed that the company underwrite the salaries of both English and Dutch Calvinist clergymen. Governor Stuyvesant and the burgomasters supported these proposals heartily. But if the Classis acted upon the pastor's recommendations, it had no effect at all upon the West India Company. Instead, the directors admonished the governor sharply that the religious toleration which had drawn so many useful citizens to old Amsterdam would be their policy for the new.[33]

When the English captured New Netherland in 1664, the Duke of

---

of Early Virginia, 1606-1625 (New York, 1907), 263-264; see also Miller, *Errand,* 139-140.

[31] "The Virginia Planters' Answer to Captain Butler, 1623," Tyler, ed., *Narratives of Early Virginia,* 415.

[32] R. G., *Virginia's Cure . . .* (London, 1662), 6, and *passim,* reprinted in Peter Force, ed., *Tracts and Other Papers Relating Principally to . . . North America* (Washington, 1836-46) III, no. 15.

[33] See Revs. Megapolensis and Drisius to the Classis of Amsterdam, Oct. 25, 1657, Jameson, ed. *Narratives of New Netherland,* 399-402; and William H. Kilpatrick, *The Dutch Schools of New Netherland and Colonial New York* (U. S. Bureau of Education, *Bulletin, 1912,* no. 12 [Washington, 1912]), 72, 93-94, 99, 107, 199-224.

York proclaimed a religious establishment which was similar in aim to the plan which Megapolensis had urged upon the Dutch authorities a decade before, but which took fully into account the fact of religious diversity. The freeholders of each village were to choose their faith and elect a pastor, but the public treasury would support him. Whenever a dissenting group in any community became numerous enough, they were to be free to organize their own congregation, and have their minister also placed on state support. Though Anglicanism gained a foothold through the operation of this system, it was neither in form nor in purpose an outgrowth of English tradition, but a new departure designed to deal practically with the problem of social order in a pioneer society. The Duke's Laws in fact paved the way for the development of several denominations in the colony during the succeeding century.[34]

Pennsylvania passed through the same cycle somewhat more rapidly. William Penn was as troubled as any man of the time by the disintegration of family life which poverty and the increasing instability of village social life had produced.[35] Yet he was opposed on principle to any effort by the state to impose a uniformity of faith. To be sure, Penn had no fears for the survival in America of his own sect. The Society of Friends had learned in England and elsewhere to rely upon the traveling ministry, the circulation of letters from George Fox and other leaders, and the system of monthly, quarterly, and yearly meetings to maintain congregational discipline and family order among a mobile and minority people.[36] But what of the other wanderers who, he hoped, would find their way from Britain and Germany to the colony which bore his name?

Penn concluded that a commonwealth founded on the principle of brotherly love must provide by law a framework of community which would stand above the differences in religion that every settlement was bound to display. He announced in 1681 that his lands in the New World would be sold in such a way as to require people to settle in hamlets of at least ten families, situated in the midst of townships containing 5,000

[34] Thomas Jefferson Wertenbaker, *The Founding of American Civilization; The Middle Colonies* (New York, 1938), 82-85, tells the story but with a different conclusion.

[35] "Some Account of the Province of Pennsilvania, by William Penn, 1681," Myers, ed., *Narratives of Early Pennsylvania*, 203-205, 209-210; and "Letter from William Penn to the Committee of the Free Society of Traders, 1683," *ibid.*, 238.

[36] Frederick B. Tolles, *Quakers and the Atlantic Culture* (New York, 1960), 1-35.

acres.[37] Of this requirement, Penn wrote four years later, "I had in my view Society, Assistance, Busy Commerce, Instruction of Youth, Government of Peoples manners, Conveniency of Religious Assembling, Encouragement of Mechanicks, distinct and beaten Roads, and it has answered in all those respects, I think, to an Universall Content."[38] Penn appealed to neither English tradition nor Quaker theory in justifying this close regulation of community life. He simply feared that without it, a dissolution of social bonds would occur, giving rise to conditions that would "tempt the people to frivolity."[39] Enforcement of the requirement, however, did not outlast the first generation. Like subsequent efforts to establish community by decree in South Carolina and Georgia, Penn's
100 framework succumbed to the confusion of economic with idealistic motives, the rivalry of religious and national traditions, the reluctance of Englishmen to transfer control of communal matters from local to central authorities, and the democratic tendencies of popular political sentiment.[40]

Behind these factors lay also a larger obstruction: laws and decrees, however reasoned, could not reach the men of Penn's generation at the deeper emotional levels where the problem of community had to be worked out. Nor did the cultivation of a distinctive language or national culture, as at Germantown, prove an adequate substitute; for the Germans were themselves sharply divided in their religious loyalties. A sense of spiritual and moral kinship, rooted in voluntary adherence to a congregation, was to remain throughout the eighteenth century and long beyond the key to neighborhood stability, ordered family life, and the education of children.[41] Legislation having proved inadequate, pastors and lay lead-

[37] "Some Account by Penn," Myers, ed., *Narratives of Early Pennsylvania,* 208-209.

[38] "A Further Account of the Province of Pennsylvania, by William Penn, 1685," *ibid.,* 263.

[39] See "Description of Pennsylvania," *ibid.,* 377, 380, 407, 438-439.

[40] *A Description of the Province of South Carolina . . . 1731,* 3-5, reprinted in Force, ed., *Tracts,* II, no. 11; Daniel J. Boorstin, *The Americans: The Colonial Experience* (New York, 1958), 80-96; and William P. Holcomb, *Pennsylvania Boroughs* (Herbert B. Adams, ed., *Johns Hopkins University Studies in Historical and Political Science,* 4th Ser., IV [Baltimore, 1886]), 146-147.

[41] For a variety of examples, see Andrew Burnaby, *Travels Through the Middle Settlements in North-America in the Years 1759 and 1760 . . . ,* 2d ed. (London, 1775), 107-108, 125-126; "Extracts from the Minutes of the Shearith Israel Congregation Concerning Its Religious School," for 1731-68, in Alexander M. Dushkin, *Jewish Education in New York City* (New York, 1918), 449-450; Backus, *Baptists,* I, 490; John Lawson, *History of North Carolina . . . ,* ed. Frances L. Harriss (Rich-

ers of each persuasion united to form an inter-colonial association to counter the weaknesses stemming from the diversity and mobility of the membership of congregations. These associations, later called denominations, became in the eighteenth century the mainstay of beleaguered local brotherhoods. Not until the end of the War for Independence, however, did Americans realize fully what had happened. The actions which they took then in ecclesiastical and constitutional conventions, and the debates which attended those actions, ratified in both law and ideology the system of denominationalism that had been for decades a central fact of their social experience.

A farsighted Englishman, Thomas Bray, was the first clergyman in the state-church tradition to grasp fully the new situation. He organized the Society for Promoting Christian Knowledge in 1699, to give permanence to his earlier program of raising funds for parish schools and libraries in Britain and America. Then, after a tour of duty in Maryland as commissary for the Bishop of London, he founded in 1701 the Society for the Propagation of the Gospel in Foreign Parts. The aim of this second organization was to raise money in the homeland to support clergymen and schoolmasters in colonial parishes. Some of Bray's disingenuous successors, and many of the clergymen whom the society subsidized, used the resources of both organizations in vain efforts to promote an establishment of religion in America. But the main thrust of Anglican activity in the eighteenth-century colonies was consistent with the emerging denominational principle that education and evangelism, in which different communions would both cooperate and compete, must propagate the Christian faith independently of civil power.[42]

---

mond, 1951), xxv, 6-7; Gotthardt D. Bernheim, *History of the German Settlements and of the Lutheran Church in North and South Carolina* . . . (Philadelphia, 1872), 205-216; I. Farmer, "Churches and Ministers in New Hampshire," Massachusetts Historical Society, *Collections*, 2d Ser., IX (Boston, 1832), 367; and, for the Presbyterians of the Shenandoah Valley, the John Brown-William Preston Correspondence, Documents 2QQ, 3QQ, 4QQ, 5QQ, Wisconsin State Historical Society, Madison.

[42] Bernard C. Steiner, ed., *Reverend Thomas Bray: His Life and Selected Works Relating to Maryland* (Baltimore, 1901), 101-122, 174-176, and *passim;* Joseph, Lord Bishop of Gloucester, *A Sermon Preached Before the Incorporated Society for the Propagation of the Gospel in Foreign Parts . . . 1725* (London, 1726), 17-21; and Ernest Hawkins, *Historical Notices of the Missions of the Church of England . . .* (London, 1845), 85-86, for light on efforts to sustain congregational life in North Carolina.

The impetus to centralized order in other churches that had enjoyed legal establishment in Europe came not from the homeland but from the colonies. As early as 1709, the Presbytery of Philadelphia began sending annual appeals for aid to the dissenting clergymen of London, the Synod of Glasgow, and the Presbytery of Dublin. The Pennsylvania preachers recounted "the desolate condition of sundry vacant places" and pointedly reminded the Presbyterians in Scotland of the generosity and zeal of the Anglican society. In 1719, having had little success, they set out to collect money from their stronger congregations in America, thus initiating the Presbyterian Ministers Fund.[43] The pattern of native denominationalism took shape rapidly thereafter in declarations of doctrinal uniformity, in
102 concern for the proper preparation of ministers, and in the establishment of a synod for the New World. In 1734, at the behest of Gilbert Tennent, the synod resolved, in order "to revive the declining power of godliness," to inquire carefully of each pastor whether and how he discharged his duty towards the young people of his congregation, "in a way of catechizing and familiar instruction," and whether and in what manner he visited his flock and instructed them from house to house.[44] The spiritual awakening which followed these and other measures as Tennent and his log-college preachers sought out the Scotch-Irish on rural as well as urban frontiers is a familiar story. The emotions which they discovered in themselves and in their hearers signified more than simply a resurrection of Old World faith and discipline. As in the earliest colonial congregations, a reconstruction of family and community life was in progress; now, however, denominational order, rather than the decrees of a godly commonwealth, was helping to make it possible.[45]

Precisely the same thing happened earlier when the Classis of Amsterdam sent Theodore J. Frelinghuysen to New Jersey, in response to an appeal from Dutch Reformed congregations struggling to establish themselves in the Raritan Valley. Pastors of the wealthy Dutch churches in New York City protested Frelinghuysen's direct and earnest evangelism. Looking to the past instead of the future, they sought to have him re-

[43] See William M. Engles, comp., *Records . . . Embracing the Minutes of the Presbytery of Philadelphia, from A.D. 1706 to . . . 1758 . . .* (Philadelphia, 1841), 21, for the quotation, and, in general, 16, 20, 33, 37, 39, 53, 58, 142.

[44] *Ibid.*, 105, 111, and, for background, 94-95. See also Leonard J. Trinterud, *The Forming of An American Tradition: A Re-examination of Colonial Presbyterianism* (Philadelphia 1949), 40-[illegible].

[45] Trinterud, *Forming of an American Tradition*, 53-85.

called. Although the fathers in Amsterdam deferred action for a time, they at last concluded that voluntary structure and revival fervor must go hand in hand, and supported Frelinghuysen heartily.[46]

The story of the Baptists, who were everywhere a minority group, without a formally educated clergy, and in principle opposed to centralized direction, illustrates nascent denominationalism at the opposite ecclesiastical pole. The social and spiritual conditions of their progress in America made each Baptist congregation the center of a familial community. Closed communion, the kiss of charity, the rite of immersion, and, in some places, the admission to membership of "devoted children" explicitly affirmed the individual believer's identity with his spiritual kin.[47] Yet associations slowly became the rule, following the early example of Rhode Island and Philadelphia.

A contemporary description of the ritual by which new congregations were formed in eighteenth-century North Carolina illustrates how the interdependence of Baptist churches emerged. The ritual echoed the marriage ceremony in the *Book of Common Prayer.* A group of members either living or planning to move a distance from the meetinghouse first requested permission to establish a new church. This voted, the entire parent congregation assembled on a day appointed for fasting and prayer, during which the prospective members presented their names and their individual certificates of dismissal. The minister then solemnly inquired whether they desired to become "a church," whether their habitations were "near enough to each other, conveniently to attend church conferences," whether they were "so well acquainted with each other's life and conversation as to coalesce into one body, and walk together in love and fellowship," and whether it was "their intention to *keep up a regular discipline* agreeably to the scriptures." These questions having been answered in the affirmative, the members of the new group repeated and signed a covenant, pledging themselves not only to observe the usual religious duties but "in brotherly love to pray for each other, to watch over one another, and if need be, in the most tender and affectionate manner to reprove one another." The minister then said, mentioning each person

[46] Wertenbaker, *Middle Colonies,* 85-98.

[47] Morgan Edwards, "Materials Towards a History of the Baptists in Virginia to 1772," 2-4, 11, 18, 27, 32, 34, American Baptist Historical Society, Rochester, New York; Robert B. Semple, *A History of the Rise and Progress of the Baptists in Virginia,* ed. G. W. Beale, rev. ed. (Richmond, 1894), 76-79.

individually, "In the name of our Lord Jesus Christ, and by the authority of our office, we pronounce you . . . a true *gospel church*."[48]

Obviously, the farmer-preachers had not found this ritual in the New Testament; it represented, rather, a folk accommodation to geographic mobility which was by then an established Baptist tradition. On all the American frontiers, "mother" congregations exercised spiritual discipline over their "daughter" churches during the years when regional associations were weak or nonexistent. Traveling Baptist evangelists, as in the case of the Society of Friends, provided additional direction, as did the circulation of approved books and tracts. None of these measures, however, violated the principle of congregational autonomy. Thus emerged
104 out of necessity and experience a denomination whose cohesion has ever since belied the apparent lack of formal ties.

Congregations of the German "sects"—Mennonite, Dunker, Amish, and Moravian—had learned by long experience in Europe similar ways of protecting their members from the perils of the wilderness errand. As with the Baptists, initiation to their circles of familial fellowship came by way of both birth and the new birth. Love feasts, foot washings, the holy kiss, and rigid rules of dress and behavior separated the true believers from the unordered and hence "sinful" world outside.[49]

Moravian history illustrates the connection between such intimate congregational practices and the development of a denominational consciousness. In 1722, Count Zinzendorf invited Brethren who were suffering persecution to settle on his estate near Berthelsdorf, in Moravia. The refugees soon discovered that the parish church nearby must continue to serve the needs of the local peasantry, rather than the gathered community. They began meeting separately, therefore, first for "love feasts," then in intimate groups called "bands" or "classes." Households of unmarried men and unmarried women soon appeared, testifying to the disintegration of family life which their migration had involved. Shortly, also, an elaborate program of missions to the world outside signaled their recognition that the spiritual community had a function, a peculiar calling, in

[48] Lemuel Burkitt and Jesse Read, *A Concise History of the Kehukee Baptist Association* . . . (Halifax, N. C., 1803), 174-175, and covenant, 30-31.

[49] See descriptions of familial customs in Dunker and Mennonite congregations in John W. Wayland, *The German Element of the Shenandoah Valley of Virginia* (Charlottesville, 1907), 120, 125-129; and Samuel Kercheval, *A History of the Valley of Virginia* (Winchester, Va., 1833), 50-61.

an age when men at all social levels suffered from the dissolution of custom and kinship. Once created, such a community was itself exportable, mobile; its roots were not in the soil of Bohemia but in the souls of troubled men. In the 1730's Peter Bohler drew together a company of such migrants in London. A few years later, on board a vessel bound for Pennsylvania—a moving frontier if ever there was one—Bohler organized the "First Sea Congregation" to maintain discipline and cultivate brotherly love until the group reached the wilderness Zion which Zinzendorf was preparing for them at Bethlehem.[50]

By contrast, few ministers of the Lutheran or German Reformed churches accompanied redemptioners of their faith as they passed through what Oscar Handlin has called the "brutal filter" of migration to the New World. In small groups at best, sometimes singly or by individual families, they departed on foot from their villages for the ports of embarkation. Then followed anxiety and often illness aboard the immigrant ships, and the pathetic but what they hoped would be temporary separation of families by the sale of their labor under articles of indenture at dockside in Philadelphia or Charleston.[51] The reunion of these fragmented families after their years of service were over, their journey a short distance into the wilderness, and the discovery of their fellows in the newly joyous emotions of congregational life all took place without the help of the clergymen they had relied upon in Europe.[52] They often built schoolhouses before they erected chapels, pressing into service teachers of varying degrees of worthiness, not infrequently indentured servants as they had themselves recently been. The schoolmasters taught the children to read, write, and sing and, in time-honored German fashion, led the

[50] J. Taylor Hamilton, *A History of the Church Known as the Moravian Church . . . During the Eighteenth and Nineteenth Centuries* (Bethlehem, Pa., 1900), 40-49, 109-110.

[51] Gottlieb Mittelberger, *Journey to Pennsylvania*, eds. and trans. Oscar Handlin and John Clive (Cambridge, Mass., 1960), x-xi, 14-15; Oscar Handlin, *The Uprooted* (New York, 1951), 61.

[52] See contemporary descriptions in reports of Rev. John Philip Boehm to the Synods, Oct. 18, 1734, Jan. 14, 1739, July 8, 1744, William J. Hinke, ed., *Minutes and Letters of the Coetus of the German Reformed Congregations in Pennsylvania, 1747-1792 . . .* (Philadelphia, 1903), 1-3, 6-13, 27-31; Henry M. Muhlenberg, *The Journals . . .*, trans. Theodore G. Tappert and John W. Doberstein (Philadelphia, 1942-50), I, 141-142, 223; and, on the Palatine community in Virginia, William J. Hinke and Charles E. Kemper, eds., "Moravian Diaries of Travels through Virginia," *Virginia Magazine of History and Biography*, XI (1903-04), 229-230, 376-377.

hymns at worship, cleaned and warmed the church, and in the absence of a clergyman read the liturgy as well.[53]

John Philip Boehm, one of the most able of these schoolmasters, later told how, being unordained, he had for five years resisted the pleas of three Pennsylvania settlements of Reformed Germans to become their pastor, only to see the people become "much scattered," like "wandering sheep having no shepherd." He relented finally, in a tearful scene when, as he said, "With humbleness of heart I addressed myself to the Lord's work, and drew up with my brethren, as well as we could, a Constitution of the church, so that all things might be done in good order. . . . when the Constitution had been presented to and accepted by the whole people
106 I was regularly elected by each one of the congregations, and a formal call was extended to me by the elders. Whereupon I began the ministry of the Lord in his name."[54] Clearly, in such a body, pietistic sentiments would prevail whatever the beliefs of the members had been before they left Europe. And democratic church government was a natural corollary of the brotherly emotions at work.

Boehm wrote repeatedly to the Classis of Amsterdam during these years, imploring them to send ministers and schoolmasters to Pennsylvania. A young Swiss clergyman, Michael Schlatter, finally arrived in response to these pleas in 1747. Meanwhile, Lutheran congregations in Pennsylvania, Virginia, and the Carolinas sent representatives to Germany seeking similar aid. The result was the establishment of another missionary center, at the University of Halle; from there Henry Melchior Muhlenberg came to Philadelphia in 1742. Both Schlatter and Muhlenberg arrived armed with funds to subsidize the salaries of pastors and teachers. Both sent back immediate and urgent appeals for much greater assistance.[55] As a result of their labors, churches from Pennsylvania to Georgia pledged themselves by families to the support of the ministers they hoped to receive, revised both their doctrines and their practices to

[53] Hinke and Kemper, eds., "Moravian Diaries," 232-234; Muhlenberg, *Journals*, trans. Tappert and Doberstein, I, 84, 120-121, 170, 213, 526, 533, 576, 606, 725; Bernheim, *German Settlements*, 187-188; and Boehm's reports Jan. 13, 1739, July 8, 1744, Hinke, ed., *Minutes of the Coetus*, 13, 20-25.

[54] Hinke, ed., *Minutes of the Coetus*, 17-18.

[55] Michael Schlatter, "A True History of the Real Condition of the Destitute Congregations in Pennsylvania," Henry Harbaugh, *The Life of Rev. Michael Schlatter* . . . (Philadelphia, 1857), 205, 217-219; Muhlenberg, *Journals*, trans. Tappert and Doberstein, I, 85, 88, 121, 141-142, 145.

harmonize with denominational objectives, and willingly placed themselves under the supervision of authorities three thousand miles away.[56]

The emotions with which isolated Lutheran and Reformed congregations received the ministry of these missionaries from their homeland produced scenes like those which in other communions have been ascribed to the Great Awakening. At Frederick, Maryland, for example, on his first tour of the Potomac region, Schlatter found a Reformed group worshiping in their schoolhouse and erecting a church building, though they had never had a pastor. He returned a few weeks later to preside at the dedication of the sanctuary. "When I was preparing myself for the first prayer," he wrote his sponsors in Amsterdam, "and saw the tears of the spiritually hungry souls roll down over their cheeks, my heart was
singularly moved and enkindled with love, so that I fell upon my knees . . . the whole congregation followed me, and with much love and holy desire I . . . wrestled for a blessing from the Lord upon them." After the sermon, he administered communion to ninety-seven members, baptized several children and older persons, married three betrothed couples, and installed new elders and deacons. This congregation owed much of its health to the schoolmaster, he declared, the best one he had met in America.[57] By 1751, Schlatter had taken forty-six congregations under his care, all of them having been born of lay initiative, and many of them served previously by ministers whom neither God nor man, seemingly, had ordained. Through the years, their people had clung to one another steadily, finding fellowship and identity through a familiar tongue and ritual in a world where all else was strange.[58]

Schlatter made important departures from European customs of church government in the process of creating the German Reformed denomination in America. He invariably dealt first with whole congregations, rather than with a board of deacons or elders. Like the pastors whom he placed elsewhere, he was himself called to his Philadelphia charge by vote of all the adult male members. He defended this procedure, in a letter to the Classis in Amsterdam, by reference to the "custom

[56] Hinke, ed., *Minutes of the Coetus,* 40-45; Bernheim, *German Settlements,* 46-49, 151-154, 243-259.

[57] See Harbaugh, *Life of Schlatter,* 171, and for the quotation, 176-177; see generally 134-135, 140, 153-154, 157-159, and, for other descriptions of emotional responses, 130, 143, 148, 205.

[58] *Ibid.,* 137, 157-159, 203-204.

of taking a vote prevalent in Switzerland in great state assemblies, in which a majority of raised hands decides the question at issue."[59] Such a statement might pass at face value among advocates of the germ theory of history. But democratically-governed congregations were implicit in the American religious situation from the beginning. That denominational structures eventually arose in response to the demands of such congregations strengthened the democratic tendency in all communions. And the emotional scenes which accompanied these developments seemed to participants to sanctify the whole.

Viewing in retrospect the entire history of colonial Protestantism, I think the use of the term "Great Awakening" to describe the wide-spread
108 effort to solve the problems of evangelism, of education, and of congregational order which took place in the eighteenth century serves more to confuse than to clarify our understanding of what was happening. What we have called the "Awakening" certainly occurred at widely separated times and places. It began, perhaps we may say, with Frelinghuysen's labors in New Jersey, and it burned out (or, possibly, simply took off across the mountains) on the Carolina frontier in the 1790's. With a little more imagination, one might say it began with John Cotton's arrival in Boston and continued, but did not stop, with Daddy Grace.

Another and less mysterious way of looking at these events would be to say simply that revivalism in American history has generally served communal purposes. Its major achievement has been to forge the links which bound together the two kinds of new voluntary associations that have provided for the people's religious needs: first congregations, and then, denominations. What was called an "effusion of the Holy Spirit" signified to participants a divine sanction upon their new arrangements,[60] and meanwhile convinced onlooking members of other evangelical sects that the new organization should be recognized as a member of the family of Christian communions. The result, in the long succession of events, was to nurture the American Protestant consensus, the community of feeling and aspiration which in the nineteenth century helped give the nation itself a sense of oneness.

In summary, then, it seems to me that the colonists' departure from the society of village and kin-group they had known in Europe, and the es-

[59] *Ibid.*, 130; see generally, 131-135, 166-167.

[60] Alan Heimert and Perry Miller, eds., *The Great Awakening* (Indianapolis, 1967), 178, 189, 389.

tablishment and repeated disruption of new patterns of family and neighborhood life in the wilderness, made the quest of community a central feature of early American experience. For large numbers of settlers, that quest was essentially religious. The worshiping brotherhood became the pivot upon which both tradition and innovation turned. Congregations, new and fragile, could not stand alone, however. They first looked to the colonial governments to strengthen and support them, thus reaffirming the interdependence of state and church which many of them professed to have sought by migration to escape. By the end of the first century of colonization, however, increasing diversity of belief made legislation in matters of religion impractical, while political and theological conviction made it unacceptable. Early in the eighteenth century, therefore, voluntary national associations of congregations recognizing a similar European background took over from the provincial governments the task of providing support and discipline for local religious communities. This happened at the prompting of the congregations themselves, and without regard to the doctrines of church government they had espoused before. The emotional fervor of religious revivals, whether regarded hitherto as a part of the so-called "Great Awakening" or not, cemented these new unions, making organizations organisms, denominations, "communions."

Neither revivalism nor denominationalism was an exclusively New World plant, to be sure. Both simply flowered earlier and more luxuriantly in America. The new institutional forms that they sustained—missionary funds and boards, charity schools, publishing societies, denominational academies and colleges, and techniques of supervising congregational life—were in fact the inventions of European churchmen who were concerned for the welfare of their uprooted brethren, in the homeland as well as overseas. By the nineteenth century, the quickening pace of urbanization made it clear that the migrations which had begun in the sixteenth and seventeenth centuries had prompted in both the Old World and the New an extensive reorganization of Protestant religious life. Its basis was consent. Persuading men to make and keep the commitments necessary to voluntary association was now the churches' central task.

The

AMERICAN HISTORICAL REVIEW

110 VOLUME LXXV, NUMBER 2 DECEMBER 1969

Political Mimesis: A Consideration of the Historical and Cultural Roots of Legislative Behavior in the British Colonies in the Eighteenth Century

JACK P. GREENE

UNTIL comparatively recently, most investigations of government and politics in the eighteenth-century American colonies concentrated upon the recurrent contests between governors and elected lower houses of assembly and "the growth of colonial self-government" as reflected in the repeated triumphs of the assemblies in those struggles. There was an almost total consensus, as Charles M. Andrews wrote in 1943 after a lifetime of study, that "the most conspicuous feature" of "the political and institutional aspects . . . of the eighteenth century . . . was the rise of the colonial assembly with its growth to self-conscious activity and *de facto* independence of royal control."[1] Perhaps because the focus in these studies was primarily upon institutional development and the process by which

► *Mr. Greene is a professor at Johns Hopkins University. At Duke University, where he received his Ph.D. in 1956, he worked with John R. Alden. One of his publications is* The Quest for Power: The Lower Houses of Assembly in the Southern Royal Colonies, 1689–1776 *(Chapel Hill, N. C., 1963). He presented a shorter version of this paper to the London conference of the International Commission for the History of Representative and Parliamentary Institutions, July 19, 1968.* *He wishes to thank Professors William W. Freehling, Caroline Robbins, Thad W. Tate, and Corinne Comstock Weston for their helpful suggestions. The title and central conception of the article were suggested by a passage in Herman Merivale's 1839–1841* Lectures on Colonization and Colonies *(3d ed., London, 1928), 74–75.*

[1] The quotations are from Charles M. Andrews, *The Colonial Background of the American Revolution: Four Essays in American Colonial History* (New Haven, Conn., 1924), 30, and "On the Writing of Colonial History," *William and Mary Quarterly*, 3d Ser., I (Jan. 1944), 39.

the assemblies increased their authority, none of the studies made much attempt to handle the problem of motivation, to explain in any detail why the assemblies acted as they did. The early assumption of nineteenth-century patriotic American historians that the assemblies, obviously representing the natural desire of all men to be free, were fighting for liberty and democracy against executive oppression and tyranny simply gave way to the equally vague and untestable supposition of H. L. Osgood, Andrews, and their students. They contended that the assemblies, responding to environmentally induced social and intellectual tendencies that diverged sharply from those of the mother country, were seeking to secure as much self-government as possible, to attain, in the words of one writer, "the largest measure of local home rule compatible with whatever might be necessary to retain the advantages of the British connection."[2]

Around the beginning of this century, a few historians adopted a more promising line of investigation by focusing upon the political divisions that existed in almost every colony at many points during their history and that invariably cut across institutional boundaries. Because these historians often sought to explain those divisions in terms of a crude social dichotomy between upper and lower classes, the earliest of their studies did not much advance our understanding of the psychology of colonial politics. But they did show, as Andrews acknowledged late in his career, that any complete explanation of colonial political life required an "understanding of the social and propertied interests involved, class distinctions and personal rivalries, the motives of majorities, and the ambitions of political leaders."[3] Despite the often fragmentary records of colonial politics, many detailed studies written during the past twenty-five years have provided a wealth of solid information on the nature of political rivalries, the social, economic, and religious motivation that lay behind those rivalries, and the substantive issues in dispute. In the process, they have shifted attention almost entirely away from the emergence of the assemblies, but they have revealed that rivalries were so diverse, motivation so complex, and issues so varied—not only from colony to colony but also from time to time within colonies—that it has been extremely difficult to construct an alternative general framework of interpretation that has so comprehensive an applicability.[4]

Bernard Bailyn has considered this problem at some length in his recent

[2] See *ibid.*, esp. 40–41, and Charles M. Andrews, "The American Revolution: An Interpretation," *American Historical Review*, XXXI (Jan. 1926), 219–32. For more extensive discussion of these traditions and citations to some of the principal works, see Jack P. Greene, *The Quest for Power: The Lower Houses of Assembly in the Southern Royal Colonies, 1689–1776* (Chapel Hill, N. C., 1963), vii–ix, 4–7, and *id.*, review of F. G. Sprudle, *Early West Indian Government: Showing the Progress of Government in Barbados, Jamaica and the Leeward Islands, 1660–1783* (Palmerston, N.Z., 1963), in *William and Mary Quarterly*, 3d Ser., XXII (Jan. 1965), 147–48. The quotation is from Charles Worthen Spencer, "The Rise of the Assembly, 1691–1760," in *History of New York State*, ed. Alexander C. Flick (10 vols., New York, 1933–37), II, 196.

[3] Andrews, "On the Writing of Colonial History," 40.

[4] For an extended discussion of these works, see Jack P. Greene, "Changing Interpretations of Early American Politics," in *The Reinterpretation of Early American History*, ed. Ray A. Billington (San Marino, Calif., 1966), 151–72.

studies of the relationship among society, politics, and ideology in the eighteenth-century colonies. Earlier writers had described many of the central ingredients of colonial political thought and had pointed out the remarkable degree to which they were "a proudly conscious extension of political thought in England,"[5] but Bailyn was the first to try to show which strands of English political thought were most important in the colonies and how those strands affected colonial political behavior. In the introduction to the first volume of his *Pamphlets of the American Revolution* he analyzed in greater detail than any previous scholar the intellectual content of American arguments against British policy between 1763 and 1776. He found that, although Americans drew heavily upon the heritage of classical antiquity, the writings of Enlightenment rationalism, the tradition of the English common law, and the political and social theories of
112 New England Puritanism, it was the writings of "a group of early eighteenth-century radical publicists and opposition politicians in England who carried forward into the eighteenth century and applied to the politics of the age of Walpole the peculiar strain of anti-authoritarianism bred in the upheaval of the English Civil War" that dominated revolutionary political thought, "shaped it into a coherent whole," and, to a remarkable degree, determined the ways American leaders interpreted and responded to British regulatory and restrictive measures after 1763.[6] In a new and expanded version of this work Bailyn argued on the basis of an investigation of earlier political writings that this same "configuration of ideas and attitudes . . . could be found [in the colonies] intact—completely formed—as far back as the 1730's" and "in partial form . . . even . . . at the turn of the seventeenth century."[7]

That this opposition vision of politics—this pattern of thought that viewed contemporary Britain "with alarm, 'stressed the dangers to England's ancient heritage and the loss of pristine virtue,' studied the processes of decay, and dwelt endlessly on the evidences of corruption . . . and the dark future these malignant signs portended"[8]—was the single most important intellectual ingredient in "American politics in its original, early eighteenth-century form" has subsequently been contended by Bailyn in a series of recent essays. He seeks to explain why this conception of politics acquired in the colonies a place in public life far more significant than it had ever had in England, why it became so "determinative of the political understanding of eighteenth-century Americans" that it formed the "assumptions and expectations" and furnished "not merely the vocabulary but the grammar of thought, the apparatus by which the world was perceived." In constructing an answer to this question, Bailyn manages to weave "into a single brief statement of explanation" his own findings on political ideology, many of

[5] The most important is Clinton Rossiter, *Seedtime of the Republic: The Origin of the American Tradition of Political Liberty* (New York, 1953), 139–47; the quotation is from p. 140.

[6] Bernard Bailyn, *Pamphlets of the American Revolution, 1750–1776* (1 vol. to date, Cambridge, Mass., 1965–), I, 20–89; the quotations are from pp. ix, 28.

[7] *Id., The Ideological Origins of the American Revolution* (Cambridge, Mass., 1967), xi, 45–52.

[8] *Ibid.*, 46.

the discoveries of those writers who stressed the rise of the assemblies, and the conclusions of the students of internal political divisions. What gave the opposition view of politics a "sharper relevance" in America, according to Bailyn, was the "bitter, persistent strife" that characterized colonial politics, strife between executives and legislatures and, infinitely more important, among the chaotic and continually shifting factions that, he suggests, were endemic to colonial life. This strife was rooted in two anomalies. First, while the theoretical powers of colonial executives were greater than those of their English counterparts, their actual powers were much smaller because they had at their disposal few of the "devices by which in England the executive" exerted effective political control. Second, the intense competition for status, power, and wealth generated by an unstable economic and social structure made what in England were only "theoretical dangers" appear in the colonies to be "real dangers" that threatened the very essentials of the constitution and created an atmosphere of suspicion and anxiety that made the opposition vision of politics seem especially appropriate.

Although the interpretation presented by Bailyn in *The Origins of American Politics* accommodates more aspects of colonial political life than any previous explanation, it is not, by itself, a sufficient explanation. Above all, it is insufficient because it does not fully take into account or put in clear perspective one of the main features of colonial political life, the very feature almost invariably singled out for comment by contemporaries in the colonies and subsequently treated as the central theme of colonial political development by so many later historians: the persistent preoccupation of colonial legislators with the dangers of prerogative power. Bailyn is, to be sure, at some pains to show the excessiveness, by English standards, of the governors' assigned powers. But he pays little attention to the colonial response to this situation. Instead, he stresses the executive weakness and the economic and social instability that made public life so brittle as presumably to give the opposition's frenzied charges of influence, conspiracy, and ministerial corruption such extraordinary explanatory power in the colonies. But this neglect and this emphasis were, in large measure, predetermined by Bailyn's research design. Limiting his investigation mostly to pamphlets and newspaper essays and ignoring other relevant sources such as legislative journals, he approached his study of early eighteenth-century political thought in search of the intellectual *origins* of the American Revolution and the *origins* of mid-eighteenth-century American politics, and he found precisely what he was looking for: instances of colonial use of the writings of John Trenchard and Thomas Gordon, Viscount Bolingbroke, and other writers of the opposition to Sir Robert Walpole, and the colonial conditions that made the message of those writers so congenial. The result of this focus is that his study is both incomplete and, to the extent that it does not give adequate attention to other, perhaps more central aspects of early eighteenth-century politics, anachronistic. Specifically, in relation to the subject of this article, it does not consider changes in the nature and content of colonial political thought over time. It neither explores older intellectual and political traditions that preceded colonial acceptance of the Walpolean opposition conception of politics nor seeks to explain under what conditions and to what extent newer conceptions replaced those older traditions. What Bailyn has failed to do for the early eighteenth century is thus precisely what he has correctly accused earlier writers of not doing for the revolutionary era: he has not been sensitive to what colonial political leaders "themselves . . . professed to be their own motivations." He has not considered the importance of how they saw themselves and how they conceived of the dimensions and function of the political roles into which they were cast.[9]

It is this problem as it specifically relates to the behavior of colonial legislators during the eighteenth century that I shall attempt to explore. My argument is
114 that colonial legislative behavior was initially and deeply rooted in an older political tradition. I shall try to identify and explain the nature of that tradition, the sources and ways through which it may have been transmitted to the colonies, the intellectual and institutional imperatives it required of its adherents, the internal political and social circumstances that contributed to its acceptance and perpetuation in the colonies long after it had spent most of its force in England, and the extent to which it continued to inform and shape colonial legislative behavior right down to the American Revolution.

The older political tradition to which I refer is, of course, the seventeenth-century tradition of opposition to the Crown as it developed out of the repeated clashes between the first two Stuarts and their Parliaments during the first half of the century and, even more important because it occurred during a formative period in colonial political life, out of the Whig opposition to Charles II and James II in the 1670's and 1680's. Initially emerging from attempts by James I to challenge some of the "ancient Privileges" of the House of Commons, this tradition, as Thornhagh Gurdon remarked in the early eighteenth century, was a product of the "Apprehensions and Fears" among "Parliament and People . . . that instead of the ancient Constitution of *England*, a Monarchy limited by original Contract, between the ancient Princes and their People, established, and known by Custom and Usage," James "aimed at a . . . despotick Government." The ensuing "Strife and Debate," as eighteenth-century opposition writers were fond of pointing out, could be interpreted, fundamentally, as another effort in behalf of liberty in its age-old struggle against arbitrary power from whatever source it emanated. But because the Crown in this instance was the offending party and the House of Commons was still conceived of as the chief bulwark of the people's liberties, the contest became a fight by the House of Commons

[9] Bernard Bailyn, *The Origins of American Politics* (New York, 1968), esp. the preface and Chaps. I and II. This work was previously published in *Perspectives in American History*, I (1967), 9–120. The quotations are from p. ix, 10, 53, 56, 63, 96, 160.

to restrain the prerogative of the King, an attempt by the Commons to define what one later writer described as "the just Limits between Prerogative and Privilege."[10] The specific issues in dispute changed from Parliament to Parliament under the early Stuarts, but the debate over them was almost invariably cast in this form. Even after the contest had escalated in the early 1640's to the point where the ultimate issue became whether King or Parliament would exercise sovereign power, parliamentary leaders tended to see and to justify their actions as necessary protests or preventive measures against arbitrary use of royal prerogatives.[11]

In part because Parliament itself had been so obviously guilty of abusive use of governmental power during the Civil War and Interregnum and in part because Parliament's existence no longer appeared to be in jeopardy, the conditions under which Charles II returned to the throne created strong pressures toward cooperation between King and Parliament. For a decade and a half after the Restoration, the opposition talked not about the dangers of excessive prerogative but about the potential evils of royal influence in the second Long Parliament. But as the "prerogative reached unparalleled heights"[12] in the late 1660's and as the very existence of Parliament increasingly seemed to the emerging Whig opposition "to be far too precarious and desperately in need of stronger protection,"[13] the "uneasy co-operation of the first few years after the Restoration gave way, in the 1670s to a series of charges by the Commons that the King was acting unconstitutionally." It was widely assumed, as a later speaker declared, that the King had had "a surfeit of Parliaments in his father's time, and was therefore extremely desirous to lay them aside."[14] Moved by the same old fears that had plagued its predecessors during the first half of the century, the House of Commons once again "leapt at any chance to question the royal prerogative" and to demand "constitutional safeguards . . . to protect the role of Parliament."[15] As Betty Kemp has pointed out, the last six years of the reign of Charles II "and the whole reign of James II, showed that the more fundamental dangers of dissolution and absence of parliament had not passed" with the significant result that the Commons was "recalled . . . from a seemingly premature concern with influence to their earlier concern with prerogative."[16] Opposition writers reminded their readers that the history of relations between Crown and Commons had been a "Series of . . . Invasions upon the *Privileges of Parliaments*" by the

[10] The quotations are from Thornhagh Gurdon, *The History of the High Court of Parliament* (2 vols., London, 1731), II, 415–16, 506–508.

[11] For discussions of the varied content of opposition thought under the first two Stuarts, see Margaret Atwood Judson, *The Crisis of the Constitution: An Essay in Constitutional and Political Thought in England 1603–1645* (New Brunswick, N. J., 1949).

[12] Caroline Robbins, *The Eighteenth-Century Commonwealthman: Studies in the Transmission, Development and Circumstance of English Liberal Thought from the Restoration of Charles II until the War with the Thirteen Colonies* (Cambridge, Mass., 1961), 26.

[13] J. H. Plumb, *The Origins of Political Stability: England 1675–1725* (Boston, 1967), 32.

[14] Betty Kemp, *King and Commons 1660–1832* (London, 1957), 3, n. 21.

[15] Plumb, *Origins of Political Stability*, 50–51.

[16] Kemp, *King and Commons*, 23–24.

Crown[17] and dilated upon the theme that, in the later words of Thomas Hanmer, it was not cooperation with but "distrust of the executive" that was the chief "principle on which the whole of our Constitution is grounded."[18] Although the conviction that "serious restrictions" had to be imposed "on the King's prerogative in relationship to Parliament" was inextricably intertwined with fears of popery and concern over the Crown's arbitrary interference with all sorts of established institutions, and although it was held in check by vivid memories of what happened when Parliament went too far in its assault upon the Crown in the 1640's,[19] it was central to Whig and parliamentary opposition under the last two Stuarts and was one of the primary justifications for the Revolution of 1688.[20] Once these restrictions had been achieved by the settlement of 1689, they provided the
116 basis for working out in the eighteenth century those methods "for co-operation between King and Commons" described by Betty Kemp, J. H. Plumb, and others.[21] Though the fear of prerogative always lurked not far beneath and occasionally even appeared above the surface of political life, it ceased to be an animating force in English politics. Opposition writers concerned themselves instead with the dangers of ministerial influence and corruption.[22]

In the colonies, by contrast, the seventeenth-century opposition tradition, with its overriding fear of prerogative power and its jealous concern with protecting the privileges and authority of the House of Commons, continued to occupy a prominent place in politics at least until the middle of the eighteenth century and did not entirely lose its force until after the Declaration of Independence.

Any explanation for this phenomenon must at this point be highly tentative. A partial explanation is to be found, however, in the powerful mimetic impulses within colonial society. At work to some extent in all areas of colonial life from the beginning of English colonization, these impulses are another example of the familiar tendency of provincial societies to look to the cultural capital for preferred values and approved models of behavior. If, as Peter Laslett has remarked, English colonization contained within it a strong urge to create in America "new societies in its own image, or in the image of its ideal self,"[23]

[17] See, e.g., the title to Pt. 2 of William Petyt, *Jus Parliamentarium: or, the Ancient Power, Jurisdiction, Rights and Liberties, of the most High Court of Parliament, Revived and Asserted* (London, 1739). This work was first published in 1680.

[18] As quoted in Kemp, *King and Commons*, 4–5.

[19] O. W. Furley, "The Whig Exclusionists: Pamphlet Literature in the Exclusion Campaign, 1679–81," *Cambridge Historical Journal*, XIII (No. 1, 1957), 19–36; J. R. Jones, *The First Whigs: The Politics of the Exclusion Crisis* (London, 1961). The quotation is from Kemp, *King and Commons*, 8.

[20] For the Whig opposition program, see Betty Behrens, "The Whig Theory of the Constitution in the Reign of Charles II," *Cambridge Historical Journal*, VII (1941), 42–71, esp. 61–63. A clear analysis of events is provided by Clayton Roberts, *The Growth of Responsible Government in Stuart England* (Cambridge, Eng., 1966), 197–244.

[21] Kemp, *King and Commons*, 8; Plumb, *Origins of Political Stability*, *passim*.

[22] Robbins, *Eighteenth-Century Commonwealthman*, 56–319; Bailyn, *Ideological Origins*, 34–54; and Isaac Kramnick, *Bolingbroke and His Circle: The Politics of Nostalgia in the Age of Walpole* (Cambridge, Mass., 1968).

[23] Peter Laslett, *The World We Have Lost* (New York, 1965), 183.

the impetus among the colonists to cast their societies in that same ideal image was (except in places like Massachusetts Bay, where men actually hoped to improve upon and not merely to duplicate English patterns) infinitely more powerful. Conditions of life in new and relatively inchoate and unstable societies at the extreme peripheries of English civilization inevitably created deep social and psychological insecurities, a major crisis of identity, that could be resolved, if at all, only through a constant reference back to the one certain measure of achievement: the standards of the cultural center. The result was a strong predisposition among the colonists to cultivate idealized English values and to seek to imitate idealized versions of English forms and institutions.[24]

These mimetic impulses, which became increasingly intense through the eighteenth century and, ironically, were probably never greater than they were on the eve of the American Revolution, were given more power and made more explicit by two simultaneous developments in the late seventeenth and early eighteenth centuries. The first was the emergence of recognizable and reasonably permanent colonial elites with great political influence, whose economic activities carried them directly into the ambit of English society and thereby subjected them, to an even greater degree than earlier colonials, to the irresistible pull of English culture.[25] The second was the extensive expansion of English governmental influence into the colonies after the Restoration and the largely successful attempt by imperial authorities to substitute something resembling an English model of government for a welter of existing political forms that had grown up in the colonies.[26]

That this model was only superficially English, that the analogy between King, Lords, and Commons in England on the one hand and the governors, councils, and assemblies in the colonies on the other was so obviously imperfect only stimulated the desire of colonial political leaders to make it less so.[27] Nowhere was this desire more manifest than in the behavior of the lower houses of assembly and of the men who composed them. Because the governors and councils so clearly rested upon a less independent foundation, they might never be more than "imperfect" equivalents of their English counterparts. But the lower houses had so "exact" a "resemblance" to "that part of the British constitution," which they stood for in the colonies that it was entirely plausible to

[24] There is no adequate treatment of this phenomenon during the early phase of European expansion, but see Ronald Syme, *Colonial Elites: Rome, Spain and the Americas* (London, 1958), *passim*.

[25] There is no comprehensive study of this subject, but see Louis B. Wright, *The First Gentlemen of Virginia: Intellect and Qualities of the Early Colonial Ruling Class* (San Marino, Calif., 1940); Bernard Bailyn, *The New England Merchants in the Seventeenth Century* (Cambridge, Mass., 1955); and Frederick B. Tolles, *Meeting House and Counting House: The Quaker Merchants of Colonial Philadelphia* (Chapel Hill, N. C., 1948).

[26] On this point, see esp. A. P. Thornton, *West-India Policy under the Restoration* (Oxford, Eng., 1955); and Michael Garibaldi Hall, *Edward Randolph and the American Colonies, 1676–1703* (Chapel Hill, N. C., 1960).

[27] The power of this analogy is discussed, perhaps in somewhat exaggerated form, in Bailyn, *Origins of American Politics*, 59–65.

entertain the heady possibility that each of them might indeed come to be the very "epitome of the house of Commons." Because they were "called by the same authority," derived their "power from the same source, [were] instituted for the same ends, and [were] governed by the same forms," there was absolutely no reason why each of them "should not have the same powers . . . and the same rank in the system of" its "little community, as the house of Commons" had "in that of Britain."[28]

In their attempt to convert this possibility into reality, to model their lower houses as closely as possible after the English House of Commons, colonial legislators had a wide range of sources to draw upon. They had, to begin with, some of the proceedings of the House of Commons as published, for the period from 1618 to the execution of Charles I, along with many other relevant docu-
118 ments in John Rushworth's eight-volume *Historical Collections* (London, 1659–1701) and, for the 1670's and 1680's, in the separately printed journals of each session of the House. They had, as well, much of the vast literature of the Whig opposition to the later Stuarts, including both the major philosophical disquisitions of Henry Neville, Algernon Sydney, and John Locke (each of which carefully defined the functions of the House and elaborated the proper relationship between prerogative and Parliament), and many of the vast number of occasional pieces, some of which were reprinted following the Glorious Revolution in the two-volume collection of *State Tracts* (London, 1689–93) and others of which were later issued together in the sixteen-volume edition of *Somers Tracts* (London, 1748–52).[29] Finally, they had such terse and comprehensive statements of Whig theory as Henry Care's *English Liberties: or, The Free-Born Subject's Inheritance* (London, 1682), which was reprinted several times in the colonies; the Whig contributions to the extensive debate over the antiquity of Parliament;[30] early Whig histories, especially that of Paul de Rapin-Thoyras, the Huguenot who sailed with William of Orange and who interpreted the events of the seventeenth century from the perspective of the most radical wing of Whig thinkers;[31] and, probably most important of all, the several parliamentary commentaries and procedural books published in the seventeenth century, including those of William Hakewill,[32] Sir Edward Coke,[33] Henry Scobell,[34]

[28] The quotations are from *The Privileges of the Island of Jamaica Vindicated with an Impartial Narrative of the late Dispute between the Governor and House of Representatives* (London, 1766), 33–34. Similar statements are scattered throughout the literature of colonial politics.

[29] The best analyses of the content of this literature will be found in Behrens, "Whig Theory of the Constitution"; Furley, "Whig Exclusionists"; and Robbins, *Eighteenth-Century Commonwealthman*, 22–87. The best discussion of Locke's ideas is in the introduction to Peter Laslett's edition of *Two Treatises of Government* (Cambridge, Eng., 1960).

[30] The standard discussion of these writings is J. G. A. Pocock, *The Ancient Constitution and the Feudal Law: A Study of English Historical Thought in the Seventeenth Century* (Cambridge, Eng., 1957).

[31] Paul de Rapin-Thoyras, *The History of England, as well ecclesiastical as civil*, tr. Nicholas Tindal (15 vols., London, 1725–31), is the first English edition.

[32] William Hakewill, *The Manner of Holding Parliaments in England* (London, 1641).

[33] Sir Edward Coke, *The Fourth Part of the Institutes of the Laws of England* (London, 1644).

[34] Henry Scobell, *Memorials of the Method and Manner of Proceedings in Parliament in Passing Bills* (London, 1656).

Henry Elsynge,[35] and, most significantly, George Petyt.[36] Petyt's work was reprinted by Andrew Bradford in 1716 in both New York and Philadelphia and was the last such treatise of major proportions until John Hatsell published his four-volume work in 1781.[37]

As Petyt remarked in his preface, these procedural books served as a comprehensive introduction to "*the admirable method of* Parliamentary Proceedings; *the Exactness and Decency of their* Orders; *the Wisdom and Prudence of their* Customs; *the Extent of their* Powers; *and the Largeness of their* Privileges." They adumbrated in detail and cited appropriate precedents concerning mechanics of conducting elections, the necessary qualifications for members and electors, the methods of examining election returns and deciding disputed elections, the power of the House over its own members, the method of electing a speaker and the correct way for him to conduct his office, the ways of selection and the roles of other House officers, the proper procedures for passing bills and conducting debates, the several categories of committees and the structure and function of each, the customary form of a session, the privileges of members, and the usual distribution of function and patterns of relationship among the three branches of Parliament.

The importance of such manuals in the exportation of parliamentary government to distant plantations can scarcely be overemphasized. If, as Anthony Stokes later remarked, "the Journals of the Houses of Parliament" were "the precedents by which the Legislatures in the Colonies conduct[ed] themselves,"[38] these manuals provided a convenient distillation of the several pertinent matters in those journals. The extent to which colonial legislators probably used them in the process of taking, as the Pennsylvania Speaker David Lloyd phrased it, "their rules from the *House of Commons*," of copying its forms and procedures, may be inferred from the work of several earlier scholars, most notably Mary Patterson Clarke,[39] and requires no further comment here.

What has been much less clearly perceived, however, and what, in fact, has

[35] Henry Elsynge, *The Ancient Method and Manner of Holding Parliaments in England* (London, 1660).

[36] George Petyt, *Lex Parliamentaria: or a Treatise of the Law and Custom of the Parliaments of England* (London, 1689).

[37] John Hatsell, *Precedents of Proceedings in the House of Commons* (4 vols., London, 1781). Among the few pieces of literature of this genre to appear in the eighteenth century were Gurdon's *History of the High Court of Parliament;* and Giles Jacob, *Lex Constitutiones: or, The Gentleman's Law* (London, 1719), esp. Chap. III. For a discussion of the changing nature of the interest in such matters from the seventeenth to the eighteenth century, see J. Steven Watson, "Parliamentary Procedure as a Key to the Understanding of Eighteenth Century Politics," *Burke Newsletter,* III (Summer 1962), 108–28.

[38] Anthony Stokes, *A View of the Constitution of the British Colonies in North America and the West Indies, at the Time the Civil War broke out on the Continent of America* (London, 1783), 243–44.

[39] Mary Patterson Clarke, *Parliamentary Privilege in the American Colonies* (New Haven, Conn., 1943), esp. 1–13. The bibliographical note (pp. 270–87) refers to several other specialized works touching on this point. The quotation is from [David Lloyd,] *Remarks on the late Proceedings of Some Members of Assembly at Philadelphia* (Philadelphia, 1728). Among many similar statements, see [Thomas Nairne,] *A Letter from South Carolina* (London, 1710), 21–22.

been largely missed by earlier writers, is the remarkable extent to which these parliamentary commentaries and the later Stuart opposition literature shaped not merely the form and procedure of the lower houses but also the understanding and behavior of their members. For, in addition to spelling out the method and manner of parliamentary proceedings, they prescribed explicitly and in detail a whole set of generalized and specific institutional imperatives for representative bodies, a particular pattern of behavior for their members, and a concrete program of political action.

The central assumptions behind this prescription were, first, that there was a natural antagonism between the "King's Prerogative" and the "Rights, Liberties and Properties of the People," and, second, that the primary function of
120 the House of Commons, as Henry Care declared, was "to preserve inviolable our Liberty and Property, according to the known Laws of the Land, without any giving way unto or Introduction of that absolute and arbitrary Rule practised in Foreign Countries."[40] To that end the House was expected always to be careful never to relinquish possession of the "Keys to unlock Peoples Purses" and always to be on the alert for any indications of arbitrary government in order that they might be checked before they could "wound the Body Politick in a vital Part." The role of the House of Commons was thus essentially negative and defensive. To "redress Grievances, to take notice of Monopolies and Oppressions, to curb the Exorbitances of great Favourites, and pernicious Ministers of State, to punish such mighty Delinquents, who are protected by the King, that they look upon themselves too big for the ordinary reach of Justice in Courts of Common Law, to inspect the conduct of such who are intrusted with the Administration of Justice, and interpret the Laws to the prejudice of the People, and those who dispose the publick Treasure of the Nation"—these were the many grave and weighty responsibilities that fell to and could only be handled by that "great Assembly." The House was the subject's single most important governmental hedge against "arbitrary Violence and Oppression" from the prerogative or any other source and final guarantor of the liberty that was the peculiar and precious "Birth-right of Englishmen."[41]

Such extraordinary responsibilities required both a strong House of Commons and a membership devoted to maintaining that strength. Voters had, therefore, always to be especially careful to elect only such men to Parliament who had sufficient "Wisdom and Courage" that they could "not be hectored out of their Duties by the Frowns and Scowls of Men" and who were "resolved to stand by, and maintain the *Power and Privileges of Parliaments*," which were the very "Heart-strings of the Common-Wealth." It was incumbent upon all men elected to "*that honourable Station*" to make sure that they were "*thoroughly*

[40] Gurdon, *History of the High Court of Parliament*, 415–16; Henry Care, *English Liberties* (4th ed., London, 1719), 164. All citations to Care in this article are to this edition.
[41] *Ibid.*, 4, 122, 138–39; Petyt, *Lex Parliamentaria*, 19, 24.

skill'd in Parliamentary Affairs, *to know their own* Laws *and* Customs, *their* Powers *and* Priviledges, *that they may not at any time suffer Invasions to be made upon them, by what plausible* Pretences *soever.*"[42]

Because many—perhaps most—of those "Invasions" could be expected to derive directly from and even to be protected by the excessive "Privileges and Prerogatives" invested in the Crown, it was absolutely necessary that the House of Commons have sufficient powers and privileges to contest the Crown on equal, perhaps even superior, grounds. The House had to have legal guarantees that it would meet frequently, have full investigative powers, and have complete control over its own officers.[43] Its members must have freedom of speech and debate, freedom from arrest during sessions, and exemption from punishment outside the House for anything said or done in or on behalf of the House. In short, the House had to be a law unto itself responsible only to its constituents and to its own special law, the "Lex & Consuetudo Parliamenti."[44]

Bent upon turning their lower houses into "epitomes of the House of Commons," "so fond," as one Jamaica governor reported, "of the notion to be as near as can be, upon the foott of H[is] M[ajesty's] English subjects that the desire of it allmost distracts them,"[45] and prone, like all provincials, to take the ideals of their cultural capital far more seriously than they are ever taken in the capital itself, colonial representatives adopted *in toto* this entire system of thought and action along with its patterns of perception and its cluster of imperatives, roles, and conventions. This system supplied them with a special frame of reference, an angle of vision that helped them to put their own problems and actions in historical, seemingly even cosmic, perspective, gave them a standard of behavior, determined how they conceived of the lower houses and of their own political roles, and, most important, shaped into predictable and familiar forms their perceptions of and responses to political events.

So deeply was this system of thought and action imbedded in their political culture that the remembrance of the terrible excesses of Stuart despotism, of those infamous times "when prerogative was unlimited, and liberty undefined" and "arbitrary power, under the shelter of unlimited Prerogative was making large strides over the land," was throughout the eighteenth century always near the surface of political consciousness. Colonial representatives scarcely needed to be reminded of "what extraordinary Progress was made" in the attempt "to raise Royalty above the Laws and Liberties of the People, by the chimerical Ideas of Prerogative" during the "three last hereditary Reigns of the *Stuarts*, what Toil, what Fatigue, what Slaughter the Nation underwent before the Delirium of

[42] Care, *English Liberties*, 164–67; Petyt, *Lex Parliamentaria*, preface.

[43] *Ibid.*, 3, 13, 16, 30–31, 132. Petyt was clearly unhappy with the King's prominent role in the choice of speaker, noting that the selection must have been "anciently free to the *Commons*, to choose whom they would of their own House." (*Ibid.*, 132.)

[44] *Ibid.*, 9, 36–37, 81–82, 87, 139.

[45] Duke of Portland to [Lord Carteret?], *Calendar of State Papers, Colonial*, ed. William Noel Sainsbury *et al.* (43 vols., London, 1860–), *1722–1723*, 385.

Charles the 1st, could be vanquished. What Lengths were run, what large Compliances made under *Charles* the Second, . . . how near fatal the Blow was to Freedom and Liberty under his Brother *James*," and how all of these evil efforts were defeated only because they were "constantly and strictly opposed by Parliament" under the leadership of those noble House of Commons men—Sir John Eliot, Sir Edward Coke, Edward Littleton, John Pym, John Hampden, William Jones—"who stood forth at that critical period, in defense of the Constitution."[46]

With such vivid memories always before them, colonial legislators had a strong predisposition to look at each governor as a potential Charles I or James II, to assume a hostile posture toward the executive, and to define with the broadest possible latitude the role of the lower house as "the main barrier of all those
122 rights and privileges which British subjects enjoy."[47] Ever ready to stand "in the gap against oppression," they were, in the best tradition of seventeenth-century English opponents of the Crown, constantly worried lest *"Prerogative"* gain "a considerable Advantage over *Liberty*" or a governor extend "his Power, beyond what any King in *England* ever pretended to, even in the most despotick and arbitrary Reigns."[48] Especially sensitive to any encroachments "upon their jurisdiction" that might "(if submitted to) strip them of all authority, and [thereby] disable them from either supporting their own dignity or giving the people . . . that protection against arbitrary power, which nothing but a free and independent Assembly" could "give," they invariably, in imitation of the English House of Commons, opposed all attempts to make innovations "contrary to . . . the constant Practice of all English Assemblies" or "to Govern otherwise than according to the Usage and Custom of the Country since the first Settlement thereof." In the words of Elisha Cooke, Jr., they "Warily observed and tim[or]ously Prevented" any precedents that might, by making "little Changes in Fundamentals," lead to the collapse of the whole constitution.[49] In their determination to discover and root out all examples of arbitrary executive power, they were particularly concerned "to enquire into the abuses and corruptions of office, the obstructions of public justice, and the complaints of subjects, oppressed by the hand of power, and to bring the offenders in such cases to justice."[50]

[46] *Privileges of the Island of Jamaica Vindicated*, 8, 11, 13, 28, 36, 66; A New-England Man, *A Letter to the Freeholders and Qualified Voters, Relating to the Ensuing Election* (Boston, 1749), 2.

[47] Pennsylvania Assembly, *To the Honourable Patrick Gordon, Esq., Lieut. Governor* (Philadelphia, 1728), 6, as quoted by Lawrence H. Leder, *Liberty and Authority: Early American Political Ideology, 1689–1763* (Chicago, 1968), 87.

[48] *Privileges of the Island of Jamaica Vindicated*, 42; Americanus, *A Letter to the Freeholders and other Inhabitants of the Massachusetts-Bay relating to their approaching Election of Representatives* ([Boston,] 1739), 111; *A Second Letter from One in the Country to His Friend in Boston* ([Boston,] 1729), 2.

[49] *Privileges of the Island of Jamaica Vindicated*, 2; *The Remonstrance of Several of the Representatives for Several Counties of the Province of New York being Members of the Present Assembly* (New York, 1698), 1; Resolutions of the Maryland House of Delegates, Oct. 22, 1722, in St. George Leakin Sioussat, *The English Statutes in Maryland* (Baltimore, 1903), 75; Elisha Cooke, *Just and Seasonable Vindication Respecting some Affairs transacted by the late General Assembly at Boston, 1720* ([Boston, 1720]), 14.

[50] *Privileges of the Island of Jamaica Vindicated*, 51.

The governors of the colonies themselves encouraged colonial representatives in this conception of the function of the lower houses and the mode of behavior it implied. For the legislators were not the only group imprisoned by the rhetoric, anxieties, and peculiar political myopia of Stuart England. Like the Stuart monarchs and their supporters, governors, occupying similar roles in the political order, could scarcely avoid interpreting any questioning of executive actions and any opposition to gubernatorial programs or imperial directives as, covertly and fundamentally at least, a challenge to the essential prerogatives of the Crown or proprietors. From every colony came charges from the governors and their adherents that the lower houses were "exceeding their due and reasonable Bounds; strengthening themselves with pretences of publick Good and their own Privileges as the Representatives of the People." Everywhere, the executive complained that the lower houses were declaring "themselves a House of Commons," assuming "all the Privileges of it, and" acting "with a much more unlimited Authority." It was widely echoed, and believed, that the lower houses, like the first Long Parliament in the "Period that every good Man wishes could be struck out of our Annals," were actually endeavoring "to wrest the small Remains of Power out of the Hands of the Crown," "to assume the Executive Power of the Government into their own Hands," and perhaps even "to weaken, if not entirely to cast off, the Obedience they owe to the Crown, and the Dependance which all Colonies ought to have on their Mother Country." From the governors' chairs, the leaders of the legislative opposition appeared to be not patriots struggling in the glorious cause of liberty but exactly as the leaders of the House of Commons had seemed to the Stuarts: "designing and malicious Men imposing upon, and deluding the People" until they were "so far infatuated, as to seem insensible of their . . . true interest."[61] Every recalcitrant lower house appeared to be bent on pursuing "the example of the parliament of 1641" and every leader to be "a great Magna-Carta Man & Petition-of-Right-maker" determined to persuade his fellow legislators "to dance after the Long Parliament's pipe."[62] Both sides, then, were playing out roles and operating within a conception of politics that derived directly from the revolutionary situation in Stuart England, a conception

[61] The quotations are from *The Representation and Memorial of the Council of the Island of Jamaica to the Right Honourable The Lords Commissioners for Trade and Plantations* (London, 1716), ii, iv, 14; Governor James Glen to Commons House, Sept. 20, 1755, Journals of the South Carolina Commons House, Jan.–May 1754, Colonial Office Papers, Class 5/472, 6–7; and a speech of Governor Jonathan Belcher to the Massachusetts General Assembly, Oct. 2, 1730, reprinted in *Extracts from the Political State of Great Britain, December 1730* ([Boston, 1731]), 4–5. For many similar characterizations of the lower houses and their leaders by governors and their supporters, see Sir William Beeston to Board of Trade, Aug. 19, 1701, *Calendar of State Papers, Colonial, 1701*, ed. Sainsbury *et al.*, 424–25; Lord Cornbury to Board of Trade, Nov. 6, 1704, Feb. 19, 1705, *ibid., 1704–1705*, 308–309, 386; Samuel Shute to Crown, [Aug. 16, 1723,] *ibid., 1722–1723*, 324–30; Henry Worsley to Duke of Newcastle, Aug. 4, 1727, *ibid., 1726–1727*, 325–26; *The Honest Man's Interest As he Claims any Lands in the Counties of New-Castle, Kent, or Sussex, on Delaware* ([Philadelphia, 1726]), 1.

[62] Francis Lord Willoughby to King, Aug. 8, 1665, Colonial Office Papers, Class 1/19, No. 92, as quoted in Thornton, *West-India Policy*, 65; Lewis Morris to Board of Trade, June 10, 1743, *The Papers of Lewis Morris, Collections of the New Jersey Historical Society* (14 vols., Newark, 1852–1965), IV, 162.

that conditioned them to view politics as a continuing struggle between prerogative and liberty, between executive and legislative power.

For governors and legislators alike, this conception of their behavior and their disagreements gave them an enlarged purpose that transcended the narrow bounds of their several localities and, by investing their actions with national—not to say, universal—meaning, linked them directly to their cultural inheritance as Englishmen, gave them a more secure sense of who and what they were, and helped to satisfy their deepest mimetic impulses. What was equally important, at least in the case of the legislators, that enlarged purpose also supplied them and their institutions with the prestige, standing, and political power within their respective communities, which seem to be so necessary to the psychological
124 needs of emergent elites.

But the fact that this specific conception of politics had such a powerful hold on men's minds in England at exactly the same time that colonial legislators were self-consciously beginning to cultivate English political values and to imitate the procedures and behavior of the House of Commons does not completely account for the adoption of that conception in the colonies. What also accounts for its adoption as well as for its continued vitality in the colonies long after it had become in England little more than a series of political clichés and hackneyed constitutionalisms that were largely irrelevant to the realities of political life was the survival in the colonies during the eighteenth century of the very conditions and circumstances that had initially spawned it in seventeenth-century England. For, as Bailyn has recently reminded us,[53] explicit restrictions of the kind Parliament successfully imposed upon the prerogative in England following the Glorious Revolution were never achieved in the colonies. As a result, the institutional cooperation made possible by the revolutionary settlement in England was rarely attainable in the colonies, and the specter of unlimited prerogative thus continued to haunt colonial legislators.

For legislators "in love with . . . [the English] Constitution," striving diligently to achieve a "form of government" that resembled "that of England, as nearly as the condition of a dependent Colony" could "be brought to resemble, that of its mother country," and culturally programmed to be ever on guard against the dangers of unlimited prerogative,[54] this situation was a source of perpetual anxiety. Not only did it directly frustrate their mimetic impulses by blatantly reminding them of the great gap between their aspirations and reality; it also put them into continual fear lest some evil governor employ his excessive power to introduce the most pernicious form of tyranny. It seemed absolutely inexplicable, as an anonymous Jamaican declared in 1714, "that in all the Revolutions of State, and Changes of the Ministry" in England since the Restoration "the several

[53] Bailyn, *Origins of American Politics*, 66–71.

[54] Fayer Hall, *The Importance of the British Plantations in America to the Kingdom* (London, 1731), 24; *Privileges of the Island of Jamaica Vindicated*, 31.

Colonies which compose the *British* Empire in *America*" and were inhabited by supposedly freeborn Englishmen "should . . . lye still so much neglected, under such a precarious Government and greivous [*sic*] Administration, as they have, for the most part, labour'd under, both before and since the late signal Revolution."[65] Indeed, from the perspective of that Revolution in which the rights and privileges of subjects in England had been so fully "confirmed; and the knavish Chicanes, and crafty Inventions, that were introduced to deprive the Subject of his Rights . . . abolished," it seemed especially grievous—and frighteningly dangerous—"that a Governour of any Colony . . . so far distant from the Seat of Redress . . . should be vested with a Power to govern, in a more absolute and unlimited manner there, than even the Queen herself can, according to Law, or ever did attempt to exercise in *Great Britain*," that a lower house should have "less Sway and Weight" in a colony "than the *House of Commons* had in *Great Britain*."[66]

The dangers of this situation were not merely imaginary. They were vividly confirmed by the many "Instances" in which both royal and proprietary governors, lacking in many cases even a remote sense of identity of interests with the colonists, had used their preponderant powers "to gripe and squeeze the People . . . for [no] . . . other Reason, than their own private Gain," "usurped more Authority than [even theoretically] belonged to them," and attempted to exercise "Arbitrary Power, unknown in our Mother-Country since the glorious Revolution of 1688." It was well known "that all [of the many] Contentions and Animosities . . . between the Governour and Inhabitants of" the colonies took "their first Rise, from some grievous and intolerable Acts of Oppression, in the Administration." As Richard Jackson remarked, it was the governors who always acted the "*offensive Part*," who "set up unwarrantable Claims" and employed "Snares, Menaces, Aspersions, Tumults, and every other unfair Practice" in an attempt either to bully or to wheedle "the Inhabitants out of the Privileges they were born to." Like the House of Commons, the lower houses thus always acted "on the *defensive only*"; their members courageously struggled with true British patriotism against the wicked machinations of "hungry, ignorant, or extravagant" governors and their "crafty, active, knavish . . . , servile, fawning" adherents, the very "trash of mankind" who alone would enter into such unsavory alliances against the people's rights and liberties as represented by the lower houses.[67]

Whatever images they held of themselves, however, colonial representatives could not, in the situation, act "on the *defensive only*." Precisely because the

[65] *The Groans of Jamaica, Express'd in a Letter from a Gentleman Residing there, to his Friend in London* (London, 1714), iv.

[66] Daniel Dulany, *The Rights of the Inhabitants of Maryland to the Benefit of the English Laws* (Annapolis, 1728), 17; *Second Letter*, 2; *Groans of Jamaica*, vi.

[67] The quotations are from *An Essay upon the Government of the English Plantations on the Continent of America* (London, 1701), written by an anonymous Virginian and reprinted in a modern edition by Louis B. Wright (San Marino, Calif., 1945), 11, 21; A New-England-Man,

King's governors claimed to "be more Absolute in the Plantations than" the King himself was "in England," because some governors actually sought to use their exorbitant powers to increase the prerogative at the expense of liberty, and because, as a Barbadian complained in 1719, it was not always possible to secure redress against such grievances in London in face of the superior influence of the governors with men in power—for all of these reasons so "generally [well] Known in *America*" the lower houses found themselves—and were frequently and correctly accused of—trying to secure checks on the prerogative and power over executive affairs well beyond any exercised by the House of Commons. It was "a received opinion" that "Right without Power to maintain it, is the Derision and Sport of Tyrants."[58] To defend such deviations from the imperial norm, colonial legislators were forced to fall back upon that ultimate defense of
126 the seventeenth-century House of Commons, *"Perpetual Usage"* and "established custom," and to claim that, like the Commons, each legislature had a "Lex & Consuetudo Parliamenti" of its own.[59] Despite the depth and genuineness of their imitative impulses, the mimesis of the House of Commons by the colonial lower houses and of the imperial government by the several provincial governments could never be exact because of the Crown's exaggerated claims for prerogative in the plantations and the immoderate responses those claims evoked from the legislatures. The result, a source of amusement, derision, and amazement among imperial administrative supporters in the colonies, was the ironic spectacle of men determined to form their "Assemblies . . . on the Plan of an *English* Parliament" forced into defending their peculiar practices on the obvious grounds that it was "altogether . . . absurd to prescribe [exactly] the same form of government to people differently circumstanced."[60]

The lower houses in most colonies were able through such innovative practices to bridle the governors, both because, unlike the king, the governors were never protected from attack by the aura of the concept that the king could do no wrong and because, as Bailyn has so fully and effectively argued, most gov-

---

Letter to the Freeholders, 5; *Groans of Jamaica*, iv–v; [Richard Jackson,] *An Historical Review of Pennsylvania from its Origin* (Philadelphia, 1812), 378–79; *A Representation of the Miserable State of Barbadoes Under the Arbitrary and Corrupt Administration of his Excellency, Robert Lowther, Esq; the present Governor* (London, 1719), esp. 22–23; "Considerations of the present Benefit and better Improvement of the English Colonies in America," [1690's,] Historical Manuscripts Commission, *Report of the Manuscripts of the Duke of Buccleuch and Queensberry* (3 vols., London, 1899–1926), II, Pt. 2, 737; Morris to Secretary of State, Feb. 9, 1707, *Documents Relative to the Colonial History of the State of New York*, ed. E. B. O'Callaghan and Berthold Fernow (15 vols., Albany, 1856–87), V, 37.

[58] *Essay upon Government*, 17; *Representation of the Miserable State of Barbadoes*, 32–33; [Nairne,] *Letter from South Carolina*, 21–22, 26–27; A New-England-Man, *Letter to the Freeholders*, 5.

[59] Examples may be seen in Cooke, *Just and Seasonable Vindication*, 3, 9; and Henry Wilkinson, "The Governor, the Council & Assembly in Bermuda during the First Half of the Eighteenth Century," *Bermuda Historical Quarterly*, II (Apr. 1945), 69–84, esp. 81–84.

[60] The quotations are from [Lloyd,] *Remarks on the Late Proceedings*, as quoted by Roy N. Lokken, *David Lloyd: Colonial Lawmaker* (Seattle, Wash., 1959), 230; and *Pennsylvania Gazette* (Philadelphia), Mar. 28, 1738, as quoted by Leder, *Liberty and Authority*, 103; see also [Nairne,] *Letter from South Carolina*, 21–22, 25–26; and Lewis Evans, "A Brief Account of Pennsylvania," 1753, in Lawrence Henry Gipson, *Lewis Evans* (Philadelphia, 1939), 131–34.

ernors did not have at their command those "devices by which in England the executive" was able to exert its control over politics and secure its goals. But this ability to restrain the governors never completely allayed the colonial legislators' fears of prerogative power and arbitrary government. As long as the Crown or proprietors refused to abandon the claims of such extravagant powers for their governors or to recognize the actual limitations imposed upon the prerogative by the lower houses, there was always the terrifying possibility that imperial authorities might unleash the unlimited might of the parent state to enforce its claims, perhaps even by bringing the force of Parliament itself against the lower houses.[61] Although some colonial leaders wishfully hoped that "*that August Assembly*, the Protectors of English Liberties," might actually side with its sister institutions in the colonies, there was an uneasy awareness as well of "how deeply" parliamentary intervention might "enter into our *Constitution* and affect our most *valuable priviledges*." Such extreme vulnerability meant, of course, that colonial legislators could never feel entirely secure "against the assaults of arbitrary power . . . [upon] their lives, their liberties, or their properties."[62]

The resulting anxiety, only partly conscious and appropriately expressed through the classic arguments of the seventeenth-century opposition to the Stuarts, ensured that, at least until such a time as the colonies were granted "a free Constitution of Government" equivalent to that enjoyed by Englishmen at home, those arguments would continue to be especially relevant to colonial politics and to give form and coherence to much of its outward appearance. However, because those arguments and the conception of politics from which they derived were seemingly so explanatory of the peculiar circumstances of colonial politics and apparently so well suited to meet the psychological needs produced by these circumstances, they became so integral a part of colonial political culture and so determinative of the sensibilities of colonial politicians that they ran far "deeper than the Surface of things."[63] They ran so deep, in fact, that they created a strong predisposition to interpret virtually all political conflict as struggles between prerogative and liberty. Even factional fights over tangible economic issues that obviously cut across institutional lines and had nothing ostensible to do with constitutional questions were perceived as, and thereby to some extent actually converted into, such struggles.

It is important, of course, to keep in mind that in colonial, as in all, politics there was frequently, if not invariably, a considerable difference between the ostensible and the real; any comprehensive interpretation will have to distinguish between and describe both "the dress parade of debate" and "the program of

[61] Bailyn, *Origins of American Politics*, 70–105; review of Spurdle, *Early West Indian Government*, 149.

[62] *A Letter to a Gentleman Chosen to be a Member of the Honourable House of Representatives to be Assembled at Boston* ([Boston, 1731]), 7–8, 14–15; *Privileges of the Island of Jamaica Vindicated*, 27–28, 45.

[63] The quotations are from *Essay upon Government*, 20; and Isaac Norris, *Friendly Advice to the Inhabitants of Pennsylvania* (Philadelphia, 1710), 2.

opportunist political tactics" and concrete social and economic interests that lay behind that debate.[64] But it is equally important to comprehend the powerful hold of this older opposition political conception upon the minds of colonial politicians and the remarkable extent to which it conditioned them to conceive of and to explain—even to themselves—behavior and actions arising out of the most self-interested and sordid ambitions as essential contributions to the Englishman's heroic struggle against the evils of unlimited prerogative.

But the hold of this older political conception upon colonial politicians was not so powerful as to prevent them from receiving and employing later English conceptions. Through the middle decades of the eighteenth century, the economies of the home islands and the colonies became ever more tightly connected, the
128 last two intercolonial wars provided a new and compelling focus of common attention,[65] and the colonial elites developed an increasing cultural and political self-consciousness and became more aware of the great social gulf between the colonies and Britain.[66] As a result, the attractive force of English culture and the explicit desires of the elites to cultivate English styles and values and to Anglicize their societies greatly intensified. Under certain conditions, this intensification of colonial mimetic impulses led to the supplementation and, in a few cases, the virtual submersion of the older seventeenth-century political tradition by either, or parts of both, of two newer systems of political thought imported directly from Walpolean England. This process of supplementation and submersion was rendered especially easy because of the close similarity among the older and newer traditions of basic assumptions about human nature, the corrosive effects of unbridled power, the functions of governments and constitutions, and the preferred qualities for rulers.

The first of these traditions, which Bailyn has labeled "mainstream thought," was developed by administrative supporters in the half century after the Glorious Revolution and especially during Walpole's ministry. Within the House of Commons itself, this tradition was fostered by and epitomized by the behavior of Arthur Onslow, who was speaker continuously from 1727 to 1761. He enjoyed a great reputation in both Britain and the colonies and served as a model for speakers of the colonial lower houses. The nuances of this tradition cannot be described here, but its central imperative was the desirability of institu-

[64] The quotation is from Spencer, "Rise of the Assembly," 197.

[65] The role of the intercolonial wars in intensifying British patriotism and a concern for things British among the colonists is described by Max Savelle, *Seeds of Liberty: The Genesis of the American Mind* (New York, 1948); and Richard L. Merritt, *Symbols of American Community, 1735–1775* (New Haven, Conn., 1966).

[66] See the perceptive reflection by [Sir Egerton Leigh,] *Considerations on Certain Political Transactions in the Province of South Carolina* (London, 1774), 27, upon "what slow advances *Infant Societies* of Men make towards Regularity or Perfection; that in the first outset they are occupied in providing for their necessary wants, and securing their protection; the niceties and punctilios of Public Business never enter their heads, till they have brought their Colony to such an outward state that they feel some *Self-conceit* has crept into their hearts; then it is that Men begin to give polish to their Acts, and to be emulous of Fame."

tional cooperation among all branches of government.[67] Governors and administrative supporters in all the colonies cultivated this ideal in every sort of political situation. But the ideal could only become the dominant political tradition—among legislators as well as among the administration—in colonies where there was no threat from the prerogative either through direct challenges made by governors who were intent upon exercising the full range of their assigned powers or through the corruption or manipulation of the legislature through the use of patronage.

Among the mainland colonies, at least, such a situation existed only in Virginia. There, Lieutenant Governor William Gooch had practically no patronage at his disposal to raise fears of undue executive influence and had sufficiently strong connections at home to keep the Board of Trade from insisting that he take steps to obtain legislative recognition of his assigned prerogative powers. By cooperating closely with Sir John Randolph and John Robinson, two speakers of the House of Burgesses who were obviously inspired by and frequently compared to the great Onslow, Gooch managed both to extirpate faction in the colony and to gain such widespread acceptance of the theory of institutional cooperation as to avoid almost all conflict with the legislature and seriously to undermine the older conception that politics was a struggle between prerogative and liberty.[68]

The second tradition was, of course, that of the Walpolean opposition, which has been so fully and penetratingly analyzed by Bailyn, J. G. A. Pocock, Caroline Robbins, Isaac Kramnick, and others that it requires little elaboration here.[69] What I would like to call attention to, however, is the emphasis in this tradition upon the necessity of maintaining a clear separation of powers and upon the dangers of executive influence in the House of Commons. To some degree, of course, the theory of balanced government was integral to every English political tradition from the middle of the seventeenth to the early part of the nineteenth century, and colonials had conventionally employed it in political arguments. Even such a militant antiprerogative politician as Elisha Cooke, Jr., subscribed to it. In 1720 he wrote that "the Kings Prerogative when rightly used, is for the good & benefit of the People, and the Liberties and Properties of the People are for the Support of the Crown, and the Kings Prerogative when not abused."[70]

[67] This tradition has never been fully analyzed, but Kramnick, *Bolingbroke and His Circle*, 111–36, is a good brief introduction.

[68] The content of this tradition and conditions under which it took root in Virginia are described at length in the early chapters of a book I am currently preparing, in collaboration with Keith B. Berwick, on Virginia political culture in the eighteenth century. For contemporary statements, see the speeches of Randolph, Aug. 24, 1734, Aug. 6, 1736, in *Journals of the House of Burgesses of Virginia, 1727–1740*, ed. John Pendleton Kennedy and Henry R. McIlwain (Richmond, 1910), 175–77, 241–43.

[69] Bailyn, *Ideological Origins*, 22–93; J. G. A. Pocock, "Machiavelli, Harrington, and English Political Ideologies in the Eighteenth Century," *William and Mary Quarterly*, 3d Ser., XXII (Oct. 1965), 547–83; Robbins, *Eighteenth-Century Commonwealthman*, esp. 271–319; Kramnick, *Bolingbroke and His Circle*, esp. 84–110, 137–87, 205–60.

[70] Cooke, *Just and Seasonable Vindication*, 18.

Significantly, however, most colonial legislators, like Cooke, seem to have employed the idea of balance primarily as a defense of liberty and property against prerogative.[71] Confronted as they were with executive claims for such extensive prerogative powers, they manifested little interest in imposing any restraints upon their own legislative powers. Indeed, as Corinne Comstock Weston has implied in her revealing study, *English Constitutional Theory and the House of Lords, 1556–1832*, that theory seems to have been attractive primarily to groups whose powers or prerogatives were under attack and who were operating from a position of practical political weakness. Just as Charles I, seeking to stem the assault of the first Long Parliament, was chiefly responsible for popularizing and thrusting into the center of political consciousness the doctrine of balanced
130 government in England during the seventeenth century,[72] so in the colonies during the eighteenth century the governors and various administrative adherents in places where the executive was unusually weak—men such as Cadwallader Colden and Archibald Kennedy in New York and James Logan and the Reverend William Smith in Pennsylvania—were its earliest and most vociferous exponents and were most deeply committed to it.[73]

Among the colonial political community at large, however, it appears to have received primary emphasis only where the threat of administrative corruption of the legislature was sufficiently great to make the desirability of a strict separation of powers especially obvious. Such a situation seems to have existed in Maryland, where the proprietor always had extensive patronage at his command;[74] in New Hampshire, where after 1750 Governor Benning Wentworth established a powerful patronage machine;[75] in New York, where in the 1740's and 1750's James De Lancey, first as chief justice and then as lieutenant governor, managed to achieve such an invulnerable position in the government that he was able to establish a system very much resembling a "Robinarchical" corruption;[76] and, pre-eminently, in Massachusetts, where William Shirley, governor from 1741 to 1756, put together a peculiar combination of superb talents for political management, strong connections in Britain, and local patronage sufficient to enable him to secure an effective "influence" over the Massachusetts legislature.[77]

[71] It is probably also true that the balance that interested colonial legislators most was not the classic English mixture of monarchy, aristocracy, and democracy, which, because of the absence of any social base for an aristocratic branch of government in the colonies, was of doubtful applicability, but, as one anonymous South Carolinian phrased it, the "proper [for the colonies] balance of power between the crown and people." (*South Carolina Gazette* [Suppl.,] May 13, 1756.) Among many other expressions of a similar idea from widely varying sources, see Thomas Foxcraft, *God the Judge, putting down One, and setting up Another* (Boston, 1727), iii; *The Crisis* ([Boston,] 1754); and Lewis Evans, "A Brief Account of Pennsylvania," 1753, in Gipson, *Lewis Evans*, 131–34.

[72] Corinne Comstock Weston, *English Constitutional Theory and the House of Lords, 1556–1832* (New York, 1965), esp. 5–6, 26–28, 32–33.

[73] See Savelle, *Seeds of Liberty*, 298–304.

[74] See Donnell M. Owings, *His Lordship's Patronage: Offices of Profit in Colonial Maryland* (Baltimore, 1953).

[75] Jere R. Daniell, "Politics in New Hampshire under Governor Benning Wentworth, 1741–1767," *William and Mary Quarterly*, 3d Ser., XXIII (Jan. 1966), 76–105.

[76] Bailyn, *Origins of American Politics*, 107–14.

[77] John M. Murrin, "From Corporate Empire to Revolutionary Republic: The Transformation of

In such a situation the real danger of "Subversion and Change of the Constitution" derived not from "the Wantonness and Violence of Prerogative," but from "the Power of the People trusted with their Representatives," and the charges of conspiracy, corruption, and influence associated with the Walpolean opposition and the whole system of thought connected with them took on a heightened relevance. Shirley's Massachusetts provided real substance to the charge that there was a *"deep Plot"* among "all the Men *in the P—v—ce of the Massachusetts* that have grown very remarkably Rich and Great, High, and Proud, since the Year 1742," who "by Cunning, and by Power; through Lust of Power, Lust of Fame, Lust of Money," and "love of *Prerogative*"; "through Envy, Pride, Covetousness, and *violent* Ambition" were intent upon "killing . . . our CONSTITUTION," destroying the very "Freedom, the Liberty and Happiness of the People of *New-England*." In such a situation, in which a grasping administration was intent upon corrupting the whole legislature, the legislature could no longer be trusted to safeguard the constitution. That responsibility then fell directly upon the people, who were urged to bind their representatives by positive and inflexible instructions to prevent them from selling their constituents' liberty for pelf or position.[78]

The extraordinary flowering in Shirley's Massachusetts of political literature cast in the intellectual mold of the Walpolean opposition suggests the possibility that prior to 1763 the ideas of that opposition were fully relevant to and predominant in only those colonial political situations that bore some reasonable resemblance to that of Walpole's England. These were situations in which the administration actually had at its command many of the devices of the informal constitution which Walpole had used to give his administration its effective influence over Parliament and to achieve that "high degree of public harmony" and "peaceful integration of political forces" that, much to the chagrin and worry of the opposition, accounted for the stability and marked the success of his ministry. If this suggestion turns out to be true, if the acceptance and widespread utilization of the political conceptions of the Walpolean opposition prior to 1763 were concentrated in, or even limited to, those places where the governors had enough practical political power to enable them to dominate the lower houses and where an informal constitution similar to the one that existed in England was most fully developed, then Bailyn's arguments that the Walpolean opposition tradition became dominant everywhere in the colonies during the decades before the Revolution and that the "swollen claims and shrunken powers" of the executive were among the most important sources of that development may have to be substantially qualified.[79]

---

the Structure and Concept of Federalism," unpublished paper read at the Annual Meeting of the American Historical Association, New York City, Dec. 30, 1966.

[78] A New-England-Man, *Letter to the Freeholders*, 6; Vincent Centinel, *Massachusetts in Agony: or, Important Hints to the Inhabitants of the Province* (Boston, 1750), 4, 8, 9, 12; *A Letter to the Freeholders and Other Inhabitants of this Province* ([Boston,] 1742), 8.

[79] Bailyn, *Origins of American Politics*, 63, 96.

I would suggest, in fact, that before the 1760's in most colonies both the mainstream and opposition Walpolean traditions supplemented rather than supplanted the older tradition of the seventeenth-century opposition to the Stuarts. The older tradition had been so institutionalized in colonial politics and so internalized among colonial politicians that it could never really be displaced until the conditions that had given rise to and nourished it had disappeared, until "the principles of the British constitution" had been fully extended to the colonies and, as James Otis remarked as late as 1762, "all plantation Governors" had resolved to "practice upon those principles, instead (as most of them do) of spending their whole time in extending the prerogative beyond all bounds."[80] In Virginia, even while Randolph was praising Lieutenant Governor Gooch for his mild administration and dilating upon the necessity and virtues of cooperation between legislature and executive, he worried about "those Governors" elsewhere "who make Tyranny their Glory." How close the fears of unlimited prerogative remained to the surface of Virginia politics was dramatically revealed during the early 1750's in the pistole fee controversy when Gooch's successor, Robert Dinwiddie, tried to levy a fee without the consent of the House of Burgesses.[81] Similarly, in Shirley's Massachusetts the Walpolean opposition fear of the administration's influence, of "an ambitious or designing Governour" who might "be able to *corrupt* or *awe* your Representatives," was often—and probably usually—combined with the older concerns about the "large Strides Prerogative" was "daily making towards absolute and despotick Power,"[82] much in the same way that earlier in the century the apprehensions of prerogative had frequently been accompanied by complaints that avaricious courtiers were assisting prerogative in its unending efforts to "compleat" its "Conquest . . . over Liberty."[83]

What finally led to the submersion of the older opposition tradition and what rendered the Walpolean mainstream tradition totally irrelevant was the series of restrictive measures taken by Crown and Parliament against the colonies after 1763. Even farther removed from the center of politics than the English opposition, the colonists, as Bailyn has so brilliantly and convincingly argued, could only interpret British behavior in opposition terms. Even then, however, it was not the corruption of local legislatures by local executives about which they were primarily worried, nor was it the relevance of the message of the Walpolean opposition to local politics that made it so attractive to them. Rather, it was the

[80] James Otis, *A Vindication of the Conduct of the House of Representatives of the Province of the Massachusetts-Bay* (Boston, 1762), 51.

[81] Speech of Randolph, Aug. 6, 1736, *Journals of the House of Burgesses of Virginia, 1727–1740*, ed. Kennedy and McIlwain, 242. On the pistole fee controversy, see Jack P. Greene, "The Case of the Pistole Fee," *Virginia Magazine of History and Biography*, LXVI (Oct. 1958), 399–422.

[82] See, e.g., A New-England-Man, *Letter to the Freeholders;* L. Quincius Cincinnatus, *A Letter to the Freeholders and other Inhabitants of the Massachusetts Bay* (Boston, 1748); *A Letter to the Freeholders*, 9; and *The Crisis*. The quotations are from Americanus, *A Letter to the Freeholders* (1739), 5, 11. This pamphlet is an excellent example of the uneasy and even awkward superimposition of the new opposition fears of influence upon the older opposition apprehensions about prerogative.

[83] Among many examples, see *Samuel Mulfords Speech to the Assembly at New-York* ([New York,] 1714), esp. 6–7. The quotation is from *A Letter to the Freeholders* (1742), 4.

corruption of Parliament by the ministry and the extraordinary extent to which that corruption seemed to explain what was being done to the colonies by the imperial government. Even after 1763, however, the submersion of the older tradition by the newer was not total. Because so many of the objectionable measures of the British government between 1763 and 1776 stemmed directly from the Crown and were immediate challenges to the customary powers of the colonial lower houses, the old fears of unlimited prerogative persisted. The Declaration of Independence can and must be read as an indictment of not merely a corrupt Parliament under the influence of a wicked king but also of the unjust and arbitrary misuse of the royal prerogative to undermine the liberties of the people and their lower houses.[84]

The degree to which this seventeenth-century conception of politics as a continual struggle between prerogative and liberty was fundamental to the political system of the old British Empire is perhaps best indicated by the fact that the conception continued to exercise a powerful sway over men's minds and to have an important influence in political life in all of those colonies that did not revolt as long as the old pattern of political and constitutional relationships persisted. Over sixty years after the American Revolution it was still true, as Lord Durham reported in 1839, that "it may fairly be said . . . that the natural state of government in all these colonies is that of collision between the executive and representative body."[85] That such collisions were the "natural state of government" in the older colonies in the eighteenth century as well was the reason why the tradition of the seventeenth-century opposition to the Stuarts continued down to the early 1760's to be such a primary element in colonial political culture and profound shaping influence upon the behavior of colonial legislators.

[84] See Greene, *Quest for Power*, ix–x, 438–53; and, for a similar argument, Edward Dumbauld, *The Declaration of Independence and What It Means Today* (Norman, Okla., 1950).

[85] As quoted by Sir Alan Burns, "The History of Commonwealth Parliaments," in *Parliament as an Export*, ed. Sir Alan Burns (London, 1966), 20.

ECONOMIC FUNCTION AND THE GROWTH OF AMERICAN PORT TOWNS IN THE EIGHTEENTH CENTURY

134 I. Introduction*

URBAN history is very much alive today as a field of serious research and intellectual interest in Britain and America. For students of the seventeenth and eighteenth centuries, however, the results do not seem as impressive as those for some earlier and later centuries. No city of the seventeenth and eighteenth centuries has received the continuing historiographic attention bestowed upon Renaissance Florence by historians since the days of Davidsohn.[1] Scholars approaching the great towns of these centuries have most often lacked a synthetic vision or an integrative model of process and have tended to work in conceptual isolation upon one or another aspect of town life: architecture and town planning; urban political institutions and political life; demography; social structure; economic activity. It is of course all too easy to criticize: frequently the lack of previous work on the

*This paper was originally presented to the First Soviet-American Historical Colloquium held in Moscow in October 1972. With this audience in mind, the author confined his footnote references to the more important and readily available printed materials. He deliberately excluded references to manuscript sources (except for statistics), particularly eighteenth-century mercantile records which he has been studying for more than twenty years and which constitute a general background to many of his observations on mercantile practice. He is particularly indebted to his colleague Professor John Shy for many helpful suggestions. For a comparable treatment of this subject in a later period, cf. David T. Gilchrist, ed., *The Growth of the Seaport Cities, 1790–1825* (Charlottesville, Va., 1967).

1. E.g., Robert Davidsohn, *Geschichte von Florenz*, 4 vols. (Berlin, 1896–1927); Gene A. Brucker, *Florentine Politics and Society, 1343–1378* (Princeton, 1962); Marvin B. Becker, *Florence in Transition*, 2 vols. (Baltimore, 1967–1968).

town or of useful models in works on comparable towns makes such isolated topical studies a most feasible way to start. One must begin somewhere.

There are of course other traditions. Sixty years ago, Werner Sombart in *Luxus und Kapitalismus*[2] suggested summarily and somewhat impressionistically a unified way of looking at the phenomenon of the great capital cities of the sixteenth to the eighteenth centuries. The combination of essentially agricultural economies, late feudal patterns of land ownership, and centralizing 135
bureaucratic states produced the disproportionately large capital cities (Paris, Madrid, Naples) of the seventeenth and eighteenth centuries which are essentially centers of consumption not just for bureaucrats and courtiers, but for a much broader class of *rentiers* (noble, clerical, and bourgeois) with their attendant populations of purveyors, agents, and servants.

The approach of Sombart (even as developed by Weber) has not exactly founded a school. It finds echoes in Latin American studies in the broad integrative approach of Richard Morse[3] to the study of cities in colonial Latin America. James Scobie has shown that, even in the present century, comparable socio-economic circumstances can produce in Buenos Aires a city as "dominating" in the twentieth century as Naples was in the eighteenth.[4] In west European studies, examples of this approach are rarer. Perhaps the modern scholarly work which most fully explores the lines suggested by Sombart is Bartolomé Bennassar's valuable study of Valladolid, capital of Castile in the sixteenth century, a city with an "économie de consommation bien plus que de production."[5] (In-

2. Werner Sombart, *Luxus und Kapitalismus* (Leipzig, 1913); translated as *Luxury and Capitalism* (Ann Arbor, 1967), esp. pp. 21–38. The concept of the "consumer city" was subsequently (1921) given much wider currency by Max Weber in the papers published in the United States as *The City*, ed. and transl. by Don Martindale and Gertrud Neuwirth (Glencoe, Ill., 1958), esp. pp. 68–70. Weber, however, draws his examples from ancient and medieval cities, while Sombart refers specifically to the phenomenon of the seventeenth and eighteenth centuries.

3. Richard M. Morse, "Latin American Cities: Aspects of Function and Structure," *Comparative Studies in Society and History*, 4 (1962), 473–493.

4. James R. Scobie, *Argentina: A City and a Nation*, 2nd ed. (New York, 1971).

5. Bartolomé Bennassar, *Valladolid au siècle d'or* (Paris, 1967).

terestingly, there is no evidence that Bennassar ever read Sombart, but valuable ideas have lives of their own.)

In English-speaking countries, London, Dublin, and Edinburgh could all be approached in the Sombartian mode, but thus far have not been. There is a vast literature on each, including good studies of architecture and urban design, but, at the synthetic level, even the best modern work seems merely impressionistic. The literature on the smaller towns of England is rich but uneven. The older antiquarian literature fills libraries, but there is little to compare to
136 the modern, French studies (ranging from Roupnel's older study of Dijon[6] to the more recent well-known studies of Beauvais,[7] Lyons, and Amiens[8]) in which the economic and social lives of the community are integrated with imagination, erudition, and quantitative precision. Perhaps the best-studied English town in this sense is Exeter, which has attracted modern work of considerable sophistication.[9] Like Beauvais and Amiens, Exeter has the advantage of being small enough to be handled by a single scholar. For the greater towns of France, cooperative studies now seem to be flourishing. For Marseilles, we have a narrowly commercial series;[10] for Bordeaux a less detailed but more broadly conceived series that attempts to cover (if not necessarily to integrate) economic, social, political, and demographic history.[11] For Paris, as for London, there are still only the antiquarian literature and the modern impressionistic studies. For both, the monographic work (surely a collective project) has yet to be done.

6. Gaston Roupnel, *La ville et la campagne au XVIIe siècle: Étude sur les populations du pays dijonnais*, new ed. (Paris 1955).

7. Pierre Goubert, *Beauvais et le Beauvaisis de 1600 à 1730*, 2 vols. (Paris, 1960).

8. Pierre Deyon, *Amiens capitale provinciale, étude sur la société urbaine au 17e siècle* (Paris, 1967); Maurice Garden, *Lyon et les Lyonnais au XVIIIe siècle* (Paris, 1970).

9. W. G. Hoskins, *Industry, Trade and People in Exeter, 1688–1800* (Manchester, 1935); Wallace T. MacCaffrey, *Exeter, 1540–1640* (Cambridge, 1958); W. B. Stephens, *Seventeenth-century Exeter* (Exeter, 1958); Robert Newton, *Victorian Exeter, 1837–1914* (Leicester, 1968).

10. *Histoire du commerce de Marseille*, ed. Gaston Rambert, 6+ vols. (Marseilles, 1949–). For a good example of current quantitative approaches to the study of port towns, cf. Pierre Dardel, *Navires et marchandises dans les ports de Rouen et du Havre* (Paris, 1963).

11. Charles Higounet, ed., *Histoire de Bordeaux*, planned in 7 vols. (Bordeaux, 1962–). See in particular vol. IV: Robert Boutruche, ed., *Bordeaux de 1453 à 1715* (1966); and vol. V: François-Georges Pariset, ed., *Bordeaux au XVIIIe siècle* (1968).

In this paper, I shall discuss the principal towns of the thirteen British colonies in North America in the eighteenth century, the colonies that were to become the United States. I have defined the subject as those towns having populations of 8,000 or more in the first federal census of 1790: Philadelphia and suburbs, 42,520; New York, 32,328; Boston, 18,038; Charleston, 16,359; Baltimore, 13,503. I shall also have something to say about Newport, Rhode Island, which had a population of over 9,000 on the eve of the Revolution, though this had fallen to 6,716 by 1790, as well as about Norfolk, Virginia, and some of the New England coastal towns from Salem to New Haven—all in the 3,000–8,000 range.[12] All of these were ports, as were all towns in the United States in 1790 with a population of more than 4,000. The port character of the principal towns of eighteenth-century America defines the two key problems with which we shall be concerned: (1) the characteristic occupational structure of the leading port towns; and (2) commercial factors influencing the growth or stagnation of these and lesser port towns.

The principal port towns of the thirteen colonies have not suffered from a neglected past. All the older towns of the United States have received a respectable body of attention from serious antiquarians and their vulgarizers. In addition, most (though not Boston) have received the attention of historians of commerce or the mercantile community. Unfortunately, most of these commercial histories seem to have been written under the spell of A. M. Schlesinger's famous work[13] on the role of the colonial merchants in the coming of the American Revolution, for they concentrate almost uniformly on the years immediately preceding the Revolution. Thus they do not convey a sense of process, of change over

12. United States Bureau of the Census, *A Century of Population Growth from the First Census of the United States to the Twelfth*, ed. W. S. Rossiter (Washington, D.C., 1909), pp. 11, 78. For a general discussion of population and other surviving eighteenth-century data, see Stella H. Sutherland, "Colonial Statistics," *Explorations in Entrepreneurial History*, 2d ser., 5 (1967), 59–107.

13. Arthur Meier Schlesinger, *The Colonial Merchants and the American Revolution 1763–1776* (New York, 1918). Cf. also Charles M. Andrews, "The Boston Merchants and the Non-importation Movement," *Publications of the Colonial Society of Massachusetts*, XIX (*Transactions, 1916–1917*), 159–259.

time, in which the economy and life of the towns reflect changing conditions in the greater world about them. Most of these are also insufficiently quantitative in their approach: statistics are given in appendices; they are rarely integrated into the analysis. Nevertheless, such studies are useful in themselves and valuable beginnings.[14]

On quite a different level are the monumental works of Carl Bridenbaugh on the five principal colonial towns (Boston, Newport, New York, Philadelphia, and Charleston) from their beginnings until 1776.[15] Historiographically, Bridenbaugh is most im-
138 portant. He devoted twenty-five years to the study of the beginnings of town life in the United States long before urban studies were fashionable; he also pioneered "comparative studies" before that term had been invented. He brought to his work imagination and catholic interests that could find place for everything from drains to jails to theaters and a considerable erudition that absorbed all the printed sources plus the records of the towns investigated. It is unlikely that anyone else will soon attempt to do over what he has so thoroughly done. For our purposes, however, Bridenbaugh has not quite finished the job. First of all, he would himself, I think, be the first to admit that he is not particularly sympathetic toward the quantitative approach to history. If we compare Bridenbaugh's books with (for example) the Pariset volume on Bordeaux in the eighteenth century,[16] we can see what this means. The Pariset volume has the same broad focus as Bridenbaugh, with chapters on demography, intellectual, artistic, and religious life, as well as the expected politics and economics. However, when we look in particular at the elegant chapters on the port's trade by François Crouzet and on its demography by J. P. Poussou, we find not only sta-

14. Cf. Virginia D. Harrington, *The New York Merchant on the Eve of the Revolution* (New York, 1935), the best of the group with valuable statistics; Arthur L. Jensen, *The Maritime Commerce of Colonial Philadelphia* (Madison, 1963), despite its title heavily political; and Leila Sellers, *Charleston Business on the Eve of the American Revolution* (Chapel Hill, 1934).

15. Carl Bridenbaugh, *Cities in the Wilderness: The First Century of Urban Life in America 1625–1742* (New York, 1938), and *Cities in Revolt: Urban Life in America 1743–1776* (1955; 2d ed., New York, 1971). The second but not the first edition of the latter has a valuable bibliography.

16. See note 11.

tistical tables and charts but a solid quantitative substructure to the argument that is for the most part missing in Bridenbaugh. It seems likely that when young scholars in the future attempt to carry further the work of Bridenbaugh, they will, by attempting more precise quantification, find not only new materials but also new questions. Second, Bridenbaugh is essentially a social and institutional historian. He is interested in the public and private institutions of the city and how they worked, as well as in the colors, tones, sounds, and smells of the town, its layout, its buildings, the 139
pulse of its daily life, its values, and its woes. For a social historian like Bridenbaugh, the economic foundations of a community tend to be a "given," something that is there like Mount Everest, to be described as one describes the topography and climate of the town. That approach, though justified when one is simply giving "background," leaves much unexplained. In more analytical or scientific studies, a more questioning approach may be needed. Just as the geologist sees in the earth process rather than fact, so the historians of towns must see in the economic base problems not preconditions.

II. Function and Structure

THE basic problem facing the student of eighteenth-century American towns is why did the life of certain of the colonies produce relatively large towns and the life in others not. Why the relatively precocious town life of Boston, New York, and Philadelphia and the marked absence of significant towns before 1750 in the otherwise highly developed provinces of Maryland and Virginia—not to mention New Jersey and North Carolina? Why was Connecticut's pattern of several medium-sized towns so different from that of neighboring New York and Massachusetts? Why too was Boston's rapid growth stunted in the decades after 1740? Why did the Chesapeake, so bereft of towns in 1750, suddenly in the next generation produce two substantial towns (Baltimore and Norfolk) without any significant official assistance? To try to answer these questions, we must adopt a functional approach toward the life of the towns. What functions did the towns perform in their regional economies? Correlatively, what distinctive functions did the separate sections of the town's populations perform?

To many, these may not seem like real questions at all. There is a well-established tradition in international scholarship (in America associated with the name of C. H. Cooley[17]) that would explain the location and size of towns entirely in terms of the geography of production and markets and the technology of transportation. As goods move from the loci of production to markets and con-
140 sumers, geography and transport technology require that they be transshipped at certain points. Around these points, towns developed; as the physical volume of production and exchange increased, so did the size of the towns affected. All this is correct, of course, to the point of being a truism. Yet to say this is not to explain everything. One must distinguish between necessary and sufficient causes. Access to feasible trade routes with appropriate volumes of activity is a necessary condition for the development of towns of various sizes. However, the mere existence of production and exchange and suitable geographic location are not conditions sufficient to guarantee that a town of any foreseeable size will develop in any given place. If New York and Philadelphia fit everyone's preconceptions, one must also consider the unexploited possibilities at the mouths of the Connecticut and Cape Fear (North Carolina) rivers and again the urban backwardness of the populous Chesapeake. Then too, certain towns historically have developed volumes of activity which transcend geography. The greatest mart towns (e.g., Amsterdam and London) seem to attract volumes of activity which exceed mere geographic convenience. On a much smaller scale, the activity of Boston, Newport, and even New York in the eighteenth century also seems to have exceeded what might have been geographically predictable. In short, while giving due weight to geography and to the physical volume of trade, we must also consider the *quality* of economic activity in explaining

17. Charles H. Cooley, *The Theory of Transportation* (Publications of the American Economic Association, IV, no. 3 [Baltimore, 1894]), pp. 90–100. Cooley drew heavily on Roscher.

urban growth: the nature of the commodities produced and exchanged, the marketing problems they create, the institutional and legal framework within which economic activity takes place.

Functionally, we may divide the roles of preindustrial towns (i.e., towns of the seventeenth and eighteenth centuries) as follows: (1) civil and ecclesiastical administration with their attendant "court life" and demimondes; (2) maritime transport and external commercial exchange; (3) industrial production; and (4) internal services. The first three can usually be described as independent variables, while the fourth is essentially a dependent variable. That is, 141
the number of persons employed in a town in service functions (broadly conceived to include not just innkeepers, servants, tailors, dressmakers, barbers, and the like, but also petty retail shopkeepers, building trade workers, most teachers, ministers of religion, and other professionals) will vary roughly with the number of persons attracted to the town as residents or visitors by the other three functions.

It is not easy to find acceptable data that might enable one to construct functional profiles of colonial towns, measuring exactly the number of persons employed in each of the four sections just described. However, reasonable approximations can be made. Allan Kulikoff[18] has reported the number of adult males in each occupation recorded in the Boston tax records for 1790. I have reanalyzed his figures, classifying them according to the four "sectors" enumerated in the previous paragraph (Appendix C). For Philadelphia and its suburbs of Southwark and Northern Liberties, there are published and unpublished tax lists giving occupations. Sam B. Warner has supplied me with data for Philadelphia in 1774 (from tax and other official records) giving 3,793 occupations out of about 6,000 heads of household and single men listed.[19] I had

18. Allan Kulikoff, "The Progress of Inequality in Revolutionary Boston," *William and Mary Quarterly*, 3d ser., 28 (1971), 375–412, esp. 411–412. This is a valuable article, though marred by some errors in arithmetic and eighteenth-century commercial terminology.

19. For an explanation of the sources of these data (now stored in a machine archive at the Inter-University Consortium for Political Research, Ann Arbor), see Sam Bass Warner, Jr., *The Private City: Philadelphia in Three Periods of Its Growth* (Philadelphia, 1968), pp. 226–227.

earlier made a similar but less thorough calculation from the published tax lists of 1780 and 1783 giving the occupations of 3,265 adult males (also Appendix C). I have arranged these data in the same manner as I have Kulikoff's Boston data. (In both, "laborers" have been listed separately at the end as unclassified because they could not be assigned to a sector.) The results appear strikingly consistent, though there are far more unidentified people in the Philadelphia data.

I have not thus far been able to find equivalent data for other
142 towns, but have located four possible substitutes for New York: (a) the printed admissions of freemen, which I have analyzed for the twenty-five years, 1746–1770; (b) the published New York wills of the eighteenth century;[20] (c) the New York City directories available from 1786 (I have chosen that of 1790 for analysis); and (d) the published record of all persons dying in New York City during the yellow fever epidemic of 1795, containing specific occupations for 258 men. Of the four, only the wills must be totally rejected, for an experimental analysis of those for the years 1771–1776 shows them to misrepresent grossly (as one might expect) the relative weight of the wealthier inhabitants of the city, particularly merchants. The other three (summarized in Appendix D) show less obvious bias and prove relatively consistent. The admissions of freemen have hitherto been deliberately neglected by historians because there was little effective compulsion to oblige residents to take up the freedom of the city. Even so, the political life of the community seems to have been lively enough to have drawn respectable numbers in that direction, from merchants and gentlemen to common laborers. The only possible distortions apparent are the paucity of clerks and the relatively large proportion of artisans in the industrial sector, considerably higher than that shown by our later (1790–1795) data for the city. It is possible, however, that New York City had a higher proportion of artisans in 1746–1770 than in 1790–1795; i.e., as the city's commerce and population

20. *Abstract of Wills on File in the Surrogate's Office, City of New York [1665–1801]*, (*Collections of the New York Historical Society for the Year[s] [1892–1908]*, XXV–XLI [New York, 1893–1909]).

grew, its industrial sector failed to grow with it and declined in
relative importance. The 1790 directory (the fourth published) is
remarkably full and detailed, even by London standards, but it
suffers from one obvious blemish: no clerks are designated as such,
though many clerks are undoubtedly concealed among the unidentified males. By contrast, the yellow fever list of 1795, though containing far fewer names than either the freemen's registers or the
city directory, probably contains a more reasonable sample of New
York's adult male population (women and children were more
likely to have been out of town), and thus provides the best avail- 143
able picture of vocational distribution. Because of its less distorted
measurement of nonhouseholders, including clerks, this 1795 death
list is not only better than the other earlier and longer New York
lists but also probably represents nonhouseholding elements in the
population more clearly than do the Philadelphia data. Nevertheless, the sample is not perfect and has to be used with caution.

There is a further problem common to the data of all the towns. In assigning specific occupations to one or another of the sectors, certain difficult and somewhat arbitrary decisions have had to be made, for some occupations might rightly have fallen in more than one sector. Care must be taken to distribute such overlapping crafts so as not to favor any one sector. Thus, butchers and bakers (two numerous crafts) have been assigned to the service sector, where they are usually thought to belong, though many in those trades worked not for the local market alone but also for the export market and belong at least partly in the industrial sector. On the other hand, furniture makers and shoemakers (cordwainers), another numerous craft, have been placed in the industrial sector, for they made goods in job lots for external sale, but a good part of them also worked for local orders and could be put in the service sector. It is impossible, given present knowledge, to divide the totals employed in such crafts into fractions working for the local and external markets; however, it is more than likely that any overweighting caused by the assignment of certain crafts *in toto* to the external market (industrial sector) is balanced by the other overweighting caused by the assignment of other crafts *in toto* to the local market (service sector) so that the general proportions suggested by our sectoral totals are only minimally distorted.

With these data in hand, we may proceed to our sectoral analysis, starting with the service sector. Remembering the point made above that the number of service personnel (whether doctors or chimney sweeps) is ultimately dependent upon the other more independent activities in the town, the reader need not be unduly impressed by the proportions we find ascribable to this sector. From Kulikoff's data, it would appear that at least 45 percent of
144 Boston's tax-inscribed adult males in 1790 were employed in the service sector. The equivalent figures are 48.93 to 49.29 percent for Philadelphia and 46.7 to 56.59 percent for New York. In general, it seems safe to say that, in all substantial colonial towns, the service sector broadly conceived accounted for around 50 percent of the employed adult male population. (The proportion would probably be even higher in the enumerated towns if we could get accurate information on slaves and women and on apprentices and other employees who resided on the premises of their employers.) Much rigorous quantification remains to be done, but the burden of proof lies on those who would claim that other towns might have had significantly different patterns. Of course, however finely measured, the impressive size of the service sector tells us nothing about the *raison d'être* of the town or of its ultimate proportions. To understand them, we must try to measure the more independent variables: the public, industrial, and commercial sectors.

In studying the American towns of the eighteenth century, we need not concern ourselves unduly with the first function or sector: governmental and ecclesiastical administration. The clergy were broadly dispersed among the general population. There were no bishops, cathedral chapters, or other types of salaried ecclesiastical administrators in any of the thirteen colonies. Most university colleges were of course church related or church controlled, but only two of them were in large towns (New York and Philadelphia) and could not have added as much as 1 percent to the population of those places. (In smaller towns, such as Cambridge or Princeton, the presence of a college had greater economic and demographic

impact.) Nor was there much public employment created by royal, provincial, or local government. Boston, with a population of 18,000 in 1790, was the capital city of a state with a population of 378,500, yet it had only sixty-eight adult males on its tax rolls in 1790 who could be classified as "government officials," and not all of them occupied full-time remunerated positions. Our Philadelphia data are much less satisfactory than our Boston data; even so, the 2.85 percent shown in the public sector in the congressional capital of 1780–1783 is quite consistent with the 2.75 percent
shown at Boston in 1790 (Appendix C), or with the 3.49 to 3.7 *145*
percent for New York, the capital in the 1790's. Even if we were to add to the public sector schoolmasters, lawyers, and notaries, we should still have a public sector of only 4.25 percent at Boston and 3.22 (1774) or 3.73 (1780–1783) at Philadelphia.[21] Military employment can also be ignored as a contributor to town growth in the eighteenth century. Except under the extraordinary conditions preceding the American Revolution, garrisons were not normally stationed in or near large towns.[22]

The industrial sector was quantitatively a much more important element in the structure and growth of the larger eighteenth-century towns, even though we are dealing with a primarily agricultural society. Historians have long been aware of this element, if only because persons styled "artisans" or "mechanics" were sometimes mentioned as active in mobs or revolutionary societies on the eve of the Revolution.[23] However, the precise composition of this artisan or "mechanic" element has received very little sys-

21. Appendices A–C.

22. For garrison policy, see John Shy, *Toward Lexington: The Role of the British Army in the Coming of the American Revolution* (Princeton, 1965), particularly chaps. i and ii. Some historians believe that military expenditures may have been important at New York, even without a garrison.

23. There is an enormous literature on the coming of the Revolution. For the most recent treatment (with a conscious social perspective, but little quantification), see Pauline Maier, *From Resistance to Revolution: Colonial Radicals and the Development of American Opposition to Britain, 1765–1776* (New York, 1972), esp. pp. 297–312. Cf. also Edmund S. Morgan and Helen M. Morgan, *The Stamp Act Crisis: Prologue to Revolution* (Chapel Hill, 1953), chap. x; Merrill Jensen, *The Founding of a Nation: A History of the American Revolution, 1763–1776* (New York, 1968); and Richard Walsh, *Charleston's Sons of Liberty: A Study of the Artisans* (Columbia, S.C., 1959).

tematic analysis. The Boston data for 1790 show that persons who can be considered to belong to the "industrial sector" constituted 26.6 percent of the tax-inscribed adult male population in 1790; our rough equivalent data for Philadelphia show 26.81 percent (1774) or 27.31 percent (1780–1783) in the same classification—not a significant difference, though Philadelphia has commonly been thought of as being much more "industrial" than Boston (Appendix C). However, when we look at the 664 individuals at Boston or the 1,017 at Philadelphia who constituted the "industrial" sector,
146 we find them a rather disparate lot. Some of them, particularly the shoemakers, metal craftsmen, and cabinetmakers, must have been working for a predominantly local clientele and could arguably have been enrolled at least in part in the "service" sector. If the largest group in the industrial sector at Philadelphia were the leather workers processing the hides produced on the farms of Pennsylvania and New Jersey, the largest at Boston consisted of those in shipbuilding and shipfitting work. These last could with justice be ascribed in good part to the "commercial-maritime" sector, for much of their work consisted of building and repairing ships for Boston's own commercial fleet and fisheries; only a part of their output was for the market.[24] Were we to transfer from our "industrial sector" some shoemakers and the like to the service sector and some shipwrights, ropemakers, and such to the commercial sector, those left in the more strictly defined "industrial sector" (i.e., those making goods for outside markets) would be a smaller proportion of the whole—perhaps only 10 or 15 percent instead of the 26–27 percent originally shown.

At New York, the "industrial "sector appears to decline from 32 percent in the midcentury freemen's register to only 16.67 percent in the yellow fever sample of 1795, compared to the 26.6 to 27.3 percent for Boston and Philadelphia. This is the largest discrepancy produced by our sectoral comparisons. Other nonquantitative data suggest a large variety of crafts in mid-eighteenth-

24. For the structure of Boston's shipbuilding and shipowning at the beginning of the century, see Bernard Bailyn and Lotte Bailyn, *Massachusetts Shipping 1697–1714: A Statistical Study* (Cambridge, 1959).

century New York, consistent with the freemen's data.[25] At the same time there is reason to believe that the proportions inferred from the yellow fever data may be close to the truth for 1795. New York did not have the distilling or shipfitting activities of Boston or the leather and metal activity of Philadelphia. This is obviously another question on which much work remains to be done.

The data on the industrial sector contained in Appendices C and D permit us to scrutinize more critically some commonly accepted statements about colonial towns. We are sometimes told that Boston had lost much of its industry between 1740 and 1775 and on the 147
eve of the Revolution was much more a "consumer" town (in the Weberian sense) and much less a productive town than New York, Philadelphia, or perhaps even Baltimore. Yet the data in Appendices C and D show the proportions of the male population engaged in the industrial sector just after the Revolution to be approximately equal at Boston and Philadelphia—and both considerably higher than at New York. If Philadelphia had a much higher proportion of its employment in the leather and fur-using trades, Boston still had proportionately more in shipbuilding and shipfitting: even if Philadelphia had more shipwrights[26] than Boston, the latter had a wider representation of ropemakers, sailmakers, and the like.

Finally, there remains that section of the leading towns' populations that was engaged in maritime commerce and fisheries. Our picture of them is relatively consistent: 25.64 percent of the studied population were so employed at Boston, 23.26 percent at New York (1795), and 22.73 percent (1774) or 20.61 percent (1780–1783) at Philadelphia. Although none of these figures can be taken too literally, the general picture is clear. The Philadelphia proportion for 1780–1783 is probably a little too low because of the war and be-

25. Newspaper notices of various arts and crafts have been reprinted in *The Arts and Crafts in New York 1726–1776: Advertisements and News Items from New York City Newspapers* (*Collections of the New York Historical Society*, LXIX, for 1936 [New York, 1938]).

26. For the social and political importance of the Philadelphia shipwrights, see James H. Hutson, "An Investigation of the Inarticulate: Philadelphia's White Oaks," *William and Mary Quarterly*, 3d ser., 27 (1971), 3–25. On Boston as a "consumer city," cf. Kulikoff, "The Progress of Inequality," pp. 376–379.

cause the Philadelphia data (all from tax records) probably failed to identify merchants' clerks to a greater degree than did the data used for Boston or even New York. (The clerks of course were not heads of firms and, usually being young, were infrequently heads of residential households.) However, even if we should triple the number of clerks in Philadelphia in 1780–1783 we should not raise the weight of this sector to much over 22 percent, suggesting that the maritime sector was indeed marginally less important at Philadelphia than at the somewhat smaller New York and Boston. At
148 all three places, local employment data would tend to underrepresent grossly the number of sailors employed on the town's ships. Unless married and maintaining local households, they must have escaped the tax surveys almost completely.

In summary, then, our quite disparate and shaky data on the occupational distribution of the port towns suggest a pattern more remarkable for its consistencies than for its differences.

Table I

Sector	*Boston* (*1790*)	*Philadelphia* (*1774*)	*Philadelphia* (*1780–1783*)	*New York* (*1795*)
Governmental	2.75%	1.53%	2.85%	3.49%
Service	45.01%	48.93%	49.29%	56.59%
Industrial	26.60%	26.81%	27.31%	16.67%
Maritime	25.64%	22.73%	20.54%	23.26%

Transcending, however, this pattern of seeming consistency lies a dynamic of inconsistency. These towns did not grow at a uniform rate. As is well known, early in the nineteenth century New York was to pass Philadelphia and never look back. In the eighteenth century, both started out well behind Boston but caught up during the third quarter of the century. Boston, the first in the colonies almost from its founding (1630) until about 1755, stagnated from about 1740 until after 1790 (Appendix B). Why? As all our towns were port towns, we must turn for an answer to the structure and marketing conditions in the trades which animated their commercial lives.

III. Commercial Factors in the Growth of the Principal Port Towns of British North America, Particularly before 1776

WHEN one talks of traders and trading towns even in an early modern primarily agricultural society, one uses very general terms to embrace a considerable variety of phenomena. Traders range from petty hucksters doing a few shillings' worth of business a day to great merchants trading for tens of thousands of pounds sterling. At the lowest level were petty retailers, peddlers, 149
and hucksters (hawkers) who sold for cash or cash credit only. They were of no great importance outside the few large towns. At the next higher level were what I shall call the *primary traders* or country storekeepers[27] who bought the goods produced by the agricultural sector and supplied farmers and planters with most of the manufactured and foreign goods they required. At a slightly higher level were *secondary traders* or wholesalers who, in addition to performing the same functions for farmers and planters, also acted as wholesale suppliers to the primary traders, taking their agricultural purchases in return. They traded over a larger area than the primary traders and, when not themselves located in major ports, maintained trading connections with one or more ports through which their supplies might be obtained and their purchases marketed. They might even order goods from Britain and pay for them with cash or bills of exchange, but they did not really *trade* overseas, i.e., venture their wealth abroad; all their "effects" were "in the country." These secondary traders might be styled "merchants" in America, but were not strictly so in English usage. At a still higher level, we find the *tertiary traders* or merchants proper, who, in the narrow English usage of that term, had to be "traders by sea." They did venture their effects abroad and thus took much greater risks for themselves and those who advanced them credit. We may also

27. The terms "shop" and "store" are used almost interchangeably in the United States today, if not in Great Britain. In the eighteenth century, however, the term "store" suggested something larger than a shop, a trading station where goods were bought as well as sold.

distinguish between limited and general merchants, merchants who dealt with only one geographic area or commodity group and merchants who dealt with all areas and in all goods significant for the economies of their home regions. In America this distinction separated the smaller merchants who dealt only with the West Indies from their bigger confreres who traded to Europe.

This hierarchy of traders created a hierarchy of trading towns. Primary traders tended to scatter across the countryside where they would be accessible to their agricultural customers. Secondary
150 traders, however, tended to congregate along main trading routes in places convenient for their customers, the primary traders, and with easy access to the major ports. Except for a few spots such as Lancaster, Pennsylvania, the seats of these secondary traders were almost entirely in riverine and coastal ports. While any hamlet or country crossroad or public warehouse in the Chesapeake might do for the site of the "store" of a primary trader, secondary traders tended to be found in towns and townlets of 1,500–4,000 population, which as ports and county seats often attracted more traffic than their modest size would suggest. Merchants properly so called tended to congregate in coastal or river ports which could handle ocean-going vessels, had easy access to the full variety of goods needed for their export trades, and were convenient to markets for their imported goods.[28]

Even so, not all the ports where mercantile activity took place performed the same functions. (1) Some were mere *shipping points*, where goods were loaded and unloaded, while others were *processing centers* where goods received some manufacture in transit. (2) Some merely received ships sent to them, but others were *shipping centers and markets* where ships could be built, outfitted, repaired, and bought, sold, or chartered, and sailors hired. (3) While some were only *limited marts*, where only the most restricted range of goods could be bought and sold, others were more *general marts* where a great variety of goods (by no means all of local produce)

28. For a related but different analytical system by a geographer, see James T. Lemon, "Urbanization and the Development of Eighteenth-Century Southeastern Pennsylvania and Adjacent Delaware," *William and Mary Quarterly*, 3d ser., 24 (1967), 501–542.

could be purchased and almost anything disposed of. (4) Some had
only limited and indirect communication with the outside world,
while others functioned as *communications centers*, with relatively
easy communications to all the areas with which they traded. (It
was no small boon to New York to be made the America terminus
of the official mail packet boats from England.) (5) Finally, some
gave little evidence of capital accumulation or sophisticated credit
and other financial facilities, while others were more fully developed *financial centers* (relatively speaking) where capital could be
raised for a wide variety and substantial scale of shipbuilding and 151
trading ventures, where credit could be obtained for ventures
overseas, where bills of exchange on a wide variety of places could
be bought and sold, and where insurance could be obtained.

The degrees of functional development or underdevelopment in a port are not to be understood merely as *givens*, but were derivatives or reflections of the character of the trade of the port and of the institutional arrangements produced by the marketing requirements of the goods traded.

That Boston was the principal town and port of British North America until ca. 1755 is an historical fact but hardly a self-evident proposition. The capital of the province of Massachusetts Bay had some but not many natural advantages. Geography had endowed it with an excellent, deep, sheltered harbor with moderate tidal range. This excellent haven was not, however, particularly well situated to serve any obvious trade routes, lacking as it did any significant riverine connection with the interior of the continent. The immediate hinterland of Boston, its natural trading domain—the country for about forty miles around—was a land of forest and tidal marshes. There was some natural meadow and open land usable for unimproved pasture; hence grazing was an early profitable activity: horses and cattle, salted beef, pork, butter, and cheese were early exports. However, the soil of the region, as of almost all of eastern New England, was mediocre. This inadequate soil made the Boston region, as indeed all of New England except Connecticut, a net importer of cereals, reportedly even in the seventeenth century, but definitely and consistently in the eighteenth. By 1768–

1772 this dependence of Massachusetts, Rhode Island, and New Hampshire on cereal imports from New York, Pennsylvania, and Maryland had become quite marked.[29] Thus there were no agricultural riches for the infant town of Boston to exploit.

Yet Boston had another hinterland: the long strip of coastal settlements from Cape Cod in the south to the frontier of habitation in Maine on the north. This hinterland had two great natural endowments: fish and timber. The founders of Boston had not thought of themselves as coming three thousand miles across the
152 ocean to found a fishing village; indeed they had the lowest opinion of the manners and morals of the fishermen they found already active on the coast of Massachusetts Bay. Yet necessity forced many in the Bay Colony to become fishermen, and its proudest houses were founded by traffickers in cod. It was not for nothing that a stuffed cod was placed ceremoniously over the speaker's chair in the Massachusetts legislature. Cod from off the colony's own coasts or from the Nova Scotia and Newfoundland banks[30] was the one locally available commodity which could be readily sold almost anywhere—in the colonies to the southward, in the West Indies (where the poorer grades could be sold for the use of the slaves), and in Spain and Portugal. Earnings from sales to the mainland colonies to the southward paid for the cereals and provisions needed in New England; sales to the West Indies paid for imports of sugar, molasses, and other tropical produce; sales to Spain and Portugal and their "Wine Islands" paid for imports of wine and the salt so vital to the fisheries; surplus earnings from the West Indies and Iberia could be remitted to England in commodities or bills of exchange to pay for the European and Asian produce and manu-

29. Public Record Office, London [hereafter PRO] Customs 16/1. This volume contains full data on intercolonial trade, 1768–1772. The data were rather fully analyzed by Max G. Schumacher in an unpublished thesis, "The Northern Farmer and His Markets During the Late Colonial Period" (University of California, Berkeley, 1948), particularly pp. 151–173. His work has been carried further in David Klingaman, "Food Surpluses and Deficits in the American Colonies, 1768–1772," *Journal of Economic History*, 31 (1971), 553–569.

30. In addition to the cod taken by their own fishermen, New England traders acquired much of the cod taken by fishermen resident in Newfoundland; this they usually sent directly to markets in southern Europe.

factures which all the colonies were obliged to buy only from the mother country whether or not they had anything to sell which the mother country wanted to buy.

The opportunities created by the fisheries called into existence at Boston almost from the beginning of settlement a shipbuilding industry, to supply fishing craft, then coastal craft, then sloops and schooners for the West Indies trade (important by the 1640's), and finally the larger brigantines, snows, and ships suitable for the trade to Spain and Portugal. The merchants of Massachusetts soon found
that they could sell these larger vessels advantageously in Spain and 153
Portugal and in Britain as well. While oak was expensive in England and the pine planks and deals for shipbuilding there had to be imported from Norway and the best masts from Riga, the shipbuilders of New England had close at hand inexpensive supplies of adequate oak and splendid pine for both planks and masts. Profits from the sale of ships in the ever fluctuating market in Europe constituted the most attractive "windfall profits" of the fish export trade and must have played an important part in capital accumulation among merchants and shipowners in the seventeenth century.[31]

Although dozens of seaside villages in Massachusetts, Maine, and New Hampshire participated in the fisheries, and Salem and Marblehead exported fish in quantity, only Boston developed the full panoply of trade based on the fishing-shipbuilding complex. There were economies of scale in these trades and the greater amounts of capital required for the longer voyages to Europe were probably not available at first in the lesser ports. But part of the concentration at Boston must be seen as arising from the very complexity of the trade. If the New England colonies' trade had been a simple bilateral trade with the mother country, it is possible that several Massachusetts havens might have participated as soon as volume justified. However, the complexity of the trade required a "comprehensive entrepôt" and not simply a "shipping point" for fish. Sloops going southward in the coastal trade carried not just fish but other New England produce (including some crude manufactures)

31. Cf. note 24 for data on shipbuilding in Massachusetts at the beginning of the century.

plus manufactures from Britain and salt from either Iberia or the West Indies. Sloops in the West Indies trade carried fish, horses, flour, and provisions (including some bought from the more southerly colonies) and manufactures and wine from Europe. To England went not only the furs and forest products (particularly turpentine) of New England[32] but sugar from the West Indies and tobacco from the Chesapeake. With trade of this complexity, there were advantages in concentration in a single mart town, or general entrepôt, where one man's surplus could fill another's vessel, and
154 external economies of linkages be realized.

The earliest surviving shipping (naval officer's) accounts for Boston, showing imports and exports on every vessel, date from the 1680's.[33] By then, even before Philadelphia was founded, Boston was a general entrepôt, a miniature Amsterdam or London, with a trade marked by extreme complexity if not necessarily great volume by the standards either of what was to follow shortly or of contemporary European ports. Boston was at the height of its relative importance in the small world of North American commerce from the 1680's to the 1730's. As other colonies developed their own agriculture and commercial activities, they might compete with Boston in the West Indian trades, yet become markets for Boston's fish, turpentine, rum, and European goods.

After 1740, however, Boston's population ceased to grow (Appendix B): from 1740 to 1775, it remained steady at ca. 15,000–17,000 (and only reached 18,000 in 1790), while its principal rivals, New York and Philadelphia, tripled and quadrupled in size. This stagnation has long intrigued historians and its true character has yet to be established—partly for lack of statistical data on Boston's trade. While Boston stagnated, everything about it seemed to be growing. The population of the future United States quadrupled between 1740 and 1790, while that of Massachusetts (without Maine) more than doubled (Appendix A). All commodity export

32. For the New England naval stores trade, see Joseph J. Malone, *Pine Trees and Politics: The Naval Stores and Forest Policy in Colonial New England 1691–1775* (London, 1964).

33. In PRO; I have used for Boston the extracts assembled by Prof. L. A. Harper at the University of California, Berkeley.

indices show healthy rates of growth in these decades, though we lack a good series for fish and shipbuilding. English exports to the thirteen colonies were 4.6 times as much in 1772–1774 as they had been in 1737–1739, while those to New England alone had increased 3.73-fold (real values).[34] All indications are that the coastal trade of Massachusetts as a whole was growing throughout the century.[35] Yet, Boston's own commerce did not fully participate in this growth. Its tonnage cleared out in 1754–1755 was hardly higher than it had been in 1714–1717, though by 1772 it had increased about 60 percent over its 1754 level. (A more marked in- 155
crease could be shown if we used the inward tonnage.)[36]

Paradoxically, then, while Boston's population stagnated after 1740, its commerce and that of Massachusetts Bay continued to grow, if somewhat irregularly. Whatever retardation Boston's seaborn commerce experienced in the 1740's and early 1750's was amply compensated for thereafter. Analytically, Boston seems to have been affected by a combination of temporary misfortunes and more lasting structural change. The start of the British-Spanish war in 1739 probably affected Massachusetts more than any other continental colony, for Spain was such an important market for New England fish. With the loss of this market, Boston's merchants would have lost part of the wherewithal to purchase European goods; at the same time, owing to the severe winters and bad harvests in western Europe in 1739–1741, the cereal-exporting colonies to the southward were earning unprecedentedly large balances in Europe and the means thereby to make their own purchases directly in Britain without going through Boston. Once the merchants of New York, Philadelphia, and elsewhere had expanded the connections necessary for acquiring goods directly in Britain, it was to prove almost impossible to force them to give up these efficient

34. John J. McCusker, "The Current Value of English Exports, 1697 to 1800," *William and Mary Quarterly*, 3d ser., 28 (1971), 624–625. The better-known official values (from Whitworth) can be found in U. S. Bureau of the Census, *Historical Statistics of the United States* (Washington, D.C., 1960), p. 757.

35. Klingaman, "Food Surpluses and Deficits," pp. 563–565.

36. *U. S. Historical Statistics*, p. 759.

channels of trade. Thus, in the 1740's, English exports to New England declined while those to all the other colonies increased.

Table II

ENGLISH EXPORTS TO NORTH AMERICA, 1737–1749

		To New England	*To All Colonies*
		(in thousands of pounds sterling)	
156	1737–1739	179 p.a.	583 p.a.
	1740–1745	149	690
	1740–1749	165	729

Though Boston's shipping activity resumed its growth in the generation 1755–1775, it was almost inevitable that Boston would lose its place as the leading American port, if only because wheat and flour passed fish as the leading export of the northern and middle colonies both generally and to southern Europe. In this, North American production was reacting to the expansion of population in Europe and the higher prices for cereals that characterized the last third of the eighteenth century. Thus, by 1765–1772, Philadelphia, which had long since passed Boston in population, also passed it marginally in shipping volume. The Philadelphia lead was most pronounecd in the trade to the West Indies and southern Europe, both of which took its flour, but Boston still led in the direct trade with Britain, suggesting that there was still life left in its old trade of reexporting goods from Britain to the other colonies.

Boston's problems were not confined to the rise of independent general entrepôts in New York and Philadelphia which could dispense with its services as intermediary. Within Massachusetts, its position in the simpler trades was also challenged by lesser ports which eventually seemed able to operate on a competitive scale at lower costs. The old bases of the area's ocean-borne commerce, fishing and shipbuilding, had never been Boston's monopoly: From the earliest days of settlement the lesser ports to the north and south of Boston had participated in these activities, though Boston marketed much of their fish and commissioned or bought much of the

output of their shipbuilding yards.[37] Salem and (after 1717) Marblehead had long been major exporters of cod to Iberia but failed to develop much of an import trade from Britain.[38] By the third quarter of the eighteenth century most fishermen had long since deserted expensive Boston. Between 1771 and 1775, 121 vessels (14,020 tons) with 4,059 men were engaged in the Massachusetts whale fishery: of these, only five vessels (700 tons) with 260 men came from Boston.[39] During 1765–1775, 665 vessels (25,630 tons) with 4,405 men were engaged in the Massachusetts cod fishery: of
these *none* were of Boston.[40] Marblehead and Gloucester to the 157
north continued the great centers of the cod fishery, while Salem shared in its export trade. With the growing volume of the fishery, local traders had gradually been accumulating the capital and commercial knowledge which by the 1740's enabled them to act independently of their erstwhile great friends in Boston. By the 1760's these ports shipped all their cod directly to southern Europe and the West Indies (as Salem had been doing for a century) and not through Boston. What little cod the Boston port district did export must have come from the fishing villages to the southward or been purchased in Newfoundland. Boston merchants may have had an interest in these shipments from Gloucester and Marblehead and Salem, as they had in some from Newfoundland to Iberia, but this created little activity or employment at Boston.[41]

Boston's slippage was less marked in shipbuilding than in fishing. The Bailyns have analyzed the Boston shipping register of 1697–

37. Cf. note 24.

38. On Salem and vicinity, see William I. Davisson and Dennis J. Dugan, "Commerce in Seventeenth-Century Essex County, Massachusetts," *Essex Institute Historical Collections*, 107 (1971), 113–142.

39. Timothy Pitkin, *A Statistical View of the Commerce of the United States of America* (Hartford, Conn., 1816), pp. 78–79. By 1787–1789, employment in the Massachusetts whale fishery had declined to 1,611 men, of whom 78 served on Boston vessels. Appendix C shows only 37 fishermen on Boston's tax lists in 1790. They probably worked close by for the local market.

40. *Ibid.*, p. 74.

41. During 1768–1772 the customs district of Salem and Marblehead sent 103,700 quintals of dried fish p.a. to southern Europe, while Boston sent only 10,321; the former sent 87,904 qu. p.a. to the West Indies, while the latter sent only 58,193. The shipments from Boston came not from the town but from the fishing villages to the southward in the same customs district. PRO Customs 16/1.

1714: they show Massachusetts (without Maine) shipbuilding averaging 3,094 tons p.a. in 1697–1704 and 4,246 tons in 1705–1714.[42] By 1769–1771, Massachusetts shipbuilding averaged 7,667 tons p.a., an increase of about 150 percent since the beginning of the century (1697–1704).[43] This is not a very high rate of growth when we consider that Massachusetts' population increased by about 320 percent between 1700 and 1770. Yet in 1769–1771 Massachusetts accounted for about one-third of the tonnage built in the colonies. In all probability her share had been between half and two-thirds
158 at the beginning of the century. A good example of the new competition Massachusetts had to face comes from our New Hampshire data. In 1697–1714 the Boston registry shows shipping built in New Hampshire of only 3,245 tons, or 4.75 percent of the 68,311 tons built in Massachusetts. (There was no separate registry in New Hampshire.)[44] By 1769–1771, shipping was being built in New Hampshire at the rate of 3,675 tons p.a. or about half the Massachusetts figure.[45] Within Massachusetts, shipbuilding had always been dispersed. The Bailyns reported that only 25 percent of the Massachusetts registered fleet of 1698 had been built in Boston. However, in succeeding years, Boston's shipbuilding activity increased so that 40 percent of all vessels registered through 1714 were built in Boston.[46] We lack accessible data at the present time (though the problem is not insoluble), but it seems unlikely that as much as 40 percent of the Bay Colony's shipbuilding remained in the confined and expensive site of Boston throughout the century.[47] The same cost-cutting forces that encouraged shipbuilding in New Hampshire would have encouraged it elsewhere in Massachusetts proper and in Maine (then part of Massachusetts). However, even if Boston's share of Massachusetts shipbuilding slipped somewhat from the 40 percent of 1674–1714, this would not have

42. Bailyn and Bailyn, *Massachusetts Shipping*, pp. 102–105.

43. John, Lord Sheffield, *Observations on the Commerce of the American States*, 6th ed. (London, 1784), p. 96.

44. Bailyn and Bailyn, *Massachusetts Shipping*, pp. 106–109.

45. See note 43.

46. Bailyn and Bailyn, *Massachusetts Shipping*, p. 50.

47. This problem could be solved by sampling the shipping records ("naval officers' reports") in the PRO.

meant any absolute decline, for the total volume of activity was increasing. Throughout the century a significant shipbuilding trade remained in Boston, probably specializing in larger vessels and leaving the fishing and coastal craft to the lesser ports. Some of these larger vessels were produced on order from merchants in Britain and others were sold in Britain or elsewhere in Europe after their first voyage. For example, of a group of 36 vessels of which we have information, carrying tobacco from Virginia to Britain in 1774, 13 were built in Massachusetts: 11 at Boston, 1 at Charlestown across the harbor, and 1 at Newbury on the Merrimack. All 159
were registered, hence owned, at Glasgow.[48] By contrast, there were only one Philadelphia-, one Maryland-, and no New York-built ships in this trade. In short, it would appear that the Boston shipbuilding industry was very much alive and competitive in 1775, though it no longer accounted for as large a share of American shipbuilding as it had in the much smaller world of 1675. This would help to explain why in the previous section we found the shipbuilding group accounting for a somewhat larger share of the employed population in Boston than in Philadelphia or New York.

In shipping activity, Boston also came to share somewhat more with the lesser ports in Massachusetts. Between 1699 and 1714, the Bailyns report that Boston accounted for 83.8 percent of Massachusetts ship registrations by number and 89.7 percent by tonnage.[49] By the end of the century (1798), however, Boston accounted for only 37.5 percent of Massachusetts' registered tonnage.[50] This trend was probably of long standing for in 1768–1772 the port district of Salem and Marblehead already accounted for about 34 percent of the province's shipping activity, and it was to account for 34.6 percent of registration in 1798.[51] Before 1775 these home rivals had invaded all of Boston's trades except that to England.

48. Naval officers' (inspectors of navigation) accounts in PRO: T.1/506 ff. 1–2, 5, 7, 10, 13v; T.1/512 ff. 196, 198, 201v, 204, 207 (excluding Rappahannock as imprecise).

49. Bailyn and Bailyn, *Massachusetts Shipping*, p. 44.

50. Samuel Eliot Morison, *The Maritime History of Massachusetts 1783–1860* (Boston, 1921), p. 378.

51. *Ibid.*; PRO Customs 16/1.

To summarize, on the basis of an initially favorable position in fish and shipbuilding Boston had by the end of the seventeenth century an extensive and elaborate general entrepôt position touching all the colonies. In the eighteenth century, it lost the cod fishery and most of the fish export trade to lesser rivals within Massachusetts, and its relative position in shipbuilding declined, leaving it dependent on its rather artificial entrepôt trades. Except for the difficult years 1740–1755 these trades continued to grow down to the Revolution, though declining in relative importance as other
160 ports, particularly New York and Philadelphia, through increased exports to the West Indies and southern Europe were increasingly able to finance their own imports from Britain without going through the Boston entrepôt. Boston's greatest weakness throughout remained the limitation of its immediate hinterland and the closeness of rival ports, which probably explains why its service sector and (except for shipbuilding and distilling) its manufacturing sectors were relatively less important than those of Philadelphia.

Newport's economy was a reduced and somewhat bizarre version of that of Boston. Located on the original island of Rhode Island, it too was endowed with an excellent harbor but only the most minimal natural hinterland in southern New England. It could, however, draw on the agricultural surpluses of the Connecticut River valley, but had to compete for them with New York and eventually with the petty Connecticut river and shore towns that also ventured into the West India trade. It did, however, have certain political advantages. In the seventeenth century, extreme religious toleration drew to it various Protestant sectarians who did not find easy toleration in the tight Calvinist-Congregationalist world of Massachusetts or Connecticut. Quakers and Jews were quite conspicuous there in the eighteenth century. By then, however, its most important political advantage was its virtually self-governing status. Alone of the colonies, Connecticut and Rhode Island chose their own governors and thus were effectively free of close imperial inspection. In practical terms this meant that it was easier to disregard imperial tax (customs) and trade regulations in Newport than in any other major commercial center. This perhaps

explains why Newport more than any other colonial port seemed drawn to illicit trade—not simply trade to the Dutch and French islands, which was only technically illegal, but the smuggling in of European and Asian goods from the Dutch islands and from Holland itself. The more legitimate trade of Newport consisted of exporting fish, provisions, and local horses to the West Indies, and —rarely—to southern Europe. It was very much a busy entrepôt, for almost everything it exported it had to obtain from other colonies—fish from Newfoundland, flour and provisions from Connecticut and the colonies to the southward. Lacking natural en- 161
dowments in its hinterland or any commercial imperative for its existence, Newport grew by pushing the most marginal trades, including the whale fishery. Its only significant industry was making whale-oil candles and distilling rum from the molasses it imported from the West Indies, much of it improperly. Most of this rum was sold in New England and to the southward, but Rhode Island also had the largest African trade of any of the colonies.[52] Rum purchased the slaves which in turn purchased the molasses and provisions needed by Newport. Newport could also supply all its own shipping, the Rhode Island shipbuilding industry being third among the colonies, after Massachusetts and New Hampshire. There was a significant surplus ship production available for sale in England, though small compared to that of Massachusetts. By the generation preceding the Revolution, Newport was earning enough sterling exchange on its West Indian and other trades to obtain its European goods directly from England (when it did not obtain them surreptitiously from Holland) rather than get them at second hand from Boston or New York.[53]

Though Newport was never again so prosperous as just before

52. PRO Customs 16/1. More than half of all rum exported from the colonies to Africa in 1769 came from Rhode Island. Only Boston was also active in this trade.

53. There is no full-scale study of Newport's commerce. The main lines can be derived from Bridenbaugh (note 15) or from the documents published in *Commerce of Rhode Island 1726–1800* (*Collections of the Massachusetts Historical Society*, 7th ser., IX [Boston, 1914]). The latter show, for example, Newport merchants in the 1770's sending ships to Philadelphia to purchase flour for shipment to Lisbon. This type of speculative activity is hard to trace in shipping records.

the American Revolution, its position was entirely artificial. Its trade was based upon no imperatives of geography but upon a series of historic accidents that brought together a trading population there and facilitated the accumulation of capital and entrepreneurial and technical skills. Even it in hour of prosperity, Newport's position was being undermined by the development of Providence at the head of Narragansett Bay on the mainland. Providence's trade to the West Indies and southern colonies inevitably intercepted much of Newport's trade from its very limited natural hin-
162 terland. The American Revolution dispersed the trading community at Newport and dissipated much of their capital, and the town was never again to be a serious commercial center. (Needless to say, it could not have, under the new federal government of 1789, the advantages of inefficient tax collection it had enjoyed when part of the British Empire.)

Philadelphia's position was as natural as that of Newport was artificial. While the New England commercial centers, starting with Boston and Newport, had trading hinterlands that hugged open coastlines and the valleys of navigable rivers and so were open to the intrusion of such rival, upstart port towns as Salem, Providence, and New London, the richest hinterland of Philadelphia lay inland from the town—to the west and northwest—and for long had access to no other large port town where its produce could be vended. Only after the zone of settlement in Pennsylvania expanded to the west of the Susquehanna River did the farmers and traders of central Pennsylvania have the option of sending their produce southward to the rival port of Baltimore. This alternative, however, became real only after the American Revolution.[54]

Between Philadelphia and the Susquehanna River lay a territory of superior soil, well suited to growing wheat. On this soil settlement became relatively thick in the eighteenth century, particularly that of German immigrants. In addition to raising wheat and hogs, they fattened cattle, including many driven in from the more outlying sections of Pennsylvania and up from the south along a drove

54. For the later story, see James Weston Livingood, *The Philadelphia-Baltimore Trade Rivalry 1780–1860* (Harrisburg, Pa., 1947).

road that extended from the interior of North Carolina through the valley of Virginia into Maryland and Pennsylvania. Closer to Philadelphia a large number of mills were set up along the streams flowing into the Delaware to grind the wheat into flour,[55] while the remarkably large number of bakers in Philadelphia (Appendix C) is some evidence of the important trade of baking this flour into biscuit for use on shipboard and in the West Indies. Similarly, the abnormally large number of butchers also shown in our occupational data for Philadelphia is evidence of the substantial trade there in slaughtering and packing beef and pork for exportation. 163

From the time of its foundation, in the 1680's, Philadelphia had an active trade, exporting its flour and provisions to the West Indies. This appears to have been a rather simple bilateral trade for the most part, supplemented by occasional shipments of wheat and flour to southern Europe as market conditions there justified. Although Philadelphia did supply West Indian and European goods to adjacent parts of New Jersey and Maryland, there is very little sign of a real entrepôt at Philadelphia in the first seventy years or so of its existence.[56] The volume of its imports from England was quite low[57] (Appendix E). This is not simply because Pennsylvania's population was still low (Appendix A), reflecting the later date of its foundation. (Pennsylvania did not pass Maryland in population until ca. 1760.) Although Pennsylvania passed New York in population in 1730, during the next thirty years New York regularly imported more goods from Britain than Pennsylvania did. This left no significant surplus for an entrepôt trade in European goods. Rather, Philadelphia appears to have continued to import such goods from Boston and other New England ports in payment for the provisions sold the New Englanders. This rather simple pattern of trade seems to have encouraged the development of a large community of small merchants in Philadelphia, big enough to trade to the West Indies but not very venturesome out-

55. Cf. Bridenbaugh, *Cities in Revolt*, pp. 50–51, 57, 75, 265, 268.

56. W. I. Davisson may not agree. Cf. his "The Philadelphia Trade," *Western Economic Journal*, 3 (1965), 310–311.

57. *U. S. Historical Statistics*, p. 757.

side those familiar waters, all too glad to sell wheat and flour and provisions to New England craft that visited their haven in return for fish and European goods, but not too inclined to send their own craft to New England or Newfoundland and only rarely to England.

Matters began to change in Philadelphia in the early 1750's, about the time the young Robert Morris started in business. During the Seven Years' War (1756–1763), a substantial British military effort to drive the French out of Fort Duquesne (Pittsburgh)
164 led to considerable army expenditures in Pennsylvania on supplies. This gave the merchants of Philadelphia unprecedentedly large supplies of bills of exchange on London at the time when military business was increasing the volume of direct sea traffic between England and their port. (Part of this military business continued after the peace of 1763.) During these same war years, cereal prices in Europe began that secular upswing that was to last until ca. 1815. A series of bad harvests in the late 1760's and early 1770's not only greatly expanded markets for North American wheat and flour in the familiar markets at Lisbon and Cadiz, but encouraged North American ships to venture more frequently into the Mediterranean, to Barcelona in particular, and even carried them to France ca. 1770.[58] Britain, a cereal exporter since ca. 1689, but now feeling the pressure of rising population, was forced to open its harbors to grain imports in the bad years of the late sixties and early seventies. Philadelphia, as the principal flour exporter in North America, profited particularly from these changes in the European markets. Its flour exports increased almost sixfold between 1730–1731 and 1773–1774. Four times as many vessels went from Philadelphia to the continent of Europe in 1768 as in 1733–1734 and six times as many in 1769 and 1770. Tonnage to Britain in 1768 was 126 percent above that in 1765–1766.[59] Higher prices for cereals and flour made overland transportation to Philadelphia economic from a

58. Ports inside the Mediterranean were long known to New England ships in the fish trade. Cf. note 38.

59. *U. S. Historical Statistics*, pp. 759–760; Jensen, *Commerce of Philadelphia*, p. 292. Cf. Donald Grove Barnes, *A History of the English Corn Laws from 1660–1846* (1931; New York, 1961), pp. 38–43.

wider geographic area and greatly encouraged the settlement of the Pennsylvania frontier, made safe by the defeat of the French and their Indian allies.

At Philadelphia these same developments meant changes of scale and style for the mercantile community. The profits (often windfall profits) of the flour trade greatly facilitated the accumulation of capital. By the early 1770's Philadelphians were investing eleven times as much per annum in new shipping as they had in the 1720's and supplied almost all their shipping needs. The town's mercantile fleet was now worth about £500,000 sterling. The average 165
ship sent to Britain or southern Europe in the 1770's was considerably larger than the average of those sent as recently as the 1750's.[60] With these developments went a change in scale of mercantile operations at Philadelphia and an articulation within the mercantile community. Larger firms emerged (of whom perhaps the best known is Willing and Morris) with correspondents in every major port between Barcelona and Amsterdam. In order to undertake very risky operations, these firms had to know the credit of great speculators in London who might send them purchase orders totaling tens of thousands of pounds sterling, as well as the creditworthiness of the houses at Lisbon, Barcelona, and Leghorn who would handle their flour sales and remit the proceeds to London. In many senses, the establishment of such liaisons by great merchants like Robert Morris was a commercial prerequisite of the American Revolution.

With such vastly increased earnings from military supplying and the flour trade, Philadelphia was able to multiply its imports from Britain and more than free itself from any dependence on New England. While the combined population of Pennsylvania and its dependency, Delaware, increased about 160 percent between 1740 and 1770, English exports to the same areas increased by more than a thousand percent. (In the same period, English exports to all the colonies increased by only 360 percent.) Philadelphia had by this

60. John J. McCusker, "Sources of Investment Capital in the Colonial Philadelphia Shipping Industry," *Journal of Economic History*, 32 (1973), 151–152. See also Jensen, *Commerce of Philadelphia*, p. 290.

time more than freed itself from dependence on Boston for any European supplies and was extending its own trading sphere southward into the backcountry of Maryland and Virginia. While the entrepôt trades of Boston and Newport show up very clearly in the records of ports up and down the coast, most of Philadelphia's went by wagon and has left less record. References in surviving mercantile correspondence leave no doubt, however, that by 1765–1776 merchants throughout Maryland and Virginia were much aware of the presence of Philadelphia. (The coastal export trade of
166 Philadelphia with other colonies was largely in flour, West Indian sugar, and New England rum.)[61]

The "Conestoga" wagons and wagoners must have been a very important part of the life of Philadelphia. Bridenbaugh has vividly described the great files of these enormous wagons lumbering into Philadelphia along the Lancaster Road, sometimes a hundred or more a day.[62] In our discussion of the population structure of Philadelphia in the previous section, we noted that it had a somewhat larger service sector than Boston, and part of this must be ascribable to the wagon traffic. To move a given tonnage by wagon required a greater quantity of labor accompanying the goods than did moving the same tonnage by sailing vessels (perhaps ten times as much). Philadelphia at times must have been filled with wagoners, and despite Bridenbaugh's insistence on the thrift and abstinence of the "Pennsylvania Dutch" farmer-wagoners, this congregation must have created an enormous amount of business for innkeepers, tavernkeepers, harnessmakers, wheelwrights. Since the wagoners were often themselves farmers of the interior, they must have taken advantage of their stay in Philadelphia to make a wide variety of purchases for their families and neighbors at prices that of necessity were less than those charged by the country storekeepers (our primary traders) in their neighborhoods—even when they as carters were working for interior traders. Thus both the retail and wholesale trading areas of Philadelphia probably extended far deeper into

61. *U. S. Historical Statistics*, p. 757; Jensen, *Commerce of Philadelphia*, pp. 70–84.
62. Cf. note 55.

the interior than did that of any of its competing towns: hence the larger "service sector."

To compare Philadelphia and New York is to raise an obvious question. Early in the nineteenth century New York passed Philadelphia, to become the principal port and largest city in the United States. In the early eighteenth century New York was already larger and busier than Philadelphia but lost that edge by 1750 and did not recover it until early in the next century. Why did New York not grow as rapidly as Philadelphia in the decades after 1740? The answer probably lies in the difference between immediate and 167
ultimate geographic advantage. In the long run New York had a more advantageous situation than Philadelphia, particularly before the construction of railroads, for the Hudson is more navigable than the Delaware and with its tributary the Mohawk opens up a larger and richer hinterland. This, however, was well in the future in 1740. The valley of the Mohawk and western New York were closed to significant European settlement by hostile Indians and their French allies. The valley of the Hudson south of Albany was safer but was geographically confined and had only limited agricultural possibilities. What counted in the 1740's was the immediate hinterland of the two ports, the areas within a fifty- or sixty-mile radius—and by this criterion Philadelphia was better endowed. In addition to the Hudson Valley, New York could draw on Long Island and adjacent parts of New Jersey and Connecticut (subject to competition from Newport) but this added up to less than Philadelphia's western breadbasket. Between 1730 and 1780 the population of New York province increased from 48,594 to 210,541 (333 percent) while Pennsylvania increased from 51,707 to 327,000 (533 percent). The slower growth of New York City is the slower growth of its region.

There may, however, be a slight pro-Philadelphia bias in accounts that compare the growth of Philadelphia with that of New York. Bridenbaugh (Appendix B1) suggests that Philadelphia in 1775 was 60 percent larger than New York City (40,000:25,000). However, in 1790 the first census (Appendix B2) showed Philadelphia only 28 percent larger than New York (42,444:33,131).

If, instead of using Bridenbaugh's figures for 1775, we use the older figures of Rossiter (Appendix B2), we find that Philadelphia's lead over New York in 1770 was only 33 percent (28,000:21,000). Recently, Warner has investigated the population of Philadelphia and calculated that it was only 23,739 in 1775. Part of this great difference is due to the previous use of high multipliers (ca. 6.3) when converting the number of houses into heads of population. Warner has calculated that the multiplier in the 1770's was only 4.44; hence his much lower population figure.[63] Although the last word has
168 probably not been said on this subject, it is apparent that part of the supposed lead of Philadelphia over New York may be a statistical illusion.

At first glance, New York was very similar to Philadelphia in its commerce and population structure, though closer inspection reveals some marked similarities to Boston. Although it continued to count furs among its significant exports longer than any other northern colony—owing to the great Indian trade at Albany—its principal exports in the eighteenth century were, like Philadelphia's, flour and provisions. The general volume of its maritime activity was, however, less than that of any other major port.

Table III

AVERAGE SHIPPING TONNAGE
CLEARED OUTWARD P.A.
1768–1772

Philadelphia	42,790 tons
Boston	37,842
Charleston	31,075
New York	26,278

CF. *U. S. Historical Statistics*, pp. 759–760.

In value, all of New York's exports in 1769 were worth only £231,906 while Pennsylvania's, essentially Philadelphia's, were worth £410,757; its imports were valued at only £188,976, Penn-

63. Warner, *The Private City*, pp. 11–12, 225–226.

sylvania's at £399,821.[64] New York's trade to southern Europe was quite undeveloped relative to Philadelphia's. In a peak year for that trade, 1769, New York sent only 2,039 tons of flour and biscuit to southern Europe, Philadelphia 15,206 tons. (In addition, New York sent 79,565 bushels of wheat, while Philadelphia sent 165,-315.)[65] All of New York's exports to southern Europe that year were in one estimate valued at £52,199, Pennsylvania's at £204,-313: by a modern calculation they were worth only £37,810, Pennsylvania's £183,760.[66] New York's West Indian trade was also 169
considerably smaller than that of Philadelphia or Boston.

Table IV

VALUES OF IMPORTS AND EXPORTS TO WEST INDIES, 1769

	Exports		*Imports*
Pennsylvania	£178,331	(123,557)	£180,592
Massachusetts	123,394	(101,569)	155,387
New York	66,325	(53,241)	97,420

NOTE: The figures in parentheses are Shepherd, "Commodity Exports," estimates.

SOURCE: *U. S. Historical Statistics*, p. 758; Shepherd, "Commodity Exports," pp. 32–33.

Yet, despite these relatively unsuccessful branches, New York by complicated entrepôt functions was able to send far more to Britain and Ireland than Pennsylvania and to maintain a favorable balance of trade with the mother country, something no other northern colony did. The £113,382 worth of goods which New York sent the British Isles in 1769[67] consisted of its own wheat, whale oil, flax-seed (in demand in Ireland), iron and ashes, plus Caribbean sugar, annatto (a cheese dye), logwood, and other dyes, Honduras

64. *U. S. Historical Statistics*, p. 758. For a full breakdown of colonial exports, 1768–1772, with somewhat different values, see the valuable long paper of James F. Shepherd, "Commodity Exports from the British North American Colonies to Overseas Areas, 1768–1772: Magnitudes and Patterns of Trade," *Explorations in Economic History*, 8 (1970) 5–76.

65. PRO Customs 16/1 (L. A. Harper's abstracts); Shepherd, "Commodity Exports," pp. 32–33.

66. *U. S. Historical Statistics*, p. 758; Shepherd, "Commodity Exports," pp. 32–33.

67. £65,016 before shipment, in a modern estimate. *Ibid.*

mahogany, and Carolina rice and naval stores.[68] In other words, because flour and provisions, "natural" endowments, were not available in sufficient quantities, even under the high prices prevailing ca. 1768–1774, New York was forced, much as was Boston, into a complex entrepôt trade. Its merchants were probably as adept as those of Boston; like those in Boston and Philadelphia, they had mastered, for example, the intricacies of underwriting marine insurance.[69] They enjoyed one marked advantage in having their port as the American terminus of the official British trans-
170 atlantic packet boat. Getting mail early was no small commercial advantage. Although there was no Robert Morris in New York then, when the French government was forced—in the *pacte de famine* crisis of 1770—to purchase wheat and flour in North America, the French agents in London (Bourdieu & Chollet) chose to work through Wallace & Company of New York rather than through a Philadelphia house.

New York was significantly behind Boston and Philadelphia in one further respect; the shipbuilding of the province (essentially the town's) as of 1769–1771 was less than one-fifth that of Massachusetts and only 70 percent of Pennsylvania's, essentially Philadelphia's (Appendix F). New York's shipbuilding fell below that of less urban colonies such as New Hampshire, Rhode Island, Connecticut, Maryland, and Virginia. This is probably a significant explanation of why, as noted earlier (Appendix D), the manufacturing sector in the population of New York City, even if measured in 1795, was significantly below that of Boston and Philadelphia.

Before closing our discussion of the three great commercial centers of colonial America—Boston, New York, and Philadelphia—something ought to be said about the alleged independent character of their mercantile communities. Most people who write about

68. Harrington, *New York Merchant*, pp. 165–172. A more recent work confirming the "entrepôt" version of New York trade is William I. Davisson and Lawrence J. Bradley, "New York Maritime Trade: Ship Voyage Patterns, 1715–1765," *New York Historical Society Quarterly*, 55 (1971), 309–317.

69. It is noteworthy that ports as small as Boston, New York, and Philadelphia developed maritime insurance from the 1740's. Cf. Bridenbaugh, *Cities in Revolt*, pp. 93, 287. Even Charleston obtained an insurance office in 1761, though most of its insurance was made in London.

these three ports take it for granted that their trade was entirely in the hands of their own merchants on whose account (i.e., with whose capital and at whose risk) both exports and imports were made. There is evidence that, during the great boom in the wheat and flour trade in the 1760's and 1770's, big London grain speculators or French agents sent purchase orders to New York, Philadelphia, and perhaps Maryland. There is also better-known evidence (in standard accounts and unpublished sources) of British merchants sending goods to those centers on their own account to be 171
sold on commission.[70] This means that, for a part of their business, the merchants of New York and Philadelphia and perhaps even Boston were acting as the agents or factors of metropolitan merchants to whom the risks and the profits belonged. If this was true in the 1760's and 1770's, might it not also have been true earlier? How did all those new houses in New York and Philadelphia get started between the 1720's and the 1760's? Finally, there is the matter of auctions. In the years after 1815 one of the characteristic institutions of British-American trade was the import auction, particularly at New York. British manufacturers who had surplus stocks or needed cash in a hurry bypassed the export merchants and sent their goods directly to New York to be auctioned on arrival, usually for cash. It is clear, however, from the monographic literature on the colonial period that similar auctions were being complained of in New York and Philadelphia in the 1760's and 1770's. But we are told nothing of the persons who sent such goods for auction—though we get tantalizing hints of direct contact with Manchester.[71] Then too we know all too little about the internal history of the businesses in these places. We have been told where the capital for their ships came from, but not the capital for the firms themselves. These are some of the problems that will have to be solved before we can understand fully the inner dynamics of the mercantile communities in those port towns.

70. E.g., Jensen, *Philadelphia Commerce*, pp. 17–19, 96–97; Harrington, *New York Merchant*, pp. 67–72.

71. Harrington, *New York Merchant*, pp. 92–93; Bridenbaugh, *Cities in Revolt*, pp. 78–79, 276–277; and, particularly, Jensen, *Philadelphia Commerce*, pp. 123–124.

The last of the great commercial centers of colonial America was Charleston in South Carolina. At the beginning of the eighteenth century it was important only for its Indian trade, though it enjoyed a small trade with the West Indies in forest products and provisions. In the eighteenth century it developed two great agricultural staples: rice (after 1710) and later indigo, both grown by slave labor in the coastal districts near Charleston. These trades reached impressive proportions. In 1769, rice exports from the thirteen colonies (83 percent originally from Charleston) were
172 worth £340,693, making this the fourth most valuable export of British North America just after fish (tobacco and the wheat-flour group being first and second). At the same time, indigo exports from the same colonies (almost all originally from Charleston) were worth £131,552, the fifth most valuable export from the colonies.[72] More than half the rice went to Great Britain with a large fraction also going to southern Europe and the West Indies and lesser quantities to the other mainland colonies. (Large but unknown quantities, were retained in South Carolina for local consumption.) As provided by law, almost all the indigo went to Britain, where it was valued for the textile industries.

One of the striking features of South Carolina colonial life was the degree to which the single port of Charleston was able almost to monopolize the import and export trade of that colony and even of nearby Georgia. While New York and Pennsylvania really had room for only one significant port at the mouth of each of their great rivers, South Carolina had a number of river valleys and possible harbor sites. Nevertheless, river and coastal communication was easy and a very high proportion of the external commerce of South Carolina became concentrated in Charleston, which also handled some of the trade that emanated from North Carolina and Georgia. This pattern began in the first half century of settlement, when the settled areas all lay close to Charleston, but persisted after

72. *U. S. Historical Statistics*, pp. 761–762, 767–768. For the five years, 1768–1772, Shepherd ("Commodity Exports," p. 65) estimates annual average value of colonial exports at: tobacco, £766,000; flour and biscuit, £412,000; rice, £312,000; dried fish, £287,000; indigo, £117,000.

dispersion. From the early dangerous days down to midcentury, when relations with the Indians were not peaceful, many large planters chose to live in Charleston for safety's sake. This pattern persisted afterwards partly because the planting regions were unhealthy, partly because they were populated predominantly by slaves, and partly out of habit and convenience. This gave Charleston a significant population of resident gentry, a social phenomenon known in the West Indies but unusual in North America. With a significant number of planters spending at least part of the year in
Charleston, it became the inevitable center of consumer handicrafts 173
in the colony and of the import trade. That it also became a center of the export trade suggests that for its commodities, there were no ultimate economies in a more dispersed pattern. By concentrating export commodities in one place, larger vessels could be used and turn-around time for even large ships reduced.

Charleston never developed a significant shipbuilding industry. Its exports to England were generally carried in English-owned vessels employed in a bilateral service back and forth to England.[73] Charleston was also frequently visited by smaller craft from the northern colonies that may have carried a significant part of the colony's exports to the Caribbean. Shipping movements and rice exports to southern Europe fluctuated considerably from year to year depending upon the price of cereals in those parts. The picture is not clear. but British shipping probably also handled a good part of that trade. All of this added up to a considerable volume of activity. Charleston was a busier port than New York on the eve of the Revolution.

Despite this activity, Charleston did not have as large an autochthonous business community as the northern centers. In the early days many of her traders were factors sent there by firms in England. On the eve of the Revolution, we find some big firms in Charleston that are in effect branches of houses in London or Liverpool under the management of a local resident partner. There were of course locally based organizations as well but they never succeeded

73. Even after the Revolution, for a time the majority of vessels entering South Carolina ports were British.

in dominating trade as indigenous firms did in the northern ports. It was, of course, precisely because Charleston offered commodities desired in England (rice and indigo) that British merchants were attracted more toward this trade than toward that of the northern ports. This pattern tended to reduce Charleston to the level of a mere "shipping point" rather than a real "commercial center" or a "general entrepôt." Entrepreneurial decisions were made in Britain, capital was raised there, ships were built or chartered there and outfitted there, insurance was made there—all for the South Caro-
174 lina trade. There was nothing conspiratorial in this, nor anything to be taken as evidence of the feckless character of the Charleston mercantile community. It was rather a rational adaptation to market conditions and comparative costs, given the commodities traded and the markets available to them. Nevertheless, this "colonial" character of Charleston's commercial life helps to explain why Charleston with a larger volume of tonnage and more valuable imports and exports than New York had only half the population of New York City in 1770.

The last remaining area to be discussed is perhaps the most paradoxical in colonial America: the Chesapeake Bay colonies of Virginia and Maryland. Virginia was the most populous continental colony, or state, from its foundation until passed by New York in 1820. Virginia and Maryland together accounted for over 30 percent of the population of the thirteen colonies in 1770. Their chief product, tobacco, was the most valuable export of North America for more than a century preceding the Revolution. In 1770, exports were estimated to be worth over £900,000 sterling. They were also major exporters of wheat. Yet down to 1750 or 1760 they had no town with a population of as much as 3,000. This was partly corrected in the years 1760–1775 by the rise of Baltimore and Norfolk, but on the eve of the Revolution the former had only 5,934 inhabitants and latter about 6,250. Williamsburg, the capital of Virginia (not a port but a *Residenzstadt* like Karlsruhe or Wolfenbüttel), then had a population of only 2,000 and Annapolis, the capital of Maryland, both a port and a capital, only 3,700.[74]

74. Bridenbaugh, *Cities in Revolt*, p. 217.

Without major centers almost to the eve of the Revolution, Virginia and Maryland were not without town life. The maps are filled with places that contemporaries considered towns. If most of the county seats (or "Court Houses") in Virginia were little more than hamlets, there were somewhat more substantial commercial towns at the mouths of rivers (Norfolk and Yorktown) and more characteristically at the limits of navigation of the principal rivers: Alexandria on the Potomac (population 2,748 in 1790), Fredericksburg on the Rappahannock (1,485 in 1790), Richmond on the James (under 2,000 in 1775), and Petersburg on the Appomattox 175
(2,828 in 1790 but the most important tobacco shipping center), as well as Georgetown in Maryland. There were also even smaller but fairly busy little port towns along the rivers that handled local traffic and ships that could not or did not wish to venture up to the "heads" of navigation: Port Tobacco in Maryland, Dumfries on the Virginia side of the Potomac, Hobbs Hole on the Rappahannock. Busy or not, none of this latter group attracted very much of a population.

The failure of Virginia and Maryland to develop any large commercial centers before 1775 (or even any middling centers before 1750) has long perplexed historians and geographers. Moreover, it perplexed the people and leaders of the two colonies themselves in the seventeenth and eighteenth centuries. In general, royal policy favored town growth, and the legislatures of the two colonies passed numerous acts intended to encourage town growth, but all to very little effect.

The most common explanation for the lack of towns in the Chesapeake has been geographical. According to this explanation, towns did not develop in Virginia and Maryland because the area was so well endowed with waterways, the great Bay of Chesapeake itself, two hundred miles long, with the many rivers that flow into it, great and small, and the numerous tributaries of those rivers. Ships could come from Britain or other colonies and deliver goods and pick up tobacco at the wharf of the individual planter or country storekeeper. There was thus no need for a compulsory point of transshipment as at Philadelphia where wholesale dealers and greater

merchants might congregate and services usefully be centralized. I have never been quite satisfied with this argument. (1) It seems to place location before activity, saying that, if there had been towns in Virginia, there would have been more merchants, wholesale dealers, and manufacturing artisans. Is it not, however, sensible to assume that, if there were merchants and wholesale traders and artisans in the Chesapeake, they would have found some convenient place to settle? The relevant question then becomes, Why were there not more merchants, traders, and artisans in the Chesapeake?
176 (2) Another assumption of the geographical argument is that ease of transportation leads to population dispersal: thus because the Chesapeake had the greatest ease of internal transportation it had the most dispersed population. However, in studying other regions and other times we are commonly told that ease of transportation leads to greater urban concentration, that it allows a single town to serve a larger area, to reach a larger market, that railroads in the nineteenth century greatly encouraged the growth of large towns by extending their trading areas. We have seen, even in the eighteenth century, how ease of coastal transport greatly extended the trading areas of Boston and Charleston and helps to account for much of their commercial success. Let us therefore recognize geography as an ever present element in any economic explanation, but not make it into the single grand touchstone of analysis that alone solves all problems.

If we are to analyze more exactly the factors retarding town growth in the Chesapeake, we must look more closely at its economy. It was an agricultural economy dominated almost entirely in the seventeenth and eighteenth centuries by a single commodity, tobacco. After 1750, wheat exports were also increasingly important but never rivaled tobacco. In 1770, overseas wheat exports from Virginia and Maryland were worth only £92,776 while tobacco shipments totaled £900,000.[75] By law, all tobacco in Vir-

75. PRO Customs 16/1; *U. S. Historical Statistics*, p. 761. Tobacco counted then for 27 percent of all native produce exported from the continental colonies. To the above figure of wheat exports, about 37 percent should be added for exports to other colonies. The wheat and Indian corn crops were, or course, much more valuable than suggested here if one considers the amounts raised for local consumption. Cf. David Klingaman,

ginia (from 1730) and Maryland (from 1747) had to be sent to public warehouses for inspection and storage. These were all located on navigable water. In the tidewater or low-country sections of Virginia and Maryland, tobacco could often be sent to the warehouse by water or by road carriage of not more than ten miles or so. From the inland areas of Virginia and North Carolina, however, carriage to the warehouse often involved wagon trips of fifty or seventy-five miles. The hogsheads were commonly sold unopened in the warehouse by the transfer of warehouse receipts. From the warehouse, the tobacco was generally taken in lighters or 177
other craft directly to ocean-going vessels lying in the river nearby or some miles downstream. Tobacco was sufficiently bulky, with hogsheads weighing about one thousand pounds in the 1770's, so that all unnecessary handling was avoided. At the same time, tobacco was sufficiently valuable to make it worthwhile to keep ships waiting while cargoes were assembled from a number of warehouses. The tobacco trade in the first instance was in the hands of primary traders, rural storekeepers, scattered over the countryside, who in return provided the planters with imported salt, sugar, rum, tea, and European manufactures. Some of these storekeepers were employees of British (particularly Scottish) firms; others were indigenous independent traders. The latter obtained their imports from and sold their tobacco to the Scottish stores, or dealt with larger indigenous trader/merchants settled in the principal river townlets (but relatively scattered for the convenience of their customers, the primary traders). These indigenous merchants or secondary traders carried on some Caribbean trade and ordered their manufactures from Britain, which they generally paid for with bills of exchange obtained from their West Indian trade and by selling their tobacco to the Scots and others. Before the 1760's very little tobacco arrived in Britain on the account of these native "merchants," for they were characteristically short of capital and

---

"The Significance of Grain in the Development of the Tobacco Colonies," *Journal of Economic History*, 29 (1969), 273–274. For the five years, 1768–1772, Shepherd estimates that Virginia and Maryland wheat exports were worth £84,085 compared to £756,129 for tobacco. Shepherd, "Commodity Exports," tables I-III.

did not ship unless they could not dispose of their tobacco in any other way.

If any of these indigenous traders in the Chesapeake thought of going into the tobacco shipment business in a large way, they would immediately have run into a number of difficulties. The most obvious resulted from the effects of the English Acts of Trade and Navigation, which required that all tobacco had to be exported either to Great Britain or to other British colonies in America; in fact, over 99 percent was shipped to Great Britain. Demand for
178 Chesapeake tobacco was quite limited in the Caribbean owing to the small populations there and to the availability of much-esteemed tobaccos and snuffs from Cuba, Venezuela, and Martinique, not to mention the substantial production of Brazil. Thus, small men in the Chesapeake area could not start out in tobacco exporting on a modest scale to the West Indies or southern Europe as small dealers in fish, flour, or provisions did elsewhere.

If the indigenous merchant in the Chesapeake thought of sending tobacco to Britain, the only available market, he would of course have to compete with British merchants already in the trade. This was most difficult for a variety of reasons. (1) When the tobacco got to Britain, about 15 percent—the best in quality—was retained for home consumption, while the remaining 85 percent was reexported, primarily to France, the Low Countries, and Germany. Before sale, the tobacco had to be carefully examined and graded according to type and quality; certain types and qualities could usefully be sold promptly for the ready cash that merchants always needed, others were best held back until the right buyer came along. These were difficult decisions to make three thousand miles away and left one uncomfortably dependent upon one's correspondent. (2) Tobacco was very heavily taxed in Britain—200 to 300 percent *ad valorem*. Even though tobacco reexported recovered the taxes after 1724, deposits had to be made and bond for the duties given. Giving and discharging bonds was a rather technical business and required finding others to sign one's bonds as sureties. All this created cash-flow and credit problems for new firms in the trade. (3) The goods sent out from Britain to America in return for the

tobacco were normally bought on long credit from middle men (linendrapers, ironmongers) who obtained them from the manufacturers. These middle men were unlikely to supply such goods on long credit to any firm that did not have a partner or agent resident in Britain who was of good credit and personally guaranteed repayment. (4) Since there was a lot of competition in the Bay area to get tobacco to fill ships, prices there tended to approach European prices very closely and remittances of tobacco to Britain were often made at a bookkeeping loss. The great profits of the trade in Virginia and Maryland came not from sending tobacco to 179
Britain but from importing European goods which could be sold at very great "advances." Thus when traders in the Bay did get tobacco into their hands, they characteristically preferred to sell it "in the country" and remit bills of exchange to London to pay for European goods ordered. (5) Finally, there existed in both tobacco colonies a class of middling and large planters who in varying degrees from year to year preferred not to sell their tobacco to nearby stores but to remit it to London, Bristol, or Liverpool and have it sold there by commission merchants who would pay them the proceeds in cash (by accepting bills of exchange) or in goods purchased for them. Such consignments probably did not account for more than one-fifth of the crop by the 1770's but they removed some of the best tobacco from the grasp of the indigenous traders.

Putting all the bits of evidence together, one gains the impression that the trade to Britain was not a very attractive proposition for persons with money in the tobacco colonies. For the small man with limited capital it was much easier to enter into the West Indian provision trade, just as it was for his sort in the northern colonies. For wealthier persons, there were the rival attractions of land speculation or perhaps acting as sales agent for an English slave dealer, or even iron making or shipbuilding. When Virginians or Marylanders did build ships (and each colony built more than New York did), they usually found it to their advantage to sell their larger vessels after their first or second voyage to Britain rather than try to keep them in what was obviously only a marginally attractive trade. Finally, when a Virginian or Marylander of means decided despite all to go into the tobacco trade, more often than not he moved to London or sent a partner there. The trade could obviously be carried out much more efficiently from there.

Nevertheless, there were changes underway in the Chesapeake in the years from 1750 to 1775. The corps of indigenous traders was growing in both Virginia and Maryland. Some of them were not satisfied with the limited and highly competitive trade to the West Indies and sought entry to the vaster trade to Britain. Many were able to do so through the "cargo system" that flourished in
180 the decade preceding the Revolution. Rich merchants in London, acting as factors (or agents on commission) for these smaller houses in the Chesapeake would buy "cargoes" of assorted goods for them from London middlemen on one year's credit and ship those goods out with the understanding that remittances would be made in tobacco or bills of exchange before the year's credit was up. These new indigenous houses were now indeed trading to Britain, but they were trading on other people's capital and credit and often in other people's ships. They were thus still closer to being "secondary traders" than real merchants. Nevertheless, much of the life in the new little towns of the interior of Virginia (Petersburg, Richmond, and the like) came from these new native firms trading precariously under the "cargo system." That those towns were not larger says something about the scale and nature of their operations.

Much more innovative in these years was the growth of Norfolk and Baltimore from mere hamlets to towns of about six thousand inhabitants and active commercial centers—larger than anything else in the Chesapeake. The important thing about them is that neither had very much to do with tobacco, that staple so little conducive to town growth. Norfolk, near the mouth of Chesapeake Bay, was in the southeastern corner of Virginia; its hinterland there and in the adjacent parts of North Carolina was a land of forest and swamp and marginal agriculture. It produced a limited amount of tobacco of no very great repute and abundant forest products (pitch, tar, and lumber) plus some Indian corn, pork, and beef suitable for the West Indies. With these endowments, Norfolk came to specialize in the West Indian trade. Because of the volume of

this activity, Norfolk attracted a certain amount of the surplus provisions, etc., from elsewhere in Virginia though all the major rivers and havens of Virginia and Maryland continued to have their own West Indian trade, and New Englanders continued to bring West Indian produce into the Bay. Similarly, when traders elsewhere in the Bay were short of sugar, molasses, and rum, they knew they could always order some from Norfolk, where there were large distilleries.[76] Norfolk also became a major exporter of Virginia wheat to southern Europe though other districts also did their own wheat exporting.[77] The one thing that Norfolk did not 181
handle very much of was tobacco.[78] With the surplus earnings of its sales to the West Indies, Norfolk imported manufactured goods from Britain, most of which were sold in its natural hinterland in southeast Virginia and adjacent North Carolina, but some of which were also sold elsewhere in Virginia.

In short, the not very impressive trade of Norfolk to the West Indies and southern Europe made possible a larger town than the infinitely more valuable tobacco export trade of the rest of Virginia did. Norfolk's size was consistent with that of other towns specializing in the West Indian trade, e.g., Providence, New London, New Haven. To be active in its trades, Norfolk had to be a smaller-scale Philadelphia, a city of mariners, shipwrights, small merchants, butchers, tanners, and shopkeepers.

The case of Baltimore is even clearer. Baltimore sits on a minor branch of the Patapsco River, one of the less important rivers flowing into the Chesapeake Bay, about two hundred miles north of Norfolk, and at the extreme northern limits of the tobacco producing zone. Nearby, on the main branch of the Patapsco River, was the hamlet of Elk Ridge where there was a public tobacco inspection warehouse—as there was at Balitmore. Elk Ridge tobacco

76. Thomas J. Wertenbaker, *Norfolk Historic Southern Port*, ed. Marvin W. Schlegel, 2d ed. (Durham, N.C., 1962), pp. 1–47.

77. PRO Customs 16/1.

78. *Ibid.*; for the years 1745–1756, see Edward D. Neill, *The Fairfaxes of England and America* (Albany, 1868), p. 225. Tobacco shipments from the Norfolk district may have risen significantly in the early 1770's, but still remained much less than that of any of the tobacco-producing districts.

had a very good reputation and often fetched a superior price. Tobacco growers round about preferred therefore to sent their tobacco to Elk Ridge and little came to Baltimore. In 1750 it was a totally insignificant place. In the next quarter century, however, it came alive. Baltimore sat near the geological line dividing lowland or "tidewater" Maryland, the land of tobacco, from the upcountry or "piedmont" region better suited to wheat. In fact, the back country of western Maryland was an extension southward of the wheat-producing lands of adjacent Pennsylvania. In the years after
182 1750, as wheat prices rose in Europe, there was a great incentive to settle these areas, and Scotch-Irish and German farmers from Pennsylvania pushed southward to take up lands in hitherto neglected western Maryland. Baltimore was most conveniently situated to serve these new wheat-producing areas. Flour mills were established and soon Baltimore was attracting wheat shipments not only from western Maryland but also from the adjacent parts of central Pennsylvania west of the Susquehanna River. A distinct mercantile community came into existence at Baltimore to handle wheat exports, for tobacco traders were not interested in a product whose markets fluctuated radically from year to year and were quite different from their own. Shipyards were set up in and near Baltimore to build the sloops, schooners, and ships needed to take Baltimore's wheat, flour, and provisions to the West Indies and southern Europe. They also built some larger tobacco vessels for sale in Britain. Her trade and occupational configuration were quite similar to those of Philadelphia, and Baltimore was becoming Philadelphia's keenest rival.[79] In the years after the American Revolution, Baltimore became much more of a general entrepôt, sending its wheat to Britain and importing all sort of merchandise from there. The tobacco regions of lowland Maryland which before the Revolution had ignored Baltimore now began to feel its pull and sent their tobacco too for sale there. By then, of course, the Acts of Trade and Navigation no longer affected American commerce, and Baltimore

79. Cf. Clarence P. Gould, "The Economic Causes of the Rise of Baltimore," *Essays in Colonial History Presented to Charles McLean Andrews by His Students* (New Haven, 1931), pp. 225–251.

merchants were free to send this tobacco to its best markets in the Low Countries and Germany.[80] But Baltimore's export trade consisted primarily of wheat and flour.

In short, most areas of Virginia and Maryland did not develop significant towns in the eighteenth century because they produced tobacco. Where alternative productions predominated, significant towns grew up—at Norfolk and Baltimore on the fringes of the tobacco regions but outside the grip of that staple trade. This was partly the result of the Navigation Acts. Because Britain had its own agriculture to protect, most of the products of North America 183
were not affected by those acts. The exempted products included fish, some forest products, wheat, Indian corn, pork, beef, dairy products, and the like. Rice could be exported directly to southern Europe but, if destined for northern Europe, had to be landed in Britain first. Only tobacco and indigo of major North American produce definitely had to be landed in Britain. These two products could not, therefore, generate the flocks of small traders who appeared quite early at Philadelphia, Boston, and New York trading in small sloops to the West Indies and from whose numbers emerged the larger merchants of the next generation who traded in larger vessels to Europe and Africa.

However, too much should not be ascribed to the Navigation Acts. After the American Revolution, when those British laws no longer directed American commerce, the greater part of the tobacco of the Chesapeake still continued to find its way to Britain. And, as of 1790, the only two states that still had more British than American ships entering their harbors were South Carolina and Virginia—precisely those whose maritime economies had been most directed toward Britain and by British interests before the war. In other words, market forces strengthened the thrust of the Navigation Acts but had a life of their own that outlived these acts. Thus, the low degree of urbanization cannot be blamed simply on the Navigation Acts, any more than it could be blamed simply on geography, but represents the interaction of geography, legisla-

80. Cf. Stuart Weems Bruchey, *Robert Oliver, Merchant of Baltimore 1783–1819* (Baltimore, 1956).

tion, and forms of commercial organization rationally responsive to market conditions.

In summary, then, suitable geographic position was one necessary precondition for the development of a significant port town in eighteenth-century America as anywhere else. An appropriate volume of export trade was another. But these two preconditions were not sufficient in themselves to determine the size of a port town. Had they been, Charleston would not have been only half as big as New York, and Norfolk would have been bigger than
184 Boston. When the entrepreneurial decision-making center of a trade was in a port, it necessitated the presence there of a population of sailors, shipwrights, sailmakers, ship chandlers, and the like, as well as specialist brokers, insurance underwriters, and often a manufacturing population to process goods in transit. Without such "entrepreneurial headquarters effect," the port need have been little more than a "shipping point" whose urban configuration would not reflect its shipping volume. With such entrepreneurial activity, the port could attract entrepôt business that enabled it to transcend the limits of the activity arising from its immediate hinterland. The precise locus of entrepreneurial activity was not primarily a cultural phenomenon (i.e., reflecting a different business ethos in different places), but represented to a considerable degree a rational adaptation to the availability of capital and other resources and the marketing problems of specific commodities.

The West Indian trade could apparently be carried on efficiently in towns in the 4,000–8,000 range: Providence, Rhode Island; the Connecticut towns, Norwich, New London, New Haven; and Norfolk. A significant export trade to Europe with substantial imports from Great Britain implied a size of 6,000–12,000 on the eve of the Revolution: Newport, Baltimore, Charleston. The functions of a "general entrepôt" went with a size of 15,000–30,000: Philadelphia, New York, Boston. Though we do not have all the data we need, the occupational/sectoral profiles of all the principal towns would appear to be similar, with the local service sector about twice the size of the maritime sector. The only variations that appear were in the manufacturing or industrial sector. Where the town was particularly active in shipbuilding (e.g., Boston) or in processing local products (e.g., Philadelphia's leather crafts), the industrial sector might appear slightly larger than elsewhere, but we do not have enough data to say with assurance what was normal.

APPENDIX A

Estimated Population of American Colonies, 1610–1780

Series No.	Colony	1780	1770	1760	1750	1740	1730	1720	1710	1700	1690	1680	1670	1660	1650	1640	1630
	WHITE AND NEGRO																
1	Total	2,780,369	2,148,076	1,593,625	1,170,760	905,563	629,445	466,185	331,711	250,888	210,372	151,507	111,935	75,058	50,368	26,634	4,646
2	Maine (counties)[1]	49,133	31,257	...	...	...	...	...	...	...	...	...	...	...	1,000	900	400
3	New Hampshire	87,802	62,396	39,093	27,505	23,256	10,755	9,375	5,681	4,958	4,164	2,047	1,805	1,555	1,305	1,055	500
4	Vermont	47,620	10,000	...	...	...	...	...	...	...	...	...	...	...	...	...	...
5	Plymouth[2]	...	...	...	...	...	...	...	...	...	7,424	6,400	5,333	1,980	1,566	1,020	390
6	Massachusetts[1,2]	268,627	235,308	222,600	188,000	151,613	114,116	91,008	62,390	55,941	49,504	39,752	30,000	20,082	14,037	8,932	506
7	Rhode Island	52,946	58,196	45,471	33,226	25,255	16,950	11,680	7,573	5,894	4,224	3,017	2,155	1,539	785	300	...
8	Connecticut	206,701	183,881	142,470	111,280	89,580	75,530	58,830	39,450	25,970	21,645	17,246	12,603	7,980	4,139	1,472	...
9	New York	210,541	162,920	117,138	76,696	63,665	48,594	36,919	21,625	19,107	13,909	9,830	5,754	4,936	4,116	1,930	350
10	New Jersey	139,627	117,431	93,813	71,393	51,373	37,510	29,818	19,872	14,010	8,000	3,400	1,000	...	...	...	...
11	Pennsylvania	327,305	240,057	183,703	119,666	85,637	51,707	30,962	24,450	17,950	11,450	680	...	...	...	...	...
12	Delaware	45,385	35,496	33,250	28,704	19,870	9,170	5,385	3,645	2,470	1,482	1,005	700	540	185	...	...
13	Maryland	245,474	202,599	162,267	141,073	116,093	91,113	66,133	42,741	29,604	24,024	17,904	13,226	8,426	4,504	583	...
14	Virginia	538,004	447,016	339,726	231,033	180,440	114,000	87,757	78,281	58,560	53,046	43,596	35,309	27,020	18,731	10,442	2,500
15	North Carolina	270,133	197,200	110,442	72,984	51,760	30,000	21,270	15,120	10,720	7,600	5,430	3,850	1,000	...	...	...
16	South Carolina	180,000	124,244	94,074	64,000	45,000	30,000	17,048	10,883	5,704	3,900	1,200	200	...	...	...	...
17	Georgia	56,071	23,375	9,578	5,200	2,021	...	...	...	...	...	...	...	...	...	...	...
18	Kentucky	45,000	15,700	...	...	...	...	...	...	...	...	...	...	...	...	...	...
19	Tennessee	10,000	1,000	...	...	...	...	...	...	...	...	...	...	...	...	...	...
	NEGRO																
1	Total	575,420	459,822	325,806	236,420	150,024	91,021	68,839	44,866	27,817	16,729	6,971	4,535	2,920	1,600	597	60
2	Maine (counties)[1]	458	475	...	...	...	...	...	...	...	...	...	...	...	...	...	...
3	New Hampshire	541	654	600	550	500	200	170	150	130	100	75	65	50	40	30	...
4	Vermont	50	25	...	...	...	...	...	...	...	...	...	...	...	...	...	...
6	Massachusetts[1]	4,822	4,754	4,866	4,075	3,035	2,780	2,150	1,310	800	400	170	160	422	295	150	...
7	Rhode Island	[3]2,671	3,761	3,468	3,347	2,408	1,648	543	375	300	250	175	115	65	25	...	...
8	Connecticut	[3]5,885	5,698	3,783	3,010	2,598	1,490	1,093	750	450	200	50	35	25	20	15	...
9	New York	21,054	19,112	16,340	11,014	8,996	6,956	5,740	2,811	2,256	1,670	1,200	690	600	500	232	10
10	New Jersey	10,460	8,220	6,567	5,354	4,366	3,008	2,385	1,332	840	450	200	60	...	...	...	...
11	Pennsylvania	7,855	5,761	4,409	2,872	2,055	1,241	2,000	1,575	430	270	25	...	...	...	...	...
12	Delaware	2,996	1,836	1,733	1,496	1,035	478	700	500	135	82	55	40	30	15	...	...
13	Maryland	80,515	63,818	49,004	43,450	24,031	17,220	12,499	7,945	3,227	2,162	1,611	1,190	758	300	20	...
14	Virginia	220,582	187,605	140,570	101,452	60,000	30,000	26,559	23,118	16,390	9,345	3,000	2,000	950	405	150	50
15	North Carolina	91,000	69,600	33,554	19,800	11,000	6,000	3,000	900	415	300	210	150	20	...	...	...
16	South Carolina	97,000	75,178	57,334	39,000	30,000	20,000	12,000	4,100	2,444	1,500	200	30	...	...	...	...
17	Georgia	20,831	10,625	3,578	1,000	...	...	...	...	...	...	...	...	...	...	...	...
18	Kentucky	7,200	2,500	...	...	...	...	...	...	...	...	...	...	...	...	...	...
19	Tennessee	1,500	200	...	...	...	...	...	...	...	...	...	...	...	...	...	...

Series No.	Colony	1620	1610
	WHITE AND NEGRO		
5	Plymouth	102	...
14	Virginia	[4]2,200	350

[1] For 1660–1760, Maine Counties included with Massachusetts.
[2] Plymouth became a part of the Province of Massachusetts in 1691.
[3] Includes some Indians.
[4] Includes 20 Negroes.

SOURCE: United States Bureau of the Census, *Historical Statistics of the United States, Colonial Times to 1957* (Washington, D.C., 1960), p. 756.

APPENDIX B

Population of Eighteenth-Century American Towns

	Philadelphia	*New York*	*Boston*	*Newport*	*Charleston*	*Baltimore*
			(1. Bridenbaugh)			
1680	0	3,200	4,500	2,500	700	0
1685	2,500	—	—	—	900	0
1690	4,000	3,900	7,000	2,600	1,100	0
1700	5,000	5,000	6,700	2,600	2,000	0
1710	6,500	5,700	9,000	2,800	3,000	0
1720	10,000	7,000	12,000	3,800	3,500	0
1730	11,500	*8,622*	13,000	*4,640*	4,500	—
1740	—	—	*17,000*	—	—	—
1742	13,000	11,000	*16,258*	6,200	6,800	—
1760	23,750	18,000	*15,631*	7,500	8,000	—
1775	40,000	25,000	16,000	11,000	12,000	*5,934*
			(2. Rossiter)			
1700	4,400	ca. 4,900	6,700	—	—	0
1710	—	5,840 (1712)	9,000	*2,203* (1708)	—	0
1720	—	7,248 (1723)	11,000	—	—	0
1730	8,500	8,500	13,000	*4,640*	—	—
1740	10,500	11,000	17,000	—	—	—
1750	13,400	11,300	15,731	*6,508* (1748)	—	—
1760	18,756	14,000	15,631	*6,753* (1755)	8,000	—
1770	28,000	21,000	15,520	9,000	10,863	—
ca. 1775	34,400	—	—	9,209 (1774)	12,000 (1773)	5,934
1780	30,000	18,000	10,000	5,530 (1782)	10,000	8,000
1790	*42,444*	*33,131*	*18,038*	*6,716*	*16,359*	*13,503*

(3. Population of other towns)

	Bridenbaugh	*1790 census*
New Haven, Conn. (1771)	*8,295*	*4,487*
Norwich, Conn. (1774)	*7,032*	—
Norfolk, Va. (1775)	ca. 6,250	*2,959*
New London, Conn. (1774)	*5,366*	—
Salem, Mass. (1776)	5,337	*7,921*
Lancaster, Pa. (1776)	ca. 5–6,000	*3,762*
Hartford, Conn. (1774)	4,881	*4,072*

	Bridenbaugh	*1790 census*
Middletown, Conn. (1775)	4,680	*5,298*
Portsmouth, N.H. (1775)	4,590	*4,720*
Marblehead, Mass. (1776)	4,386	*5,661*
Providence, R.I. (1774)	4,361	*6,380*
Albany, N.Y. (1776)	ca. 4,000	*3,498*
Annapolis, Md. (1775)	3,700	—
Savannah, Ga. (1771)	ca. 3,200	—

SOURCES: Bridenbaugh, *Cities in the Wilderness*, pp. 6, 143, 303; *idem*, *Cities in Revolt*, pp. 5, 216–217; Rossiter, *Century of Population Growth*, pp. 11, 78; *Return of the whole number of persons within the . . . United States* (Philadelphia, 1791), pp. 12, 23–24, 34, 37, 39, 45, 47, 50. For 1790, the last publica-
188 tion differs from Rossiter in giving 42,520 for Philadelphia and 32,328 for New York. Census-type data shown in italics; estimates in roman face.

APPENDIX C

A Sectoral Analysis of the [Tax-Assessed] Population of Boston (1790) and Philadelphia (1774, 1780–1783)

	Boston (1790)	*Philadelphia (1774)*	*Philadelphia (1780–1783)*
I. Government	68 (2.75%)	58 (1.53%)	93 (2.85%)
A. Foreign diplomats	—	—	3
B. Federal or congressional	11	—	6+
C. State or provincial	13	23	16+
D. Local and law enforcement	44	34	15+
E. "Esquires" unidentified	—	—	34
F. Military	—	1	19
II. Service sector	1115 (45.01%)	1856 (48.93%)	1608 (49.29%)
A. Professional	102 (4.12%)	129 (3.4%)	94 (2.88%)
1. apothecary, druggist	17	10	10
2. architect	1	—	—
3. dentist	1	—	—
4. doctor, physician	26	38	41
4a. surgeon	—	2	2
4b. midwife	—	1	—
5. lawyer, attorney, conveyancer	21	17	13
5a. notary public	—	4	2

	Boston (*1790*)	*Philadelphia* (*1774*)	*Philadelphia* (*1780–1783*)	
6. minister	20	13	8	
7. schoolmaster	16	43	14	
7a. schoolmistress	—	—	1	
8. surveyor	—	1	3	
B. Retailers and local wholesalers, etc.	243 (9.81%)	301 (7.94%)	336 (10.3%)	
1. auctioneer, vendue cryer	7	7	1	
2. bookseller	2	2	2	
3. cyderman, cider cooper	—	1	1	189
4. grocer	33	17	93	
5. hardware dealer, ironmonger, iron merchant	12	1	8	
6. hosier	—	—	6	
7. jeweler	3	3	2	
8. lemon dealer, lime-seller	10	1	1	
9. lumber merchant, board merchant	5	5	14	
10. milkman	—	11	—	
11. oysterman	—	1	1	
12. peddler, huckster	10	39	8	
13. retailer, shopkeeper, storekeeper	133	195	153	
14. shoe dealer	6	—	—	
15. slop-shop keeper	4	—	—	
16. stationer	5	—	5	
17. tallow chandler	—	11	8	
18. trader, dealer, jobber	13	2	32	
18a. horsedealer	—	1	—	
19. wine cooper, liquor seller	—	1	1	
19a. meadseller	—	3	—	
C. "Retail" crafts	201 (8.11%)	495 (13.05%)	446 (13.67%)	
1. bacon smoker	1	—	—	
2. baker, biscuit baker	64	124	98	
2a. gingerbread baker, pastry cook	2	1	—	
3. butcher	10	121	89	
4. confectioner	1	1	1	
5. mustardmaker	—	1	—	

	Boston (*1790*)	*Philadelphia* (*1774*)	*Philadelphia* (*1780–1783*)
6. bookbinder	3	9	2
7. furrier	3	—	—
8. tailor	100	190	207
8a. breechesmaker	—	26	17
8b. mantua-maker, muffmaker	—	2	—
9. tobacconist, snuffmaker	17	20	32
D. Building crafts	250 (10.09%)	428 (11.28%)	263 (8.06%)
190 1. carpenters, house carpenters	140	178	133
1a. fence-maker	—	—	2
1b. joiner	5	94	59
2. contractor, bead builder	5	—	2
3. glazier	12	2	1
4. mason, bricklayer	44	70	31
5. millwright	—	—	1
6. painter	34	27	16
7. paver	—	1	2
8. plasterer	—	19	4
9. plumber	—	2	1
10. sawyer, woodsawyer, woodcutter	7	20	5
11. stonecutter, marble quarrier	3	13	4
12. wharfbuilder	—	2	2
E. Travel and transport services	187 (7.55%)	382 (10.07%)	385 (11.8%)
1. blacksmith, smith, farrier	59	125	116
2. carter, cartman, truckman	59	40	49
3. chaise-letter	3	—	—
4. coach-driver, coachman	6	6	5
5. drayman	—	—	2
6. drover	—	1	—
7. hack-driver	7	—	—
8. innkeeper, innholder, boarder-keeper	24	73	92
8a. lodging-house keeper	—	3	2
8b. waiter	—	—	2

	Boston (1790)	*Philadelphia (1774)*	*Philadelphia (1780–1783)*	
9. stable-keeper, livery-stable-keeper	3	2	8	
10. tavern-keeper, taverner, dram shop keeper	26	97	70	
11. waterman, boatman, flatman	—	23	32	
11a. ferryman	—	3	5	
11b. shallopman	—	9	2	
F. Other services	132 (5.33%)	121 (3.19%)	84 (2.58%)	191
1. barber, hairdresser	42	39	41	
2. chimney sweeper	6	1	—	
3. gravedigger	—	2	—	
4. lightman	7	—	—	
5. limner (portrait painter)	—	—	2	
6. musician, fiddler	3	3	3	
6a. dancing master	—	—	2	
7. servant, porter	63	70	35	
7a. overseer	—	2	—	
8. sexton	11	1	1	
9. razor grinder	—	2	—	
10. washerwomen	—	1	—	
III. Industrial	659 (26.6%)	1017 (26.81%)	891 (27.31%)	
A. Textile trades	54 (2.18%)	110 (2.9%)	59 (1.81%)	
1. calico printer	—	—	1	
2. duckcloth maker	24	—	—	
3. dyer, silkdyer, blue dyer	3	10	3	
4. fuller	—	4	—	
5. lacemaker	—	—	1	
6. linen manufacturer, flax dresser	—	2	2	
7. spinner	—	1	—	
8. stocking weaver, stocking knitter, knitter	—	59	17	
9. threadmaker	—	1	—	
10. weaver	3	32	31	
10a. clothier	—	—	1	
11. woolcardmaker, card-maker	24	--	1	
12. woolcomber	—	1	2	

	Boston (*1790*)	*Philadelphia* (*1774*)	*Philadelphia* (*1780–1783*)
B. Leather and fur-using trades	136 (5.49%)	385 (10.15%)	349 (10.7%)
1. currier	—	6	4
2. glover	—	—	1
3. harnessmaker, whipmaker	—	9	4
4. hatter	29	72	57
5. leather dresser, skinner, skindresser	13	30	22
6. leather merchant	—	1	—
7. saddler, saddlemaker	6	32	20
192 8. shoemaker, cordwainer	78	198	206
9. tanner	10	37	35
C. Food and drink processing	59 (2.38%)	56 (1.48%)	35 (1.07%)
1. brewer, beer house	—	19	19
2. chocolate maker	—	3	3
3. distiller	47	17	7
4. miller, bran flourer, flour-maker	4	11	4
5. sugarboiler, refiner, sugarbaker	8	6	2
D. Shipbuilding and fitting crafts	213 (8.6%)	187 (4.93%)	169 (5.18%)
1. blockmaker	16	7	8
2. boatbuilder	—	13	16
3. caulker	14	14	7
4. mastmaker	7	5	2
5. oarmaker	1	—	—
6. pumpmaker	4	2	4
7. rigger	11	4	10
8. ropemaker	42	13	14
9. sailmaker	30	17	15
10. sea cooper	16	—	—
11. shipcarpenter, -joiner, -wright	72	112	93
E. Metal crafts (except blacksmiths)	80 (3.23%)	103 (2.72%)	118 (3.62%)
1. brassfounder, founder	15	4	6
2. bucklemaker, buttonmaker	—	1	2
3. clockmaker	—	8	2

	Boston (1790)	Philadelphia (1774)	Philadelphia (1780–1783)
4. coppersmith	4	9	10
5. cutler	—	10	6
6. file cutter	—	—	1
7. goldsmith	23	7	8
8. gunsmith	1	5	14
9. instrument maker	3	1	1
10. locksmith	—	3	1
11. nailor, nailsmith, nailmaker	—	7	6
12. pewterer	6	3	1
13. plane-maker, sawmaker	—	3	2
14. silversmith	5	15	28
15. tinner, tinker, tinman, whitesmith	15	20	21
16. watchmaker	8	7	8
16a. watchcase maker	—	—	1
F. Furniture trades	35 (1.41%)	34 (0.9%)	39 (1.19%)
1. cabinetmaker	15	—	2
2. carver	4	11	2
3. chairmaker	11	—	19
4. turner	1	17	15
5. upholsterer, upholder	4	6	1
G. Miscellaneous trades	82 (3.31%)	142 (3.74%)	122 (3.74%)
1. brickmaker	—	5	6
2. brushmaker	—	4	7
3. chaisemaker, coachmaker	16	29	13
4. paperstainer, papermaker	3	4	2
5. potter	—	24	23
6. printer, engraver	17	21	21
7. soapboiler, soap chandler	6	2	3
8. whalebonecutter, comb-maker, staysmaker	4	15	14
9. wheelwright	8	20	11
10. other trades	28	18	22
IV. Commerce (maritime) and fisheries	635 (25.64%)	862 (22.73%)	670 (20.9%)
A. Mariners	231 (9.33%)	331 (8.73%)	228 (6.99%)
1. sea captain, master mariner	114	83	71
2. mate	20	3	—
3. pilot	2	22	6
4. sailor, seaman, mariner	58	199	140
5. fisherman	37	24	11

	Boston (*1790*)	*Philadelphia* (*1774*)	*Philadelphia* (*1780–1783*)
B. Merchants and supporting personnel	404 (16.31%)	531 (14.00%)	442 (13.55%)
1. accountant	3	1	—
2. banker	1	—	—
3. broker, scrivener	16	6	10
4. chandler, ship chandler	17	15	13
5. clerk, scribe	66	34	28
6. cooper	70	142	56
7. corn dealer, flour mer-	—	2	3
194 chant/seller			
8. merchant	206	329	331
9. stevedore, trimmer	—	2	—
10. underwriter	1	—	—
11. wharfinger	24	—	1
I–IV TOTAL	2477	3793	3262
V. Unclassified			
A. Agricultural			
1. ditcher	—	1	—
2. farmer, yeoman	—	111	79
3. goat keeper	—	1	—
4. gardner	15	17	4
5. grazier	—	11	9
6. welldigger	—	2	—
B. Laborers (unassignable to sector)	157	614	371
C. Unemployed and retired (including gentlemen)	106	—	68
D. Women head of household without occupation			
1. widows	—	105	266
2. other	—	72	226
E. Males, without stated occupation	—	—	1332
1. married man	—	635	—
2. single man	—	612	—
F. Negro heads of household without stated occupation	—	—	28
G. Illegible and not indicated	—	40	—

APPENDIX D

Three Estimates of the Sectoral Distribution of the Employed Adult Population of New York City, 1746–1795

	Freemen Admitted 1746–1770[a]	*Directory 1790*[b]	*Yellow Fever Deaths, 1795*[c]
Government	0.7%	3.7%	3.49%
Service Sector	46.7%	59.9%	56.59%
Industrial Sector	32.0%	22.9%	16.67%
Maritime-mercantile Sector	20.6%	13.5%	23.26%

[a]"The Burghers of New Amsterdam and the Freemen of New York, 1675–1863," *Collections of the New York Historical Society, XVIII for 1885* (New York, 1886). Cf. Beverly McAnear, "The Place of the Freeman in Old New York," *New York History*, 21 (1940), 418–430.

[b]*The New York Directory and Register for the Year 1790* (New York, 1790): analysis based on 2,000+ names on pp. 1–70.

[c]New York Municipal Archives: MS, "Record of Persons who have died in the City of New York of the putrid bilious or Yellow Fever in 1795 as reported by Health Committee," printed, with the omission of some slaves and foreigners, as "New York Deaths," *New York Genealogical and Biographical Record*, 81 (1950), 146–155, 203–206.

APPENDIX E

A Sectoral Analysis from a Sample of New York City Population, 1795

I. Government		9 (3.49%)
A. Federal	4	
B. State	0	
C. Local	5	
II. Service Sector		146 (56.59%)
A. Professional	10	
B. Retailer	30	
C. Retail crafts	23	
D. Building crafts	39	
E. Travel and transport services	27	
F. Other services	17	
III. Industrial sector		43 (16.67%)
A. Textile	2	
B. Leather and fur trades	17	

C. Food and drink processing 1
D. Shipbuilding 12
E. Metal crafts 4
F. Furniture trades 2
G. Miscellaneous trades 5

IV. Commerce (maritime) and fisheries 60 (23.26%)
A. Mariners, etc. 24
B. Merchants and supporting service 36
I–IV 258 (100%)

V. Other (occupation unknown) 427
A. Men and boys 221
196 B. Women and girls 206

APPENDIX F

Colonial Shipbuilding, 1769–1771

TS=top sail ships, snows, etc.
S+S=sloops and schooners

	1769			*1770*			*1771*		
	TS	*S+S*	*tons*	*TS*	*S+S*	*tons*	*TS*	*S+S*	*tons*
Newfoundland	0	1	30	0	0	0	0	4	50
Canada	0	1	60	0	1	15	4	3	233
Nova Scotia	0	3	110	1	2	200	1	3	140
New Hampshire	16	29	2,452	27	20	3,581	15	40	4,991
Massachusetts	40	97	8,013	31	118	7,274	42	83	7,704
Rhode Island	8	31	1,428	16	49	2,035	15	60	2,148
Connecticut	7	43	1,542	5	41	1,522	7	39	1,483
New York	5	14	955	8	10	960	9	28	1,698
New Jersey	1	3	83	0	0	0	0	2	70
Pennsylvania	14	8	1,469	18	8	2,354	15	6	1,307
Maryland	9	11	1,344	7	10	1,545	10	8	1,645
Virginia	6	21	1,269	6	15	1,105	10	9	1,678
North Carolina	3	9	607	0	5	125	0	8	241
South Carolina	4	8	789	0	3	52	3	4	560
Georgia	0	2	50	0	3	57	2	4	543

SOURCE: John Baker Holroyd, 1st earl of Sheffield, *Observations on the Commerce of the American States*, 6th ed. (London, 1784), p. 96.

APPENDIX G

Annual Averages of Values of American Colonial Exports 1768–1772 (Shepherd est.)

(1) by origin and destination

(in thousands of pounds sterling)

TO:	*Great Britain*	*Ireland*	*S. Europe and Wine Islands*	*West Indies*	*Africa*	TOTAL
FROM:						
Canada, etc.	36.8	4.8	133	12.2	0	186.8
New England	86.8	1.4	66.2	303.4	19.2	477
Middle Colonies	75	54.2	185	244.2	1	559.4
Virginia and Maryland	931.4	30.4	100.4	100	0	1,162.2
Carolina and Georgia	435	1.4	54.6	111.8	0.4	603.2
Florida, Bahamas, and Bermuda	22.6	0	0	3.2	0	25.8
TOTALS	1,587.6	92.2	539.2	774.8	20.6	3,014.4

(2) by commodities

tobacco	£766,000
bread and flour	412,000
rice	312,000
dried fish	287,000
indigo	117,000

SOURCE: adapted from James F. Shepherd, "Commodity Exports," pp. 55–56, 65.

Adolescence in Eighteenth-Century America

N. RAY HINER

Children should be seen and not heard—at least according to the traditional maxim. Unfortunately, in the work of most American historians children and youth are not only silent, they are rarely even seen. Children and youth have been granted little more than cameo roles in the drama of American history. Although a scarcity of sources has contributed to this lack of attention, American historians have too often failed to take children and youth seriously, and this failure has had lamentable consequences. Historians have been unable to grasp the full significance of generational factors in American history; and social and behavioral scientists have thereby been denied an indispensable historical perspective from which to assess the validity and universality of their theories of personality development. Only recently, when, as Leon and Marion Bressler remind us, many young people have made themselves increasingly visible and highly audible, have American historians begun to give more careful attention to this neglected group. However, the appearance of *The History of Childhood Quarterly*, and the publication of a three-volume documentary history of *Childhood and Youth in America*, along with several recent articles and monographs in family and social history, all testify to the growing vitality of the new historiographical interest in childhood and youth in America.[1]

The new history of childhood and youth will no doubt develop in several directions, but one especially promising topic which deserves

more attention from historians is adolescence. In their studies of adolescence, psychologists have generally concentrated on biological and maturational factors and thus tend to stress its near universality as a stage of life.[2] Anthropologists and sociologists, on the other hand, usually argue that the cultural and social conditions of premodern or traditional societies precluded the appearance of adolescence as we know it until very recent times.[3] On the rare occasions when historians have treated this question, they tend to agree with the social scientists and emphasize the historicity and culture-bound nature of adolescence. John Demos probably expressed the prevailing opinion among American historians when in a recent article he (and his wife) declared, "The con- 199
cept of adolescence, as generally understood and applied, did not exist before the last two decades of the nineteenth century."[4] This statement by Demos, a specialist in seventeenth-century family history, has been echoed somewhat by Joseph Kett, who writes primarily on the nineteenth century. According to Kett, "a class of books aimed specifically at youth" did not appear until the nineteenth century. He notes that Cotton Mather published several sermons on the rising generation in the early eighteenth century, but Kett says he was "left with a feeling that Puritans used 'youth' more as a noun than as a concept." The Puritans, declared Kett, "hardly believed that individuals moved through stages of life." Kett doubts that teenagers became "truly conspicuous" in America before the teenage conversions of the Second Great Awakening led to "the emergence of a conviction among evangelicals that adolescence was the ideal time to induce religious conversion."[5]

The importance of the nineteenth century in the development of the modern concept of adolescence cannot be disputed, but do we know enough about the history of childhood and youth to justify such sweeping statements? Can we say with such certainty that nothing like modern adolescence existed before the nineteenth century? Lloyd deMause has pointed out that the notion of youth as a part of the "Ages of Man" concept has existed for centuries, and recent studies such as those by Steven Smith of seventeenth-century England and Natalie Davis' work on sixteenth-century France directly challenge the standard view that adolescence evolved rather late in European history.[6] My own analysis of essays on youth published in New England during the first three decades of the eighteenth century also raises serious questions about the validity of the views expressed by Demos, Kett, and others. Young people were very much on the minds of the adults of New England during this period. Scarcely a year passed that did not bring forth a large number of sermons and essays concerning youth, their behavior, their social and psychological characteristics, and their spiritual needs. The unprecedented quantity and remarkable sophistication of this body of

literature requires a fundamental revision of the belief that adolescence either did not exist or was little noticed or understood in America before the late nineteenth century. Modern adolescence and colonial "youth" are certainly not synonymous, but, as Ross Beales has suggested, their similarities are at least as striking as their differences.[7] If adolescence in the social-psychological sense is "the experience of passing through the unstructured and ill-defined phase that lies between childhood and adulthood,"[8] if it is a period in which a young person struggles to acquire psychological autonomy and self control,[9] and seeks to create a sense of identity within a context of prolonged economic
200 and social dependence,[10] then it existed in early eighteenth-century New England, and it occupied a central place in the thought of those leaders who sought to maintain the efficacy of traditional values in a society undergoing profound social and cultural stress.

When the spiritual leaders of New England surveyed the social and cultural landscape at the beginning of the eighteenth century, they saw an increasingly complex, fluid, heterogeneous, and secular society. By 1700, Boston, the primary mercantile center of New England, possessed the beginnings of what Richard Brown has called the basic characteristics of an urban society: "communication, heterogeneity, cosmopolitanism, and choice."[11] After 1700 Boston's urban character became more pronounced, and during the 1720's a striking increase in crime, violence, economic distress, epidemics, bitter disputes in the press, and defiance of authority forced even Boston's most optimistic citizens to fear for the continued health and stability of their community. Noting the great tension and unrest in Boston during this period, Gerald B. Warden declared that it was "something of a miracle" that no revolution occurred.[12]

Not even the rural communities of New England were able to escape the pressures of social change. By 1700, the stable hierarchical and patriarchical character of the towns of the first two generations was being undermined by the dynamic vicissitudes of an expanding society. The primary culprits in this historical drama seem to have been population growth and migration, the development of a commercialized economy, ecclesiastical disputes, and political factionalism. For whatever reason, by the 1720's life in rural New England was profoundly unsettled and shared to some degree with Boston the effects, if not the characteristics, of a society in the early stages of modernization. Puritan culture was fast becoming Yankee culture.[13]

For anyone seriously concerned with preserving Puritan values, there was real cause for alarm. Many Puritan leaders sensed that they were losing control of their collective spiritual destiny and failing in their traditional mission to maintain a holy commonwealth in New

England. How could New England be protected from the ravages of secularization? How could these trends be stopped or reversed? Like many others in times of social and cultural stress, Puritan leaders looked to their children and youth as both a source of many of their problems as well as the key to their solution. Writing in 1705, Solomon Stoddard explained that although "the example of other neighboring nations, the temptations of wealth," and "the evil opinions" of others had no doubt contributed to the spiritual decline of New England, he was convinced that "the main reason of the degeneracy" was the lack of conversion of the new generation. Increase Mather agreed: nothing would contribute more to the reformation of society than a revival of piety in the 201
rising generation. William Williams concluded that if the people of New England feared the Lord, if they hoped to preserve their society from spiritual destruction, then their faith had to be "transmitted carefully to posterity, and be upheld from generation to generation."[14]

Puritan writers on youth during this period were sensitive to the complex and delicate nature of their situation. They knew the conversion of young people was problematical, and they realized they had to gain a deeper understanding of their youth. Hence, they undertook a comprehensive and systematic analysis of the physical, psychological, social, and spiritual characteristics of youth by (1) searching the scriptures, (2) examining their own experience, and (3) studying the lives of individual young persons. The insights produced by this inquiry were woven into the basic fabric of their essays and sermons on youth. Often addressed to young people, these essays had both didactic and analytic purposes, but the promotion of the spiritual growth and conversion of youth was paramount.[15]

Concern for the conversion of the rising generation was of course not new in New England; for decades Puritan ministers had made it a fundamental theme of their Jeremiads. Yet the statements by Stoddard, Mather, and Williams, and many others were earnest and contained an element of urgency which should not be ignored. As Stoddard pointed out, they could have turned to other equally logical means of explaining and solving their problems. However, by concentrating on the conversion of the rising generation during this critical, transitional stage in New England's development when a wider range of life choices were becoming available to young people, Puritan leaders had perhaps unknowingly placed an enormous amount of psychological power in the hands of their youth. Only young people, it seemed, had the ability to save their communities from corruption; their parents or ministers could not do it; the decision and the power was theirs![16] Thus by simply refusing to act, by choosing not to enter into the difficult, intense, and often painful quest for psychic transformation, the young could assert

their independence from adult authority. There is in fact some evidence that many Puritan children in the seventeenth century had found it difficult if not impossible to experience conversion until after their fathers had died or unless they left home and settled in new communities. As John Murrin has put it, "a son who did not love his father could not easily persuade himself that he loved God." And "dead fathers," he concludes "were easier to love than live ones." In a hierarchical society where even a hint of overt resistance to parental or adult control had often been suppressed, this more subtle, less direct, perhaps unconscious, but quite profound form of resistance must have continued to
202 be very attractive to those young people who harbored conscious or unconscious resentments toward their parents or elders.[17]

If Puritan young people possessed a significant amount of psychological leverage, they also carried an enormous psychological burden. They were reminded incessantly, and in very clear language, that they had not only the power but, more importantly, the responsibility to save their communities from corruption. Benjamin Colman, speaking in 1720, asked a group of young people to remember that

> We have spoken to you in your own languages, to your capacity when babes, and to your ability to receive words in your childhood. And since that you have been charged by parents, by ministers, by guardians, and friends, that you remember and keep in mind what you have learnt of God and your souls. . . . Yea it may be your dying as well as living parents have charged you. . . . They have prayed over you many a time, and you have heard them; they have wept for you and over you, and begged of you, yea entreated you—about your souls and your duty to God, and that you might be blessed of him.

"Will you not obey their voice?," asked Colman. If they did not obey, if they remained unconverted, Colman assured his young audience that they stood condemned as a corrupt, perverse, and ungrateful generation. Better, he warned, if they had been born heathen and never known God.[18] Young people had to realize that they faced a basic choice in their lives: they could become "children of God" or "children of the Devil." No young person could escape this fundamental decision.[19]

It would be easy to assume that the young people of the early eighteenth century did not take this responsibility seriously. But it is possible, even likely, that many unconverted youth experienced a strong sense of conscious or unconscious guilt for their failure. By remaining unconverted they damned themselves to eternal punishment and threatened the spiritual health and safety of their communities. At the very least the intense social and psychological pressure applied to Puritan youth by their parents and ministers must have reinforced a deep ambivalence within them between the urge to submit to adult authority and internalize the traditional values and norms of Puritan culture, and an equally strong temptation to resist this pressure, assert their personal autonomy, and thereby gain a degree of power over those who exercised authority over them.[20]

So ambivalence and choice lay at the very heart of the relationship between Puritan adults and their youth. The writers on youth sensed this, and this awareness permeated their descriptions of the essential character of youth as a stage of life. "The time of youth," wrote Israel Loring in 1718, "is the time of a man's choice."[21] In a more compre- 203
hensive but no less representative statement, Benjamin Colman emphasized the same theme when he spoke to young people in 1720:

> Now O young people is your chusing time, and commonly your fixing time; and as you fix now, it is like to last. Now you commonly chuse your trade; betake yourselves to your business for life, show what you incline to, and how you intend to be employ'd all your days. Now you chuse your master and your education or occupation. And now you dispose of yourself in marriage ordinarily, place your affections, give away your hearts, look out for some companion of life, whose to be as long as you live. And is this indeed the work of your youth.[22]

Colman and his fellow ministers realized that the character of youth as a stage of life was defined in part by the social and cultural context in which it existed. The economic system, the family system, and the educational system converged to force young people to make several very significant decisions regarding their futures. Choice and youth seemed almost synonymous.

In Boston, and by the 1720's even in the towns of New England, the educational and occupational choices available to youth had increased, but the capacity of families or kinship units to guarantee a secure economic and social status for their children had weakened considerably.[23] In 1715, Josiah Franklin found that he could not afford to keep Benjamin, his tenth and youngest son, in the Boston Grammar School, so he enrolled him in George Brownell's school for writing and arithmetic. A year later, at the age of ten, Benjamin's formal education ended, and he was put to work making candles for his father. Benjamin tells us in his autobiography that he was dissatisfied with this arrangement and wanted to go to sea instead. Benjamin notes that his father, fearing that if he did not put him to a "more agreeable" trade that "I should break loose and go to sea, as my brother Josiah had done, . . . sometimes took me to walk with him and see joiners, bricklayers, turners, braziers, etc., at their work that he might observe my inclination and endeavour to fix it

on some trade that would keep me on land." Josiah later placed Benjamin with a cutler for a short time, but decided the fee for the apprenticeship too high. Benjamin was finally "persuaded" at the age of twelve to sign an indenture with his brother to serve as an apprentice printer until he was twenty-one. Five years later, in 1723, he ran away to Philadelphia, and after an adventure in London eventually returned to Philadelphia where he married and settled down to become a successful printer.[24] The experiences of the precocious, venturesome Franklin were certainly not typical, but they do illustrate dramatically the range of vocational and educational choices becoming available to New England young people and the tensions and problems these new alternatives could create in
204 the relationship between parents and children. Basic life choices were becoming more contingent and problematical for the individual, and youth as a stage of life was coming to be characterized by a unique tentative quality.

Furthermore, youth as a stage of life was increasing in length; all of the major indices of maturity during this period show that New England youth entailed a long period of dependence and marginality. Throughout the first half of the eighteenth century, New England's young people were generally converted after marriage, and most delayed their marriage until their middle twenties. Adult legal and political status also came late, and the attainment of complete economic independence occurred even later.[25] J. M. Bumstead's observation concerning youth in Norton, Massachusetts seems applicable to New England as a whole: "The problem was not that upward progress and the achievement of full recognition as an adult member of the community did not come, but rather that a number of interrelated steps were involved in the process. A man was usually in his thirties before everything had fallen into place."[26] Growing up was a slow and difficult process. But contrary to the pattern in most traditional societies, recent studies show that New England young people also experienced expanded vocational choice, greater privacy, increasing rates of literacy, and a widening range of formal educational alternatives.[27] Thus, biologically and intellectually mature young people were expected to accept several years of social and economic dependence even though their awareness of the possibilities for autonomous behavior was growing. Youth was beginning to take on the character of a moratorium with its opportunities for intellectual and psychological growth, and its potential for tension, ambiguity, and uncertainty.

The tentativeness and uncertainty of youth both frightened and encouraged Puritan leaders. If youth was a stage of life when the individual was forced to concentrate on making educational, vocational, and marital choices, it threatened to divert the attention of the young person from his spiritual development. Yet, it also gave the young person more time to work on this problem. So Benjamin Colman asked young people to consider if youth was not above all else the

> time for you to fix too in your general calling, your heavenly calling? Your Father's business and the working out of your salvation? .... You are to chuse for life, and to dispose of yourself for eternity! Whose and where and what you will be! How dreadful is the thot! Dispise heaven and eternal glory? And cast away thyself into the arms of the world, the flesh, and the Devil! And into the flames of Hell forever! God forbid it! Wherefore now in thy chusing time remember thy creator and chuse the ways of God the things that please him.[28] *205*

Colman and his colleagues hoped to persuade young people to place spiritual matters at center stage during this critical period of their lives when they were making many irreversible decisions concerning their identities. Only if they kept their spiritual calling uppermost in their minds could they resist the seductive enticements of a worldly life, realize their full potential as children of God, and protect their community from moral corruption and decay.

Important as they were, the external pressures of vocation, education, and marriage were not the only threats to the spiritual welfare of youth. A far greater danger, the ministers believed, lay deeply embedded in the hearts and souls of the youths themselves. Every person, young and old, bore the mark of original sin, so even "the very best of young people," warned Cotton Mather, "have a corrupt nature in them."[29] Although persons of every age were thought to be naturally corrupt and therefore vulnerable to all the temptations of a sinful life, the writers of this period also believed that each stage of life was characterized more by some sins than others. "The different ages of men," declared Thomas Foxcroft in 1719, "have their divers lusts and various corruptions. The impure streams run in distinct channels agreeing to the differing complexions of men in the several stages of life."[30] Thus "stubborness" and "falsness" were often identified as the special sins of childhood; "ambition" was called "the predominant vice of middle age"; and "covetousness" was described as "the more peculiar lust of old age." The two sins that seemed to "hang upon youth and dogg that season of life more than any other" were "pride" and "sensuality."[31]

Neither pride nor sensuality could claim unanimous support as the most characteristic or dangerous sin of youth. Each offense was thought to be deeply rooted in the basic nature of young people: youthful pride was seen as a fresh reassertion of man's original rebellion against God's authority, and the sensuality of youth was viewed as an outgrowth of man's natural lust for things of the flesh reinforced by the strength and vigor of the young person's maturing faculties. Both sins created major,

almost insurmountable barriers to the conversion of youth, for each was the parent of many other sins. Thus, out of pride grew disobedience, apostasy, rebellion against family government, anger, self-conceit, boasting, sabbath breaking, swaggering and vaporing, scoffing at religion, vain and profane mirth, and extravagant attire, to name a few.[32] According to Thomas Foxcroft, pride caused many youth to become "impatient of family government, and by an affection of lawless liberty, bro't them into snare and ruin."[33] Pride, echoed Daniel Lewes, too often made young people "impatient under restraint, disrespectful to their superiors, and apt to slight the grave and wholesome advice that is
206 given to them by those that will them well. . . ."[34] Joseph Sewall agreed that young persons were "apt to be conceited, and to magnify themselves, to be desirous of vain glory and ambitious of more honor and respect than they deserve." Many young people, he charged, demonstrated this ambition in their "looks, gestures, and carriage," and therefore resembled "the Daughters of Zion," who "were haughty and walked with stretched forth necks."[35] In short, youth were often so "puffed up with pride" that they were unwilling to submit to the will of their earthly or heavenly fathers and therefore unable to begin the painful and humiliating quest for their own regeneration.[36]

Sensuality, the second major sin of youth, spawned its own dangerous offspring: immodest dress, night revels, filthy songs, chambering, tipling, frolicking, wanton dalliances, masturbation, fornication and adultery, among others.[37] Joseph Sewall cautioned a young audience in 1721 that they were likely to have "the highest quest and relish for and the most exquisite sense of carnal pleasure."[38] Daniel Lewes also warned that during youth "sensual pleasures relish well, and the gaities of the world are apt to charm persons in this age, and to make them forget God and the duty which they have unto him.[39] Furthermore, Satan knew of youth's natural sensuality and used it as a snare and trap for their souls.

Sometimes the danger was very close at hand. Cotton Mather was troubled by an apparently increasing auto-eroticism among Puritan youth, and, in 1723, he published one of the first essays on the subject of masturbation.[40] Writing anonymously to "My Son," Mather condemned the "libidinous practices" of those "who do evil with both hands" and "have the cursed way of procuring a discharge, which the God of nature has ordered only to be made in a way which a lawful marriage leads unto." Onanism, warned Mather, could have dreadful consequences: impotence, sterility, or "offspring that shall prove a grief of mind." Mather prescribed several specific antidotes for the young person who had fallen into such a lewd and dangerous habit. Since "Christ and sin will never dwell together," Mather reasoned that one of the most effective things a young person could do to resist such "libidinous tendencies" was to

> Think on a Christ. His glorious person, His natures, His offices, His benefits, His maxims, His patterns, what He has done for His people, and what He will do for them. And if these thoughts are in an ejaculatory way darted up to the heavens, they may still be more effectual to quench the fiery darts of the wicked one, which are fastening upon you.

If the young person nevertheless found himself on "the brink of a precipice, and upon the point of doing what is done by none but the fools of Israel," then Mather advised him to stop and ask himself: "Is not the eye of glorious God upon me!"; "Am I not a spectacle to angels who may be near unto me!" And even if the young person was weak and finally succumbed to his sinful urges, Mather implored him not to despair, but realize that he could with God's help be "finally victorious."[41]

Some Puritan youth were apparently more interested in the genitals of the opposite sex than their own. In 1717, Solomon Stoddard expressed his concern that young men and women were too often in the evenings "in company together, toying and dallying," and "stirring up corruption with one another." There were, he lamented, many "awful instances" where "whoredom" was the result of these "wanton dalliances."[42] Some young people even had the audacity to cite Holy Scripture in support of premarital sexual intercourse. In response to these heretical arguments, Samuel Phillips commented publicly on the meaning of a passage from Paul's First Letter to the Corinthians:

> But if any man think that he behaveth himself uncomely toward his virgin, if she pass the flower of her age, and need so require, let him do what he will, he sinneth not: let them marry.[43]

Phillips insisted that it was absurd and perhaps malicious to suggest, as did some young people, that Paul had granted young couples the liberty "to come together as man and wife before marriage." This interpretation was based on an obvious "misunderstanding of that text." Phillips assured youth that Paul's words were "directed to the father of the virgin, and not to the young man who makes suit of her."[44] Joseph Sewall also warned young people that "for persons that contract an intimate acquaintance with a purpose of marriage to come together before it is consumated" is "not to be accounted a small sin: No! It is a dishonour to God, a scandal to religion. . . ." And it was dangerous![45] All fornicators and adulterers were well advised to heed the admonition offered by Cotton Mather when he described a machine constructed "in the shape of a beautiful woman, and contrived with such exquisite art that it would rise up and embrace the person that approached unto it, and at the same time stab them with a multitude of mortal wounds, when it grasped them in its iron arms." Such a fate, concluded Mather, was the inevitable product of all forms of unchastity.[46]

Thus the Puritan writers considered vigorous sexual drives to be a natural but dangerous feature of their young people's developing personalities which, if uncontrolled, could interrupt or even terminate their spiritual development and undermine the social stability and spiritual health of their communities. Hence they were frightened and appalled by what they believed was a shocking increase in promiscuous behavior
208 among their youth. Their fears were not entirely unfounded. Recent studies by Daniel Smith and Michael Hindus reveal that there was a striking increase in premarital pregnancy in New England during this period. Beginning in the late seventeenth century, premarital pregnancies rose from under ten percent of first births to around thirty percent by the end of the next century. (By the mid-nineteenth century they fell to close to ten percent, only to rise again to around twenty to twenty-five percent by the mid-twentieth century.) This phenomenon may have been the American version of what Edward Shorter has described as a change among the lower classes of Europe from manipulative to expressive sexuality, but Smith prefers to explain it as one product of the special transitional character of eighteenth-century New England. According to Smith, the surge in premarital pregnancies was part of a larger shift from the traditional, well-integrated rural society of the seventeenth century which emphasized external controls, to the dynamic, expanding society of the nineteenth century which depended more on voluntary, internal means to regulate the behavior of its young people. By the eighteenth century, Smith suggests, social and demographic change had weakened parental or communal controls over young people, but the voluntary, internal controls we associate with Victorian morality were not yet effective. Traditional family patterns and relationships were therefore left exposed, and young couples, when faced with parental restraints and the custom of late age for marriages, may have resorted to premarital conception as a weapon to force their parents to consent to the marriage and provide economic support. In this context, then, the sexuality of Puritan youth was not only viewed as a threat to their spiritual development, but had also become an implicit factor in the struggle of the rising generation for greater social and economic autonomy.[47]

In addition to pride, sensuality, and the external pressures of vocation, education, and marriage, the ministers believed that there remained one other important obstacle to the spiritual growth of their young

people. Sociability, a distinctive though not inherently sinful characteristic of youth, when found in concert with pride or sensuality, was thought to make young people highly vulnerable to Satan's effort to gain control over their souls.[48] Warnings against bad company were therefore ubiquitous, and concern about this problem prompted Josiah Smith to urge parents to keep their children and youth at home because, as he said, "the times are so degenerate that 'tis hardly safe to trust them anywhere, from your own inspection and care without danger to their morals."[49] In 1717, Soloman Stoddard decried the tendency of the young to gather together in "the evenings, on wet days, and on public days" to engage in "a great deal of vain worldly, proud discourse, and 209
corrupt communication."[50] Israel Loring was even more adamant. Writing in 1718, he declared,

> When children and young people are suffered to haunt the taverns, get into vile company, rabble up and down in the evening, when they should be at home to attend family worship; in the dark and silent night, when they should be in their beds, when they are let alone to take other sinful courses without check or restraint, they are then on the high road to ruin.[51]

Cotton Mather summed up the feelings of his colleagues on the problem when he wrote: "Man is both a sociable and an imitable creature. Experience of all sorts hath made it a proverb among us: one scabbed sheep will infect a flock." "What then," he asked, "would become of one sheep in a scabbed flock?[52]

What indeed! Mather's own son Increase succumbed to the dangerous infection of evil company. From the beginning, Mather labored diligently to instruct his son in the faith and sought good companions for him, but as early as 1711, when Increase was twelve years of age, Cotton wrote in his diary that he was "full of distress concerning my little son Increase; lest some vicious and wicked lads do corrupt and ensnare him." This fear was apparently justified, for six years later, in 1717, Mather confided to his diary that the evil he had feared had come to pass: "an harlot big with bastard, accuses my poor son Cressy, and layes her belly to him. . . ." Mather confessed he was at a loss to know what to do for "the foolish youth." Cressy continued to disappoint his father and in 1721, Mather exclaimed in sorrow: "My miserable, miserable, miserable son Increase! The wretch has brought himself under public trouble and infamy by bearing a part in a night-riot, with some detestable rakes in the town." Finally in 1724, after continued troubled relations with his son, Mather learned that a ship on which Cressy was returning from a trip to England had sunk and that he had drowned. Perhaps to work through his grief, Mather composed some sermons in

Cressy's memory. In one he included what were supposed to be excerpts from Cressy's private notes concerning the dangers of evil company.[53]

There is more than a little irony in Increase Mather's delinquency, for his father was one of the first New England ministers who sought to use young people's natural sociability as a constructive educational tool. As early as 1694, five years before Increase was born, he gave enthusiastic support to those young people who met "every week, to seek the face, and sing the praise, and repeat the word of God. . . ." He campaigned for the formal establishment of young men's associations for this purpose and published a model charter which could be used as a
210 guide for such groups. This proved to be a popular idea: the number of young men's associations grew rapidly and became an important feature of the religious education of New England youth. Unfortunately, in his son's case, Mather's labors seem to have borne little fruit except to provide evidence for the validity of his own warnings against the serious consequences of misdirected sociability among even the "best" Puritan youth.[54]

Cotton Mather's didactic use of his own son's misfortunes was not so unusual. In fact, the writers on youth during this period rarely missed an opportunity to demonstrate in concrete terms how the special sins and characteristics of youth could endanger their souls. Thus, they often encouraged young people who had been convicted of serious crimes to provide a detailed account of how and why they had arrived at their shameful condition. These accounts were sometimes published and no doubt offered powerful object lessons for those youth who heard or read them. One of the most dramatic—one might even say sensational—accounts was that of Esther Rogers, a twenty-one year old woman who was executed in 1701 for murdering her two illegitimate children at birth.[55] In her autobiographical confession she recalled that she had been apprenticed at thirteen, taught to read, and had learned Cotton's catechism. But she admitted that she was "a careless hearer of sermons," and had failed to keep up her secret prayers. "At about the age of seventeen," she confessed, "I was left to fall into the foul sin of uncleaness, suffering myself to be defiled by a Negro lad living in the same house." After learning she was pregnant, she decided to kill the infant if it were born alive. "Being delivered of a living child," she continued, "I used means presently to stop the breath of it, and kept it hid in an upper room till the darkness of night gave advantage for a private burial in the garden."

Esther claimed this was all accomplished in secret and that no one, not even the father, knew she had the child. However, in her next sexual adventure she was not so fortunate. After moving to another house, she began to practice her "old trade of running out at nights," and "entertaining" her "sinful companions in the back part of the house." And, she lamented, she fell once more "into the horrible pit . . . of carnal pollution with the Negro man belonging to that house." Again she became pregnant and when the time for birth arrived, she explained: "I went forth to be delivered in the field, and dropping my child by the side of a little pond (whether alive or still born I cannot tell) I covered it with dirt and snow and speedily returned home again." This time, however, she was suspected and questioned about her absence, and the following morning the child was discovered by some neighbors and brought before her to her "terrible shame and terror." This tragic story ended on the steps of the ladder to the gallows where Esther turned to the multitude around her, admonished young people to take warning from her example, and urged them to be obedient to their parents, to stay in at nights, and avoid bad company.

Approximately three decades later (1733), another unfortunate young woman, twenty-seven year old Rebekah Chamblit, was executed at Boston for "concealing the birth of her spurious male infant, of which she was delivered when alone . . ., and was afterwards found dead."[56] Although she may have given birth prematurely, Rebekah confessed that she threw the newly born infant into a vault "about two or three minutes after it was born," not knowing whether it was dead or alive. Her autobiographical statement, published as a broadside, also included a brief description of her childhood and youth. She said she had been "very tenderly brought up, and well instructed" in her father's house until she was twelve years old. When about sixteen, she was baptized, but within two years she confessed she was "led away into the sin of uncleaness, from which time I think I may date my ruin for this world." Rebekah also felt obligated to offer some "dying advice" to young people. She said she regretted the lies she had told, the sabbaths she did not keep, the prayers she did not offer, and the religious instruction she did not utilize. She also admonished young people not to be complacent, for hardly a year before, she had felt as "secure" as many of them, but, alas, "lust when it has conceived bringeth forth sin, and sin when it is finished bringeth forth death, it exposes the soul not only to temporal, but to eternal death." If young people were wise, advised Rebekah, they would heed her warnings, immediately "foresake the foolish and live."[57]

The message to be drawn from the lives and deaths of Increase Mather, Esther Rogers, and Rebekah Chamblit was clear: if young people ignored the instruction and authority of their elders and abandoned themselves to a life of pride, sensuality, and evil company, they would face physical or spiritual death, or both. The wages of sin, even for youth, were certain.

Although Puritan ministers spent a great deal of time and energy describing the sins of youth, they by no means ignored their positive qualities or denied their potential for spiritual growth. These writers certainly cannot be accused of ascribing to the modern cult of youth, but they did find many of the characteristics of youth quite attractive and promising. If youth was depicted as "a chusing time" which could lead a person into rebellion, profligacy, and dissoluteness, it was also described as "the choice time," "the flourishing time," "the flower of our time," "the time of pleasures," the time in which "health and strength, and complexion" was "in its verdue," when a person's "faculties and powers" were "lively and vigorous," and when his "capacity to learn"
212 was "in its blooming."[58] In the words of Thomas Foxcroft, youth was the age

> most capable of instruction, most flexible to convictions, most susceptible of impressions. Now the understanding is ordinarily most ready and perceptive, the will most obsequious, the affections and passions most governable, the memory most deeply retentive, and all the faculties of life most apt and able for service and employment. For youth is the age of business (as well as tractableness), the morning of our day, the excellency of our strength, the spring of life, most free and vigorous for labour, dispos'd to action, and admirable at dispatch. Now the faculties of soul and body are in their prime, most capable of bearing the difficulties and doing the duties that attend the work of sanctification. . . .[59]

Samuel Moody agreed with Foxcroft that youth was "the very best season" that a person "can ever have" to begin to come to Christ. Then, he declared, the heart was "most tender, the affections most lively and flowing; the conscience most wakeful and the will most pliable to the motions of the Holy Spirit; which are now most frequent and powerful."[60] In short, the characteristics of youth which if uncontrolled could lead to a life of sin, could if properly directed lead in precisely the opposite direction—to salvation. If young people nurtured the "motions of the Holy Spirit," if they turned their developing, invigorated senses toward God and waited carefully for his instruction and guidance, they would find their quest for spiritual transformation much easier during youth than later in life when they had become hardened sinners. Young people obviously possessed great spiritual potential.

This attitude represented a significant change from the opinion commonly expressed in the seventeenth century that middle age, not youth, was the best time for conversion.[61] By the eighteenth century, ministers had become convinced that if a young person were not converted before he chose his vocation, education, and mate, then he was far more susceptible to the temptations of the secular world. In the words of

William Cooper, a young person who delayed his decision about his spiritual identity had "put that last which should be first."[62] Once spiritual identity was established, however, one could rest assured that a young person would make other decisions wisely and develop his full potential as a person.

So for every Esther Rogers, Rebekah Chamblit, or Increase Mather who failed to realize this great potential there were many others who were converted, who made the right choices, and who made God the guide of their youth. When one of these saintly young people died, it was customary to publish a eulogy which occasionally included extensive excerpts from the diary or spiritual autobiography of the deceased youth. One such youth was John Coney, "a very hopeful and pious young man," who after a brief illness died in 1726 at the age of twenty-five.[63] According to William Cooper, who preached his eulogy, Coney began very early to seek God. Apprenticed at thirteen, by sixteen he had become "deeply convinced that if he did not leave his sins and turn to God, he should not be saved." Then, after a period of unproductive praying and attending to religious duties, he read Mr. Shepard's *Sincere Convert* which brought him to understand that he had been trusting too much in his own works and not enough in Christ.[64] Thereafter religion "became his business"; he chose good companions and he joined a religious society of young men who met "every Lord's Day evening for the exercise of religion." When John was eighteen he made a "solemn profession of religion" and was admitted to Cooper's church. Cooper reported that Coney was a very faithful member: he loved sermons about Christ, and he enjoyed religious conferences, "not only with those of his own age, but with some elder christians that knew and valu'd him." John was also very concerned about the salvation of others, but as Cooper explained, his piety was "unaffected," and he was "not showery in any of this."[65]

Coney was indeed a remarkable young man. During the last five years of his life (beginning during the last year of his apprenticeship), he kept a spiritual diary and also recorded his thoughts on a variety of religious topics. Cooper reprinted long excerpts from these documents in an appendix to his eulogy, and they reveal a young man driven by an intense desire for spiritual growth and a gritty determination to keep his natural but corrupt tendencies under control.[66] At one point John resolved to keep his heart "in an affectionate frame," because he found it "easiest to keep the heart with God, when the natural affections being sanctified are carried out toward God." Yet John knew that these "natural affections" could also turn his attention away from God if not carefully controlled. For that reason he often engaged in private fasting and prayer, and in his diary he recorded his struggle to suppress the anger that rose in his heart against "a person that spoke against me."

He also reminded himself to control his eyes lest they lead him astray, for, as he confessed, "The world is wooing and enticing my heart to draw it from God, and I am sometimes almost overcome." John eventually decided that it was better to stay at home than "to wander abroad at night." After he completed his apprenticeship, and began to think about "the marriage state," John convinced himself that "in all probability it will be considerable time before I shall be settled in a way of business, it may be several years, and for me to keep company with a person so long may have great inconveniences attending it." In any event, he concluded, "I do not look upon myself capable as yet, of
214 making judicious choices; being biased more by fancy than judgement." Coney's remarkable self-discipline contrasted sharply with the sensual abandon of Esther Rogers.

Even so, Coney's struggle for spiritual meaning was not easy. At times he reached heights of religious ecstasy. On January 16, 1722 he recorded in his diary that in his morning prayer he was "serious and affectionate." "O how sweet is such a frame," he exclaimed. But little more than a month later, on February 25, he was depressed, and in "a dull frame." "I fear," he wrote, that "I am losing my first love, and that God's spirit is withdrawing from me, but I desire to return to God as the rest of my soul, in whom alone I find by experience, true solid comfort, delight and satisfaction are to be found." Yet Coney never abandoned his quest for his first love. The last words in his diary were: "But O my God, do thou quicken me!" And according to Cooper, Coney testified on his deathbed that his hope was still built "upon Christ, the Rock of Ages." Cooper doubted it was possible to find a better example of "an improved experienced Christian." Coney's life, declared Cooper, should be "a little glass in which to distinguish between the vital power of religion, and the dead image of it. . . ." To Cooper at least, Coney's life proved that "strict religion" was "possible and pleasant" for young people.[67]

Hardly less inspiring was the life and testimony of Mercy Wheeler.[68] Born in 1706, the fourth of ten children, Mercy was in good health until her twentieth year when she "was taken sick of the burning augue. . . ." By 1727 she was confined to her bed, eventually subsisting almost entirely on a liquid diet. After almost five years, in April, 1732 she regained her lost power of speech and began to praise God and offer advice and counsel to young people. Some of her comments were taken down by Samuel Stearns and printed in 1733 as a pamphlet for youth.[69] Mercy implored those of her generation to remember that "tho' youth be indeed the flower of the age, yet it is the most dangerous season of the mind." She asked them to think of her condition as an example of what could happen to their strength and vigor. Finally, she urged every young person to "run to Christ" and save their souls.

Christ was so "lovely" that Mercy could not find words adequate to describe the great blessings that he could bring to young people.[70]

When Puritan ministers reflected upon the lives of saintly young people such as John Coney and Mercy Wheeler, they became effusively optimistic about the spiritual capabilities of youth. "Lovely, lovely the young people," exclaimed Cotton Mather, "who so love God, and seek him early."[71] Young people did not have to surrender to their naturally corrupt urges; they could with the guidance of the Holy Spirit use their abundant energy to do God's will and thereby become the beautiful persons God had intended. To be sure, the writers of this period were often fearful and ambivalent in their attitudes toward young people— 215
they spent more time describing the sins of youth than listing their virtues, and when they saw the pride, sensuality, and misguided sociability of their youth, they feared for their souls and the fate of their communities. This is hardly surprising, given the unstable social conditions, the didactic purpose of their essays, and the nature of their theology. Youth in their "natural" state were viewed as sinful beings because without Christ they were unfinished, incomplete beings. Young people could never reach their potential unless they confronted their own incompleteness. By forcing youth to look at their sins and reflect on the direction of their lives, the ministers hoped to start young people on this spiritual odyssey. So what appears at first glance to be a pessimistic and morbid preoccupation with the depravity of youth can also be viewed as an important element in an optimistic program to promote their spiritual development. Puritan writers on youth remained hopeful, perhaps unrealistically so.

As we look back to the 1730's, the secularization of New England society and culture appears inevitable, but it did not seem so to these leaders who lived at the time. They continued to hope, and some even believed, that their young people would turn to God, affirm their commitment to the faith of their fathers, and thereby restore the health of their communities. When that happy event occurred, promised Daniel Baker, "then shall our peace be as a river; and then, may we hope that the Lord will return in mercy, and not only grant us a little reviving, but establish us a quiet habitation. . . ."[72] Very soon, many New England young people would indeed embrace their father's religion, and for a brief time during the Great Awakening peace did flow as a river across New England. The spiritual leaders rejoiced; God had blessed their efforts; their young people had come home.[73]

However, contrary to the millennial expectations of the New England clerics, it is doubtful that the Great Awakening wrought any fundamental or long-lasting change in character of youth as a stage of life in New England. We have little if any reason to believe that it caused any permanent alterations in the social, demographic, economic, or political

conditions which might have reduced the period of dependence for young people or made the transition from childhood to adulthood any less difficult. Although the average age of conversion did drop noticeably during the Awakening, it apparently soon reverted to its pre-awakening levels. We also know that although the average age of marriage declined somewhat, it remained relatively high and that both the rate of literacy and premarital pregnancies continued to rise until the end of the century.[74] In other words, the young people of New England were forced to continue to accept a social and economic position which was to some extent inconsistent with their intellectual and sexual maturity. When a New England child reached puberty, he still faced an ex-
216 tended period of marginality and dependence before he would be allowed to assume the role of an adult. And even if he were converted before he chose his vocation or mate, the experience of John Coney suggests that these years were not necessarily free of uncertainty, ambivalence, or even conflict. Early eighteenth-century New England was clearly not an adolescent-free society in which the "coming of age" coincided with an individual's assumption of work and family responsibilities.

On the other hand, there are important differences between New England youth and modern adolescence. If choice was characteristic of New England youth, the enormous scope and complexity of industrialized society has made it an omnipresent feature of modern life; what must have been a challenging task for New England youth, has become a confusing burden for modern adolescents who must find their way through a bewildering maze of educational and vocational alternatives before they attain adulthood.[75] And if New England youth were able on occasion to band together and escape the immediate supervision of their elders, the adolescent peer group of today has become a subculture which both insulates young people from the intrusion of adults and at times protects them from an awareness of their own marginality and redundancy.[76] In addition, New England young people, unlike modern youth, never developed an articulated self-consciousness; nor did they ever become so alienated from traditional values that they became openly rebellious, although in at least one instance, they may have come close.

In 1715 John Tufts, a young Harvard graduate, published a pamphlet calling for the reform of the method of singing in New England churches.[77] Unlike the ordered psalmody of the first generations, by the eighteenth century it had deteriorated to the point that after a tune was "lined out" by an appointed deacon, each person proceeded according to his own time and pitch. The result was a cacophony which could have brought pleasure and spiritual sustenance only to those who were musically deaf or whose aesthetic sense had been dulled by the effects of years of repetition. Tuft's proposal was simple but revolutionary: congregations should sing together according to the tune provided for each psalm. Other ministers, especially younger ones, joined Tufts in his campaign and young people, who were attracted by its novelty, flocked to special classes established to teach "regular singing."[78] Many older people in New England congregations were extremely reluctant to give up their traditional style of singing and they expressed their deep resentment at "being turned out of their old way" just "to gratify the younger generation."[79] Nathaniel Chauncy, a supporter of the new way, reminded these elders that "as old men are not always wise, so young men are not always fools."[80] The bitter dispute over this matter did not end until the late 1720's. The importance of this controversy can be exaggerated, but as Ola Winslow has pointed out, it was "a battle of generations" in which parental authority could be defied.[81] Normally, however, the rebellion of New England youth tended to be less direct, more subtle and individualistic, and therefore at times even more difficult for adults to comprehend than the open defiance of modern adolescents.

Still, the essential characteristics of youth as described by the writers of the early eighteenth century have a familiar ring to students of modern adolescence. Pride, sensuality, sociability, and spiritual promise are nicely paralleled by modern portrayals of youth as defiant, sexually active, peer-oriented, and idealistic; and the delay of consummation of genital maturity may have produced the regressive revival of autoeroticism, grandiosity, and playfulness among New England youth in much the same way that Erik Erikson claims it does in today's young people.[82] Moreover, the basic developmental tasks of adolescence as described by modern psychologists would have been acceptable at least in part to the Puritan analysts: (1) self control (sublimation and neutralization of libidinal and aggressive drives); (2) independence (detachment from infantile object ties); and (3) identity (consolidation and integration of personality, and the organization of behavior into available social roles).[83] The Puritans were no doubt more concerned with the development of self control in their youth than independence, but they would have heartily agreed with Erikson's emphasis on the importance of identity formation, the concomitant danger of identity diffusion, and his contention that the formation of identity and ideology are two indispensable parts of the same process.[84] Finally, the ambivalence which is so characteristic of adult-youth relations today was clearly present in the eighteenth century. Fear and hostility, optimism and love—these are perennial feelings which reverberated between young and old in the eighteenth century as they do today.[85]

But it is not only in their broad outlines that New England youth and contemporary adolescence are similar. They also resemble each

other in many of their more precise features, in the kind of adjustments that specific young people made to this stage of life. The unrestrained impulsivity and poor reality testing of Esther Rogers and Rebekah Chamblit; the delinquency of Increase Mather, the minister's son; the inhibited, perhaps neurotic religiosity of Mercy Wheeler, the ascetic intellectualism and idealism of John Coney, and even the egocentric rationalism of the run-away Benjamin Franklin—all have their counterparts in the adjustment repertoires of modern youth. New England young people masturbated; they engaged in fantasy; they became withdrawn and depressed; they loved and hated their parents; they sought
218 out each other's company as an escape from parental authority and control; they acted out sexually and socially; they employed the full range of classical defenses to control their impulses and prevent regression; but in the end most of them persevered and made the difficult transition from childhood to adulthood with relatively intact, healthy personalities which, like those of young adults today, were neither the exact replicas nor the complete opposites of their parents'.[86]

Thus the standard view that nothing like modern adolescence emerged before the late nineteenth century must be revised. In the unstable social conditions they faced, in their prolonged dependence and marginality, in their psychological characteristics, in their relations with their elders, and in the specific adjustments they made as individuals, the youth of early eighteenth-century New England had a great deal in common with today's adolescents. Did this similarity continue after the Great Awakening through the Revolution and beyond, or was it only the temporary product of the special transitional character of New England between 1700 and 1730? Was the strikingly modern character of youth in early eighteenth-century New England only an aberration which soon disappeared, or did it remain to shape the character of life in revolutionary America? The answer to these questions must await a more comprehensive investigation—an investigation informed by the insights of modern psychology and the new social history and guided by the empathetic conviction that the youth of the past can be heard if we learn how to listen. Only then will youth find their proper place in the history of the eighteenth century.

Ray Hiner is Associate Professor of History and Education at the University of Kansas. He is currently on leave as a Fellow in the Program for Interdisciplinary Studies at the Menninger Foundation where he is studying theories of human development and their implications for the history of childhood and youth.

REFERENCES

The research for this essay was supported in part by grants from the University of Kansas General Research Fund and the National Endowment for the Humanities. I also wish to acknowledge the helpful comments offered by Alan S. Horlick, Paul W. Pruyser, and Irvin A. Rothrock.

1. Leon Bressler and Marion Bressler (eds.), *Youth in American Life* (New York: 1972), p. 2; Robert H. Bremner, et al. (eds.), *Children and Youth in America: A Documentary History*, 3 vols. (Cambridge, Massachusetts: 1970, 1974); and Lloyd deMause, "The History of Childhood: The Basis for Psychohistory," *History of Childhood Quarterly*, I (Summer, 1973), 1-3. For examples of recent family and social history which include discussion of children and youth, see Michael Gordon (ed.), *The American Family in Social-Historical Perspective* (New York: 1973); the Autumn, 1971 issue of *Journal of Interdisciplinary History;* the August, 1973 issue of the *Journal of Marriage and the Family;* and Philip J. Greven, *Four Generations; Population, Land, and Family in Colonial Andover, Massachusetts* (Ithaca: 1970); also see James Axtell, *The School Upon a Hill: Education and Society in Colonial New England* (New Haven: 1974); Ross W. Beales, "Cares for the Rising Generation: Youth and Religion in Colonial New England" (Ph.D. dissertation, University of California, Davis, 1971); Lawrence Cremin, *American Education: The Colonial Experience, 1607-1783* (New York: 1970); John Demos, *A Little Commonwealth: Family Life in Plymouth Colony* (New York: 1970); Lloyd deMause (ed.), *The History of Childhood* (New York: 1974); Oscar Handlin and Mary F. Handlin, *Facing Life: Youth and the Family in American History* (Boston: 1971); Philip J. Greven (ed.), *Child Rearing Concepts: Historical Sources* (Itasca, Illinois: 1973); Wilson Smith (ed.), *Theories of Education in Early America, 1655-1819* (Indianapolis: 1973); and Bernard Wishy, *The Child and the Republic: The Dawn of Modern American Child Nurture* (Philadelphia: 1968). Of course interest in children and youth among American historians is not entirely new. For example of earlier works, see Grace Abbott, *The Child and the State*, 2 vols. (Chicago: 1938); Alice Earle, *Child Life in Colonial Days* (New York: 1899). Sanford Fleming, *Children and Puritanism* (New Haven, 1933); Monica Kiefer, *American Children Through Their Books, 1700-1835* (Philadelphia: 1948); and Edmund S. Morgan, *The Puritan Family* (Boston: 1944).
2. Rolf E. Muuss, *Theories of Adolescence* (second edition; New York: 1968); pp. 36-40; Peter Blos, *On Adolescence: A Psychoanalytic Interpretation* (New York: 1962), p. 9; Norman B. Atkins, "The Oedipus Myth, Adolescence, and the Succession of Generations," *Journal of the American Psychoanalytic Association*, XVIII (October 1970), 860-861. The works of Erik Erikson, Kenneth Keniston, and J. H. van den Berg are obvious exceptions and represent efforts to integrate the perspectives of psychology, social science, and history. See especially Erikson, "Youth: Fidelity and Diversity," *The Challenge of Youth* (Anchor Books edition; Garden City, New York: 1965), 1-28; van den Berg, *The Changing Nature of Man: Introduction to a Historical Psychology* (New York: 1961); and Keniston, "Psychological Development and Historical Change," *Journal of Interdisciplinary History* II (autumn, 1971), 329-345.
3. Muuss, *Theories of Adolescence*, pp. 68-80; John Middleton (ed.), *From Child to Adult: Studies in the Anthropology of Education* (Garden City, New York: 1970), p. xv; Victor Barnouw, *Culture and Personality* (Revised edition; Homewood, Illinois: 1973), 113-127, 129-136; Hans Sebald, *Adolescence: A Sociological Analysis* (New York: 1968), pp. 1-24. S. N. Eisenstadt provides a clear exception to the generalization concerning sociologists; see his *From Generation to Generation* (New York: 1956), pp. 31, 92, 258, 270.
4. John Demos and Virginia Demos, "Adolescence in Historical Perspective," *Journal of Marriage and the Family*, XXXI (November 1969), 332.
5. Joseph Kett, "Adolescence and Youth in Nineteenth-Century America,"

Journal of Interdisciplinary History, II (autumn 1971), 285-290; and his "Growing Up in Rural New England, 1800-1840," *Anonymous Americans: Explorations in Nineteenth-Century Social History*, Tamara K. Hareven, editor (Englewood Cliffs, New Jersey: 1971), pp. 1-16. In the latter essay Kett argues (p. 13) that even though "adolescence as we know it did not exist in 1820, boys did experience an intermediate period between childhood and adulthood" during which they were semi-dependent. In his recent study of colonial education, James Axtell accepts the standard interpretation of the late origins of adolescence with one "major exception." He points to the college students of colonial America who, he says, "were the only adolescents in a culture that did not know adolescence, and the anomaly of their condition created socially disruptive tensions, which were not relieved until they had contributed to the outbreak of revolution and shared in its success." See Axtell, *The School upon a Hill*, p. 202.

220 6. Lloyd deMause, "The Evolution of Childhood," *History of Childhood Quarterly*, I (Spring 1974), 507, 559 (n. 21); Steven R. Smith's two articles: "Religion and the Conception of Youth in Seventeenth-Century England," *History of Childhood Quarterly*, II (Spring 1975), 493-516; "The London Apprentice as Seventeenth-Century Adolescent," *Past and Present*, LXI (November 1973), 149-161; and Natalie Z. Davis, "The Reasons of Misrule: Youth Groups and Charivaris in Sixteenth-Century France," *Past and Present*, L (February 1971), 40-75. For the standard view of the origins of adolescence in Europe, see F. Musgrove, *Youth and the Social Order* (Bloomington, Indiana: 1965), pp. 13, 33-38; and Philippe Aries, *Centuries of Childhood: A Social History of Family Life*, Robert Baldick, trans. (New York: 1962), pp. 25-30.

7. Beales, "Cares for the Rising Generation," pp. 10-23. After an extended discussion of law, catechizing, economic status, and age of marriage, Beales concludes (p. 20) that young people in New England experienced "a prolonged 'adolescence' or 'youth.' "

8. Sebald, *Adolescence*, p. 11; and Eisenstadt, *From Generation to Generation*, pp. XIII-XIV.

9. Edith Jacobson, *The Self and the Object World* (New York: 1964), p. 161; Anna Freud, "Adolescence," *Psychoanalytic Study of the Child*, XIII (1958), 268-274; Ernest Jones, "Some Problems of Adolescence," *Papers on Psycho-Analysis* (Fifth edition; Baltimore: 1948), pp. 399, 400-403; and Alexander Aarons, "Normality and Abnormality in Adolescence," *Psychoanalytic Study of the Child*, XXV (1970), 315-320.

10. Erik Erikson, "The Problem of Ego Identity," *Identity and Anxiety*, Maurice Stein, et al., editors (New York: 1960), p. 52; Blos, *Adolescence*, p. 12; and Musgrove, *Youth and the Social Order*, pp. xvii-xviii.

11. Richard D. Brown, "The Emergence of Urban Society in Rural Massachusetts, 1760-1820," *Journal of American History*, LXI (June 1974), p. 31; and Carl Bridenbaugh, *Cities in the Wilderness: The First Century of Urban Life in America, 1625-1742* (New York: 1938, 1964), p. 139.

12. Gerald B. Warden, *Boston: 1689-1776* (Boston: 1970), pp. 80-101; Bridenbaugh, *Cities in the Wilderness*, pp. 140-300; Gary B. Nash, "The Transformation of Urban Politics, 1700-1765," *Journal of American History* LX (December 1973), 612-624; and H. B. Parkes, "New England in the Seventeen-Thirties," *New England Quarterly*, III (July 1930), 397-419.

13. Richard L. Bushman, *From Puritan to Yankee: Character and Social Order in Connecticut, 1690-1765* (New York: 1970); Kenneth Lockridge, *A New England Town: The First Hundred Years* (New York: 1970); James A. Henretta, *The Evolution of American Society, 1700-1815: An Interdisciplinary Analysis* (Lexington, Massachusetts: 1973), pp. 36-37; Edward Cook, "Changing Values and Behavior in Dedham, Massachusetts, 1700 to 1775," *William and Mary Quarterly*, XXVII (October 1970), 578-580; J. M. Bumsted, "A Caution to Erring Christians: Ecclesiastical Disorder on Cape Cod, 1717 to 1738," *William and Mary Quarterly*, XXVIII (July 1971), 411-438; Timothy H. Breen and Stephen Foster, "The Puritans Greatest Achievement: A Study

of Social Cohesion in Seventeenth-Century Massachusetts," *Journal of American History*, LX (June 1973), 20-22; Greven, *Four Generations*, pp. 103-172; and Jack P. Greene, "Autonomy and Stability: New England and the British Colonial Experience in Early Modern America," *Journal of Social History*, VII (Winter 1974), 187-192.

14. Solomon Stoddard, *The Danger of Speedy Degeneracy* (Boston: 1705), pp. 6-7; Increase Mather, in the preface to *A Course of Sermons on Early Piety* (Boston: 1721), pp. i-v; William Williams, *The Duty of Parents to Transmit Religion to Their Children* (Boston: 1721), p. iii. Also see Benjamin Wadsworth, "A Sermon Sitting Forth the Nature of Early Piety," *A Course of Sermons on Early Piety*, pp. 29-30; and Cotton Mather, "What the Pious Parent Wishes For," in *Ibid.*, p. 2.
15. William Cooper, *Serious Exhortations Address'd to Young Men* (Boston: 1732), i-ii. Also see Greven, *Child Rearing Concepts*, pp. 5-6; and Smith, *Theories of Education in Early America*, pp. xiv-xvi.

16. Thomas Foxcroft, "Exhortations and Directions to Young People," *A Course of Sermons on Early Piety*, p. 21; Solomon Stoddard, *The Danger of a Speedy Degeneracy*, pp. 23-26; and Joseph Sewall, "Sober-mindedness Explain'd as a Necessary Part of Early Piety," *A Course of Sermons on Early Piety*, pp. 5-6, 25-26.
17. John Murrin, Review essay in *History and Theory*, XI (1972), pp. 237-238.
18. Benjamin Colman, *Early Piety Again Inculcated* (Boston: 1720), pp. 35-36. Also see Wadsworth, "A Sermon Setting Forth the Nature of Early Piety," p. 29; Daniel Lewes, *The Joy of Children Walking in Truth* (Boston: 1723), pp. 12-17; and Benjamin Colman, "The Nature of Early Piety as It Respects Men," *A Course of Sermons on Early Piety*, pp. 23-24.
19. [Cotton Mather], *Youth Under Good Conduct* (Boston: 1704), p. 9.
20. John W. Walzer believes that ambivalence characterized parent-child relations throughout the eighteenth century. See his "A Period of Ambivalence: Eighteenth Century American Childhood," *The History of Childhood*, pp. 351-375. Also see Bushman, *From Puritan to Yankee*, p. 187; John Demos, "Underlying Themes in the Witchcraft of Seventeenth-Century New England," *American Historical Review*, LXXV (June 1970), 1325-1326; and Blos, *Adolescence*, pp. 109-110.
21. Israel Loring, *Duty and Interests of Young Persons* (Boston: 1718), p. 18.
22. Benjamin Colman, *Early Piety Again Inculcated*, pp. 32-34. For similar statements, see William Cooper, *Serious Exhortations Address'd to Young Men*, pp. 20-21; and [Cotton Mather], *Cares About Nurseries* (Boston: 1702), pp. 52-53, 72, 81-88. Excerpts from Mather's essay are reprinted in Wilson Smith, *Theories of Education in Early America*, pp. 11-24. For briefer characterizations of youth during this period, see William Williams, *The Obligations of Baptism and the Duty of Young Persons to Recognize Them*, p. 2 (This sermon is bound with Williams' *The Duty of Parents to Transmit Religion to Their Children* and has separate pagination); William Cooper, *The Service of God Recommended to the Choice of Young People* (Boston: 1726), p. 24; and Samuel Wigglesworth, *The Pleasures of Religion* (Boston: 1728), p. 30.
23. Henretta, *The Evolution of American Society*, pp. 25-31; Greene, "Autonomy and Stability," pp. 187-192.
24. L. Jesse Lemisch (ed.), *Benjamin Franklin: The Autobiography and Other Writings* (New York: 1961), pp. 22-27, 33-39, 63, 81.
25. Daniel Scott Smith, "The Demographic History of Colonial New England," *The American Family in Social-Historical Perspective*, p. 406; Robert Higgs and H. Louis Stettler, III, "Colonial New England Demography: A Sampling Approach," *William and Mary Quarterly*, XXVII (April 1970), 284-285; Henretta, *The Evolution of American Society*, pp. 12, 25; Greven, *Four Generations*, pp. 117-121, 208-209; Beales, "Cares for the Rising Generation," pp. 12-19, 32-57; and Gerald F. Moran, "Conditions of Religious Conversions in the First Society of Norwich, Connecticut, 1718-1744," *Journal of Social History*, V (Spring, 1972), 332-338.

26. J. M. Bumsted, "Religion, Finance and Democracy in Massachusetts: The Town of Norton as a Case Study," *Journal of American History*, LVII (March 1971), p. 824.
27. David H. Flaherty, *Privacy in Colonial New England* (Charlottesville: 1967, 1972), pp. 17-18, 244-245; Kenneth A. Lockridge, *Literacy in Colonial New England* (New York: 1974), pp. 13, 21, 27, 57, 98; John Teaford, "The Transformation of Massachusetts Education, 1670-1780," *History of Education Quarterly*, X (Fall 1970), pp. 298-301; and Cremin, *American Education: The Colonial Experience, 1607-1783*, pp. 519-520.
28. Benjamin Colman, *Early Piety Again Inculcated*, pp. 33-34. Also see William Cooper, *Serious Exhortations Address'd to Young Men;* Josiah Smith, *The Young Man Warn'd* (Boston: 1730); and Daniel Lewes two essays: *The Sins of Youth Remembered* (Boston: 1725), pp. 15-16; and *The Joy of Children Walking in Truth*, p. 25.

222 29. [Cotton Mather], *The Young Man's Preservative* (Boston: 1701), p. 4. Similar statements can be found inSolomon Stoddard, *The Danger of Speedy Degeneracy*, p. 10; Samuel Moody, *The Vain Youth Summoned* (Boston: 1707), p. 4; and Joseph Belcher, *Two Sermons Preached in Dedham* (Boston: 1710), pp. 15-19.
30. Thomas Foxcroft, *Cleansing Our Way in Youth* (Boston: 1719), p. 16.
31. *Ibid.*, Samuel Moody, *The Vain Youth Summoned*, p. 4; John Rogers, *Death the Certain Wages of Sin* (Boston: 1711); Joseph Belcher, *Two Sermons Preached in Dedham*, p. 18; Daniel Lewes, *The Sins of Youth*, pp. 6-8; James Allin, *Evangelical Obedience, the Way to Eternal Life* (Boston: 1731), p. 18; and William Cooper, *Serious Exhortations Address'd to Young Men*, pp. 18-19. For a bibliography of the "Ages of Man," see Frank Boll, *Die Lebensalter: Ein Beitrag zur antiken Ethologie und zur Geschichte der Zahlen* (Leipzig and Berlin: 1913), cited in deMause, "The Evolution of Childhood," p. 559 (n. 21). Philippe Aries includes a discussion of the "Ages of Man" in his *Centuries of Childhood* (pp. 18-25), but after noting that the French language of the sixteenth century had names for only three of the seven ages discussed in Latin treatises, he concludes, "People had no idea of what we call adolescence, and the idea was a long time in taking shape" (pp. 25-30).
32. The literature describing these sins is too voluminous to cite here. For representative examples see John Rogers, *Death the Certain Wages of Sin*, pp. 97-104; [Cotton Mather], *Nicetas* (Boston: 1705), pp. 34-37; Samuel Moody, *The Vain Youth Summoned*, pp. 4-6; Solomon Stoddard, *Three Sermons Lately Preached at Boston* (Boston: 1717), pp. 104-108; Daniel Lewes, *The Sins of Youth*, pp. 6-9; Samuel Phillips, *Advice to a Child* (Boston: 1729), pp. 7-49; and Joseph Sewall, "Sobermindedness Explained as a Necessary Part of Early Piety," pp. 6-20.
33. Thomas Foxcroft, *A Lesson of Caution to Young Sinners* (Boston: 1733), p. 35.
34. Daniel Lewes, *The Sins of Youth*, p. 6.
35. Joseph Sewall, "Sober-mindedness Explain'd as a Necessary Part of Early Piety," p. 7.
36. Samuel Phillips, *Advice to a Child*, p. 28. Also see William Cooper, *How and Why Young People Should Cleanse Their Way* (Boston: 1716), pp. 10-11, 27-28; and Benjamin Wadsworth, *Exhortations to Early Piety* (Boston: 1702), p. 7.
37. See the references in note 31.
38. Joseph Sewall, "Sober-mindedness Explain'd as a Necessary Part of Early Piety," p. 11.
39. Daniel Lewes, *The Joy of Children Walking in Truth*, p. 25.
40. [Cotton Mather], *The Pure Nazarite* (Boston: 1723). Mather's essay was the first published on this subject by an American author. There was, however, an anonymous pamphlet published in Europe in the 1720's or earlier and reprinted in Boston for American readers. See *Onania; or the Heinous Sin* (Tenth edition; Boston: 1724). Mather may have read this pamphlet before he wrote his own, but there is little internal evidence that it directly influenced him. Mather certainly did not see fit to repeat one of the suggested remedies mentioned in the European publication: ". . . when all else fails,

and you have even had emissions in your sleep, you should tie a string around your neck and the other end about the neck of your penis, which when an erection happens, will timely awaken you and put an effectual stop to the seminal emission." (p. 44). For a discussion of the early scientific literature on masturbation, see E. H. Hare, "Masturbatory Insanity: The History of an Idea," *The Journal of Mental Science* (January 1962), 1-25.

41. Mather, *The Pure Nazarite*, pp. 2, 8, 10-16. For modern discussions of Masturbation, see Jeanne Lampl-DeGroot, "On Masturbation and Its Influence on General Development," *Psychoanalytic Study of the Child*, V (1950), 153-174; Steve M. Dranoff, "Masturbation and the Male Adolescent," *Adolescence*, IX (Summer, 1974), 169-176; and Blos, *Adolescence*, pp. 159-169. Blos views masturbation as a normal part of adolescent development, but also stresses that "by its very nature" it is "defensive" and "tends to act against progressive development and to affirm regressive and fixating influences." (pp. 167-168). In his review of recent literature, 223
Dranoff also stresses the normality of adolescent masturbation, but warns that it "should be realized that overindulgence in masturbation and its accompanying fantasy cause a preoccupation with sex in the adolescent. This can result in avoiding and rejecting personal relationships, thus leading to isolation. In this way, overindulgence certainly can stunt normal adolescent development." (p. 174).
42. Solomon Stoddard, *Three Sermons Lately Preached at Boston*, pp. 106-107.
43. 1 Corinthians 7:37 (King James Version).
44. Samuel Phillips, *Advice to a Child*, p. 42. Modern biblical scholars do not agree that the meaning of this passage is as clear as Phillips believed. See Charles M. Laymon (ed.), *The Interpreters One-Volume Commentary on the Bible* (Nashville: 1971), pp. 802-803.
45. Joseph Sewall, "Sober-mindedness Explain'd as Necessary for Early Piety," p. 19.
46. Cotton Mather, *Nicetas*, pp. 40-41; and Daniel Lewes, *The Joy of Children Walking in Truth*, p. 25.
47. It should be noted that the increases in premarital pregnancy described by Smith, Hindus, and Shorter may have reflected at least in part a decline in infanticide. However, there is little reliable evidence concerning changes in the incidence of infanticide in colonial America, so this issue must remain unresolved, at least for the present. See Daniel Scott Smith and Michael S. Hindus, "Premarital Pregnancy in America, 1640-1971: An Overview and Interpretation," *Journal of Interdisciplinary History*, (Spring 1975), 537-538, 548-560; and Edward Shorter, "Illegitimacy, Sexual Revolution, and Social Change," *The American Family in Social-Historical Perspective*, pp. 296-320; and Daniel Scott Smith, "Parental Power and Marriage Patterns: An Analysis of Historical Trends in Hingham, Massachusetts," *Journal of Marriage and the Family*, XXXV (August 1973), 419-428
48. Cotton Mather, *Nicetas*, p. 34; Samuel Moody, *The Vain Youth Summoned*, p. 54; Solomon Stoddard, *Three Sermons Lately Preached at Boston*, pp. 104-107; Thomas Foxcroft, "Exhortations and Directions to Young People," *A Course of Sermons on Early Piety*, pp. 40-41; and Samuel Phillips, *Advice to a Child*, p. 14.
49. Josiah Smith, *The Young Man Warn'd*, p. 28.
50. Soloman Stoddard, *Three Sermons Lately Preached at Boston*, pp. 105-107.
51. Israel Loring, "Duty and Interest of Young Persons," p. 24.
52. Cotton Mather, *The Young Man's Preservative*, p. 28.
53. Worthington Chauncy Ford (ed.), *The Diary of Cotton Mather* (repr. New York: n.d.), Vol. II, pp. 76, 92, 195, 212-213, 447, 484, 611, 753, *et passim;* Kenneth Silverman (comp.), *Selected Letters of Cotton Mather* (Baton Rouge: 1971), p. 378; and Cotton Mather, *Words of Understanding* (Boston: 1724), pp. 98-103. Also see Elizabeth Bancroft Schlesinger, "Cotton Mather and His Children," *William and Mary Quarterly*, X (April 1953), 181-189.
54. Cotton Mather, *Early Religion Urged* (Boston: 1694), pp. 30-31, 115-117. An extraordinarily large number of sermons were preached before meetings of young persons and later published. For examples, see Cotton Mather, *The*

Young Man's Preservative; Joseph Belcher, *Two Sermons Preached in Dedham;* Jeremiah Shepard, *Early Offerings Best Accepted* (Boston: 1712); William Cooper, *How and Why Young People Should Cleanse Their Way;* John Webb, *The Young Man's Duty Explained* (Boston: 1718); Thomas Foxcroft, *Cleansing Our Way in Youth;* Daniel Lewes, *The Sins of Youth;* Benjamin Colman, *The Duty of Young People to Give Their Hearts Unto God* (Boston: 1728); Samuel Wigglesworth, *The Pleasures of Religion;* and John Cotton, *The Ministers of Christ Should Be Speedy and Earnest in Speaking to Young People* (Boston: 1729). Also see Sanford Fleming, *Children and Puritans*, pp. 146-148.

55. See the preface to John Rogers, *Death the Certain Wages of Sin.* All the statements by Esther Rogers cited below are taken from her confession and autobiographical statement which is included in the essay by John Rogers (pp. 121-147).

56. *The Declaration, Dying Warning, and Advice of Rebekah Chamblit* (Boston:
224 1733). All of the statements by Rebekah Chamblit cited below are taken from this broadside.

57. The history of infanticide is discussed in Joseph E. Illick, "Child-Rearing in Seventeenth-Century England and America," *The History of Childhood*, pp. 303-350; William Langer, "Infanticide: A Historical Survey," *History of Childhood Quarterly*, I (Winter, 1973), 353-366; and Lloyd deMause, "The Evolution of Childhood," *History of Childhood Quarterly*, I (Spring, 1974), 527-534.

58. Benjamin Wadsworth, *Exhortations to Early Piety*, pp. 5-6; Cotton Mather, *Vita Brevis* (Boston: 1714), pp. 11-13; Israel Loring, *Duty and Interest of Young Persons*, p. 11; John Webb, *The Young Man's Duty Explained*, pp. 23-30; Daniel Lewes, *The Sins of Youth*, pp. 11-13; Thomas Prince, *Morning Health* (Boston: 1727), p. 6; and Samuel Wigglesworth, *The Pleasures of Religion*, p. 2.

59. Thomas Foxcroft, *Cleansing Our Way in Youth*, p. 27; and his "Exhortations and Directions to Young People," *A Course of Sermons on Early Piety*, pp. 14-16.

60. Samuel Moody, *The Vain Youth Summoned*, p. 29; and Israel Loring, *Duty and Interest of Young Persons*, pp. 12-15.

61. Ross Beales, "Cares for the Rising Generation," pp. 32-57; and Edmund S. Morgan, *Visible Saints: The History of a Puritan Idea* (Ithaca, New York: 1963, 1965), p. 127.

62. William Cooper, *The Service of God Recommended to the Choice of Young People* (Boston: 1726), p. 24.

63. *Ibid.*, p. 26.

64. Thomas Shepard, *The Sincere Convert* (Cambridge: 1664).

65. Cooper, *The Service of God Recommended*, pp. 26-31.

66. All of the statements by Coney cited below are from the appendix to *Ibid.*, pp. 6-7, 13-14, 17-19, 30-39.

67. Cooper, *The Service of God Recommended*, pp. 31-33; and Cooper's conclusion to the appendix, pp. 82-84.

68. Mercy Wheeler, *Address to Young People* (Boston: 1733).

69. See Stearn's preface to *Ibid.*

70. *Address to Young People*, pp. 1-5, 9. The lives of other saintly young people are described in [Cotton Mather], *Memorials of Early Piety* (Boston: 1711); Benjamin Colman, *A Devout Contemplation on the Meaning of Divine Providence in the Early Death of Pious and Lovely Children* (Boston: 1714); and Cotton Mather, *Vita Brevis*, pp. 30-31.

71. [Cotton Mather], *Youth Under A Good Conduct* (Boston: 1704), p. 13.

72. Daniel Baker, *Two Sermons* (Boston: 1728), p. 88.

73. William Williams, *The Duty and Interest of a People* (Boston: 1736); Edwin Scott Gaustad, *The Great Awakening in New England* (Chicago: 1957, 1968); and Beales, "Cares for the Rising Generation," pp. 92-122.

74. *Ibid.*, p. 121; J. M. Bumstead, "Religion, Finance, and Democracy in Massachusetts," p. 828; Gerald Moran, "Conditions of Religious Conversions in the

First Society of Norwich, Connecticut, 1718-1744," p. 333; Daniel Smith, "The Demographic History of Colonial New England," p. 406; James Walsh, "The Great Awakening in the First Congregational Church of Woodburg, Connecticut," *William and Mary Quarterly*, XXVII (October 1971), 550; Philip Greven, *Four Generations*, pp. 208-209; Daniel Smith and Michael Hindus, "Premarital Pregnancy in America, 1640-1971," p. 21; and Kenneth Lockridge, *Literacy in Colonial New England*, pp. 21, 98.

75. Kenneth Keniston, "Youth: A 'New' Stage of Life," *American Scholar*, XXXIX (Autumn 1970), 633-635; and James S. Coleman, et al., *Youth: Transition to Adulthood*, Report of the Panel on Youth of the President's Science Advisory Committee (Chicago: 1974), pp. 64-72.
76. *Ibid.*, pp. 112-125; Urie Bronfenbrenner, *Two Worlds of Childhood: U.S. and U.S.S.R.* (New York: 1970), pp. 99-109, 115-116; and Mark G. Field, "The Child as Father to What Kind of Man," *Psychiatry and Social Science Review*, IV (November 10, 1970), 2-6.
77. John Tufts, *An Introduction to the Singing of Psalm-Tunes* (Boston: 1715). 225
78. For a perceptive discussion of this entire controversy see Ola Elizabeth Winslow, *Meetinghouse Hill, 1630-1783* (New York: 1952, 1972), pp. 150-170.
79. Peter Thacker, John Danforth, and Samuel Danforth, *An Essay by Several Ministers of the Gospel . . . Concerning the Singing of Psalms* (Boston: 1723), p. 8; and Josiah Dwight, *An Essay to Silence the Outcry That Has Been Made in Some Places Against Regular Singing* (Boston: 1725), p. 10.
80. Nathaniel Chauncy, *Regular Singing Defended* (New Haven: 1728), pp. 48-49. Cited in Winslow, *Meetinghouse Hill*, p. 163.
81. *Ibid.*, pp. 159, 163.
82. Erikson, "Youth, Fidelity, and Diversity," *The Challenge of Youth*, p. 11. Also see van den Berg, *The Changing Nature of Man*, pp. 111-114.
83. Blos, *On Adolescence*, pp. 75-76, 111, 118, 129-136; Gisela Konopka, "Requirements for Healthy Development of Adolescent Youth," *Adolescence*, VIII (Fall 1973), 298-300; Aarons, "Normality and Abnormality in Adolescence," p. 315; Anna Freud, "Adolescence," pp. 260, 268-275; Jacobson, *The Self and the Object World*, p. 161; E. Jones, "Some Problems of Adolescence," pp. 401-403; and Erikson, "The Problem of Ego Identity," p. 52. The concepts of identity and self are somewhat controversial. For two different approaches, see Roy Schafer, "Concepts of Self and Identity and the Experience of Separation-Individuation in Adolesceice," *Psychoanalytic Quarterly*, XLII, No. 1 (1973), 42-59; and Sandor M. Abend, "Problems of Identity: Theoretical and Clinical Applications," *Psychoanalytic Quarterly*, XLIII, No. 4 (1974), 606-637.
84. Erikson, "The Problem of Ego Identity," pp. 55, 73, 81.
85. Therese Benedek, "Parenthood as a Developmental Phase," *Psychoanalytic Investigations: Selected Papers* (New York: 1973), pp. 377-401; and Blos, *On Adolescence*, pp. 73, 109-110.
86. Stanley H. King, "Coping and Growth in Adolescence," *Seminars in Psychiatry*, IV (November 1972), 355-366; and Blos, *On Adolescence*, pp. 155-156.

The Economic Development of the Thirteen Continental Colonies, 1720 to 1775

Marc Egnal*

THE last decade has been marked by a quiet renaissance in early American economic history. Numerous articles and several books have reexamined the colonial period with an approach that emphasizes the use of quantitative data and modern theory. One important topic, however, remains little explored: economic development. Much of the writing on this question has been avowedly impressionistic and serves to underscore Ralph Andreano's pronouncement about American colonial growth that "no period of our national development remains as untouched by testable generalizations as does this one."[1] Several descriptive essays, while listing such valid reasons for growth as abundant land and a rapidly growing population, shed little light on variations in the pace of expansion or on the relationship between the thirteen colonies and the Atlantic economy.[2] At a methodological extreme from such survey articles is a recent econometric model of colonial growth. But this construct is highly abstract and not closely related to the evidence available for the colonial period; the authors confess that "it is not a theory to be tested in this book."[3] A detailed examination of colonial

* Mr. Egnal is a member of the Department of History, York University. He wishes to thank Joseph A. Ernst for his useful suggestions and comments.

[1] Ralph L. Andreano, ed., *New Views on American Economic Development: A Selective Anthology of Recent Work* (Cambridge, Mass., 1965), 42.

[2] See George Rogers Taylor, "American Economic Growth Before 1840: An Exploratory Essay," *Journal of Economic History*, XXIV (1964), 427-444; Stuart Bruchey, *The Roots of American Economic Growth, 1607-1861* (New York, 1965), 1-73; Douglass C. North, *Growth and Welfare in the American Past: A New Economic History* (Englewood Cliffs, N. J., 1966), 1-49; and Robert E. Gallman, "The Pace and Pattern of American Economic Growth," in Lance E. Davis *et al.*, eds., *American Economic Growth: An Economist's History of the United States* (New York, 1972), 15-25. One of the better accounts of colonial economic development is James A. Henretta, *The Evolution of American Society, 1700-1815: An Interdisciplinary Analysis* (Lexington, Mass., 1973), Chap. 2. See my review of Henretta's work in the *William and Mary Quarterly*, 3d Ser., XXXI (1974), 510-511.

[3] James F. Shepherd and Gary M. Walton, *Shipping, Maritime Trade, and the Economic Development of Colonial North America* (Cambridge, 1972), Chaps. 2-3, quotation on p. 25, n. 1.

economic development is, however, a feasible undertaking. There exists a surprising amount of quantitative and qualitative data, as well as demographic and regional studies, on which to base a synthesis.

Any discussion of colonial economic development inevitably will be read in the context of another question, that hardy perennial, "Were the Navigation Acts a Burden to the Thirteen Colonies?" Much has been written on this issue, generally in the framework of "counterfactual analysis." This approach compares the total income of the colonies in a given year, say 1770, to an income computed for the same year with the assumption that the Acts of Trade did not exist.[4] But such analysis is mired in difficulties, and ultimately does not elucidate the basic issue —the impact of membership in the British Empire on the colonies. The selection of a proper counterfactual is one problem. The derivation of statistics to show how the international economy would function under hypothetical circumstances is another. And a static emphasis—a focus on a single year rather than on long-term growth—is a further difficulty. Ultimately, figures computed for the cost of routing exports through Britain or for the net gain from bounty payments provide only limited information about the situation the colonists faced. The present discussion of colonial growth suggests a new approach: only by examining the process of development and only by focusing on a lengthy span of years can the effects of the linkages with Britain be judged fully.

This article offers a broad framework for analyzing the economic development of the thirteen colonies between 1720 and 1775. Growth took place because of two related sets of conditions. One was the increase in population and the accompanying expansion of total output; the other was the rise in per capita income or, equivalently, in per capita product or in the standard of living. This second category is often referred to simply as economic growth. The data suggest that colonial growth—both of population and of per capita income—was neither smooth nor uniform. Rather, two periods or "long swings" emerge, one lasting from 1720 to 1745, and the other from 1745 to 1775.[5] The first period was

[4] The contributions to this debate include Lawrence A. Harper, "The Effects of the Navigation Acts on the Thirteen Colonies," in Richard B. Morris, ed., *The Era of the American Revolution* (New York, 1939), 3-39; Oliver M. Dickerson, *The Navigation Acts and the American Revolution* (Philadelphia, 1951), 5-91; Robert Paul Thomas, "A Quantitative Approach to the Study of the Effects of British Imperial Policy upon Colonial Welfare: Some Preliminary Findings," *Jour. Econ. Hist.*, XXV (1965), 615-638; and Peter D. McClelland, "The Cost to America of British Imperial Policy," *American Economic Review*, LIX (1969), 370-381.

[5] For a definition and discussion of the equivalent concepts of national income

marked by growth during the 1720s and early 1730s, with stagnation apparent by the 1740s. The second period was characterized by expansion from 1745 to 1760, with a gradual slowdown after 1760. The increase in population was slightly more vigorous during the first long swing than during the second, but the rise in the standard of living was more notable in the years following 1745.

An emphasis on long swings is not meant to deny the role played by short-run fluctuations in the well-being of the colonies. King George's War, the French and Indian War, and the nonimportation agreements of 1766 and 1769-1770 were among the events that had an important,
228 immediate impact on economic life in North America. More generally, the colonists were affected by recurrent periods of prosperity and depression. In analyzing economic development, these year-to-year changes have not been ignored, but have been incorporated into a larger picture. Wherever possible, averages based on a five-year period, for example, 1758-1762, have been used in identifying a trend, and reliance on a single year, such as 1760, has been avoided. Wartime booms, postwar slumps, and nonimportation agreements at times reinforced and at times retarded broader developments. These short-run changes, however, must be set in a larger context if the process of growth is to be understood.[6]

The growth of population, which provided the basis for the increased output of the colonies, was rapid. Although the available statistics are estimates, they are derived from a broad variety of sources and may be relied upon to indicate orders of magnitude. Between 1720 and Independence the number of colonists rose about 35 percent a decade, or

---

and national product see Simon Kuznets, *Economic Change: Selected Essays in Business Cycles, National Income, and Economic Growth* (New York, 1953), Chaps. 6-7. Kuznets's analysis is of particular value for colonial historians because it stresses the problems of dealing with a developing agricultural society. On the same question see also Robert E. Gallman, "The Statistical Approach: Fundamental Concepts as Applied to History," in George Rogers Taylor and Lucius F. Ellsworth, eds., *Approaches to American Economic History* (Charlottesville, Va., 1971), 63-64. For a theoretical discussion of the concept of "long swings" consult Simon Kuznets, *Secular Movements in Production and Prices: Their Nature and Their Bearing upon Cyclical Fluctuations* (Boston, 1930), 59-69, 324-325.

[6] For a discussion of short-run fluctuations in the colonial period see Marc Egnal, "The Pennsylvania Economy, 1748-1762: An Analysis of Short-Run Fluctuations in the Context of Long-Run Changes in the Atlantic Trading Community" (Ph.D. diss., University of Wisconsin, 1974), esp. Chap. 3; John M. Hemphill II, "Virginia and the English Commercial System, 1689-1733: Studies in the Development and Fluctuation of a Colonial Economy under Imperial Control" (Ph.D. diss., Princeton University, 1964); and William S. Sachs, "The Business Outlook in the Northern Colonies, 1750-1775" (Ph.D. diss., Columbia University, 1957).

roughly 3.0 percent a year. The total population, black and white, grew from 466,000 to about 2,500,000.[7]

For the white population, natural increase was more important than immigration. Natural increase involves the interaction of two components —the birth rate and the death rate. Writers frequently commented on the high American birth rate. Peter Kalm, who visited the northern colonies at mid-century, recorded in his journal under the heading "Large Families": "It does not seem difficult to find out the reasons why the people multiply faster here than in Europe. As soon as a person is old enough he may marry in these provinces without any fear of poverty. There is such an amount of good land yet uncultivated that a newly married man can, without difficulty, get a spot of ground where he may comfortably subsist with his wife and children."[8] Although firm data are lacking for the colonial birth rate, the magnitude and trend of later statistics suggest an unusually high level in the eighteenth century. Between 1800 and 1940 the United States birth rate declined steadily, beginning with about 50 births per 1,000 population in 1800. The reasons commonly set forth for the high American birth rate in the nineteenth century—a large and prosperous portion of the population engaged in farming and a relative lack of urbanization—suggest that the colonial birth rate was equal to or greater than that of 1800. A rate of over 55 per 1,000 is unlikely, however; this figure is close to the observed limit of reproduction in any large group.[9]

[7] U. S. Bureau of the Census, *Historical Statistics of the United States, Colonial Times to 1957* (Washington, D. C., 1957), 7, 743-744, 756. For many of the component series from which these estimates were derived see Evarts B. Greene and Virginia D. Harrington, comps., *American Population Before the Federal Census of 1790* (New York, 1932).

[8] Adolph B. Benson, ed., *Peter Kalm's Travels in North America: The English Version of 1770*, I (New York, 1937), 211.

[9] Our knowledge of colonial vital statistics is decidedly uneven. We know a great deal about several New England settlements but too little about aggregate patterns for any of the colonies, particularly those outside New England. For a useful introduction consult the review article by Philip J. Greven, Jr., "Historical Demography and Colonial America," *WMQ*, 3d Ser., XXIV (1967), 438-454; John Demos, "Families in Colonial Bristol, Rhode Island: An Exercise in Historical Demography," *ibid.*, XXV (1968), 40-57; and Daniel Scott Smith, "The Demographic History of Colonial New England," *Jour. Econ. Hist.*, XXXII (1972), 165-183. For information on the birth rate in the colonial and early national period see *Historical Statistics*, 23; J. Potter, "The Growth of Population in America, 1700-1860," in D. V. Glass and D. E. C. Eversley, eds., *Population in History* (London, 1965), 667; Ansley J. Coale and Melvin Zelnik, *New Estimates of Fertility and Population in the United States* (Princeton, N. J., 1963), 33-36; Yasukichi Yasuba, *Birth Rates of the White Population in the United States, 1800-1860: An Economic*

Estimates of the death rate for the white population must be conjectural. Again the trend of statistics for subsequent periods sheds light on the colonial era. Between the 1790s and the end of the nineteenth century the mortality rate in the United States fell gradually from roughly 25 deaths per 1,000 population to about 19 per 1,000. Demographic studies of several colonial communities suggest that the death rate was only slightly higher between 1720 and 1775 than in the 1790s; in the computations below a figure of 27 deaths per 1,000 is used. This rate is plausible when viewed in a world context. It means that colonial America had roughly the same mortality rate as Scandinavia, a relationship
230 between the two areas that held true in the late eighteenth and nineteenth centuries.[10]

As for the immigration of white settlers, only a rough estimate of its magnitude is possible. Colonial governments kept few records of new arrivals, and the early tabulations that survive are fraught with uncertainties. Net immigration may be computed indirectly, however, by determining the difference between natural increase and the overall growth of colonial population. Assuming a rate of natural increase of 23 per 1,000 population (that is, a birth rate of 50 and a death rate of 27), computations based on Stella Sutherland's population data suggest that between 1720 and 1770 roughly 270,000 settlers arrived. The actual number could well have been 10 percent larger or smaller. Immigrants accounted for perhaps 20 percent of the growth of white population. Of course, new arrivals made a greater contribution to some regions than to others. New England and the upper South recorded only moderate net gains from immigration, while the middle colonies and the lower South received large numbers of new settlers.[11]

Study, The Johns Hopkins University Studies in Historical and Political Science, LXXIX (Baltimore, 1962), 158-159; and W. H. Grabill *et al., The Fertility of American Women* (New York, 1958), 5-8. Eighteenth-century statistics for other countries are summarized in Simon Kuznets, *Modern Economic Growth: Rate, Structure, and Spread* (New Haven, Conn., 1966), 42-44.

[10] For information on the death rate in 18th- and 19th-century America see Grabill *et al., Fertility of American Women,* 5-8; Simon Kuznets, "Long Swings in the Growth of Population and in Related Economic Variables," American Philosophical Society, *Proceedings,* CII (1958), 37-41; Kenneth A. Lockridge, *A New England Town, The First Hundred Years: Dedham, Massachusetts, 1636-1736* (New York, 1970), 67-69; John B. Blake, *Public Health in the Town of Boston, 1630-1822* (Cambridge, Mass., 1959), 247-250; Potter, "Population in America," in Glass and Eversley, eds., *Population in History,* 655-663; *Historical Statistics,* 30; and Maris A. Vinovskis, "Mortality Rates and Trends in Massachusetts Before 1860," *Jour. Econ. Hist.,* XXXII (1972), 195-202. For Scandinavian data see Kuznets, *Modern Economic Growth,* 42.

[11] Computed from data in *Historical Statistics,* 756. For other estimates see

TABLE I

AVERAGE ANNUAL PERCENTAGE INCREASE IN WHITE POPULATION, 1720 TO 1775

Period	Northern Colonies	Upper South	Lower South	All Colonies
1720-1735	3.89	3.96	6.18	4.04
1735-1745	3.39	1.98	5.38	3.13
1745-1760	3.47	2.83	4.88	3.42
1760-1775	3.07	2.66	6.66	3.43

Source:
U. S. Bureau of the Census, *Historical Statistics of the United States, Colonial Times to 1957* (Washington, D. C., 1960), 756. The figures exclude trans-Appalachian population. Midpoints between decennial years are computed with the assumption that 0.46 of the incremental population had arrived by the fifth year.

Fluctuations in white immigration to the thirteen colonies map out a pattern that seems closely related to the pace of economic growth. The statistics underlying any investigation of new arrivals are admittedly imprecise. But only the broad ebb and flow of immigration is important here—whether, for example, more settlers arrived during the 1750s or 1760s. With reservation, we may examine the evidence on this question. Assuming a constant rate of natural increase, figures for changes in the size of the population may be read as indicators of fluctuations in the number of new arrivals (see Table I). Based on these data, the two long swings for each of the regions may be set forth as follows: (1) brisk immigration between 1720 and 1735, with fewer settlers arriving from 1735 to 1745; (2) a marked influx between 1745 and 1760, slackening after 1760. This pattern is in accord with the growth of per capita income discussed below. The figures thus suggest that in the eighteenth century, just as (according to recent studies) in the nineteenth, the "pull" of

Shepherd and Walton, *Shipping*, 31-37; Potter, "Population in America," in Glass and Eversley, eds., *Population in History*, 645-646; James G. Leyburn, *The Scotch-Irish: A Social History* (Chapel Hill, N. C., 1962), 179-183; and Ian Charles Cargill Graham, *Colonists from Scotland: Emigration to North America, 1707-1783* (Ithaca, N. Y., 1956), 19, 185-189. For a review of some of the quantitative data on immigration consult Abbot Emerson Smith, *Colonists in Bondage: White Servitude and Convict Labor in America, 1607-1776* (Chapel Hill, N. C., 1947), 307-337. Throughout this article, New England and the middle colonies are designated "northern colonies"; "upper South" refers to Maryland and Virginia; "lower South" includes the Carolinas and Georgia.

favorable conditions in the host country played a more significant role in stimulating immigration than the "push" of adverse conditions in the donor land.[12] An exception reinforces the rule. The lower South was the one area in which white population grew more rapidly after 1760 than between 1745 and 1760. As will be discussed below, this was the only region to experience stronger economic growth in the decade and one-half before Independence than in the 1750s.

The black population expanded at an even higher rate than the white population. In 1720 blacks constituted 15 percent of colonial inhabitants, in 1770, 21 percent. Most blacks lived in the southern colonies; in 1770
232 only 11 percent were in the provinces north of Maryland. In the lower South the importation of slaves made a greater contribution to black population growth than did natural increase. The slow growth of the native-born slave population reflected the high mortality rate suffered by slaves engaged in rice planting. In the upper South slaves were healthier, and natural increase was more important. The arrival of new slaves, however, accounted for roughly 40 percent of black population growth in the tobacco colonies between 1720 and 1770.[13]

Like long swings in white immigration, fluctuations in the importation of slaves and in the increase of black population appear to have been in accord with the pace of economic growth. In the northern colonies, the expansion of black population followed the broad changes in per capita income, at least after 1745. Moreover, the distinct pattern of economic growth exhibited by the lower South—strong growth between 1720 and 1735, which slowed between 1735 and 1745, and more rapid expansion after 1760 than between 1745 and 1760—was true for the growth of slave population as well as for white. Fluctuations in the importation of blacks into the upper South are less easily correlated with changes in that region's economy. After 1750 the black population grew more slowly, and the number of new arrivals declined. This did not re-

[12] For a similar conceptual approach to immigration, emphasizing "long swings" in the American economy rather than cyclical fluctuations, see Brinley Thomas, *Migration and Economic Growth: A Study of Great Britain and the Atlantic Economy* (Cambridge, 1954), esp. Chap. 7. Thomas provides a yardstick, "immigrants arriving per 1,000 native population," that is more useful than absolute numbers in dealing with fluctuations. This concept underlies my discussion of the pace of immigration. See also Simon Kuznets and Ernest Rubin, *Immigration and the Foreign Born* (New York, 1954), 1-49.

[13] *Historical Statistics*, 756, 769-770; Lewis Cecil Gray, *History of Agriculture in the Southern United States to 1860* (Washington, D. C., 1933), I, 363; Philip D. Curtin, *The Atlantic Slave Trade: A Census* (Madison, Wis., 1969), 73. Extrapolations from data on slave imports were made following the procedures discussed *ibid., passim.*

flect the retardation of per capita growth in the region. The standard of living in Virginia and Maryland rose markedly during the 1750s (although there was little further progress in the 1760s). Rather, declining slave imports after mid-century mirrored the comparatively slow growth of tobacco production in a regional economy where the cultivation of foodstuffs became ever more important.[14]

A growing population, both black and white, made possible a remarkable growth in the total output of the colonies. The availability of abundant, rich land meant that each new settler could hope to become an independent producer. The total output of the colonies rose rapidly. Between 1730 and 1750 the number of inhabitants in Pennsylvania, for example, increased by about 130 percent and the volume of flour, bread, and wheat exported from Philadelphia grew roughly 120 percent.[15] Total output also increased remarkably in the southern colonies. The increase, however, cannot be judged fully by the expansion of staple exports. Between 1730 and 1750 the population of Virginia and Maryland increased by over 80 percent, while that of South Carolina more than doubled. At the same time, shipments of tobacco rose only 52 percent, and those of rice about 80 percent.[16] But these cash crops are only partial indicators of the growth of total output. Many agriculturalists, especially as settlement in the backcountry increased, raised little rice or tobacco, but much wheat, corn, and other foodstuffs. Most of these crops never reached the ports and so are unnoticed in British customs records. If James Lemon's data for Pennsylvania are applicable to other colonies, the typical family on a small grain farm consumed 60 percent of the foodstuffs it raised. In the southern colonies a significant portion of the marketable surplus, rather than entering the export trade, went to feed those who lived on the plantations.[17]

[14] *Historical Statistics*, 756, 769-770; Curtin, *Atlantic Slave Trade*, 136-145; David Klingaman, "The Significance of Grain in the Development of the Tobacco Colonies," *Jour. Econ. Hist.*, XXIX (1969), 268-278. Changes in the upper South are discussed more fully below.

[15] *Historical Statistics*, 756; Anne Bezanson *et al.*, *Prices in Colonial Pennsylvania* (Philadelphia, 1935), appendix; Helen L. Klopfer, "Statistics of Foreign Trade of Philadelphia, 1700-1860" (Ph.D. diss., University of Pennsylvania, 1936), 173.

[16] Based on annual averages for the periods 1728-1732 and 1748-1752. *Historical Statistics*, 756, 766-768; Jacob M. Price, *France and the Chesapeake: A History of the French Tobacco Monopoly, 1674-1791, and of Its Relationship to the British and American Tobacco Trades* (Ann Arbor, Mich., 1973), II, 843-844.

[17] James T. Lemon, *The Best Poor Man's Country: A Geographical Study of Early Southeastern Pennsylvania* (Baltimore, 1972), 180-181; David Klingaman, "Food Surpluses and Deficits in the American Colonies, 1768-1772," *Jour. Econ.*

Between 1720 and 1775 the growth of population was the most important reason for the increasing total output of the colonies. The rise in per capita product, which will be examined in the remainder of this article, made a comparable contribution to total output only between 1745 and 1760.

Per capita income increased between 1720 and 1775 for several reasons. Three developments had a particularly important, positive impact on the colonial standard of living. First, new techniques enhanced productivity and made the effort of individual laborers more rewarding.
234 Second, the market value of the goods the colonists produced climbed more than the cost of the wares they bought. Third, the amount of capital available to each white colonist increased, making greater investments and higher levels of income possible. The second and third developments were by far the more significant and underlay the period of most rapid growth—1745 to 1760. Between 1760 and 1775 changes in import and export prices and increases in capital invested per capita were of a lesser magnitude and had less influence on the economy. New forces making for per capita growth, however, became evident during the decade and one-half before Independence. These new developments, which collectively had only a moderate effect on the economy, will be considered at the end of this article.

Before examining these reasons for expansion in more detail, statistics suggesting the size of the "growth rate" (the annual change in per capita income or product) may be set forth (see Table II). These data serve as an introduction to and summary of the discussion that follows. Colonial growth rates must of necessity be conjectural; information about total income or product is lacking. The numbers presented in Table II are no more than estimates that comport with the data discussed in the text and notes. In addition to rates covering shorter periods, a figure for average annual growth between 1720 and 1775 is presented: 0.5 percent. This figure is in accord with statistics indicating long-term changes in individual income (for example, British imports per capita) as well as with statistics suggesting long-term changes in individual product (for example, per capita value of major staple exports). Such data make clear that the growth rate in the half-century before Independence was well below the pace of 1.6 percent per year which the United States economy averaged between 1840 and 1960.[18]

Hist., XXXI (1971), 553-569; Klingaman, "Significance of Grain," *ibid.*, XXIX (1969), 273-274.

[18] Sources for statistics on British imports per capita are given in the note

TABLE II

RATE OF ANNUAL GROWTH OF PER CAPITA INCOME IN THE THIRTEEN CONTINENTAL COLONIES, 1720 TO 1775

(growth rate as a percentage)

Period	Northern Colonies	Upper South	Lower South	Thirteen Colonies
1720-1735	0	-2.0 to 0	+5.0	0
1735-1745	-2.0 to 0	+1.0	-4.0 to -3.0	-1.0
1745-1760	+3.0 to +5.0	+2.0 to +3.0	+1.0 to +2.5	+3.0
1760-1775	-1.0 to +1.0	-3.0 to -1.0	+1.5 to +3.0	-1.0 to 0
1720-1775				+0.5

Sources:

These figures are estimates based on changes in per capita exports and per capita imports. For imports see U. S. Bureau of the Census, *Historical Statistics of the United States, Colonial Times to 1957* (Washington, D. C., 1960), 757; Customs 14, P.R.O.; and David Macpherson, *Annals of Commerce . . .* , III (London, 1805), 339-599. For exports see *Historical Statistics*, 757-772; Jacob M. Price, *France and the Chesapeake: A History of the French Tobacco Monopoly, 1674-1791, and of Its Relationship to the British and American Tobacco Trades* (Ann Arbor, Mich., 1973), II, 843-844, 852; James F. Shepherd and Gary M. Walton, *Shipping, Maritime Trade, and the Economic Development of Colonial North America* (Cambridge, 1972), 168-171; William S. Sachs, "The Business Outlook in the Northern Colonies, 1750-1775" (Ph.D. diss., Columbia University, 1957), 174-175, 271-276; Helen L. Klopfer, "Statistics of Foreign Trade of Philadelphia, 1700-1860" (Ph.D. diss., University of Pennsylvania, 1936), 173-207; and Marc Egnal, "The Pennsylvania Economy, 1748-1762: An Analysis of Short-Run Fluctuations in the Context of Long-Run Changes in the Atlantic Trading Community" (Ph.D. diss., University of Wisconsin, 1974), appendixes. Relevant price data are presented in the above sources and in Arthur Harrison Cole, *Wholesale Commodity Prices in the United States, 1700-1861: Statistical Supplement* (Cambridge, Mass., 1938). For population see *Historical Statistics*, 756.

The introduction of new or improved techniques made a noticeable, if minor, contribution to per capita income. Farming was the most important colonial occupation, and was the chief employment of be-

accompanying Figures 1-3. For data on per capita staple exports consult *Historical Statistics*, 757, 759, 765-768; Klopfer, "Statistics of Foreign Trade," 173-207; and Arthur Harrison Cole, *Wholesale Commodity Prices in the United States, 1700-1861: Statistical Supplement* (Cambridge, Mass., 1938), 6-70. Data on United States growth after 1840 are conveniently summarized in Simon Kuznets, "Notes on the Pattern of U. S. Economic Growth," in Robert William Fogel and Stanley L. Engerman, eds., *The Reinterpretation of American Economic History* (New York, 1971), 17-24.

tween 80 and 90 percent of the working population.[19] Agriculturists in the northern colonies and southern backcountry cultivated grains and raised livestock. Fragmentary evidence suggests that in these areas there was an increased use of horsepower. There was also some improvement in hand tools. The introduction of the "cradle" scythe at mid-century allowed the farmer to reap his grain more efficiently. Irrigation was used more widely. But despite certain improvements, basic methods remained more or less unchanged between 1720 and 1775. Throughout these years husbandmen depleted rich soils, made little use of fertilizers, and implemented only rudimentary schemes of crop rotation. The quan-
236 tity of foodstuffs produced per acre and the number of acres worked by the individual farmer in the 1770s were probably only slightly greater than in the 1720s.[20]

In southern plantation agriculture, new techniques had a somewhat greater impact on output. The most important advances in agricultural productivity occurred in the lower South. Although conclusions must be tentative, the quantity of rice produced per slave appears to have risen markedly between 1720 and 1775 as a result of improvements in irrigation and the migration of the crop from comparatively elevated ground to tidal and river swamplands.[21] The wasteful methods of tobacco cultivation, however, appear to have changed little during the period. Scattered figures for pounds of tobacco produced per slave suggest that there was no increase during the eighteenth century, and perhaps even a

[19] The data presented by Greene and Harrington, *American Population,* suggest that over 10% of the settlers in the North dwelt in towns and cities (as distinct from rural areas or agricultural villages). Moreover, a portion of those in rural areas were not farmers. See Lemon, *The Best Poor Man's Country,* 7-9, and Jackson Turner Main, *The Social Structure of Revolutionary America* (Princeton, N. J., 1965), 7-67. Estimates for the early national period of the portion of the labor force engaged in agriculture also suggest a range of 80-90% for the colonial era. See Stanley Lebergott, *Manpower in Economic Growth: The American Record since 1800* (New York, 1964), 510-511, and Paul A. David, "The Growth of Real Product in the United States Before 1840: New Evidence, Controlled Conjectures," *Jour. Econ. Hist.,* XXVII (1967), 166.

[20] Gray, *History of Agriculture,* I, 194-199; Lemon, *The Best Poor Man's Country,* 164-183; Benson, ed., *Peter Kalm's Travels,* I, 162; Percy Wells Bidwell and John I. Falconer, *History of Agriculture in the Northern United States, 1620-1860* (Washington, D. C., 1925), 84, 103, 123-125; Rodney C. Loehr, "Arthur Young and American Agriculture," *Agricultural History,* XLIII (1969), 43-46. This number of *Ag. Hist.* is devoted to articles on 18th-century agriculture.

[21] *Historical Statistics,* 756, 767-768; Gray, *History of Agriculture,* I, 279-297; William A. Schaper, *Sectionalism and Representation in South Carolina* (New York, 1968 [reprinted from *Annual Report of the American Historical Association for the Year 1900,* I]), 50-54.

decline from the levels reached just before the turn of the century.[22]

The effects of innovation on colonial industries varied. Some enterprises were little affected. Among these was household manufacture of textiles and implements, which was probably the colonies' most important industrial activity. In the northern colonies and southern backcountry virtually every farm family produced woolen or linen cloth and made simple tools. Although the organization of cloth and footwear production changed during the late colonial period (and will be discussed later), technological improvement in home industry was slight.[23] Ranked by value of product, shipping and shipbuilding were probably the second colonial industry, employing thousands of sailors, carpenters, and kindred laborers. Unit costs and methods of building vessels seem to have changed little during the period. Some gains were recorded in the productivity of shipping as a result of the use of increasingly larger vessels and the reduction of the average time spent idle in port, but the largest advances came before 1720, because of efforts to eliminate piracy, and after 1775, because of faster vessels and better market organization.[24]

Other industries benefited more significantly from new techniques. Milling became more efficient, especially near the end of the colonial period. By 1775 the flour mills in Pennsylvania, Delaware, and Maryland were probably among the most advanced in the world. Innovations, such as the mechanical elevation of wheat and new methods of cleaning the grain, increased the capacity of mills and reduced manpower. Price data suggest the timing of these gains in productivity. The unit cost of converting wheat into flour, as reflected by the price of the raw material (wheat) and the finished product (flour), fluctuated with no trend between 1720 and the early 1760s, and then declined markedly in the decade before Independence. The productivity of sawmills also rose. Such

[22] Gray, *History of Agriculture*, I, 218-219, 446; Aubrey C. Land, "The Tobacco Staple and the Planter's Problems: Technology, Labor, and Crops," *Ag. Hist.*, XLIII (1969), 79-80.

[23] Victor S. Clark, *History of Manufactures in the United States* (Washington, D. C., 1929), I: *1607-1860*, 160, 223; David J. Jeremy, "British Textile Technology Transmission to the United States: The Philadelphia Region Experience, 1770-1820," *Business History Review*, XLVII (1973), 24-52.

[24] Douglass C. North, "Sources of Productivity Change in Ocean Shipping, 1600-1850," in Fogel and Engerman, eds., *Reinterpretation of American Economic History*, 163-174; Shepherd and Walton, *Shipping*, Chaps. 4, 5. Shipping and shipbuilding are usefully considered together because much of the income flow from freight charges went to pay the costs of construction and repair. Shepherd and Walton's estimate of this income flow is inflated. *Ibid.*, 135. Colonial shippers regularly failed to cover freight costs, particularly in the West Indian trade. See Egnal, "Pennsylvania Economy," 130-139, 273-290.

laborsaving techniques as mechanical log carriers were American in origin. Information on rum distilling suggests few increases in efficiency. Analysis of molasses and rum prices, which are available for the Boston area between 1750 and 1775, indicates no reduction in processing costs. The production of naval stores and pig iron appears to have changed little.[25] In sum, new or improved techniques had only a minor impact on the colonial economy.

A far more important stimulus for economic growth came from two other developments: the price of the goods the colonists sold rose more than the cost of the wares they bought, and more capital was made
238 available to planters, merchants, and small farmers. Both developments involved America's economic relations with Great Britain, and both were much affected by the mother country's rapid expansion after 1745. Thus an analysis of the pace of colonial development requires a brief examination of the reasons for and the nature of Great Britain's growth between 1720 and 1775.

During the eighteenth century, the British economy grew in two long swings—one lasting from 1720 to 1745, and the next from 1745 to 1783. The first cycle was characterized by slow growth. The second was marked by strong expansion. The growth phase of the second cycle stretched from 1745 to 1760; after 1760 growth gradually was dampened.

Agriculture played a pivotal role in Britain's growth. Although overseas demand was important for England's and Scotland's manufactures, the home market—a free trade area encompassing over 7,000,000 people at mid-century—was even more significant. In large part, the level of consumer demand depended on conditions in the countryside. Between 1720 and 1745 Britain's farm economy was depressed because of overproduction. Various techniques had increased output, while at the same time population grew slowly. Exports of foodstuffs to Europe provided some, but not sufficient, relief. As a result, agricultural prices fell, and the disposable income of individual farmers decreased. After 1745 rural

[25] Bezanson *et al.*, *Prices in Colonial Philadelphia*, appendix; Cole, *Wholesale Commodity Prices: Supplement*, 31-69. Calculations of unit costs are based on the assumption that, in the long run, competition among mills and distilleries encouraged entrepreneurs to pass along productivity gains to consumers in the form of lower costs. See also Clark, *History of Manufactures*, I, 165-181; William B. Weeden, *Economic and Social History of New England, 1620-1789*, II (Boston, 1891), 501-503; and Robert Plumstead to John Scott, Sept. 3, 1757, Robert Plumstead Letter-book, Cambridge University Library. For a different view of progress in flour milling before 1776 consult Greville and Dorothy Bathe, *Oliver Evans: A Chronicle of Early American Engineering* (Philadelphia, 1935), 1-18. The Bathes minimize the technical advances occurring before Evans's inventions in the early 1780s.

depression yielded to recovery and then prosperity. Landowners benefited from the rise in population. In the 1740s the death rate began to fall, possibly because of improved midwifery and the establishment of lying-in hospitals. Although farm output continued to rise, demands from a growing population pushed up prices and brought new wealth to husbandmen and landowners. As a result of increased domestic consumption of foodstuffs, Britain's agricultural exports to overseas markets, which had reached record levels at mid-century, gradually declined. By the 1760s the growth of agricultural output had slowed, and Britain became a net importer of certain foodstuffs such as wheat.[26]

Britain's industries responded to these changes in rural conditions. 239
Between 1720 and 1745 agricultural depression circumscribed the expansion of manufacturing. Overseas demand (especially European) for the products of Britain's mines and manufactures, it is true, exhibited moderate growth, particularly in the 1720s and early 1730s. This provided a stimulus for some industries (such as tin mining and the production of wrought iron), but not an impetus for general growth. Between 1745 and 1760 British industry expanded rapidly in response to strong demand from the agricultural sector and from foreign (particularly colonial) markets. The rise in both home and overseas consumption of manufactures, as will be discussed below, was not coincidental; one was closely tied to the other. A broad spectrum of industries in England and Scotland increased their output during this period. After 1760 the continued rise of food prices and the slower growth of the agricultural sector helped brake industrial expansion. Only in the 1780s would the economy surge ahead as new industries such as cotton textiles and ferrous metals provided an impetus for growth.[27]

[26] My discussion of British growth follows the outlines of the argument presented in Phyllis Deane and W. A. Cole, *British Economic Growth, 1688-1959: Trends and Structure* (Cambridge, 1962), Chaps. 1-3. For modification and amplication see B. R. Mitchell and Phyllis Deane, *Abstract of British Historical Statistics* (Cambridge, 1962), 94-95, 468-469, 486-487; F. Crouzet, "England and France in the Eighteenth Century: A Comparative Analysis of Two Economic Growths," in R. M. Hartwell, ed., *The Causes of the Industrial Revolution in England* (London, 1967), 139-174; E. L. Jones, "Agriculture and Economic Growth in England, 1660-1750: Agricultural Change," *Jour. Econ. Hist.*, XXV (1965), 1-18; A. H. John, "Aspects of English Economic Growth in the First Half of the Eighteenth Century," *Economica*, XXVIII (1961), 176-190; J. T. Krause, "Some Aspects of Population Change, 1690-1790," in E. L. Jones and G. E. Mingay, eds., *Land, Labour and Population in the Industrial Revolution* (London, 1967), 193-201; and J. H. Plumb, *England in the Eighteenth Century* (Baltimore, 1950), 78.

[27] Deane and Cole, *British Economic Growth*, 50-75, 94-97; Mitchell and Deane, *British Historical Statistics*, 312; L. S. Pressnell, *Country Banking in the*

This analysis of the British economy helps us to understand a second reason for colonial economic growth: the price of many of the agricultural commodities that Americans exported rose more rapidly than the cost of the manufactures that they purchased from abroad. These price movements produced a significant increase in the standard of living. For example, where the 100 bushels of wheat produced by a small farm in the mid-1740s could command 150 yards of woolen cloth, the same 100 bushels could be traded for over 250 yards of cloth in the early 1760s.[28]

These price movements were closely connected to the growth of the mother country, both as a supplier of finished goods and as a market
240 for raw materials. Overwhelmingly, the manufactures that the colonists bought from overseas were made in Britain. The Navigation Acts prohibited the direct importation of finished wares from the continent of Europe, and these strictures generally were obeyed. Furthermore, most of the goods shipped by British exporters were of British origin. For example, between 1751 and 1774 only 21 percent of New York's imports from England were manufactures that had been made in other European countries.[29] The colonists were fortunate in their links with an industrializing nation. Because of improvements in technology and business organization, British manufacturers were able to increase output (particularly after 1745) and maintain low prices. Price data for the years between 1720 and 1745, although sparse, suggest that the market price of finished goods remained level or declined slightly. Information for the period between 1745 and 1775 is fuller and indicates that the cost of important manufactured commodities, while fluctuating widely, rose only slightly—about 10 percent.[30]

In its capacity as a market, the expanding British economy helped raise the prices of certain North American exports. The commercial ties between Britain and the northern provinces, however, differed from those between Britain and the southern colonies. The provinces from Pennsylvania north sent only a small portion of their commodities "home," because the Caribbean was always the most important destination and

---

Industrial Revolution (Oxford, 1956), 1-44.

[28] Available price series for English manufactures are marred by lacunae and are heavily dependent on institutional purchasing. See Mitchell and Deane, *British Historical Statistics*, 465-469, 499. New statistics which are based on mercantile records and which detail the price movements of 10 textiles are presented in Egnal, "Pennsylvania Economy," appendix G. See also Deane and Cole, *British Economic Growth*, 84. For colonial produce prices see Bezanson *et al.*, *Prices in Colonial Pennsylvania*, appendix.

[29] *Historical Statistics*, 758; Dickerson, *Navigation Acts*, 69-78.

[30] Mitchell and Deane, *British Historical Statistics*, 468-469. See also n. 28 above.

FIGURE 1

Northern Colonies: Per Capita Imports from Great Britain

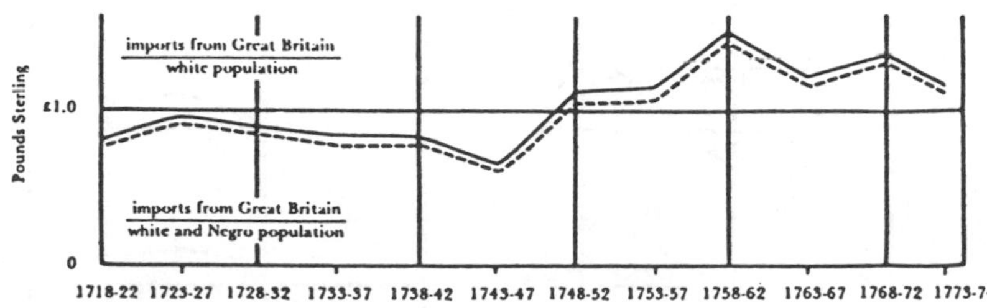

FIGURE 2

Upper South: Per Capita Imports from Great Britain

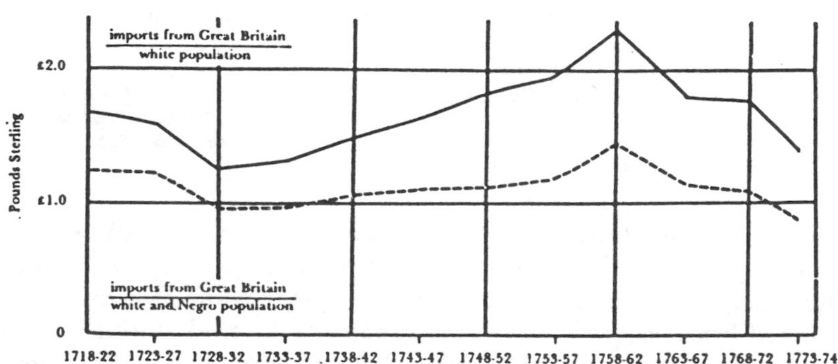

absorbed well over one-half the total value shipped to overseas markets. The southern colonies directed most of their commodities to England and Scotland.[31] Despite seemingly closer links between the South and Great Britain, the North was more affected by increases in British demand.

The West Indies provided the nexus which linked the growth of the northern colonies with that of Britain and which helps explain the trend of northern export prices before and after 1745. Between 1720 and 1745 the English economy grew slowly, English demand for sugar and rum

[31] The portion of northern exports directed toward the Caribbean declined during the 18th century, but was still over one-half in the years before Independence. *Historical Statistics*, 759-761; Sachs, "Business Outlook," 175-188; and for new tonnage statistics see Egnal, "Pennsylvania Economy," appendix I. Consult also Shepherd and Walton, *Shipping*, 115, 160, and Customs 16/1, Public Record Office.

FIGURE 3
Lower South: Per Capita Imports from Great Britain

Sources for Figures 1-3:
U. S. Bureau of the Census, *Historical Statistics of the United States, Colonial Times to 1957* (Washington, D. C., 1960), 756-757, 766, 768; Customs 14, P.R.O.; David Macpherson, *Annals of Commerce . . .*, III (London, 1805), 339-599. Imports from Scotland before 1955 are extrapolated based on colonial exports.

increased only slightly, and the British islands in the Caribbean suffered a prolonged depression. The quantity of tropical produce sent from the sugar islands to England increased before 1745, but the growth of trade reflected lower rum and sugar prices, not strengthened British purchasing power. Depression in the British Caribbean meant that West Indian demand for northern foodstuffs grew slowly. The price of the commodities, such as flour and meat, that North Americans sold to the islanders did not rise between 1720 and 1745.[32] The French plantations, which expanded more rapidly than the English during these years, provided some impetus for northern growth. But the English islands were

[32] For England's imports of tropical produce see Elizabeth Boody Schumpeter, *English Overseas Trade Statistics, 1697-1808* (Oxford, 1960), 60-62. For sugar prices see R. B. Sheridan, "The Sugar Trade of the British West Indies from 1660 to 1756 with Special Reference to the Island of Antigua" (Ph.D. diss., University of London, 1951), appendix; "An account of what his Majesty's muscovado sugars . . . sold for . . . from Christmas 1727 to Christmas 1752," T. 64/276B, 387, P.R.O.; David H. Makinson, *Barbados: A Study of North-American–West-Indian Relations, 1739-1789* (London, 1964), 34. On Caribbean conditions see Frank Wesley Pitman, *The Development of the British West Indies, 1700-1763* (New Haven, Conn., 1917), 133-136, 243-246; Sheridan, "Sugar Trade," 331-343; and Petition of merchant-planters trading to . . . British Sugar colonies, endorsed Mar. 14, 1739, C.O. 152/23, 203, 210, P.R.O.

the more valuable customers even though by mid-century the French plantations were the more important suppliers of tropical produce.[33] As a consequence of hard times in the West Indies, economic growth in the northern colonies lagged. Per capita consumption of British goods, one rough indication of individual prosperity, fell in value steadily between 1725 and 1745 (see Figure 1).

From 1745 to 1760 the Caribbean provided the stimulus for rising northern export prices and hence for improvement in the standard of living. During these years the British economy grew rapidly, British demand for rum and sugar soared, and production in the English sugar
plantations, largely based on the spread of cane culture in Jamaica, ex- 243
panded.[34] The French Antilles experienced a similar surge of growth.[35] Expansion in the islands meant new calls for North American grain, lumber, meat, and fish; the result was a strong rise in the prices of those staples. These higher prices helped produce a significant increase in per capita income in the northern colonies. Although the worth of rum and sugar rose markedly at this time, the cost of English manufactures increased only slightly.[36] Consequently, per capita consumption of imported manufactures in the northern colonies rose steadily, climbing from an annual average of £0.65 sterling per person in 1743-1747 to £1.49 in 1758-1762 (see Figure 1).

[33] For the magnitude of trade with the English and French islands see "Calculations of Sugars made in the different isles . . . ," 1747, Add. MSS 38, 331, fol. 97, British Museum; "An Inquiry into the Causes of the Present Scarcity of Money . . . ," Jamaica, 1750, Add. MSS 30, 163, fols. 13-14, Brit. Mus.; "Memorial respecting the trade carried on by his Majesty's subjects to the French settlements in Hispaniola . . . ," Dec. 1760, C.O. 137/60, 321-330; "An estimate of the tea, sugar, and molasses illegally imported . . . ," ca. 1764, Add. MSS 38, 335, fol. 243, Brit. Mus.; "Calculations concerning the molasses duty," ca. 1766, T. 1/434, 52.

[34] Schumpeter, *English Overseas Trade Statistics,* 60-62; Charles Whitworth, *State of the Trade of Great Britain* . . . (London, 1776), 47-89; Mitchell and Deane, *British Historical Statistics,* 309-311.

[35] Noel Deerr, *The History of Sugar,* I (London, 1949), 193-201, 235-240; [Ambroise Marie] Arnould, *De la balance du commerce et des rélations commerciales exterieures de la France* . . . , III, 2d ed. (Paris, 1795 [orig. publ. 1791]), plates 10-13; Richard Pares, *War and Trade in the West Indies, 1739-1763* (Oxford, 1936), 364-365; Curtin, *Atlantic Slave Trade,* 52-84. Expansion in the French West Indies reflected and helped promote a pace of economic growth in France which paralleled that of England. Crouzet, "England and France," in Hartwell, ed., *Causes of the Industrial Revolution,* 145-149.

[36] For the volume of trade between the mainland colonies and the West Indies see Sachs, "Business Outlook," 273; Shepherd and Walton, *Shipping,* 169-171; Egnal, "Pennsylvania Economy," appendix I; and John James McCusker, Jr., "The Rum Trade and the Balance of Payments of the Thirteen Continental Colonies, 1650-1775" (Ph.D. diss., University of Pittsburgh, 1970). New price series for the British West Indies are presented in Egnal, "Pennsylvania Economy," appendix H. For other price data see the sources cited in nn. 28 and 32.

After 1760 West Indian growth slackened, reflecting weakened British demand, and the prices of most northern exports leveled off or declined. Per capita consumption of British goods fell slightly. Of the traditional northern exports, only the prices of wheat, bread, and flour soared to new heights in the late colonial period. The rise in grain prices was the result not of additional West Indian purchases, but of England's transition from grain exporter to grain importer and of new calls from markets, particularly Portugal, which Britain had traditionally supplied.[37]

While British growth after 1745 helped raise prices and the standard
244 of living in the northern colonies, the impact of British growth on southern prices and per capita income was less pronounced. The chief southern exports—tobacco, rice, and indigo—were sent directly to the mother country. But these staples, excepting indigo which was the least valuable, were only in part destined for British consumers. Over 70 percent of the tobacco and rice sent "home" was reexported to the European continent.[38] Trends in these continental markets and their effect on southern prices and standard of living may be briefly outlined.

The value of rice, the chief export of the lower South, was linked closely to the European market. Between 1720 and 1740 European demand was strong and rice production in South Carolina boomed. The quantity shipped more than doubled each decade. Permission to send rice directly to southern Europe, which Parliament granted in 1730, provided a further stimulus. (Less than one-fourth of the crop, however, was sent directly to Portugal and the Mediterranean lands, while more than one-half usually was shipped to Britain for reexport.) South Carolina prices, expressed in sterling, rose to ten shillings for a hundredweight of rice in the 1730s, from a low of about five shillings in the early 1720s. Prosperity in the Carolinas during the 1720s and 1730s was reflected by a sharp rise in per capita imports of British goods (see Figure 3). The War of the Austrian Succession, which stretched from 1740 to 1748, disrupted trade with the European continent, sent the value of rice tumbling to below two shillings a hundredweight, and plunged Carolina into depression. Per capita imports fell. Sales recovered during the 1750s, but

[37] Mitchell and Deane, *British Historical Statistics,* 285-291, 309-311; Whitworth, *State of Trade,* 49-50, 57-58; Cole, *Wholesale Commodity Prices: Supplement,* 32-71; Egnal, "Pennsylvania Economy," appendix I. For the effect of these changes on the commerce of one colony see Marc Egnal, "The Changing Structure of Philadelphia's Trade with the British West Indies, 1750-1775," *Pennsylvania Magazine of History and Biography,* forthcoming.

[38] On rice see Harper, "Effect of the Navigation Acts," in Morris, ed., *Era of the American Revolution,* 23; on tobacco see *Historical Statistics,* 766.

notable upward movement in prices and volume of exports was not apparent until the 1760s. By the early 1770s prices were over eleven shillings a hundredweight. Changes in the standard of living appear to have mirrored the success of rice production. The lower South, alone of the colonial regions, experienced a larger increase in per capita imports during the 1760s than during the 1750s.[39]

Indigo was the second most valuable export of the lower South and the only one of the leading southern staples whose prices reflected the pull of the British market. The plant was used to make a blue dye for textiles, and its cultivation was tied to the strong growth of British industry after 1745. Indigo was virtually uncultivated before 1745; after that date production and prices quickly soared. South Carolina's exports of indigo increased over sixfold between 1747-1749 and 1757-1759. A bounty of sixpence sterling per pound (on a product that sold in the 1750s for about four shillings a pound) provided a strong stimulus. Paralleling developments in Britain, prices declined and the expansion of indigo cultivation was markedly slower after 1760, but compared to the rice crop, changes in the profitability of indigo cultivation appear to have had only a minor effect on the standard of living in the lower South.[40]

The price of tobacco, the chief crop of the upper South and the most valuable colonial export, was affected not only by fluctuations in European demand but also by important changes in British marketing arrangements. Demand for this weed expanded steadily, if moderately, during the eighteenth century. Between 1720 and 1775 colonial shipments to Britain increased an average of roughly 25 percent a decade. Little of the crop was destined for consumers in the realm; British merchants generally reexported between 80 and 90 percent of the hogsheads they received.[41] World prices, which had been unusually high

[39] The basic series for Carolina rice quotations used here is that in Cole, *Wholesale Commodity Prices: Supplement*, 15-69. Interpolations and extrapolations of missing data have been made using another Charleston series for rice in Gray, *History of Agriculture*, I, 277-290, II, 1030, with occasional reference to the Philadelphia statistics in Bezanson *et al.*, *Prices in Colonial Pennsylvania*, appendix. Carolina pounds have been reduced to sterling by using a par of 700 except where data suggested fluctuations from this mark. Joseph Albert Ernst, *Money and Politics in America, 1755-1775: A Study in the Currency Act of 1764 and the Political Economy of Revolution* (Chapel Hill, N. C., 1973), 378; John Sinclair to John Reynell, Nov. 20, 1751, Apr. 11, 1752, Reynell Papers, Historical Society of Pennsylvania, Philadelphia; James & Drinker to John Clitherall, May 9, 1760, James & Drinker Letterbook, *ibid.*

[40] Gray, *History of Agriculture*, I, 290-297; *Historical Statistics*, 745-746, 762; Bezanson *et al.*, *Prices in Colonial Pennsylvania*, appendix.

[41] *Historical Statistics*, 765-767; Price, *France and the Chesapeake*, II, 843-844, 849.

during the first decades of the century, dropped sharply during the 1720s. Tobacco quotations also fell in the upper South at this time, and this drop most likely underlay the decline in Virginia's and Maryland's per capita imports of British goods between 1720 and 1730. By the late 1720s the decline in world tobacco prices had ceased, and the market value of tobacco, while fluctuating, was marked by a level trend. Both in Europe and in the Chesapeake, prices varied about an unchanged mean between 1730 and 1745. Although tobacco cultivation spread in the upper South during this period, there seem to have been only small gains in per capita income.[42]

246 Between 1745 and 1770 the trends of tobacco prices in Europe and the upper South diverged: European prices continued to exhibit a level trend, while the value of the weed in Virginia and Maryland gradually rose. According to available evidence, between 1740-1744 and 1760-1764 colonial prices for tobacco increased 34 percent. These higher valuations appear to have been the product of a new, more efficient marketing structure, and of increased competition among British houses. Prior to 1745 English merchants and the consignment system dominated the purchase and reshipment of tobacco. The planter directed his produce to a particular London house, and the English firm marketed the hogsheads and advanced credit to finance cultivation of the following crop. This system catered to the larger planters who could assemble a consignment of several dozen hogsheads and who could readily secure a "London

[42] The lack of a long-run, internally consistent series for Chesapeake tobacco prices is a major handicap for economic historians. Virginia and Maryland price data and series covering short periods are presented in Calvin Brewster Coulter, Jr., "The Virginia Merchant" (Ph.D. diss., Princeton University, 1944), *passim;* Samuel Michael Rosenblatt, "The House of John Norton & Sons: A Study of the Consignment Method of Marketing Tobacco from Virginia to England" (Ph.D. diss., Rutgers University, 1960), *passim;* Ronald Hoffman, "Economics, Politics and the Revolution in Maryland" (Ph.D. diss., University of Wisconsin, 1969), appendix D; Shepherd and Walton, *Shipping,* 208-209. These quotations must be adjusted for serious fluctuations in the exchange rate. See Ernst, *Money and Politics,* 376-377. With corrections drawn from these sources, I have used Philadelphia tobacco prices presented by Bezanson *et al., Prices in Colonial Pennsylvania,* appendix. The sensitivity of Pennsylvania prices to changes in other regional markets is suggested by a comparison of Philadelphia and Charleston rice quotations, and by a comparison of Philadelphia and Boston wheat prices. Cole, *Wholesale Commodity Prices: Supplement,* 6-69. For Amsterdam tobacco prices see Nicolaas Wilhelmus Posthumus, *Inquiry into the History of Prices in Holland* (Leiden, 1946), 202-203. Scottish prices are presented in Price, *France and the Chesapeake,* II, 671-677. Price also presents data for Amsterdam. See p. 852. On conditions in the upper South between 1720 and 1745 see Jacob M. Price, "The Economic Growth of the Chesapeake and the European Market, 1697-1775," *Jour. Econ. Hist.,* XXIV (1964), 497-498, and *Historical Statistics,* 756, 769.

credit." Frequently, these wealthy landowners also handled the output of their less affluent neighbors. Consignments persisted after 1745, but a new method of marketing, based on direct purchases by local factors, became increasingly important and helped raise Chesapeake prices. The parent firms for most of these factors were in Glasgow, and the growth of direct purchasing reflected the strong expansion of the Scottish economy after 1745. The factors could offer higher prices because they made more efficient use of shipping (factors were able to load vessels more rapidly than could the consigning planters; the voyage to Glasgow was quicker than that to London) and because they dealt directly with the region's numerous small planters and eliminated the large planter as a middleman. Moreover, vigorous competition among British tobacco houses meant that economies were passed along to planters in the form of higher prices.[43]

Rising tobacco prices had their most significant impact on per capita income in the upper South between 1745 and 1760. Higher quotations increased individual purchasing power and helped raise the level of per capita imports of British manufactures (see Figure 2). But these advances must not be overstated. The rise in tobacco prices was less than the gains recorded by foodstuffs sent to the Caribbean. Between 1740-1744 and 1760-1764, the value of tobacco rose 34 percent, but wheat prices increased 59 percent, flour 54 percent, and pork 48 percent. During this period, the market for produce expanded more vigorously. The quantity of flour shipped from Philadelphia increased about 200 percent while Chesapeake tobacco exports rose less than 50 percent.[44]

Tobacco prices continued to move upward between 1760 and 1775, but higher quotations did not readily translate into an improved standard of living. While the rise in prices between 1745 and 1760 seems to have been the product of genuine gains in the efficiency of marketing and

[43] Jacob M. Price, "The Rise of Glasgow in the Chesapeake Tobacco Trade, 1707-1775," *WMQ*, 3d Ser., XI (1954), 179-199; Samuel M. Rosenblatt, "The Significance of Credit in the Tobacco Consignment Trade: A Study of John Norton & Sons, 1768-1775," *ibid.*, XIX (1962), 383-399; *Historical Statistics*, 766; Shepherd and Walton, *Shipping*, 59-60; Aubrey C. Land, "Economic Base and Social Structure: The Northern Chesapeake in the Eighteenth Century," *Jour. Econ. Hist.*, XXV (1965), 649; Ronald Hoffman, *A Spirit of Dissension: Economics, Politics, and the Revolution in Maryland* (Baltimore, 1973), 22-25.

[44] Bezanson *et al.*, *Prices in Colonial Pennsylvania*, appendix; *Historical Statistics*, 765-767; Klopfer, "Statistics of Foreign Trade," 173. On the increase in per capita income in the upper South see Aubrey C. Land, "The Tobacco Staple and the Planter's Problems: Technology, Labor, and Crops," *Ag. Hist.*, XLIII (1969), 76-79, and D. Alan Williams, "The Small Farmer in Eighteenth-Century Virginia Politics," *ibid.*, 93-95.

of vigorous competition among British buyers, the price rise after 1760 was more the result of a run of short crops and of brief spurts of speculative buying. Between 1763 and 1769, the quantity of tobacco shipped from the Chesapeake to Britain declined from 98,000,000 pounds to about 70,000,000 pounds, limiting the gains that might have resulted from higher quotations. During 1770, 1771, and 1772 planters enjoyed favorable crops and high prices as a wave of speculative purchasing increased the worth of tobacco. This wave of buying was halted abruptly, however, and prices plummeted when financial crisis shook the British economy and particularly the tobacco houses.[45] As a result of short crops, the
248 vicissitudes of speculative purchases, and the trouble that planters had in obtaining capital after 1760 (a problem that is examined below), higher tobacco prices between 1760 and 1775 did not mean prosperity for planters. One indication of the problems planters faced was the sharp decline in per capita imports of British wares after 1760 (see Figure 2).

Because of only moderate growth in the demand for and price of tobacco between 1745 and 1775, planters explored the possibility of raising other crops that would allow them to benefit from the post-1745 expansion of the British economy. A slump in tobacco sales in the mid-1750s spurred experimentation. Some planters diverted resources to hemp production. Others made a trial of indigo, although this was short-lived.[46] Most notable was the spread of Indian corn and wheat production in the upper South. The region had always produced significant amounts of these crops, but only after 1745 did output increase sharply. Between 1745 and 1760 the expansion of corn and wheat production and the strong rise in the price of these commodities helped boost the region's per capita income. After 1760 the market value of wheat continued to rise, chiefly because of the growth of the southern European market, but the price of corn, which was less affected by Iberian demand, recorded no further gains after the early 1760s. Moderate corn prices tended to limit increases in per capita income.[47]

[45] *Historical Statistics*, 766; Bezanson *et al.*, *Prices in Colonial Pennsylvania*, appendix; Price, *France and the Chesapeake*, II, 671-677, 852; Gray, *History of Agriculture*, I, 274-275; Hoffman, *Spirit of Dissension*, 96-103; Rosenblatt, "Significance of Credit," *WMQ*, 3d Ser., XIX (1962), 393-396.

[46] George M. Herndon, "The Story of Hemp in Colonial Virginia" (Ph.D. diss., University of Virginia, 1959); Coulter, "Virginia Merchant," 122, 140-142; *Historical Statistics*, 745-746, 762; Bezanson *et al.*, *Prices in Colonial Pennsylvania*, appendix; Andrew Burnaby, *Travels Through the Middle Settlements in North-America in the Years 1759 and 1760*, 3d ed. (New York, 1970 [orig. publ. 1798]), 59-60.

[47] Hoffman, "Economics," 118-122, appendix D; James H. Soltow, *The Eco-*

In sum, and excepting the lower South, the economic growth stimulated by higher export prices was most notable between 1745 and 1760, and was much less pronounced between 1760 and 1775.

Per capita income rose for a third reason: the amount of capital available to each white settler increased. Those wishing to borrow funds found them easier to obtain. This enabled the colonists to enjoy a higher standard of living. For example, planters found the acquisition of slaves easier, merchants could expand their sphere of activities, and small farmers found local shopkeepers more liberal in selling dry goods or farm implements. The chief source of capital was the increasing amount of credit which Britain extended to the colonies. The growth of colonial capital resources, like changes in export and import prices, was tied closely to the expansion of the British economy. By the late colonial period the value of colonial indebtedness to Britain was sizable. Barlow Trecothick, a leading London "North American" merchant, reported to the House of Commons in 1766:

The Committee of the Merchants of London trading to North America . . . do unanimously authorize me to give it as their opinion, that at the lowest compilation there is due the merchants of London only	£2,900,000
The agent for the merchants in Bristol authorizes in the same manner to say that there is due that town	800,000
Ditto from Glasgow (Virginia and Maryland only)	500,000
Ditto from Liverpool	150,000
Ditto from Manchester	100,000
	£4,450,000

Besides sums due to Lancaster, Whitehaven, Birmingham, Sheffield, Leeds, Norwich, Wakefield, Halifax, and other manufacturing towns, which must considerably augment the balance due from North America.[48]

---

nomic Role of Williamsburg (Charlottesville, Va., 1965), 75-97; Price, *France and the Chesapeake*, II, 669-670; Shepherd and Walton, *Shipping*, 167-171; Bezanson *et al.*, *Prices in Colonial Pennsylvania*, appendix; Klingaman, "Significance of Grain," *Jour. Econ. Hist.*, XXIX (1969), 268-278. For exports of Virginia's port districts for the selected period, 1771-1775, see T. 1/482, 239, T. 1/484, 54, and T. 1/506, 2-13.

[48] "Trecothick's Observations on the Merchants' Petition," 1766, Add. MSS 33,030, fol. 215, Brit. Mus.

The extension of British credit to the American colonies may be most usefully examined with a twofold division: those areas where British funds were channeled through the coastal merchants (that is, the northern colonies and lower South); and that area where British houses or their factors dealt directly with the colonists (that is, the upper South).[49]

The value of English capital extended to the merchants in the northern colonies and lower South increased remarkably, especially between 1745 and 1760. Easier credit for the colonies was closely tied to the growth of the mother country's economy. The English shipper relied on various financial intermediaries. As the British economy expanded after 1745
250 and the banking structure improved, exporting houses could offer more generous credit terms. One manifestation of the increased liberality of credit between 1745 and 1760 was the gradual extension of the credit period. In the mid-1740s goods were shipped typically on six months' credit. Gradually this interval lengthened, so that in 1760 a Philadelphia trader could state firmly: "From London we have twelve months' credit for our goods."[50] A second indication of the increased flow of funds to the New World was the willingness of English houses to grant credit to more individuals within each port city. Shopkeepers and vendue-masters, traditionally excluded from direct dealings with overseas houses, now found themselves beset by offers from London and Bristol. While this development angered the established American merchants, it meant that more individuals in each colonial port city could extend credit to local shopkeepers, who in turn could credit farmers and city dwellers.[51]

After 1760 the growth of the English economy slackened and English exporters became more wary of extending capital to colonial merchants. The credit period, which had reached one year by 1760, was not extended

[49] The impact of changes in the "visible" money supply (chiefly specie and paper money) on the development of the colonial economy was relatively slight. For a full discussion of this issue and a review of the historiographical debate see Ernst, *Money and Politics,* Chap. 1, and Egnal, "Pennsylvania Economy," 258-260.

[50] James & Drinker to John Lindoe, Aug. 26, 1760, to William Neate, June 21, 1759, to Daniel Mildred, Aug. 25, 1760, James & Drinker Letterbook; Joseph Broadbent to John Pemberton, Nov. 26, 1753, Pemberton Papers, Hist. Soc. Pa.; Thomas Crowley to Thomas Wharton, Aug. 6, 1754, Wharton Correspondence, *ibid.;* John Kidd to Neate & Neave, Dec. 28, 1758, Kidd Letterbook, *ibid.;* Arthur L. Jensen, *The Maritime Commerce of Colonial Philadelphia* (Madison, Wis., 1963), 99-101. Individual British houses occasionally pursued credit policies that differed from the norm.

[51] British mercantile practices in the northern colonies are examined at length in Egnal, "Pennsylvania Economy," Chaps. 3-6. For information on the lower South see the letters from John Guerard to Robert Stebbing, 1748-1761, Round Papers, Essex Record Office, Chelmsford, Eng.

further. Indeed, several English houses discussed the possibility of returning to a shorter period. The practice of offering credit to shopkeepers and vendue-masters was less evident after 1760. Only during a brief upswing in the English economy in the early 1770s did colonial merchants complain about these problems. Rather, traders in the colonial port cities were troubled by a series of credit contractions during the 1760s and during 1772 and 1773. The steps that British exporters took to draw in their affairs were soon felt up and down the chain of credit. Farmers and artisans found imported manufactures more difficult to obtain, and this helped check the rise in the colonial standard of living.[52]

The increased flow of British capital to the New World also helped 251
increase per capita income in the upper South. As in those areas served by port cities, improvement was most apparent between 1745 and 1760. The rise of the Scots factors in Virginia and Maryland after 1745 was accompanied not only by intense competition for the tobacco crop but also by a great expansion of credit. The benefits of the credit expansion were felt particularly by the small tobacco planters. Before 1745, English funds had been available only to the large planters and planter/merchants. Individuals who held less than three hundred acres and one or two slaves had been excluded from direct dealings with the London houses. These smaller planters became the chief debtors of the Scottish firms. The average sum owed to two large Glasgow houses in the late colonial period was £29, and 94 percent of those indebted owed less than £100. By contrast, the amount due six English firms averaged £664, and one-half the debts were over £100. Although the average amount loaned by the Scots was small, aggregate indebtedness was large. Competition among British firms also meant that credit terms became increasingly generous. Overdue debts rarely led immediately to lawsuits. More commonly, the factor allowed the debt to be bonded, or accepted a mortgage as surety. Consequently, a portion of the short-term debt formally became long-term indebtedness and was an important addition to the colonists' working capital.[53]

[52] David & John Barclay to James Pemberton, Jan. 14, 1771, Pemberton Papers; Christopher Rawson to T. Wharton, July 19, 1773, Wharton Correspondence. For credit contraction in the Carolinas see the valuable letters of William Pollard, Jan.-Feb. 1774, Pollard Letterbook, Hist. Soc. Pa.; Sachs, "Business Outlook," Chaps. 5-7; and Ernst, *Money and Politics, passim.*

[53] Richard B. Sheridan, "The British Credit Crisis of 1772 and the American Colonies," *Jour. Econ. Hist.*, XX (1960), 179-181; Testimony of Barlow Trecothick before Committee of Parliament, Feb. 11, 1766, Testimony of John Glassford, Feb. 13, 1766, Add. MSS 33,030, fols. 104, 160-163, Brit. Mus.; Soltow, *Economic Role of Williamsburg*, 140-144; Aubrey C. Land, "Economic Behavior in a Plant-

Between 1760 and 1775 the pace of growth of the British economy slowed and British creditors were more reluctant to extend credit to the tobacco colonies. Although there were periods when British houses were willing or even eager to enlarge their affairs in the Chesapeake, as during the late 1760s and in 1770 and 1771, these houses evinced greater caution than between 1745 and 1760. Twice, in 1762 and again in 1772-1773, British firms contracted their affairs sharply, calling in old debts and causing the planters much hardship. Virginians and Marylanders were forced to redirect funds from purchases to the reduction of indebtedness. As in the northern colonies and lower South, this credit contraction
252 worked to retard improvement in the standard of living.[54]

Although new dimensions to the economy became evident after 1760, they did not compensate for the slowdown in the upward movement of export prices or for the reduced influx of British capital. The other reason for economic growth discussed above—increases in productivity brought about by new techniques—was evident after 1760 as before, but made only a minor contribution to improving the colonial standard of living.

New forces for economic growth, although too weak to assure an increase in per capita income, offered encouragement to colonists between 1760 and 1775. One stimulus was the growing demand of southern Europe for American grain. The other reasons related to the domestic economy and foreshadowed later patterns of American development—the strengthening of the home market, the expansion of textile and shoe production, and the acquisition and exploitation of western lands. These four developments, their strengths and limitations, may be examined in turn.

First, southern European demand for colonial grain expanded rapidly in the mid-1760s, helping to raise the price of wheat, bread, and flour, and consequently the standard of living in the wheat-growing colonies. The growth of this market reflected the disappearance of Britain's grain surpluses and the need of Iberian importers to seek another source of supply. Although this expanded commerce was important for the middle colonies, and particularly for Pennsylvania, its general impact on the North American economy was less noteworthy. Between 1768 and 1772, when shipments to southern Europe were most significant,

---

ing Society: The Eighteenth-Century Chesapeake," *Journal of Southern History*, XXXIII (1967), 476-479.

[54] Sheridan, "British Credit Crisis," *Jour. Econ. Hist.*, XX (1960), 174-185; Hoffman, *Spirit of Dissension*, 96-103; Soltow, *Economic Role of Williamsburg*, 154; Gray, *History of Agriculture*, I, 274-275; Ernst, *Money and Politics*, 66-68;

only 15 percent of colonial exports were directed to that market.[55]

Second, and more portentous for the future growth of per capita income, was the gathering strength of intercolonial trade and the increasing importance of the market within the thirteen colonies. In terms set down by Adam Smith, a larger market allowed increased specialization and tended to make every individual more productive. Trade statistics suggest the magnitude of intercolonial exchanges and the growing importance of local consumption. Between 1768 and 1772, 54 percent of the tonnage clearing Boston was destined for other mainland ports. The comparable figure for New York was 35 percent, for Philadelphia, 30 percent, and for Charleston, 16 percent. Tonnage figures drawn from the years between 1720 and 1759 indicate that these percentages marked not only significant absolute gains, but also (with the exception of New York) notable increases in the portion of shipping involved in the coasting trade. New England rum and fish, bread and flour from the middle colonies, corn from the upper South, and Carolina rice found a growing market in other colonies.[56] Yet despite its importance, such trade was not yet large enough or rich enough to sustain growth. Each province still relied more heavily on earnings from foreign commerce and, except for Pennsylvania's grain exports and the rice shipments of the lower South, these were slack after 1760.[57]

Pollard to Benjamin & John Bower, July 24, Sept. 27, 1773, Pollard Letterbook.

[55] In the middle colonies, gains from higher wheat, bread, and flour prices after 1760 were partially cancelled by declining mercantile profits. Most of the grain shipped from New York and Pennsylvania was directed to the West Indies, and sugar planters frequently could not afford to pay higher first costs and also provide the exporter with an adequate return. The upper South sent a larger portion of its grain to Iberia and so was less affected by worsening conditions in the Caribbean. Middle colony shipments, however, were far more valuable than grain exports from the Chesapeake. Egnal, "Pennsylvania Economy," 291-300; Shepherd and Walton, *Shipping*, 115, 160, 211-225; Bezanson *et al.*, *Prices in Colonial Pennsylvania*, appendix; Sachs, "Business Outlook," 140-143, 187, 274-275; Hoffman, "Economics," 393-400.

[56] Adam Smith, *An Inquiry into the Nature and Causes of the Wealth of Nations* (London, 1776), Book I, chaps. 1-3; *Historical Statistics*, 759-760; Sachs, "Business Outlook," 175-188, 273-276; James G. Lydon, "Philadelphia's Commercial Expansion, 1720-1739," *PMHB*, XCI (1967), 415; James F. Shepherd and Samuel H. Williamson, "The Coastal Trade of the British North American Colonies, 1768-1772," *Jour. Econ. Hist.*, XXXII (1972), 783-810; Klingaman, "Food Surpluses," *ibid.*, XXXI (1971), 553-569. During the period 1720-1775 the increase in the percentage of tonnage involved in the coasting trade was most marked for Philadelphia and Boston.

[57] For an approach emphasizing the importance of the export trade for the early stages of development see Melville H. Watkins, "A Staple Theory of Economic Growth," *Canadian Journal of Economics and Political Science*, XXIX (1963), 141-158.

Third, the rise of textile and shoe production provided another stimulus for economic growth after 1760. An increase in the percentage of the work force engaged in manufactures meant not only the diversification of the colonial economy, but also a significant gain in product per capita. Studies of early nineteenth-century craft industries show that the value added by each industrial worker was substantially greater than the value added by each agricultural worker. If these findings hold for the colonial period—and the activities involved are similar—then any shift in the labor force from agriculture to industry meant a rise in the average standard of living.[58]

254 An increasing number of people became involved in textile production both in the countryside and in the towns after 1760. Spinning and weaving expanded in rural areas for several reasons. Farmers responded to patriotic appeals for domestic manufactures; the post-1760 credit contraction and the nonimportation agreements made the purchase of imported goods more difficult; and growing inequalities of wealth in the settled areas created a labor force willing to embrace cottage industry. A Pennsylvanian observed in 1773 that "many thousands, rather than go farther back into the country where lands are cheap or undertake the arduous task of clearing new lands, turn to manufacturing, and live upon a small farm, as in many parts of England."[59] Manufacturing was important in some towns even before this period. Andrew Burnaby, who visited the colonies in 1760, reported that "above 60,000 pair" of stockings were made in a year at Germantown, near Philadelphia.[60] During the 1760s Boston, New York, and Philadelphia all established large manufactories. Each of the institutions coordinated the work of several hundred spinners and of more than a dozen weavers.[61] Advances also were recorded in the southern lowcountry. Traditionally, southern planters had imported virtually all the cloth they needed, manufacturing only a small amount of coarse fabric for the slaves. After 1760, while still behind the North and local backcountry, spinning and weaving became

[58] David, "Growth of Real Product," *Jour. Econ. Hist.*, XXVII (1967), 168-171.

[59] Pollard to Benjamin & John Bower, Apr. 6, 1773, Pollard Letterbook; Arthur Meier Schlesinger, *The Colonial Merchants and the American Revolution, 1763-1776* (New York, 1917), 64-67, 77, 109-111, 122-124, 130-131.

[60] Benson, ed., *Peter Kalm's Travels*, I, 93.

[61] These met with mixed success, but failure often was followed by the establishment of another, larger manufactory. Rolla Milton Tryon, *Household Manufactures in the United States, 1640-1860* (Chicago, 1917), 86-88, 245-246; T. Wharton to Benjamin Franklin, Apr. 26, 1766, in Leonard W. Labaree *et al.*, eds., *The Papers of Benjamin Franklin* (New Haven, Conn., 1959-), XII, 252. See also *ibid.*, XI, 314-316.

more common on the plantations. Progress seems to have been most notable in Virginia and least marked in the rice lands of South Carolina and Georgia.[62]

The production of footwear also expanded during the late colonial period, and a growing number of individuals were involved in this enterprise, particularly in the coastal towns of the northern colonies. Lynn, Massachusetts, for example, produced about 80,000 pairs of shoes in 1767. In New England, American-made shoes not only predominated in the rural areas, but also gradually replaced shoes of British manufacture in the trading towns where imported goods were plentiful.[63]

The growth of colonial manufacturing had a significant impact on the 255
standard of living in the different regions and on the subsequent course of economic development. Home and town industry helped raise per capita income in the northern colonies. Thus, while southern whites generally imported more British goods per capita than northern whites, this distinction cannot be taken as proof of northern backwardness (see Figures 1, 2, and 3). More plausibly it suggests the importance of textile and other manufacturing in the North.[64] This local production provided an important base for industrial development in subsequent decades. There is a direct line from the manufactories of the 1760s, which organized the work of numerous spinners, to the spinning mills of the 1790s, which distributed machine-spun thread to local weavers, to the establishment of complete factories, based on the power loom, beginning in 1815.[65]

[62] Tryon, *Household Manufactures*, 4, 102-103, 110-111, 177-178; Clark, *History of Manufactures*, I, 209; Gray, *History of Agriculture*, I, 454.

[63] Tryon, *Household Manufactures*, 200; Clark, *History of Manufactures*, I, 116, 207-208; Gov. William Stuart to Secretary of State Dartmouth, Dec. 24, 1773, C.O. 71/4, 71; James & Drinker to Thomas Evans, Dec. 3, 1761, James & Drinker Letterbook. Other American manufactures expanded between 1760 and 1775, particularly iron, alkalies, and whale products. *Historical Statistics*, 757, 761-765, 771; Sachs, "Business Outlook," 188-192.

[64] Even before the Revolution, domestic manufactures in the northern colonies had eliminated certain British products from the market. Thus Pennsylvania-refined sugar replaced that baked in England. John Kidd to Rawlinson & Davison, May 2, 1751, Kidd Letterbook; Bezanson *et al.*, *Prices in Colonial Pennsylvania*, 180. Similarly, low grades of English cloth were eliminated by homespun. Thomas Willing to Burrow & Edwards, Apr. 6, 1755, Willing Letterbook, Hist. Soc. Pa.; James & Drinker to David Barclay & Sons, Nov. 4, 1761, James & Drinker Letterbook. It should be noted that the difference between northern and southern per capita consumption of British imports persists even if one assumes that a portion of goods purchased from England was consumed by the slave population.

[65] Tryon, *Household Manufactures*, 171-177; Clark, *History of Manufactures*, I, 438-463.

Fourth, Britain's acquisition in 1763 of the land between the Appalachians and the Mississippi provided the colonists with a rich territory that seemed to be a guarantee of future economic growth. For some, this land also held the promise of immediate returns. Eventually western lands yielded rich profits to settlers, speculators, and the federal government, but during the late colonial period the territory proved a troublesome asset for those seeking immediate gains. Several companies, based for the most part in Virginia and Pennsylvania, projected schemes for the development of the West. These plans ran afoul of British desires to contain colonial expansion and reduce the costs of dealing
256 with the Indians. The western lands perhaps were most important for the encouraging cast they gave to the nation's future.[66]

The impetus for growth in per capita product provided by southern European demand, the home market, manufacturing, and western lands, although important, was not sufficient to make the late colonial period one of buoyant expansion. Movements in world prices and fluctuations in the flow of British capital were all-important for the American economy, and these were not favorable between 1760 and 1775. By 1800, economic historians have suggested, America's own productivity and resources, and not the stimulus of an international economy, had become the main source of economic growth.[67] But in the late colonial period the home market and domestic resources were not yet sufficiently developed.

Nonetheless, a significant reweighting of the forces for growth had occurred in the years following 1760, and this change had serious ramifications. The domestic economy had become more important; the beneficial effects of the British Empire had been brought into question. This new economic balance helped shape the outlook of the Revolutionary generation. British restrictions on the local economy were questioned seriously, in many cases for the first time. Colonial pamphleteers and editorialists noted that royal proclamations and Parliamentary enactments prevented Americans from establishing private banks, disposing of western lands, imposing tariffs or navigation acts, or effectively regu-

[66] Merrill Jensen, *The Founding of a Nation: A History of the American Revolution, 1763-1776* (New York, 1968), 386-399; Jack M. Sosin, *Whitehall and the Wilderness: The Middle West in British Colonial Policy, 1760-1775* (Lincoln, Neb., 1961).

[67] David, "Growth of Real Product," *Jour. Econ. Hist.*, XXVII (1967), 151-197. For a contrasting approach to growth during the early 19th century see Douglass C. North, *The Economic Growth of the United States, 1790-1860* (Englewood Cliffs, N. J., 1961). North emphasizes the role played by the export trade.

lating local currency. Some individuals observed that the lack of a unified colonial government hindered development. The sovereignty that Americans gained with Independence and the unity they secured with the Constitution would be of singular help in promoting economic growth.[68]

The paradigm, or model, of colonial economic development set forth above is clearly a tentative one, and the reasons offered for the nature and timing of population increase and for changes in per capita income must bear the scrutiny of future empirical research. It is hoped, however, that the pattern of explanation presented here will help raise the debate over economic development to a higher level. With further studies we can draw still closer to an understanding of how the colonies grew and how that process affected the Revolutionary movement.

[68] For example, Charles Thomson to Cook, Lawrence & Co., Nov. 9, 1765, "Thomson Papers," New-York Historical Society, *Collections*, XI (1878), 8-11; Franklin to Lord Kames, Feb. 25, 1767, in Labaree *et al.*, eds., *Franklin Papers*, XIV, 69-70; Richard Waln, Jr., to Nicholas Waln, June 25, 1764, Richard Waln Letterbook, Hist. Soc. Pa. See also Marc Egnal and Joseph A. Ernst, "An Economic Interpretation of the American Revolution," *WMQ*, 3d Ser., XXIX (1972), 3-32, and Merrill Jensen, *The Articles of Confederation: An Interpretation of the Social-Constitutional History of the American Revolution, 1774-1781* (Madison, Wis., 1940), Chaps. 4-8.

Angels' Heads and Weeping Willows: Death in Early America

258 MARIS A. VINOVSKIS

Most recent studies of America's past can be placed into one of two distinct and sometimes hostile camps. Traditional historians have continued to rely almost exclusively on literary sources of information. As a result, their work has focused on the ideology and attitudes of early Americans. On the other hand, a small group of historians, borrowing heavily from the other social sciences, have undertaken to recreate the behavioral patterns of American society in the past. Though these two approaches are potentially complementary to each other, there has been very little effort made to integrate them.

This bifurcation of approaches to the study of American history is quite evident in the recent efforts to analyze the role of death in America. Traditional historians have begun to examine the writings of early Americans in order to recreate their attitudes and images of death. Historical demographers have exploited the censuses and vital records to calculate the incidence and timing of death in early America.

This paper was presented as a public lecture at the American Antiquarian Society on May 22, 1974, while the author was the Rockefeller Fellow in the History of the Family Program at Clark University and AAS. The author is deeply indebted to Andrew Achenbaum, Georgia Bumgardner, Ronald Formisano, Tamara Hareven, John Hench, Kathryn Sklar, Mary Vinovskis, and John Zeugner for their helpful comments and suggestions.

But no one has attempted to explore systematically the relationship between attitudes toward death and the actual levels and trends in mortality in early America. In part, this is the result of the assumption by most historians that the attitudes toward and the incidence of death in America were identical.

In this essay we will demonstrate that most colonists did not accurately perceive the extent of mortality in their society. We will suggest some of the reasons for their misperception. Hopefully this essay will encourage other scholars to integrate attitudinal and behavioral approaches to the study of American history.

Most of us have certain preconceived notions about death in colonial America. We envision the early settlers of our country facing such a multitude of hazards that death at a fairly early age was practically inevitable. We also imagine that persons surviving to old age were quite rare and extremely fortunate in having escaped the continuous waves of famine and pestilence which swept through the population. The idea that high mortality rates prevailed in colonial America has been reinforced by the numerous instances of entire families or communities perishing in the hostile environment of the New World.

Nearly all of us are familiar with the tragic experiences of the Pilgrims who landed at Plymouth on November 11, 1620. Though only one of the 102 passengers aboard the *Mayflower* perished at sea, the eleven-week journey had left the rest of them weak, exhausted, and unprepared for the coming winter. Bradford noted their ordeal in his diary: '. . . But that which was most sadd & lamentable was, that in 2. or 3. moneths time halfe of their company dyed, espetialy in Jan: & February, being the depth of winter, and wanting houses & other comforts; being infected with the scurvie & other diseases, which this long vioage & their inacomodate condition had brought upon them; so as ther dyed some times 2. or 3.

of a day, in the foresaid time; that of 100 & odd persons, scarce 50 remained. . . .'[1]

Even those settlers who survived the rigors of the first year in the New World faced unforeseen epidemics which took very heavy tolls of the inhabitants—especially in urban areas such as Boston and Salem. In 1721 there was an outbreak of smallpox in Boston in which over fifty percent of its eleven thousand inhabitants contracted the disease. In that year the Boston death rate soared to an incredible 103 deaths
260 per thousand population. Thus, over ten percent of the city's population died within the space of one year.[2] Only the very small percentage of the people daring enough to try the new technique of inoculation managed to escape the high death rate among those who had smallpox.[3]

Smaller communities were not safe from the terrors of epidemics. For example, in the parish of Hampton Falls in New Hampshire the 'sore-throat distemper' in 1735 nearly decimated the population. This epidemic, later identified as diphtheria, resulted in the deaths of 210 persons—or over one-sixth of the entire population of that parish. The outbreak of diphtheria caused fatalities particularly among young people—ninety-five percent of those who died in Hampton Falls were under the age of twenty. Nearly twenty families buried all of their children that year.[4]

Any person still skeptical of the existence of high mortality in early America would certainly be convinced by one of the

[1] William Bradford, *Of Plymouth Plantation*, Harvey Wish, ed. (New York, 1962), p. 70. For a more detailed discussion of the experiences of the Pilgrims, see George D. Langdon, Jr., *Pilgrim Colony: A History of New Plymouth, 1620–1691* (New Haven, 1966).

[2] On the extent of mortality in Boston, see John B. Blake, *Public Health in the Town of Boston, 1630–1882* (Cambridge, Mass., 1952).

[3] Blake, *Public Health*, pp. 74–98; John Duffy, *Epidemics in Colonial America* (Baton Rouge, 1953), pp. 16–112.

[4] Duffy, *Epidemics*, pp. 117–18; Ernest Caulfield, 'A History of the Terrible Epidemic, Vulgarly Called the Throat Distemper, as It Occurred in His Majesty's New England Colonies between 1735 and 1740,' *Yale Journal of Biology and Medicine* 11(1938–39),219–72, 277–335.

few extant life tables for that period—the Wigglesworth Life Table of 1789. Edward Wigglesworth, Hollis Professor of Divinity at Harvard, became interested in life tables when he was advising the Massachusetts Congregational Charitable Society on how to establish an annuity fund for the widows of ministers. At that time there were no life tables available for the United States from which to estimate the life expectancies of the ministers and their wives. Therefore, Wigglesworth collected bills of mortality from various New 261
England towns with the active cooperation of the newly established Academy of Arts and Sciences in Boston. From the sixty-two bills of mortality returned, Wigglesworth constructed a life table in 1789. He calculated that the average person in New England could expect to live only 35.5 years—thus reinforcing our grim image of health conditions in early America.[5]

Most writers have argued that death rates in seventeenth- and eighteenth-century New England were very high, and there is also a consensus that life expectancy improved significantly in the first half of the nineteenth century. This interpretation is based on a comparison of Wigglesworth's Life Table of 1789 and Elliott's table of 1855 for Massachusetts. On the basis of these two tables, it appears that the average person in the Commonwealth could expect to live an additional 4.3 years by 1855.[6]

[5] Edward Wigglesworth, 'A Table Shewing the Probability of the Duration, the Decrement, and the Expectation of Life, in the States of Massachusetts and New Hampshire, formed from sixty two Bills of Mortality on the files of the American Academy of Arts and Sciences, in the Year 1789,' *Memoirs of the American Academy of Arts and Sciences*, 2, pt. 1(1793):131–35. For an analysis of the gathering of that data as well as its utilization, see Maris A. Vinovskis, 'The 1789 Life Table of Edward Wigglesworth,' *Journal of Economic History* 31(1971):570–90.

[6] Warren S. Thompson and P. K. Whelpton, *Population Trends in the United States* (New York, 1933), pp. 228–40. A more recent interpretation of mortality trends by Yasukichi Yasuba argues that death rates probably were increasing just prior to the Civil War because of the increase in urbanization and industrialization. Yasukichi Yasuba, *Birth Rates of the White Population in the United States, 1800–1860: An Economic Study*, The Johns Hopkins University Studies in Historical and Political Science, vol. 79, no. 2 (Baltimore, 1962), pp. 86–96.

Thus, the traditional picture of mortality in early America is one of high death rates in the seventeenth and eighteenth centuries followed by a marked improvement in the nineteenth century. A sociologist has recently summarized the extent of mortality in early America as follows:

> Although precise statistical evidence is lacking, the little that
> scientists have been able to compile from various anthropological
> and archaeological sources indicates that throughout most of his
> existence man has had to contend with an extremely high death
> 262 rate. The brutally harsh conditions of life in the pre-industrial
> world made human survival very much a touch-and-go affair.
> A newborn infant had no more than a fifty-fifty chance of surviving to adulthood; the average life expectancy of primitive man was probably not much in excess of twenty-five or thirty years. Even more significant, the survival situation was not a great deal better as recently as the middle of the eighteenth century. Early records for the state of Massachusetts, for example, indicate that average life expectancy in colonial America was still somewhat less than forty years.[7]

Most studies of Puritan attitudes toward death have accepted the notion that death rates in early New England were very high. In fact, the imminence of death in Puritan society is often used by historians to explain the preoccupation of early Americans with the process of dying.

Recent work in historical demography, however, raises serious questions about the validity of the traditional view of death in early America. During the last ten years historical demographers have used family reconstitution techniques to provide a very different interpretation of mortality levels in New England.[8]

[7] Edward G. Stockwell, *Population and People* (Chicago, 1968), p. 26.

[8] Philip Greven, Jr., *Four Generations: Population, Land, and Family in Colonial Andover, Massachusetts* (Ithaca, N.Y., 1970); John Demos, *A Little Commonwealth: Family Life in Plymouth Colony* (New York, 1970); Susan L. Norton, 'Population Growth in Colonial America: A Study of Ipswich, Massachusetts,' *Population Studies* 25(1971):433–52; Kenneth A. Lockridge, 'The Population of Dedham, Massachusetts, 1636–1736,' *Economic History Review*, 2d ser. 19(1966):318–44; Daniel Scott

This recent work verifies that death rates were very high in urban areas in colonial New England. Boston deaths averaged thirty to forty per thousand population during the years 1701 to 1774. Furthermore, there were large fluctuations in the death rates in Boston. Most of the sudden rises in the death rate in 1702, 1721, 1730, and 1752 were the result of epidemics that ravaged that busy seaport (see fig. 1).

The newer work also shows that death rates in urban areas such as Boston or Salem were not typical of the rest of the 263
population. In most rural communities, the settlers who managed to survive the hardships of the early years could look forward to many more years of life in the New World. Though data on mortality levels are very scarce for the colonial period, historical demographers have been able to provide some estimates by relying on the reconstitution of families from the vital records of the community. On the basis of detailed investigations of Andover, Dedham, Hingham, Ipswich, and Plymouth, it now appears that life expectancy was much higher in rural New England than was previously believed. These communities experienced death rates of fifteen to twenty-five per thousand rather than the higher mortality rates in Boston or Salem. Since most people in America in the seventeenth and eighteenth centuries lived in small, rural communities, not unlike these five Massachusetts towns, it is likely that most Americans did not have the same frequent encounter with death that residents of commercial centers did.

Since most seventeenth- and eighteenth-century Americans

Smith, 'The Demographic History of New England,' *Journal of Economic History* 32(1972):165–83; Maris A. Vinovskis, 'American Historical Demography: A Review Essay' *Historical Methods Newsletter* 4(1971):141–48; Maris A. Vinovskis, 'Mortality Rates and Trends in Massachusetts before 1860,' *Journal of Economic History* 32(1972):184–213.

These generalizations only apply to the New England area. Mortality rates in the colonial South were considerably higher according to some of the recent work in that area. Irene Hecht, 'The Virginia Muster of 1624/5 as a Source for Demographic History,' *William and Mary Quarterly*, 3d ser. 30(1973):65–92; Lorena S. Walsh and Russell R. Menard, 'Death in the Chesapeake: Two Life Tables for Men in Early Colonial Maryland,' *Maryland Historical Magazine* 69(1974):211–27.

Figure 1

NUMBER OF DEATHS PER THOUSAND POPULATION IN BOSTON, 1701–74

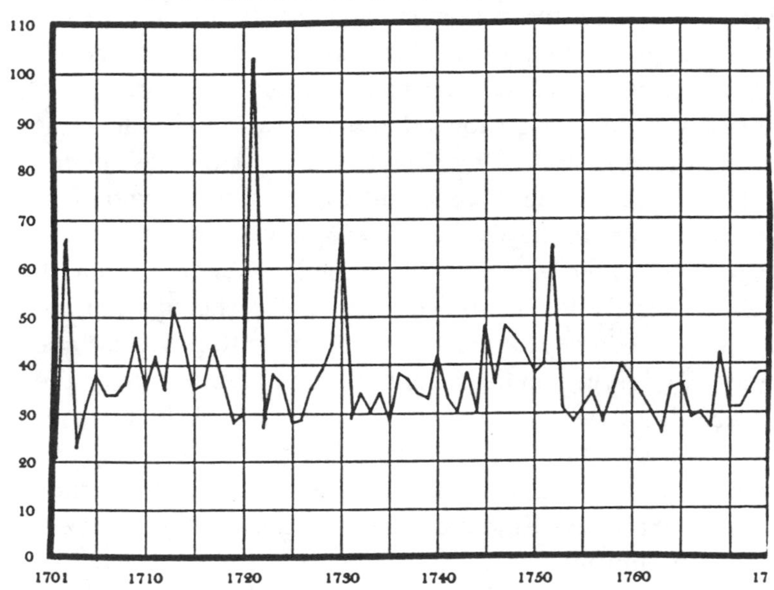

SOURCE: John B. Blake, *Public Health in the Town of Boston* (Cambridge, Mass., 1959), pp. 247–49.

SOURCE: John B. Blake, *Public Health in the Town of Boston* (Cambridge, Mass., 1959), pp. 247–49.

were English or were at least influenced by an English heritage, it is useful to compare the death rates in the New and Old Worlds. Generally, death rates in America were lower than in Europe. Death rates for infants in Andover and Ipswich were significantly lower than those in Europe, while infant mortality rates in Salem were comparable to those in Europe. Similarly, death rates after the age of twenty were lower in most Massachusetts communities than in Europe.

These findings appear to be in direct contradiction to the expectation of life according to the Wigglesworth Life Table of 1789. A detailed examination of that life table, however, reveals serious methodological flaws in its construction and coverage. Wigglesworth's table is based only on the ages at death obtained from bills of mortality. Since he did not have data available on the population who were liable to die in that period, he was forced to assume that the age-distribution of the deaths in the bills of mortality approximated the actual 265
age-distribution of the entire population. Though Wigglesworth realized that this crucial assumption was incorrect, his attempts to adjust his stationary population model must be viewed as intelligent guessing at best. Furthermore, his sample of towns was not representative of the entire region. Most of his data came from towns which were more urban than the area as a whole and consequently probably exaggerated the extent of colonial mortality. As a result, his estimate of life expectancy in colonial New England is probably too low and therefore does not invalidate the results from the family reconstitution studies.[9]

Another problem with many of the interpretations of living conditions in colonial America is that they are based on a faulty understanding of life tables. If the expectation of life at birth is 40.0 years, it means that the average person could expect to live that long. It does not mean, however, that once this average person had reached age twenty-one that he had only nineteen years remaining. When an individual had survived the perils of early childhood and the rigors of early adulthood, his or her chances of continuing to live were actually increased.[10] For example, the average male at age twenty-one in seventeenth-century Plymouth could expect another

[9] Vinovskis, 'The 1789 Life Table of Edward Wigglesworth.'

[10] For an introduction to the use and interpretation of life tables, see Louis I. Dublin, Alfred J. Lotka, and Mortimer Spiegelman, *Length of Life: A Study of the Life Table* (New York, 1949).

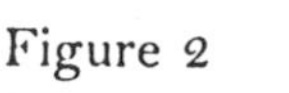

Figure 2

LIFE EXPECTANCY OF ADULTS
IN SEVENTEENTH-CENTURY PLYMOUTH

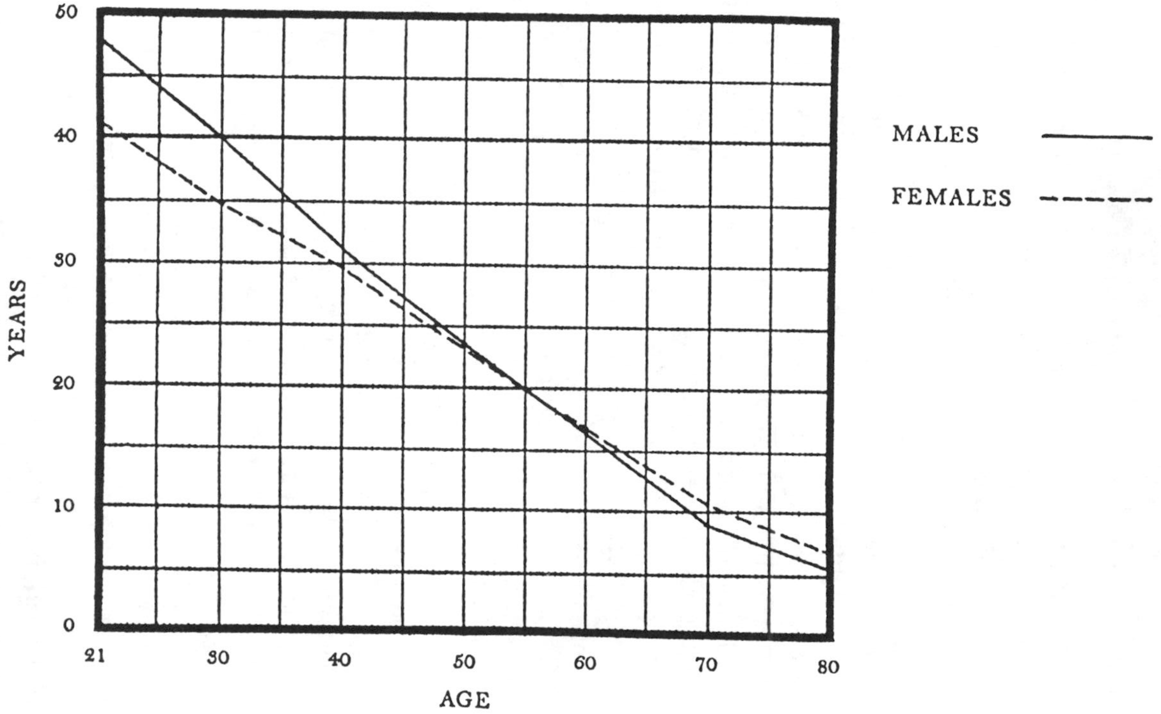

SOURCE: John Demos, *A Little Commonwealth: Family Life in Plymouth Colony* (New York, 1970), p. 192.

48.2 years of life and the average female at the same age another 41.4 years (see fig. 2).

Most of the differences in life expectancy between colonial Americans and Americans of today are due to the much higher rate of infant and child mortality in the past. Adults in colonial New England often could anticipate lives almost as long as each one of us today—especially if they were male. The average male at age twenty-one in seventeenth-century Plymouth had a life expectancy only one year less than the typical American male today. The average female at age twenty-one in seventeenth-century Plymouth, however, could expect to live 14.6 years less than her counterpart today—in large measure because maternal mortality rates in colonial America were very high.

Death rates in early America did not remain constant. In the seventeenth century there were large rural-urban differences in mortality in Massachusetts since small agricultural communities such as Dedham, Plymouth, Andover, Hingham, and Ipswich had relatively high life expectancies whereas Boston and Salem had much lower ones. The eighteenth century witnessed the convergence of these rates as mortality rose slightly in some of the smaller towns while death rates fell in Salem. Boston continued to have very high death rates throughout the eighteenth century. In the early nineteenth century there was a further convergence as Boston death rates dropped to around twenty per thousand while mortality in rural areas remained fairly steady.[11]

In order to analyze the level of mortality in nineteenth-century America in more detail and to look especially at the rural-urban differences, life tables for various Massachusetts towns in 1860 have been calculated from the federal census and the state vital records. Since the only previous life table for this period that might be of use to us, Elliott's Life Table of 1855, is inadequate because of several methodological short-

[11] Vinovskis, 'Mortality Rates and Trends.'

Figure 3

LIFE EXPECTANCY AT BIRTH IN MASSACHUSETTS TOWNS IN 1860

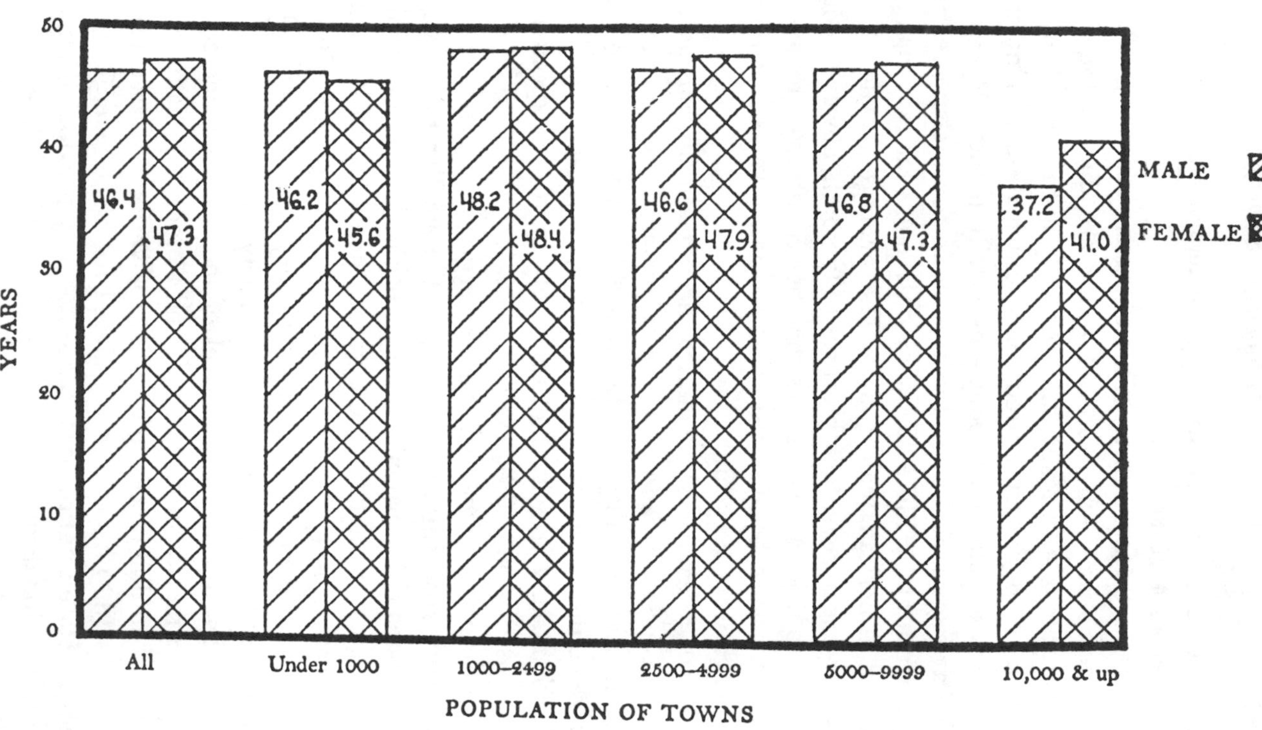

SOURCE: Maris A. Vinovskis, 'Mortality Rates and Trends in Massachusetts before 1860,' *Journal of Economic History* 32(1972):211.

comings, these tables provide an unusual opportunity to assess the presence of death in mid-nineteenth-century society.[12]

Life expectancy at birth in Massachusetts in 1860 was relatively high compared to most European countries. The average male at birth had a life expectancy of 46.4 years while the average female could look forward to 47.3 years of life (see fig. 3).

Contrary to the assertions of most other scholars, there was very little difference in mortality between rural and ur- 269
ban areas in Massachusetts. The major difference according to town size was between towns with populations under 10,000 and those with populations over 10,000. Furthermore, socioeconomic differences among these towns could not account for a large proportion of the differences in mortality. In a multiple regression analysis where the age-standardized death rate was the dependent variable and a variety of socioeconomic characteristics of those towns were the independent variables, the resultant equation for the state accounted for less than fifteen percent of the variance in the death rates. Put more simply, our detailed statistical analysis of mortality levels among Massachusetts towns in 1860 displayed a remarkable similarity amongst themselves.[13]

Compared to England and Wales in 1838–54, life expectancy in Massachusetts in 1860 was significantly higher for both males and females (see fig. 4). It is interesting to observe the generally similar pattern in life expectancy for both areas. If an American, English, or Welsh child survived the

[12] Ibid.

[13] Ibid. The results of this regression analysis have not been published yet. However, the use of the 1860 standardized mortality in a regression analysis of fertility differentials in Massachusetts is reported in Maris A. Vinovskis, 'A Multivariate Regression Analysis of Fertility Differentials among Massachusetts Towns and Regions in 1860,' a paper presented at the Conference on Early Industrialization, Shifts in Fertility, and Changes in the Family Structure at Princeton University, June 18 – July 10, 1972 (forthcoming in a volume of the conference proceedings to be edited by Charles Tilly).

LIFE EXPECTANCY IN MASSACHUSETTS IN 1860 AND IN ENGLAND AND WALES IN 1838–54

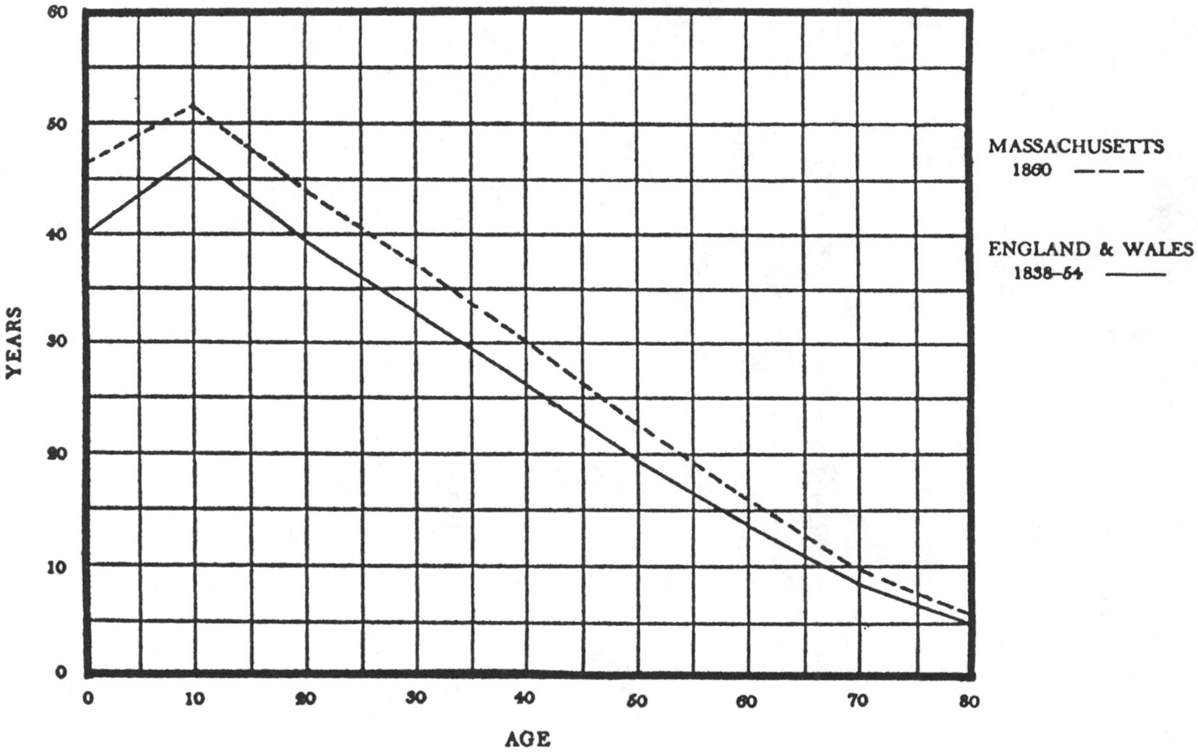

YEARS: 0, 10, 20, 30, 40, 50, 60

AGE: 0, 10, 20, 30, 40, 50, 60, 70, 80

MASSACHUSETTS 1860 – – – –

ENGLAND & WALES 1838–54 ———

SOURCES: Maris A. Vinovskis, 'Mortality Rates and Trends in Massachusetts before 1860,' *Journal of Economic History* 32(1972):211; Louis I. Dublin, Alfred J. Lotka, and Mortimer Spiegelman, *Length of Life* (New York, 1949), p. 346.

high levels of infant and child mortality, his life expectancy increased dramatically.

Though the overall level of mortality in colonial New England was probably much lower than previously estimated, it does not mean that death was not a serious problem—particularly for the young. Adults in rural New England could anticipate reasonably long lives but their children faced much worse odds. Infant mortality rates in colonial America ranged from 115 per thousand births in seventeenth-century Andover to 313 per thousand for females and 202 per thousand for males in seventeenth-century Salem. In other words, ten to thirty percent of the children never survived for the first year of life. In the United States in 1974, on the other hand, the infant mortality rate was 16.5 per thousand—or almost ten times less than that of the colonial period.

The higher mortality rate among children in the past can be illustrated by comparing the expectation of life for males in Massachusetts in 1860 with those of males in the United States in 1969 (see fig. 5). At the later ages the expectation of life for both groups is very similar, but there is a very substantial difference at birth. The average male child at birth today can expect to live to age 67.8; if he survives to age ten, he increases his total life expectation by only 1.8 years. On the other hand, the average male child in Massachusetts born in 1860 could anticipate 46.4 years of life; if he survived to age ten, his total life expectancy would increase by 16.6 years.

In addition, since the average family in colonial New England usually had three times as many children as we have today, there was a high probability that most families would experience the loss of at least one child during their lifetimes. The combination of high infant mortality rates and high birth rates increased the likelihood that the typical family in early America would have had to deal with the death of a member of their nuclear family.

LIFE EXPECTANCY IN MASSACHUSETTS IN 1860 AND IN U.S. IN 1969

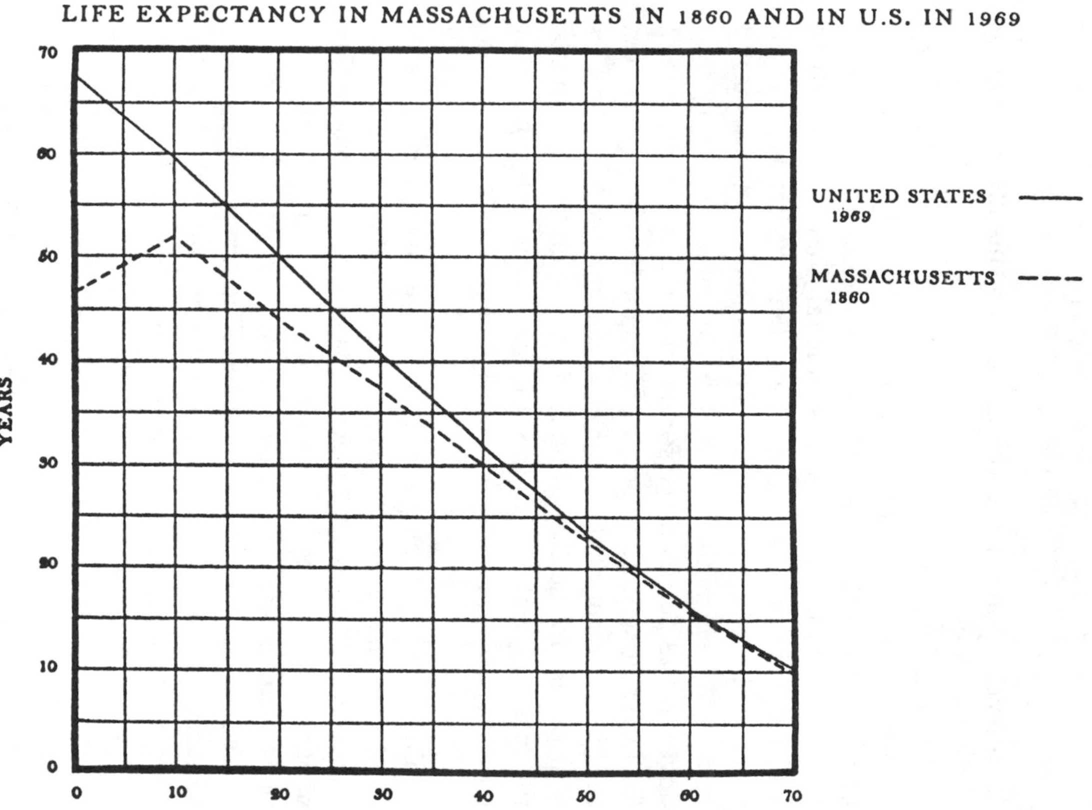

SOURCES: Maris A. Vinovskis, 'Mortality Rates and Trends in Massachusetts before 1860,' *Journal of Economic History* 32(1972):211; U.S. Bureau of the Census, *The American Almanac: The U.S. Book of Facts, Statistics & Information*, 1973 (New York, 1973), p. 56.

Our analysis of mortality levels and trends in New England before 1860 suggests that most individuals, especially those who had survived the dangers of early childhood, could look forward to reasonably long lives. Therefore, we might expect that our Puritan ancestors would not have been very concerned or worried about mortality—especially about deaths among adults. Yet New England society seemed obsessed with death despite the moderate mortality rates for that period. Even more astonishing is the fact that most people in 273
those days greatly overestimated the extent of mortality in their society.

Some colonists, such as Edward Wigglesworth, did realize that death rates in the New World were somewhat lower than in England. But even Wigglesworth, the foremost expert on colonial mortality, seriously underestimated the expectation of life in early New England. The general populace seemed convinced that death rates were very high. Anyone reading through the diaries of these people is immediately struck by the fascination and concern with death. The image of early American society one receives from these writings is that of a very unhealthy environment in which each individual anticipates his demise at any moment.[14]

For example, Samuel Rodman began to keep a diary at age twenty-nine in 1821. He was a very scientifically oriented man who collected weather data from 1812 to 1876 and was generally calm about discussions of death throughout his diary during the next thirty-eight years. But it is very interesting to observe how he misperceived the dangers to his life even well into the nineteenth century.

Rodman often mentions how he should devote more attention to his spiritual needs because he anticipates he may die

[14] Various scholars have commented on the preoccupation of early Americans with the issue of death in their writings. For example, see Charles Allen Shively, 'A History of the Conception of Death in America, 1650–1860,' (Ph.D. diss., Harvard University, 1969); Lewis O. Saum, 'Death in the Popular Mind of Pre-Civil War America,' *American Quarterly* 26(1974):477–95.

at any moment. In 1838 he celebrates his birthday by noting in his diary that 'this is the 46th anniversary of my birth. I have lived therefore already considerably beyond the average of human life.'[15] Three years later, he repeats the general theme: 'I should not conclude this note without attesting to the fact that this is my 49th anniversary, and that I have entered on my 50th year. It seems a matter of surprise that I have lived so long, and without yet any material change. I have actually passed beyond the period of youth and middle
274 age and may justly be classed among the old.'[16]

If Rodman had had the benefit of our life tables for 1860, he could have taken comfort in the fact that he was likely to survive at least another twenty years at age fifty. The intriguing question is why Rodman, an unusually intelligent and perceptive man, should have underestimated so greatly the extent of longevity in his society. Why did he and so many other diarists of the period feel that death was imminent when in fact the death rates for adults in their communities were not very high?

Perhaps the misperceptions of the extent of mortality in New England society were due to the unusual life experiences of those individuals who kept diaries. Maybe they were less healthy and/or came from families which had experienced higher mortality than the rest of the population. Keeping a diary might be part of an attempt to introduce order and stability in a life that was constantly overshadowed by the presence of death.

In the case of Samuel Rodman, this interpretation does not appear to be valid. Despite his frequent anticipations of dying, he managed to survive to age eighty-four and his wife lived to be eighty-two. Though two of their eight children did die early, at ages one and three, the remaining six lived to

[15] Zepharriah Pease, ed., *The Diary of Samuel Rodman: A New Bedford Chronicle of Thirty-Seven Years: 1821–1859* (New Bedford, Mass., 1927), p. 180.

[16] Ibid., p. 218.

the ages of twenty-three, sixty-one, seventy-seven, seventy-eight, eighty-seven, and ninety-one. One might properly object that these figures are misleading because Samuel Rodman had no way of knowing how long he or his offspring would survive. Perhaps he was merely reacting to the much higher mortality of his parents and siblings. Yet his father lived to age eighty-two and his mother to age ninety-five. Furthermore, his sisters survived to the ages of thirty-one, sixty, seventy-eight, and eighty-one while his brothers died 275
at ages twenty-four, sixty-eight, and eighty-one.[17] In other words, whatever indications of low life expectancy that Rodman had, they probably did not come mainly from the experiences of his immediate family.

Though our analysis of Rodman's own longevity suggests that his anticipation of imminent death probably was not based on his own physical frailty, we should be careful not to generalize about the relationship between personal health and preoccupation with death among diarists on the basis of just one individual. Kathryn Kish Sklar has coded data from published diaries of seventy-one American women who lived in the eighteenth and early nineteenth centuries. These data are of particular interest to us because many historians have remarked on the preoccupation of women with items about health and death in their diaries. We already know that women who kept diaries were more educated than the rest of the population and probably came from more affluent backgrounds. Using her data, it is possible to calculate age at death for forty of these women.[18] Therefore, one is now able to estimate the life expectancy of these women who kept diaries.

Of the forty women, the average age at death was 56.4 years. This compares very favorably with the expectation of

[17] Ibid.

[18] I am deeply indebted to Kathryn Kish Sklar of the University of California, Los Angeles, for allowing me to use her data for these calculations.

Figure 6

DISTRIBUTION OF AGES AT WHICH WOMEN BEGAN TO KEEP THEIR DIARIES IN THE EIGHTEENTH AND NINETEENTH CENTURIES

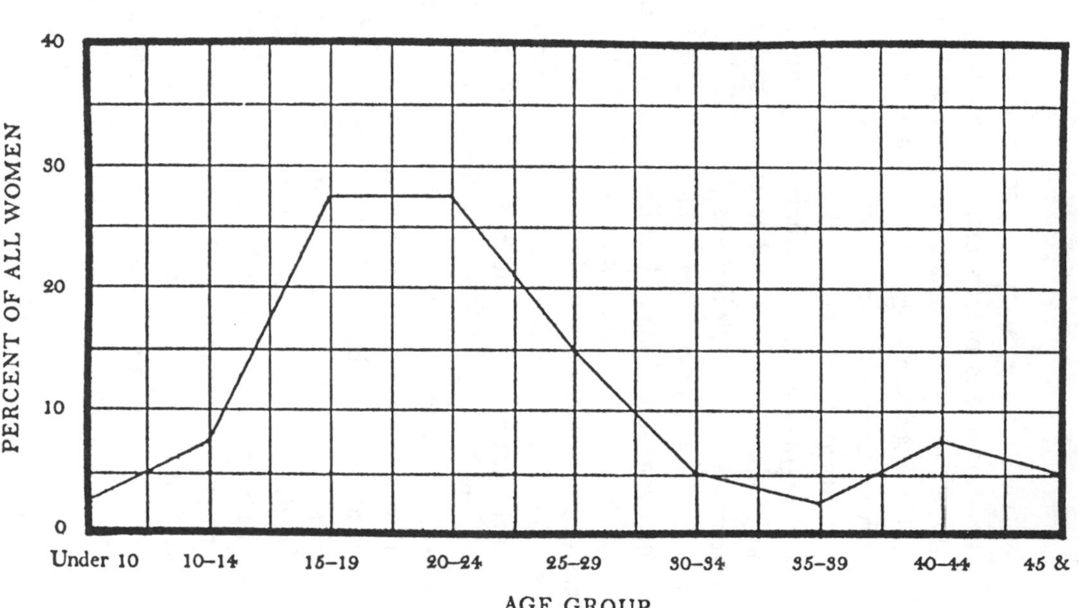

SOURCE: Calculated from data on American diaries collected by Kathryn Kish Sklar of the University of California, Los Angeles.

life at birth for Massachusetts women in 1860 of 47.3 years. This is a very misleading comparison, however, because most women did not begin to keep diaries until they had already survived the perils of early childhood (see fig. 6).

Instead, we need to take into consideration the ages at which these women began their diaries before calculating their life expectancies. Now we can compare their expectation of life to that of women in the general public (see fig. 7).

The results indicate that women who kept diaries were in fact less healthy than Massachusetts women in 1860—particularly at ages twenty and thirty. Though this does reinforce the argument that unhealthy people were more likely to keep diaries, it is important to bear in mind that the average woman who kept a diary at age twenty could expect to live another 35.5 years. Thus, most women who kept these diaries were actually quite healthy and their own prospect of dying in the very near future was not very likely despite their utterances to the contrary in those diaries.

Since we cannot account for the misperceptions of the level of mortality in early New England in terms of the colonists' personal encounters with death, we need to look at the general context of life in that period to see what factors encouraged people to imagine such high death rates—especially among the adult population. Though death is a biological phenomenon, the reactions of people to it are largely defined by the manner in which society handles its dying. It is my contention that the great emphasis placed on death in early New England led people to overestimate the extent of its occurrence in their communities and lives.

Americans today are remarkably unwilling to discuss death. Our society refuses to face the issue of death openly—thus, death has replaced sex as the major taboo. Geoffrey Gorer in a very insightful essay has argued that 'In the 20th century there seems to have been an unremarked shift in prudery;

Figure 7

LIFE EXPECTANCY OF MASSACHUSETTS FEMALES IN 1860 AND EIGHTEENTH- AND NINETEENTH-CENTURY FEMALE DIARISTS

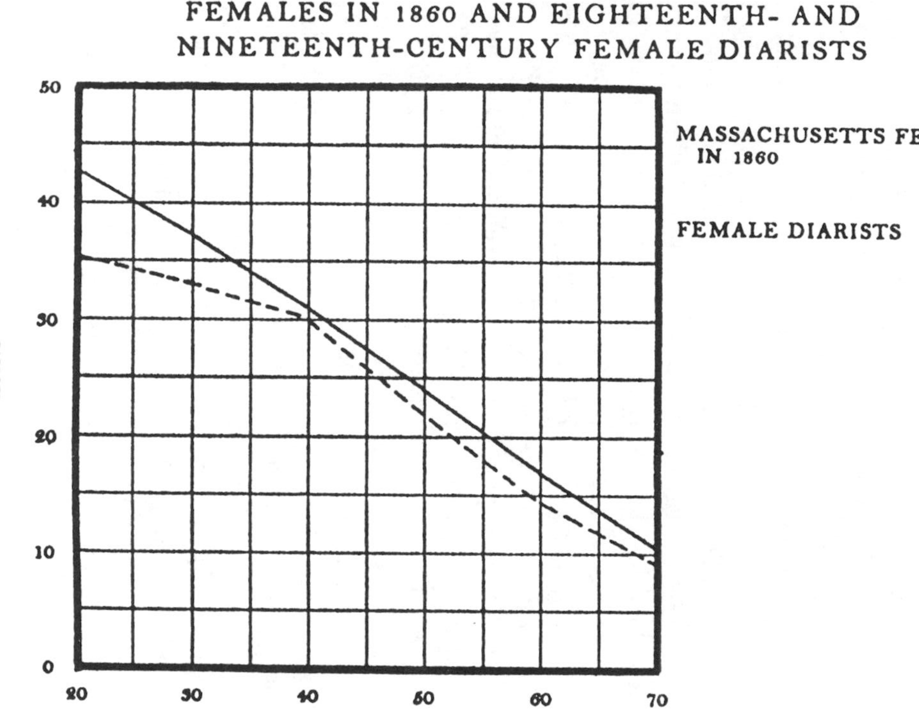

SOURCE: Calculated from data on American diaries collected by Kathryn Kish Sklar of the University of California, Los Angeles

whereas copulation has become more and more mentionable, particularly in the Anglo-Saxon societies, death has become more and more unmentionable as a natural process.'[19]

Puritan society had a very different attitude toward death —there was a great fascination and interest in that subject and people were encouraged to discuss it amongst themselves. Furthermore, the very process of dying in early New England forced people to come to terms with death rather than being able to pretend that death did not really exist.[20] 279

The location in which an individual dies is important because it determines the access his relatives and friends will have to him during that time. In addition, the place where a person dies also influences the amount of exposure the rest of society will have to the process of dying.

Today there is a debate over whether it is better to die at home or in a hospital. Some elderly actually prefer to die away from home in order to avoid becoming burdens to their families. Yet when one dies at home he or she is in familiar surroundings and among friends. A patient who is hospitalized is largely removed from the help and care of his family.

Public opinion in America has gradually shifted away from the idea of dying at home. Less than a third of the public now would prefer to have someone die at home. In 1968 a public opinion poll asked: 'Do you feel that if an individual is dying and is beyond any available medical aid, that it is more desirable to remove the person to a hospital or other institution, rather than have them remain at home?' The replies were as follows:[21]

[19] Geoffrey Gorer, *Death, Grief, and Mourning* (Garden City, N.Y., 1965), pp. 192–99.

[20] For analyses of the reactions of Puritans to death, see David E. Stannard, 'Death and Dying in Puritan New England,' *American Historical Review* 78(1973):1305–30; Shively, 'History of the Conception of Death.'

[21] Glen M. Vernon, *Sociology of Death: An Analysis of Death-Related Behavior* (New York, 1970), p. 110. For a more general discussion of American attitudes toward death, see Richard G. Dumont and Dennis C. Foss, *The American View of Death: Acceptance or Denial?* (Cambridge, Mass., 1972).

	N	*Percent*
Yes, this is best for all concerned	669	34.1
No, death should be at home if at all possible	553	28.2
Undecided	692	35.3
No answer	47	2.4

This change in attitudes has been accompanied by a shift in the actual location of dying. In 1963, fifty-three percent of all
280 deaths occurred in a hospital and many others in nursing homes or as a result of accidents outside the home.[22] As a result, most Americans today do not often see the process of dying firsthand. This isolation from death is compounded by the development of 'retirement cities' in the United States where the elderly are in effect segregated from the rest of society. As Robert Fulton has so aptly put it, 'Here for the first time modern man is able to avoid almost entirely the grief and anguish of death. By encouraging the aged members of the society to congregate in segregated communities, familial and friendship commitments are made fewer by time and distance, and emotional and social bonds are loosened. Physically and emotionally separated from those most likely to die, the modern individual is freed of the shock he would otherwise experience from their death. Herein may lie a form of man's "conquest" of death.'[23]

The colonists died mainly in their own homes since there were few hospitals or other institutions in which the aged could be placed. In the absence of a specialized nursing profession, relatives and neighbors attended to the needs of the dying—thus increasing the amount of contact between the living and the dying.

The homes of the early colonists were very small com-

[22] Robert L. Fulton, 'Death and the Self,' *Journal of Religion and Health* 3(1964): 354.

[23] Ibid., p. 367.

pared to today—especially those built in the early years of settlement. According to the probate inventories, the average number of rooms per house in rural Suffolk County, Massachusetts, rose from 4.3 in 1675–99, to 5.7 in 1700–19, and to 6.0 in 1750–75.[24] Thus, there was relatively little privacy available in these homes to shield the dying person from the rest of the family even if the colonists had desired to isolate him.

Finally, since there were no funeral homes in the seven- 281
teenth and eighteenth centuries, the dead person remained in his own home where friends and neighbors could view him. As the art of embalming was still in its infancy in colonial America, very little effort was made to preserve or repair the dead body. People were forced to see the dead persons as they were rather than having them cosmetically preserved or improved to enhance their appearance in death.[25]

The funeral itself encouraged people to come into intimate contact with death. At first funerals in colonial America were simple affairs since there was an effort to avoid the excesses of English funeral practices. One contemporary observer of early colonial funerals described them: 'At Burials nothing is read, nor any funeral sermon made, but all the neighborhood or a goodly company of them come together by tolling of the bell, and carry the dead solemnly to his grave, and then stand by him while he is buried. The ministers are most commonly present.'[26]

Gradually funerals became more elaborate and expensive. The practice of distributing gifts of gloves, rings, or scarfs to participants at funerals was a custom brought over from Eng-

[24] For a description of the development of embalming in America, see Robert W. Habenstein and William M. Lamers, *The History of American Funeral Directing* (Milwaukee, 1955).

[25] David H. Flaherty, *Privacy in Colonial New England* (Charlottesville, Va., 1972), p. 39.

[26] Thomas Lechford, *Plain Dealing or News from New England*, ed. J. Hammond Trumbull (Boston, 1867), pp. 87–88.

land and which flourished in New England in the late seventeenth and eighteenth centuries. The practice quickly became excessive as the quality of the gifts distributed was supposed to reflect the social status of the deceased. At the funeral of Governor Belcher's wife in 1736, over 1,000 pairs of gloves were distributed. Ministers, who usually received gifts at all the funerals they attended, often accumulated large quantities of such items. For example, Andrew Eliot, minister of the North Church in Boston received 2,940 pairs of funeral
282 gloves in his thirty-two years in the pulpit. Rather than allow such gifts to overwhelm his household, Reverend Eliot sold them to supplement his modest salary.[27]

As the costs of these funeral items rose, there were numerous attempts by the General Court as well as individual citizens to curtail funeral expenses. None of the proposed measures, however, succeeded because our colonial ancestors were just as determined to have extravagant funerals then as we are today.[28]

But these social aspects of funerals provided still greater encouragement for people to attend them. It was expected in the small rural communities of New England that everyone would attend the funerals of any of their townsmen. Given the death rate of that period, it was likely that in a small village of a thousand inhabitants, there would be at least ten to twenty-five funerals each year. Since most burials were handled by the neighbors and friends rather than by a professional undertaker, the significance of each funeral became even more important to the living. Thus, there was a constant reminder to the entire community of the presence of

[27] For a description of the extravagant expenditures on early funerals, see Alice Morse Earle, *Customs and Fashions in Old New England* (New York, 1894).

[28] Though Jessica Mitford argues that the excesses in funeral expenditures are only a recent phenomena, there is ample evidence that often the colonists also spent large sums on their funerals. Jessica Mitford, *The American Way of Death*, paperback ed. (Greenwich, Conn., 1963).

death whereas today most of us are not affected by the deaths of anyone except very close friends or relatives.

Finally, the practice of giving funeral sermons became established by the early eighteenth century. Ministers now used the occasion of the gathering at the grave to preach to the living the importance of coming to terms with the inevitability of death. Increasingly these sermons were published and distributed to the congregation as a remembrance of the departed and a reminder of the frailty of life.[29] 283

The awareness of death by an individual in colonial America did not end with the lowering of the body into the grave. The grave as well as the burial place continued to further the notion of the shortness of life on earth for the survivors. Scholars such as Harriette Forbes, Allan Ludwig, and Dickran and Ann Tashjian have already explored the artistic and symbolic implications of the early gravestones that are dotted throughout the countryside. Rather than simply repeat their insightful analyses of the meaning of these early artifacts, we will try only to reconstruct how these images of death might have influenced the perceptions of our ancestors about the extent of mortality in their communities.[30]

Before 1660, graveyards in New England were quite plain. Often people were buried in convenient locations near their homes rather than being interred in burial grounds near the churches. We can understand this casual attitude toward the burial site better if we recall that in England the common practice had been to bury many different individuals on the same plot of land. No effort was made to keep a separate spot for each person who died—rather bodies were buried with the expectation that someone else would share that same

[29] On the evolution of Puritan attitudes and practices at funerals, see Shively, 'History of the Conception of Death.'

[30] Harriette Merrifield Forbes, *Gravestones of Early New England and the Men Who Made Them, 1653–1800* (New York, 1927); Allan I. Ludwig, *Graven Images: New England Stonecarving and Its Symbols, 1650–1815* (Middletown, Conn., 1966); Dickran and Ann Tashjian, *Memorials for Children of Change: The Art of Early New England Stonecarving* (Middletown, Conn., 1974).

area as soon as the previous occupant had been decomposed sufficiently. Thus, the church of St. John the Baptist in Widford, Hertfordshire, buried nearly 5,000 people in a plot of less than half an acre in area. Usually these early English burials did not include even placing the deceased in a coffin.[31]

Gradually the burial places became more important to the Puritans as a reminder of the presence of death. As efforts were made to preserve the memory of those who had de-
284 parted, gravestones were used to identify the bodily remains as well as to provide inspiration for the living. Partly for ornamental reasons but mainly for instructing the living, colonial gravestones began to depict the reality of death.

These symbolic illustrations of death were significant reminders of the frailty of life in a society in which many of its citizens were illiterate and therefore unable to read the messages about death from the inscriptions on the gravestones. These grim symbols of death were meant to remind the living that the day of judgment was coming and that all would be called upon to account for their lives.[32]

The symbolic messages of the early New England gravestones were usually simpler and plainer than those on the religious art works of Europe at that time. The Puritans were very anxious to avoid duplication of symbols that were commonly identified with the Roman Catholic Church. The imagery of the early New England gravestones ranged across a wide variety of themes—from emblems of death to symbols of resurrection. Furthermore, there was an evolution in gravestone imagery over time—from the vivid and often harsh depiction of death by the use of death's heads to the more cheerful and subtle representations of death by winged cherubs and weeping willows in the late eighteenth and early nineteenth centuries.[33]

[31] Habenstein and Lamers, *History of American Funeral Directing*, pp. 91–191.

[32] On the extent of illiteracy in early New England, see Kenneth A. Lockridge, *Literacy in Colonial New England* (New York, 1974).

[33] Ludwig, *Graven Images*; Tashjian, *Memorials for Children of Change*.

Probably the single most important factor in reminding early New Englanders of the presence of death was their religion which placed such great emphasis on death and an afterlife for those who had been saved. Ministers preached with great frequency about death and the demise of any member of the congregation was seen as an opportunity to remind the living of the proper ways of serving God.[34]

Ministers tried to encourage everyone in their congregations to think about the meaning of death. Thus, Cotton 285
Mather in his work *A Christian Funeral* advises the survivors that 'when any Person known to me *Dies*, I would set my self particularly to consider; *What lesson of goodness or Wisdom I may learn from any thing that I may observe in the Life of that Person.*'[35] And in his *Death Made Easie & Happy*, Mather implores his readers to remind themselves each day that 'he is to die shortly. Let us look upon everything as a sort of Death's-Head set before us, with a *Memento mortis* written upon it.'[36]

In the early decades of settlement, church leaders were relatively matter-of-fact about the presence and inevitability of death. But as the children of the original settlers gradually turned away from the church, there was a widespread fear that their errand in the wilderness might fail. Ministers now seized upon the terrors of death to persuade their sinful townsmen to return to God's way. Thus, Solomon Stoddard in his *The Efficacy of the Fear of Hell to Restrain Men from Sin* wrote, 'Many seem to be Incorrigible and Obstinate in their Pride and Luxury and Profaness . . . they are afraid of Poverty, and afraid of Sickness, but not afraid of Hell; that

[34] On the importance of religion during this period, see John Higham, 'Hanging Together: Divergent Unities in American History,' *Journal of American History* 61(1974):5–29. For a very useful analysis of the role of liberal clergymen in emphasizing death in the mid-nineteenth century, see Ann Douglass, 'Heaven Our Home: Consolation Literature in the Northern United States, 1830–1880,' *American Quarterly* 26(1974):496–515.

[35] Cotton Mather, *A Christian Funeral* (Boston, 1713), p. 27.

[36] Cotton Mather, *Death Made Easie & Happy* (London, 1701), p. 94.

would restrain them from sinful Practices, Destruction from God would be a Terrour to them.'[37]

Increasingly these ministers directed their message to young children. From a very early age, Puritan children were admonished to think of their impending doom in hell unless they were saved by God's grace.[38] This message can be seen in an anonymous broadside of that period:

> My Cry's to you, my Children . . .
> Be wise before it be too late.
> 286 Think on your latter end.
> Though you are young and yet you must die,
> and hasten to the Pit.[39]

People were also encouraged to keep diaries in which they recorded their spiritual progress and failings. There seems to have been much emphasis on continually thinking about the shortness of one's own life. Therefore, it is not surprising that the death of anyone in the community often stimulated these diarists to reflect on their own precarious situation even though the actual conditions of life in that society were much healthier than they imagined.

Perhaps now we are in a better position to account for the misperceptions of early New Englanders of the level of mortality in their society. They came from England where mortality rates were very high. Their expectations of continued high mortality in the New World were reinforced by the difficulties of the early years of settlement, the uncertainty of life due to the presence of periodic epidemics, and the particularly high mortality of their children. Though their chances of survival in America were actually much better than those of

[37] Solomon Stoddard, *The Efficacy of the Fear of Hell to Restrain Men from Sin* (Boston, 1713), p. 10.

[38] The best account of death and young children in early American society is by David E. Stannard, 'Death and the Puritan Child,' *American Quarterly* 26(1974): 456–76.

[39] Quoted in Shively, 'History of the Conception of Death,' p. 52.

their relatives and friends in the old country, they usually did
not realize this fact because of the great emphasis that was
placed on death by their religion. The continued reminder of
the shortness of their lives whenever anyone died made it
difficult for the average person to comprehend the changes in
the overall mortality level that had occurred. Furthermore,
their incessant preoccupation with death helps to explain
why most scholars of colonial history thought that there was
such a high death rate in the seventeenth and eighteenth cen- 287
turies. Since most of these historians relied only on literary
evidence, there was no reason for them to suspect that the
colonists had incorrectly assessed the living conditions in
early New England.

The Fabrication of Identity in Early America

Michael Zuckerman

In the study of the American character there have been two primary positions. One has emphasized the ascendancy of individualism, with its values of self-interest and self-reliance. The other has stressed the sway of the community, with its corollaries of sociability, conformism, and endemic insecurity of self. Exponents of each have been indisposed to take seriously the claims of the other, and advocates of the only significant alternative have taken them both too seriously, by setting those static characterizations in historical sequence.

Consider, for instance, the recent historiography of the New England town. Almost every examination of the subject that has not affirmed an abiding communalism or an irrepressible individualism has described an evolution, or devolution, of close communal modes into more modern individuality. And on just that account such studies constitute, collectively, an advancing embarrassment. The ones among them that predicate either a constant corporate or a constant liberal inclination among the townspeople simply talk past one another, while, taken together, the ones that posit a passage from a self-subordinating to a self-seeking orientation place that passage in every generation from the founding of the colonies to the middle of the twentieth century.

Darrett Rutman affirms a transformation of communal ideals and the emergence of a profusion of private purposes and practices in the very first decade of settlement. William Haller presumes the persistence of more medieval ways through the first generation and argues their abandonment only after 1660. Kenneth Lockridge insists that the ancient frame of values remained intact through the second generation but not the third. Richard Bushman postulates a pristine traditionalism clear through the seventeenth century and asserts its erosion in the Great Awakening. John J. Waters alleges a placid homogeneity through the revivals and portrays its irrevocable

Michael Zuckerman is a member of the Department of History, the University of Pennsylvania. He wishes to thank the National Endowment for the Humanities for the Senior Fellowship that enabled him to prepare this essay, which constitutes something of the conceptual foundation for a book in progress on character and community in colonial America.

impairment in the period of the Revolution. Benjamin Labaree maintains that customs of corporate solidarity survived the Revolution but not the depression of the early nineteenth century and the War of 1812. And others extend the same paradigm through the nineteenth century, into the twentieth, and indeed into our own age.[1]

Amid differences so protracted and inconclusive, it might be wise to suppose that every side brings out at least an aspect of the truth. On such a supposition it would be less urgent to ascertain and account for the priority of communalism or individualism than to plot the pattern within which both could burgeon at once. It would then be immensely suggestive that, exactly in the years through which America was first colonized by Englishmen, both 289
the self-awareness and self-assertion that inform the modern psyche and the coercive mutuality that marks the modern community achieved something of their subsequent scope. Even as the settlers of the seventeenth century craved self-suppressive communalism, they also sought larger liberties for themselves and drew distinctions between social role and a sense of inner identity. Like many in the mother country, they established elaborate geographies of consciousness on the basis of a "separation between the behaving and the scrutinizing self."[2]

[1] Darrett B. Rutman, *Winthrop's Boston: Portrait of a Puritan Town, 1630-1649* (Chapel Hill, N.C., 1965); William Haller, Jr., *The Puritan Frontier: Town-Planting in New England Colonial Development, 1630-1660* (New York, 1951); Kenneth A. Lockridge, *A New England Town, The First Hundred Years: Dedham, Massachusetts, 1636-1736* (New York, 1970); Richard L. Bushman, *From Puritan to Yankee: Character and the Social Order in Connecticut, 1690-1765* (Cambridge, Mass., 1967); John J. Waters, Jr., *The Otis Family in Provincial and Revolutionary Massachusetts* (Chapel Hill, N.C., 1968); Benjamin W. Labaree, *Patriots and Partisans: The Merchants of Newburyport, 1764-1815* (Cambridge, Mass., 1962). For successive generations in the 19th and 20th centuries see, for example, Michael B. Katz, *The Irony of Early School Reform: Educational Innovation in Mid-Nineteenth Century Massachusetts* (Cambridge, Mass., 1968); Leonard L. Richards, *"Gentlemen of Property and Standing": Anti-Abolition Mobs in Jacksonian America* (New York, 1970); Michael H. Frisch, *Town into City: Springfield, Massachusetts, and the Meaning of Community, 1840-1880* (Cambridge, Mass., 1972); Stephan Thernstrom, *Poverty and Progress: Social Mobility in a Nineteenth Century City* (Cambridge, Mass., 1964); W. Lloyd Warner and J. O. Low, *The Social System of the Modern Factory. The Strike: A Social Analysis*, Yankee City Series, IV (New Haven, Conn., 1947); William M. Dobriner, "The Natural History of a Reluctant Suburb," *Yale Review*, N.S., XLIX (1960), 399-412.

[2] David Riesman *et al.*, *The Lonely Crowd: A Study of the Changing American Character* (New Haven, Conn., 1950), 44. For a recent discussion of the antithesis between the "inner man" and the "outer man" see Norman S. Fiering, "Will and Intellect in the New England Mind," *William and Mary Quarterly*, 3d Ser., XXIX (1972), 515-558. For a similar distinction as indigenous to English Protestantism, and indeed to Christianity itself, see Charles H. and Katherine George, *The Protestant Mind of the English Reformation, 1570-1640* (Princeton, N.J., 1961), 295-297, and

The early colonists were at once more free and more controlled, more concerned about themselves and more attentive to the opinions of their neighbors, than their European forebears had been; and Americans since have carried these fissions further. Like the men and women who planted the first colonies, they have continued to have two revolutions in train, in opposite directions, at the same time. They have grown more individuated *and* more regimented, more tolerant *and* more repressive. They have come increasingly to move, as Philip Rieff has said, in a milieu "of orgy and routine which constitutes modernization."[3]

290 Modernization may, indeed, afford a context in which it is possible to comprehend both the communal and the individualistic elements of American life. For in such a context these tendencies do not appear as antithetic as they have ordinarily done. On the contrary, they seem more nearly to have been inseparable expressions of a single dislocation, each destined to grow with the other.

It would be rash to hold that the individual's relation to society has ever been anything but problematic in the career of western Christendom, but it would be myopic not to notice that that relation became markedly more tortured in the late sixteenth and seventeenth centuries. Something seems then to have come unhinged in the ways people were wont to live with one another and in their aspirations for, and anxieties about, group life. Something seems to have driven them simultaneously to seek a new purity of personal identity and covenanted community alike.

Interpretation of the early modern character must accordingly comprehend the sources of such centrifugality, for western men had not always been impelled to those extremities. In the Middle Ages they had admitted oppositions, but "the distinctive feature of medieval thought" was that it absorbed "contrasts which later were to be presented as irreconcilable antitheses." The medieval church was "more ecumenical, more genially encompassing, more permissive doctrinally, than either the sixteenth-century Protestant churches or the post-Trentine Catholic Church." It allowed degrees of dissident freedom, in mysticism and in the religious orders, which Protestant congregations of the early modern era, organized as they were in antagonism to such catholicity, contracted to counterposed options of conformity or secession.[4]

Robert N. Bellah, "Religious Evolution," *American Sociological Review*, XXIX (1964), 358-374.

[3] Philip Rieff, *Fellow Teachers* (New York, 1973), 113.

[4] R. H. Tawney, *Religion and the Rise of Capitalism: A Historical Study* (New York, 1926), 20; Eugene F. Rice, Jr., *The Foundations of Early Modern Europe, 1460-1559*, in Felix Gilbert, ed., *The Norton History of Modern Europe* (New York, 1971), 147.

The pluralism of medieval proclivities was sharply at odds with the dichotomous ordering of experience that emerged after the Reformation. Men and women of the Middle Ages did not distinguish as strenuously as their descendants would between work and leisure, madness and sanity, or youth and maturity. They did not set apart as scrupulously the spheres of religion, science, and magic, or "rationalize" as relentlessly the realms of the economy, the polity, and the society. They did not isolate conscience from temporal affairs, as Luther would, and they did not segregate science from morality or natural law from revelation, as Bacon would. Indeed, they did not sunder nature and grace, and they did not even separate any too carefully the domains of the sacred and the secular. Pilgrimages were pretexts for 291
lovers' trysts; prostitutes pursued their trade in the churches; the earthiest of erotic relations were depicted in the most elevated of religious terms. And in discounting all these differentiations, people tended, as Huizinga said, to "reduce all things to a general type," so that "the power to discern and describe individual traits was never attained."[5]

Such diffusion suggests patterns of muffled individuality to which we also have testimony from present-day tribal societies around the globe. Among the Samoans of the South Pacific, for instance, Margaret Mead reported a similar disinclination to acknowledge individual differences or admit any consequential "consciousness of personality." Among the Balinese of Indonesia Clifford Geertz discovered a comparable "anonymization of persons." Among peoples as far-flung and diverse as the Dinka of the Sudan, the Wintu of northern California, and the Amahuaca of the upper Amazon, anthropologists have found evidence of individuation underdeveloped by modern Western standards—a lesser presence, in language and often in life, of an idea of each human being as a center of personal agency, of a valuation

[5] J. Huizinga, *The Waning of the Middle Ages: A Study of the Forms of Life, Thought and Art in France and the Netherlands in the XIVth and XVth Centuries* (London, 1924), 196. This paragraph follows Huizinga more generally; see, for example, pp. 44, 111, 137, 140-141, 142, 144-145, 195, 196, 207-208, 236-237, and also Keith Thomas, *Religion and the Decline of Magic* (New York, 1971); Philippe Ariès, *Centuries of Childhood: A Social History of Family Life* (New York, 1962); and Michel Foucault, *Madness and Civilization: A History of Insanity in the Age of Reason*, trans. Richard Howard (New York, 1965). On the significance of the recognition of the sacred for individuation see Benjamin Nelson in "Perspectives on the Therapeutic in the Context of Contemporary Sociology: A Dialogue between Benjamin Nelson and Dennis Wrong," *Salmagundi*, XX (1972), 186. On the centrality of casuistry as an institutional expression of the connectedness of nature and grace, and of the temporal and spiritual realms in the Middle Ages, and on the attenuation of the practice of casuistry among the early Protestants, see *ibid.*, 169-170, and Benjamin Nelson, "Self-Images and Systems of Spiritual Direction in the History of European Civilization," in Samuel Z. Klausner, ed., *The Quest for Self-Control: Classical Philosophies and Scientific Research* (New York, 1965), 61-72.

of each as unique, and, in truth, of the very "concept of an established separate self."[6]

In such settings, in which the individual finds his social environment "emotionally continuous with himself," the self is, as Benjamin Nelson has said, "an intermittent emergent."[7] And if the early modern epoch was the

[6] Margaret Mead, *Coming of Age in Samoa: A Psychological Study of Primitive Youth for Western Civilisation* (New York, 1928), 224, 215, and chap. 13, *passim.* Clifford Geertz, *Person, Time, and Conduct in Bali: An Essay in Cultural Analysis,* Yale University Southeast Asian Studies Cultural Report Series, No. 14 (New Haven, Conn., 1966), 54; Dorothy Lee, "The Conception of Self among the Wintu
292 Indians," *Journal of Abnormal and Social Psychology,* XLV (1950), 539. On the Dinka see Mary Douglas, *Purity and Danger: An Analysis of Concepts of Pollution and Taboo* (New York, 1966), 84; on the Wintu see Lee, "Conception of Self," *Jour. Abn. Soc. Psych.,* XLV (1950), 538-543, and D. Demetracopoulou Lee, "Linguistic Reflection of Wintu Thought," *International Journal of American Linguistics,* X (1944), 181-187; on the Amahuaca see Manuel Córdova-Rios and F. Bruce Lamb, *Wizard of the Upper Amazon* (New York, 1971), and Andrew Weil, *The Natural Mind: A New Way of Looking at Drugs and the Higher Consciousness* (Boston, 1972), 184. See also, for example, Douglas, *Purity and Danger,* 88; Nelson in "Perspectives on the Therapeutic," *Salmagundi,* XX (1972), 186; Bellah, "Religious Evolution," *Am. Sociol. Rev.,* XXIX (1964); Colin M. Turnbull, "Human Nature and Primal Man," *Social Research,* XL (1973), 528-530; Francis L. K. Hsu, "Kinship and Ways of Life: An Exploration," in Hsu, ed., *Psychological Anthropology* (Homewood, Ill., 1961), esp. 418, hereafter cited as Hsu, "Kinship"; Helen Merrell Lynd, *On Shame and the Search for Identity* (New York, 1950), 157-159; Richard N. Henderson, *The King in Every Man: Evolutionary Trends in Onitsha Ibo Society and Culture* (New Haven, Conn., 1972), 13, 124, 503-504; Donald N. Levine, *Wax and Gold: Tradition and Innovation in Ethiopian Culture* (Chicago, 1965), 238-286; and a host of older if somewhat disreputable assertions of similar points by Edward Tylor, James Frazer, Emile Durkheim, Lucien Lévy-Bruhl, and Marcel Mauss.

The issue of the premodern personality is vastly vexed, since some degrees and types of self-awareness seem to be present in, and essential to, even the most primitive societies. For suggestive efforts to explicate differences of quality and quantity despite such minima see Levine, *Wax and Gold,* 239-241; Turnbull, "Human Nature," *Soc. Res.,* XL (1973), 528-530; Geertz, *Person, Time, and Conduct,* 43, 53-55, 58-59, 69-70; and Edward Shorter, "Comment," *History of Childhood Quarterly,* I (1973-1974), 593-594. On the basis of these analyses it seems plausible to suppose that other cultures, including most Western cultures before the early modern era, may have afforded no very notable scope for the express cultivation of the individuality they did contain. In that light it is striking that the word "self" was not compounded as a prefix in English before the late 16th and early 17th centuries. See Logan Pearsall Smith, *The English Language* (London, 1912), 236-237.

[7] Dorothy Lee, "Are Basic Needs Ultimate?" *Jour. Abn. Soc. Psych.,* XLIII (1948), 393; Nelson in "Perspectives on the Therapeutic," *Salmagundi,* XX (1972), 184. On emergent individuation among the ancient Greeks see, for example, E. R. Dodds, *The Greeks and the Irrational* (Berkeley and Los Angeles, 1951), and Bruno Snell, *The Discovery of the Mind: The Greek Origins of European Thought* (Cambridge, Mass., 1953); among the early Christians see Bellah, "Religious

time of the self's decisive emergence in the West, the origins of that development are probably to be traced to the ways in which men and women of that era were wrenched loose from customary contexts of community and domesticity. For as Philippe Ariès, Michel Foucault, and Marshall McLuhan, among others, have shown, the rage for categorization and compartmentalization that shaped the new bourgeois culture of the seventeenth century made distinctions central that had scarcely been salient for medieval folk, embedded as they were in a more intricate and multifarious web of human relations.

The society of the Middle Ages was at once intensely immediate and
immensely complex. The mass of men and women lived in an intimate world 293
in which kinfolk, neighbors, and unnumbered ancient customs mediated the impingement of more distant authorities. Central government was hardly able even to curb local magnates, let alone control townspeople and villagers in the disparate jurisdictions of the realm. Peasants shielded themselves from the exactions of lords by recourse to prerogatives of ancestral usage and by enrollment under multiple masters, as well as by reliance upon their legitimate rights as members of a village and a family. For every sphere of medieval existence conferred its distinctive entitlements and exemptions, and "according to the different departments of their activity, men passed from one to the other of these zones of law." Family law, agrarian law, the customary law of the manor, the regulations of the community, and contractual obligations all cut across one another; and this multiplicity of legal codes was paralleled by a proliferation of courts to administer them. Even in the England of the Plantagenets, where royal courts and a kind of national law were relatively effective, a profusion of local tribunals persisted. Manorial, borough, county, and ecclesiastical courts preserved "a flourishing life of their own." And the administration of the law was but one aspect of the life of a myriad of counties, hundreds, villages, manors, towns, boroughs, guilds, bishoprics, abbeys, parishes, monasteries, and chapters which maintained a substantial measure of self-determination. Each regulated its own life in accordance with its venerable customs and entitlements and its current exigencies. Each possessed and protected its own privileges and immunities, in a medieval universe both personal and pluralistic.[8]

Evolution," *Am. Social. Rev.*, XXIX (1964), and Gustav Mensching, "Folk and Universal Religion," in Louis Schneider, ed., *Religion, Culture and Society: A Reader on the Sociology of Religion* (New York, 1964), 254-261; and in the "twelfth-century renaissance" see M. D. Chenu, *Nature, Man and Society in the Twelfth Century: Essays on New Theological Perspectives in the Latin West*, trans. and eds. Jerome Taylor and Lester K. Little (Chicago, 1968); Colin Morris, *The Discovery of the Individual, 1050-1200* (London, 1972); and the introduction to John F. Benton, ed., *Self and Society in Medieval France: The Memoirs of Abbot Guibert of Nogent: (1064?-c. 1125)*, rev. ed. (New York, 1970), 7-33.

[8] Marc Bloch, *Feudal Society*, trans. L. A. Manyon (Chicago, 1961), 112;

Modernization represented, in many respects, an abandonment of the richness and complexity of this medieval round of life. Like the nativistic revivals sometimes seen among tribal populations, it simplified a "gigantic game" grown "over-complicated" and altogether "too much for people." Men and women of the early modern age meant to tame what E. M. W. Tillyard called the "bursting and pullulating world" of their ancestors. They aimed to "hack their way through" what Perry Miller called "the scholastic undergrowth" of "the fifteenth-century morass." And in their readiness to renounce the multiplicity of the medieval habit, they gave up as if gladly that panoply of intermediate agencies of authority and objects of affection that
294 had hedged their parents' lives.[9]

In crucial measure, the movement toward modernity was encompassed in this stripping down of the old plenitude of powers, and in the attendant transition from ways of plurality to ways of polarity. In politics, kings began to level the realm, imposing new norms of uniformity of rights and obligations on what had been an extravagantly irregular system of baronial prerogatives and local privileges. In religion, Protestants set out to level the cosmos itself, denying the efficacy of the Virgin, the angels, the saints, the pope, and a vast variety of magical forces to intervene between God and human beings. A new-fledged passion for books and words initiated an unprecedented contraction of the very modalities of the senses. The medieval church had assumed, in its ritual and its elaborate trappings, that all its worshippers' senses were to be served. The dissenting offshoots of the early modern age declared, in their insistence on plainness, that the sensory range of their congregations' response was to be stringently restricted. Catholic exegesis had proliferated meanings. Protestant explication of texts afforded as far as possible only single meanings, so as to provide unequivocal instruction. The Christianity of the Middle Ages affirmed that its mystery was the richer

---

Michael R. Powicke, *The Community of the Realm, 1154-1485* (New York, 1973), 45. See, more generally, Joseph Strayer, "The Development of Feudal Institutions," in Marshall Claggett *et al.*, eds., *Twelfth-Century Europe and the Foundations of Modern Society* (Madison, Wis., 1961), and Bloch, *Feudal Society*, 63-64, 65, 66, 75, 82-83, 111, 116, 125-130, 185, 211, 212, 242, 264, 359, 360, 361-362, 363, 364, 367, 370-371, 382, 409. A convenient recent summary is Powicke, *Community of the Realm*, chaps. 3 and 4.

[9] E. M. W. Tillyard, *The Elizabethan World Picture* (London, 1943), 4, 92-93; Perry Miller, *The New England Mind: The Seventeenth Century* (New York, 1939), 157; Michael Walzer, *The Revolution of the Saints: A Study of the Origins of Radical Politics* (Cambridge, Mass., 1965), 151-152; and cf. Michel Foucault, *The Order of Things: An Archaeology of the Human Sciences* (New York, 1970). On the notion of nativistic revivals see James Mooney, *The Ghost-Dance Religion*, in Smithsonian Institution, Bureau of Ethnology, *Fourteenth Annual Report* (Washington, D.C., 1896); Ralph Linton, "Nativistic Movements," *American Anthropologist*, N.S., XLV (1943), 230-240; and Anthony F. C. Wallace, "Revitalization Movements," *ibid.*, LVIII (1956), 264-280.

for its ambiguity. The religion of the Reformers favored didactic sermons and allegories over such ambiguity, appending marginal notes even to its allegories lest those limited meanings be missed.[10]

In the family a similar and still more central transformation took place. For it was in the late sixteenth and seventeenth centuries that, according to Ariès, the conjugal unit began to set itself off in sensibility from the surrounding society. It was in the same period that, according to J. Hajnal, Europeans first diverged from a marital pattern which they had maintained in common with the rest of the world and began to marry much later in life, under conditions of greater domestic isolation. And it was at the same time, too, that individuals began to stand forth distinctively from their families, especially at the critical junctures of birth, marriage, and death, as their families stood forth from the wider social fabric. Newborn children of the seventeenth century invariably received their own specific names, where siblings had shared forenames as late as the Elizabethan era. Young men and women assumed a significant initiative in their choice of a marriage partner, where they had submitted to the marital arrangements of their parents in an earlier time. And mortals met their eternal fate alone and unaided at the advent of predestinarian Protestantism, where formerly they had been able to attach themselves to kinfolk by whose good works their souls could still be saved after death in the Catholic conception of purgatory.[11]

In the community as well, it was most momentously in the early modern era that the immemorial traditions came undone. English men and women experienced immense social dislocations under the Tudors and the first

[10] Walzer, *Revolution of the Saints*, 151-152; Thomas, *Religion and the Decline of Magic*, 639, 637; Larzer Ziff, *Puritanism in America: New Culture in a New World* (New York, 1973), 6, 14-15; cf. Rice, *Foundations of Early Modern Europe*, 147; Richard Slotkin, *Regeneration through Violence: The Mythology of the American Frontier, 1600-1860* (Middletown, Conn., 1973), 65-66; and Sacvan Bercovitch, *The Puritan Origins of the American Self* (New Haven, Conn., 1975), 110-111. In science, too, men first imagined with Bacon and then achieved with Newton a mechanistic reduction of the teeming natural world of their medieval predecessors. E. A. Burtt, *The Metaphysical Foundations of Modern Physical Science*, 2d ed. rev. (Garden City, N.Y., 1954), 238-239. As the historian of the Royal Society reported proudly at mid-17th century, English scientists had returned "to the primitive purity" of a "naked, natural way of speaking" and had succeeded in "bringing all things as near the mathematical plainness as they can." Floyd W. Matson, *The Broken Image: Man, Science and Society* (New York, 1964), 26.

[11] Ariès, *Centuries of Childhood;* J. Hajnal, "European Marriage Patterns in Perspective," in D. V. Glass and D. E. C. Eversley, eds., *Population in History . . .* (Chicago, 1965), 101-143; Daniel Scott Smith, "Child-Naming Patterns and Family Structure Change: Hingham, Massachusetts, 1640-1880" (paper delivered at the Clark University Conference on the Family and Social Structure, Worcester, Mass., Apr. 1972), 7; Lawrence Stone, *The Crisis of the Aristocracy, 1558-1641* (Oxford, 1965), chap. 11; Hsu, "Kinship," 422-423.

Stuarts. Population doubled in a little more than a century before the Civil War. The economy was transformed by crown confiscation and subsequent sale of monastic and chantry property, by an expansion of overseas commerce that made the cloth trade a national preoccupation, by enlargement of internal trade and specialized markets, by a dramatic reduction of interest rates, by the institutionalization of a money market, and above all by the creation of proto-capitalistic relations of production in agriculture. The tens of thousands of small-holders displaced by enclosure and its attendant alterations set in motion a geographic mobility generally apprehended as ominous and a social mobility nearly "unique in English history."[12]

296 The vagabonds, rogues, and roaring lads who stirred such anxiety in the England of Elizabeth and James were but the most visible embodiment of the throng that was loose upon the land. Towns and villages were roiled by migrations of remarkable extent.[13] And such mobility betokened even more extensive upheavals. Puritans, for example, set such high priority on dismantling the rituals and routines that helped sustain the medieval community that Keith Thomas has insisted on reckoning the "true significance" of Puritanism less in terms of its putative relation to capitalism than in its "implacable hostility to [the] more primitive society" of the Middle Ages. And Puritans were by no means alone in their antipathy to conventions of collective sentiment. They assailed those ceremonies of solidarity—the hagiography and festivals, the sports and dancing, the magic and taboos—with special vigor, but a wide spectrum of English society conspired in their dissolution. Many communal usages were already declining if not disappearing before the Marian exiles ever departed the realm. Many others

[12] Lawrence Stone, *The Causes of the English Revolution, 1529-1642* (London, 1972), 110, and see generally pp. 58-117. See also Carl Bridenbaugh, *Vexed and Troubled Englishmen, 1590-1642* (New York, 1968).

[13] E. E. Rich, "The Population of Elizabethan England," *Economic History Review*, 2d Ser., II (1949), 247-265; Peter Laslett and John Harrison, "Clayworth and Cogenhoe," in H. E. Bell and R. L. Ollard, eds., *Historical Essays, 1600-1750: Presented to David Ogg* (London, 1963), 157-184; S. A. Peyton, "The Village Population in the Tudor Lay Subsidy Rolls," *English Historical Review*, XXX (1915), 234-250; Julian Cornwall, "Evidence of Population Mobility in the Seventeenth Century," *Bulletin of the Institute of Historical Research*, XL (London, 1967), 143-152; Peter Clark, "The Migrant in Kentish Towns, 1580-1640," in Peter Clark and Paul Slack, eds., *Crisis and Order in English Towns, 1500-1700: Essays in Urban History* (London, 1972), 117-154; Stone, *Causes of the English Revolution*, 110-111; Bridenbaugh, *Vexed and Troubled Englishmen*, 21-22; Alan Everitt, *Change in the Provinces: The Seventeenth Century* (Leicester, Eng., 1969); E. A. Wrigley, "A Simple Model of London's Importance in Changing English Society and Economy, 1650-1750," *Past and Present*, XXXVII (July 1967), 45-49. On the implications of such mobility for the ancient web of kinship and community, mediated as it was by marriage, see Bridenbaugh, *Vexed and Troubled Englishmen*, 35-36, 40-41, 153-154, 368, 373.

waned without any apparent relation to the distinctive pressures of the movement the exiles ignited on their return.[14]

As ancient cords of kinship and community frayed, men and women began to counterpose things that had been better integrated for their parents and to schematize things that had been full of the stuff of life. As the depth and enduringness of primary relationships diminished, individuals began to depend both more and less than they had before on the old centers of the common life. And as they did, those centers could no longer hold so compellingly. The family could not remain an unconsidered matter of course when its members began to set themselves apart from it and, at the same time, make demands and place burdens upon it which it had never borne 297 before. The community could not continue to engage its inhabitants as a matter of casual necessity when they began to refuse its social and economic confinements while, at the same time, clinging the more tenaciously to a mental image of it as a deliberate ideal.

From these beginnings the English would be impelled by contrapuntal forces of excess and insufficiency, exaggerated and attenuated fellowship. And this impulsion, with the disturbances and intensifications of local life that accompanied it, is essential to an understanding of the emergence of American individuality and the conditions of American community.

Social psychologists have held that among persons for whom "doubt" has replaced "basic trust" in "the way of one's social group or in one's place in it," such doubt may "undermine the sense of one's own identity." They have suggested the salience, in the precipitation of what they call an "identity struggle," of a "sense of being expendable."[15] In early modern England, with its unemployed and underemployed masses, its conviction of overpopulation, its official complicity in the departure of its offscourings for the colonies, and its apprehension of declension and even of impending apocalypse, men and women might readily have received the impression that they were not needed and thereby found occasion for doubting their own identity.

[14] Keith Thomas, "History and Anthropology," *Past and Present*, XXIV (Apr. 1963), 3-24, quotation at p. 8. See also Charles Pythian-Adams, "Ceremony and the Citizen: The Communal Year at Coventry, 1450-1550," in Clark and Slack, eds., *Crisis and Order in English Towns*, 57-85; John Dolan, "Religious Festivities during the Reformation and Counter-Reformation: Challenge and Response," *Societas*, II (1972), 95-120; Alan Macfarlane, *Witchcraft in Tudor and Stuart England: A Regional and Comparative Study* (London, 1970).

[15] Lynd, *On Shame*, 46-47; Anthony F. C. Wallace and Raymond D. Fogelson, "The Identity Struggle," in Ivan Boszormenyi-Nagy and James L. Framo, eds., *Intensive Family Therapy: Theoretical and Practical Aspects* (New York, 1965), 396-397.

In such situations of endangered identity people often project onto others the characteristic they fear may be their own: an "incompetence for civilized living" associated with their anxiety at being supernumerary in their society.[16] They are driven to define others as adversaries, as if to vindicate their own uncertain worth by assaults on those around them. Certainly many seemed so driven in a nation paranoid in its abhorrence of popery, fanatical in its execration of the French and Spanish, and, withal, sufficiently insatiable for contrariety to sustain a civil war for a dozen years and more.[17]

In situations of disruption of basic trust people often express their fearfulness of life by exaggerated emphasis on morality and heightened
298 hatred of "sin."[18] They embrace identities defined primarily by their aversion to iniquity, as if to salvage a satisfactory sense of self in circumstances in which that sense is imperiled. Assuredly, a host of men and women embraced such identities in seventeenth-century England. Their exquisite concern for the determination of the boundaries of sin betrayed the *ressentiment* implicit in their "disinterested tendency to inflict punishment."[19] Their fixation on salvation, damnation, and the separation of sheep from goats suggested their profound need to achieve a new basis for trust, in an eternal order if not a temporal one.

[16] Wallace and Fogelson, "The Identity Struggle," in Boszormenyi-Nagy and Framo, eds., *Intensive Family Therapy*, 396-397. Wallace and Fogelson associate such phenomena with "technologic society" and insist that its attendant prejudices "have not (despite the cross-cultural ubiquity of ethnocentrism) been in any degree as savagely and indiscriminately destructive in nonindustrial societies as they have been in the technologic societies of the past four hundred years." They deny that there are any comparable confrontations of identity in most primitive groups; see p. 388. Hsu, too, has argued the affinity of early modern Europeans for religious persecution. He maintains that such abstract struggles may flare briefly in societies with denser kinship ties but that they are "neither long lasting nor widespread" in those settings. Hsu, "Kinship," 412, 423.

[17] Stone, *Causes of the English Revolution*, 121. The Georges argue that indeed "the Protestant mind came into being" in England during the assault on Catholicism; George and George, *Protestant Mind*, 12-13. And see more generally William Haller, *The Elect Nation: The Meaning and Relevance of Foxe's "Book of Martyrs"* (New York, 1964); William M. Lamont, *Godly Rule: Politics and Religion, 1603-1660* (New York, 1969); William S. Maltby, *The Black Legend in England: The Development of Anti-Spanish Sentiment, 1558-1660* (Durham, N.C., 1971); Carol Z. Weiner, "The Beleaguered Isle: A Study of Elizabethan and Early Jacobean Anti-Catholicism," *Past and Present*, LI (May 1971), 27-62. Weiner is especially sensitive to the counterposition of order and adventure in the fragile but strident nationalism of the time. For the ubiquity of the impulse to affirmation by negation see Christopher Hill, *Antichrist in Seventeenth-Century England* (London, 1971).

[18] Lynd, *On Shame*, 47.

[19] Svend Ranulf, *Moral Indignation and Middle Class Psychology* (Copenhagen, 1938), 1 and *passim*.

These stresses had their origins in the mother country before the first British ship ever anchored in the James, but they were felt most forcefully in the colonies. Modernization proceeded most unimpededly in America because the intricate webs of kinship and vicinage that were already disintegrating in England came quite apart in the New World. Traditional familial ideals and communal norms could be carried intact across the Atlantic and reconstituted in America from the models in the colonists' minds, but such deliberate recourse to tradition was, at bottom, the very antithesis of tradition. The rich particularity of the past could not be remade from models.

Indeed, the very effort to preserve traditional precepts and practices 299
provoked innovation. The people who projected colonies and crossed an ocean to establish them may have acted defensively, in regressive determination to resist the centralizing initiatives of the Stuarts in England. Some of them—the Puritans who fled the alluring corruption of their native land, the would-be patroons of New York, the Catholics who envisioned a feudal retreat in Maryland, Shaftesbury and his gifted secretary who set forth the Fundamental Constitutions of Carolina—may have aimed to arrest the changes that were undermining older ways. But in their endeavors to defend that traditional insularity, they shattered the continuity with the past that was a hallmark of the English localism they sought to conserve. For the communities which could be constructed on a wilderness coast were wholly new communities, without indigenous customs, without elders who had lived there all their lives, without ancient burying grounds or even any old buildings. Traditional ends had therefore to be achieved under novel circumstances by novel means. In the exigencies of existence three thousand miles from kings and archbishops, and in the cause of conserving ancient ideals, the colonists improvised a variety of new institutional arrangements unparalleled since the Norman conquest.[20]

Modernization also began most unobstructedly in America because a secure sense of social place could not be sustained in the strange land. Some people in some degree discovered their superfluousness in the mother country, but men and women in the colonies came face to face, inescapably, with the evidence of their own dispensability, simply by being where they were, an ocean apart from all they took to be civilized.[21]

[20] T. H. Breen, "Persistent Localism: English Social Change and the Shaping of New England Institutions," *WMQ*, 3d Ser., XXXII (1975), 3-28. See also Philip J. Greven, Jr., "Historical Demography and Colonial America," *ibid.*, XXIV (1967), 438-454, and Darrett B. Rutman, *American Puritanism: Faith and Practice* (Philadelphia, 1970), chaps. 2-3.

[21] The evidence of the impact of this discovery is inferential and not equally extensive for all the colonists. The surviving sources inevitably reflect disproportionate articulateness about self and society, and an incapacity to commit that

A few of the colonists accepted that evidence and gave vent to an answering savagery in themselves, but most of them made other, more poignant adjustments to their inconsequence. A Marylander, pleading Lord Calvert's case in London, conceded that his patron's province was "not a place any way considerable or worth his Highness' trouble." A "simple cobbler" of Aggawam, patching "all the year long, gratis," resigned himself "never to be paid for his work" in the wilderness. A Puritan chronicler admitted the dismay of the first planters at their "perpetual banishment from their native soil," in a "desert's depth where wolves and bears abide." The proprietor of Pennsylvania confessed his own colony "a desert of original
300 wild people . . . [and] wild beasts."[22] And creole colonials betrayed still deeper doubts. Cotton Mather was merely one of the first among many to lust after English acclaim on a suspicion that American accolades did not count, offered as they were in a "wilderness, in the ends of the earth," whose brave beginnings had "come to nothing."[23]

Mather could hardly admit even to himself his grim apprehension that the American experiment had fallen into "outer darkness" in remote regions "which the unprofitable are there condemned unto." But English men and women at home could and did entertain such notions, in disparaging images of the New World that inevitably offered emigrants a disturbing impression of their own undesirability by the very fact of their departure for such places.

---

articulateness to print that leaves the exposition which follows consistently overattentive to certain elites and sometimes overmindful of New England.

[22] John Langford, *A Just and Cleere Refutation of a False and Scandalous Pamphlet Entituled Babylons Fall in Maryland* . . . (1655), in Clayton Colman Hall, ed., *Narratives of Early Maryland, 1633-1684*, Original Narratives of Early American History (New York, 1910), 262; Theodore de la Guard (Nathaniel Ward), *The Simple Cobler of Aggawam in America* . . . (1647), in Peter Force, comp., *Tracts and Other Papers Relating Principally to the Origin, Settlement, and Progress of the Colonies in North America* . . . , III (Washington, D.C., 1844 [orig. publ. London, 1713]), no. 8 [1]; J. Franklin Jameson, ed., *Johnson's Wonder-Working Providence, 1628-1651*, Original Narratives of Early American History (New York, 1910), 53, 112; Gary B. Nash, *Quakers and Politics: Pennsylvania, 1681-1726* (Princeton, N.J., 1968), 162. See also John Pory to Sir Dudley Carleton, Sept. 30, 1619, in Louis B. Wright, ed., *The Elizabethans' America: A Collection of Early Reports by Englishmen on the New World* (Cambridge, Mass., 1965), 253-254. These and subsequent quotations are modernized.

[23] Cotton Mather, *Magnalia Christi Americana; or, the Ecclesiastical History of New-England* . . . , I (Hartford, Conn., 1855), 26, 27. See also [Henry Hartwell, James Blair, and Edward Chilton], "An Account of the Present State and Government of Virginia," Mass. Hist. Soc., *Colls.*, V (1798), 127; Louis B. Wright, ed., *The Prose Works of William Byrd of Westover: Narratives of a Colonial Virginian* (Cambridge, Mass., 1966), 19, 22-23, 345, 368. Three of the four narratives that were best-sellers in New England between 1680 and 1720 were captivity narratives, which Richard Slotkin takes to be paradigms "of the self-exile of the English Israel from England" (*Regeneration through Violence*, 94-96).

A promotional tract for the Chesapeake colonies admitted that "the country [was] . . . reported to be an unhealthy place, a nest of rogues, whores, dissolute and rooking persons; a place of intolerable labor, bad usage and hard diet, etc." Friends of New England recognized that the reputation of the Puritan outposts quickly came to "stink everywhere." And a popular saying abroad in England suggested that South Carolina was proverbial for its unsavoriness; men and women in the mother country measured the distastefulness of their circumstances by whether they "would rather live and die in Carolina."[24]

The effect of such conceptions was that an aura of outcast infelicity hung over the seaboard settlements, to color the migrants' ideas of their destina- 301
tions before they came or, indeed, to discourage their coming. The colonies standing "not handsomely in England, very few of good conversation would adventure thither" to "join with such an indigent and sottish people as were reported to be in Virginia." And in truth, relatively few of the indigent and sottish would adventure there either. People chose to "beg, steal, rot in prison, and come to shameful deaths," to "stuff Newgate, Bridewell, and other jails with their carcasses, nay cleave to Tyburn itself," before they would cross the ocean. The awareness of such choices detracted still further from the image of America, and consequently of themselves, which colonists could hold.[25]

Men and women who came in the face of such forbidding knowledge had, or quickly acquired, other reasons as well for doubting that they were wanted or of worth. Some, such as the Puritans, Catholics, and Quakers, were derelicts of religious devotion, forced from England because "every corner" of the country "was filled with the fury of malignant adversaries."

[24] Mather, *Magnalia*, I, 27; John Hammond, *Leah and Rachel, or, the Two Fruitfull Sisters Virginia and Mary-land* . . . (1656), in Hall, ed., *Narratives of Early Maryland*, 284; George Downing to John Winthrop, Aug. 26, 1645, *Winthrop Papers* (Mass. Hist. Soc., *Colls.*, 4th Ser., VI [Boston, 1863]), 537; Peter H. Wood, *Black Majority: Negroes in Colonial South Carolina from 1670 through the Stono Rebellion* (New York, 1974), 66-67. South Carolina's proverbial bad name persisted in England. As an 18th-century saying had it, "Whoever desires to die soon, just go to Carolina." Louis B. Wright, *The Colonial Search for a Southern Eden* (University, Ala., 1953), 44. For Bermuda's reputation as "the Devil's Islands," a "hideous and hated place" shunned by mariners "as they would shun the Devil himself," see Wright, ed., *Elizabethans' America*, 194, 196-197.

[25] Hammond, *Leah and Rachel*, in Hall, ed., *Narratives of Early Maryland*, 287, 286, 281, 296. See also, for example, *ibid.*, 283, 285, 299-300; "Extracts from the Annual Letters of the English Province of the Society of Jesus . . . ," *ibid.*, 123; Wood, *Black Majority*, 133n; Samuel Wilson, *An Account of the Province of Carolina, in America* . . . (1682), in Alexander S. Salley, Jr., ed., *Narratives of Early Carolina, 1650-1708*, Original Narratives of Early American History (New York, 1911), 164; John Archdale, *A New Description of that Fertile and Pleasant Province of Carolina* . . . (1707), *ibid.*, 295.

They had fled with "breast-breaking sobs" and "bowel-breaking affections" for friends and relatives left behind, and they clung to their attachment to England even in flight. It was, as one of them said, "for England's sake" that they were "going from England." A majority of the rest, such as younger sons or persons otherwise in "extreme misery" or "reduced to . . . poverty," were servants, forced to sell themselves into bondage to come to the colonies at all. The terms of their transplantation made plain that they had no attractive alternative in England. The often ruthless exploitation to which they were subjected in the New World disabused them of any hopes they might have held of a new and better home. Like the religious refugees who
302 soon began to ask "how shall we go to England?" as well as "how shall we go to heaven?," many of those servants came to "cry out day and night, oh that they were in England without their limbs and would not care to lose any limb to be in England again, yea though they beg from door to door."[26]

And in fact many did return, or attempted to. The very first English settlement in North America, at Roanoke, failed because Ralph Lane refused to wait for a promised supply that was actually on its way and chose instead to put his entire expedition aboard Drake's ships and go home. The survivors among the first settlers of Virginia were under sail on the James when, by almost incredible coincidence, they met Lord De la Warr and were persuaded to remain. A few years later the Virginia Company sent its storied shipload of women because the young men of the plantation were staying only "to get something, and then to return for England." A few years after that, and after the demise of the Company, the governing council of the colony also acknowledged that what settlers sought in Virginia was still, essentially, "a present crop, and their hasty return." More than one hundred of the first migrants to Massachusetts went back to the mother country within a year of the arrival of the Winthrop fleet, despite the desperate entreaties of their governor, and they were merely the beginners of what became a great remigration in the years of Cromwell's Commonwealth. And

[26] Jameson, ed., *Johnson's Wonder-Working Providence*, 23, 51-52, 53; "Letters of the Society of Jesus," in Hall, ed., *Narratives of Early Maryland*, 118-119, 122; "Roger Clap's Memoirs," in Alexander Young, ed., *Chronicles of the First Planters of the Colony of Massachusetts Bay* (Boston, 1846), 354-355; Richard Frethorne to his parents, Mar. 20, Apr. 2, 3, 1623, in Warren M. Billings, ed., *The Old Dominion in the Seventeenth Century: A Documentary History of Virignia, 1606-1689* (Chapel Hill, N.C., 1975), 305. See also, for example, John Smith, *Advertisements For the unexperienced Planters of New-England, or any where . . .* (1631), in Edward Arber and A. G. Bradley, eds., *Travels and Works of Captain John Smith: President of Virginia, and Admiral of New England, 1580-1631*, II (Edinburgh, 1910), 954; Perry Miller and Thomas H. Johnson, eds., *The Puritans* (New York, 1938), 119, 122; Jameson, ed., *Johnson's Wonder-Working Providence*, 45; Wood, *Black Majority*, 54n; Billings, ed., *Old Dominion*, 140; and Edmund S. Morgan, "The First American Boom: Virginia 1618 to 1630," *WMQ*, 3d Ser., XXVIII (1971), 169-198.

among the colonists of the Caribbean the very "mark of a successful . . . planter was his ability to escape from the island and retire grandly to England."[27]

Nonetheless, we would miss much of the inner meaning of modernization if we were to take these sources of the sense of displacement too straightforwardly. For the self-diminution that attended the recognition of dispensability evoked its own contravention in other, more expansive ways in which men and women apprehended their situation. In religious terms, New Englanders took the lead. Their jeremiads lamented the unworthiness of their land, but they also took the Lord's afflictions to prove His continuing concern for its inhabitants, in circularities that were ultimately as self-serving as self-abasing. Jonathan Mitchell called his fellow colonists "a small, weak . . . and despised people," but he did so by deliberate analogy to the chosen people of the Bible who also suffered such oppression. Cotton Mather trembled for New England's fate, but his very trepidation impelled him to an opposite verge of compensatory consecration and sublime certainty of its glorious destiny. When he declared, in the introduction to the *Magnalia*, that "whether New England may live anywhere else or no, it must live in our history," he expressed exactly the depth of his doubt and the outlandishness of his aspiration. His ambivalence articulated at once his exaggerated anguish that the errand might have gone for naught in the wilderness and his equally exaggerated determination that it survive, inviolate, in the American imagination.[28]

In realms other than religion, other colonies were at least as presumptuous as New England. Extravagant derogation of the rude settlements was met, in the colonial promotional literature, by correspondingly extravagant inflation of New World excellences and opportunities. If the image of America as hell on earth disposed English men and women to scorn the plantations, the counter-images of the country as Canaan or even Eden must have carried people's minds to states of voluptuous anticipation. Almost every

[27] Edmund S. Morgan, *American Slavery—American Freedom: The Ordeal of Colonial Virginia* (New York, 1975), 41, 111, 112; Susan Kingsbury, ed., *The Records of the Virginia Company of London,* I (Washington, D.C., 1906), 256; "Dudley's Letter to the Countess of Lincoln," in Young, ed., *Chronicles of the First Planters of Massachusetts,* 315; Thomas Hutchinson, *The History of the Colony and Province of Massachusetts-Bay,* ed. Lawrence Shaw Mayo, I (Cambridge, Mass., 1936), xxix; William Sachse, "The Migration of New Englanders to England, 1640-1660," *American Historical Review,* LIII (1948), 251; Richard S. Dunn, *Sugar and Slaves: The Rise of the Planter Class in the English West Indies, 1624-1713* (Chapel Hill, N.C., 1972), 116 and, for quantitative data, 111. For the same situation in Virginia by the second half of the 17th century see Morgan, *American Slavery—American Freedom,* 191, 200, 206.

[28] Miller and Johnson, eds., *The Puritans,* 239; Mather, *Magnalia,* I, 27. See also Bercovitch, *Puritan Origins of the American Self,* chap. 4, esp. 132-134.

promotional tract held out prospects of gold, or silks, spices, and wines, or health and long life, or spiritual fulfillment, or peace, or a passage to India, in innumerable alluring combinations. One Virginia production of the seventeenth century actually advanced Sir Walter Ralegh's mystic conviction that God had placed His earthly paradise on the 35th parallel of north latitude, in what was then part of Virginia. And like the assumption of God's cherishing faith in the jeremiads, the promulgation of these Edenic images in the promotional works offset the negative notions of the day without ever annulling them.[29]

In regard to servitude, too, the exploitation endured by inferiors was only
304 one side of a disjunctive development of the institution in the New World. As much as servants became mere commodities in the colonies, they were also indispensable on the virgin continent, where labor was everywhere in short supply. Consequently, the ones who stayed and survived cultivated cunning in turning their advantageous situation to account and acquired a sense of self-importance and worth in the course of doing so. Masters in New England grumbled that servants learned "to live idly, and work when they list." Manor lords in New York complained of their tenants' "hopes of having land of their own and becoming independent of landlords." Planters in Virginia had to exempt white servants from the slavishness of their original legal lot and afford them the prerogatives of a racial upper class. As the younger Thomas Shepard explained, men and women of the most servile status came in America to "desire liberty."[30] Every colony was obliged ultimately to gratify that desire in some degree—by legislation, adjudication, or common custom—in order to attract inhabitants at all. In every colony there were "laboring men, who had not enough to bring them over, yet now worth scores, and some hundreds of pounds." And in some colonies, such as Pennsylvania and New York, rival publicists vied in promoting their own province as the "best poor man's country," in an odd conflation of poverty and prepotency that was itself indicative of the antipodal tensions of early American life.[31]

These antithetic images and experiences of indispensability and ex-

[29] Wright, *Search for a Southern Eden*, 37; see also Louis B. Wright, *The Dream of Prosperity in Colonial America* (New York, 1965).

[30] Ziff, *Puritanism in America*, 86, 87; Patricia Bonomi, *A Factious People: Politics and Society in Colonial New York* (New York, 1971), 195; Oscar and Mary Handlin, "Origins of the Southern Labor System," *WMQ*, 3d Ser., VII (1950), 199-222; Edmund S. Morgan, "Slavery and Freedom: The American Paradox," *Journal of American History*, LIX (1972), 5-29.

[31] Jameson, ed., *Johnson's Wonder-Working Providence*, 212; James Lemon, *The Best Poor Man's Country: A Geographical Study of Early Southeastern Pennsylvania* (Baltimore, 1972), xiii, 229; Bonomi, *A Factious People*, 196. See also Wilson, *Account of Carolina*, in Salley, ed., *Narratives of Early Carolina*, 167.

pendability, that jostled each other in uneasy irresolution, affected the dominant classes of colonial society, too. As if driven to exorcise the demons of their unnecessariness and prove that they did belong despite their transplantation, the very men and women who had come most effectively to terms with the New World engaged in a prodigious variety of exaggerated affirmations of their Englishness. In the tropical islands of the Caribbean they wore English woolens and worsteds and put up lodgings that resembled London row houses. In the forest clearings of New England they perpetuated classical learning. And in the presence of marauding Powhatans in the Chesapeake they pursued an English gentry ideal so ardently that even in the declining days of the Virginia Company, when sickness, starvation, and death stalked the straggling settlements, the town cow-keeper and the wife of a collier still decked themselves out in modish silks.[32]

In their importunate desire for the amenities of the mother country, the colonists exhibited a disposition to conceive the world in dualistic terms, as though to redeem their own enigmatic identities by disparaging the identities of others, in the peculiar logic of negation and self-salvage imposed by the identity struggle. The early settlers were, as Winthrop Jordan has said, "especially inclined to discover attributes in savages which they found first but could not speak of in themselves." They were disposed to defend their civility by comparing their own skin color and social customs with those of the Indians and Africans. Yet the very comparison that spared them the strain of dwelling on the disparity between their own practices and those they had left behind, and the contraposition that sustained their psychic equilib-

[32] Dunn, *Sugar and Slaves,* chap. 8; Kenneth A. Lockridge, *Literacy in Colonial New England: An Enquiry into the Social Context of Literacy in the Early Modern West* (New York, 1974); Robert Middlekauff, *Ancients and Axioms: Secondary Education in Eighteenth-Century New England* (New Haven, Conn., 1963); John Pory to Sir Dudley Carleton, Sept. 30, 1619, in Lyon Gardiner Tyler, ed., *Narratives of Early Virginia, 1606-1625,* Original Narratives of Early American History (New York, 1907), 284-285. A suggestive expression of this effort to imitate the English, or outdo them on their own terms, was the obsessive comparison the colonists forced between English and American flora and fauna, as if the settlers had to defend against a haunting fear that things American were offscourings of the earth as well as of England. For the first generations see Miller and Johnson, eds., *The Puritans,* 382; William Wood, *New Englands Prospect* (Boston, 1865), 14; Thomas Morton, *New English Canaan . . .* (1637), ed. Charles Francis Adams (Prince Society, *Publications,* XIV [Boston, 1883]), 180-183, 185-190, 193, 194, 201-203; Jameson, ed., *Johnson's Wonder-Working Providence,* 91, 99, 210; Archdale, *New Description of Carolina,* in Salley, ed., *Narratives of Early Carolina,* 288. For the persistence of such fears to the end of the 18th century see Henry Steele Commager and Elmo Giordanetti, *Was America a Mistake?: An Eighteenth-Century Controversy* (New York, 1967), and Gordon S. Wood, ed., *The Rising Glory of America, 1760-1820* (New York, 1971), 14-16.

rium by reassuring them of who they were when they were a long way from home, also compounded their dilemma. For those contrasts intensified their conviction that they were poised on the edge of an abyss of barbarism. They reinforced their disjunctive definition of the colonial situation as one in which civilized virtue stood always in awful temptation of descending into savage vice.[33]

Inhabitants of the southern colonies yielded to the temptation most nearly, in exploiting their slaves, and at the same time resisted it most stridently, in drawing a dichotomous color line between themselves and the Africans. Whereas settlers of the other European nations in the New World
306 apprehended color categories in continua that reflected initial African diversity and subsequent racial interbreeding, the English who colonized America acknowledged only the polarized alternatives of white and black. Whereas Spaniards and Portuguese evolved elaborate vocabularies that recognized the complexity of racial realities, Virginians and Carolinians put themselves radically apart from their slaves. Drawing a line that denied all gradation or degree, they defied the abundant actuality of miscegenation and the evidence of the varied complexions before their eyes.[34]

Settlers of the northern as well as the southern colonies drew a clear line of demarcation between themselves and the other people they found tempting them to savagery, the Indians. Few frontier dwellers would have disputed Samuel Purchas's description of the indigenous inhabitants of the eastern woodlands as "bad people, having little of humanity but shape, ignorant of civility, or arts, or religion; more brutish than the beasts they hunt, more wild and unmanly than that unmanned wild country, which they range rather than inhabit." And the few who did see the natives differently could not defend their vision in the face of open strife between the two cultures and the consequent extinction of sympathy for the Indians. Virginians accepted the Indian incursion of 1622 in grim exultancy, "because now we have just cause to destroy them by all means possible." New Englanders improved

[33] Winthrop D. Jordan, *White over Black: American Attitudes Toward the Negro, 1550-1812* (Chapel Hill, N.C., 1968), 40, and see 97-98, 110, 119-120, 143-144, 193 for discussion of specific spheres—religion, law, community, and family—in which racial comparisons enabled the colonists to cling to their self-conception as Englishmen in otherwise unconvincing circumstances.

[34] There was, to be sure, a more elaborate and complex set of color categories in the British West Indies than in the British colonies on the mainland; see, for example, Winthrop D. Jordan, "American Chiaroscuro: The Status and Definition of Mulattoes in the British Colonies," *WMQ*, 3d Ser., XIV (1962), 183-200. But this is, in the exact sense of the phrase, the exception that proves the rule, since even in the British islands the intermediate categories were less elaborately and more grudgingly applied than in the French, Spanish, and Portuguese colonies. See, for example, Donald Horowitz, "Color Differentiation in the American Systems of Slavery," *Journal of Interdisciplinary History*, III (1973), 509-542, esp. 518-520.

King Philip's provocations as a pretext "to extirpate the enemy in holy war." Indeed, almost the only relations with the Indians that New Englanders could even imagine were the antagonistic ones of war and captivity.[35]

New Englanders drew other lines as well. They drew them deliberately, pervasively, and at the highest levels of conscious culture, for they, pre-eminently among the settlers of early America, distilled dichotomies out of the traditional multiplicities of medieval pluralism. The logic of Ramus on which their formal thought depended was a logic that displaced the profuse categories of Aristotle and exalted instead "the doctrine of contraries." It postulated that every art and science fell "of itself into dichotomies," and accordingly it took the task of thought to be the successive bifurcation of its subject into "serried ranks of opposites" so as to trace that subject to its elemental units. John Cotton exemplified the letter of the method in the opening exposition of a sermon in which he explained that "all the men in the world are divided into two ranks, godly or ungodly, righteous or wicked; of wicked men two sorts, some are notoriously wicked, others are hypocrites; of hypocrites two sorts . . . some are washed swine, others are goats." Michael Wigglesworth exemplified the spirit that lay behind the letter in his simple resolution to wage "spiritual war against sin." And similar martial metaphors entered into innumerable Puritan preachings and utterly shaped such statements as Edward Johnson's *Wonder-Working Providence*, which set dichotomy at the heart of history just as others had established it at the center of logic. Johnson viewed all the modern history of Europe as a contest between men pursuing the reformation of religion and men opposing that pursuit. He saw the history of New England, in particular, as just such a series of battles between saints seeking "to batter down, root up, and quite destroy all heresies and errors" and the motley minions of Antichrist.[36]

Settlers west of the Connecticut were less relentlessly preoccupied with heresy and error, but English settlers everywhere understood themselves in absolute antitheses. Saved and damned, Christian and heathen, civilized and savage, white and black were counterpositions that came congenially and, indeed, compellingly to the colonists, at the Chesapeake as much as at

[35] Gary B. Nash, "The Image of the Indian in the Southern Colonial Mind," *WMQ*, 3d Ser., XXIX (1972), 222-223, 218-219; Slotkin, *Regeneration through Violence*, 83-195. See also Ziff, *Puritanism in America*, 171-172; Roy Harvey Pearce, *Savagism and Civilization: A Study of the Indian and the American Mind*, 2d rev. ed. (Baltimore, 1965); and Francis Jennings, *The Invasion of America: Indians, Colonialism, and the Cant of Conquest* (Chapel Hill, N.C., 1975).

[36] Miller and Johnson, eds., *The Puritans*, 32-33; Miller, *New England Mind: The Seventeenth Century*, 127; Miller and Johnson, eds., *The Puritans*, I, 314; Edmund S. Morgan, ed., "The Diary of Michael Wigglesworth," Colonial Society of Massachusetts, *Publications*, XXXV (Boston, 1951), 326; Jameson, ed., *Johnson's Wonder-Working Providence*, 189, and see also 269; Mather, *Magnalia*, I, 25-26.

Massachusetts Bay. And in such counterpositions, and the counteridentities they betokened, were the seeds of a new individuality and a new community alike.

Individual settlers, unable to accept fully their disordered experience in the New World, confined its complexity in disjunctions and then deliberately disdained one side of the disjunctions. They attained identity by denying the undisciplined and undifferentiated impulses that plagued them and by disowning the abundant opportunities that tempted them. Thomas Morton of Merry Mount caught their character in his offhand observation that "he that played Proteus (with the help of Priapus) put their noses out of joint."
308 Virginians illustrated his insight—that the orthodox subordinated even their animus against phallic license to their abhorrence of unfixed identity—in their repeated resentment of men with more power than breeding and in their revulsion from the Indians as "most treacherous people" because "inconstant in everything." New Englanders were even more vehement. Nathaniel Ward raged revealingly against the Apocrypha in the Bible, foreigners in his country, counterfeit coins, and religious toleration as the four things his heart "naturally detested." All four were emblems of the adulteration of homogeneous substance; and Ward, who pronounced "polypiety" the "greatest impiety in the world," found "mixtures pernicious" and "power" only in "purity."[37]

In significant measure, individuals such as Ward came to know themselves by their negations. They forged their identities as one might make a silhouette, establishing a boundary about themselves and appearing as what was inside without having to say exactly what that was. In their logic they distinguished ideas "by setting them against their opposites." In their lives they discerned themselves by setting their assumptive civility against the unconditional abandon—the "license, sedition, and fury" of the "inordinate soul," as the Virginia Company put it—which they ascribed to others. They achieved a sense of their own moral ideal by conjuring a contrast to "the Indian as a symbol of that . . . degradation to which the spiritual thralls of the wilderness are brought." They preserved an assurance of their religious aspiration by emphasizing, as Roger Williams noted of the New Englanders, that they were "no Jews, no Turks . . . nor Catholics," despite "their own formal dead faith," or by supposing, as Jordan suggests of the early Virginians, that they were not so "*totally* defective" as their African slaves, despite

[37] Morton, *New English Canaan*, 281; John Pory, "A Report of the Manner of Proceeding in the General Assembly . . . 1619," in Wright, ed., *Elizabethans' America*, 243; William Strachey, *History of Travel into Virginia Britannia*, *ibid.*, 218; [Ward], *Simple Cobler*, 7. For Puritan detestation of the "mixed multitude" of the English parish before the great migration to New England see David D. Hall, *The Faithful Shepherd: A History of the New England Ministry in the Seventeenth Century* (Chapel Hill, N.C., 1972), 25.

their own deficiencies of Christian piety.[38] And so they defined themselves less by the vitality of their affirmations than by the violence of their abjurations. Their apprehension of their individuality came to be encapsulated in such counter-identity and in the "identity-work" by which they managed the modicum of their inclinations that they could accept and the rest that they rejected.[39]

The very counter-identifications that forced a more straitened and simplified fixing of the individual forced also a more deliberate fixing of the terms of his associations. For a man's phobias did not sustain him, or enable
him to solve the problem of his endangered identity, unless he could share 309
them with others. An individual whose identity was established primarily by purification, as an integrity achieved by putting many inclinations apart, was an individual impelled to dissolve old tolerances and old ties of family and propinquity, and consequently to search for "wider circles of solidarity."[40]

The search was most manifest among the Puritans of Massachusetts and Connecticut, for whom its result was, inevitably, to expose the individual to the strictures of those he embraced as brothers. His very attachment to them placed his outward behavior under their ceaseless surveillance and made his most inward experience, the vicissitudes of his regeneration, subject to their scrutiny. He could not count his own conversion complete or authentic until he had confessed its course to their satisfaction.

The result of his search was also to impose upon the individual a range of reciprocal obligations of intrusion and examination into the affairs of his fellows. Once admitted to a congregation of visible saints, he had in his turn to hear the confessions of other candidates. He had to know himself precisely in order to obtain a "standard of sanctity" by which to judge the experience of others and carry on relations with his spiritual kinsmen. He had to display a daily "zeal for the morality of others" in order to uphold the social covenant on which he predicated the temporal prosperity of the community and in order to be confident of the covenant of grace on which his own eternal destiny depended. For his alacrity in overseeing the reformation of his neighbors was a test of the efficacy of his conversion. "Whatever sins come within [the true convert's] reach," Thomas Hooker averred, "he labors the

[38] Miller and Johnson, eds., *The Puritans*, 33, 480; *A True Declaration of the estate of the Colonie in Virginia . . .*, in Force, comp., *Tracts*, III, no. 1, 15; Slotkin, *Regeneration through Violence*, 86; Jordan, *White over Black*, 98.

[39] On the concept of "identity work" see Anthony F. C. Wallace, "Identity Processes in Personality and in Culture," in Richard Jessor and Seymour Feshbach, eds., *Cognition, Personality, and Clinical Psychology* (San Francisco, 1967), 62-89.

[40] Hsu, "Kinship," 421. On the notion of purified identity see Richard Sennett, *The Uses of Disorder: Personal Identity and City Life* (New York, 1970), esp. chap. 1.

removal of them, out of the families where he dwells, out of the plantations where he lives, out of the companies and occasions, with whom he hath occasion to meet and meddle at any time."[41]

The imperative to be his brother's keeper also provided the Puritan with a way of alleviating his unease at the inevitable impurities of his community. For even in his expectation "that wicked men will be mixed with the godly," he believed with Samuel Willard that, by a suitable surveillance, he could mingle with the multitudes and still preserve a sense of social purity. "When [the wicked] are not countenanced, but due testimony is born against them; when they are contemned in the places where they live, and a note of infamy
310 and scandal is put upon them; this will not be charged on [the saints] for apostasy."[42]

Puritans were therefore driven to demand a close association with their godly brethren and prohibited any comparable tie to the ungodly. Exactly as believers, they faced always the "double requirement" of an "ardor of intimacy" within the fellowship and a fierce "heat of hostility" outside it, amid "the circling mass of enemies." Their communities were never merely places where babies were born and people died. The land they consecrated was God's country.[43]

Some of the most sophisticated students of Puritanism have recognized this power of the movement simultaneously to individuate and aggregate. Michael Walzer has observed the "constant tendency" of the saints to "turn the theology of salvation into a sociology" in which the very voluntarism of private allegiance led to "a collective discipline" that "created bonds in many ways more intensive than those of blood and nature." Perry Miller marked the concomitance between "a piety in which the individual was the end of creation" and "a social philosophy in which he was subordinate to the whole." Max Weber pointed to the propensity of Reformed religion to plunge men and women into "inner isolation" and, at the same time, "the undoubted superiority of Calvinism in social organization."[44]

Nonetheless, few of these dispositions and disjunctions were unique to the New England Puritans. Many of them were developed even more fully

[41] George and George, *Protestant Mind,* 102-103; Morgan, ed., "Diary of Wigglesworth," Col. Soc. Mass., *Pubs.,* XXXV, 316-317. See also Edmund S. Morgan, *Visible Saints: The History of a Puritan Idea* (New York, 1963).

[42] Miller and Johnson, eds., *The Puritans,* 374-375.

[43] George and George, *Protestant Mind,* 103-104; Bercovitch, *Puritan Origins,* esp. chap. 4.

[44] Walzer, *Revolution of the Saints,* 170; Miller, *New England Mind: The Seventeenth Century,* 462; Max Weber, *The Protestant Ethic and the Spirit of Capitalism* (New York, 1958), 108. See also Morgan, ed., "Diary of Wigglesworth," Col. Soc. Mass., *Pubs.,* XXXV, 315, for a characterization of an ideal-typical Puritan as a "selfish busybody."

among the Quakers,[45] and most of them were evident in some measure in all the colonies. For early English Protestantism in its entirety was at once a renewal of the old tribal temper and a symptom of the decay of the common life of preceding centuries. It brought both a new scrupulousness in the reconnaissance of conduct and a new freedom from such scrutiny. And it subjected settlers of every plantation to more and, concurrently, less control than they had known in the land of their nativity.[46]

In all the colonies the first settlers were disproportionately composed of Englishmen impatient of conventional social ties and disproportionately disposed to set their own advantage before the public good. In Massachusetts as much as in Virginia or Carolina, authorities had to contend with "self-
love" that "forgot all duty" and with men who "neither feared God nor man." Indeed, such men often took their cues from the authorities themselves. Thomas Weston "pursued his own ends" assiduously in the Plymouth enterprise. Gov. George Yeardley gave an impression of being "wholly addicted to his private" in Virginia. And leading men and lesser men alike found "their own conceived necessity" a "warrant sufficient" to take up lands where they pleased and to plant crops as they pleased, even if their fellows implored and the laws enjoined otherwise.[47]

At the same time, such determined affirmations of personal liberty evoked equally determined assertions of social control. The imbalance of bachelors among the early settlers was offset by the assignment of such potentially reckless young men to reputable families in New England and by the confinement of such potentially dissolute young men to grinding servitude in Virginia. Enticements to self-interest were counteracted by exemplary

[45] Quakers legitimated "personal authoritative revelation" as the Puritans never did, and at the same time secured an even more encompassing "system of discipline and church control" with a thoroughness the Puritans never managed. J. William Frost, *The Quaker Family in Colonial America: A Portrait of the Society of Friends* (New York, 1973), 49. A similar simultaneity shapes almost every recent account of colonial Quakerism; for example, see Richard Bauman, *For the Reputation of Truth: Politics, Religion, and Conflict among the Pennsylvania Quakers, 1750-1800* (Baltimore, 1971); Susan Forbes, " 'As Many Candles Lighted': The New Garden Monthly Meeting 1718-1774" (Ph.D. diss., University of Pennsylvania, 1972); Sydney V. James, *A People among Peoples: Quaker Benevolence in Eighteenth-Century America* (Cambridge, Mass., 1963); and Frederick B. Tolles, *Meeting House and Counting House: The Quaker Merchants of Colonial Philadelphia, 1682-1763* (Chapel Hill, N.C., 1948).

[46] George and George, *Protestant Mind*, 82-83, 84. See also Nelson, "Self Images and Systems of Spiritual Direction," in Klausner, ed., *Quest for Self-Control*, 70-71, for a comparable connection in early Lutheranism.

[47] William Bradford, *Of Plymouth Plantation, 1620-1647*, ed. Samuel Eliot Morison (New York, 1952), 54, 107, 254; "A True Declaration of the estate of the Colonie of Virginia . . . ," in Force, comp., *Tracts*, 18; Morgan, *American Slavery—American Freedom*, 123n.

penalties imposed on worldlings as different as Robert Keayne and Thomas Morton. And inclinations to go off from settled society—ultimately, to go off to the Indians—were fought with maledictions on the wilderness and grisly executions of recaptured renegades "to terrify the rest for attempting the like."[48]

Religious controls also evolved in the face of unprecedented freedom from religious sanctions. In every colony on the North American continent, religious and lay leaders became uneasy as farms spread scatteringly and the nearby woods whispered of the possibilities of privacy;[49] and in every colony an ansering church discipline of a strikingly similar sort emerged. Quakers
312 did not maim and kill to maintain their way, as New England Puritans sometimes did, but Quakers, Puritans, and Anglicans alike appointed ecclesiastical agents to pry into personal lives and attempt the repression of iniquity, under conditions of tribal exclusivity and congregational communalism. For without effective bonds of episcopal order, individual churches everywhere in British America functioned essentially by themselves. They were not enmeshed in national or papal hierarchies, and they were not organized as inclusive parishes. On the contrary, they were gathered by spiritual affinity out of much larger local populations. They reflected both the heightened individuality that led people to separate themselves from society at large and the augmented intensity of community life that was embodied in the very churches in which they set themselves off.[50]

[48] Morgan, *American Slavery—American Freedom,* 74. Under Gov. Dale, some who tried to go off to the Indians were "appointed to be hanged, some burned, some to be broken upon wheels, others to be staked, and some to be shot to death." *Ibid.* And at least as revealing was the cautionary tale told by William Strachey of the fate that Englishmen might expect if they did succeed in getting to the Indians: "When [Powhatan] would punish any notorious enemy or trespasser, he causeth him to be tied to a tree, and with mussel-shells or reeds the executioner cutteth off his joints one after another, ever casting what is cut off into the fire; then doth he proceed with shells and reeds to case the skin from his head and face, after which they rip up his belly, tear out his bowels, and so burn him with the tree and all. Thus themselves reported that they executed an Englishman . . . whom the women enticed up from the barge unto their houses at a place called Appocant" (*History of Travel,* in Wright, ed., *Elizabethans' America,* 209).

[49] On the significance of scattered settlement for privacy see David H. Flaherty, *Privacy in Colonial New England* (Charlottesville, Va., 1972).

[50] Laymen gained control of all these churches, most completely, perhaps, among the Quakers and pietist sectarians, and more completely, in many ways, in the officially Anglican South than in ostensibly Congregational New England, where ministers maintained occasional synods and rather regular consociations, and asserted a sacerdotal authority over the laity which would have been inconceivable in the Quaker colonies and was literally laughable in Virginia. See Paul Lucas, *Valley of Discord: Church and Society along the Connecticut River, 1636-1725* (Hanover, N.H., 1976); Hall, *Faithful Shepherd;* and on the derision of such pretensions in Virginia, Wright, ed., *Prose Works of Byrd,* 344.

Political controls also expanded and contracted concurrently, and expectations and assumptions of both individuals and the organized community underwent a simultaneous inflation. Government was notoriously harsh in almost all the early settlements, while the governed were notoriously unruly and even rebellious. Virginia oscillated incessantly between the libertinism of the first planters and the brutal leadership necessary to contain it. Governors imposed martial law on the populace or were "thrust out" for trying to impose it. The air rang with recriminations of "extreme choler and passion" and "tyrannical proceeding" on one side and "mutinous meetings" and "treason" on the other. "Giddy headed and turbulent persons" rose repeatedly against the "oppressions" of "men in authority and favor," burning 313
Jamestown itself to the ground in Bacon's Rebellion; and men in authority responded as repeatedly and heatedly, executing the rebels for treason.[51]

And though Virginia was perhaps the most sorely torn of all the colonies, similar cleavages appeared everywhere. In Massachusetts the public affairs of the first decades were occupied with a periodic sparring between magistrates insistent upon an extensive discretionary sphere and more popular forces adamant in their demand for legal guarantees of local rights and liberties. In New York political volatility was "chronic and inherent," and governors found their subjects so "contentious" and recalcitrant that one observer was "sure if the Roman Catholics have a place of purgatory, it's not so bad as [this] place is under my Lord's circumstance." In Carolina a succession of smaller "broils," as John Archdale called them, was punctuated by a number of serious collisions such as the one in which a "loose and extravagant spirit . . . got head in the government of James Colleton" and provoked "the common people" to choose representatives "to oppose whatsoever the governor requested." In Maryland an atmosphere of intrigue prevailed from the time of Baltimore's first instructions and exploded over the next two decades in "illegal executions and murders," "seditions and mutinies," and "malicious plots and conspiracies" on the part of both antagonists and adherents of the proprietor. In Ingle's rebellion and in the affair of the Parliamentary commissioners, the colony was twice "deflowered, by her own inhabitants, stripped, shorn, and made deformed," even before the battle at the Severn in 1655.[52]

[51] "The Thrusting Out of Sir John Harvey," in Billings, ed., *Old Dominion,* 252, 253, 255; "The Surry County Court's Verdict, January 6, 1673/74," *ibid.,* 265; "Bacon's 'Manifesto,' " *ibid.,* 278; see, generally, *ibid.,* 236-287. Howard Mumford Jones, *O Strange New World: American Culture, The Formative Years* (New York, 1964), 277-278; Morgan, *American Slavery—American Freedom.* For a suggestive study of the extensive detachment of individuals from familial moorings in the early years of colonization, with implications for both collective instability and the necessity for oppressive authority, see Irene W. D. Hecht, "The Virginia Muster of 1624/5 as a Source for Demographic History," *WMQ,* 3d Ser., XXX (1973), 65-92.

[52] Bonomi, *A Factious People,* 138, 11; Archdale, *New Description of Carolina,*

In all of these struggles the modernizing logic of polarization that shaped the fray was apparent in the pronouncements of the partisans. Lord Baltimore's opponents charged that he "ruled in Maryland in such an absolute way and authority, as no Christian prince or state in Europe exercises the like," yet they were so little daunted by his "absolute" power that they were able to resist it effectively for more than twenty years. Proponents granted that the Calverts claimed prerogatives "not . . . convenient for any one man to have in England," yet they added in the very next breath that the freemen of the colony also possessed political privileges exceeding those current in the mother country. And even in Pennsylvania, where the Quaker leadership was
314 preoccupied with peace, Isaac Norris was obliged to acknowledge that, from the first, the government was unable to attain to a middle ground "between arbitrary power and licentious popularity."[53]

Indeed, in their most idealistic envisionings of an appropriate public order in the New World, men seemed incapable of imagining a regime that did not augment at once the authoritarian and the libertarian tendencies of the time. The "true and absolute Lords proprietors" of Carolina might wish to "avoid erecting a numerous democracy," and set forth on that account Fundamental Constitutions that provided for a hereditary nobility and leet-men whose children would be leet-men "to all generations," but they also operated under a charter that promised the inhabitants "full and free license" in religious affairs and extensive rights in the political process. The proprietors of New Jersey might proclaim their lordly powers in the most "full and ample manner," but they also issued Concessions and Agreements that allowed their colonists "liberty of conscience," generous terms of landed settlement, and a representative assembly with decisive control over provincial taxation; and the purchasers of their privileges in West Jersey issued further Concessions and Agreements that renewed the assurance of "full liberty of religious faith and worship," offered elaborate protections against corruption of the electoral process, and guaranteed that representatives would "act nothing in that capacity but what shall tend to the fit service and behoof

in Salley, ed., *Narratives of Early Carolina*, 282, 295; *Instructions 13 Novem: 1633 directed by the Right Hon[ora]ble Cecilius Lo: Baltimore and Lord of the Provinces of Mary Land and Avalon* . . . (1633), in Hall, ed., *Narratives of Early Maryland*, 16-17; *Virginia and Maryland, or The Lord Baltamore's printed CASE, uncased and answered*. . . . (1655), *ibid.*, 201; "Letter of Governor Leonard Calvert to Lord Baltimore" (1638), *ibid.*, 152; "Extract from a Letter of Captain Thomas Yong to Sir Toby Matthew" (1634), *ibid.*, 56; Hammond, *Leah and Rachel*, *ibid.*, 300.

[53] *Virginia and Maryland*, in Hall, ed., *Narratives of Early Maryland*, 199, 191; *The Lord Baltemore's Case, Concerning the Province of Maryland* . . . (1653), *ibid.*, 174; Nash, *Quakers and Politics*, 292-293. Nash depicted early Pennsylvania politics as "a make-believe world" in which "words became more important than actions," which is striking in the light of Hsu's point that, in the absence of a dense social web, people are more prone to be "pulled asunder by abstract issues." Hsu, "Kinship," 409; cf. 423.

of those that send and employ them." William Penn's charter for Pennsylvania might confer upon him a "free, full, and absolute power" of superintendency over his province, but his Frames of Government made every inhabitant a member of the assembly for the first year of the venture, provided for annual elections of as many as five hundred representatives thereafter, and established a representation not only proportional to population but also rotated so that "all may be fitted for government, and have experience of the care and burden of it." In all these colonies, then, and in the others as well, the government grew more ambitious of control than the state was at home even as it afforded its citizens a more effective participation in authority than they had at home. Discipline and autonomy developed apace.[54] 315

The coming apart of the old connectedness of self and society was simultaneously a coming into being of new unities of covenanted community and purified personality.[55] But the new unities betrayed their basis in the initial partitioning. Communities made excessive claims of concord for themselves and then fell into a dismayed sense of declension whenever they failed to sustain such ideological aspirations.[56] Individuals defined sanctified reaches of being for themselves and then found themselves drawn—even driven—to the very impurities they professed to have put aside. They did not cease to be susceptible to the terrors of the irrational merely because they distinguished

[54] William MacDonald, ed., *Select Charters and Other Documents Illustrative of American History: 1606-1775* (New York, 1899), 122, 150, 151, 154, 123-125, 140, 142-143, 146, 176, 180-181, 186, 197, 202-203, 194, 201. Similar tensions appeared even earlier, as in George Donne's design for the reconstitution of Virginia, with its plea for stronger government *and* for a more sturdily self-reliant citizenry. These tensions persisted far into the 18th century, as in Benjamin Franklin's plan for a colony of Vandalia, with its provision for an appointed governor of feudal proclivities *and* for the happy mediocrity and republican simplicity that were hallmarks of his "Virtuous Order." See T. H. Breen, "George Donne's 'Virginia Reviewed': A 1638 Plan to Reform Colonial Society," *WMQ*, 3d Ser., XXX (1973), 449-466, and Paul W. Connor, *Poor Richard's Politicks: Benjamin Franklin and His New American Order* (New York, 1965), 143-144.

[55] This may seem like an application of the Parsonian logic of functional differentiation; see Neil J. Smelser, *Social Change in the Industrial Revolution: An Application of Theory to the British Cotton Industry* (Chicago, 1959). But where that logic posits mere dispersion of a persistent set of functional imperatives, the argument of the present paragraph goes beyond such segmentation of old responses and responsibilities to the creation of responses and responsibilities quite new and unprecedented.

[56] At the local level such sentiments often serve as evidence in studies such as the ones cited in n. 1 above. At the provincial level Bernard Bailyn has traced the structure and consequences for colonial politics of a comparable caesura of overinflated ambition and underdeveloped aptitude. See Bailyn, *The Origins of American Politics* (New York, 1968), chap. 2.

themselves in terms of an exaggerated sanity. They did not divest themselves of carnal desire merely because they conceived themselves as civilized white men and projected their sensuality upon the "savage" blacks. They had to have their counterposed impurities, in order to complete themselves.[57] They had to have those they scorned—the blacks, the Indians, and all the idle, dissolute, and damned—to maintain the boundaries of their increasingly brittle identities. Precisely because they found themselves, and in truth created themselves, in their counteridentities, they required for their very sense of selfhood the outcasts they purported to abhor.[58]

These oppositional notions of social and personal identity set the contexts
316 within which the colonists of the seventeenth century moved. And these notions were given substance and force in the narrow nuclear families of the early modern era, which were at once the loci of the new lust for aversive classification and the crucibles of the new identity. Purified personality became possible under the aegis of their interdicts as it has never been possible amid the extended networks of traditional families. Guilt became important to people whose personalities were forged in such fear and denial as it had never been important amid the diffuse ties of traditional communities.

For guilt is an issue of boundaries. It is essentially a transgression. It can begin to be crucial only for people whose rage for categories and classifica-

[57] On the asymmetry of the civilized man's need for the idea of the "savage" and the lack on the part of the "savage" of any analogous need for the civilized see Stanley Diamond, ed., "Introduction: The Uses of the Primitive," *Primitive Views of the World* (New York, 1969), v-xxix.

[58] The notion of boundary maintenance is derived from Durkheim; for an instance of its application in a colonial setting see Kai T. Erikson, *Wayward Puritans: A Study in the Sociology of Deviance* (New York, 1966). Such dependence on counter-identities was sometimes a source of genuine dilemmas of identity. The settlers' emphasis on the heathenism of other races helped reassure them of their Christian character in the wilderness. It also obliged the settlers to convert the heathens and risk eradicating the very contrast on which they predicated that Christian conception of themselves. Michael Kammen, *People of Paradox: An Inquiry Concerning the Origins of American Civilization* (New York, 1972), 142.

The promotional efforts of the colonists often exaggerated the differences between the old world and new world in order to attract immigrants. This dichotomous advertising often carried over into the self-justifications the colonists composed for themselves, as in Cotton Mather's celebration of "the wonders of the Christian religion, flying from the depravations of Europe to the American strand." But the gratification the colonists found in differentiating themselves from the Europeans by the opposition of innocence and corruption simultaneously jeopardized the identity they claimed as Europeans in opposition to the "innocent" denizens of the New World, the Indians. Martin E. Marty, "Reinterpreting American Religious History in Context," in Jerald C. Brauer, ed., *Reinterpretation in American Church History* (Chicago, 1968), 200-204.

tions is sufficiently strong to focus their psychic energies on barriers which might be violated. And just where the care of a previous era had been to ascertain the similitude of things, the intellectual enterprise of the early modern age was to discriminate the differentness of things.[59] In many ways it was from such concern for distinguishing, say, the saved from the damned or the civilized from the savage, and upon the structures of guilt which were built on that concern, that the modern idea of the self emerged.

Americans sensitive to such distinctions struggled unendingly against what they took to be their own lower nature and thereby doomed themselves to ravages of guilt when they crossed the line between what they conceived to be spirituality and what they consigned to the sphere of sensualism. In the 317
first decades in Virginia, for instance, John Rolfe underwent a "mighty war in [his] meditations" before convincing himself that he could marry Pocahontas with "an unspotted conscience." He knew that others would believe him to be acting from a "hungry appetite, to gorge [him]self with incontinency," and, more than that, he was uncertain in his own mind for a time whether he proceeded from an "unbridled desire of carnal affection." Indeed, even after he had persuaded himself that his marriage to the Indian princess would be a "godly labor" in converting the heathen, he still felt compelled to plead the "clearness of his conscience" and the "pious duties of a Christian" in his appeal for the approval of the governor. Earlier, other adventurers in the Virginia Company blamed the distress of the first settlers on "idleness and bestial sloth" and insisted that the colonists were "conscious and guilty . . . of their own demerit and laziness." A few years later, Company officials attributed the massacre of 1622 to the vengeance of God upon the "enormous excesses of apparel and drinking" among the Virginians, "the cry whereof cannot but have gone up to heaven." And a few years after that, the burgesses enacted legislation establishing churchwardens to enforce moral regulations, lest the colony "answer before God for such evils and plagues wherewith almighty God may justly punish His people for neglecting" His "good and wholesome" commandments.[60]

In the first years of settlement in New England, the same anxieties arose from the same dichotomies. Men and women like Michael Wigglesworth searched their own "vile heart." People like Thomas Hooker discovered

[59] Gerhart Piers and Milton B. Singer, *Shame and Guilt: A Psychoanalytic and Cultural Study* (Springfield, Ill., 1953), 11; Foucault, *Order of Things*, 42-43.

[60] "John Rolfe Requests Permission to Marry Pocahontas (1614)," in Billings, ed., *Old Dominion*, 217-219; David Bertelson, *The Lazy South* (New York, 1967), 24. Perry Miller, *Errand into the Wilderness* (Cambridge, Mass., 1956), 120, 120n. See also Bertelson, *Lazy South*, 28; Miller, *Errand*, 109, 118-119, 126. For the persistence of such values to the end of the century see the analysis of Robert Beverley's *History and Present State of Virginia* (1705), a Virginia jeremiad, in Bertelson, *Lazy South*, 67-68.

there their "inordinate and raging lusts." And like Thomas Shepard, they trembled at the discovery, for they could see "no wrath like this, to be governed by [their] own lusts for [their] own ends." They therefore cultivated the "strong exercises of conscience" that attended the accession of grace and enabled them to bow before their Lord and "bid farewell to all the world." And increasingly over the years, they came to seek such submissive dedication in dread of God's retribution if they failed to keep their covenants with Him. Their guilt-ridden recognition that they had in fact failed expressed itself obsessively in the jeremiads of the second generation and achieved its culminating articulation in the fulminations of the third, espe-
318 cially of Cotton Mather. Assailing the "torrent of wickedness" all about him, Mather demanded of his followers that they be always "full of self-abasing and self-abhorring reflections" by "loathing of [themselves] continually."[61]

Haltingly, and despite such derogations of self, colonists came to an awareness of their susceptibility to these compunctions of conscience which carried them toward a new vision of individual freedom as atomism. For it is only in societies where such a vision obtains that "guilt, a separate, individual act that transgresses a barrier, attracts more attention than shame, a falling short of ideals," and it is only in such societies that men and women view their fellows so focally as threats to their own freedom. It is, in truth, "a special version of life which regards society as external to the individual."[62]

To this day, Americans remain heirs to that early modern sense of antagonism between self and society. With Calvin, they continue to counterpose self-love and the love of others, sanctions of guilt and sanctions of shame. And their very conception of such counterpositions, in which the society always encroaches on the self, is in its own right a reflection of the

[61] Morgan, ed., "Diary of Wigglesworth," Col. Soc. Mass., *Pubs.*, XXV, 328; Miller and Johnson, eds., *The Puritans,* 306; Michael McGiffert, ed., *God's Plot: The Paradoxes of Puritan Piety, Being the Autobiography & Journal of Thomas Shepard* ([Amherst, Mass.], 1972), 116; John Winthrop, "John Winthrop's Christian Experience," *Winthrop Papers,* I (Boston, 1929), 155-156; *Diary of Cotton Mather* (Mass. Hist. Soc., *Colls.*, 7th Ser., VIII, pt. II [Boston, 1911]), 27, 69. By their disjunctions of spirituality and sensualism the New Englanders were drawn inevitably into the tangled paradoxes of polarity. Wigglesworth, for example, could scarcely sustain an unequivocal conception of himself for a single sentence in his diary. He would begin in disgust—"I am vile, I desire to loathe myself"—and then confess at once his countervailing and apparently invincible self-love—"(O that I could!)." Or, conversely, he would start from "pride"—"instead of admiring God I admire myself"—and then admit immediately his revulsion—"for this I loathe myself." Morgan, ed., "Diary of Wigglesworth," Col. Soc. Mass., *Pubs.*, XXXV, 323, 327. And of course his professed self-love was unloving, his purported self-loathing proud and satisfied. See also McGiffert, ed., *God's Plot,* and Rutman, *American Puritanism,* 126.

[62] Lynd, *On Shame,* 158-159.

primacy among them of boundary-maintenance. For on that conception guilt actually augments the autonomy of the self. The boundaries on which it is based not only define but also limit the individual's obligation to society. To the extent that he does not overstep its limits, his society can make no claims upon him whose force he is inwardly driven to acknowledge. And so a process initiated in early modern Europe, in the erosion of an old integrity of clan and congregation, has persisted quite beyond that original fission and indeed persists today, in its ever more intensive elaboration of individuation and its ever more extensive exposure of the individual to the surveillance and sanctions of others.

Journal of Interdisciplinary History, VII:4 (Spring 1977), 559–581.

Gloria L. Main

Inequality in Early America: The Evidence from Probate Records of Massachusetts and Maryland

Inequality in Early America: The Evidence from Probate Records of Massachusetts and Maryland The distribution of wealth in America is highly unequal now and was even more unequal a hundred years ago. If the distribution of slaves in 1790 is a trustworthy guide, inequality, in the South at least, was already high in the earliest years of the Republic (see Table 1). A careful
320 probing of the census data on wealth-holding for the years 1850, 1860, and 1870 persuaded one investigator that the distribution of wealth was highly *stable* as well as unequal. The relatively slight decline in inequality registered by a 1962 survey, he argues, was almost entirely attributable to such demographic factors as the aging of the general population, its geographical redistribution, and the virtual closing-off of foreign immigration.[1]

Because this limited but weighty evidence strongly suggests that the structure of wealth-holding in America may have long been frozen at a high level of inequality despite enormous economic and social change, one wonders whether the condition is somehow inevitable and therefore irreversible. One approach to the issue is to investigate the distribution of wealth in the more distant past to discover if, indeed, inequality has always been high. This essay first reviews existing studies for the period prior to 1860 and then introduces new evidence. The focus throughout is on the *course* of inequality over time. If it did change significantly, can the timing of such changes reveal their origins? The paper contributes both to the history of the distribution of wealth in America, and more ambitiously, toward an understanding of the nature of inequality itself.

Gloria L. Main is currently working on a book describing the changes in the wealth and standard of living of farmers in colonial Massachusetts and Maryland.

Members of the Columbia University Seminar in Early American History and Culture in 1974 and of the Cliometrics Conference at the University of Wisconsin, Madison in 1976 heard and commented on earlier versions of this article. The author wishes to thank them and, in addition, John McCusker, Richard Rapp, Jackson T. Main, James Shepherd, and anonymous reviewers of this Journal.

1 Lee Soltow, *Men and Wealth in the United States, 1850–1870* (New Haven, 1975), 60, 123, 177, 182, 183.

Table 1 Indices of Inequality in the American Past

RURAL AREAS OF THE NORTH	YEARS	DATA SOURCE	%SSTT	GINI
Chester Co., Pa.	1693	Tax Records	24½	.27
"	1715	"	26	.32
"	1730	"	29	.39
"	1748	"	29	.35
"	1760	"	30	.44
"	1782	"	34	.50
	1800–02	"	38	.56
Essex Co., Mass.[a]	1635–60	Probate Records	36	.54
"	1661–81	"	49	.62
Vermont Townships	1860	Census	38	.53
Tremeauleau Co., Wis.	1860	"	39	.48
CITIES OF THE NORTH				
Salem, Mass.	1635–60	Probate Records	31	.51
"	1661–81	"	59	.69
New York, N.Y.	1675	Tax Records	51	n.a.
"	1695	"	45	.60
"	1701	"	46	.59
"	1735	"	45	.55
"	1789	"	54	.67
"	1796	"	61	.72
Boston, Mass.	1687	"	47	.70
"	1771	"	63½	.73
"	1790	"	65	.79
"	1820	"	50	.65
"	1830	"	66	.78
"	1845	"	73	.91
"	1860	Census		.94
REGIONAL AGGREGATES				
Middle Colonies	1774	Probate Records		.51
New England	1774	"		.55–.62
South (Slaves)	1790	Census		.83
South (Slaves)	1860	"		.93
United States, North	1860	"		.81
"	1870	"		.82
United States, South	1860	"		.84
"	1870	"		.87
United States	1962	Survey, Households		.76(.79)[b]

a Includes Salem.
b Figure in parentheses adjusts for changes in definitions.
SOURCES: Chester Co., Pa.: James T. Lemon and Gary B. Nash, "The Distribution of Wealth in Eighteenth-Century America: a Century of Change in Chester County, Pennsylvania, 1693–1802," *Journal of Social History*, II (1968), 13; Essex Co. and Salem, Mass.: Donald Warner Koch, "Income Distribution and Political Structure in Seventeenth-Century Salem, Massachusetts," *Essex Institute Historical Collections*, CV

Table 1 summarizes the current literature on the distribution of wealth in America's past, using as measures of inequality two of the more commonly used indices: the size share of the top 10 percent of all potential wealth-holders, "SSTT," and the Gini coefficient of inequality.[2] The latter index ranges from 0.00 to 1.00 and measures the degree to which any distribution departs from absolute equality of wealth shares among all potential wealth-holders. The greater the level of inequality, the higher the value of the Gini coefficient. The size share of the richest decile is especially useful when the data sources omit or overlook those
322 with little or no property, because it is particularly sensitive to changes in the wealth of the rich. As we shall see later, alterations in the relative fortunes of those at the top played a significant role in determining the level of inequality in the past.[3]

The evidence assembled in Table 1 suggests that inequality was generally lowest in simple farming communities, higher in

---

(1969), 57, 59; Vermont and Trempeauleau Co., Wis.: Merle Curti, *The Making of an American Community* (Stanford, 1959), 78; New York, N.Y.: 1676, Robert C. Ritchie, "The Duke's Province: A Study of Proprietary New York, 1664–1685," unpub. diss. (UCLA, 1972), 244; 1695, Joyce D. Goodfriend, "'Too Great a Mixture of Nations': The Development of New York City Society in the Seventeenth Century," unpub. diss. (UCLA, 1975), 163; 1701–1796, Bruce M. Wilkenfeld, "The Social and Economic Structure of the City of New York, 1695–1796," unpub. diss. (Columbia Univ., 1973), 22, 58, 59, 80, 122, 158, 192; Boston, Mass.: 1681, 1771, James A. Henretta, "Economic Development and Social Structure in Colonial Boston," *William and Mary Quarterly*, XXII (1965), 80, 82; 1790; Alan Kulikoff, "The Progress of Inequality in Revolutionary Boston," *ibid.*, XXVIII (1971), 380; 1820, 1830, 1845, computed from grouped data in Lemuel Shattuck, *Report to the Committee of the City Council Appointed to Obtain the Census of Boston for the Year 1845 . . .* (Boston, 1846), 95; 1860, Soltow, "The Wealth, Income, and Social Class of Men in Large Northern Cities of the United States in 1860," in James D. Smith (ed.), *The Personal Distribution of Income and Wealth* (New York, 1975), 236; Middle Colonies and New England, 1774: Alice Hanson Jones, "Wealth Estimates for the New England Colonies about 1770," *Journal of Economic History*, XXXII (1972), 119; South (Slaves), 1790: Soltow, "Economic Inequality in the United States in the Period from 1790 to 1860," *ibid.*, (1971), 838; South (Slaves), 1860: Soltow, *Men and Wealth*, 136; United States, North and South, 1860 and 1870: *ibid.*, 103; United States, 1962: Dorothy S. Projector and Gertrude S. Weiss, *Survey of Financial Characteristics of Consumers* (Washington, D.C., 1966), 30; adjustment to these data for comparison with the 1860 census data, in Soltow, *Men and Wealth*, 183.

2 For mathematical explorations of inequality, two classical articles are Joseph E. Stiglitz, "The Distribution of Income and Wealth Among Individuals," *Econometrica*, XXXVII (1969), 382–399; Anthony B. Atkinson, "On the Measurement of Inequality," *Journal of Economic Theory*, II (1970), 244–263. A useful formula for computing Gini coefficients for grouped data may be found in Charles M. Dollar and Richard J. Jensen, *Historian's Guide to Statistics* (New York, 1971), 124.

3 See text below, 570, 581.

urban areas, lower in the colonial period, and much higher since then. The evidence is not wholly without ambiguity, however. The Chester County series, for instance, reveals some increases in concentration during the eighteenth century, but the tax base had also expanded in the meanwhile, encompassing a greater variety of property with each change in the statutes. A more significant contribution toward rising inequality in Chester County came with the appearance of several very wealthy individuals after the Revolution. The largest assessment there rose from £180 in 1748 to £5,298 in 1782 and again to $39,666, equivalent to £11,000 at 6 shillings to the dollar, in 1800–1802.[4]

Early probate records from Essex County, Massachusetts, exhibit levels of inequality similar to those found in the wealth censuses of Vermont townships and a frontier county in Wisconsin two centuries later. The growth of Salem, Essex's major port, substantially altered the distribution of wealth in the county's probate records, lending support to the notion that urbanization does contribute toward greater inequality.

Urbanization is a complex process and is itself a symptom of economic change. One would expect the distribution of wealth to vary somewhat from city to city according to its principal source of income and relative occupational structure, but inequality also varied within cities. The tax structure of colonial New York City, for instance, was less unequal than Boston's and grew even less concentrated between 1675 and 1735. Both cities experienced greater inequality after the Revolution, but Boston's tax data, on the whole, show a relatively narrow range of fluctuation until 1845. Both cities experienced strong surges in inequality between the tax lists of circa 1830 and 1845.[5]

Taxable wealth is not total wealth, and the difficulties in establishing the degree of comparability between tax lists over several years or between different jurisdictions make any conclusions

4 James T. Lemon and Gary B. Nash, "The Distribution of Wealth in Eighteenth-Century America: a Century of Change in Chester County, Pennsylvania, 1693–1802," *Journal of Social History*, II (1968), 11, 13.

5 The top 1% of taxable households in New York City owned 29% of private taxable wealth in 1828 and 40% in 1845. The equivalent group in Boston owned 33% in 1833 and 37% in 1848. Edward Pessen, *Riches, Class, and Power Before the Civil War* (Lexington, Mass., 1973), 33–34, 39.

based on them highly tentative.[6] If inequality rose *within* cities over time, however, the growth of inequality in the North sometime after the Revolution cannot be attributed solely to the growth of cities themselves. Urbanization and growing inequality are both products of the same underlying processes.

The story for the South features a different plot. The study of the 1850–1870 censuses referred to above bluntly attributes the higher levels of inequality there to the presence and consequences of slavery.[7] Since the Gini coefficient for inequality of slaveholding was already high in 1790, it seems that inequality in the colo-
324 nial South rose with slavery and that the two are necessarily intertwined. Such a possibility demands investigation.

Table 1 furnishes the elements for plotting a profile over time of the level of inequality in the American past. The gaps between points are great, however, and there are very few points for the early colonial period. The need for more data, particularly in continuous series form, is readily apparent. Because of the relative absence of other sources, this need can be met only by probate records. Before proceeding, however, some description and discussion of their limitations is in order.

Inventories of estates list and evaluate in monetary terms the personal and, in New England, the landed possessions of deceased property holders, most of whom died intestate. Accounts of administration of probated estates, which survive for a substantial minority of them, often provide additional information such as the value of harvested crops, loans recovered, and debts paid. Obviously these records draw from a sharply restricted sector of society—deceased property holders who were mostly free white males in the older age brackets. Inherent biases due to age and wealth, therefore, may seriously distort the inventories' picture of society and its material possessions.[8]

6 By demonstrating the different assessment bases of the 1687 and 1771 tax schedules, for instance, G. B. Warden effectively destroyed their implication of a long-term trend toward greater concentration of wealth in colonial Boston. G. B. Warden, "Inequality and Instability in Eighteenth-Century Boston: A Reappraisal," *Journal of Interdisciplinary History*, VI (1976), 585–620. Warden's recalculations register a slight *decline* in the level of inequality for Boston between 1687 and 1771. *Ibid.*, 602.

7 Soltow, *Men and Wealth*, 133–134.

8 Early inventories of Maryland and Virginia valued personal property in pounds of tobacco. For a fuller description of these records, see Gloria L. Main, "Probate Records as a

The difficulties of correcting for these biases are considerable but not insuperable, and their burden should not outweigh in the reader's mind the priceless nature of the new information to be gained in the process. Successful studies based on them have begun to appear in print, their authors having grappled critically and substantively with the problems of bias.[9] Indeed, it may well be that historians have reserved for these records a sensitivity toward biased origins which might profitably be applied to more traditional sources.

Inferences about trends in the distribution of probate wealth
will not require any adjustment of the data if the sources of bias
remain constant. Recent work in Connecticut probate records demonstrates the validity of this statement. A rich variety of genealogical materials and town tax schedules enabled the author to determine the extent of probate coverage among adult males and the relative wealth of those missing, and to measure the distortion introduced by the lopsided age structure of adult decedents.[10] Table 2 reproduces from that study the mean personal wealth, deflated to current money circa 1700, the size shares of the top 10 percent of probated estates, and the estimates of these based on corrections for the living population of adult free men.

As the Hartford, Connecticut, study shows, the higher average age of the adult male decedents raised average wealth but did not affect the level of inequality. The distribution of values merely moved up the scale. The shape of the distribution of probate wealth, however, approximates that of the living population only so long as the missing propertyless are not too numerous. One must attempt to estimate the degree of coverage and gauge the proportion of young in order to adjust for missing estates. This

---

Source for Early American History," *William and Mary Quarterly*, XXXII (1975), 89–99. *Idem*, "The Correction of Biases in Colonial American Probate Records," *Historical Methods Newsletter* 8 (1974), 10–28; Daniel Scott Smith, "Underregistration and Bias in Probate Records: an Analysis of Data from Eighteenth-Century Hingham, Massachusetts," *William and Mary Quarterly*, XXXII (1975), 100–110.

9 Alice Hanson Jones pioneered the measurement and correction of biases in probate records in "Wealth Estimates for the American Middle Colonies, 1774," *Economic Development and Cultural Change*, XVIII (1970), 1–172; "Wealth Estimates for the New England Colonies about 1770," *Journal of Economic History*, XXXII (1972), 98–127.

10 Jackson T. Main, "The Distribution of Property in Colonial Connecticut," in James Kirby Martin (ed.), *The Human Dimension of Nation Making: Essays on Colonial and Revolutionary America* (Madison, 1976), 54–104.

Table 2 Average Personal Wealth[a] and the Size Share of the top 10% of Probated Estates and of Living Adult Males, Hartford[b], 1650–1774

YEARS	AVERAGE ESTATE (£)	PER LIVING MAN (£)	SSTT, ESTATES (%)	SSTT, LIVING (%)
1650–1669	209	167	45	45½
1670–1679	170	126	48	43
1680–1689	145	87	47	47
1690–1699	146	109	49	43
1700–1709	134	109	47½	46
1710–1714	176	140	47	45
1715–1719	159	131	43½	43½
1720–1724	142	108	49	45½
1725–1729	124	115	37	42½
1730–1734	165	130	44	48
1735–1739	132	108	32	33
1740–1744	132	98	41	44
1745–1749	118	98	45	43
1750–1754	120	98	37	39
1755–1759	107	94	35	34
1760–1764	125	99	43½	47
1765–1769	203	174	45	48½
1770–1774	163	132	50	45½

a Personal wealth deflated to level of inventory prices c. 1700.
b The Hartford probate district covered an area larger than the present-day county.
SOURCE: Jackson T. Main, "The Distribution of Property in Colonial Connecticut," 88.

rough procedure will produce an adequate degree of comparability for probate data of diverse origins if one does not lean too heavily on small differences between sets.

Probate records are a principal source material for exploring the early history of the distribution of wealth in America. Inventories from Maryland and Massachusetts, supplemented by the data from Hartford, provide important new evidence for the seventeenth and eighteenth centuries, while published summaries of such records from nineteenth-century Massachusetts carry forward the story for that state. Federal and state censuses offer a valuable opportunity to test the effects on inequality in individual counties of Massachusetts of the growth of cities, manufacturing, and foreign immigration.

Table 3 summarizes the colonial and early national findings, showing the size shares of the top 10 percent, SSTT, and the Gini coefficients of inventoried estates of adult males in six coastal counties of Maryland from 1674 through 1719 and again during a four-year period at mid-century, 1750–1753.[11] Tax data from 1783 supply a limited comparison with the probate data and with the census data on slaveholding.[12]

Two large geographical areas of early Massachusetts are represented in the inventories of Suffolk and Hampshire Counties the populations of which constituted almost a third of the colony's total in 1690.[13] Although the probate records of Suffolk County 327
actually begin as early as 1638, they are too few before 1650 to support inferences about the course of inequality in those early years. The table distinguishes between Boston and the rest of the county's towns, here grouped under the rubric, "Rural Suffolk." Much of Hampshire County remained exposed frontier throughout the years 1666 to 1719, but even by the middle of the eighteenth century, little change marked the personal belongings of the deceased male residents of this extensive farming region. The western part of Suffolk County was set off as Worcester County in 1721, and inventories of this region are represented in the table for the years after 1760.

Two sets of contrasts mark the early data: North versus South and urban versus rural. Although such contrasts will evoke

11 See note "a" to Table 3 about the geographical makeup of the six-county sample from Maryland. Menard, Harris, and Carr found no trend in the distribution of wealth in the inventories of their counties, two of which overlap with those of the present set. Their choice of measure for inequality, the distance between the median and the mean, did not permit the inclusion of their results in Table 1. Russell R. Menard, P. M. G. Harris, and Lois Green Carr, "Opportunity and Inequality: the Distribution of Wealth on the Lower Western Shore of Maryland, 1638–1705," *Maryland Historical Magazine*, LXIX (1974), 181.

12 Incomplete schedules for four of the six counties indicate a size share for the richest 10% of taxables, including those excused from payment, of about 60% of total taxable property, which included land, slaves, livestock, money, silverplate, and unspecified "other." Sixty percent is a conservative estimate of the true size share because I made no effort to link properties owned by the same person in separate districts, although Charles Carroll of Carrollton and John Ridgely were so conspicuous on the lists that I was able to identify and combine the values of their holdings for the lists I did examine. The method of noting down the largest values in each schedule and the summed assessments has only convenience and speed to recommend it. It forecloses any possibility of computing a Gini coefficient because it does not take account of the remainder of the distribution.

13 Evarts B. Greene and Virginia D. Harrington, *American Population Before the Federal Census of 1790* (New York, 1932; reprinted Gloucester, Mass., 1966), 19–21.

Table 3 Indices of Inequality among Inventoried Males, 1650–1788

328

YEARS	MARYLAND[a] SSTT	MARYLAND[a] GINI	BOSTON SSTT	BOSTON GINI	R. SUFFOLK[b] SSTT	R. SUFFOLK[b] GINI	HAMPSHIRE[c] SSTT	HAMPSHIRE[c] GINI	WORCESTER[d] SSTT	WORCESTER[d] GINI
1650–64	—	—	.60	.73	.37	.50	—	—	—	—
1665–69	—	—	.64	.74	.37	.54	.30	.47	—	—
1670–74	—	—							—	—
1675–79	.49	.60	.59	.70	.38	.53	.38	.54	—	—
1680–84	.51	.64							—	—
1685–89	.53	.61	.46	.61	.34	.46	.37	.51	—	—
1690–94	.55	.64							—	—
1695–99	.53	.66	.50	.64	.36	.48	.35	.49	—	—
1700–04	.56	.68							—	—
1705–09	.54	.65	.55	.66	.33	.45	.38	.48	—	—
1710–14	.65	.74							—	—
1715–19	.65	.74	.54	.68	.31	.44	.52	.58	—	—
1750–54	(.66	.80)	.53	.67	.31	.46	.41	.54	—	—
1760–69	—	—	.53	.68	.38	.50	—	—	.39	.50
1782–88	(.60)[e]	—	.56	.72	.42	.53	—	—	.43	.55

a Six counties only: Anne Arundel, Baltimore, Calvert, Charles, Kent, and Somerset. Boundary alterations took place periodically making somewhat imprecise the geographical area included in the jurisdiction of the six probate courts. Only personal wealth was included in the inventories of Maryland. Data for 1750–54 corrected for under-reporting. See appendix (available on request from the author) for details.

b Rural Suffolk County originally stretched from the coast to the borders of Hampshire. The creation of Worcester County defined Suffolk's western border but excluded very few settlements in the process since most of this interior upland country remained empty until well into the eighteenth century. When Boston and its suburbs were set off as Suffolk County in the nineteenth century, the remainder of the old Suffolk County became Norfolk. "Rural Suffolk" is roughly contiguous with the latter.

c Hampshire County included the entire Connecticut River valley from Suffield, Connecticut, northward until 1790 when Franklin County was established and 1830 when Hampden County was set off.

d Worcester County was set off from Suffolk in 1721.

e Taxable wealth in 1783 included both real and personal property. The schedules are on microfilm and are incomplete. Those analyzed for the present work were all the surviving schedules from the counties of Anne Arundel, Baltimore, Calvert, Kent, and Worcester (formerly part of Somerset County). None survived from Somerset and only one did so for Charles.

SOURCES: Maryland: *Inventories*, I–III, 43–60; *Accounts*, I–IV, 27–32; miscellaneous will books, county records, and testamentary proceedings. All in Hall of Records, Annapolis. Tax Assessment Schedules, 1783: microfilm copy, Institute for Colonial Studies, SUNY-Stony Brook. Massachusetts: Suffolk County Probate Court Records, I–XXII, 50–54, microfilm copy, Institute for Colonial Studies, SUNY-Stony Brook; LXIII–LXXI, 81–87, manuscript notes, courtesy of Jackson T. Main. Hampshire County Probate Court Records, I–IV, 7–8, microfilm copy, Institute for Colonial Studies, SUNY-Stony Brook. Worcester County Probate Records, VIII–X, 18–21, manuscript notes, courtesy of Jackson T. Main.

no surprise among readers, their appearance at so early a date is clearly a matter of great interest and significance. The size share of the top 10 percent of male decedents in the relatively more urbanized Hartford district averaged about 45 percent of personal wealth, but the same decile in "Rural Suffolk" seldom reached as high as 40 percent. Maryland's richest 10 percent, however, engrossed shares comparable to those of urban Boston's top decile.

Differences in the demographic structures of the regions created the initial gap between the levels of inequality displayed by the two agricultural regions, but the story grows more complicated with the passage of time. In order to probe these sectional differences more fully, we will first examine the history of Maryland's wealth-holding patterns and then apply the implications of that state's experience to the rest of the upper South.

MARYLAND To a degree unknown in colonies to the north, and 329
perhaps as a case more comparable to that of the West Indies, young males rather than family groups dominated white immigration into the Chesapeake for most of the years between settlement and the virtual cessation of such movements after 1687.[14] The heavy mortality sustained by new arrivals and the continuing influx from abroad during much of the seventeenth century created a population with rather bizarre characteristics: foreign-born, heavily male, and concentrated in the 16 to 40 age group. These characteristics did not subside until the formation of family units in sufficient numbers eventually permitted population growth through natural reproduction. Such a transition took place in Maryland somewhere between 1690 and 1710 when fewer young men came and more left, thus impelling the age distribution toward stability. A long depression in the European tobacco market combined with improvement in labor opportunities in

14 The following description of the demographic history of Maryland rests on the work of Carr, Harris, Menard, Walsh, and their colleagues on the St. Mary's City Commission staff who have explored public records of every description in order to reconstruct the demographic experience of this colony. They are not responsible for any errors in my interpretation of their work. Lorena S. Walsh and Russell R. Menard, "Death in the Chesapeake: Two Life Tables for Men in Early Colonial Maryland," *Maryland Historical Magazine*, LXIX (1974), 211–227; Menard, "Immigration to the Chesapeake Colonies in the Seventeenth Century: a Review Essay," *ibid.*, LXVIII (1973), 323–329. See also Wesley Frank Craven, *White, Red and Black: The Seventeenth-Century Virginian* (Charlottesville, 1971), 1–37; Darrett B. Rutman and Anita H. Rutman, "Of Agues and Fevers: Malaria in the Early Chesapeake," *William and Mary Quarterly*, XXXIII (1976), 31–60. On the demographic experience of the British West Indies in the seventeenth century, see Carl and Roberta Bridenbaugh, *No Peace Beyond the Line: the English in the Caribbean, 1624–1690* (New York, 1972), chs. 1 and 2; Richard S. Dunn, *Sugar and Slaves: the Rise of the Planter Class in the English West Indies, 1624–1713* (Chapel Hill, 1972), chs. 8 and 9.

England to shut off the stream of immigration from the mother country, while out-migration to the flourishing new settlements of Pennsylvania during the middle 1690s and again after 1703 balanced the sex ratio by reducing the preponderance of young men in the population. Blacks, who had played only a minor role in Chesapeake demography until 1690, then began to grow rapidly in number as planters attempted to replace their vanishing labor supply.

Maryland's demographic history has relevance for our purposes because it goes far toward explaining the early high levels of
330 inequality in the probate records—high by comparison with those of the rural North. The immigrant background of the overwhelming majority of white adults in Maryland during these years explains both their poverty and the greater weight enjoyed by the rather small number of men whose relative wealth and social prominence nominated them for positions of public responsibility and authority.[15] For the majority of the foreign-born, however, the years of servitude rendered in their youth prolonged the stage of legal dependence, shortening thereby the number of years during which accumulation out of current income could take place. Native-born residents, on the contrary, were thrice-blessed. They gained independence at an earlier age than their immigrant predecessors, tended to live longer, and, since the sex ratio was naturally balanced among them, wives were more readily available as the native-born replaced the immigrants. Thus proportionately more men were able to live longer working lives and enjoy their earnings earlier. Native-born fathers, by marrying younger and living longer, were better able to help their sons to make a start in life, thus extending the time horizon of the family by perpetuating the gains of one generation in the income potential of another.[16]

For the seventeenth century, then, the presence in the colony's population on the one hand of large numbers of freed servants born overseas and on the other of a very small group of men

15 Lois Green Carr and David William Jordan, *Maryland's Revolution of Government 1689–1692* (Ithaca, 1974), ch. 6 and the appendix, "Biographies of the Members of the Associators' Convention," 232–288.

16 References to grandchildren are uncommon in Maryland wills before 1700: Gloria L. Main, "Personal Wealth in Colonial America: Explorations in the Use of Probate Records from Maryland and Massachusetts, 1650–1720," unpub. diss. (Columbia Univ., 1972), 41.

of some means produced a relatively high level of inequality in Maryland's probate records. Other things being equal, the replacement of the former by a native-born population free of contract obligations and capable of enjoying the fruits of their own labor plus some of their parents' as well, should have tended to reduce inequality. On the contrary, the inventories show an increase in the size share of the richest 10 percent and in the Gini coefficient of inequality, particularly after 1710.[17]

A solution to the paradox of rising inequality in the face of declining proportions of immigrants and freed servants in the white population lies in the growth of great fortunes during these years despite the secular depression in the tobacco market. Valuable clues to the origin of this wealth lie in the inventoried assets themselves, because one characteristic common to the majority of personal estates worth £1,000 sterling or more is the involvement of their owners in mercantile and financial activities.[18] Occupational versatility, not specialization in tobacco culture, marked the careers of Maryland's richest men.[19]

Although the rapid growth of slavery in the Chesapeake during these years coincided with the emergence of great wealth, the latter permitted the former and was not caused by it. From the point of view of Maryland's economic elite, slaves as well as land

17 A moderate contraction in the probate coverage of free adult male decedents may have taken place during the decade after 1704, but it cannot explain this increase because the missing tended to come from the poorer ranks of society and their greater relative absence would decrease inequality rather than the reverse.

18 On the depression in tobacco output, see the export statistics in U.S. Bureau of the Census, *Historical Statistics of the United States, Colonial Times to 1970, Part 2* (Washington, D.C., 1975), 1189–1190. Tobacco production stagnated between 1697 and 1727 while population in the two Chesapeake colonies more than doubled in size. For a discussion of the sources of the depression in the market for tobacco, see Jacob M. Price, "The Economic Growth of the Chesapeake and the European Market, 1697–1775," *Journal of Economic History*, XXIV (1964), 496–511. Aubrey C. Land first pointed out the strong association between wealth and mercantile activity in the inventories of colonial Maryland planters in "Economic Base and Social Structure: the Northern Chesapeake in the Eighteenth Century," *Journal of Economic History*, XXV (1965), 647.

19 The variety of occupations pursued by Maryland's residents included many which, in the North, concentrated in cities or port towns. Earle's study shows how an extensive system of natural waterways, the ease of making roads over level, sandy soil, and an abundance of sturdy little horses enabled men pursuing "urban" occupations to spread out over the land in order to supervise their farming enterprises. Carville V. Earle, *The Evolution of a Tidewater Settlement System: All Hallow's Parish, Maryland, 1650–1783* (Chicago, 1975), ch. 5.

were merely investments of capital involving less risk than alternative but potentially more lucrative forms of economic activity.

Access to mercantile enterprise provided the key to great wealth in the South and slaves the means by which to preserve it. Most men, however, had to farm land in order to gain any income at all. The question of trends in landholding looms importantly in this agricultural society, but firm evidence on land use and ownership remains elusive. Leasing through some form of sharecropping provided many freed servants the wherewithal eventually to purchase their own acreages in the seventeenth century.
332 Evidence from one Maryland parish suggests that the rate of tenancy probably rose in the Tidewater regions of the Chesapeake during the course of the eighteenth century as population growth placed greater pressure on the land despite substantial levels of emigration.[20]

The only colony-wide evidence on the pattern of landholding in the early Chesapeake comes from a Virginia quitrent roll of the year 1704. Of 5,501 individuals named on the roll, the top 10 percent owned approximately half the acreage included, but the number of free adult males owning no land is unknown. County militia lists supply an absolute minimum of 31 percent of all white adult males without land, but the true figure may be close to double that if the militia lists excluded as many as did those in Maryland.[21]

Depending on the estimated proportion of men owning on land at all, the top 10 percent of all potential land-holders in the Chesapeake owned half to two-thirds of the available acreage in the opening years of the eighteenth century. Eighty years later the landowning elite probably controlled about two-thirds of the

20 Menard, "From Servant to Freeholder: Status Mobility and Property Accumulation in Seventeenth-Century Maryland," *William and Mary Quarterly*, XXX (1973), 52. Earle, *All Hallow's Parish*, 206–207.

21 Thomas J. Wertenbaker, *The Planters of Colonial Virginia* (Princeton, 1922), appendix. A minimum estimate of white adult males without land comes from the membership figure for the militia: 7,972 minus 5,501 landowners equals 2,471, or 31% without land. Greene and Harrington, *American Population*, 149–150. A Maryland governor enumerated the "Christian" men and women in the colony in addition to white servants and slaves. His report of the size of the militia was fully one-fifth smaller than the number of "Christian" men and fewer than three-fifths of all white men in the colony. William Hand Browne, *et al* (eds.), *Maryland Archives*, XXV (Baltimore, 1905), 258.

land, given the proportion of landless men found in the tax schedules for Virginia in 1787: 48.5 percent of free males aged 16 and over in the state's Piedmont area and 57 percent in the old Tidewater section.[22] These figures approach the upper limit of the equivalent range in 1704 and lend support to the idea that the distribution of land in the colony as a whole altered little in the course of the century.

The level of inequality marking the distribution of both personal and real property in the Chesapeake was high around 1700 and bore a strong resemblance to the distribution of slaves in the 1790 census and to the distribution of wealth in the South in the 333
census of 1860. Because Maryland's economy diversified in the nineteenth century, it ceased to conform to the rural southern pattern, and we will not follow the state's history further. Maryland's colonial experience does serve, however, to confirm our doubts about a pristine egalitarian past for at least that section of early America.

MASSACHUSETTS AND CONNECTICUT We have argued that Maryland's distribution of wealth was more unequal than that of the rural areas of the North, at first because of continuing immigration of indentured servants, and then in even greater degree because of the expanding wealth of a few families. No such great change took place in New England, according to the probate data from two counties in Massachusetts and one large district in Connecticut.

The distribution of wealth in colonial New England seems to have remained stable under conditions of a rapidly growing population and with little gain in productivity per capita attributable to technological improvements. Expanding markets for their manufactures and shipping services permitted economic growth to raise the standard of living without also enhancing inequality.[23]

Despite poor farming conditions and rapid population growth, the New England economy proved flexible. The older towns exported their surplus young men to the port cities and the

22 Jackson T. Main, "The Distribution of Property in Post-Revolutionary Virginia," *Mississippi Valley Historical Review* XLI (1954), 243–248.

23 Shuttle-style shipping to myriads of small ports lowered the possibility for economies of scale and this may have placed a ceiling on the growth of individual fortunes.

frontier, where the founding of new towns proceeded apace after 1720.[24] Although such an out-migration undoubtedly served to suppress the level of inequality in the older settlements, a simultaneous restructuring of the occupational makeup of the labor force took place as well.[25] Sons of farmers combined farming with artisanal work or even specialized in the latter entirely, merely supplementing this income with the produce of a garden and a cow.

Trade abroad, then, had provided a diversity of occupational opportunity and enabled a multiplying population to live on
334 shrinking units of land. Growing commercial competition with ports to the south, coupled with steadily advancing costs of farmland, may have increasingly troubled parts of New England as the eighteenth century wore on, but the degree of inequality in wealth-holding did not worsen.[26] On the contrary, it merely fluctuated within a rather narrow range. In Hartford, the corrected size share of the richest 10 percent peaked at 48 percent in the first half of the 1730s and again in the 1760s. It touched bottom at 33 percent in the second half of the 1730s and at 34 percent in 1755–1759. Such fluctuations resulted as much from accident as from real cause, since the timing of a rich man's death could place his estate in one five-year period rather than another: in 1734, for example, instead of 1735. Close examination of the probate evidence for New England simply will not support the thesis that some irresistible force levered open a widening gap between rich and poor.

NINETEENTH-CENTURY MASSACHUSETTS Measured in terms of its distribution of probate wealth, society in eighteenth-century New England appears positively egalitarian compared to the degree of

24 Lois Kimball Mathews, *The Expansion of New England: The Spread of New England Settlement and Institutions to the Mississippi River 1620–1865* (Boston, 1909), ch. 4.

25 Jackson T. Main, "Distribution of Property in Colonial Connecticut," 89.

26 See Kenneth Lockridge, "Land, Population and the Evolution of New England Society, 1630–1790," *Past & Present*, 39 (1968), 62–80; Alan Kulikoff, "The Progress of Inequality in Revolutionary Boston," *William and Mary Quarterly*, XXVIII (1971), 392, 404, 409–411; James Henretta, "Economic Development and Social Structure in Colonial Boston," *ibid.*, XXII (1965), 88–92, *idem*, *The Evolution of American Society, 1700–1815: an Interdisciplinary Analysis* (Lexington, Mass., 1973), *passim*. G. B. Warden and Jacob Price treat this view with great skepticism: Warden, "Inequality and Instability in Boston," *Journal of Interdisciplinary History* VI (1976), 585–613; Jacob M. Price, "Quantifying Colonial America: A Comment on Nash and Warden," *ibid.*, 707–708.

inequality which one encounters in Massachusetts in the following century. Table 4 shows the corrected size shares of the richest 10 percent of Massachusetts estates and Gini coefficients of inequality for four time periods of three years each at intervals scattered throughout the nineteenth century. The unadjusted indices are given in Table 5.

The data in Table 4 required correction for differences in the rate of coverage of adult male decedents, since the years from 1859 to 1861 and after show sharp declines in the proportion of inventories to estimated deaths.[27] Because the corrections merely amplified differences already large, it seems reasonable to conclude 335
that the sharp rise in inequality revealed there was a real

Table 4 Indices of Inequality among Inventoried Males, 1829–1891

	1829–31		1859–61		1879–81		1889–91	
COUNTY	SSTT	GINI	SSTT	GINI	SSTT	GINI	SSTT	GINI
Boston	.83	.86	.94	.95	.84	.90	.86	.91
Norfolk	.59	.69	.75	.82	.74	.81	.81	.85
Worcester	.50	.63	.57	.73	.66	.77	.69	.80
Barnstable	.52	.63	.56	.69	.94	.95	.61	.69
Berkshire	.40	.56	.69	.81	.64	.75	.61	.71
Bristol	.57	.68	.73	.80	.80	.85	.65	.75
Dukes	.32	.44	.45	.51	.62	.68	.43	.61
Essex	.73	.80	.65	.77	.82	.87	.68	.78
Franklin	.41	.56	.50	.66	.39	.57	.58	.69
Hampden	.67	.79	.47	.63	.72	.82	.71	.81
Hampshire	.44	.56	.57	.69	.72	.81	.38	.56
Middlesex	.57	.69	.60	.71	.78	.86	.70	.80
Nantucket	.64	.72	.47	.65	.31	.54	.81	.81
Plymouth	.40	.54	.45	.56	.54	.66	.62	.72
State	.70	.77	.74	.82	.80	.86	.75	.83

SOURCE: Bureau of Statistics of Labor, *Twenty-Fifth Annual Report* (Boston, 1895), 238–267; see also appendix to this article, available on request from the author.

27 An appendix gives the details. The correction procedure estimated the differences in the recording rates, adjusted for those whose estates were probated but not inventoried, and filled in as zeroes the remaining number of "missing." Because of space constraints a note on the methodology of the correction procedures does not appear with the article. Copies of this appendix are available on request from the author.

Table 5 Unadjusted Indices of Inequality among Inventoried Males, 1829–1891

COUNTY	1829–31 SSTT	1829–31 GINI	1859–61 SSTT	1859–61 GINI	1879–81 SSTT	1879–81 GINI	1889–91 SSTT	1889–91 GINI
Boston	.81	.83	.80	.86	.76	.83	.78	.84
Norfolk	.59	.69	.73	.80	.73	.79	.81	.84
Worcester	.49	.63	.51	.62	.61	.71	.63	.73
Barnstable	.52	.63	.56	.69	.94	.95	.61	.69
Berkshire	.40	.56	.64	.72	.62	.73	.61	.71
Bristol	.57	.68	.70	.77	.80	.85	.65	.75
Dukes	.32	.44	.45	.51	.62	.68	.43	.61
Essex	.73	.80	.60	.72	.80	.85	.65	.74
Franklin	.71	.56	.47	.59	.39	.57	.58	.69
Hampden	.55	.76	.43	.53	.69	.78	.68	.76
Hampshire	.44	.56	.55	.63	.70	.78	.38	.56
Middlesex	.57	.68	.60	.71	.71	.80	.69	.77
Nantucket	.64	.72	.47	.65	.31	.54	.81	.77
Plymouth	.40	.54	.45	.56	.54	.66	.62	.72
State	.67	.76	.70	.78	.77	.83	.74	.80

SOURCE: *Twenty-fifth Annual Report*, 238–267.

phenomenom. By 1830, therefore, Massachusetts had undergone a transformation in its distribution of wealth which resulted in an increase in the Gini coefficients from about .55–.62 to one of .77. By 1860, the index had again risen to .825. As a basis for comparison, the census data for the North that year yielded a coefficient of .81 and for Boston, .94 (see Table 1).

The major problem raised by the Massachusetts probate data is to explain the timing of that transformation in its distribution of wealth. The first step is to test the impact of demographic changes, for marked alterations in the makeup of the state's population did take place. However, the modifications of the age composition of the adult population actually militated *against* increases in inequality. The proportion of adult American males aged 20–29 declined from 41 percent in 1830 to 36 percent in 1860, and it continued to decline thereafter, dropping to 32 percent in 1900, and to 26 percent by 1970.[28] In short, shrinkages in the youngest and

28 Oscar Handlin, *Boston's Immigrants, 1790–1880: A Study in Acculturation* (Cambridge, Mass., 1959; rev. ed.), 242, 262; Frank L. Mott, "Portrait of an American Mill Town:

poorest age bracket could only have tended to lower the level of inequality.

But the growth of cities and of foreign immigration certainly exerted a contrary effect. The percentage of people living in cities, however, rose significantly *after* 1830, not before. Moreover, inequality *within* cities also jumped, *before,* as well as after, 1830. As to immigration, little occurred until after 1847, so it could not have caused either the initial increase in the concentration of wealth or the rise within the cities subsequent to 1830. The great waves of Irish and others only further supported a level of inequality already high. 337

The same conclusion emerges from a county-by-county analysis. Those counties whose populations contained the largest proportions of foreign-born did not uniformly exhibit the greatest degrees of concentration in probate wealth. Table 6 ranks the individual counties by their proportion of foreign-born in the year 1870, compares their levels of inequality a decade before and a decade after that year, and also lists other information, including the percentage population change between 1860 and 1880, the relative proportion of the population employed in manufacturing, and the size of manufacturing establishments as measured by their capital investment. Those counties with a fifth or more of their population born outside of the country showed considerable variation in their rates of growth, in the importance of manufacturing, and in the distribution of their probate wealth.

Immigration, urbanization, population growth, and manufacturing employment are obviously interrelated developments, and disentangling their effects on the level of inequality would require much more data and the application of sophisticated mathematical analysis. Certain observations might prove useful, nevertheless. First, foreign immigration wielded only minimal impact on inequality in areas showing levels which were already high. Second, manufacturing appears to have raised inequality

Demographic Response in Mid-Nineteenth Century Warren, Rhode Island," *Population Studies,* XXVI (1972), 147–157; Stephan Thernstrom, *The Other Bostonians: Poverty and Progress in the American Metropolis 1880–1970* (Cambridge, Mass., 1973), 33. The proportion of Boston's labor force in unskilled occupations grew from 13% in 1830 to 16% in 1840, but then vaulted to 30% in 1850 at the height of the Irish immigration. By 1860, however, it was already dropping, reaching 15% in 1880 and 12% in 1900. Peter Knights, *The Plain People of Boston* (New York, 1971), 84; Thernstrom, *Other Bostonians,* 272.

Table 6 Massachusetts Counties and Inequality, 1860 and 1880, Ranked by % Foreign-born

GINI 1860	COEFF. 1880	COUNTY	FOREIGN-BORN, %[a]	POPULATION GROWTH %[b]	WORKERS MANUFAC.[c]	CAPITAL PER ESTB.[d]
.63	.82	Hampden	26½	81½	216	32½
.71	.86	Middlesex	26	47	181	27
.73	.77	Worcester	24	42	221	16
.81	.75	Berkshire	23	25	143	20
.80	.85	Bristol	23	48	261	34
.77	.875	Essex	22	48	262	20
.82	.81	Norfolk	22	−12[e]	168	14½
.69	.81	Hampshire	20	25	139	15
.66	.57	Franklin	11	14½	96	11
.66	.66	Plymouth	10	14	181	9
.69	.95	Barnstable	6	−11	67	13
.65	.54	Nantucket	5	−39	54	6
.51	.68	Dukes	3	−3	30	10
.95	.90	Boston	34	101[e]	128	13

a For the year 1870.
b Between 1860 and 1880.
c Average number of workers per 1,000 population, 1860 and 1880.
d $1,000's, average invested per manufacturing establishment, 1860 and 1880.
e County boundaries redefined between two census dates.
SOURCES: Various federal census publications and Table 7.

most substantially in those counties into which it had newly penetrated. The economies of Bristol, Essex, Hampden, and Middlesex had based themselves on manufacturing early in the century, but the growth of manufacturing and of relatively large establishments reshaped the distribution of wealth only in those counties which had been previously dependent on agriculture: Worcester by 1860, and Berkshire and Hampshire by 1880.[29]

The shift out of agriculture appears to have been a crucial first step in the direction of rising inequality, but insufficient in itself. Manufacturing on a small scale appeared early in the eastern part of the state and in the older settlements of Connecticut with no visible effect on the distribution of wealth. The introduction of the factory system, or of heavy machinery, may have played the critical roles of catalysts, but the relationship between the size of the

29 *The Census of Manufactures* (Washington, D.C., 1810) provides the earliest profile of county economies. Soltow, *Men and Wealth*, 10.

manufacturing sector, the capital investment per establishment, and the Gini coefficient of inequality in probate records of individual Massachusetts counties does not support any position which pins the tail on these particular donkeys. Essex County, for instance, waited until the 1840s to reorganize its shoe industry, yet the Gini coefficient in the probate records of that county was higher before than after this technological change had taken place.

A final and fundamental characteristic of the Massachusetts probate data is the dramatic increase in the relative frequency of very large estates over the course of the century. The gap between poor and rich appeared at the upper end of the distribution before 339
it widened at the bottom. Although the definition of what constituted a "large" estate must be arbitrary, an examination of the "Rural Suffolk"/Norfolk inventories from 1750 to 1890 provides an illustration of the progression into higher classes of estate wealth over the years. Table 7 gives the frequency distributions as well as the total number of inventories in each period, their mean value in pounds both in current money and deflated to sterling, and two measures of inequality.

Norfolk County's distribution of wealth in successive time periods is characterized by a rising trend in inequality which accelerated in the forty years between the final data from the eighteenth century and the earliest for the nineteenth. Although the level of inequality continued to rise even further in the course of that century, the annual rate of increase in the size shares of the richest 10 percent of estates slowed in the second half as the central tendency of the distribution moved up out of the lower class values. Estates valued under £300 or $1,000 made up 43 percent of all the inventories in the eighteenth century but declined to just under 40 percent in 1830, 27 percent in 1860, and 20.5 percent in 1890. Although this decline in the poorer estates did curb the progressive increases in the level of inequality in Norfolk's inventories, the size share of the richest 10 percent leveled off after 1860, primarily because the growth in numbers of the largest fortunes had also leveled off.

The largest estates in colonial Boston had never reached as high as £20,000 sterling, or $66,667. Even estates of £5,000 sterling were rare there during the colonial period and virtually nonexistent in the rural inventories. By contrast, the first half of the nineteenth century witnessed a great advance in the numbers and

Table 7 Distribution of Total Estate Values in Rural Suffolk/Norfolk County (Males, %)

CLASSES IN $	EQUIVALENT IN £	1750–53	1763–69	1783–88	1829–31	1859–61	1889–91
Under 500	Under 150	20.9	21.85	24.5	26.5	15.1	10.6
500–999	150–299.7	22.7	21.1	18.4	13.2	11.6	9.9
1,000–4,999	300–1,499.7	53.5	48.15	48.2	38.8	39.4	46.5
5,000–9,999	1,500–2,999.7	2.9	6.7	6.4	12.3	13.7	14.65
10,000–24,999	3,000–7,499.7	—	2.2	2.1	5.5	10.6	9.4
25,000–49,999	7,500–14,999.7	—	—	0.35	1.8	4.1	4.3
50,000–99,999	15,000–29,999.7	—	—	—	1.4	2.5	1.4
100,000–199,999	30,000–59,999.7	—	—	—	0.5	2.1	1.7
200,000–299,999	60,000–89,999.7	—	—	—	—	0.4	0.3
300,000–399,999	90,000–119,999.7	—	—	—	—	—	0.2
400,000–499,999	120,000–149,999.7	—	—	—	—	0.2	—
500,000 and over	150,000 and over	—	—	—	—	0.4	1.2
Total Number Estates		172	270	280	219	518	587
Mean Value £ (current)		486	598	623	1442	4039	5669
Deflated £ (sterling)		376	464	417	966	2706	4394
Size Share Top 10%		31.0	38.0	42.4	59.5	72.9	80.8
Gini Coefficients		.456	.503	.532	.692	.796	.844

Deflators: 1750–53, 0.775; 1763–69, 0.775; 1782–88, 0.67; 1829–31, 0.67; 1859–61, 0.67; 1889–91, 0.775. Those for the eighteenth century are based on wholesale commodity price index numbers for the month of June, compiled by Ruth Crandall. Arthur H. Cole, *Wholesale Commodity Prices in the United States 1700–1861* (Cambridge, Mass., 1938), 118. Deflators for 1829–91 are based on wholesale commodity prices in Philadelphia, *Historical Statistics* (Washington, D.C., 1962), 116, and on the Warren and Pearson wholesale commodity price index, *ibid.*, 119.

SOURCE: Suffolk County Probate Records, C–CIV, CXIII–CXXI, CXXXI–CXXXVII; *Twenty-Fifth Annual Report*, 256–258.

wealth of those at the top. Whereas immigration and industrial development wielded their greatest impact on the level of inequality in the former agricultural counties, growth in the numbers of the very rich provided the all-important upward thrust in those areas where manufacturing and commerce had long served as the major sectors of employment.

Close attention to the history of the distribution of wealth in the probate records of three states has yielded valuable insights into the nature of inequality and its range of behavior. In the rural
communities of the preindustrial Northeast, from colonial times 341
to the Civil War, a relatively egalitarian distribution prevailed. Even those historically low levels of inequality, however, suggest that a natural floor existed beneath which inequality could not go. The effect of the life cycle on wealth accumulation is that men in their fifties and early sixties owned more property than men in their twenties.

For Maryland, and, by extension, for the South, the picture was different from the start. In the seventeenth century, immigration and disease combined to keep a major portion of the population in the younger and poorer age brackets. The practice of indenturing servants, which paid the transportation costs of this mass movement, placed a majority of these men further behind in the process of economic accumulation compared to even the poorest among the native-born. A few men of substance and connection migrated as well and, with their families, founded a small and not very opulent upper class whose life style differed little from their neighbors. Thus in the early South, a large class of poor and a small class of well-to-do characterized a society the wealth distribution of which was more unequal than in the rural North.

As the eighteenth century got well underway, a handful of Maryland planters who had hitherto been only well-to-do grew quite rich. The source of their new wealth lay not in raising tobacco, although that crop continued to offer steady employment for their capital, but in trade and money lending, "urban" activities which were dispersed over the countryside rather than centered in cities.

Colonial cities of the North exhibited greater levels of inequality than did their rural hinterlands, because opportunity, the sources of credit, and the mobile poor concentrated there. Although that level fluctuated with trade conditions, no long-term trend emerged before the Revolution. Viewed in the aggregate, the distribution of wealth in the colonial North proved stable, producing a size share for the richest 10 percent of about 45 percent and a Gini coefficient probably in the range of .55–.60.

Sometime after the Revolution cracks appeared in the picture of stability. In Massachusetts by 1830 the level of inequality as measured by the Gini coefficient had climbed by some twenty points. It would climb only a little further in the years thereafter
342 despite the steady and rapid advance of industrial progress and its demographic accompaniments.

As in Maryland's case much earlier, the growth of wealth at the top rather than the expansion of the propertyless provided the impetus for Massachusetts' sudden jump in inequality. Whatever the source of that great new wealth, it was before the Industrial Revolution and before the great growth of the cities that the distribution of wealth in Massachusetts took what now appears an irreversible leap forward in the degree of its concentration.

ANNOUNCEMENT

Power and Precedent in the Creation of an American Impeachment Tradition: The Eighteenth-Century Colonial Record

Peter C. Hoffer and N. E. H. Hull

"TO understand what the Framers [of the Federal Constitution] had in mind," Raoul Berger has written of impeachment in America, "we must begin with English law, for nowhere did they more evidently take off from that law than in drafting the impeachment provisions."[1] Following similar reasoning, historians have ransacked Stuart parliamentary and American constitutional records for impeachment precedents and commentary. Six neglected eighteenth-century colonial impeachments are here added to this inquiry. These cases, all *causes célèbres* in their day, raised basic issues of intra-governmental balance of power, recording the colonial assemblies' efforts to counter royal executive and judicial power. The cases transmitted an essentially political impeachment tradition to the framers of the Constitution.

Though the political substance of the cases varied—personal, factional, and anti-imperial motives being mixed with disinterested concern for the public weal—their political significance is nevertheless clear. Conscious of the power which impeachment gave to the lower house, factions in the assemblies learned to use the process to resist proprietary and royal executive and judicial officeholders. In their relationship to imperial authority, the colonists in 1700 differed greatly from their predecessors of even a generation before. Crown reorganization of the imperial bureaucracy, revision of colonial charters, and improved customs and legal supervision after 1696 gave Americans a sense of the vast powers lodged in the hands of the home government. At the same time, lower houses in every colony groped toward greater autonomy. At the intersection of these opposing political movements

Mr. Hoffer is a member of the Department of History at the University of Georgia, Athens. Ms. Hull is a doctoral candidate at Columbia University. They are collaborating on a book entitled *Republican Impeachment: The Origins of Impeachment in America, 1635-1805*. The authors wish to thank Alden T. Vaughan, M. L. Benedict, Bradley Chapin, Milton Klein, Richard B. Morris, Paul Kurtz, and R. Clayton Roberts for their assistance during the preparation of this article.

[1] Raoul Berger, *Impeachment: The Constitutional Problems* (Cambridge, Mass., 1973), 54.

lay the conditions for impeachment of proprietary and royal officials. The political impact of these cases was cumulative, and it pointed toward a final repudiation of imperial rule.[2]

Even as colonial assemblies applied this expedient, partisan check upon external authority, they drew consciously and respectfully from parliamentary impeachment precedent. Without the force of the English example—the assumption that the process was shared by all adherents of the British constitution—impeachment would forfeit its legitimacy. Colonial reception and transformation of English practices passed through two stages. In the seventeenth century, colonial legislators employed impeachment as an experimental criminal process, following the letter (if not the spirit) of the
344 Stuart Commons. The growing intrusiveness of English imperial officers, in the next century, offended colonial legislative spokesmen and steered the latter into consciously political impeachments. A sense of the solemn importance of constitutional precedent still informed these proceedings. In the face of otherwise uncontrollable royal appointees in the colonies, eighteenth-century American legislators adopted impeachment, the constitutional right of the English Commons—the "grand inquest of the nation"—to seek out and indict otherwise untouchable wielders of royal power in the realm. In these six colonial cases one finds a synergism of politics and law, in which partisanship fostered adaptation of parliamentary precedent, and that precedent, in turn, furnished a larger constitutional rationale for indictment of royal wrongdoing. Ultimately impeachment became a fundamental part of republican law.

Because particular political circumstances provided the opportunity for these impeachments, we must first turn to political narrative. In the impeachments of Massachusetts merchant captains Samuel Vetch, John Borland, William Rouse, and Roger Lawson (1706), a primarily political interpretation of impeachment in America began to emerge from its quasi-criminal predecessor. Impeachment in the lower house of Parliament was in form a criminal action, meant for prosecution before the Lords, on clearly defined criminal charges, ending in criminal sentences. Seventeenth-century colonial impeachment managers adopted this mechanism, though with mixed results.[3] On the surface, the Vetch case also followed this rule. The charges

[2] Charles M. Andrews, *The Colonial Period of American History*, IV: *England's Commercial and Colonial Policy* (New Haven, Conn., 1938), 375, 377; Michael Garibaldi Hall, *Edward Randolph and the American Colonies, 1676-1703* (New York, 1960), 213; David S. Lovejoy, *The Glorious Revolution in America* (New York, 1972), 377; Jack P. Greene, *The Quest for Power: The Lower Houses of Assembly in the Southern Royal Colonies, 1689-1776* (New York, 1972), 206-207.

[3] The English precedent and the 17th-century colonial cases are discussed in Peter C. Hoffer and N. E. H. Hull, "The First American Impeachments," *William and Mary Quarterly*, 3d Ser., XXXV (1978), 653-667.

against the merchants had a clear criminal basis in a violation of statutory provisions against trading with an enemy in time of war. The General Court intended to try the impeachments before the Council, as the Commons did before the Lords, and to punish by criminal penalties. At the same time, the real target of the lower house was political: to check the overbearing, corrupt royal governor, Joseph Dudley. Dudley's opponents in the assembly sought to impeach and try him, albeit by proxy, for abuse of the powers of his office. The latter action was a political impeachment, without trial or criminal penalties, in which the most the prosecutors could expect was Dudley's ultimate loss of office.

The affair began in 1691, when the second charter of Massachusetts Bay stripped the General Court of its judicial powers. Under the old charter the 345
General Court acted as the highest bench in the province. Bay Colony law explicitly permitted the General Court to "impeach" criminals. The new royal charter forced assembly and assistants to surrender their jurisdiction to a separate court system, whose justices were appointed by the crown. The old Puritan "country party" in the General Court resented this loss of judicial power. The arrival of Dudley, a fierce partisan and soon the leader of a "court party," further inflamed these animosities.[4]

While Dudley was a native New Englander and perhaps as committed to the welfare of his colony as any of the royal governors, he still expected to gain what he could from his post. Trade with the enemy was a treasonable offense, but one widely practiced and very profitable. Dudley allied himself in this enterprise with Samuel Vetch, a Scots immigrant who had established himself in the lucrative French Canadian trade earlier in the century. These ventures attracted a number of other local traders, including Borland, Lawson, and Rouse.[5]

In March 1706, assembly agents intercepted Vetch's *Flying Horse* on its way to French Acadia and discovered incriminating documents and cargo on board. The assembly detained Vetch for "impeachment" on a charge of treason and placed his suspected co-conspirators under large bonds. In its eagerness to defend the colony against the ostensible danger of smuggling

[4] On the judicial powers of the General Court see Edwin Powers, *Crime and Punishment in Early Massachusetts, 1620-1692* (Boston, 1966), 45-76. On the activity of the "country party" see T. H. Breen, *The Character of the Good Ruler: A Study of Puritan Political Ideas in New England, 1630-1730* (New York, 1974), 234. Everett Kimball, "The Public Life of Joseph Dudley, 1672-1715" (Ph.D. diss., Harvard University, 1904), 62; and Clifford K. Shipton, ed., *Sibley's Harvard Graduates* (Cambridge, Mass., 1873-), IV, 43-45, describe the governor and his party. Dudley's rapport with the General Court suffered from his involvement in the Andros government. See Lovejoy, *Glorious Revolution*, 147-148, and *passim*.

[5] This was but one form of the smuggling activities of New England's rising commercial entrepreneurs. Bernard Bailyn, *The New England Merchants in the Seventeenth Century* (New York, 1964), 127. On Vetch see G. M. Waller, *Samuel Vetch: Colonial Enterpriser* (Chapel Hill, N.C., 1960), 30-93.

and the hidden danger of Dudley's unscrupulous conduct, the lower house reached for its defunct judicial powers, only to learn, in the middle of its deliberations, that under the new charter the General Court could only vote a "High Misdemeanor" against the criminals. In August the General Court belatedly asked for the legal opinion of the Council. Councillor Samuel Sewall, chief justice of the Superior Court and an enemy of Dudley, concluded that the assembly had no jurisdiction in the case, but Dudley, possibly to keep the case out of the Superior Court, where treason was still punishable by death, barely persuaded the Council to urge that the impeachment continue. The assembly impeached the four captains and asked the Council to sit as a court; the councillors found the defendants guilty. Here the problem
346 of a punishment arose, and in a novel hybrid solution—not quite a sentence nor really an attainder—a joint committee of the two houses voted a "bill of punishment," including fines and imprisonment.[6]

In England, the Board of Trade, confronted with Dudley's report, Vetch's testimony, and pamphlets by Dudley's antagonists, Cotton Mather and Francis Higginson, suggested a new trial in the regular courts. The Privy Council, acting in its capacity as the appellate court for the colonies, invalidated the bill of punishment and freed the defendants. The Privy Council had perhaps seen danger in colonial lower house use of impeachment. In the middle 1760s Thomas Hutchinson, lieutenant governor, chief justice, and foremost historian of the Massachusetts Bay colony, set down similar conclusions on the impeachment of 1706. Hutchinson judged that this case set a precedent that any loyal crown official must reject. The General Court had not only contravened the power of the governor but had also questioned the entire structure of imperial rule. The revolutionary potential of the precedent was not lessened because the General Court had not chosen to follow the logic of its lese majesty to its ultimate conclusion.[7]

The second eighteenth-century impeachment fell upon James Logan, William Penn's protégé, Pennsylvania's provincial agent, and secretary of the colony's Council. It became a struggle between branches of government—

[6] Waller, *Samuel Vetch*, 30-93; Kimball, "Public Life of Dudley," 76-84. Sewall's misgivings about the conduct of the trial, later exacerbated by his discovery that Dudley was indeed involved in the crime, are recorded in the *Diary of Samuel Sewall* (Massachusetts Historical Society, *Collections*, 5th Ser., V-VI [1878-1882]), II, 64.

[7] *A Memorial of the Present Deplorable State of New-England* . . . (Boston, 1707) (Mass. Hist. Soc., *Colls.*, 5th Ser., VI [1878-1882]), II, 49-50; [Cotton Mather], *A Modest Inquiry into . . . A Late Pamphlet, Entitled, A Memorial of the Present Deplorable State of New-England* (London, 1707), *ibid.*, 65-95; [Nathaniel Higginson], *The Deplorable State of New England* . . . (London, 1708), *ibid.*, 99-131; *Diary of Sewall*, *ibid.*, II, 200-201; Kimball, "Public Life of Dudley," 78-80; Thomas Hutchinson, *The History of the Colony and Province of Massachusetts-Bay*, ed. Lawrence Shaw Mayo (Boston, 1936), II, 155.

one representing local, elected officials; the other, English executive appointees—over the practical balance of power. When Penn returned to England in 1684, he left Logan in charge of the key executive offices of proprietary finance. Logan plunged into his responsibilities with tactless vigor. In so doing, he clashed with David Lloyd, a Welsh lawyer whose talents induced Penn to appoint him attorney general, councillor, and clerk of the provincial court in 1686. Amity between Penn and Lloyd dissolved by 1688, and in 1693 Lloyd entered the assembly as a leader of the antiproprietary party, shortly thereafter becoming assembly speaker.[8]

Animosity between Lloyd and Logan flared into a broader contest between the assembly and the colonial executive during debate over the
Judiciary Act of 1706. The crux of the dispute was the prerogatives each 347
branch claimed for itself. On November 28, 1706, Logan fumed: "The Case is short and plain: The Assembly requests several Things to be granted away from the Proprietary and Governor, which are now his Right, and to this he will not agree." The day after receiving the governor's veto of the courts bill, with Logan's explanation, the legislature resolved unanimously that it had the right "to address and advise the Governor to turn out or displace for Misdemeanour, any Magistrate or other Officer constituted by the Governor." It further asserted *nem con dicente* that "if any such Magistrate or Officer shall be impeached by the Assembly for official Misdemeanour, such Magistrate or Officer, upon Proof made of such Charge, ought to be removed or displaced at the Instance of the Assembly." The house, led by Lloyd, correctly assumed that Logan's "pernicious Counsel" induced Lieutenant Governor John Evans to threaten to constitute the courts himself in the absence of an acceptable courts bill. It resolved finally "that an humble Address be made to the Governor, to remove the said *James Logan* from his Council and presence." When Logan, replying on behalf of the lieutenant governor, ignored the assembly's charges, the house voted "that a Committee be appointed to draw up a certain Articles of Impeachment against *James Logan.*"[9]

With this step, the assembly turned from an "address" to the executive

[8] On Logan see Irma Jane Cooper, *The Life and Public Services of James Logan* (New York, 1921); Joseph Esrey Johnson, "A Statesman of Colonial Pennsylvania: A Study of the Private Life and Public Career of James Logan to the Year 1726" (Ph.D. diss., Harvard University, 1942); Frederick B. Tolles, *James Logan and the Culture of Provincial America* (Boston, 1951), 63-69; and Albright G. Zimmerman, "James Logan, Proprietary Agent," *Pennsylvania Magazine of History and Biography,* LXXVIII (1954), 143-176. On Lloyd see Roy N. Lokken, *David Lloyd: Colonial Lawmaker* (Seattle, Wash., 1959), 3-187.

[9] Samuel Hazard *et al.*, eds., *Votes and Proceedings of the House of Representatives of the Province of Pennsylvania* (*Pennsylvania Archives,* 8th Ser. [1852-1859]), I, 630-631, 714, 652, hereafter cited as *Votes and Proceedings;* Cooper, *Life and Services of Logan,* 210.

for removal of an erring minister, common in the colonies and England, to the wholly distinct process of impeachment. Although the two were entirely different, it is possible that Lloyd believed impeachment to be the logical sequel to an ineffectual appeal. He knew that the bringing of impeachment charges unified the lower house in defense of its privileges against the executive. He had before him one clear precedent—the 1685 impeachment of Chief Justice Nicholas More in Pennsylvania—and perhaps a second—the Vetch case. In Pennsylvania, the lower house's right to impeach appeared in the original charter, saw use in the More case, and was reaffirmed in 1688; it reappeared in the new 1701 charter, though no provision was made for trial. One might infer from the assembly's boast "that the People of *Massachu-*
348 *setts,* in *New-England,* could not pretend to greater Privileges than the Proprietary granted to the Purchasers and Adventurers here . . ." that information on the Vetch affair had reached Philadelphia.[10]

The assembly prepared thirteen "articles of impeachment" against Logan. The first accused him of using his influence with the Proprietor to "insert a certain Salvo [that is, a rider] . . . in the Proprietary's Commission to his Lieutenant-Governor, whereby the final Assent to all such Bills as he was to pass into Laws in this Province, is absolutely lodged in the proprietary." The second also objected to a clause in Evans's commission that gave him the power "to call Assemblies, and . . . to prorogue or dissolve" them at his pleasure—a clause, the assembly maintained, that had been inserted at Logan's behest. The next four articles were indictments of Logan's performance as land commissioner, faulting him for not providing copies of patents for tenants, for charging excessive and unfair quit-rents, for extending the period for resurvey of lands "whereby divers of the Queen's Subjects have been disquieted in their Lawful Possessions," and for dividing up and redistributing lands illegally. The seventh article accused Logan of deliberately concealing from the assembly various objections of the Board of Trade to the earlier version of the courts bill, leading the assembly to write new bills that would be equally and embarrassingly unacceptable to the Board of Trade. There followed other objections to his conduct in land transactions. The twelfth article charged Logan with "a wicked Intent to create Divisions and Misunderstandings between him and the people," and the last accused him of interfering with the election of sherriff John Budd.[11]

Dissatisfied with Logan's brief reply, issued in the Council, the assembly insisted on its right to prosecute him and requested that the lieutenant

[10] Tolles, *Logan and Culture of America,* 65; *Votes and Proceedings,* I, 102, 660. On the More case see Hoffer and Hull, "First Impeachments," *WMQ,* 3d Ser., XXXV (1978), 653-667.

[11] *Votes and Proceedings,* I, 715-719; *Minutes of the Provincial Council of Pennsylvania* (Philadelphia, 1852-1853), II, 352, 356, hereafter cited as *Pa. Council Mins.*

governor act as judge and jury, the Frame of Government of 1701 having abolished the legislative power of the upper house. Trial was arranged for May 12, 1707. The speaker and assembly arrived en masse—literally following English precedent whereby the Commons prosecuted as a body—presented the articles of impeachment, and asked Logan to plead. The lieutenant governor demurred that his powers were not comparable to those of the House of Lords in England, repeating a consensus reached that morning in the Council. Lloyd retorted that the charter gave the assembly the power to impeach and that although the Frame of Government did not spell out the trial procedure, there was the precedent of the More case to follow. The lieutenant governor conceded the point by ordering the trial to continue. Logan admitted his ignorance of the law, and gave a graphic demonstration 349
by asking to hear the evidence against him before pleading to the charges. Caught between the secretary, whom he wished to protect, and an implacable assembly, Evans declared an adjournment until the next morning.

When the trial reconvened, no doubt after Evans and Logan met in serious conference, the lieutenant governor reiterated his initial aversion to presiding over an impeachment trial. He informed the lower house that "the Governor and Council have declared their Opinion fully to the Assembly, that they are not qualified to hear and judge of the Articles exhibited against the Secretary of an Impeachment, according to the parliamentary Proceedings of *England*; and being no judicial Court, they cannot oblige him to plead in any Form." The lieutenant governor offered to receive any complaints against Logan in the usual form, that is, as an appeal to the judgment of the executive. Public opinion in the colony soon shifted to Logan's side, and Lloyd lost his seat in the assembly. Yet precedent had been created which, when the venerated William Penn no longer lived, could be used in a sweeping assault upon proprietary rule.[12]

In the Carolinas, as in early eighteenth-century Massachusetts and Pennsylvania, individuals and factions in the assembly saw in impeachment a tool to check the power of externally appointed executive and judicial officials. In 1719 the assembly of South Carolina waited anxiously for the

[12] *Pa. Council Mins.*, II, 355-357; *Votes and Proceedings*, I, 751-756. Evans's hesitation may have been based upon his belief that the colonial upper houses, unlike the House of Lords, were never intended to be courts and therefore could never exercise the powers to sentence and punish criminals as all courts (including the Lords) could. American colonial precedent went against Evans's ruling, for the upper house in Pennsylvania, as well as those of her neighbors, acted as an appellate court in criminal cases.

For the denouement of the case see James Logan to William Penn, Jan. 2, 1706/7, in Edward Armstrong, ed., *Correspondence between William Penn and James Logan, . . . and Others, 1700-1750 . . .*, II (Historical Society of Pennsylvania, *Memoirs*, X [1872]), 194-197; Johnson, "Statesman of Colonial Pa.," 349-385; and Lokken, *David Lloyd*, 186-187.

proprietors to assent to four bills intended to give it greater control over land grants, Indian policy, elections, and prices. When the proprietors vetoed the entire package, the planters who led the lower house correctly suspected that Chief Justice Nicholas Trott had undermined their case in England. For covert political opposition to the assembly, no less than for the malfeasance in office named in the charges against him, Trott was impeached.[13]

Trott's uncontrolled power in the courts of the colony invited legislative scrutiny. He had been trained at the Inner Temple and had served in South Carolina as attorney general and judge of the vice-admiralty court before his elevation to the Council and appointment as chief justice in 1703. He had once been an ally of the assembly but, by 1703, was firmly in the proprietary
350 camp. Although Trott performed genuine services for the bench and bar in the colony, he was an autocratic and avaricious political operator. Holding multiple positions as chief justice, sole judge of common pleas and king's bench, and leader of the vice-admiralty and chancery courts, Trott stood almost above the law. He could not be charged with being the proprietors' pawn, but he could be accused of misusing his judicial powers. In April 1719, thirty-one articles of impeachment were presented in the assembly, charging that Trott "had been guilty of many partial judgments" and "that he had contrived many ways to multiply and increase his fees, contrary to Acts of Assembly, and to the great grievance of the subjects." Trott was accused of creating new fees for himself, delaying cases and giving legal advice in court, and drawing up legal documents while acting as a judge.[14]

The assembly impeached Trott but then could find no way to try him. He insisted to his accusers that he held his commissions at the pleasure of the proprietors. In 1707, when Trott stood on friendlier terms with the assembly, the Council had asked that he be impeached for judicial misconduct. At that time the assembly had replied that the Council "were not a House of Lords nor a proper jurisdiction" before which the assembly could prosecute a case. Twelve years later, Trott used the assembly's old ruling against its new leaders. The assembly, reversing its position, asked the governor and Council to try him, but the Council, advised by Trott, decided that it had no power to

[13] Edward McCrady, *The History of South Carolina under the Proprietary Government, 1670-1719* (New York, 1897), 627-680; W. Roy Smith, *South Carolina as a Royal Province* (New York, 1903), 12-13.

[14] Francis Yonge, *A Narrative of the Proceedings of the People of South Carolina, In the Year 1719 . . .* (London, 1726), in Peter Force, ed., *Tracts and Other Papers, Relating Principally to . . . North America*, II (Washington, D.C., 1838), no. 10, 1-39, hereafter cited as Yonge, *Narrative of S.C.* See also L. Lynn Hogue, "Nicholas Trott: Man of Law and Letters," *South Carolina Historical Magazine*, LXXVI (1975), 25-34; M. Eugene Sirmans, *Colonial South Carolina: A Political History, 1663-1763* (Chapel Hill, N.C., 1966), 72-79; David Ramsay, *History of South Carolina from Its First Settlement in 1670 to the Year 1808*, II (Newberry, 1858), 275; and McCrady, *History of S.C.*, 690-693.

try an impeachment case. When the assembly pressed the Council to take the issue to higher authority, Governor Nathaniel Johnson refused to shield the defendant. Instead, he sent councillor Francis Yonge to the proprietors with a "letter of grievances" againt Trott, along with the assembly's "remonstrance" against the veto of the four acts. The assembly, governor, and Council recommended that Trott be either removed or at least limited to one of his offices. What began as an impeachment had temporarily become an appeal.[15]

For three months Yonge pleaded for an audience before the proprietors. When at last the proprietors heard his petition, they found the presumption of the assembly alarming. Yonge returned to the colony bearing the proprietors' praise of Trott and instructions for the formation of a new, pro-
Trott Council. The assembly refused to accept this mandate. Johnson called 351
for new elections, and the proprietary party was overwhelmed at the polls. In the chaotic weeks that followed, an ad hoc "Association" replaced the assembly and chose a Council to its taste, which then tried and removed Trott from office. Political exigency—the proprietors still ruled in South Carolina—prevented a more sanguinary punishment. The Trott impeachment became entangled in the larger contest between the assembly and the proprietors, though it had not originated as an attack upon the proprietary. As he fell, Trott reached out for support from England and, like Logan, ended by threatening to topple the men whom he served.[16] Penn's stature in his own colony, compared to the weakness of the remaining Carolina proprietors, had much to do with the contrasting outcomes of these two impeachments.

Two decades later a futile attempt to impeach the chief justice of North Carolina, William Smith, proved that marginal political support in the colony and able political maneuvering by the accused could derail impeach-

[15] On the 1707 espisode see Mary Patterson Clarke, *Parliamentary Privilege in the American Colonies* (New Haven, Conn., 1943), 42-43. The records of the assembly for the years 1718-1720 are no longer in existence. See Verner W. Crane, *The Southern Frontier, 1670-1732* (Durham, N.C., 1928), 217n.

[16] Yonge, *Narrative of S.C.*, 160-183; McCrady, *History of S.C.*, 692-699; Hogue, "Nicholas Trott," *S.C. Hist. Mag.*, LXXVI (1975), 30-34. Recoiling from their actual impeachment of Trott for trial in the upper house, the newly established royal lower house contented themselves with a petition to the Board of Trade for the removal of Councillor Middleton in 1725. Two years later, they imprisoned Chief Justice Smith for judicial irregularities. Both these men were "impeached," but not for trial by the upper house. The former had the force and form of an "appeal," and the latter of a censure. Of course, both actions were designed to demonstrate assembly feeling toward George I's ministers in London. See George Chalmers, *Introduction to the History of the Revolt of the American Colonies,* II (Boston, 1845), 99-103. Roger Foster, *Commentaries on the Constitution of the United States, Historical and Juridical,* I (Boston, 1895), 635, incorrectly identifies these as parliamentary impeachment precedents.

ment in the assembly. Smith, an educated English lawyer, received appointment as a councillor and chief justice shortly after arriving in the newly reorganized royal colony. He got along famously with Governor Gabriel Johnston and, with the governor's aid, set about establishing himself as a landed squire. By the end of the decade, he had over 7,000 acres in the colony and an annual income of £550. Smith wished to incorporate his holdings into a township to be called Wilmington, but families already established in the region resisted. Led by the Moores, influential landholders in the south of the colony, anti-Smith forces tried to prevent Council confirmation of the incorporation of Wilmington. The chief justice would not permit his dream of landed nobility to be shattered so easily. Again with
352 Johnston's consent, he declared himself the possessor of a double vote in the Council and there blocked opposition to incorporation.[17]

In the fall of 1738, Smith's opponents, led by Sir Richard Everard, Samuel Swann, and Maurice Moore, proposed seventeen articles of impeachment aganst the chief justice. They believed they had a chance of success in the lower house, though Smith's influence in the Council and with the governor would have rendered the trial verdict a foregone conclusion. Even nominal victory over Smith was denied by another of the chief justice's strategems. According to depositions collected in 1749, ten years after the affair, Smith and Speaker John Hodgson managed to convince northern county assemblymen to absent themselves from the November 1738 session. North-south rivalry within the colony was lively, and Smith had earlier defended the interests of the northern counties. Without these members, the assembly lacked a quorum and had to adjourn. The newly elected assembly that gathered in February 1739 to weigh the evidence against Smith was, according to Smith's enemies, packed with his supporters.[18]

The journal of the lower house records the brief and unsuccessful impeachment attempt. The whole process, from the reading of the seventeen articles through the issuing of warrants for evidence and witnesses to the final vote, took only three days. According to the journal, every assistance was afforded the complainants by the Speaker, and the dismissal of the charges by a majority of six votes exonerated Smith. The chief justice informed the Council that the assembly had fully vindicated him. "After nine hours of

[17] William K. Boyd, ed., *Some Eighteenth Century Tracts Concerning North Carolina* (Raleigh, N.C., 1927), 3-6; William D. Price, Jr., " 'Men of Good Estates': Wealth among North Carolina's Royal Councillors," *North Carolina Historical Review*, XLIX (1972), 75, 79; Hugh Williamson, *The History of North Carolina*, II (Philadelphia, 1812), 43; William L. Saunders, Walter Clark, and Stephen B. Weeks, eds., *Colonial Records of North Carolina* (Raleigh, Winston, Goldsboro, and Charlotte, 1886-1914), III, 342-343, 552, 600, 607, IV, 449-450, 457, hereafter cited as *N.C. Recs.*

[18] *N.C. Recs.*, IV, 1207-1209; William S. Price, Jr., "A Strange Incident in George Burrington's Royal Governorship," *N.C. Hist. Rev.*, LI (1974), 149-158.

debate," he wrote in 1740, the assembly "were so sensible of that Gentleman's Integrity and faithfulness in the Discharge of his office [and] were so fully convinced of what was at the bottom of their design to put in a tool of a Chief Justice in order to get the Supreme Court of Justice and consequently the whole property of the province under their own management . . . [that] the fullest house that was ever known . . . Rejected . . . their infamous accusation."[19] Unlike Trott, Smith maintained some support in the lower house, and, equally important, the royal authorities in England, unlike Trott's patrons among South Carolina's proprietors, gave Smith powerful backing. These internal and external friends insulated Smith from his partisan opponents and preserved his powers in the courts and on the Council.

After their defeat, the anti-Smith faction prepared *A True and Faithful* 353
Narrative of the Proceedings of the House of Burgesses of North Carolina . . . to vindicate their case. They accused Smith of using illegal tactics to prevent a quorum in the fall 1738 session of the assembly. The authors attacked the speed of the 1739 inquiry, engineered by Speaker Hodgson, for preventing the complainants from gathering all their witnesses and materials. The journal neither specified the charges nor printed any of the evidence, an omission which the *Narrative* claimed to correct. If true, the charges show a pattern in Smith's judicial irregularities. The first article was a general condemnation of the "violent, arbitrary, and illegal manner" with which Smith rendered judgments. The second argued that he swore to call juries by ballot but was actually calling them by "venire" (*venire facias juratores,* that is, bidding the sheriff select a jury and bring them to court, rather than by random selection of eligible jurors by ballot). The third and fourth articles accused Smith of holding courts where he pleased and executing criminals when he pleased, contrary to assembly laws and common law precedents. The next three articles detailed incidents in which Smith imposed penalties without regard to the law or the rights of the defendants; and articles eight, nine, and ten documented the chief justice's appetite for extorting fees. In the next two articles, the legal chicaneries Smith employed to funnel court fees into his own pocket were revealed. The last five articles found him guilty of bad temper and violent personal feeling against anyone who dared chide him for errors—among whom was Sir Richard Everard.[20] In all these ways,

[19] *N.C. Recs.,* IV, 501-514, 459. In an earlier episode of turbulence in 1711 in North Carolina, the lower house "impeached" one Cary upon learning that he had raised a rebellion in the colony. He was later arrested by Gov. Spotswood of Virginia and sent to England for trial. "Impeachment" in this case merely meant "accused of crime," and the assembly had no intention of having Cary tried by an upper house in the province. Foster, *Commentaries on the Constitution,* I, 635, again erroneously treats this as an impeachment precedent.

[20] *A True and Faithful Narrative of the Proceedings of the House of Burgesses of North Carolina* . . . (n.p., 1740), in Boyd, ed., *Some Eighteenth Century Tracts,*

Smith used the courts to personal advantage. Great latitude was conferred on magistrates, from local justices of the peace to high court judges, in the English common law tradition. If these allegations were true, Smith had truly stretched the bounds of magisterial authority. What emerges from the *Narrative* might, perhaps, include some evidence of felonious activity, but primarily it is a portrait of the creation of a powerful, unscrupulous, and self-serving political machine. Unable in the Council to prevent Smith's political empire-building, his opponents brought an impeachment in the assembly on malfeasance charges.

The Vetch, Logan, Trott, and Smith cases all involved, in addition to personal animosities, broad inter-branch struggle between locally elected
354 assemblies and appointive royal or proprietary officeholders. The political contest remained within the confines of the colony, except when one of the parties sought assistance or refuge in England. Colonial impeachment managers appear to have realized that English authorities had the power to block or reverse colonial impeachments and elected not to challenge their opponents across the sea. Indeed, in all four of the cases, lower house impeachment leaders took pains to profess loyalty to their English overlords.

The impeachment of Pennsylvania county judge William Moore introduced a new pattern. From the first, it was an assault upon the powers of the proprietor in England and his supporters in the colony. Given the nature of Pennsylvania politics at mid-century, such a case may have been inevitable. By the 1750s, confrontation between the proprietor in England and his provincial assembly was characteristic of Pennsylvania politics. Defeats in western Pennsylvania at the start of the Great War for Empire added new urgency to the old hostilities. From 1755 to 1756, the war party—the proprietary forces led by Lieutenant Governor Robert Hunter Morris, the western settlers, and the Anglican establishment—fumed, while anti-proprietary forces in the assembly fussed.[21]

The bitterness of political infighting became apparent in the estrangement of Benjamin Franklin and the Reverend William Smith, leading in tortuous fashion to the impeachment of William Moore. With Franklin's assistance, the young, newly arrived Smith founded the Philadelphia Academy. War partisanships separated the patron and his protégé. By the winter of 1755-1756, Smith championed the proprietary cause and Franklin advocated the assembly position. When Franklin journeyed to England as colonial

10-52; Julian P. Boyd, "The Sheriff in Colonial North Carolina," *N.C. Hist. Rev.*, V (1928), 151-180.

[21] On wartime politics in Pennsylvania see Lawrence Henry Gipson, *The Great War for the Empire: The Years of Defeat, 1756-1757*, The British Empire before the American Revolution, VI (New York, 1946), 66-69; and James H. Hutson, *Pennsylvania Politics, 1746-1770: The Movement for Royal Government and Its Consequences* (Princeton, N.J., 1972), 13-40.

agent, his defense of assembly rights was perpetuated by his lieutenants in the lower house. In 1757 the assembly struck boldly against Smith and the proprietary government, using Moore as a tool.[22]

Moore was a Chester County landholder, militia leader, and justice of the peace. He strongly supported the war effort, for which he was rewarded on February 22, 1757, with a proprietary commission as the head judge of the Chester County court. In the summer and fall of 1757 the assembly reported receiving petitions from Chester County plaintiffs declaring that Moore had set aside jury verdicts, delayed executions of judgments, and refused to pay his personal debts. When the assembly called Moore to account for his behavior, he refused to appear. The assembly could not force him to resign because his commission was at the pleasure of the king. On September 28, 355
1757, it sent the first of many requests to Lieutenant Governor William Denny that Moore be removed from his offices. Unwilling to give the assembly cause to upset the delicate negotiations over the war supply bill, Denny convened a formal inquiry. On October 20, 1757, Moore testified to his grievances against the assembly's war policy and denied that he had ever been formally summoned to appear before the assembly. Satisfied with Moore's account, or hoping that inaction was a safe course, the lieutenant governor permitted the matter to rest without a decision. Moore was not as sensible. When the assembly adjourned for the winter of 1757-1758, he published an accusation in the *Pennsylvania Journal* that the lower house had manufactured evidence against him. Although Moore had secured permission from outgoing Speaker Isaac Norris to print the defense, the new assembly took official umbrage. The first order of business for the new Speaker, Thomas Leech, was to arrest Moore for libel.[23]

To embarrass the assembly and assist a political ally, Smith published Moore's defense. Though Smith prudently waited until the *Journal* and the equally prestigious *Pennsylvania Gazette* had published similar accounts, his caution was unavailing. He was detained for contempt of the assembly at the same time that Moore was arrested. Joseph Galloway, Franklin's chief aide, directed the prosecution. Galloway intended the indictment of Moore to lead to the suppression of the far more dangerous Smith, and the latter was duly

[22] On the Smith-Franklin controversy see Ralph L. Ketcham, "Benjamin Franklin and William Smith: New Light on an Old Philadelphia Quarrel," *PMHB*, LXXXVIII (1964), 142-163; Verner W. Crane, *Benjamin Franklin and a Rising People* (Boston, 1954), 78-97; and Horace W. Smith, ed., *Life and Correspondence of Rev. William Smith*, I (Philadelphia, 1879), 167.

[23] A critical account of the assembly action against Moore is William Renwick Riddell, "Libel on the Assembly: A Prerevolutionary Episode," *PMHB*, LII (1928), 176-192, and for the *Pa. Journal* accounts see *ibid.*, 225. Some of the petitions against Moore are displayed in *Votes and Proceedings*, VI, 4682-4683, See also *Pa. Council Mins.*, III, 764-768.

convicted of contempt. Smith's influence with the governor and Chief Justice William Allen enabled the prisoner to plead his case before the Privy Council, which ordered his freedom before the year was out. Moore was less fortunate, for, as in the Trott case, his impeachment on charges of judicial corruption was still possible. And unlike the South Carolina assembly, the Pennsylvania lower house aimed at the heart of proprietary power from the inception of their proceedings against Moore.[24]

When Denny refused to remove Moore on the petition of the new assembly, the lower house formally impeached the judge. If criminal impeachment, followed by trial, was its aim, the assembly had before it an impossible task: to convince Denny to disregard his own inquiry, in effect to
356 repudiate his power to hold such investigations, and instead to sit as judge and jury in an impeachment trial. In the process, he would also have to render a formal decision on Moore's guilt. Galloway and the assembly party were too experienced to expect such a turnabout. From the first, their aim was not to convict the defendant but to challenge the proprietary system itself. They therefore placed their argument on the highest ground—the English constitution. The assembly told the lieutenant governor that its power to impeach was "strictly agreeable to the Usage of Parliament, and Customs of our Mother Country," as well as "incontestably in the Assembly, by the Charter of Privileges, and an established Law of the Province." It warned Denny that any attempt by him to circumvent the impeachment would be "an Innovation in the Constitution, as it would be erecting a new Court of Judicature, unknown in the Government before."[25]

Though Denny knew that the assembly sought to embarrass the proprietary, he still hoped that it would assist the war effort. He had to find some reason to bar himself from sitting in judgment on the impeachment, while avoiding an open feud with the legislature. Looking to the English constitution, he cited the parliamentary principle, established by 1715, that an executive did not have and could not assume the powers of a House of Lords or Council. Denny, in effect, adopted Evans's argument, which he had read closely. In England, the impeachment trial always took place before this "middle branch,"—the Lords—but in Pennsylvania, Denny wrote, the legislature was unicameral. He reasoned that he had no power to stand in the stead of the Council or upper house: "No such jurisdiction is given him by the Words of the Charter, or elsewhere, that I can find, on the strictest Scrutiny." He added that this was a wise precaution, for should such a power

[24] Theodore Thayer, *Pennsylvania Politics and the Growth of Democracy, 1740-1776* (Harrisonburg, 1953), 68-69; Ernest H. Baldwin, "Joseph Galloway, the Loyalist Politician," *PMHB*, XXVI (1902), 174-176.

[25] Assembly Message to Gov. Denny, Jan. 10, 1758, *Votes and Proceedings*, VI, 4683-4685.

fall upon one man, he might overthrow the rights and liberties guaranteed by the English constitution. Denny's reasoning was sound, and his use of English theory and precedent correct, but the assembly had no patience with his stand.[26]

On January 17 the assembly rebuked Denny for rejecting a basic charter right of the lower house. The assembly had reread the Logan case, and took a very different view of a lieutenant governor's refusal to try impeachments. It found Evans "a Gentleman remarkable for being destitute of every Virtue, either moral, political, or religious. The Government was in a continual Ferment during his whole Administration: The Rights of the People in perpetual Jeopardy by his arbitrary and unjust Invasions." The assembly then broadened its arguments to include the entire range of political issues in 357
contention. "The principal Powers of our Assemblies are, those of making Laws, granting Aids to the Crown, and redressing the Grievances and Oppressions of the People. The first, you well know, is highly invaded, and greatly diminished, by arbitrary Proprietary Instructions, now in your Possession. . . . The second has been greatly violated by the frequent and constant Amendments in our Money bills."[27] The third of these grievances was the Moore case, and it was the effect, not the cause, of the larger breach between the governor and the lower house.

In 1759 the Privy Council, in ruling on the Moore case, denied the assembly the right to imprison for a libel against a previous assembly, and by implication also denied that the assembly possessed parliamentary privileges. including the power to impeach. Moore was fully exonerated and restored to his offices the same year. Despite this, the Moore impeachment broadened the assembly's own conception of its authority and made it more jealous of the powers of the governor. The assembly had grown aware of the difference between its interests—conceived to be identical with the interests of the people—and the interests of the proprietors and their agents.[28]

A similar anxiety over external restraint propelled the Massachusetts General Court in 1773 into its second impeachment effort. The target was Chief Justice Peter Oliver, and the object of attack was royal control over the superior court of the colony. The issue was as old as the Vetch case. When, in the early 1760s, Thomas Hutchinson attacked the General Court's encroachment of 1706 upon the king's courts, he was battling his own General Court for control over the judicial branch. The lower courts were still not

[26] Gov. Denny to Assembly, Jan. 13, 1758, *ibid.*, 4693-4696.

[27] Assembly to Gov. Denny, Jan. 17, 1758, *ibid.*, 4697-4703. Here the assembly had reference to the Logan impeachment arguments made by Lloyd in 1707. See *ibid.*, I, 753.

[28] Joseph W. Smith, *Appeals to the Privy Council from the American Plantations* (New York, 1950), 149.

very responsive to the nominal supremacy of the governor and Council, representing the king, over the judiciary. Hutchinson wished to anglicize these provincial arrangements. He told the Suffolk grand jury repeatedly that the bench must be modelled upon and responsible to English authority. Rival politicians in the General Court suspected a hidden design in Hutchinson's plans for the courts: the corruption of an independent judiciary by a combination of royal patronage and Hutchinson family alliances. Hutchinson's appointment of his in-law Oliver as chief justice of the superior court gave substance to the legislators' fears and eventuated in the impeachment of Oliver.[29]

When Hutchinson was elevated from the lieutenant governorship to
358 replace Governor Francis Bernard, he needed a loyal replacement in the chief justiceship. He turned first to Benjamin Lynde, Jr., who accepted but, sensing the coming storm, soon resigned. Hutchinson next offered the post to Oliver, recommending him to the home government as "the man most likely to resist popular pressure." Oliver, the youngest son of a great mercantile family, fit easily into the elite of the colony's officialdom. He was related to Hutchinson by marriage once in his own generation and twice in the generation of his children, and his brother, Andrew, was Hutchison's lieutenant governor. Though Oliver had been an associate justice of the superior court for almost twenty years, he preferred to remain at home in Plymouth County, tending to his lands, his library, and his iron works, rather than ride circuit. The status of the chief justice's office, the promise of a fair salary, and his unswerving filial devotion to Hutchinson finally led him to accept the higher post. The new chief justice soon became a weak pawn in the power struggle between the royal governor and the rebellious assembly.[30]

Hutchinson and the General Court were deadlocked on the judiciary issue until the rumor that the English government might fund the salaries of

[29] William E. Nelson, *Americanization of the Common Law: The Impact of Legal Change on Massachusetts Society, 1760-1830* (Cambridge, Mass., 1975), 32-33. The three first-hand accounts of this era include sections on the judicial issue. See Lyman H. Butterfield *et al.*, eds., *Diary and Autobiography of John Adams,* III (Cambridge, Mass., 1961), 299-300; Hutchinson, *History of . . . Massachusetts-Bay,* ed. Mayo, III, and Douglass Adair and John A. Schutz, eds., *Peter Oliver's Origin and Progress of the American Rebellion: A Tory View* (San Marino, Calif., 1961).

[30] Shipton, ed., *Sibley's Harvard Graduates,* VI, 255, VIII, 748. Lynde was so wary of political complications that he avoided mentioning his resignation in his diary. Fitch Edward Oliver, ed., *The Diaries of Benjamin Lynde and of Benjamin Lynde, Jr.* (Boston, 1880). The description of Oliver comes from the Hutchinson-Oliver Papers, III, Manuscript Collection, Mass. Hist. Soc. Citations can be found in Natalie Hull Hoffer, "The Origin and Progress of Peter Oliver, Portrait of a Loyalist" (Sr. Thesis, Ohio State University, 1974). See also Robert McCluer Calhoon, *The Loyalists in Revolutionary America, 1760-1781* (New York, 1965), 234-243.

the superior court justices gave the assembly a popular rallying point. While Hutchinson advocated royal salaries to bring order and dignity to the court, the legislature feared that with the end of its own grants to support the judges would come the end of the court's sensitivity to local rights. At the opening of the 1773 term the General Court made crown salaries for the justices the focal point of its assault, warning the governor that "the people without doors are universally alarmed" about the threat. When Hutchinson finally reported that Lord North's ministry had indeed ordered that the justices be paid from customs receipts, the lower house told the chief executive: "We conceive that no Judge who had a due regard to Justice, or even to his own Character, would chuse to be placed under such an undue bias as they must be under, in
the Opinion of the House, by accepting of and becoming dependent for their 359
Salaries upon their Crown. Had not his Majesty been misinformed with Respect to the Constitution and Appointment of our Judges by those who advised to this Measure, we are persuaded he would never have passed such an Order."[31] The governor was safe from the General Court so long as he did not displease his English masters, but the superior court judges might be brought to heel. This was the assembly's next move.

The assembly baited its trap for the justices by voting a grant of £300 for Chief Justice Oliver, for a year's service already passed, and £200 for the associate justices for the same term. The treasurer was to determine whether the justices accepted and used the General Court salary. In June the treasurer reported that Oliver and associate justices Foster Hutchinson, Nathaniel Ropes, and William Cushing had used only half of the grant. The General Court then changed its warning into an ultimatum. Should the justices accept a crown salary in lieu of the assembly grant, they would violate the "most important Clause in the Charter," whereby the assembly was empowered to pay for the services of government. That was on June 25; three days later, the assembly told the justices "without Delay, explicitly to Declare" whether they would accept a crown salary.[32]

All the justices complied, save Oliver. When Oliver told the assembly that he would accept the crown salary, the legislators moved articles of impeachment against him. They declared that he had permitted himself to be bought by a salary "unjustly and unconstitutionally levied and extorted from the Inhabitants of the American Colonies" and that he had acted "against the known Sense of the Body of the People of this Province." For these alleged abuses the assembly asked the governor and Council to try Oliver

[31] Bernard Bailyn, *The Ordeal of Thomas Hutchinson* (Cambridge, Mass., 1974), 118, 127; *Journal of the Honorable House of Representatives of . . . Massachusetts Bay* (Boston, 1773-1774), Feb. 3, 1773, 206, Feb. 15, 1773, 224, June 23, 1773, 275.

[32] *Jour. Mass. Bay,* June 25, 1773, 86-88, June 28, 1773, 94.

and, if found guilty, to remove him without delay from his judicial offices. Asking Hutchinson to sit as a judge in a case against his hand-picked successor and political supporter was a perversion of the impeachment process; it would make trial a mockery. But the request forced the governor to either defend the unpopular chief justice or accede to the demand for a trial.[33]

Caught in the storm, Oliver was reduced to pleading that "I can with the strictest truth assert, that I have suffered since I have been upon the bench of the Superior Court, in the loss of my business and not having sufficient to maintain my family."[34] Hutchinson, for his part, told the General Court he could not judge the chief justice because "if I should comply with your
360 request or take any steps in order to the Removal of the Chief Justice, from this place, merely for receiving what is thus granted him by the King, I should make *myself* chargeable with counteracting his Majesty and endeavoring to defeat his Royal Intentions expressly signified to *me*."[35]

The pleading of Oliver and the legalisms of Hutchinson could not detract from the victory of the assembly. Their indictment of Oliver was tried in the court of public opinion. While the majority of the patriot faction was not yet ready for violent resistance, impeachment of the chief justice was an effective weapon against royal government. As a consequence of the impeachment, the Suffolk grand jury refused to meet, preventing the justices of the Superior Court from meeting. The rights of Massachusetts men and women, the jurors declared, were "not the gifts of kings."[36] Impeachment permitted the lower house to gain some control over untouchable political opponents in royal executive and judicial offices.

Behind this partisan effort to check and balance royal government stood a larger constitutional achievement. Consensus among the legislators and their constituents upon the appropriateness and the force of the impeachment of a public official for violation of a public trust bespoke firm commitment to certain constitutional assumptions. Bound to an ideology of legislative privilege, impeachment moved from an expeditious tactic to a fixture of American government. The origin of the consensus on the legitimacy of colonial impeachment lay in the colonists' understanding of the English precedent.

[33] *Ibid.*, Feb. 2, 1774, 117-118, Feb. 8, 1774, 137-139, Feb. 11, 1774, 146-148.

[34] Oliver to General Court, Feb. 3, 1774, Miscellaneous Bound MSS, Mass. Hist. Soc.

[35] Thomas Hutchinson, "Reply to Remonstrance of February 12, 1774," Feb. 15, 1774, Massachusetts Colonial Papers, Mass. Hist. Soc. Italics added.

[36] Order to Council, Mar. 7, 1774, Mass. Colonial Papers; Adair and Schutz, eds., *Oliver's Origin and Progress*, 111-115; Grand Jury of Suffolk Co., Aug. 30, 1774, in Peter Force, ed., *American Archives: Consisting of a Collection of Authentick Records* . . . , 4th Ser., I (Washington, D.C., 1838), 74.

While political circumstances dictated the use of impeachment in the eighteenth-century colonies, the lower houses never lost sight of the fact that impeachment was a legal remedy for wrongdoing, whose precedent lay in the experience of the English Parliament. When Americans impeached malefactors, the prosecutors drew consciously and proudly from English sources. From those sources and from their experience Americans created their own impeachment rationale.

Eighteenth-century colonists' knowledge of English precedent was not exhaustive, but it exceeded the groping approximations of their seventeenth-century predecessors. Americans could learn about Stuart impeachments from a number of written sources. Of these, the most widely distributed and cited
were John Rushworth's eight-volume *Historical Collections* (1659) and John 361
Selden's terse, technical *Of the Judicature in Parliament* (1681). Rushworth, a parliamentary follower, included detailed and supportive documentation of the Commons' defense of law and liberty against Stuart tyranny. Selden's posthumous work judiciously reaffirmed the Commons' power to inquire into royal wrongdoing. Both works were available in public and private colonial libraries throughout the century. Standard manuals of English law also described the impeachment process in terms of the initiative and latitude of the Commons. John Adams's copy of Giles Jacob's *A New Law-Dictionary* defined impeachment as "the Accusation and Prosecution of a Person for Treason, or other Crimes and Misdemeanors. Any Member of the House of Commons may not only impeach any one of their own Body, but also any Lord of Parliament, etc. And thereupon *Articles* are exhibited on the Behalf of the Commons, and Managers [are] appointed to make good their charge and accusation. Which being done in the proper Judicature, Sentence is passed, etc." Thomas Wood's equally popular *Institutes of the Laws of England* also mentioned the law of impeachment. "The Commons," Wood noted, "have often Impeached several Persons before the House of Lords, and have prosecuted them to judgment. For the Commons, coming from all Parts, are the General inquisitors." Sir Matthew Hale's *History of the Common Law* (1713), in colonial libraries by the 1740s, added judicial authority to the same message: the Commons, as the grand inquest of the nation, could impeach for illegal acts in the kingdom.[37] Absent from these accounts was the emphasis upon criminal procedures so evident in the Stuart

[37] For Giles Jacob, *A New Law-Dictionary* . . . , 5th ed. (London, 1744), see L. Kinvin Wroth and Hiller B. Zobel, "Editorial Note on the Case of Field *v.* Lambert," in L. H. Butterfield *et al.*, eds., *The Earliest Diary of John Adams* (Cambridge, Mass., 1966), 86, n. 15; Thomas Wood, *An Institute of the Laws of England* . . . , 7th ed. (London, 1745), 478; Matthew Hale, *The History of the Common Law of England*, ed. Charles M. Gray, Classics of British Historical Literature (Chicago, 1971), 35. On Rushworth and Selden see Hoffer and Hull, "First American Impeachments," *WMQ*, 3d Ser., XXXV (1978), 653-667.

parliamentary cases. The vital role which the Lords played in impeachment episodes, not only as a trial court but as the Commons' tutor on the law of impeachment, is nowhere apparent.

The colonists also witnessed a series of English impeachments during the period 1701-1715. These cases were highly political in origin and purpose, often ending, by design, not with trial in the Lords but with the accused's flight or loss of influence at court. The crimes of Somers in 1701 and of Oxford in 1715 amounted to no more than giving bad advice to the crown. This was often included in Stuart impeachment charges, but never without other, more substantial criminal allegations. Observations of these cases, coupled with the written accounts available, had the inevitable effect of
362 stressing the political rather than the quasi-criminal facets of impeachment in the minds of Americans. If one may credit later colonial commentators, the American student of English impeachment saw it as the highest form of political act: the defense of the public interest against private ambition, corruption, and blundering.[38]

The only extended colonial essays on the law of impeachment—a 1768 article in the *Boston Gazette* by Josiah Quincy, Jr., and John Adams's dinner table dissertation during the Oliver case—dwelt upon the elevated political duties of the lower house. Quincy, one of the leading legal authorities among the anti-Hutchinson faction, noted that "a short attention to the following extracts [from Rushworth and Selden] will convince every intelligent mind, that, while the first principles of our constitution . . . are adhered to, no subject . . . is beyond the reach of a strict examination into his conduct, or out of Danger of a scourge for his crimes." The remedy was simple: " 'A peer of the Realm may be impeached in Parliament,' " and so, by implication, might a malefactor in the colonial lower house. Adams, many years later, claimed that in 1773 he had suggested impeachment of the justices who accepted royal salaries. In his autobiography he recalled that he had dined with members of the General Court and "other gentlemen" during the salary crisis and agreed with them that royal payment "would be the Ruin of the Liberties of the Country." "I believed," Adams recalled, "there was one constitutional Resource . . . Several Voices at once cryed out, a constitutional Resource! what can it be? I said it was nothing more nor less than an Impeachment of the Judges by the House of Representatives before the Council. An Impeachment! Why such a thing is without Precedent. I believed it was in this Province: but there had been precedents enough, and by much too many in England."[39] Neither Quincy nor Adams discussed the

[38] Clayton Roberts, *The Growth of Responsible Government in Stuart England* (Cambridge, 1966), 308-315.

[39] The first colonial impeachment study was Josiah Quincy, Jr., *Boston Gazette*, Jan. 4, 1768, in Samuel H. Quincy, ed., *Reports of Cases . . . Superior Court of Judicature of the Province of Massachusetts Bay* . . . (Boston, 1861), Appendix IV,

criminal aspects of parliamentary impeachment: limitation of charges to illegal acts, prosecution and trial before the Lords, the power of the Lords to correct the Commons, or the imposition of criminal penalties. The two American commentators conferred upon the provincial lower houses the jurisdiction which the Commons had as the "grand inquest of the nation" over men in high places, without also requiring the entire panoply of English quasi-criminal procedures.

Quincy and Adams were, with or without full cognizance of the fact, merely reporting established American precedents.[40] While all charges made in eighteenth-century American cases had precedents in English cases, the former, unlike the latter, rarely led to criminal trials or penalties. Vetch and Dudley had been no less guilty of betraying the colony to its enemies than 363
Buckingham had England in 1626, but Dudley never faced trial and Vetch eluded punishment. Strafford had given no more "illegal" advice to Charles I than Logan had to Evans and Penn, but Logan kept his head. Chief Justice North faced impeachment in 1680 for impeding an election—no greater offense than Trott's. Trott, however, returned to South Carolina a free man.

580-584; and Butterfield *et al.*, eds., *Diary and Autobiography of Adams*, III, 298-302.

[40] Neither Adams nor Quincy cited any American colonial precedent to support their arguments. Were they unaware of any of the American cases? Hutchinson was wary of the Vetch precedent, and his work, published in the colony a year before Quincy's article, was supposedly closely read by the patriot faction in the General Court. It is unlikely that Quincy and Adams missed that earlier case. They may have elected to use English precedent because it was stronger or more convincing. Adams, it should be noted, did not mention to his dinner partners that Quincy had written about impeachment, nor did he add this fact to his recollection of the entire Oliver episode.

The General Court did mention impeachment at least once between the Vetch case and the Oliver episode. On January 18, 1732, the lower house addressed Gov. Jonathan Belcher: "The Representatives who raise the money [for the colonial treasury] and whose constituents pay it, have no sort of remedy [for misuse of funds] . . . for we cannot impeach, as is the usage of the House of Commons in such cases." The issue before the General Court was the governor's right to disperse colonial funds without their consent, and Belcher had urged lower house acquiescence in this with an explicit analogy to parliamentary practice. To reject this argument, the assembly had to show that the parallel failed, for it had not the power to prosecute wrongdoing in the executive. See Lawrence H. Leder, *Liberty and Authority: Early American Political Ideology, 1689-1763* (New York, 1976), 112-113. Laying this point to one side, one can see that the thrust of the General Court argument was entirely in the opposite direction—that the colonial lower house had the same higher duty as the Commons. The General Court, acting as a grand inquest, was charged by the people with preventing misuse of public funds. There was no need to claim the specific right of impeachment, because, as yet, there was no culprit and no crime. Demand for the abstract right of impeachment would have been bootless in these circumstances.

Smith and Moore were accused of corruption and of exceeding their powers as judges; Chief Justice William Scroggs faced similar charges in 1680, but, unlike the American defendants, would have suffered severely if proven guilty. Oliver had obeyed the orders of his king and was impeached, but never came to trial; for a similar violation of public trust the "ship money" justices were impeached, tried, and severely fined. Oliver suffered, too—not for his conviction on the charges but for his loyalism. As in the English cases, the American lower house went through the steps of bringing an indictment to the upper house, but the prosecutors of Logan and Moore knew that the Council had no power to try, the accusers of Vetch and his fellow sea captains were aware that the Council did not want to try, and the impeachers of Trott
364 had to create a new Council to finish the process.[41]

Even in extreme spasms of political factionalism, English parliaments stayed closer to the original criminal forms of impeachment than did their provincial counterparts. The Commons found some statutory or "constructive" basis for charges, but American lower houses, with the exception of the Vetch case, which according to the Massachusetts courts bill of 1696 should have gone to the superior court or an admiralty court in the first instance, did not require such statutory basis. The Commons impeached private citizens as well as officeholders; the American lower houses, again with the exception of the Vetch case, a transitional episode, concerned themselves only with officeholders. In the English cases, a criminal penalty resulted from conviction. In the American cases, with the Vetch exception, no criminal penalty was attached to the impeachable offenses, though the defendant might be imprisoned for a time during the crisis. Such differences between colonial and English practices as did occur were inadvertant results of local conditions and necessity in the seventeenth century. The earliest colonial lower houses tried to follow the letter of parliamentary practice, with all its quasi-criminal forms, although the Commons often deviated from this path. The persistence of these differences into the eighteenth-century colonial cases suggests a conscious desire to create a native impeachment tradition, proof of which lies in the American legislators' approach to the question of jurisdiction—that is, their right to impeach at all.[42]

In English law, only the Commons, sitting at Westminster, was the "grand inquest of the nation." The Commons alone, representing the colonies "virtually," had the power to impeach and prosecute abuses of public power. Colonial assemblies had not the jurisdiction over local affairs, much less over officers of the crown in colonial posts, that the Commons had in the

[41] Roberts, *Responsible Government in Stuart England,* 60-61, and *passim.*

[42] The essential criminal nature of the Stuart impeachments is made clear in Clayton Roberts, "The Law of Impeachment in Stuart England: A Reply to Raoul Berger," *Yale Law Journal,* LXXXIV (1975), 1419-1439.

realm. Seventeenth-century assemblies may have pleaded ignorance on this point, but their eighteenth-century counterparts could not do so. From the time of the Vetch case, whenever American impeachments came to the attention of the Privy Council, crown lawyers denied the assemblies the right to impeach anyone for anything. No document or decision—charter, regulation, act, or instruction—that imperial officials drafted gave any colony the right to impeach. Two statutory provisions for lower house impeachment, one in the Massachusetts judicial code before 1684 and the other in the Pennsylvania charter of 1682, escaped crown lawyers for a time, but both loopholes were closed by the turn of the century. It is not clear whether these provisions were ever meant to sanction impeachment like that of the Commons. "Impeachment" also had the more general meaning of "indictment," 365
which seventeenth-century colonial councils, doubling as high courts, might hear on appeal. Beyond the absence of specific grants of impeachment power to the assemblies, crown lawyers could raise a broader theoretical objection. The model of colonial charters, and hence of colonial government, was the English borough charter. It followed that the colonial legislatures had no more right to impeach royal officers than London's council had to impeach the lord chancellor.[43]

Crown officials noted that the correct alternative to impeachment in America was recourse to executive or judicial authority in England. Appeal, petition, remonstrance, and address to the crown, its Privy Council, or its administrative offices were all courses sanctioned in imperial usage and statute. The colonies lay in the king's domain, and removal and punishment of his officers could be effected through these channels. This argument formed the basis of Chief Justice Hutchinson's reply to Quincy's essay on impeachment. Hutchinson told a grand jury in 1768 that, in cases of official misconduct, "we must seek relief from Great Britain. If our Governor acts in an illegal Manner, we have a good King, and can easily have him removed. Upon a just complaint, we may have a Governor ordered to Westminster and there tried and punished." Hutchinson urged appeal to the king, instead of impeachment of the king's officers.[44]

[43] Smith, *Appeals to the Privy Council,* 4, and *passim.* For the Massachusetts law see *An Abridgement of the Laws in Force and Use in Her Majesty's Possessions* (London, 1704), "New England," 14. On Pennsylvania see "Penn's Charter of Liberties (1682)," in Francis Newton Thorpe, ed., *The Federal and State Constitutions, Colonial Charters, and Other Organic Laws . . . of the United States . . . ,* V (Washington, D.C., 1909), 3051. The meaning of impeachment in general (that is, as a synonym for indictment) is discussed in Clarke, *Parliamentary Privilege,* 39, and Henry Campbell Black, *Black's Law Dictionary . . . ,* 4th rev. ed. (St. Paul, Minn., 1968), 886.

[44] Thomas Hutchinson, "Charge to the Grand Jury, 3 Geo. III (1768)," in Quincy, ed., *Reports of Cases,* 267-268. The "normal" channels of removal or

The colonial reply to this argument, implicit in every impeachment episode and explicit in the Oliver case, was that, as Englishmen, gathered in representative bodies, the colonial legislators had all the rights of the Commons in Westminster. The argument reduced to a "belief in a fundamental correspondence," as Bernard Bailyn elucidates it, "between the English constitution and the separate colonial constitutions." John Adams assumed this fact when he argued, "But whence can We pretend to derive such a Power? From our Charter, which gives Us . . . all the Rights and Priviledges of Englishmen: and if the House of Commons in England is the grand Inquest of the Nation, the House of Representatives is the Grand Inquest of this Province." It was a natural assumption—the form and
366 language of American legislative process paralleling that of Parliament—and hardly novel or naive. In the first place, the American claim to the basic rights of English parliaments, to wit, to control their own affairs and to inquire into the safety of their constituents, was enunciated as early as the first meeting of the Virginia Burgesses and the first sessions of the Massachusetts General Court. In the second place, the colonists had before them the continuing English example, "the very definite and very bitter struggle . . . which parliament was simultaneously carrying on . . . against prerogative in England," to remind them of their rights. Impeachment leaders realized that it was this struggle against prerogative that, historically, had led Stuart parliaments to reassert their old right of impeachment. And even if the connection with the English constitution should fail, as it did in the final Revolutionary crisis, the lower houses could argue that their right to impeach inhered in the very nature of a popular representative government. Such a right need not be granted by imperial law or written in any charter. It was this right, apart from a specific grant of jurisdiction, that permitted colonial legislators to adopt parliamentary impeachment precedent.[45]

When one looks at the American cases in this light, one can see the departures from the English precedents as systematic—part of a larger pattern of the americanization of impeachment. The absence of the criminal process, criminal penalties, and criminal trial, though forced upon the lower houses by political circumstances, was turned to specific purpose. Impeach-

---

punishment for royal officers were very often used. See, for example, discussion in Bradley Chapin, *The American Law of Treason: Revolutionary and Early National Origins* (Seattle, Wash., 1964), 8, and *passim.*

[45] Bernard Bailyn, "The Origins of American Politics," *Perspectives in American History,* I (1967), 48; Butterfield *et al.*, eds., *Diary and Autobiography of Adams,* III, 300; Clarke, *Parliamentary Privilege,* 60. On early colonial assumptions about the rights of assemblies see Alden T. Vaughan, *American Genesis: Captain John Smith and the Founding of Virginia* (Boston, 1975), 117; and Richard S. Dunn, *Puritans and Yankees: The Winthrop Dynasty of New England* (New York, 1971), 24.

ment became a political check of the lower house upon the executive and judicial branches when no other, regular appeal sufficed. Colonial impeachments thus anticipated and, if one gives due weight to the Oliver case, helped to create the comprehensive system of checks and balances of the state constitutions. The imperial system did not permit the colonial lower houses such a check upon executive and judicial officers. The Revolutionary constitutions did. The eighteenth-century colonial impeachments were precedent for this.

The pattern of adoption and wording of impeachment provisions in the first state constitutions strongly suggest that the eighteenth-century precedents were remembered after 1776. Every state whose colonial legislature had attempted an impeachment in the preceding seventy-five years reiterated that 367
right in its constitution. The Massachusetts compact of 1780 termed impeachment "the grand inquest" of the people, and the Pennsylvania framers conferred on the assembly a power "to impeach criminals." North and South Carolina included similar statements in their constitutions. Only New York, Georgia, New Hampshire, and Delaware, among former colonies without an impeachment precedent, conferred it on the lower house during the Revolutionary era. New Hampshire and Delaware so perfectly copied the language of Massachusetts and Pennsylvania, respectively, as to suggest that they were drawing upon the experience of the latter. Among the states that had no eighteenth-century impeachment experience, Virginia, Maryland, and New Jersey did not mention this right, and Connecticut and Rhode Island added it only in the mid-nineteenth century. The earliest of these incorporations of impeachment law occurred sixty years after the last of the impeachments of Queen Anne's reign and ten years before the impeachment of Warren Hastings in Parliament. Whenever the state constitutions detailed the process, it was restricted to officeholders for nonspecific violations of public trust. Conviction in the upper house brought only loss of office, following the precedent of the colonial cases.[46]

What emerged from these cases, then, was an American impeachment tradition—a tradition embodied in Article 2, section 4, of the United States

[46] Thorpe, ed., *Federal and State Constitutions*, III, Art. V, 1899 (Mass.), V, Art. XI, 3085 (Pa.), and Art. IX, 2787 (N.C.), VI, Art. XI, 3253 (S.C.), V, Art. XXXII, 2635 (N.Y.), II, Art. III, 784 (Ga.), IV, Art. VI, 2462 (N.H.), I, Art. XXIII, 566 (Del.), I. Impeachment cases under these provisions soon occurred, to the authors' knowledge, in Massachusetts and South Carolina, both states with previous colonial impeachment experience. See Octavius Pickering and William Howard Gardiner, *Report of the Trial by Impeachment of James Prescott . . . with an Appendix of Previous Impeachments . . . in Massachusetts* (Boston, 1821), 212-219; and James W. Ely, Jr., "Judicial Impeachments and the Struggle for Democracy in South Carolina" (Paper delivered to the American Society of Legal History, Nov. 9, 1973), 3.

Constitution. It is true that the language used there is reminiscent of English terminology, and in the Constitutional Convention the framers cited only early Stuart cases and the contemporary case of Warren Hastings. One nevertheless ought to ask if, on the subject of impeachment law, the framers deserted their commitment to American political experience. Surely the Federalists must have had some notion of the American tradition, if only from the Oliver case. Would they return to imitation of the Commons' practice when a fully developed precedent existed in America? The colonial assemblies, one notes, also stayed close to English terminology, even as they struck out against the criminal steps at the heart of parliamentary practice. It is probable that the framers, like the colonial lower-house leaders, simply
368 gave their own meaning to the English terms. Evidence for this interpretation lies in Article 2, section 4, and in Article 1, section 3. The English impeachment cases which the framers cited were criminal proceedings, used against any powerful individual, ending in criminal punishment. The House of Lords was instrumental in the process, defining the law as well as trying the accused. By contrast, in Article 2, section 4, and Article 1, section 3, the proceeding was political; it was restricted to officeholders and ended only with removal from office. Article 1, section 2, implied that the Senate, unlike the Lords of England, was to leave matters of legal definition to the initiative of the House. The differences between the English precedents of 1621-1715 and the Federal Constitution had origins in the eighteenth-century colonial cases.[47]

One may propose a number of reasons why the framers cited English rather than American impeachment precedents. Strong Federalists, committed to the new national government, may not have wished to elevate colonial precedents to the level of federal law. The use of local precedents might also have strengthened the hands of the direct inheritors of colonial government, the Antifederalists in the state governments. Instead, the architects of Article 2, section 4 compared the federal system to the most stable and powerful of its predecessors. English precedents had an aura of authority that colonial precedent did not. At the same time, the colonial episodes may have been so well known that reference to them was unnecessary. Certainly, the political circumstances in which the last of them took place were well understood. The framers may have wished to convey a less partisan and turbulent message to ratifiers of the Constitution, in effect to play down the manifestly political purpose of Article 2, section 4. One sees this in the *Federalist Papers*' stress on the gravity and impartiality of a trial in the

[47] See Gordon S. Wood, *The Creation of the American Republic, 1776-1787* (New York, 1972), 261, 555, on the American views of the British constitution in the months preceding the Philadelphia convention and during ratification.

Senate, a shield against the "political animosities" which Alexander Hamilton admitted every impeachment expressed.[48]

In the early 1800s the Jeffersonian Republicans attempted to apply the eighteenth-century American impeachment precedents to their contest with the Federalist judiciary. Their doctrine that impeachment was a purely political step, a check the Congress had upon the other branches, logically emerged from the colonial practice. The accused had to be guilty of misuse of power, corruption, or incompetence, though not necessarily of a statutory or criminal offense. Impeachable offenses, in this view, could be, but did not have to be, indictable in a court. Jefferson and his party were merely applying the doctrine of the Oliver case.[49]

In the years since the failure of the Jeffersonian impeachment of Justice 369
Samuel Chase the colonial tradition has faded from view. But these precedents should not be forgotten, if only for the part impeachment played in the Revolution. Impeachment conferred great power upon the representatives of the people in the lower houses of the legislature to check abuse of power in other branches of government. The legacy of those cases is not that impeachment may be undertaken frivolously, through malice only, or to gain a partisan advantage, but that when abuse of power does not fall into recognizably criminal categories, the lower house may still bring impeachment. The Revolutionaries well knew that power corrupts and that power in high places may corrupt an entire government. For the framers of the Constitution, impeachment was one remedy for this danger.

[48] See James Madison, *The Journal of the Debates in the Convention . . . May-September, 1787*, ed. Gaillard Hunt, II (New York, 1908), 15-16, 335-338; and Edward M. Earle, ed., *The Federalist Papers* (New York, 1938), No. 65, 423-427.

[49] Richard E. Ellis, *The Jeffersonian Crisis: Courts and Politics in the Young Republic* (New York, 1974), 75.

Church Adherence in the Eighteenth-Century British American Colonies

Patricia U. Bonomi and Peter R. Eisenstadt

"TIS natural," wrote William Byrd II in 1728, "for helpless man to adore his Maker in some form or other." Byrd had made the disturbing discovery that many North Carolina Anglicans, finding themselves destitute of ministers and the comforts of their own liturgy, were converting to Quakerism, and he concluded that "people uninstructed in any religion are ready to embrace the first that offers."[1] Byrd's assumption that religious sentiments should be nurtured within the framework of an organized church or sect reflected the world as he knew it, for it was the exceptional person in any colony who deliberately stood apart from the fellowship of a religious community.

The evidence is ample and widespread. Pennsylvania churches in the early eighteenth century were crowded with "hearers that . . . constantly attend Divine Service," some of whom had to ride twenty miles to worship; Congregational church foundings increased sharply in New England after the turn of the century; and in a 1710 account from a North Carolina parish a minister noted "one Quaker, and five or six of no professed religion; the rest all join with me in our [Anglican] Church service."[2] The colonists continued to support their religious institutions in the decades that followed. From 1700 to 1780 the number of churches in

Patricia U. Bonomi is a member of the Department of History at New York University. Peter R. Eisenstadt is a doctoral candidate at New York University. An earlier version of this essay was presented in March 1980 to Michael Zuckerman's Philadelphia Area Group for Colonial Studies.

[1] William Byrd, *History of the Dividing Line betwixt Virginia and North Carolina Run in the Year of Our Lord 1728*, in Louis B. Wright, ed., *The Prose Works of William Byrd of Westover* (Cambridge, Mass., 1966), 193.

[2] David Humphreys, *An Historical Account of the Incorporated Society for the Propagation of the Gospel in Foreign Parts . . .* (London, 1730), 178; Harold Field Worthley, *An Inventory of the Records of the Particular (Congregational) Churches of Massachusetts, Gathered 1620–1805*, Harvard Theological Studies, XXV (Cambridge, Mass., 1970); Edwin Scott Gaustad, *Historical Atlas of Religion in America*, rev. ed. (New York, 1976), 15; James Adams to the Secretary, Mar. 27, 1710, in William L. Saunders, ed., *The Colonial Records of North Carolina*, I (Raleigh, N.C., 1886), 722.

seven of the largest Protestant denominations increased over sevenfold,[3] while the overall rate of congregation building rose in closer ratio to population growth than is commonly supposed.[4]

It is curious, in light of such indications of robust growth, that the traditional view of eighteenth-century American church life has emphasized lassitude and indifference. The conventional wisdom holds that within a few decades after first settlement, religious fervor began a decline that continued until the Great Awakening. The tumult of the Awakening, according to this view, revived religious feeling, but before long Americans were resuming their former unconcern. Thus in eighteenth-century New England, the section generally acknowledged to have been the most devout, at best one person in five is supposed to have been a church member; in the Middle Colonies the ratio dropped to one in fifteen; and 371
in the southern colonies hardly one person in twenty is thought to have belonged to any church. Provincial America, so it would appear, had come to contain "a greater proportion of unchurched in the population than existed in any other country in Christendom."[5]

This view of eighteenth-century religious culture—which pervades the literature—is based on a number of factors: the absence of an established church in nearly half the colonies, confusion created by the babel of competing sects, the dispersal of population across an expanding frontier, the growth of rationalism and materialism, and the paucity of trained

[3] Gaustad (*Atlas*, 3-4) defines a church as any autonomous congregation, whether meeting at a church, chapel, mission, or regular preaching place (*ibid.*, x; see also n. 119). The seven denominations are the Anglican, Baptist, Congregational, Dutch Reformed, German Reformed, Lutheran, and Presbyterian. Missing from the list is the Society of Friends (which by 1750 was about level with the Lutherans and Baptists in number of churches [*ibid.*, 26]), because Gaustad does not include any of the sects in his charts.

[4] White population increased 888% between 1700 and 1780. According to Gaustad, the number of churches (including the Roman Catholic but not the Quakers, Mennonites, or other pietistic sects) rose from 373 to 2,731, or 632%, during the same interval. U.S. Bureau of the Census, *Historical Statistics of the United States, Colonial Times to 1970* (Washington, D.C., 1975), Pt. 2, 1168; Gaustad, *Atlas*, 3-4. Using Charles O. Paullin's figure of 3,228 churches in 1775-1776 (which includes the Quakers and other sects), we determine that congregation building rose 765% between 1700 and the Revolution (*Atlas of the Historical Geography of the United States*, ed. John K. Wright [Washington, D.C., 1932], 49-50).

[5] Most commonly quoted for this view are W. W. Sweet, "The American Colonial Environment and Religious Liberty," *Church History*, IV (1935), 43-56; Sidney E. Mead, "From Coercion to Persuasion: Another Look at the Rise of Religious Liberty and the Emergence of Denominationalism," *ibid.*, XXV (1956), 317-337, quotation on p. 329; and Clinton Rossiter, *Seedtime of the Republic: The Origin of the American Tradition of Political Liberty* (New York, 1953), 36-43—all of whose estimates are conjectural. For more recent versions see Richard Hofstadter, *America at 1750: A Social Portrait* (New York, 1971), xv-xvi, 181-182, and Jon Butler, "Magic, Astrology, and the Early American Religious Heritage, 1600-1760," *American Historical Review*, LXXXIV (1979), 317-318.

ministers. Further evidence of decline is drawn from the clergy's own testimony, not only from the jeremiads of New England divines but from critical observations of the southern and middle colonies as well. Anglican ministers arriving in the early eighteenth century were shocked by the "indifferency, carelessness, [and] unconcernedness" of Maryland worshippers, and by Virginia parishioners who were "wofully ignorant" of basic doctrine.[6] Gottlieb Mittelberger remarked that Pennsylvania clergymen were hired by the year, "like cowherds in Germany," making that colony "hell for . . . preachers." New Light ministers repeatedly charged that before the Great Awakening religion was "dying, and ready to expire." And J. Hector St. John Crèvecoeur observed that whatever religious belief the colonists retained after exposure to America's "strange religious
372 medley" tended to evaporate "in the great distance it has to travel" on the frontier.[7]

Such comments indicate that religious life in the colonies was disconcertingly unstable, but it is not at all clear that large numbers of Americans responded by rejecting the institutional church. True, one finds many reports of religious "indifference," but in the eighteenth century this usually meant religious impartiality, or a blindness to the fine points of doctrine that differentiated one denomination from another. Thus a South Carolina Anglican reported in 1728 that his parishioners were "true blue Protestants of the modern Stamp, or Latitudinarian in Protestantism . . . and do not imagine much real difference in Principle 'twixt Churchmen & Dissenters of all Denominations." And a group of Lutheran ministers, noting in 1760 that their parishioners lived among and intermarried with members of various sects, warned that "a dangerous indifferentism is easily occasioned; therefore it is necessary at times to point out the differences, as otherwise the suspicion of indifference may also fall upon the preacher."[8] But it was the absence of doctrinal rigor that was being deplored, not religious apathy.[9] Furthermore, many of the severest critics

[6] Bernard C. Steiner, ed., *Rev. Thomas Bray: His Life and Selected Works Relating to Maryland* (Baltimore, 1901), 139; John Lang to the bishop of London, Feb. 7, 1726, Fulham Papers, XI, 97-98, Lambeth Palace Library, London (World Microfilm Publications).

[7] Mittelberger, *Journey to Pennsylvania*, ed. Oscar Handlin and John Clive (Cambridge, Mass., 1960), 47-48; Joseph Tracy, *The Great Awakening: A History of the Revival of Religion in the Time of Edwards and Whitefield* (Boston, 1841), 20, 26; Crèvecoeur, *Letters from an American Farmer* (New York, 1904 [orig. publ. London, 1782]), 65-66.

[8] Mr. Hunt to the Secretary, May 6, 1728, Records of the Society for the Propagation of the Gospel in Foreign Parts, Letterbooks Series A, XXI, 97-104, London (Micro Methods, Ltd.); *Oxford English Dictionary*, s.v. "indifference." The Lutheran ministers are quoted in Stephanie Grauman Wolf, *Urban Village: Population, Community, and Family Structure in Germantown, Pennsylvania, 1683-1800* (Princeton, N.J., 1976), 242.

[9] Crèvecoeur found that in America "all sects are mixed as well as all nations; thus religious indifference is imperceptibly disseminated from one end of the continent to the other" (*Letters from an American Farmer*, 61-66, quotation on p. 66).

were either newcomers or sojourners who inevitably compared the colonial churches with their parent institutions at home. The same newly arrived Anglican ministers who disapproved of the low church preferences of Americans were relieved to discover that "many Thousands" were nonetheless "very Zealous for our Holy Church" and "in a happy Disposition to embrace" it.[10] The Lutheran minister Henry Melchior Muhlenberg had been in Pennsylvania but a short time before he came to see that "European standards . . . do not always fit the complicated conditions in America." Pastors who could adjust to American ways—as Muhlenberg and a host of others learned to do—soon wished that they could "divide . . . [themselves] in pieces" the better to serve their rapidly proliferating congregations.[11]

The slightest shift of perspective will reveal other aspects of provincial 373
culture that support a far more positive impression of the place religion occupied in the lives of eighteenth-century Americans. One thinks of the congregations that gathered spontaneously for informal services before ministers became available to serve them or of the passion that New Englanders invested in squabbles about psalm singing or the location of churches. And though denominational pluralism may have confused some colonials, such diversity also promoted competition and sharpened loyalties. As for apathy on the frontier, we know that many backcountry settlements were clannish enclaves of immigrant coreligionists who promptly reconstituted their churches in the wilderness.[12] Finally, when New Light preachers described religion in pre-Awakening America as dead or dying, they meant that the churches were dead by *their* definition; that is, dead to the central importance of the conversion experience. Even George Whitefield acknowledged that American churches were "externally" active.[13]

Our purpose in this essay is to reconsider the question of church adherence in the eighteenth-century mainland colonies. Several aspects of the question will be explored. We will first reexamine the standard generally used by historians to determine whether a colonist was "churched," and propose a new definition that is more in harmony with eighteenth-century practices. Using this definition we will then estimate the percentage of adherents in a number of Anglican parishes in 1724,

[10] Steiner, ed., *Life and Works of Bray,* 159; Lang to the bishop of London, Feb. 7, 1726, Fulham Papers, XI, 97-98 (microfilm).

[11] Muhlenberg, *The Journals of Henry Melchior Muhlenberg,* trans. Theodore G. Tappert and John W. Doberstein (Philadelphia, 1942), I, 249, 235.

[12] On congregation formation see Presbytery of Donegal Minutes, 1732-1752, Vols. I, II, Presbyterian Historical Society, Philadelphia. New England squabbles are discussed in Ola Elizabeth Winslow, *Meetinghouse Hill, 1630-1783* (New York, 1952), chaps. 7, 10. Regarding pluralism and the frontier consult Carl Bridenbaugh, *Myths & Realities: Societies of the Colonial South* (Baton Rouge, La., 1952), 178-181, and Timothy L. Smith, "Congregation, State, and Denomination: The Forming of the American Religious Structure," *William and Mary Quarterly,* 3d Ser., XXV (1968), 155-176.

[13] Tracy, *Great Awakening,* 104-105.

drawing on responses to a questionnaire, or church census, that was initiated by the bishop of London. This census—to our knowledge the only systematic survey of church adherence in eighteenth-century America—provides information on all sections of the colonies, though by far the largest number of responses came from the southern provinces where the Church of England was established. Since the South has been described by colonists and historians alike as the least churched section,[14] and since religious apathy was most pronounced—according to the traditional view—in the two or three decades preceding the Great Awakening, the 1724 survey provides a unique opportunity to test church affiliation at a time and place in which it was allegedly at low ebb. Following this, we will
374 discuss the effect of the frontier on religious life and examine churchgoing in the Middle Colonies and New England. Finally, we will offer some general estimates of church adherence in the colonies from 1700 to the Revolution.

Much of the confusion about church adherence stems from the common assumption that only those who had participated in a formal rite of admission were considered to be "churched." Yet churches did not hold to a single standard for identifying adherents in the eighteenth century any more than they do today. Then, as now, membership was defined so differently—in some instances reflecting passage through a formal program of catechization and induction, in others including all who were baptized or attended church regularly—as to deny the term a common usage.[15] Nor can adherence be determined by counting communicants, since procedures governing admission to the sacrament of the Lord's Supper also varied widely.[16] A number of churches modified their practices over time, as rigid standards and categories proved difficult to maintain in the fluid New World environment.

The best-documented example is that of the Congregational churches, which initially imposed a strict test for admission. After the adoption of the half-way covenant by the synod of 1662, many congregations continued to resist the inclusion of baptized but unconverted persons. This slowed the growth of some churches, but in others the number of full communicants increased steadily.[17] By the 1680s the barriers to half-way

[14] As William Smith, Jr., of New York observed in 1757: "In matters of religion we are not so intelligent, in general, as the inhabitants of the New-England colonies; but both in this respect and good morals, we certainly have the advantage of the southern provinces" (*The History of the Province of New-York*, ed. Michael Kammen, I [Cambridge, Mass., 1972], 244).

[15] Leo Rosten, ed., *Religions of America . . . A New Guide and Almanac* (New York, 1975), esp. chap. 12.

[16] The term "communicant" may in some cases, however, identify the more orthodox churchgoers.

[17] Robert G. Pope, *The Half-Way Covenant: Church Membership in Puritan New England* (Princeton, N.J., 1969); Ross W. Beales, Jr., "The Half-Way Covenant and Religious Scrupulosity: The First Church of Dorchester, Massachusetts, as a

membership were rapidly breaking down, and a few ministers even welcomed to the Lord's Supper all who wished to partake. Another late seventeenth-century innovation was mass renewal of the baptismal covenant, in which entire congregations, adults and children alike, were "required to stand and renew" their pledges of faith. After 1690 some clergymen also encouraged townspeople with no formal church connection to participate in these renewals, which then qualified them for half-way membership.[18] In some towns, extension of the covenant meant that "virtually no member of the rising generation would be excluded from the benefits of both church discipline and the preaching of the gospel."[19] Perhaps this explains why that inveterate quantifier, Ezra Stiles, when computing New England church membership in 1760, simply subtracted an estimate of dissenters from the total population and came up with the
figure of 445,000 Congregationalists.[20]

Presbyterians defined their communion more flexibly than did Congregationalists. Ministers and elders briefly examined a prospective member's faith and life, but the church's embrace tended to be inclusive. Most congregants participated in the Lord's Supper.[21] Nor did the New Side evangelists narrow membership by insisting on proof of conversion before granting admission to church or sacrament. All who considered themselves ready to participate were encouraged to do so, and only the "flagrantly unworthy" were barred.[22]

A similar latitude characterized the Lutheran church during the mid-century years of rapid expansion under Muhlenberg. Though Muhlenberg would have preferred that adherents undergo a formal test, he had to be content with their understanding "the most necessary things in outline" before making a public profession of faith, and he found it hard to refuse the sacrament of communion when people "yearningly request[ed] it."

Test Case," *WMQ*, 3d Ser. XXXI (1974), 465-480. In Milford, Conn., where the half-way covenant was not adopted until 1730, approximately 46% of the male inhabitants and an even higher percentage of the women were nonetheless full communicants of the church at the end of the 17th century; a low point had been reached in 1669, when but 36% of the adult males were in full communion (Gerald F. Moran, "Religious Renewal, Puritan Tribalism, and the Family in Seventeenth-Century Milford, Connecticut," *ibid.*, XXXVI [1979], 245-246).

[18] Perry Miller, *The New England Mind: From Colony to Province* (Cambridge, Mass., 1953), 112-118. See also Paul R. Lucas, *Valley of Discord: Church and Society along the Connecticut River, 1636-1725* (Hanover, N.H., 1976), 232, 242, and Pope, *Half-Way Covenant*, 246. The Great Awakening was in part a protest against such practices, but once set in motion they proved difficult to rescind.

[19] Beales, "Half-Way Covenant," *WMQ*, 3d Ser., XXXI (1974), 480.

[20] Franklin Bowditch Dexter, ed., *Extracts from the Itineraries and Other Miscellanies of Ezra Stiles* . . . (New Haven, Conn., 1916), 92-93, hereafter cited as *Stiles Itineraries*.

[21] Leonard J. Trinterud, *The Forming of an American Tradition: A Re-examination of Colonial Presbyterianism* (Philadelphia, 1949), 17-19.

[22] Gilbert Tennent, *The Duty of Self-Examination* . . . (Boston, 1739); Trinterud, *Forming of an American Tradition*, 181-182.

Practices in the German and Dutch Reformed churches were much the same.[23] The Society of Friends in America required neither a relation of spiritual "convincement" nor adherence to a formal creed from candidates for membership. When George Keith attempted to impose both tests in 1690, arguing that meetings ought "first to prove Men before they own them as fellow members of Christ's body," the effort was firmly rejected. By the late seventeenth century, birthright membership was automatically granted to all Quaker children.[24] To be sure, a departure from Quaker principles might cause a member to be disciplined or even disowned, but all those who attended meeting regularly were considered members in good standing.[25]

Even the Baptists, though more doctrinaire than most other churches
376 regarding membership, were inconsistent about enforcing standards. The separate Baptists usually required applicants to relate their conversion experiences and gain approval from the body of members before baptism and affiliation were granted.[26] But the regular Baptist congregations were often of "mixed communion"—that is, they included some who had received infant baptism only or had not undergone a full test of faith by the church.[27]

[23] Muhlenberg, *Journals*, trans. Tappert and Doberstein, I, 194-195, 118, 157. The German Reformed leader, Michael Schlatter, tried to hold a preparatory service before each communion, but this proved difficult. Schlatter recorded one instance when he preached to a "congregation" of 600, of whom 500 were "members" and 100 took communion. *The Journal of Rev. Michael Schlatter*, in Henry Harbaugh, *The Life of Rev. Michael Schlatter* (Philadelphia, 1857), 154-155, 158, hereafter cited as *Schlatter's Journal*. Theodore Frelinghuysen reserved communion for those who had experienced saving grace, but most of his Dutch Reformed colleagues found this practice too harsh (James Tanis, *Dutch Calvinistic Pietism in the Middle Colonies: A Study in the Life and Theology of Theodorus Jacobus Frelinghuysen* [The Hague, 1967], 136, 143-149).

[24] Jon Butler, "'Gospel Order Improved': The Keithian Schism and the Exercise of Quaker Ministerial Authority in Pennsylvania," *WMQ*, 3d Ser., XXXI (1974), 438; J. William Frost, *The Quaker Family in Colonial America: A Portrait of the Society of Friends* (New York, 1973), 68-69, 89.

[25] Richard Bauman, *For the Reputation of Truth: Politics, Religion, and Conflict among the Pennsylvania Quakers, 1750-1800* (Baltimore, 1971), 36-37; Rufus M. Jones, *The Quakers in the American Colonies* (New York, 1966 [orig. publ. London, 1911]), 449-450, 551-552; Frost, *Quaker Family*, 54-57.

[26] Robert B. Semple, *A History of the Rise and Progress of the Baptists in Virginia*, ed. G. W. Beale (Philadelphia, 1894), 72, 274; C. C. Goen, *Revivalism and Separatism in New England, 1740-1800: Strict Congregationalists and Separate Baptists in the Great Awakening* (New Haven, Conn., 1962), 159-164.

[27] Goen, *Revivalism and Separatism*, 258-264. Disagreements between separate and regular Baptists in Virginia were finally resolved by allowing each church to decide its own policy on "covenanting" (Semple, *History of the Baptists*, ed. Beale, 72). In New England mixed or "open" communion declined after 1754 when all Baptist factions united around the doctrine of adult baptism as the central practice that differentiated them from the Congregationalists (William G. McLoughlin, *New England Dissent, 1630-1833: The Baptists and the Separation of Church and State* [Cambridge, Mass., 1971], I, 305-311, 424-439, 447-453).

If the community of Anglicans had been strictly defined, the church would indeed have been reduced to a shadow, since only a bishop could confirm new members and no bishop ever set foot in the colonies. The colonists were thus "absolutely deprived of Confirmation for all their Youth."[28] Yet provincial ministers and schoolmasters continued to teach the catechism, and when young people attained sufficient knowledge to satisfy their ministers, they apparently made a confession of faith and were admitted to communion. The lack of official confirmation kept some Anglicans from the communion table out of "fear or ignorance," and it may have contributed to the low church tendency of American Anglicanism. One minister reported, for example, that "in some parishes where the people have been used to receive the communion in their seats (a custom introduced for . . . such as are inclined to Presbytery . . .) it is not an easy 377
matter to bring them to the Lord's Table decently upon their knees." Thus had sacramental practice, as well as membership standards, been shaped to suit "the conveniency and nature" of the colonists.[29]

The widely variant but usually nonexclusive ways in which the churches defined their constituencies suggest that to classify as churched only those who were communicants or formal members, however defined, would eliminate many whom the clergy themselves counted as faithful adherents. Perhaps only for the Congregational churches, where membership lists were often kept by ministers, is membership, in the strict sense, even quantifiable.[30] A more meaningful measure, and one that comports with

[28] "Some Considerations humbly offered by Thomas [Sherlock] Bishop of London relating to Ecclesiastical Government in his Majesty's Dominions in America," [1749?], Papers of the SPG, Lambeth Palace Library, X, 120-135, London (World Microfilm Publications).

[29] Hugh Jones, *The Present State of Virginia . . .*, ed. Richard L. Morton (Chapel Hill, N.C., 1956), 97-98, 95; Francis LeJau, *The Carolina Chronicle of Dr. Francis LeJau, 1706-1717*, ed. Frank J. Klingberg (Berkeley, Calif., 1956), 150.

[30] Several other denominations attempted to list members, but record keeping was haphazard and lists often include only church officers or heads of families. See *Schlatter's Journal*, 170, 189, and William J. Hinke, ed., "Church Records of the New Goshenhoppen Reformed Congregation . . . Pennsylvania," Pennsylvania German Society, *Proceedings and Annual Report*, XXVIII (1917), 274-277. The Baptists, and especially the record-conscious Quakers, kept some membership lists. See Phebe R. Jacobsen, *Quaker Records in Maryland*, The Hall of Records Commission, State of Maryland, XIV (Annapolis, Md., 1966), and McLoughlin, *New England Dissent*, II, 1285-1287. The best records were kept by the Congregational churches. See Edward M. Cook, Jr., *The Fathers of the Towns: Leadership and Community Structure in Eighteenth-Century New England*, Johns Hopkins University Studies in Historical and Political Science, XCIV (Baltimore, 1976), 119, 121, 226, n. 2. Few, however, compare with the detailed membership lists (1673-1741) maintained by the Mathers and their successors at Boston's Second Church (Manuscript Records of the Second Church [Boston], Massachusetts Historical Society). (We thank Kenneth Silverman for sharing his microfilms of the Second Church records with us.) Where such records exist they repay study, but since the information varies greatly from denomination to denomination, and comprehen-

the ministers' interchangeable use of the terms *member, adherent, parishioner,* and *auditor,* is regular church attendance. The validity of attendance as an index of church adherence will become apparent as we take a closer look at the Anglican survey of 1724.

In 1724 the bishop of London sent a list of "Queries" to the ministers of every Anglican parish in the English colonies. In this survey—a substitute for diocesan visitation—the bishop asked, among others, three key sets of questions: (1) "Of what Extent is your Parish, and how many Families are there in it?" (2) "How oft is divine Service performed in your Church? And what Proportion of the Parishioners attend it?" (3) "How oft is the Sacrament of the Lord's Supper administered? And what is the usual
378 Number of Communicants?" At least eighty responses were received from the mainland colonies, with the most complete series of sixty answers coming from Virginia, Maryland, and South Carolina.[31] The responses lack a uniform style, and some do not answer all the questions completely (see Appendix). But despite their shortcomings, the answers provide the most detailed picture we have of participation in the colonial Anglican church before the Great Awakening. Historians have made occasional use of the responses, especially those from Virginia, but have never examined them systematically for information about adherence.[32]

The written questionnaire addressed directly to parish priests was an innovation of the eighteenth century begun by Bishop Wake of Lincolnshire in 1706. Almost every query sent to parishes in England asked for a report on the number of communicants, a significant gauge of piety in the

---

sive lists are extremely rare outside New England, they do not offer sufficient data for a colonies-wide analysis of membership, even if the term could be given a common meaning.

[31] For the printed Queries see the 80 responses in the Fulham Papers. World Microfilms Publications includes the following responses: Connecticut, I, 209; Delaware [Pennsylvania], II, 7-8; Maryland, III, 48-71; Massachusetts, IV, 150-152; Rhode Island, VIII, 188-191; South Carolina, IX, 160-171; Virginia, XII, 41-84. The seven New York responses have recently been microfilmed for Vol. LXI. For New Jersey and Pennsylvania see Library of Congress Transcripts, Great Britain, Fulham Palace Manuscripts, New York, New Jersey, Rhode Island, New Hampshire, 171-173, and Pennsylvania, 59. Some responses have been printed, with a few errors, in William Stevens Perry, ed., *Historical Collections Relating to the American Colonial Church* (Hartford, Conn., 1870), as follows: Virginia, I, 261-334; Massachusetts, III, 147-152; Maryland, IV, 190-223. The West Indian replies (Barbados, XV, 201-214; Jamaica, XVII, 211-235; Leeward Islands, XIX, 116-120, Fulham Papers [microfilm]), not analyzed here, indicate substantially lower Anglican adherence in the islands than in the southern mainland colonies.

[32] The fullest analysis is George M. Brydon, *Virginia's Mother Church and the Political Conditions Under Which It Grew*, I (Richmond, Va., 1947), 361-395. See also Nelson Waite Rightmyer, *Maryland's Established Church* (Baltimore, 1956), 72-74, and Richard Beale Davis, *Intellectual Life in the Colonial South, 1585-1763* (Knoxville, Tenn., 1978), II, 672-673.

mother country where bishops were present to confirm new members.[33] But only in the colonial query of 1724 was the question on attendance asked, apparently because the bishop recognized that the number of communicants alone would provide an inadequate measure of church strength in the colonies.

Looking first at the responses from the southern parishes, we can extract meaningful data despite variations in reporting style, once certain standard definitions have been established. The number of families reported was based on censuses and the official county list of tithables, the latter being constructed from vital statistics registered by the parish clerk.[34] We cannot know for certain how attendance estimates were reached, but eighteenth-century ministers, like those of today, must have had a good idea of how many people their churches would hold.[35] The responses indicate that they reported only adult churchgoers, aged sixteen and above. Small children usually did not go to church, and older youths went mainly during the Lenten season for catechization.[36] Some slaves and indentured servants attended, but nothing suggests that their numbers were significant.[37] The typical pattern of early Maryland churchgoing was

[33] For a discussion of the visitation tradition, with copies of queries circulated to English parishes in the early 18th century, see Lincoln Record Society, *Publications*, IV (1913), Pt. I, and Norman Sykes, *Church and State in the XVIIIth Century* (New York, 1975), 137-139.

[34] Jones, *Present State of Virginia*, ed. Morton, 96.

[35] Many Virginia churches and chapels were 60′ × 30′ or larger by the 1720s; with galleries added and single pews made double, they could seat several hundred people. A Gloucester County church raised in 1723 measured 74′ × 34′; Christ Church in Lancaster County, built in 1732, was 70′ × 70′. Bruton Parish Church, built in 1715 and somewhat enlarged in 1752, seats nearly 500. George Carrington Mason, "The Colonial Churches of Christ Church Parish, Middlesex County, Virginia," *WMQ*, 2d Ser., XIX (1939), 8-24, and "The Colonial Churches of Gloucester County, Virginia," *ibid.*, 325-346; Davis, *Intellectual Life in the Colonial South*, III, 1174-1176. Maryland churches were often 40′ or 50′ × 25′ and larger, and South Carolina churches, sometimes constructed of brick by the 1720s, were the same. William Hand Browne *et al.*, eds., *Proceedings and Acts of the General Assembly* (*Archives of Maryland*, I-LXXII [Baltimore, 1883-1972]), LIX, LXI, hereafter cited as *Md. Archs.*; SPG Records, Letterbooks Series A, XX, 98-104, 110-115 (microfilm).

[36] See the reports from Portobacco and Durham Parish and St. Michael's Parish, Maryland, and from Henrico Parish, Virginia, and *passim*, Fulham Papers.

[37] The 1724 reports describe ministers' attempts to catechize and convert slaves. Masters in South Carolina and Virginia frequently refused to support these efforts; Maryland masters seemed more willing to send their slaves for instruction. See also Peter H. Wood, *Black Majority: Negroes in Colonial South Carolira from 1670 through the Stono Rebellion* (New York, 1974), 133-142; Brydon, *Virginia's Mother Church*, I, 392-403; and Albert J. Raboteau, *Slave Religion: The "Invisible Institution" in the Antebellum South* (New York, 1978), chap. 3. In what was apparently a typical pattern, John Harrower, an indentured servant and tutor on a Virginia plantation, attended church only 14% of the time. More than once he stayed at

recalled by Thomas Bray in 1723: "I found the Good People, Masters and Heads of Families (Servants & Children, God help them, must remain at Home) Ride Fifteen Miles on the Sunday Morning to Church."[38] If we posit a mean family size of six persons in Maryland and Virginia and five in South Carolina, and assume that about half of the family members were adults,[39] we arrive at a figure of three churchgoers per family in Maryland and Virginia and 2.5 per family in South Carolina. Eighteenth-century Anglican ministers counted two to three persons in each family church party.[40]

Because the ministers reported not only Anglican but all white families resident in their parishes, corrections must be made for the sizable number of dissenters in some areas. Virginia was the most uniformly
380 Anglican colony in 1724, though the parishes of Lawnes Creek, Henrico, Southwark, and Upper Parish (Isle of Wight) contained some Quaker families. The only Baptist congregation in Virginia before 1743 was also located in Upper Parish, which may in part account for the exceptionally low Anglican attendance reported there in 1724.[41] Because dissenters

---

home "because I hade no saddle to go to the Church with"; at other times he was "teaching Brooks," his charge (Edward Miles Riley, ed., *The Journal of John Harrower: An Indentured Servant in the Colony of Virginia, 1773-1776* [Williamsburg, Va., 1963], 79, 62-63).

[38] Bray to the bishop of London, Oct. 28, 1723, Fulham Papers, XXXVI, 50-53.

[39] A standard estimate of colonial family size is six (Evarts B. Greene and Virginia D. Harrington, *American Population before the Federal Census of 1790* [New York, 1932], xxiii). Robert V. Wells finds 5.9 whites per family in Maryland in 1704 (*The Population of the British Colonies in America before 1776: A Survey of Census Data* [Princeton, N.J., 1975], 156-157). An analysis of the 1790 census provides the following estimates of family size: South Carolina, 5.42; North Carolina, 5.6; Maryland, 6.04 (Philip J. Greven, Jr., "The Average Size of Families and Households in the Province of Massachusetts in 1764 and in the United States in 1790: An Overview," in Peter Laslett, ed., *Household and Family in Past Time* [London, 1972], 552). For five as the standard figure in South Carolina, see Wood, *Black Majority*, 147. Detailed white population counts in several South Carolina parishes in the 1720s show between four and five members per family (see n. 44). According to a 1726 enumeration of families in St. George's Parish, South Carolina, approximately half of the family members were under age 16 (SPG Records, Letterbooks Series A, XIX, 104-108 [microfilm]). Wells finds around 47% under 16 in early 18th-century Maryland and approximately 42% in South Carolina in 1708 (*Population before 1776*, 152, 168).

[40] Ministers typically counted "three to a Family to attend Divine Worship" (Mr. Ross, New Castle, Pa., History of His Church, Mar. 1, 1724, SPG Records, Letterbooks Series A, XX, 162, United SPG Archives, London). For the Rev. Charles Woodmason's count of two or three members per family party see Richard J. Hooker, ed., *The Carolina Backcountry on the Eve of the Revolution: The Journal and Other Writings of Charles Woodmason, Anglican Itinerant* (Chapel Hill, N.C., 1953), 26. (Ezra Stiles found somewhat larger church parties—between 3.7 and 4.1 persons per Anglican family—in New England [*Stiles Itineraries*, 32-33, 69].)

[41] In an extended reply to the 1724 questionnaire, the Rev. Alexander Forbes noted, "We have sundry Dissenters . . . Anabaptists and Quakers, and also others

were a tiny minority at that time, however, no corrections have been made in our computations for Virginia. Catholics and Protestant dissenters represented a significant element in Maryland, where one-sixth or more of the population may have been nonconformist in the early eighteenth century.[42] In the 1724 survey Maryland ministers noted an abundance of "papists" and Quakers in some parishes. Owing to the irregular pattern of distribution, we correct for nonconformists only where their presence is well documented. The Anglican church was established in South Carolina in 1706 over the strenuous protests of dissenters, whose meetings then outnumbered Anglican churches by three to one, though the Anglicans may have drawn equal or gained a slight majority of adherents by 1730.[43] Fortunately, periodic reports from South Carolina by missionaries of the
Society for the Propagation of the Gospel in Foreign Parts indicate the 381
ratio of Anglicans to dissenters in each parish.[44]

One way to estimate Anglican adherence in 1724, working from the foregoing premises, is to examine only the twenty-six responses from Virginia, Maryland, and South Carolina that provide figures in two prime categories: the number of families residing in each parish, and the number of persons attending church on a typical Sunday.[45] Table I indicates that in seven Maryland parishes a mean of 58 percent of the adult parishioners attended regularly; for eight South Carolina parishes the figure is 61 percent; and for eleven Virginia parishes, it is 56 percent. These percentages may be conservative, since the total pool of regular churchgoers was larger than the number in church on any given Sunday. Evidence shows

---

that care little for any religion" (Forbes to the bishop of London, July 21, 1724, Fulham Papers, XII, 60-72 [microfilm]). Stephen B. Weeks finds up to 20 Quaker meetings in Virginia before 1724 (*Southern Quakers and Slavery* [Baltimore, 1896], Appendix III). See also Brydon, *Virginia's Mother Church*, I, 260, 394, n. 18.

[42] According to a 1708 census, Maryland was 10% Catholic in that year (*Md. Archs.*, XXV, 258). Quakers were said to constitute less than 1/12 of the population in 1700, though they were increasing rapidly (*ibid.*, 93). See also George B. Scriven, "Religious Affiliation in Seventeenth Century Maryland," *Historical Magazine of the Protestant Episcopal Church*, XXV (1956), 220-226.

[43] Frederick Dalcho, *An Historical Account of the Protestant Episcopal Church, in South-Carolina* (Charleston, S.C., 1820), 53-69; David Duncan Wallace, *The History of South Carolina*, I (New York, 1934), 170-178, 419; M. Eugene Sirmans, *Colonial South Carolina: A Political History, 1663-1763* (Chapel Hill, N.C., 1966), 76-77.

[44] We thank Scott M. Wilds for directing us to the following SPG correspondence, which provides unusually detailed population and church statistics for South Carolina parishes in the 1720s: SPG Records, Letterbooks Series A, XV, 50-51; XVIII, 70, 77-82; XIX, 60, 68, 90-91, 104-108; XX, 98-104, 110-115; XXI, 77-87, 97-104, 108-116 (microfilm). Using information from these reports, we estimate the proportion of Anglicans in each parish as follows: St. Andrew's and St. George, 50%; Christ Church, 58.3%; St. John's, 66.6%; St. Philip's, 75%; St. James (Goose Creek) and St. James (Santee), 100%. St. Thomas had 50 Anglican families in 1724.

[45] Where a range of numbers is given an average has been used.

TABLE I
ANGLICAN CHURCH ATTENDANCE IN TWENTY-SIX SOUTHERN PARISHES, 1724

Parish (County)	*Potential White Anglican Churchgoers*	*Auditors at Church*	*Percentage of Eligibles Regularly Attending Church*
MARYLAND			
Christ Church (Kent)	300	250	83
Coventry (Somerset)	900	250	28
Dorchester (Dorchester)	600	400	67
Queen Anne's (Prince George's)	900	600	67
St. Michael's (Talbot)	750[a]	525	70
St. Paul's (Queen Anne's)	1380[a]	500[b]	36
Westminster (Anne Arundel)	300	160	53
SOUTH CAROLINA[c]			
Christ Church (Berkeley)	205	70	34
St. Andrew's (Berkeley)	225	163[d]	72
St. George's (Dorchester)	88	45	51
St. James, Goose Creek (Berkeley)	300	150[e]	50
St. James, Santee (Craven)	200	165[f]	83
St. John's (Berkeley)	133	55	41
St. Philip's (Charleston)	656	400	61
St. Thomas (Berkeley)	125	120	96[g]
VIRGINIA			
Abingdon (Gloucester)	900	200	22
Christ Church (Middlesex)	780	600	77
Henrico (Henrico)	1200	450	38
James City (James City)	594[h]	330	56

TABLE I—*continued*
ANGLICAN CHURCH ATTENDANCE IN TWENTY-SIX SOUTHERN PARISHES, 1724

Parish (County)	Potential White Anglican Churchgoers	Auditors at Church	Percentage of Eligibles Regularly Attending Church
Newport (Isle of Wight)	1200	900	75
Petsworth (Gloucester)	438	300	68
St. Anne's (Essex)	390	280	72
St. Mary's (Essex)	450	150	33
St. Peter's (New Kent)	612	175	29
Southwark (Surry)	1182	800	68
Stratton Major (King and Queen)	585	450[i]	77

Answers to the bishop of London's Queries, 1724, Fulham Papers.

[a] Number of families reduced by 1/6 owing to large numbers of Quakers and Catholics in parish.

[b] Report could be interpreted as either 500 or 900 auditors; if 900, the percentage would be 65.

[c] See n. 44 for South Carolina SPG correspondence that supplements and clarifies the 1724 responses.

[d] Minister reported that 65 (of approximately 90) Anglican families attended church regularly.

[e] Minister noted that a chapel was being built. We estimate chapel congregation at one-half that of the church.

[f] We estimate conservatively that chapel congregation was one-half that of the church.

[g] This figure may have included some French Reformed families in St. Dennis Parish, a French enclave within St. Thomas Parish.

[h] Minister's report of 78 families was apparently for Jamestown only (see Greene and Harrington, *American Population,* 149n). Figuring from number of auditors, we estimate total families in the parish at 198.

[i] With a church, chapel, and 220 communicants in the parish, this figure (based on 300 in church and 150 in chapel) may be low.

that would-be worshippers were often kept home by inclement weather, illness, business, or problems with carriages and horses.[46] In 1724 most ministers reported attendance for an average Sunday service only, rather than the larger parish total. Since it would be difficult to estimate the total pool of churchgoers, we have based our calculations on the lower Sunday averages.

[46] William Byrd II, a loyal Anglican and vestryman of Westover Parish, meticulously recorded his church attendance. During the three periods of Byrd's extant diary he attended church 45% (1709-1712), 67% (1720-1721), and 29%

The ministers of most southern parishes made additional comments in the 1724 responses that strongly support the picture of an active churchgoing majority. They tell of "large" congregations or of having "more present than there are pews for,"[47] remarks that are confirmed by the frequent enlarging of churches at that period. The report from the rector of Christ Church Parish in tidewater Lancaster County is typical: "The Church is thronged and almost all white persons in the parish (not necessarily hindered) attend divine Service." Only two of the twenty-eight Virginia respondents commented that church attendance was low. In Maryland the nearly unanimous word was that the "greatest part" or "most" of the parishioners came to church. For St. James Parish, Anne Arundel County, where many dissenters lived, the minister reported that
384 two-thirds of the parish attended, "the remainder being Dissenters (viz.), 40 families of Quakers, 5 of Papists, 1 of Presbyterians, & 1 of Anabaptists." The Maryland reports clearly convey a sense of growth and vigor in the Anglican church.[48] In South Carolina the church had benefited enormously from the work of the S.P.G., and by 1724 some services were so crowded that auditors "were forced. to stand without the door, and others hang at the windows."[49]

The ministers had little cause to inflate substantially attendance figures. The bishop of London had very limited power over the colonial clergy, the great majority of whom made permanent careers in America and therefore had nothing much to gain by falsifying their responses.[50] A few may have rounded out the figures to their own advantage, but independent evidence tends on the whole to confirm the reports. Gov. Alexander Spotswood, an objective witness, found Virginians in 1717 to be "well affected to the

---

(1739-1741) of the time, for a mean attendance of about 50%. *The Secret Diary of William Byrd of Westover, 1709-1712,* ed. Louis B. Wright and Marion Tinling (Richmond, Va., 1941); *William Byrd of Virginia: The London Diary (1717-1721) and Other Writings,* ed. Louis B. Wright and Marion Tinling (New York, 1958); *Another Secret Diary of William Byrd of Westover, 1739-1741,* ed. Maude H. Woodfin, trans. and collated by Marion Tinling (Richmond, Va., 1942). George Washington, a vestryman of Truro Parish, may have attended somewhat less frequently, but another man of affairs, Henry Laurens of South Carolina, was a "strict and exemplary" churchgoer. *The Diaries of George Washington, 1748-1799,* ed. John C. Fitzpatrick (Boston, 1925); David Duncan Wallace, *The Life of Henry Laurens* (New York, 1915), 438.

[47] Reports from St. Paul's Parish, Kent County, Md., St. Peter's Parish, Talbot County, Md., and Bristol Parish, Henrico County, Va., Fulham Papers.

[48] This is emphatically confirmed in Humphreys, *Historical Account.*

[49] Rev. Varnod to the Secretary, Apr. 1, 1724, SPG Records, Letterbooks Series B, Vol. 4, Pt. II, 173, USPG Archives. For further comments see Appendix.

[50] None of the reporting Virginia clergy, and at most three of the Maryland rectors, returned to England (Brydon, *Virginia's Mother Church,* I, 376-377; Rightmyer, *Maryland's Established Church,* 155-221). Rightmyer notes that the bishop of London "could not give, nor take away, the poorest parish" in Maryland (*ibid.,* 85). Even among the SPG respondents in South Carolina, only two returned to England (Dalcho, *Episcopal Church in South-Carolina,* 253, 289, and *passim*).

Church" and "contending [over] who shall have" the services of incoming ministers. A 1724 petition from the "Vestry, Freeholders, & Masters of Families" of Wilmington Parish, James City County, Virginia, expressed fear about "the Extirpation of Christianity" if a plan to divide their parish and annex its parts to adjacent ones (whose churches were "Scarce affording room for their own Congregations") were not defeated. The rector had counted 180 families in Wilmington Parish in response to the bishop's queries; the petition, apparently signed in a single day, carried the names of 146 men.[51] A minister newly arrived from England in 1725 had no reason to exaggerate when he observed that his Virginia parishioners seemed "Zealously affected to the doctrines of the Church, very Devout in their Devotions." Two weeks after settling in York-Hampton Parish, 385
York County, he administered the sacrament to "59 Communicants"; in answer to the 1724 queries the previous rector had counted 60 communicants.[52] Most convincing of all is the blunt and bitter letter written to the S.P.G. in 1728 by the Reverend Brian Hunt of St. John's Parish, South Carolina. (Sometime between 1724 and 1728, Hunt had been placed under censure by the S.P.G. for allegedly performing a "clandestine" marriage.) Mincing no words, Hunt listed the difficulties faced by ministers in the colonies, noting in passing that some of his parishioners "Seldom" went to church. Yet he went on to report that of 500 "Men, Women, and Children" in the parish, about 200 men and women frequented the Anglican church, and about 40 men and women attended the Presbyterian meeting. Thus 240 of the 250 adults in St. John's Parish were apparently churchgoers in 1728 (far greater than the 41 percent estimated for 1724 in Table I).[53]

Communion practices provide another measure of adherence. In Virginia and South Carolina, as in England, communion was held about four times a year.[54] Maryland parishes averaged six communion services a

[51] Spotswood to the bishop of London, Oct. 24, 1710, and June 13, 1717, in R. A. Brock, ed., *The Official Letters of Alexander Spotswood, Lieutenant-Governor of the Colony of Virginia, 1710-1722* (Virginia Historical Society, *Collections,* N.S. [Richmond, Va., 1882, 1885]), I, 27, II, 254; Petition to Bishop Gibson . . . May 23, 1724, Fulham Papers, XII, 7-10 (microfilm). (It might be noted that in accordance with the assembly's decision, Wilmington Parish was dissolved.)

[52] Richard Hewitt to Bishop Gibson, June 1, 1725, Fulham Papers, XII, 89-90 (microfilm).

[53] Hunt to the Secretary, May 6, 1728, SPG Records, Letterbooks Series A, XXI, 97-104 (microfilm). A second congregation at Strawberry, which had built "a neat Chappel at their own Charge" in 1723, may have been included in Hunt's population figure (though not the auditor count) in 1724, thereby accounting for the discrepancy. See Mr. Hunt to the Secretary, May 18, 1723, SPG Records, Letterbooks Series A, XVIII, 102-103, USPG Archives. Hunt had reported in 1724 that "not above 3 (save some hindered by great distance of way vizt 15 & 17 miles) did totally neglect coming to Church" (SPG Records, Letterbooks Series A, XVIII, 80-82 [microfilm]).

[54] Sykes, *Church and State,* 250.

year.[55] Twenty-eight southern Anglican ministers reported both the number of auditors and the number of communicants in 1724, with a median of 26 percent of the auditors present at service communicating.[56] Comparing this figure with the 56 to 61 percent adherence obtained in Table I, we find that at least 15 percent, and perhaps a much larger proportion,[57] of the adult Anglican population of the South may have been regular communicants in 1724. Scattered evidence from English parishes for the first half of the eighteenth century suggests that from 5 to 30 percent of the eligible population may have communicated regularly, though a larger percentage participated at least once a year at Easter.[58] While one could hardly claim that the Anglican church in the southern colonies was as actively supported as the church at home, the 1724 survey
386 gives no reason to suppose that it was sunk in lethargy.

Responses from the Middle Colonies and New England to the bishop's questionnaire are less informative than those from the South. The great diversity of religion in the middle region, as well as the dearth of ministers and churches in 1724, meant that some inhabitants attended the nearest church regardless of denomination, "preferring their worship to none."[59] The Anglican church gained stability in New England after 1723, when the "Connecticut Apostates" returned from England as ordained priests.[60] Yet the ministers' tendency to report about the size of their congregations in general, if often glowing, terms makes it difficult to ascertain numbers or proportions of Anglican adherents in the North. Adherence ranged from 61 to 100 percent for the three congregations for which we have

[55] Nine of the 23 parishes held communion monthly in 1724.

[56] In four congregations (14%), 45% or more of those present typically took communion; in seven (25%), 30-44% communicated; in eleven (39%), 20-29% participated; and in six congregations (22%), 19% or fewer typically took the sacrament.

[57] Semiannual reports from the Rev. Francis LeJau of St. James, Goose Creek, South Carolina, to the SPG, from 1706 to 1717, show that only about 55% of the total communicants in the parish took communion at any one service (*Carolina Chronicle*, ed. Klingberg, 58, 105, 120, 133, 145, 180, and *passim*). This percentage is confirmed by other SPG reports in the 1720s.

[58] Robert Currie *et al.*, *Churches and Churchgoers: Patterns of Church Growth in the British Isles Since 1700* (Oxford, 1977), 22: *Archbishop Herring's Visitation Returns, 1743*, ed. S. L. Ollard and P. C. Walker, Yorkshire Archeological Society Record Series (Wakefield, Eng., 1928-1931), 5 vols.; Sykes, *Church and State*, 251-253. The surge of communicants at Easter may have been a response to the Test Act and other legislation limiting the rights of nonconforming Christians (*Herring's Visitation Returns*, ed. Ollard and Walker, I, xx-xxi).

[59] William J. Hinke, ed., *Life and Letters of the Rev. John Philip Boehm ...* (Philadelphia, 1916), 27, 239. See, for example, the reports from Salem, N.J., and Rye, N.Y., Fulham Papers.

[60] Carl Bridenbaugh, *Mitre and Sceptre: Transatlantic Faiths, Ideas, Personalities, and Politics, 1689-1775* (New York, 1962), 68-72.

specific data.[61] The ratio of communicants to auditors can be computed for fourteen congregations, with the mean falling at about 17 percent.[62] But if the proportion of communicants was lower than in the South, the frequent reports of expanding congregations suggest that by 1724 Anglicanism was an attractive alternative for some northerners.[63] In both North and South, then, most Anglican ministers could report to the bishop that the colonial church was an active and growing, rather than a withered, branch of the Church of England.

The influence of the frontier on American culture and institutions is a subject of perennial interest, not least among students of religious history. Some writings on frontier religion give the impression that rapid expansion westward in the eighteenth century strained or even severed tradi- 387
tional church ties, making the frontier a kind of religious desert until the Second Great Awakening. Others show to the contrary that frontier religious leaders were exceptionally resourceful, and that churches and sects multiplied throughout the backcountry before the American Revolution.[64] Both versions agree, however, on two points: vast territories and a shortage of clergymen were the most critical factors in shaping frontier religious life. The variety of ways in which church leaders learned to manage these problems sheds light not only on the character of the religious culture but also on the question of church adherence on the eighteenth-century frontier.

Looking first at the southern backcountry in the early eighteenth century, we find that some Anglican parishes extended from sixty to over one hundred miles in length. This would certainly suggest that religious bonds underwent much strain. One respondent to the 1724 survey observed that "the distance of the way may hinder many . . . who cannot be prepared to come 10, 12, or 15 miles [to church], though they might if

[61] They are Perth Amboy, N.J. (71%), Staten Island, N.Y. (61%), and Newbury, Mass. (100%).

[62] The range is from 8 to 35%; see Appendix.

[63] George Keith had reported "not one Church of England as yet in either West or East Jersey" in 1701; by 1724 there were six "parishes" and at least 11 congregations in New Jersey, 17 churches or preaching places in Pennsylvania, and, in addition to Trinity Church, six "parishes" and seven preaching places in New York. "A Letter from Mr. George Keith to the Secretary about the State of Quakerism in North America," [1701?], Journals of the SPG, Appendix A, no. 4 (Micro Methods Ltd.); "List of Several Parishes or Places where Divine Service is performed . . . 1724," Fulham Papers, XXXVI, 54-58 (microfilm). Rhode Island ministers reported overflowing churches in 1724. The church grew more slowly in the rest of New England, though by the Revolution it encompassed "25,000 persons and 74 functioning congregations" (Bruce E. Steiner, "New England Anglicanism: A Genteel Faith?" *WMQ*, 3d Ser., XXVII [1970], 122-123).

[64] See, for example, Winthrop S. Hudson, *Religion in America: An Historical Account of the Development of American Religious Life*, 2d ed. (New York, 1973), 60-61, 132-134, and Louis B. Wright, *Culture on the Moving Frontier* (Bloomington, Ind., 1955).

they had but 5 or 6" to travel.[65] To deal with this problem Anglican vestries were constantly building chapels of ease in newly settled areas. Rectors of large parishes often kept two horses in order "to Ride into all the Parts of their Cures to Discharge their Ministerial Duties."[66] But if distance posed formidable challenges, other aspects of backcountry life encouraged close ties between inhabitants and their churches. Churches were almost invariably the first institutions organized on the southern frontier, and, pending the formation of new counties and county courts,[67] they supplied not only moral discipline but a wide range of social and civic services. Anglican ministers, usually the best educated persons in the backcountry, took up multiple roles as teachers, doctors, lawyers, and community spokesmen. Their churches became vital centers where isolat-
388 ed families not only renewed social fellowship on the Sabbath but also made contact with distant political and economic networks. Official proclamations were regularly read from the pulpit, provincial laws were posted near the church door, elections were frequently held at the church, and petitions of grievance were drafted and circulated after services.[68]

Focusing still on the first three decades of the eighteenth century, one finds the strength of religious feeling among westward-moving Anglicans further attested to by the spontaneous formation of congregations, followed shortly by the building of a church and requests for a minister to supply it.[69] Although the shortage of clergymen retarded growth, this hardly meant that the church lacked vitality. The activities of lay assistants have not been sufficiently appreciated. When a minister preached at an outlying chapel, he usually left "a Reader, to read Prayers and a Homily." Alternatively, the parish clerk might serve as "a kind of curate, performing frequently all the offices of the church, except the two sacraments and matrimony."[70] Nothing in the 1724 reports indicates that Virginia frontier

[65] Rev. Alexander Forbes to the bishop of London, July 21, 1724, Fulham Papers, XII, 60-72 (microfilm).

[66] "A Memorial Representing the Present Case of the Church in Maryland, 1700," Fulham Papers, II, 183-184 (microfilm).

[67] Because South Carolina had no county courts outside Charleston, parishes became "the most important units of local government" (Sirmans, *Colonial South Carolina,* 142-144, 250-252). In Virginia and Maryland, parishes outdistanced counties as settlement reached and then spilled over the Alleghenies in the 18th century. See Edward Lewis Goodwin, *The Colonial Church in Virginia . . .* (Milwaukee, Wis., 1927), 321-340; Arthur E. Karinen, "Maryland Population: 1631-1730: Numerical and Distributional Aspects," *Maryland Historical Magazine,* LIV (1959), 365-407; and Bridenbaugh, *Myths & Realities,* 156-157.

[68] Hooker, ed., *Carolina Backcountry,* 179, 277; Brydon, *Virginia's Mother Church,* I, 181; Bridenbaugh, *Myths & Realities,* 180-181.

[69] "Petition of the Parishioners of North Elk River [Md.] for a Minister," 1715 (Perry, ed., *Historical Colls.*, IV, 84-85), is typical of many such requests now in the SPG and Fulham Papers.

[70] Robert Beverley, *The History and Present State of Virginia,* ed. Louis B. Wright (Chapel Hill, N.C., 1947), 261; Jones, *Present State of Virginia,* ed. Morton, 96; and parish reports, *passim,* Fulham Papers.

churches were less well attended than those in more settled areas. St. Paul's Parish in Hanover County had two churches and two chapels by 1724, "all of which are generally full, no less than 200 or 300 people at a time."[71] Of the six other frontier parishes, only Upper Parish, Isle of Wight, reported a "small proportion" of the inhabitants attending church.[72] The Maryland frontier parish of King George in Prince George's County had "frequently a large auditory in both churches," and a remote chapel in Queen Anne's Parish had as many communicants as the more centrally located church.

The Yamasee War of 1715 so depopulated the South Carolina frontier that by 1730 the area had "not yet recovered from [its] ravages."[73] The parishes of St. Helena and St. Bartholomew had no ministers at all in 1724, despite their pleas to the S.P.G. St. John's and St. George's appear at the low end of the church adherence scale in Table I, though both had rebounded vigorously by 1728.[74] Conditions on the North Carolina frontier aroused the perennial concern of churchmen. Hugh Jones found Anglicanism there in a "deplorable state" in 1724, and William Byrd reported in 1728 that North Carolinians accounted themselves fortunate not to be "priest-ridden."[75] Yet one-seventh of the population was apparently Quaker as early as 1708; when John Woolman toured the area some years later, he visited a number of sizable Quaker meetings and noted that the backcountry folk were more devout than those in long-settled regions.[76] Negative comments about North Carolina almost invariably came from Anglicans, reflecting perhaps their acute anxiety about the undermanned and insecure position of their church in a colony where dissenters abounded.[77]

[71] Response to the Bishop's Queries, XII, Fulham Papers (microfilm). Hanover was the county that responded so warmly to Presbyterian revivalists from Pennsylvania in the 1750s, suggesting that, contrary to standard interpretations, the revival may have enjoyed its greatest success in areas where religious activity was high from the outset.

[72] See responses from Upper Parish, Bristol, Lawnes Creek, St. Stephen's, Southwark, and Overwharton parishes in Appendix.

[73] Humphreys, *Historical Account*, 94.

[74] Hunt to the Secretary, May 6, 1728, and Varnod to the Secretary, Apr. 3, 1728, SPG Records, Letterbooks Series A, XXI, 97-104, 77-87 (microfilm). See also n. 53 regarding a possible undercount in St. John's Parish.

[75] Jones, *Present State of Virginia*, ed. Morton, 104; Byrd, *History of the Dividing Line*, in Wright, ed., *Prose Works*, 195.

[76] Phillips P. Moulton, ed., *The Journal and Major Essays of John Woolman* (New York, 1971), 37, 69-71. The Moravian, Presbyterian, and Baptist churches also grew rapidly on the North Carolina frontier from the 1750s on. Sydney E. Ahlstrom, *A Religious History of the American People* (New Haven, Conn., 1972), 243, 319-320; Frederick Lewis Weis, *The Colonial Clergy of Virginia, North Carolina and South Carolina* (Boston, 1955), 58-70, 97.

[77] James Adams to the Secretary, Sept. 18, 1708, SPG Papers, XV; Byrd, *History of the Dividing Line*, in Wright, ed., *Prose Works*, 193; Paul Conkin, "The

During the middle third of the century, when the frontier population was greatly augmented by a stream of immigrants, we find a strong interest in congregation building evinced by Presbyterian, Lutheran, German Reformed, Huguenot, Moravian, and Quaker settlers. A few communities were predesigned as enclaves of pietists, but most congregations gathered spontaneously. Rustic, rough-hewn churches were among the first buildings erected on the middle and southern frontier, and new congregations could be found "pleading" with circuit-riding ministers to be included in their rounds. When a preacher did call, settlers so crowded the churches that barns and tents were needed to handle the overflow.[78] By the 1740s Lutheran congregations were "being formed all around," the members of one of which were "willing to sell their coats and the rest of their clothing
390 to help support a preacher."[79] A German Reformed minister had over six hundred auditors in western Pennsylvania; when he visited a frontier Maryland community in 1747, its large congregation—which probably had existed in some form since the 1720s and was still without a resident minister—"listened with tears of joy" to his sermon.[80] Nor should these outpourings be attributed solely to the Great Awakening, for the German churches, having already been influenced by pietism in Europe, received the Awakening with relative equanimity.[81] In any case, the notion that large crowds assembled only under the inspiration of the Awakening needs to be reconsidered in view of reports from ministers active in the preceding decades.

Churches serving the immigrants brought increasing numbers into formed congregations. Though reports vary, the most reliable estimate is that German Reformed members served by ministers from Pennsylvania doubled between 1730 and 1740, and doubled again to reach the approximately thirty thousand that Michael Schlatter reported he had formed into more than forty-six congregations by 1751.[82] The Lutheran

---

Church Establishment in North Carolina, 1765-1776," *North Carolina Historical Review*, XXXII (1955), 1-30. As already noted, when Anglican ministers were present in North Carolina their churches were full. See Hooker, ed., *Carolina Backcountry*, 51, 77.

[78] Donegal Presbytery Minutes, I, II, Presbyterian Hist. Soc.; Harbaugh, *Life of Schlatter*, 36-41, and *Schlatter's Journal*, 154; Dieter Cunz, *The Maryland Germans: A History* (Princeton, N.J., 1948), 62, 98, and chap. 2.

[79] Muhlenberg, *Journals*, trans. Tappert and Doberstein, I, 99, 155-156, 159, 194.

[80] *Schlatter's Journal*, 134, 154. Schlatter added: "Farther, I must say of this congregation, that it appears to me to be one of the purest in the whole country, and one in which I have found the most traces of the true fear of God" (p. 154).

[81] For another view see John B. Frantz, "The Awakening of Religion among the German Settlers in the Middle Colonies," *WMQ*, 3d Ser., XXXIII (1976), 266-288.

[82] Hinke, ed., *Life and Letters of Boehm*, 243n; *Schlatter's Journal*, 201–205. Schlatter traveled over 8,000 miles from 1747 to 1751 and preached 635 times (*ibid.*, 215).

church made an equally spectacular advance.[83] As for the Presbyterians, the westernmost Presbytery of Donegal grew from six congregations in the 1730s to thirty-three by the mid-1760s. In the South the number jumped from a few scattered congregations in the early eighteenth century to over forty-five by 1750, most of them located along the frontier, and continued to increase rapidly thereafter.[84] The Anglican church also expanded westward in these years, though its progress was greatly impeded by competition from dissenters and the reluctance of some clergy to locate in thinly settled frontier parishes.[85] But if some were unwilling, others had not lost the missionary spark, as we may see in the most detailed and surely the most spirited account of religious life on the later colonial frontier, Charles Woodmason's journal. 391

An itinerant Anglican minister in South Carolina's vast backcountry, Woodmason saw himself as the bearer of both God's true word and the civilizing seeds of English culture. His primary mission was to keep the flame of religion alive among migrating Anglicans. Yet he hoped to make converts among other folk, whom he described in rare moments of objectivity as "Sectaries of various Denominations and Countries," but more often as "a Gang of Baptists" or "the sweepings of the Jails of Hibernia."[86] Scattered among this unholy lot were but a few "serious Christians" (that is, Anglicans). That Presbyterian and Baptist preachers "infested" the backcountry by the 1760s heightened Woodmason's resolve "to disperse these Wretches" and their "Religious Foppery."[87] Disperse them he could not, but during six years in the back parts he traveled more than three thousand miles a year on horseback, organized nearly thirty Anglican congregations, and preached in every weather and season to all who would listen.

Woodmason's exasperated denunciations of "Infidels and Atheists" have sometimes been used to support claims of frontier disdain for religion, but a full reading of his journal and other writings conveys a very different impression. In one entry, for example, Woodmason complained that the backcountry was without "Law, Gospel . . . or Religious Life—No

[83] Abdel Ross Wentz's figure of 40,000 Lutherans in 1750 is more reasonable than the estimate of 60,000 sometimes attributed to Muhlenberg. Wentz, *A Basic History of Lutheranism in America* (Philadelphia, 1955); *Reports of the United German Evangelical Lutheran Congregations in North America, Especially in Pennsylvania*, trans. Jonathan Oswald (Philadelphia, 1880-1881), 2 vols.

[84] Donegal Presbytery Minutes, I, II, Presbyterian Hist. Soc.; Frederick Lewis Weis, *The Colonial Churches and the Colonial Clergy in the Middle and Southern Colonies, 1607-1776* (Lancaster, Mass., 1938).

[85] Richard R. Beeman, "Social Change and Cultural Conflict in Virginia: Lunenburg County, 1746 to 1774," *WMQ*, 3d Ser., XXXV (1978), 461-464. The Church may have been more successful in Maryland, if other congregations matched the 203 families of All Saints Parish, Frederick County, in 1756; "Petitions . . . for Division into Two Parishes," *Md. Archs.*, LII, 669-673.

[86] Hooker, ed., *Carolina Backcountry*, 85, 20, 142.

[87] *Ibid.*, 8, 78, 104.

Churches [or] Ministers." Yet he observed a few paragraphs later that "Sectaries" had settled themselves in every "Hole and Corner where they could raise Congregations . . . [had] built upwards of 20 Meeting Houses," and had "not less than 20 Itinerant Presbyterian, Baptist, and Independent Preachers." Another time he found "but one religious person" in a "Great Multitude"; read in context, this clearly means only one *Anglican*.[88] Woodmason evidently considered dissenting religion to be no religion at all.

Woodmason's attitude seems not to have diminished his appeal, for everywhere he went settlers flocked to hear him[89]—and this despite the ingenious "tricks" of some dissenters who tried to disrupt services or misinform people about the times and places he planned to appear.[90]
392 Woodmason frequently preached to gatherings of 200 to 500, or to "vast crowds" or "a great Multitude of People." On one occasion at the remote village of Waxhaws, "more than a thousand people assembled" in anticipation of his sermon were "vex'd and disappointed" when bad weather forced its cancellation. On November 20, 1767, he "gave Sermon to a Body of about 2000 arm'd" Regulators.[91] To be sure, many auditors were dissenters who came "with Itching Ears only . . . out of Curiosity, not Devotion," but Woodmason also recorded that the resident Presbyterian pastor at Waxhaws had "Seldom less than 9, 10, 1200 People assemble of a Sunday."[92]

Woodmason left no doubt that lack of ministers had done damage to the established church on the frontier. He told of reviving one congregation that was in danger of falling "from the Church to Anabaptism," in which "not one had a Bible or [Book of] Common Prayer—or could . . . hardly repeat the Creed or Lords Prayer—Yet all of 'em had been educated in the Principles of our Church." Still, their attitude toward religion was hardly apathetic, for "many of these People walk 10 or 12 Miles with their Children in the burning Sun . . . so earnest, so desirous [are they of] becoming Good Christians." And no sooner had Woodmason located in the backcountry than solicitations came from every quarter for him to preach and baptize. "The Poor People are hungry after the Word, and ready to devour Me," he noted on one occasion; on another, "Wherever you went to a House to marry or baptize, a Multitude would assemble, and

[88] *Ibid.*, 93, 239-240, 8.

[89] Woodmason's congregations ranged from 40 to 400 auditors, with a mean of about 160; see the specific figures for 26 Anglican congregations, *ibid.*, 26, 48.

[90] *Ibid.*, 35, 45. One practice of the "Holy and Devout Members of . . . [the] Kirk, was To take down the Advertisements for calling our People together, and nicely erasing the Name of the Month . . . inserting some other: By this Means, I had Journeys to no Purpose. When I came, there were no People—and on other days, the People would meet, and no Minister" (*ibid.*, 108).

[91] *Ibid.*, 6-16, 56, 13, 28.

[92] *Ibid.*, 13, 14. Woodmason noted how denominational pluralism led to latitudinarianism, or, as he put it, "the Husband a Churchman, Wife, a Dissenter, Children nothing at all" (*ibid.*, 52).

desire a Discourse." He was therefore confident that if a regular supply of ministers could be sent to the backcountry, Anglican attendance would triple.[93]

Woodmason's descriptions of his hazardous travels through the rugged countryside make clear to the modern reader why church attendance declined during bad weather. Flooded streams were the main obstacle, and one can only marvel at how many swollen creeks he was forced to swim and at how often he traveled for hours, or even days, "Wet to the Skin." As he explained, "[N]o Bridges are yet built in the Country—Nor are there any ferries or Boats—We pass at the Fords when the Waters are low—and when up, all Communication is cut off."[94] But despite these hardships, Woodmason faithfully discharged his multiple roles as minister, schoolteacher, political spokesman, and even midwife.[95] As for the 393
impudent calumnies of dissenters, these he passed over (so he tells us) "with that Christian Meekness and Compassion becoming my Function—and the Contempt and Derision befitting a Gentleman."[96]

Thus far we have drawn evidence mainly from the South and the frontier, two regions often depicted as resistant to organized religion in the eighteenth century. If church affiliation was substantially higher in those areas than the 5 to 10 percent assumed by some historians, we can expect to find churches attracting still greater support in the Middle Colonies and New England.

Though we will not undertake an equally detailed analysis of the northern denominations here, recent work in New England parish and town records tends to confirm that participation in church life was high. A number of Connecticut churches experienced periodic revivals during the early decades of the century, as exemplified by the Congregational church

[93] *Ibid.*, 60-61, 56, 15, 27. When Philip Fithian toured the Virginia and Pennsylvania frontier in 1775-1776, he found "many solid religious Characters in these Parts" and preached to "attentive" and very large congregations (*Philip Vickers Fithian: Journal, 1775-1776*, ed. Robert G. Albion and Leonidas Dodson [Princeton, N.J., 1934], 21-22, 32).

We know less about how religion fared on the northernmost frontier, though frequent petitions to create new parishes and obtain ministers for them appear in the New Hampshire and Maine records. When Samuel Libby of Scarborough, Me., was haled before the court in 1725 for two years' absence from church, his nonattendance was seen as unique in that town. *Documents and Records Relating to the Province of New Hampshire*, ed. Nathaniel Bouton (Manchester, 1869), III, 405-410 and *passim; Province and Court Records of Maine*, ed. Neal W. Allen, Jr. (Portland, Me., 1964), VI, 181, 187; Charles E. Clark, *The Eastern Frontier: The Settlement of Northern New England, 1610-1763* (New York, 1970), 273.

[94] Hooker, ed., *Carolina Backcountry*, 31-33, and *passim.*

[95] *Ibid.*, 7, 28, 53.

[96] *Ibid.*, 47.

of Woodbury.[97] Of 45 men born and raised in Woodbury around 1700, when little distinction was made between full and half-way membership, 66 percent joined the church in full communion and another 19 percent were at least half-way members. The percentage of female members would have been even higher. By 1760, after admission rules were tightened, 42 percent of the male taxpayers nonetheless joined as members in full communion.[98] In Andover, Massachusetts, where the population rose from approximately 1,000 persons in 1710 to 2,200 by 1759, 1,080 became church members in full communion and 551 became half-way members during the same interval, suggesting that most adults belonged to one or another of the town's two Congregational churches. As the distinction between full and half-way membership declined at South
394 Church in Andover between 1711 and 1749, half-way admissions rose from 20 to 50 percent.[99]

A study of New England selectmen shows that from 40 to 50 percent of these officials joined the church as full members during the eighteenth century, no doubt in part because the church was a focal point of the social and political as well as the religious community. Though the proportion of selectmen identified as full members dropped from 70 percent between 1650 and 1699 to 50 percent between 1700 and 1747, and then to 43 percent between 1750 and 1784, this probably reflects the fading distinction between full and half-way membership rather than a decline of interest in the institutional church.[100] At Boston's Second Church, Cotton Mather and his successor, Joshua Gee, admitted 559 persons between 1700 and 1729, with surges in 1700, 1714, 1725, and 1727. Mather told, moreover, of preaching to "vast congregations" (one rural gathering in

[97] James Walsh, "The Great Awakening in the First Congregational Church of Woodbury, Connecticut," *WMQ*, 3d Ser., XXVIII (1971), 543-562. "Such early revivals call into question any assumption on the part of historians that the Great Awakening appeared unexpectedly in the midst of a general decline in religious feelings" (*ibid.*, 547).

[98] *Ibid.*, 547-552. On women in the church see Mary Maples Dunn, "Saints and Sisters: Congregational and Quaker Women in the Early Colonial Period," *American Quarterly*, XXX (1978), 582-601.

[99] Philip J. Greven, Jr., "Youth, Maturity, and Religious Conversion: A Note on the Ages of Converts in Andover, Massachusetts, 1711-1749," *Essex Institute Historical Collections*, CVIII (1972), 119-134, and *Four Generations: Population, Land, and Family in Colonial Andover, Massachusetts* (Ithaca, N.Y., 1970), 176. The town contained about 465 families in 1768; 200 families belonged to North Parish Church, and 450 to 500 people attended Sabbath services at South Parish Church on June 19, 1768. In 1729, of 133 families in the northern precinct, 126 males and 200 females were members in full communion (*Stiles Itineraries*, 237, 244, 264). At the lower end of the scale, Lucas finds only one-third to one-half of the (adult?) population becoming church members in the Connecticut River Valley toward the end of the 17th century (*Valley of Discord*, 141-142, 244-245).

[100] Cook, *Fathers of the Towns*, 122-124, 131.

1698 numbered "four or five thousand Souls"). He considered a congregation of a thousand to be "Thinner . . . than Ordinary," though by the 1720s Second Church was but one of seven Congregational churches in Boston that, together with other denominations, served a population of some 15,000.[101] In 1740 George Whitefield commented that "for the Establishment of Religion" New England might exceed "all other Parts of the World."[102]

Ezra Stiles, the intrepid counter of congregations, filled his travel accounts with church statistics. In one series of reports on New England Congregational churches in the 1760s—often depicted as another low point for religion—Stiles found that the typical meeting consisted of about 160 families, with five Boston churches having a mean of 216 families.[103] He also collected information on the number of families adhering to dissenting churches. Quaker meetings ranged from 200 families in Newport, Rhode Island, to very small congregations in outlying Massachusetts towns.[104] Rhode Island Baptist congregations numbered about 150 families; those in the rest of New England averaged 29.[105] Presbyterian churches averaged about 80 families, and Anglican churches outside of Boston closer to 70.[106] In one summary computation Stiles concluded that in 1760 New England had 21,300 Baptists, 16,767 Quakers, 12,600 Anglicans, 440,000 Congregationalists, and 60,000 persons who were "reducible to no class" and apparently included 11,000 "Nothingarians" in Rhode Island.[107] This last category is of special interest, and one wishes

[101] Manuscript Records of the Second Church, Mass. Hist. Soc. (microfilm); *The Diary of Cotton Mather, 1681-1708,* ed. Worthington C. Ford, Mass. Hist. Soc., *Collections,* 7th Ser., VII (1911), 279, and *passim; Paterna: The Autobiography of Cotton Mather,* ed. Ronald A. Bosco (Delmar, N.Y., 1976), 72; Frederick Lewis Weis, *The Colonial Clergy and the Colonial Churches of New England* (Lancaster, Mass., 1936), 241-242.

[102] Edwin Scott Gaustad, *The Great Awakening in New England* (New York, 1957), 30.

[103] *Stiles Itineraries,* 98-120. A total of 1,080 families were adherents of the five Boston congregations in 1761. At 7.5 members per family in Boston (Wells, *Population of the British Colonies,* 87), the 8,100 persons associated with these five churches alone accounted for 54% of Boston's population of 15,000. There were, it might be noted, eleven Congregational churches in Boston in 1761 (Weis, *Colonial Clergy of New England,* 241-242).

[104] The mean for all Rhode Island meetings was 71 families, and for the rest of New England about 42 families (*Stiles Itineraries,* 105-106). An apparent exception to the New England pattern was Providence County, R.I., where half the population attended only the Friends Yearly Meeting. Stiles called these Quakers "stay at home Christians" (*ibid.,* 106).

[105] Stiles's estimate is somewhat lower than McLoughlin's figure for Massachusetts Baptist churches (*New England Dissent,* II, 698).

[106] For the three Boston Anglican churches Stiles reports two different totals, 360 and 500 families (*Stiles Itineraries,* 94, 101, 109).

[107] Stiles's summary total of 550,000 is about 100,000 above the usual estimates of New England population in 1760. It also differs slightly from totals mentioned

that Stiles had defined it more exactly. "Nothingarian" could mean no church connection whatever, but "reducible to no class" sounds more like the "ubiquitarians" of New Jersey, who worshipped regularly though at no single church in particular.[108] However this last group may be defined, Stiles seems to be saying that only 11 percent of the New England population could not be identified with a specific denomination.

All these estimates suggest that for New England leaders and ordinary citizens alike, Sabbath worship remained a highly significant activity. In 1740 an English visitor wrote that "their observation of the sabbath . . . is the strictest kept that ever I yet saw anywhere . . . [and the justices] compel obedience to this law."[109] For all of Dr. Alexander Hamilton's sour view of Yankee economics, he does seem to have had certain insights
396 into Yankee religion: "It is not by half such a flagrant sin to cheat and cozen one's neighbor as it is to ride about for pleasure on the sabbath day or to neglect going to Church and singing of psalms."[110]

Turning to the Middle Colonies, one finds it argued that both pluralism and the shortage of ministers crippled religious development in that region before the Great Awakening. Yet the takeoff points for expansion of the Presbyterian, Lutheran, and German Reformed denominations all occurred at least two decades before the Awakening.[111] Scores of itinerant ministers, including a number from the large city churches, worked tirelessly among the Middle Colony congregations, as did elders, deacons, and lay readers who were given enlarged responsibilities for discipline, local administration, and the conducting of services in towns where permanent clergymen were few.[112] Middle Colony churches would cer-

---

elsewhere in the *Itineraries* (pp. 92-94), but Stiles often rounded off or adjusted figures as he received new information (he also made occasional errors of addition). Nevertheless, he remains the supreme quantifier of 18th-century America.

[108] Nelson R. Burr, *The Anglican Church in New Jersey* (Philadelphia, 1954), 210. They might also have been called "indifferent" in religion.

[109] Winton U. Solberg, *Redeem the Time: The Puritan Sabbath in Early America* (Cambridge, Mass., 1977), 296-297. Massachusetts, Connecticut, Virginia, and South Carolina had compulsory church attendance laws in the 18th century. John M. Murrin, working in the court records of York [Me.], Middlesex, and Suffolk counties, Mass., for roughly 1700-1725, and A. G. Roeber, examining the Virginia county court records for 1720-1760, tell us that in those colonies a number of grand jury presentments were returned each year for nonattendance at church. Chronic offenders were the likely objects of these presentments, which apparently numbered no more than three or four per county each year. Church attendance laws, as well as those against Sabbath breaking (drinking, gaming, and other boisterous activities), may have been irregularly enforced, but they reflected the standards and expectations of 18th-century religious culture. See Solberg, *Redeem the Time*, 103-105, 194-196, 237-253.

[110] *Gentleman's Progress: The Itinerarium of Dr. Alexander Hamilton 1744*, ed. Carl Bridenbaugh (Chapel Hill, N.C., 1948), 145-146.

[111] Gaustad, *Atlas*, 18, 21, 28.

[112] This story can be traced in *Schlatter's Journal;* Hinke, ed., *Life and Letters of Boehm;* Muhlenberg, *Journals*, trans. Tappert and Doberstein, esp. vol. I; Trin-

tainly have grown in a more orderly fashion had central direction been stronger. Yet the greater degree of lay participation and leadership required in a voluntary church may also have promoted a vitality that would have been missing with better-regulated growth.

Some persons of weak conviction were undoubtedly alienated by the competition between denominations, but others were apparently invigorated by the challenge. Lewis Morris, a leading Anglican layman, was one of the latter. In a report of 1702 on the state of religion in New Jersey, Morris found both a "Hotch Potch of all Religions" and some persons of "no Religion." Observing that New Jersey had no Anglican house of worship, Morris urged leaders in England to place the church in a more competitive position.[113] The S.P.G. responded by sending missionaries.
By 1724 the colony had three Anglican churches and at least eight other 397
preaching places; ten parishes were in existence by 1740; and in 1765 New Jersey had twenty-one Anglican congregations, many of them packed to the church doors. Other denominations also did well. The historian Samuel Smith counted 169 churches in 1765 for a white population of about 97,000, or approximately one church for every 96 families.[114] This would suggest that neither diversity nor the shortage of ministers impeded the growth of organized religion in New Jersey.

The Presbyterian and German churches expanded dramatically in the middle region owing to Scotch-Irish and German immigration. The Presbyterian church grew from seven ministers and a score of congregations in 1706 to approximately 125 congregations in New York, New Jersey, and Pennsylvania by 1740; by the Revolution that number more than doubled. The Lutheran and German Reformed churches expanded by over 160 percent and 260 percent respectively between 1740 and 1776.[115] The Society of Friends continued to attract adherents; by 1775 there may have been 50,000 Quakers in 250 meetings, with over three-fifths located in Pennsylvania, New Jersey, and New York.[116]

---

terud, *Forming of an American Tradition;* and Theodore E. Schmauk, *A History of the Lutheran Church in Pennsylvania (1638-1820) from the Original Sources* (Philadelphia, 1903).

[113] The Memoriall of Col. Morris concerning the State of Religion in the Jerseys, Sept. 19, 1702, Journals of the SPG, Appendix A, no. 2, USPG Archives.

[114] List of Several Parishes or Places where Divine Service is performed . . . 1724, Fulham Papers, XXXVI, 54-58 (microfilm); Samuel Smith, *The History of the Colony of Nova-Caesaria or New Jersey . . . to the Year 1721* (Burlington, N.J., 1765), 485-500; Burr, *Anglican Church in New Jersey,* 86, 113, 213. Lester J. Cappon *et al.*, eds., *The Atlas of Early American History: The Revolutionary Era, 1760-1790* (Princeton, N.J., 1976), has 247 churches in New Jersey in 1775, or approximately one for every 80 families (p. 38).

[115] Trinterud, *Forming of an American Tradition,* 30; Weis, *Churches of the Middle and Southern Colonies,* 18; Gaustad, *Atlas,* 21, 18, 28, Appendix B.

[116] Gaustad estimates 200 meetings in 1800 (*Atlas,* 26), but Paullin gives the figure of 310 meetings in 1775 (*Atlas of Historical Geography,* ed. Wright, 50). Jones estimates 43,000 Quakers by 1780, without counting New York and New England (*Quakers in the American Colonies,* xv-xvi). Our figure of 50,000 in 1775 is an average based on these sources.

Table II
Ratio of Churches to Population, 1750

Section	*White Population*	*No. of Churches in Nine Denominations*	*Ratio of Churches to Population*
New England	349,029	576	1/606
Middle	275,723	590	1/467
South	309,588	296*	1/1046*

U.S. Bureau of the Census, *Historical Statistics of the United States,* II, 1168; Gaustad, *Historical Atlas of Religion in America,* Appendix B. The 9 denominations are the Anglican, Baptist, Congregational, Lutheran, Presbyterian, Dutch Reformed, French Reformed, German Reformed, and Roman Catholic.

398 * A detailed study of Virginia parishes now in progress suggests that Gaustad may have understated the number of Anglican congregations in 1750 by roughly 80 to 85. We thank John K. Nelson for alerting us to this possibility. Adding 80 congregations to the count of southern churches would bring the ratio to 1/823.

As for the two major cities, New York had eighteen principal churches in 1768, or one for approximately every 167 families, and Philadelphia had twenty by the Revolution for a similar ratio.[117] As early as 1744, Trinity Church in New York City had "a large congregation of above a thousand," and in 1760 the Presbyterian church there reportedly had a congregation of "12 or 1400 Souls."[118]

Two final computations will provide an overview of estimated church adherence in the eighteenth-century colonies. From Edwin S. Gaustad's colony-by-colony count of churches for 1750,[119] we can estimate the ratio of churches to population for each section at that time. (See Table II.) The closer ratio of churches to population in the Middle Colonies would be even more striking if the many Quaker meetings and other sectarian congregations in that region were included, though it may be that some newly formed Lutheran, Reformed, and Presbyterian congregations were quite small. The larger numbers of ministers in the South, and especially in New England, would also have made church practices more regular in those regions. Nonetheless, the ratios indicate that by mid-century the South had fallen behind in congregation building, a deficit that may in part explain the warm welcome given to itinerant Presbyterian and later Baptist preachers.

Table III compares the rising number of churches to the increase of

[117] Lawrence A. Cremin, *American Education: The Colonial Experience, 1607-1783* (New York, 1970), 536.

[118] Bridenbaugh, ed., *Gentleman's Progress,* 45; *Stiles Itineraries,* 71.

[119] Gaustad counts each separate preaching place as a distinct "church" (see n. 3). This definition is fully supported by our investigation, since preaching places were located approximately 10 miles apart and developed only when enough people to form a congregation had settled in an area. (For the spacing of congregations, see map in George C. Mason, "The Colonial Churches of Gloucester County, Virginia," *WMQ,* 2d Ser., XIX [1939], 324-346, and other parish histories by Mason, *ibid.,* 1938-1943, as well as the Pennsylvania map at the back of Hinke, ed., *Life and Letters of Boehm.*)

TABLE III
PROPORTION OF CHURCH ADHERENTS TO POPULATION, 1700 TO 1780

Year	*White Population*	*No. of Churches in Eight Denominations*	*Ratio of Churches to Population*	*% Church Adherents to Population at 80 Families per Church*
1700	223,071	373	1/598	80
1720	397,346	646	1/615	78
1740	755,539	1176	1/642	74.7
1750	934,340	1462	1/639	75.1
1765	1,478,037	2110	1/700	69
1780	2,204,949	2731	1/807	59*

U.S. Bureau of the Census, *Historical Statistics of the United States,* II, 1168; 399
Gaustad, *Historical Atlas of Religion in America.* The 8 denominations are the Anglican, Baptist, Congregational, Lutheran, Presbyterian, Dutch Reformed, German Reformed, and Roman Catholic.

* See note 121.

population at six points during the eighteenth century. Using a colonies-wide mean of eighty families per congregation,[120] we find that church adherence stood at 80 percent in 1700, declined but slightly to 74 percent by 1740, and rose slightly in the following decade—a pattern that indicates a remarkable stability during the first half of the century. By 1765 a distinct drop is visible, and in the midst of the Revolutionary War in 1780 church adherence seems to have declined to 59 percent.[121] This trend, if such it was,[122] would be reversed by the Second Great Awakening with the enormous expansion of the Methodist and Baptist churches.

[120] Eighty families is a reasonable average. Brydon estimates 150 families per Anglican congregation in Virginia in 1724 (*Virginia's Mother Church,* I, 380). In 1772 a Baptist reported to Stiles that the five southern colonies had about 90 full members and over 175 families adhering to each Baptist church (*The Literary Diary of Ezra Stiles,* ed. Franklin Bowditch Dexter [New York, 1901], I, 330). As early as 1731, the combined German Lutheran congregations of Philadelphia, Germantown, and Skippack embraced 200 families (Hinke, ed., *Life and Letters of Boehm,* 72). Pennsylvania Presbyterian congregations averaged about 100 families (Guy Soulliard Klett, *Presbyterians in Colonial Pennsylvania* [Philadelphia, 1937], 95-96). For New England estimates, see above, pp. 268–271.

[121] But if we used Weis's figure of 2,962 congregations in 1776, which includes all sects except the Quakers and all churches, our estimate of church adherence that year would be about 71% (*Churches of the Middle and Southern Colonies,* 18). Employing Paullin's figure of 3,228 congregations, which includes the Quakers, our estimate would rise to 77.5% in 1775-1776 (*Atlas of Historical Geography,* 49-50).

[122] Doubt has recently been cast on the notion that religious adherence declined significantly during and after the Revolution. See Douglas H. Sweet, "Church Vitality and the American Revolution: Historiographical Consensus and Thoughts Towards a New Perspective," *Church Hist.,* XLV (1976), 341-357.

The preponderant weight of the evidence we have examined indicates that the churched population of eighteenth-century colonial America was larger than the unchurched population. Overall, we estimate that from 56 to 80 percent of the population were churched, with the southern colonies occupying the lower end of the scale and the northern colonies the upper end.[123]

The Anglican survey of 1724 offers a singular opportunity to examine the pattern of affiliation for one church at a significant point of development. Our most detailed evidence indicates that Anglican adherence ranged at that time from 61 percent in South Carolina to 56 percent in Virginia. The proportion of regular communicants in established parishes, while much lower than in the modern Protestant Episcopal church,[124] may
400 not have been significantly less than the proportion of communicants in the eighteenth-century mother Church of England.

The notion that religious lethargy prevailed among settlers on the eighteenth-century frontier finds little support here. The frontier regions were underserved, but whenever a preacher visited or settled there, the almost universal report was that the people eagerly attended services, sought baptism and communion, and formed congregations with a zeal that at times surpassed that of more stable regions.

Nor do we find that the churched population was more than temporarily increased by the Great Awakening. Rapid expansion of the Anglican, German Lutheran and Reformed, and Presbyterian churches before the Awakening, as well as frequent reports of religious quickenings and strong church attendance in the decades before 1740, suggest that the Awakening's greatest impact may have fallen in a realm other than that of numbers.[125] Perhaps the character of piety, or styles of religious discourse, or popular attitudes toward authority changed, but the proportion of regular church adherents appears to have remained about the same.

The reader will have noticed that this essay makes no attempt to measure the quality or intensity of eighteenth-century religious experience. Nor have we attempted to determine what sort of people went to church, what they expected to gain by going, or how their worship affected their lives.[126] For the present, we have tried to demonstrate only that

[123] The balance has been reversed today, with the South being the best churched section (Constant H. Jacquet, Jr., ed., *Yearbook of American and Canadian Churches, 1979* [Nashville, Tenn., 1979], 263).

[124] *Ibid.*, 221.

[125] Reports from New England suggest that church attendance surged briefly at the height of the Awakening and that substantial numbers may have moved from half-way to full membership. Jonathan Edwards wrote of the Northampton revival of 1734-1735 that "the Church was very *large* before; but Persons never *thronged* into it, as they did in the late extraordinary Time" (*The Christian History . . .* [Boston, 1744], 126).

[126] Patricia Bonomi is presently completing a study of early American religious culture that will take up some of these issues.

when ministers looked down from their pulpits in eighteenth-century America, their eyes fell not on empty pews but on a numerous audience. We hope that this revised picture of church adherence will suggest new approaches to the study of religious life in colonial America. At the least, it should confirm that historians writing on religious subjects are working in the mainstream of eighteenth-century colonial history, rather than examining mere islands of zeal in a sea of religious apathy.

Appendix

Anglican Ministers' Responses to Bishop of London's Queries, 1724

Parish (County)	*Total White Families in Parish*	*No. Auditors at Anglican Services*	*No. Anglican* Communicants*	*No. Anglican Places of Worship*
THE SOUTH				
MARYLAND				
All Faiths (St. Mary's)	"152 protestants & 52 popish families"	"large number of Parishioners" attend both churches; often full in good weather	usually 50-60, "seldom fewer than 20" (total 80?)	2
All Saints (Calvert)	208	"greatest part of the Parishioners constantly attend"	"usual number about 60"	1
Christ Church (Calvert)	230	"greatest part . . . constantly attend except a few Papists & Quakers"	"usual number about 40" (total 80?)	2
Christ Church (Kent)	100	200 or 300 "in fair weather"; only Quakers and Papists "wholly absent themselves"	10-30	1
Coventry (Somerset)	300	"in summer between 2 & 300"	100	1
Dorchester (Dorchester)	400 taxables (200 families)	100 at church, 200 at chapel, 100 in the islands	few communicants	at least 4
Great Choptank (Dorchester)	1000 taxables		few communicants	4
King George's (Prince George's)	400	"Frequently a large auditory in both churches"	50 to 70 "in each place" [2 churches] (total 120+)	4

APPENDIX—*continued*

ANGLICAN MINISTERS' RESPONSES TO BISHOP OF LONDON'S QUERIES, 1724

Parish (County)	*Total White Families in Parish*	*No. Auditors at Anglican Services*	*No. Anglican* Communicants*	*No. Anglican Places of Worship*
King and Queen (St. Mary's)	200	"most part of the Parishioners attend"	"generally between 60 & 80" (total 140?)	2
Portobacco and Durham (St. Mary's)	"300 families in both parishes"	"most of the Parishioners . . . give constant attendance"	40-50 "& often more" (total 90?)	2
St. Anne's (Anne Arundel)	130		30	1
Queen Anne's (Prince George's)	300	"300 attend on Sundays" (total 600)	"about 60 . . . in each place" (total 120)	2
St. James (Anne Arundel)	150	"generally . . . near two-thirds" of parish, "remainder being Dissenters"	20-40	1
St. Michael's (Talbot)	300	"ordinarily 3 or 400" at church, "150 or 200" at chapel	60-80 at church 20-30 at chapel (total 95)	2
St. Paul's (Baltimore)	363	"for the most part a full congregation"	"seldom above 25 at a time"	1
St. Paul's (Kent)		"commonly a large Congregation"	100	1
St. Paul's (Prince George's)	220	"greatest part attend divine service"	"seldom less than 60" (total 120)	2
St. Paul's (Queen Anne's)	552	"300 . . . in the church, & in the chapels about 200" (500 to 900?)	60-70 at church, 30-40 "at a time" at chapels (total 100 to 170?)	4

St. Peter's (Talbot)	344	"on the Lord's day . . . a large Congregation"	"I always have pretty many"	1
Shrewsbury (Kent)	unknown "till the boundaries are better settled"	"Constantly & in good weather 3 or 400 attend"	100	1
Stepney (Somerset)	400	"some hundreds attend" in summer; winter congregations "small"	50 at church; "about 40" at one chapel (total 90+)	3
Westminster (Anne Arundel)	100	"every Lord's Day" 160 "or thereabouts"	16	1
William and Mary (St. Mary's)	"number of families unknown, because there are so many romans"	"about 400 [?] auditors, 300 at one church and 200 at another"	100 "at each church" (total 200)	2
SOUTH CAROLINA				
Christ Church (Berkeley)	140	"70 persons come constantly" to church	28	1
St. Andrew's (Berkeley)	180	"60 or 70 families do attend"; the rest dissenters	23 "constant communicants"	2
St. Dennis (Berkeley)	16 French families [plus 18 families in dispute with church, 1724]	"commonly between 50 and 60"	15	1
St. George's (Dorchester)	70	"40 or 50 parishioners" and "25 or 30 . . . Negroes"	"above 40, 17 being Negroes"	1
St. James, Goose Creek (Berkeley)	300 "Europeans," ages 16 to 60	"about 100 parishioners constantly attend" (total 150 to 200?)	"20 each time"	2

APPENDIX—*continued*

ANGLICAN MINISTERS' RESPONSES TO BISHOP OF LONDON'S QUERIES, 1724

Parish (County)	*Total White Families in Parish*	*No. Auditors at Anglican Services*	*No. Anglican* Communicants*	*No. Anglican Places of Worship*
St. James, Santee (Craven)	80	"ordinarily" 100 to 120 "and more"	65	2
St. John's (Berkeley)	80	"all . . . in general attend" as plantation affairs permit; "seldom less than 50 or 60"	30	2
St. Philip's (Charlestown)	350	"on Sundays seldom less than 400"	"from 30 to 50" each time; 100 at Easter	1
St. Thomas (Berkeley)	94 [and 34 French families in St. Dennis]	50 to 70 "ordinarily attend each" church (total 120)	20 each church (total 40)	2
VIRGINIA				
Abingdon (Gloucester)	300	"200 Christians generally attending"	60-70	1
Accomack (Accomack)	400-500	"all within 10 miles of each church that are capable commonly attend"; "churches cannot contain all"	200	3
Blissland (New Kent)	160	"every Sunday: the greatest part"	70	2
Bristol (Henrico and Prince George)	430	"very often more present than there are pews for"	"usual number is about 50" (total 100?)	2

Bruton (James City and York)	110	"full congregations" on Sundays	50	1
Christ Church (Lancaster)	300	"Church is thronged . . . almost all white persons in parish . . . attend"	60-80	2
Christ Church (Middlesex)	260	number attending each service "may be about 200" (total 600)	"number . . . in my parish is 230"	3
Elizabeth City (Elizabeth City)	350	"most of the parishioners attend . . . few dissenters"	"commonly 100"	1
Henrico (Henrico)	"may be 400 families"	"sometimes 100 or 200 attend" (total 450)	"20 is the greatest number that do communicate at one time" (total 60?)	3
Hungars (Northampton)	365	"scarce one third of the parishioners attend"	"in all the parish about 80"	2
James City (James City)	78 (Jamestown only)	James City Church—130; Mulberry Island—200	James City—25; Mulberry Island—50	2
Lawnes Creek (Surry)	"700 tithables"	"always . . . a full congregation"	12 at church; 30-40 at chapel	2
Newport (Isle of Wight)	400	"500 . . . constantly attending Mother Church and scarce that number at all by other places" (total approximately 900)	"40 communicants which are constant" (at mother church)	3
Overwharton (Stafford)	650	"generally as full a congregation as . . . Church or Chappel can contain"	"betwixt 80 & 100 communicants each time" (total 270?)	3

APPENDIX—*continued*

ANGLICAN MINISTERS' RESPONSES TO BISHOP OF LONDON'S QUERIES, 1724

Parish (County)	*Total White Families in Parish*	*No. Auditors at Anglican Services*	*No. Anglican* Communicants*	*No. Anglican Places of Worship*
Petsworth (Gloucester)	146	"generally speaking . . . about 300"	"upwards of 100"	1
St. Anne's (Essex)	130	"if Good weather, between 100 & 180 . . . come to church" (total 280)	"50 to 80 . . . at each Church" (total 130)	2
St. Mary's (Essex)	150	"about 150 parishioners" on Sunday	"above 100"	1
St. Paul's (Hanover)	? [torn]	churches and chapels "all . . . generally full, no less than 200 or 300 people at a time" (total 1000)	"at the Churches commonly above 100" (total 200 + chapels)	4
St. Peter's (New Kent)	204	"commonly 170 or 180 souls attend"	40-50	1
St. Stephen's (King and Queen)	300	"a good congregation"	60	1
South Farnham (Essex)	200	"the most part of the parishioners do attend"	"50 at each church" (total 100)	2
Southwark (Surry)	394	"near 300 . . . and sometimes more" at church and at one chapel; other chapel's congregation also "very large" (total approximately 800)	"40 to 70 or 80" each time (total approximately 160)	3
Stratton Major (King and Queen)	"between 190 and 200"	"in fair weather commonly about 300 and upwards attend" (total 600?)	"about 220" total	2

Upper Parish (Isle of Wight)	700 "assessed persons"	"often a small proportion of the hearers attend"	10-20	4 [?]
Washington (Westmoreland)	200	on occasion "not convenient room for them all" within the two churches	"two quarts of wine used in the administration"	2
Westover (Charles City)	233	"two-thirds of the parishioners generally attend"	"75 in the whole parish"	3
Wilmington (James City)	180	"here being no dissenters the Churches are generally well frequented"	"at all the churches . . . about 100"	3
York-Hampton (York)	200	"two thirds of my parishioners are commonly present"	60 at one church, 20 at the other	2
MIDDLE COLONIES				
NEW JERSEY				
St. John's (Elizabeth)	270	congregation from 150 to 270	12-30	?
St. Peter's (Perth Amboy)	70 Anglican families	Amboy, 150; Piscataway, 150; Woodbridge, about 50—"almost all Dissenters and violently attached to the New England Scheme"	Amboy, 20-24; Piscataway, 14-16; Woodbridge, 0	3
St. John's (Salem)	"30 Dwelling houses" in 1727	At Salem "about 70," some Anglicans, "others Independents and Presbyterians"; small congregation at Cohansic; at "Maurice's River . . . all Church People and are above 100"		3

APPENDIX—*continued*

ANGLICAN MINISTERS' RESPONSES TO BISHOP OF LONDON'S QUERIES, 1724

Parish (County)	*Total White Families in Parish*	*No. Auditors at Anglican Services*	*No. Anglican* Communicants*	*No. Anglican Places of Worship*
NEW YORK				
St. George's (Hempstead)	"parish consists of two Townships"	"commonly a large Auditory"	50	1
Grace Church (Jamaica)	409	"Not above 89 families of the 409 . . . come . . . the rest being Dutch and English Dissenters"	40 "at a time"	3
Trinity (New Rochelle)	"70 families" including some Presbyterians	"always attended by the most part of the [Anglican] parishioners	"commonly between 40 and 50"	1
Grace Church (Rye)	"200 families, or rather more"	"few are well affected to our excellent litturgy"; auditors "sometimes not 30 sometimes above 300" in good weather	26	6
St. Andrew's (Staten Island)	50-60 Anglican families	"100 persons generally attend in good weather"	9	1
Trinity (New York City)	"1600 families of English Dutch French and Jews"	"members of the Church ordinarily attend . . . on Sundays here is a great congregation"	100-200	1
St. Peter's (Westchester)	200	"70 auditors" at Westchester church; no count for others	18 at Westchester	4

PENNSYLVANIA				
St. Paul's (Chester)	"30 families who frequent service"	church full	10-15	1 [?]
St. Peter's (Lewes)	400 families; 136 of those Anglican	"Churches are full" on the Sabbath	"about 20" (total ?)	3
NEW ENGLAND				
CONNECTICUT				
Christ Church (Stratford)	50 Anglican families, Stratford; 30 Anglican families, Fairfield; same in Newtown; 10 Anglican families, West Haven	"many times an 100 or 150 . . . but sometimes not half so many, & sometimes thrice that number" (65-300?)	at each communion 30-60 in Stratford; 100 in adjacent towns	3 (church being built)
MASSACHUSETTS				
Christ Church (Boston)	"80 families belonging to this Church"	"ordinarily full with constant and transient hearers"	usual number 40	1
St. Michael's (Marblehead)	70-80 Anglican families	"generality of Parishioners attend" when home; "the men go to sea 2 or 3 months together"	usual number 30-40; "the whole consists of 50"	1
Queen Anne's (Newbury)	"about 30 [Anglican] families"	"about eight score souls" (160)	38	1

APPENDIX—*continued*

ANGLICAN MINISTERS' RESPONSES TO BISHOP OF LONDON'S QUERIES, 1724

Parish (County)	*Total White Families in Parish*	*No. Auditors at Anglican Services*	*No. Anglican* Communicants*	*No. Anglican Places of Worship*
RHODE ISLAND				
St. Michael's (Bristol)	40 Anglican families	"the Parishioners all in generall give their Constant attendance"	20-30	4
St. Paul's (Narragansett)	600-700	150 to 270 on Sundays; "Congregation every day Encreasing Especially with young people"	17	1 (and occasionally visited 5 adjacent places)
Trinity (Newport)	about 400 houses	"our people are grown so numerous, that we are now building a new and Larger Church"	"above 50 . . . properly belonging to this Church"	1 (and supplies adjacent places)
King's Church (Providence)	500	"generally above 100" at Providence; many Quakers & Anabaptists in town	10	2

* See n. 57.

Consumer Behavior in Colonial America

CAROLE SHAMMAS
University of Wisconsin—Milwaukee

A necessary step in any assessment of early national economic growth is a characterization of market development before independence from Great Britain. Drawing up such a characterization, however, presents problems as at least two different pictures of the eighteenth-century economy are currently available. One depicts the intense involvement of early Americans in markets and overseas trade, while another equally powerful image suggests a colonial landscape of sleepy villages inhabited by farmers devoid of a profit orientation and almost entirely dependent upon their own households and neighborhood reciprocity for goods and services.

What kind of economy did the new republic inherit? Can these two seemingly contradictory portrayals of colonial development be reconciled? One way to make them compatible is to assume a dual economy, two self-contained systems in the colonies: a hard-driving commercial society composed of plantations and seaport towns coexisting alongside an inland pastoral one. In fact, many history texts explicitly or implicitly adopt this position because it fits in nicely with an interpretation of Old World economic life that attributes most market activity to the citizens of towns and the upper classes, and considers the bulk of the preindustrial population—the peasantry—as "traditional" consumers with

---

Author's Note: *An earlier draft of this article was delivered at the Conference on Economic Growth and Social Change in the Early Republic, Chicago, April 24-26, 1980. I wish to thank Lorena Walsh and Daniel Scott Smith for their comments and criticisms.*

SOCIAL SCIENCE HISTORY, Vol. 6 No. 1, Winter 1982 67-86

desires that normally could be satisfied by home production. Any resources left over after basic needs had been met would not go toward consumer durables, but "into more land and cattle, or into hoards, or into new building, or even into sheer waste—gargantuan weddings, funerals, and other feasts" (Hobsbawm, 1967: 27-28).

Recently this notion that the preindustrial consumer was not much of a consumer at all has come under attack. According to some European historians, the early modern society, though still basically agrarian in nature, witnessed a continual increase in 413
consumer demand because of agricultural specialization and cottage industry (De Vries, 1974, 1975; Thirsk, 1978). The situation in America, however, remains largely unexplored. A serene rustic image of self-sufficient communities still prevails in many social histories (Merrill, 1977; Henretta, 1978; Clark, 1979; Jedrey, 1979), and the criticisms that have been voiced primarily concern the depiction of market production not consumption (Rothenberg, 1981).

Consumer demand has commonly been measured in relation to the resources a nation or an individual possesses. On the macro level, consumer expenditures are compared with disposable income over time, while for households, a cross-section of family expenditures for specific goods—food, consumer durables, and so forth—is compared to income or total expenditures. This comparison results in a figure called the "income elasticity of demand" that indicates how much consumer expenditure goes up or down as income goes up or down. An elasticity of one, or unity, implies both are increasing/decreasing at the same rate; elasticities over one imply consumer/demand is increasing/decreasing at a faster rate; and elasticities under one imply increases/decreases at a slower rate. Total consumer expenditure always has an income elasticity under one because savings (elasticity over one) are much more likely to be altered by changes in income (Suits, 1963). If savings are removed, however, and only household expenditures rather than income are counted, then individual consumer goods, especially durables, have elasticicies over one while food, as a necessity, is under one. Food expenditures level off after a point while consumer durables are less likely to behave in that manner. Engel's Law and the modifications of it made over the years define this household buying behavior (Houthakker, 1957; Williamson, 1967). Most recently, attempts have been made to chart consumer demand for social goods (education, health) and for the specific characteristics of commodities (Terleckyj, 1975).

In the preindustrial period, little in the way of income/expenditure information exists for the calculation of demand elasticities, but data on stocks of wealth are available. Probate inventories list the personalty and in some places the realty of decedents. This
414 total wealth can be separated into two categories—consumer goods and produced goods—and be used to obtain a rough indication of consumer behavior. Total inventoried wealth (i.e., consumer goods and producer goods) and the value invested in consumer goods are, of course, far from perfect operational variables for the concepts they represent. Consumer goods value is largely in durables—furniture, tableware, jewelry, and metalware—but apparel (nearly a durable in early modern society), small stocks of foods and pocket money (semidurables and perishables) are included because some inventories simply say "all the stuff in the kitchen," "all the stuff in the parlor," or "apparel and purse" (meaning cash on hand), rather than enumerating all the commodities.

There are other difficulties, too. Those stocks that constitute investment in consumer goods may have been purchased, but they also might have been inherited or made at home. The inheritance problem affects widows' inventories much more than those of any other group because these women tended to have legal title over consumer goods rather than producer. The consumer goods males inherited would be balanced by the producer goods legacies and do not create as much of a difficulty.

Homemade goods also pose a problem. While, theoretically, colonists could have manufactured all their own high quality consumer good and accumulated as valuable a stockpile as that of the person buying on the market, it would be rather unlikely that the nonspecialized home manufacturer could shine in all areas of production. In fact, most homemade items tended to be crude and cheap. In addition, by the eighteenth century, a wide array of metal, pottery, and textile items commonly found in homes could only be obtained in the marketplace. Thus, the dollar or pound sterling amount of consumer goods value is an indicator of demand even if the value found in the individual inventory is not a pure figure.

Other kinds of problems plague the estimation of the producer goods portion of total inventoried wealth. It includes financial assets, equipment, sales inventory, livestock, crops, and realty, but debts owed to others are omitted. These assets, despite the fact that they are not all "stocks" proper, had to be included, in order to reflect adequately the wealth of the decedent. Producer goods are thus a catch-all category for nonconsumer items. All of these measurement errors should be remembered as the analysis proceeds. However, historians may take some consolation in the fact that the variables used to chart modern consumer behavior are as flawed and troublesome as the preindustrial ones.[1]

What can these variables from probate inventories tell us about preindustrial consumer behavior? For one thing, they can provide some idea of the way the value of consumer goods varied with total wealth. Figure 1 displays the possible forms this relationship could assume. Would it be that of the proverbial traditional consumer? In the most extreme case, this individual would stop stocking consumer goods after all necessaries had been obtained, and put the rest of his wealth into cows, land, or gold for his lineal descendants or for the sheer joy of hoarding. This wealth-consumer goods relationship resembles a in Figure 1. On the other hand, if with each increment to wealth, people kept investing the same amount of the increment in consumer goods, then a straight line such as the one in diagram b would describe the situation.

The third relationship that might exist is one in which the value of goods continued to climb with increasing wealth, but the rate of growth was lower than that for wealth. Progressively, more additional dollars went into producer goods or savings as wealth levels climbed. For example, a family with total wealth of $10,000 might have $9,000 in consumer goods, but, if suddenly through a large salary raise, inheritance, or a winning lottery ticket family wealth shot up to $20,000, stocks in consumer goods would not

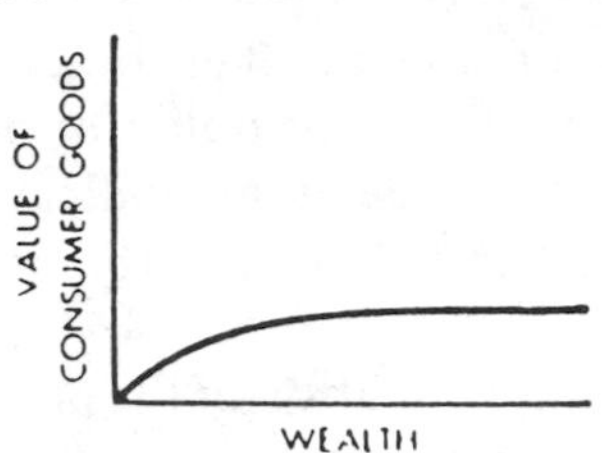

(a) SHARP LEVELLING OFF OF THE VALUE OF CONSUMER GOODS
PUTATIVE TRADITIONAL CONSUMER PATTERN

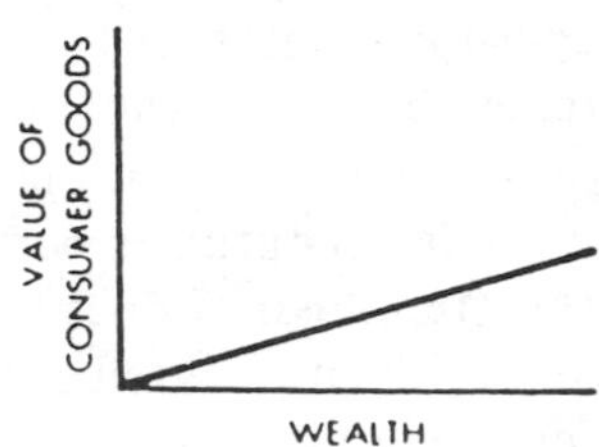

(b) STRAIGHT LINEAR RELATIONSHIP

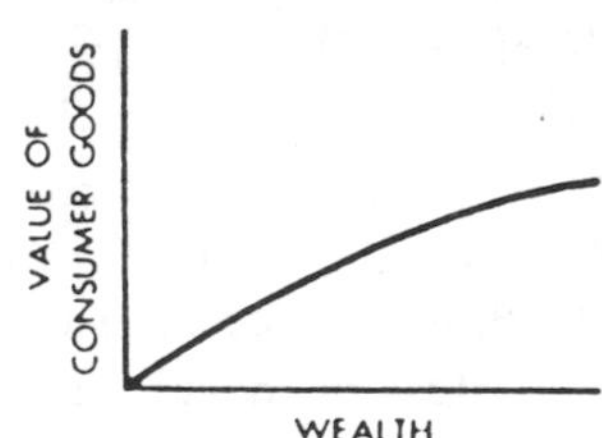

(c) PROPORTIONAL INCREASE IN THE VALUE OF CONSUMER GOODS
PUTATIVE MODERN CONSUMER PATTERN

Figure 1 Possible Relationships Between Wealth and Value of Consumer Goods

amount to $18,000. A higher portion of the increment would go to savings. What might stay constant, however, is the percentage increase in consumer goods value. So the growth in this investment, given a 100% increase ($10,000) in wealth, would be 90% of $9,000. Thus, $17,100 of the $20,000 would be in consumer goods, not $18,000. Such a relationship can be expressed as a slow curving line as the one in diagram c of Figure 1. The amount invested in consumer goods gradually—but only gradually—fell further and further behind the total wealth figure because as the latter increased by a certain amount (say 1%) the consumer goods amount went up by under 1% each time. Thus, as people grew richer, the value of consumer goods constituted a smaller and smaller proportion of total wealth. Diagram c is often assumed to be the modern relationship between consumption and total family resources, just as diagram a is a representation of what is described as traditional consumer behavior. Empirical tests of this modern relationship, of course, have been made with income and expenditure data, not stocks of wealth.

The probate inventories to be used to test the hypothesis that the total value of consumer goods leveled off as all traditional needs were met while wealth continued to climb are ones from selected counties of Massachusetts in 1774 compiled by Alice Hanson Jones.[2] She has estimated that roughly one in three of the eligible decedents (those free, over 21, and, in the case of women, unmarried) had an estate probated (Jones, 1977: 1789, 1803). While the affluent may have been overrepresented, all wealth groups appear. For the type of analysis being conducted here, it is the latter condition that is crucial.

As "peasants" are the particular group of interest, I selected for the initial analysis only those inventories belonging to yeoman, farmers, husbandmen, and dual occupationists (combination farmer and craftsmen). If the line denoting consumer goods value actually did tend toward the horizontal as wealth climbed, then a scattergram should reveal such a configuration. Diagram a in Figure 2 shows the relationship between the consumer goods value and total wealth of Massachusetts agriculturalists. While the relationship is far perfectly linear (R^2 of .449), consumer goods value does not level off. Diagram b displays the semilog transformation, which theoretically should make the data in

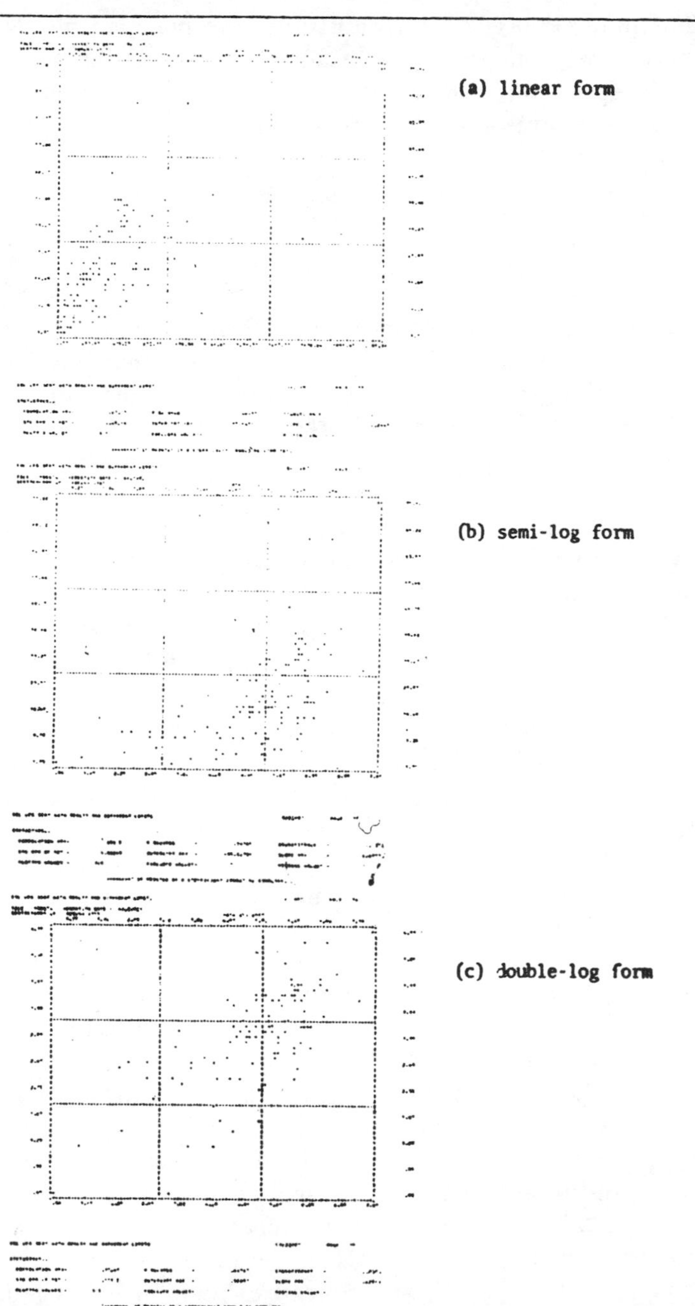

Figure 2 Actual Relationship Between Wealth and Value of Consumer Goods

diagram b more linear *if* the relationship did become horizontal with increasing wealth. Instead the semilog transformation of the data makes it less linear, turning it into a crescent (R^2 of .392). The data do not show these Massachusetts farmers following the so-called traditional consumer pattern. In fact, it is the modern pattern, the double log function seen in diagram c, that best straightens out the relationship suggesting that the most accurate way to describe the economic behavior of the colonists is that the value of their consumer goods steadily increased proportionally as wealth increased (the situation hypothesized in diagram c of Figure 1). 419

At the same time, it is clear that consumer goods value did not respond to wealth increases as closely as expenditures or consumer durables respond to income variation in twentieth-century data. About 50% of the variation in the dependent variable remains unexplained. The double log form of the equation (c in Figure 2) produced an elasticity of .425, meaning as the wealth of the farmers increased 1%, the value of consumer goods increased 4.25%. The wealth elasticity of consumer goods will always be below one or unity regardless of whether or not agriculturalists or others are being measured just as that for producer goods will be above one.[3] These conditions are the result of the fact that richer people keep a smaller proportion of their wealth in consumer goods than poorer people do. It is the shape of the curve rather than the elasticity that has concerned us here, because the elasticity will only take on meaning when estimates from other probate samples are available for comparison.

What remains to be considered is to what degree differences in early modern consumer behavior existed among households, and what determined these differences, aside from wealth. To do that, multivariate analysis of the complete data set including the nonagriculturalists is necessary. The 1774 Massachusetts sample does not encompass all areas of the colony, but does contain a mix of seaboard counties (Suffolk, Essex, and Plymouth) and interior ones (Hampshire and Worcester). If agricultural histories of New England are to be believed, the colony was a veritable land of contrasts during the colonial period, and if a dual economy existed anywhere in America, it would have existed there. While the residents of the region surrounding Boston and lesser port towns exhibited an intense commercial orientation, the farming population of the more remote inland counties is characterized as being more diversified and more self-sufficient than either its counterparts in the middle colonies or the planters of the South (Clemens, 1980). In one recent study, communities in Hampshire county have been depicted as essentially precapitalist in the eighteenth century. "Rather than relying on the market," it is claimed that

> 420 rural families supplied their wants both by producing their own goods for consumption and by entering into complex networks of exchange relationships with their neighbors and relatives in order to provide for needs that they could not or chose not to provide for themselves [Clark, 1979: 173][4]

The people are not portrayed as being poor—just self-sufficient. Presumably, if they produced most of their goods themselves, the value of their consumer durables would be lower than that of people who bought more on the market. Moreover, they would have to keep a higher proportion of their wealth in producer goods in order to manufacture a wide array of home consumed items.

The results of a regression to discover the determinants of consumer goods value, the dependent variable, appear in Table 1. If a true dual economy had existed, wealth and household size would be much less important as determinants than as indicators of economic specialization such as where people lived or their occupation. Self-sufficient households, theoretically, could possess plenty of wealth in the form of land and livestock but have little wealth in consumer products because homemade goods would be of lower value, and commodities only available through market exchange would not usually be acquired. On the other hand, if all areas were completely homogeneous commercially and enjoyed an equally high degree of market activity, wealth and household size should be able to explain almost the entire variance. Most economists, in fact, make that assumption about today's economy when studying household consumption. Table 1 shows that the value of decedents' consumer goods depended

Table 1 Determinants of Per Capita Consumer Goods Value: Massachusetts, 1774 (N = 253)

N = 253

Independent Variables	Coefficient	Standard Error	R^2	Mean[a]
Constant	.164			
(ln) per capita Wealth	.335*	.033	.272	3.391
County			.093	
Essex	-.216*	.106		.278
Plymouth	-.219	.126		.147
Hampshire	-.358*	.125		.179
Worcester	-.489*	.117		.246
Occupational Status[b]			.077	
dual occupationist	-.064	.129		.082
farmer/husbandman	.108	.121		.109
laborer/mariner	.261*	.120		.109
craftsman/tradesman	.300*	.105		.180
merchant	.689*	.248		.020
gentlemen/professional	.402*	.116		.112
woman	.577*	.145		.066
Age			.010	
25 and under	.282	.199		.029
26-45	.130	.072		.353
Literacy (owns books)	.091	.076	.003	.727
R^2 Total			.455	

SOURCE: Jones (1977).

a. The sample has been weighted by the population of each county in 1774 according to the figures furnished in Jones (1977: 1817). The means in the table reflect this weighting. The dependent variable, consumer goods value, in in natural log (ln) form.

b. Reference categories for dummy variables: county—Suffolk; occupational status—yeoman; Age—over 45; and Literacy—does not own book.

*Significant at the .05 level or better.

heavily, though not exclusively, upon inventoried per capita wealth. Because of collinearity, wealth and a measure of household size could not be run together as independent variables. Both wealth and consumer goods value, therefore, were divided by household size, as measured by beds, to obtain a per capita figure even though this combining of two independent variables lowered the R^2 about .25 points and also lowered the elasticity to .335.[5] In the resulting regression, over a quarter (27%) of the variation in consumer goods value, or 60% of the total explained variation of 45%, could be attributed to the effect of wealth, implying the absence of a dual economy.

At the same time, homogeneity did not reign either. Out of the remaining four variables—occupational status, county, age, and literacy (obtained through the proxy of book ownership)—the first two were statistically significant at the .05 level or better and
422 together explained 17% of the variation in consumer goods value. Occupational status made a difference because of the contrast between the agriculturalists and all other vocational categories. We know the yeomen and husbandmen did not stop investing in consumer goods at a certain point as the traditional peasant paradigm would have it. What one does find, however, is that their consumer good value fell somewhat below that of other occupations at every point on the wealth spectrum. In Table 1, the coefficients for dual occupationist (-.064) and farmer/husbandman (.108) clustered near the reference category of yeoman and were not significantly different from it, while merchant, gentleman/professional, craftsman/trademan, and laborers/mariners all had coefficients that added substantially more to consumer goods value, .689, .402, .300, and .261, respectively.[6] Altogether occupational status explained almost 8% of the variance in the dependent variable.

Why did farmers, other variables including wealth held constant, keep more of their resources in land, producer goods and financial assets than craftsmen and tradesmen did, who unlike the wage earning laborer, were also mainly small household "firms"? Was it the uncertainty of farming, an uncertainty arising from the dependence of agriculture on the vagaries of weather, that made farmers save more than other groups? Or was the lower consumer goods value solely a reflection of the nature of agricultural work that made it more logical for agrarian households to continue producing certain goods at home in slack periods, bringing the value of the goods down rather than buying on the market? Interestingly enough, modern farm

lower levels of consumption than do other occupational groups (Suits, 1963: 15).

Women, whose marital status rather than their trade was listed in the probate documents, registered a high coefficient, .577, out-consuming most of the male occupational groups, but as noted earlier, this situation may be a result of the inheritance practices of the time. Almost all inventoried females were widows because the property of wives upon their death automatically fell to their husbands, eliminating the necessity for probate. The inventories of widows reflected the portion of their husbands' estates that they received with no strings attached. That is, they might inherent land, producer goods, or financial assets for life only, while the property would revert directly to lineal descendants, and this wealth would not appear in their inventory. Consequently, women showed an exceptionally high percentage of wealth in consumer goods.

The fact that county in addition to occupational status proved statistically significant, explaining 9% of the variance in consumer goods value, demonstrated that differences in levels of consumer buying cannot be explained simply as a contrast between self-sufficient farmers and market oriented merchants and craftsmen. Those in agriculture could specialize also; nothing stopped a colonial artisan from possessing a garden plot, a cow, and other materials for home production. A regional variable such as county is not a variable at all, but a collection of area characteristics—physical terrain, age of settlement, population density, and transportation facilities. I will make the assumption here that these many facets of county add up to a measure of economic specialization. Certainly the coefficients for this dummy variable reconfirm the stereotypes (Zemsky, 1971; Cook, 1976) of the different counties: the sparser the population and the further away from the coast the lower consumer goods value turned out to be. The descent, however, was gradual. Suffolk County, which includes Boston, is the reference category, and its decedents, other variables held constant, had the highest consumer goods value. Essex County, where Salem is located, finished second, the noticeable gap between it and Suffolk being .216. The remaining coastal county, Plymouth, followed close

behind with –.219, before both the interior counties. Hampshire ranked fourth with a coefficient of –.358, and Worcester decedents, other variables held constant, put the least into consumer goods, having a coefficient of –.489. Although Hampshire was further inland than Worcester, it was part of the Connecticut River Valley, an area settled early and sufficiently commercialized to have produced a rich ruling class sometimes referred to as the "River Gods." Worcester on the near frontier, though closer to the coast, was actually less accessible and more thinly
424 populated. So from Suffolk County to Essex, Plymouth, Hampshire and finally Worcester there is a slow progressive diminution in consumer goods value.

The evidence from the probate inventories, then, suggests differences in the level of commercialization among different areas, but nothing as extreme as a dual system in operation. In the 1774 sample of Massachusetts counties, one does not come across a "traditional" consumer pattern in which "peasant" purchases of consumer goods leveled off at a certain point. Moreover, the major determinant of consumer goods value was wealth. While region certainly made a difference with coastal, more urbanized counties investing more than rural settlements far into the interior, no sharp dividing line existed separating market areas from nonmarket onces. Instead, one sees gradations in the value of consumer goods held, from a high in Suffolk to a low in Worcester county. The differences in the coefficients between the coastal areas of Suffolk and Essex proved greater than the spread between Essex and the interior county of Hampshire. In addition, it should be remembered that fewer people lived in those areas with lower consumer goods valuations. Of the entire population of Massachusetts, two-thirds or more dwelled along the coast or in the counties directly adjoining, and even those who lived in interior counties, such as Worcester, chose the populated enclaves, not the wilderness. The majority of colonists may indeed have resided in rural communities, but that did not mean the frontier or isolated villages. The frontier was called the frontier because almost no one lived there. Notwithstanding the testimonies of Hector St. John de Crevecoeur and other born-again backwoodsmen, it would be wrong to believe that the modal experience of most colonists on the eve of the Revolution was residence in a forest outpost or closed-off community.

The idea of colonial Americans as commercial primitives, however, has a long and proud history reaching right into the present, so that one must ask what exactly had fed and nurtured that reputation? I would argue that the impression is to a large part the result of America's colonial status. Certain sectors of the colonial economy did remain undeveloped, but this condition arose not out of a lack of market orientation, but from deep dependence on overseas commerce. The settlements established on the Atlantic coast in the seventeenth century replicated neither the home economy, nor the social structure. Rather, to be viable enterprises, the colonies had to complement the economy of the mother country. Carving out a niche in the world economy required specialization in some things and reliance on the Old World for others. Furthermore, it became the policy of the empire to maintain these areas of dependence permanently. What emerged as America's staple commodities are quite well known, but what goods and services were not developed because of their availability in England or elsewhere has been less systematically catalogued. Yet it was these areas of market dependence that gave the colonies the deceptive appearance of commercial primitiveness. To illustrate what I mean, let us consider two examples—currency/credit and textiles.

One of the practices most frequently cited in support of the view that colonists lacked a market orientation was the custom of payment in kind or in labor for goods and services. What is not mentioned or other times explained away as nothing more than a convenience is the fact that in account books these transactions were recorded in pounds, shillings, and pence. When cloth, or candles, or gunpowder was purchased from a country store, the shopkeeper entered the price in the ledger. If the customer paid in grain, the cash value based on the number of barrels and the grade was also recorded. Likewise, written agreements made between a farmer and a craftsperson for an exchange of foods and services specified the price of each. Where did these prices come from? Might not the regional, intercolonial, and even world markets have had influence on them (Rothenberg, 1981: 310-311)? Why else would it be necessary for a deal between two parties to bear a price? From figures now available on per capita income and imports circa 1770, I would estimate that roughly one quarter of yearly expenditures went toward buying goods brought in from outside of the province (Shammas, 1982).

Rather than illustrating the absence of a market mentality, payment-in-kind transactions point up the problems colonists had operating within a money market controlled from the British Isles. Specie, by law, was not to leave England, and parliament
426 tried to regulate the value of foreign monies in the colonies. Moreover, the crown opposed the issuance of paper monies and land bank projects favored by ordinary citizens. Instead, they wanted all bills and credit to materialize through the long, laborious process of seller to shopkeeper to colonial merchant to English mercantile house, and then back through the same channels. In fact, the colonies did issue paper currency, but its value fluctuated and people could never be sure it would be accepted by merchants, or that the British government would not demand the retirement of the bills. According to one historian of Massachusetts politics, the biggest problem plaguing the colonial government during the eighteenth century was the maintenance of "a viable medium of exchange," and nothing motivated the electorate to vote against a politician as much as the rumor that the candidate opposed paper money (Zemsky, 1971). It is within this context that one has to place the payment-in-kind transactions. They were makeshift arrangements that those far from the sources of power and influence in the empire had to use because they were denied proper currency and credit facilities. These same deficiencies played a large role later in rallying support for a stronger nation-state, but it took a long time for the new republic, precariously situated in the world economy, to resolve the class-infused issue of the exchange medium.

Another case in point involves textiles. The emblem for the self-sufficient early America household is homespun cloth, and many history texts leave the strong impression that most colonists manufactured almost all their own material. Certainly during the course of the eighteenth century, more American households than English did their own spinning, but, once again I would argue that this situation had more to do with colonial dependence on the world market than with the absence of a commercial orientation.

At the time the English colonized America, wool and linen cloth industries based on the putting-out system and organized by clothiers and various kinds of merchants were already established. Except in those areas where such capitalists operated, inventories show less than one in five households having spinning wheels. To give some idea of the scope of the industry by the early eighteenth century, a recent study has identified 1022 firms operating between 1730-1750 whose business was extensive enough for them to take out insurance policies (Chapman, 1973). Britain sent large amounts of textiles produced at home or obtained from the East to America, cloth being nonperishable and easily shipped, and all segments of colonial society consumed them. The mother country naturally wished to maintain this market dependence, and periodically passed legislation designed to discourage colonial cloth production.

Hampered by the advanced state of manufacturing in Britain and restrictive Parliamentary statutes, the colonies never developed much of a textile industry in which organizers put out wool or flax to be spun, furnished weavers with the yarn, and supervised the finishing processes. High prices and trade disruptions due to wars and then hostilities with England itself made it imperative that households produce some crude fabrics for daily use. In the plantation colonies, even this development did not occur until the early eighteenth century (Carr and Walsh, 1977; Walsh, 1977), but in New England these activities were underway earlier (Ulrich, 1980). Although storekeepers put out yarn and sold some domestically produced cloth, and Boston tried to establish a cloth manufactory (Tryon, 1917; Clark, 1929; Martin, 1935; Baumgarten, 1975; Nash, 1979), most of what households produced in conjunction with weavers, fullers, and whiteners probably went toward their own use. If this primitive system had met the textile needs of the colonists, then the homespun image of consumer demand would have some validity, but that does not seem to have been the case. Merchant account books indicate that the colonists continued to rely heavily on imports for all types of fabric—luxury, everyday, and material to be used for slaves. What early American households spun or wove in their homes for themselves was only the tip of the demand iceberg.

Our analysis suggests that the pre-Revolutionary legacy to the new republic was an economy in which no stark dichotomy of market versus nonmarket activity existed. Rather, in the case studied here at least, wealth was the prime determinant of the amount devoted to consumer goods, with gradual reductions
428 occurring as one moved from major seaport areas to minor, from coast to interior, from older settlements to the frontier. Part of this effect can be attributed to households engaged in farming who produced more of their own consumption items, but not all of them. Controlling for both wealth and occupational status, consumer goods value still varied from county to county; those with reputations for a high degree of economic specialization had higher sterling amounts in consumer goods investment. This relationship gives added support to the assertion that the consumer goods value variable is indeed a good measure of how much a household relied on the market. Estate inventories probably provide the best single source for the study of early American economic development.

What obscured the legacy of consumer activity in America, it would seem, was the new republic's inheritance of an economy that was *colonial* in nature, one initially shaped in response to the demands of European powers and trading interests. The Old World encouraged commercial structures overseas that were far different from its own, and when the Revolution came, some of the economic institutions most highly developed in Europe—for example, the money market and the textile industry—only existed in rudimentary form in America. Many of the major issues of the early national period—the formation of a national bank, the role of manufactures, tariff regulation, and the reliance on unfree labor—arose as a result of the conversion of America to nation-state status in the capitalist world economy, not because some new market mentality had emerged with nascent industrialization.

NOTES

1. An extensive economics literature has evolved concerning the determinants of consumption in the twentieth century, and while the two major variables in the analysis are usually expenditures and income (flows rather than the stocks measured in the data here), the ideal measure is recognized as being some form of "permanent income" rather than simple annual earnings. Corrections are frequently made with expenditures also, due to the fact that major durables purchases occur sporadically causing unsightly bulges in annual household consumption figures. In short, measures of consumer behavior may differ, but all have their problems. The possible relationships that could exist between income and expenditure, however, are rather similar to the ones between wealth and value of consumer goods. For an example of an *historical* analysis using income and expenditure see Williamson (1967).

2. The Massachusetts 1774 inventories are printed in Jones (1977). I transformed the data in several ways to make them comparable to English data sets from the sixteenth and seventeenth centuries I have been using, but those changes should not make any difference in the results here. While the value of indentured labor and slaves was subtracted from total wealth, very few Massachusetts inventories listed this type of property. The colonial country currency of Massachusetts was converted to pounds sterling. I followed the conversion rate suggested by Alice Hanson Jones: 1.33 country pound = 1 pound sterling. The pounds sterling were deflated according to the index of Phelps-Brown and Hopkins (1962) to make the sums comparable to 1660-1674 prices. To reconvert the Massachusetts data to the 1774 pound sterling figure, one would multiply by 1.177. New England is the only area where the total wealth variable includes realty.

3. In the double log form the elasticity is the same as the slope.

4. Some of the same sentiments can be found in Merrill (1977) and Henretta (1978).

5. Wealth here includes realty. I arrived at a measure for household size by multiplying the number of beds in the inventory by two, counting no bed inventories as one person households. De Vries (1974: 217-218) also uses beds as an indicator of household size. When total inventoried wealth and household size are run as separate variables, they explain much more of the variance in consumer goods value than the combined per capita wealth variable in the regression in Table 1 does, but the collinearity makes the results rather suspect.

6. The coefficients for the dummy variables, of course, must be subtracted or added to the intercept to show how they increase or decrease the consumer goods value. They cannot show how the marginal propensity consume operated across the wealth spectrum. Ideally, interaction terms would be combined with the dummies, but again, the collinearity that results makes this impossible.

REFERENCES

BAUMGARTEN, L. R. (1975) "The textile trade in Boston 1650-1700," in I.M.G. Quimby (ed.) Arts of the Anglo-American Community in the Seventeenth Century. Charlottesville: Univ. of Virginia Press.

CARR, L. G. and L. WALSH (1977) "The planter's wife: the experience of white women in seventeenth-century Maryland." William and Mary Q. 34 (July): 542-571.

CHAPMAN, S. D. (1973) "Industrial capital before the industrial revolution: an analysis of the assets of thousand textile entrepreneurs 1730-1750," pp. 113-137 in N. B. Harte and K. G. Ponting (eds.) Textile History and Economic History. Manchester: Manchester Univ. Press.

CLARK, C. (1979) "The household economy, market exchange and the rise of capitalism in the connecticut valley, 1800-1860." J. of Social History 13 (Winter) 169-189.

CLARK, V. (1929) History of Manufactures in the United States I.New York: McGraw-Hill.

CLEMENS, P. G. (1980) "Coming to terms with a new world: agricultural change and farmers in the eighteenth century." Presented at a meeting of the Organization of American Historians, San Francisco.

COOK, E. M. (1976) The Fathers of the Town. Baltimore: Johns Hopkins Univ. Press.

DE VRIES, J. (1975) "Peasant demand patterns and economic development: Friesland, 1550-1750," pp. 205-268 in N. Parker and E. L. Jones (eds.) European Peasants and their Markets: Essays in Agrarian Economic History. Princeton: Princeton Univ. Press.

——— (1974) The Dutch Rural Economy in the Golden Age 1500-1700. New Haven: Yale Univ. Press.

HENRETTA, J. (1978) "Families and farms: mentalité in pre-industrial America." William and Mary Q. 35 (January): 3-32.

HOBSBAWM, E. J. (1967) "The crisis of the seventeenth century," pp. 5-62 in Trevor Aston (ed.), Crisis in Europe 1560-1660. Garden City, NY: Doubleday.

HOUTHAKKER, H. S. (1957) "An international comparison of household expenditure patterns, commemorating the centenary of Engels' law." Econometrica 26 (October), 532-551.

JEDREY, C. M. (1979) The World of John Cleaveland: Family and Community in Eighteenth Century New England. New York: Norton.

JONES, A. H. (1977) American Colonial Wealth. New York: Arno.

MARTIN, M. E. (1935) Merchants and Trade of the Connecticut River Valley 1750-1820. Northampton, MA: Smith College.

MERRILL, M. (1977) "Cash is good to eat: self-sufficiency and exchange in the rural economy of the United States." Radical History Rev. 7 (Winter): 42-71.

NASH, G. B. (1979) "The failure of female factory labor in colonial Boston." Labor History 20 (Spring): 165-188.

PHELPS-BROWN, E. H. and S. HOPKINS (1962) "Seven centuries of the prices of consumables, compared with builders' wage-rates," pp. 179-196 in E. C. Wilson (ed.) Essays in Economic History: II.

ROTHENBERG, W. B. (1981) "The market and Massachusetts farmers, 1750-1855." J. of Economic History 41 (June), 283-314.

SHAMMAS, C. (1982). "How self-sufficient was early America." J. of Interdisciplinary History.

SUITS, D. B. (1963) "The determinants of consumer expenditure: a review of present knowledge," pp. 1-57 in Impacts of Monetary Policy. Englewood Cliffs: Prentice-Hall.

TERLECKYJ, N. E. [ed.] (1975) Household Production and Consumption. New York: National Bureau of Economic Research.

THIRSK, J. (1978) Projects and Policy: The Development of a Consumer Society in Early Modern England. Oxford: Oxford Univ. Press.

TRYON, R. M. (1917) Household Manufactures in the United States 1640-1860. Chicago: Univ. of Chicago Press.

ULRICH, L. T. (1980) "Good wives: a study in role definition in northern New England 1650-1750." Ph.D. dissertation, University of New Hampshire.

WALSH, L. S. (1977) "Charles County Maryland 1658-1705." Ph.D. dissertation, Michigan State University.

WILLIAMSON, J. G. (1967) "Consumer behavior in the nineteenth century: Carrol D. Wright's Massachusetts workers in 1875." Explorations in Entrepreneurial History 4 (Winter): 98-135.

ZEMSKY, R. (1971) Merchants, Farmers, and River Gods. Boston: Gambit.

Carole Shammas is Associate Professor of History at University of Wisconsin—Milwaukee.

The publisher and editor gratefully acknowledge the permission of the authors and the following journals and organizations to reprint the copyright material in this volume; any further reproduction is prohibited without permission:

The American Antiquarian Society for material in their *Proceedings*; *The William and Mary Quarterly*; *The Huntington Library Quarterly*; The American Historical Association for material in *The American Historical Review*; *Perspectives in American History*; The Association for Psycho-history for material in the *History of Childhood Quarterly*. MIT Press, Cambridge, Massachusetts for material in *The Journal of Interdisciplinary History*; The Social Science History Association for material in *Social Science History*.

Contents of the Set

9.
AFRICANS BECOME AFRO-AMERICANS
Selected Articles on Slavery in the American Colonies

10.
COMMERCE AND COMMUNITY
Selected Articles on the Middle Atlantic Colonies

11.
COLONIAL WOMEN AND DOMESTICITY
Selected Articles on Gender in Early America

12.
AMERICAN PATTERNS OF LIFE
Selected Articles on the Provincial Period of American History

13.
THE MARROW OF AMERICAN DIVINITY
Selected Articles on Colonial Religion

14.
AN AMERICAN ENLIGHTENMENT
Selected Articles on Colonial Intellectual History

15.
THE STRESSES OF EMPIRE
Selected Articles on the British Empire in the Eighteenth Century

16.
THE PACE OF CHANGE
Selected Articles on Politics and Society in Pre-Revolutionary America

17.
A NATION IN THE WOMB OF TIME
Selected Articles on the Long-term Causes of the American Revolution

18.
A RAGE FOR LIBERTY
Selected Articles on the Immediate Causes of the American Revolution